COLLECTED POEMS

THE MACMILLAN COMPANY
NEW YORK · BOSTON · CHICAGO · DALLAS
ATLANTA · SAN FRANCISCO

MACMILLAN AND CO., Limited
LONDON · BOMBAY · CALCUTTA · MADRAS
MELBOURNE

THE MACMILLAN COMPANY
OF CANADA, Limited
TORONTO

FROM A PAINTING BY
LILLA CABOT PERRY

COLLECTED POEMS

OF

EDWIN ARLINGTON ROBINSON

NEW YORK

THE MACMILLAN COMPANY

1946

The author begs to acknowledge his indebtedness to Messrs. Charles Scribner's Sons for permission to include in this collection the contents of the volumes entitled "The Children of the Night," and "The Town Down the River," and to Mr. Thomas Seltzer for permission to include the poem entitled "Lancelot."

CONTENTS

CONTENTS

CONTENTS

CONTENTS

CONTENTS

xi

CONTENTS

THE MAN AGAINST THE SKY

(1916)

To the Memory of
William Edward Butler

COLLECTED POEMS

Romantic attitude

FLAMMONDE

praise / sensitive parable

THE man Flammonde, from God knows where,
With firm address and foreign air,
With news of nations in his talk
And something royal in his walk,
With glint of iron in his eyes,
But never doubt, nor yet surprise,
Appeared, and stayed, and held his head
As one by kings accredited.

Erect, with his alert repose
About him, and about his clothes,
He pictured all tradition hears
Of what we owe to fifty years.
His cleansing heritage of taste
Paraded neither want nor waste;
And what he needed for his fee
To live, he borrowed graciously.

He never told us what he was,
Or what mischance, or other cause,
Had banished him from better days
To play the Prince of Castaways.
Meanwhile he played surpassing well

A part, for most, unplayable;
In fine, one pauses, half afraid
To say for certain that he played.

For that, one may as well forego
Conviction as to yes or no;
Nor can I say just how intense
Would then have been the difference
To several, who, having striven
In vain to get what he was given,
Would see the stranger taken on
By friends not easy to be won.

Moreover, many a malcontent
He soothed and found munificent;
His courtesy beguiled and foiled
Suspicion that his years were soiled;
His mien distinguished any crowd,
His credit strengthened when he bowed;
And women, young and old, were fond
Of looking at the man Flammonde.

There was a woman in our town
On whom the fashion was to frown;
But while our talk renewed the tinge
Of a long-faded scarlet fringe,
The man Flammonde saw none of that,
And what he saw we wondered at—
That none of us, in her distress,
Could hide or find our littleness.

There was a boy that all agreed
Had shut within him the rare seed
Of learning. We could understand,

4

FLAMMONDE

But none of us could lift a hand.
The man Flammonde appraised the youth,
And told a few of us the truth;
And thereby, for a little gold,
A flowered future was unrolled.

There were two citizens who fought
For years and years, and over nought;
They made life awkward for their friends,
And shortened their own dividends.
The man Flammonde said what was wrong
Should be made right; nor was it long
Before they were again in line,
And had each other in to dine.

And these I mention are but four
Of many out of many more.
So much for them. But what of him—
So firm in every look and limb?
What small satanic sort of kink
Was in his brain? What broken link
Withheld him from the destinies
That came so near to being his?

What was he, when we came to sift
His meaning, and to note the drift
Of incommunicable ways
That make us ponder while we praise?
Why was it that his charm revealed
Somehow the surface of a shield?
What was it that we never caught?
What was he, and what was he not?

How much it was of him we met
We cannot ever know; nor yet

5

Shall all he gave us quite atone
For what was his, and his alone;
Nor need we now, since he knew best,
Nourish an ethical unrest:
Rarely at once will nature give
The power to be Flammonde and live.

We cannot know how much we learn
From those who never will return,
Until a flash of unforeseen
Remembrance falls on what has been.
We've each a darkening hill to climb;
And this is why, from time to time
In Tilbury Town, we look beyond
Horizons for the man Flammonde.

THE GIFT OF GOD

BLESSED with a joy that only she
Of all alive shall ever know,
She wears a proud humility
For what it was that willed it so,—
That her degree should be so great
Among the favored of the Lord
That she may scarcely bear the weight
Of her bewildering reward.

As one apart, immune, alone,
Or featured for the shining ones,
And like to none that she has known
Of other women's other sons,—
The firm fruition of her need,
He shines anointed; and he blurs

6

THE GIFT OF GOD

Her vision, till it seems indeed
A sacrilege to call him hers.

She fears a little for so much
Of what is best, and hardly dares
To think of him as one to touch
With aches, indignities, and cares;
She sees him rather at the goal,
Still shining; and her dream foretells
The proper shining of a soul
Where nothing ordinary dwells.

Perchance a canvass of the town
Would find him far from flags and shouts,
And leave him only the renown
Of many smiles and many doubts;
Perchance the crude and common tongue
Would havoc strangely with his worth;
But she, with innocence unwrung,
Would read his name around the earth.

And others, knowing how this youth
Would shine, if love could make him great,
When caught and tortured for the truth
Would only writhe and hesitate;
While she, arranging for his days
What centuries could not fulfill,
Transmutes him with her faith and praise,
And has him shining where she will.

She crowns him with her gratefulness,
And says again that life is good;
And should the gift of God be less
In him than in her motherhood,
His fame, though vague, will not be small,

As upward through her dream he fares,
Half clouded with a crimson fall
Of roses thrown on marble stairs.

THE CLINGING VINE

"Be calm? And was I frantic?
    You'll have me laughing soon.
I'm calm as this Atlantic,
    And quiet as the moon;
I may have spoken faster
    Than once, in other days;
For I've no more a master,
    And now—'Be calm,' he says.

"Fear not, fear no commotion,—
    I'll be as rocks and sand;
The moon and stars and ocean
    Will envy my command;
No creature could be stiller
    In any kind of place
Than I . . . No, I'll not kill her;
    Her death is in her face.

"Be happy while she has it,
    For she'll not have it long;
A year, and then you'll pass it,
    Preparing a new song.
And I'm a fool for prating
    Of what a year may bring,
When more like her are waiting
    For more like you to sing.

"You mock me with denial,
    You mean to call me hard?
9

THE CLINGING VINE

You see no room for trial
  When all my doors are barred?
You say, and you'd say dying,
  That I dream what I know;
And sighing, and denying,
  You'd hold my hand and go.

"You scowl—and I don't wonder;
  I spoke too fast again;
But you'll forgive one blunder,
  For you are like most men:
You are,—or so you've told me,
  So many mortal times,
That heaven ought not to hold me
  Accountable for crimes.

"Be calm? Was I unpleasant?
  Then I'll be more discreet,
And grant you, for the present,
  The balm of my defeat:
What she, with all her striving,
  Could not have brought about,
You've done. Your own contriving
  Has put the last light out.

"If she were the whole story,
  If worse were not behind,
I'd creep with you to glory,
  Believing I was blind;
I'd creep, and go on seeming
  To be what I despise.
You laugh, and say I'm dreaming,
  And all your laughs are lies.

"Are women mad? A few are,
  And if it's true you say—

9

If most men are as you are—
  We'll all be mad some day.
Be calm—and let me finish;
  There's more for you to know.
I'll talk while you diminish,
  And listen while you grow.

"There was a man who married
  Because he couldn't see;
And all his days he carried
  The mark of his degree.
But you—you came clear-sighted,
  And found truth in my eyes;
And all my wrongs you've righted
  With lies, and lies, and lies.

"You've killed the last assurance
  That once would have me strive
To rouse an old endurance
  That is no more alive.
It makes two people chilly
  To say what we have said,
But you—you'll not be silly
  And wrangle for the dead.

"You don't? You never wrangle?
  Why scold then,—or complain?
More words will only mangle
  What you've already slain.
Your pride you can't surrender?
  My name—for that you fear?
Since when were men so tender,
  And honor so severe?

"No more—I'll never bear it.
  I'm going. I'm like ice.

CASSANDRA

My burden? You would share it?
    Forbid the sacrifice!
Forget so quaint a notion,
    And let no more be told;
For moon and stars and ocean
    And you and I are cold."

CASSANDRA

I HEARD one who said: "Verily,
    What word have I for children here?
Your Dollar is your only Word,
    The wrath of it your only fear.

"You build it altars tall enough
    To make you see, but you are blind;
You cannot leave it long enough
    To look before you or behind.

"When Reason beckons you to pause,
    You laugh and say that you know best;
But what it is you know, you keep
    As dark as ingots in a chest.

"You laugh and answer, 'We are young;
    O leave us now, and let us grow.'—
Not asking how much more of this
    Will Time endure or Fate bestow.

"Because a few complacent years
    Have made your peril of your pride,
Think you that you are to go on
    Forever pampered and untried?

11

"What lost eclipse of history,
  What bivouac of the marching stars,
Has given the sign for you to see
  Millenniums and last great wars?

"What unrecorded overthrow
  Of all the world has ever known,
Or ever been, has made itself
  So plain to you, and you alone?

"Your Dollar, Dove and Eagle make
  A Trinity that even you
Rate higher than you rate yourselves:
  It pays, it flatters, and it's new.

"And though your very flesh and blood
  Be what your Eagle eats and drinks,
You'll praise him for the best of birds,
  Not knowing what the Eagle thinks.

"The power is yours, but not the sight;
  You see not upon what you tread;
You have the ages for your guide,
  But not the wisdom to be led.

"Think you to tread forever down
  The merciless old verities?
And are you never to have eyes
  To see the world for what it is?

"Are you to pay for what you have
  With all you are?"—No other word
We caught, but with a laughing crowd
  Moved on. None heeded, and few heard.

JOHN GORHAM

"TELL me what you're doing over here, John Gorham,
Sighing hard and seeming to be sorry when you're not;
Make me laugh or let me go now, for long faces in the
    moonlight
Are a sign for me to say again a word that you forgot."—

"I'm over here to tell you what the moon already
May have said or maybe shouted ever since a year ago;
I'm over here to tell you what you are, Jane Wayland,
And to make you rather sorry, I should say, for being so."—

"Tell me what you're saying to me now, John Gorham,
Or you'll never see as much of me as ribbons any more;
I'll vanish in as many ways as I have toes and fingers,
And you'll not follow far for one where flocks have been
    before."—

"I'm sorry now you never saw the flocks, Jane Wayland,
But you're the one to make of them as many as you need.
And then about the vanishing. It's I who mean to vanish;
And when I'm here no longer you'll be done with me indeed."—

"That's a way to tell me what I am, John Gorham!
How am I to know myself until I make you smile?
Try to look as if the moon were making faces at you,
And a little more as if you meant to stay a little while."—

"You are what it is that over rose-blown gardens
Makes a pretty flutter for a season in the sun;
You are what it is that with a mouse, Jane Wayland,
Catches him and lets him go and eats him up for fun."—

13

"Sure I never took you for a mouse, John Gorham;
All you say is easy, but so far from being true
That I wish you wouldn't ever be again the one to think so;
For it isn't cats and butterflies that I would be to you."—

"All your little animals are in one picture—
One I've had before me since a year ago to-night;
And the picture where they live will be of you, Jane Wayland,
Till you find a way to kill them or to keep them out of sight."—

"Won't you ever see me as I am, John Gorham,
Leaving out the foolishness and all I never meant?
Somewhere in me there's a woman, if you know the way to find
    her.
Will you like me any better if I prove it and repent?"—

"I doubt if I shall ever have the time, Jane Wayland;
And I dare say all this moonlight lying round us might as well
Fall for nothing on the shards of broken urns that are
    forgotten,
As on two that have no longer much of anything to tell."

STAFFORD'S CABIN

ONCE there was a cabin here, and once there was a man;
And something happened here before my memory began.
Time has made the two of them the fuel of one flame
And all we have of them is now a legend and a name.

All I have to say is what an old man said to me,
And that would seem to be as much as there will ever be.
"Fifty years ago it was we found it where it sat."—
And forty years ago it was old Archibald said that

14

HILLCREST

"An apple tree that's yet alive saw something, I suppose,
Of what it was that happened there, and what no mortal knows
Some one on the mountain heard far off a master shriek,
And then there was a light that showed the way for men to
    seek.

"We found it in the morning with an iron bar behind,
And there were chains around it; but no search could ever find,
Either in the ashes that were left, or anywhere,
A sign to tell of who or what had been with Stafford there.

"Stafford was a likely man with ideas of his own—
Though I could never like the kind that likes to live alone;
And when you met, you found his eyes were always on your
    shoes,
As if they did the talking when he asked you for the news.

"That's all, my son. Were I to talk for half a hundred years
I'd never clear away from there the cloud that never clears.
We buried what was left of it,—the bar, too, and the chains;
And only for the apple tree there's nothing that remains."

Forty years ago it was I heard the old man say,
"That's all, my son."—And here again I find the place to-day,
Deserted and told only by the tree that knows the most,
And overgrown with golden-rod as if there were no ghost.

HILLCREST

(To Mrs. Edward MacDowell)

No sound of any storm that shakes
Old island walls with older seas
Comes here where now September makes
An island in a sea of trees.

15

Between the sunlight and the shade
A man may learn till he forgets
The roaring of a world remade,
And all his ruins and regrets;

And if he still remembers here
Poor fights he may have won or lost,—
If he be ridden with the fear
Of what some other fight may cost,—

If, eager to confuse too soon,
What he has known with what may be
He reads a planet out of tune
For cause of his jarred harmony,—

If here he venture to unroll
His index of adagios,
And he be given to console
Humanity with what he knows,—

He may by contemplation learn
A little more than what he knew,
And even see great oaks return
To acorns out of which they grew.

He may, if he but listen well,
Through twilight and the silence here
Be told what there are none may tell
To vanity's impatient ear;

And he may never dare again
Say what awaits him, or be sure
What sunlit labyrinth of pain
He may not enter and endure.

16

OLD KING COLE

Who knows to-day from yesterday
May learn to count no thing too strange;
Love builds of what Time takes away,
Till Death itself is less than Change.

Who sees enough in his duress
May go as far as dreams have gone;
Who sees a little may do less
Than many who are blind have done;

Who sees unchastened here the soul
Triumphant has no other sight
Than has a child who sees the whole
World radiant with his own delight.

Far journeys and hard wandering
Await him in whose crude surmise
Peace, like a mask, hides everything
That is and has been from his eyes;

And all his wisdom is unfound,
Or like a web that error weaves
On airy looms that have a sound
No louder now than falling leaves.

OLD KING COLE

In Tilbury Town did Old King Cole
A wise old age anticipate,
Desiring, with his pipe and bowl,
No Khan's extravagant estate.
No crown annoyed his honest head.
No fiddlers three were called or needed,
For two disastrous heirs instead
Made music more than ever three did.

Bereft of her with whom his life
Was harmony without a flaw,
He took no other for a wife,
Nor sighed for any that he saw;
And if he doubted his two sons,
And heirs, Alexis and Evander,
He might have been as doubtful once
Of Robert Burns and Alexander.

Alexis, in his early youth,
Began to steal—from old and young.
Likewise Evander, and the truth
Was like a bad taste on his tongue.
Born thieves and liars, their affair
Seemed only to be tarred with evil—
The most insufferable pair
Of scamps that ever cheered the devil.

The world went on, their fame went on,
And they went on—from bad to worse;
Till, goaded hot with nothing done,
And each accoutred with a curse,
The friends of Old King Cole, by twos,
And fours, and sevens, and elevens,
Pronounced unalterable views
Of doings that were not of heaven's.

And having learned again whereby
Their baleful zeal had come about,
King Cole met many a wrathful eye
So kindly that its wrath went out—
Or partly out. Say what they would,
He seemed the more to court their candor;
But never told what kind of good
Was in Alexis and Evander.

18

OLD KING COLE

And Old King Cole, with many a puff
That haloed his urbanity,
Would smoke till he had smoked enough,
And listen most attentively.
He beamed as with an inward light
That had the Lord's assurance in it;
And once a man was there all night,
Expecting something every minute.

But whether from too little thought,
Or too much fealty to the bowl,
A dim reward was all he got
For sitting up with Old King Cole.
"Though mine," the father mused aloud,
"Are not the sons I would have chosen,
Shall I, less evilly endowed,
By their infirmity be frozen?

"They'll have a bad end, I'll agree,
But I was never born to groan;
For I can see what I can see,
And I'm accordingly alone.
With open heart and open door,
I love my friends, I like my neighbors;
But if I try to tell you more,
Your doubts will overmatch my labors.

"This pipe would never make me calm,
This bowl my grief would never drown,
For grief like mine there is no balm
In Gilead, or in Tilbury Town.
And if I see what I can see,
I know not any way to blind it;
Nor more if any way may be
For you to grope or fly to find it.

19

"There may be room for ruin yet,
And ashes for a wasted love;
Or, like One whom you may forget,
I may have meat you know not of.
And if I'd rather live than weep
Meanwhile, do you find that surprising?
Why, bless my soul, the man's asleep!
That's good. The sun will soon be rising."

BEN JONSON ENTERTAINS A MAN
FROM STRATFORD

You are a friend then, as I make it out,
Of our man Shakespeare, who alone of us
Will put an ass's head in Fairyland
As he would add a shilling to more shillings,
All most harmonious,—and out of his
Miraculous inviolable increase
Fills Ilion, Rome, or any town you like
Of olden time with timeless Englishmen;
And I must wonder what you think of him—
All you down there where your small Avon flows
By Stratford, and where you're an Alderman.
Some, for a guess, would have him riding back
To be a farrier there, or say a dyer;
Or maybe one of your adept surveyors;
Or like enough the wizard of all tanners.
Not you—no fear of that; for I discern
In you a kindling of the flame that saves—
The nimble element, the true caloric;
I see it, and was told of it, moreover,
By our discriminate friend himself, no other.
Had you been one of the sad average,
As he would have it,—meaning, as I take it,

20

BEN JONSON ENTERTAINS A MAN FROM STRATFORD

The sinew and the solvent of our Island,
You'd not be buying beer for this Terpander's
Approved and estimated friend Ben Jonson;
He'd never foist it as a part of his
Contingent entertainment of a townsman
While he goes off rehearsing, as he must,
If he shall ever be the Duke of Stratford.
And my words are no shadow on your town—
Far from it; for one town's as like another
As all are unlike London. Oh, he knows it,—
And there's the Stratford in him; he denies it,
And there's the Shakespeare in him. So, God help him!
I tell him he needs Greek; but neither God
Nor Greek will help him. Nothing will help that man.
You see the fates have given him so much,
He must have all or perish,—or look out
Of London, where he sees too many lords.
They're part of half what ails him: I suppose
There's nothing fouler down among the demons
Than what it is he feels when he remembers
The dust and sweat and ointment of his calling
With his lords looking on and laughing at him.
King as he is, he can't be king *de facto*,
And that's as well, because he wouldn't like it;
He'd frame a lower rating of men then
Than he has now; and after that would come
An abdication or an apoplexy.
He can't be king, not even king of Stratford,—
Though half the world, if not the whole of it,
May crown him with a crown that fits no king
Save Lord Apollo's homesick emissary:
Not there on Avon, or on any stream
Where Naiads and their white arms are no more,
Shall he find home again. It's all too bad.
But there's a comfort, for he'll have that House—

21

The best you ever saw; and he'll be there
Anon, as you're an Alderman. Good God!
He makes me lie awake o'nights and laugh.

And you have known him from his origin,
You tell me; and a most uncommon urchin
He must have been to the few seeing ones—
A trifle terrifying, I dare say,
Discovering a world with his man's eyes,
Quite as another lad might see some finches,
If he looked hard and had an eye for nature.
But this one had his eyes and their foretelling,
And he had you to fare with, and what else?
He must have had a father and a mother—
In fact I've heard him say so—and a dog,
As a boy should, I venture; and the dog,
Most likely, was the only man who knew him.
A dog, for all I know, is what he needs
As much as anything right here to-day,
To counsel him about his disillusions,
Old aches, and parturitions of what's coming,—
A dog of orders, an emeritus,
To wag his tail at him when he comes home,
And then to put his paws up on his knees
And say, "For God's sake, what's it all about?"

I don't know whether he needs a dog or not—
Or what he needs. I tell him he needs Greek;
I'll talk of rules and Aristotle with him,
And if his tongue's at home he'll say to that,
"I have your word that Aristotle knows,
And you mine that I don't know Aristotle."
He's all at odds with all the unities,
And what's yet worse, it doesn't seem to matter;
He treads along through Time's old wilderness
As if the tramp of all the centuries

22

Had left no roads—and there are none, for him;
He doesn't see them, even with those eyes,—
And that's a pity, or I say it is.
Accordingly we have him as we have him—
Going his way, the way that he goes best,
A pleasant animal with no great noise
Or nonsense anywhere to set him off—
Save only divers and inclement devils
Have made of late his heart their dwelling place.
A flame half ready to fly out sometimes
At some annoyance may be fanned up in him,
But soon it falls, and when it falls goes out;
He knows how little room there is in there
For crude and futile animosities,
And how much for the joy of being whole,
And how much for long sorrow and old pain.
On our side there are some who may be given
To grow old wondering what he thinks of us
And some above us, who are, in his eyes,
Above himself,—and that's quite right and English.
Yet here we smile, or disappoint the gods
Who made it so: the gods have always eyes
To see men scratch; and they see one down here
Who itches, manor-bitten to the bone,
Albeit he knows himself—yes, yes, he knows—
The lord of more than England and of more
Than all the seas of England in all time
Shall ever wash. D'ye wonder that I laugh?
He sees me, and he doesn't seem to care;
And why the devil should he? I can't tell you.

I'll meet him out alone of a bright Sunday,
Trim, rather spruce, and quite the gentleman.
"What ho, my lord!" say I. He doesn't hear me;
Wherefore I have to pause and look at him.
He's not enormous, but one looks at him.

COLLECTED POEMS

A little on the round if you insist,
For now, God save the mark, he's growing old;
He's five and forty, and to hear him talk
These days you'd call him eighty; then you'd add
More years to that. He's old enough to be
The father of a world, and so he is.
"Ben, you're a scholar, what's the time of day?"
Says he; and there shines out of him again
An aged light that has no age or station—
The mystery that's his—a mischievous
Half-mad serenity that laughs at fame
For being won so easy, and at friends
Who laugh at him for what he wants the most,
And for his dukedom down in Warwickshire;—
By which you see we're all a little jealous. . . .
Poor Greene! I fear the color of his name
Was even as that of his ascending soul;
And he was one where there are many others,—
Some scrivening to the end against their fate,
Their puppets all in ink and all to die there;
And some with hands that once would shade an eye
That scanned Euripides and Æschylus
Will reach by this time for a pot-house mop
To slush their first and last of royalties.
Poor devils! and they all play to his hand;
For so it was in Athens and old Rome.
But that's not here or there; I've wandered off.
Greene does it, or I'm careful. Where's that boy?

Yes, he'll go back to Stratford. And we'll miss him?
Dear sir, there'll be no London here without him.
We'll all be riding, one of these fine days,
Down there to see him—and his wife won't like us;
And then we'll think of what he never said
Of women—which, if taken all in all

24

With what he did say, would buy many horses.
Though nowadays he's not so much for women:
"So few of them," he says, "are worth the guessing."
But there's a worm at work when he says that,
And while he says it one feels in the air
A deal of circumambient hocus-pocus.)
They've had him dancing till his toes were tender,
And he can feel 'em now, come chilly rains.
There's no long cry for going into it,
However, and we don't know much about it.
But you in Stratford, like most here in London,
Have more now in the *Sonnets* than you paid for;
He's put one there with all her poison on,
To make a singing fiction of a shadow
That's in his life a fact, and always will be.
But she's no care of ours, though Time, I fear,
Will have a more reverberant ado
About her than about another one
Who seems to have decoyed him, married him,
And sent him scuttling on his way to London,—
With much already learned, and more to learn,
And more to follow. Lord! how I see him now,
Pretending, maybe trying, to be like us.
Whatever he may have meant, we never had him;
He failed us, or escaped, or what you will,—
And there was that about him (God knows what,—
We'd flayed another had he tried it on us)
That made as many of us as had wits
More fond of all his easy distances
Than one another's noise and clap-your-shoulder.
But think you not, my friend, he'd never talk!
Talk? He was eldritch at it; and we listened—
Thereby acquiring much we knew before
About ourselves, and hitherto had held
Irrelevant, or not prime to the purpose.

25

And there were some, of course, and there be now,
Disordered and reduced amazedly
To resignation by the mystic seal
Of young finality the gods had laid
On everything that made him a young demon;
And one or two shot looks at him already
As he had been their executioner;
And once or twice he was, not knowing it,—
Or knowing, being sorry for poor clay
And saying nothing. . . . Yet, for all his engines,
You'll meet a thousand of an afternoon
Who strut and sun themselves and see around 'em
A world made out of more that has a reason
Than his, I swear, that he sees here to-day;
Though he may scarcely give a Fool an exit
But we mark how he sees in everything
A law that, given we flout it once too often,
Brings fire and iron down on our naked heads.
To me it looks as if the power that made him,
For fear of giving all things to one creature.
Left out the first,—faith, innocence, illusion,
Whatever 'tis that keeps us out o' Bedlam,—
And thereby, for his too consuming vision,
Empowered him out of nature; though to see him,
You'd never guess what's going on inside him.
He'll break out some day like a keg of ale
With too much independent frenzy in it;
And all for cellaring what he knows won't keep,
And what he'd best forget—but that he can't.
You'll have it, and have more than I'm foretelling;
And there'll be such a roaring at the Globe
As never stunned the bleeding gladiators.
He'll have to change the color of its hair
A bit, for now he calls it Cleopatra.
Black hair would never do for Cleopatra.

But you and I are not yet two old women,
And you're a man of office. What he does
Is more to you than how it is he does it,— *his work*
And that's what the Lord God has never told him
They work together, and the Devil helps 'em;
They do it of a morning, or if not,
They do it of a night; in which event
He's peevish of a morning. He seems old;
He's not the proper stomach or the sleep—
And they're two sovran agents to conserve him
Against the fiery art that has no mercy
But what's in that prodigious grand new House.
I gather something happening in his boyhood
Fulfilled him with a boy's determination
To make all Stratford 'ware of him. Well, well,
I hope at last he'll have his joy of it,
And all his pigs and sheep and bellowing beeves,
And frogs and owls and unicorns, moreover,
Be less than hell to his attendant ears.
Oh, past a doubt we'll all go down to see him.

He may be wise. With London two days off,
Down there some wind of heaven may yet revive him;
But there's no quickening breath from anywhere
Shall make of him again the poised young faun
From Warwickshire, who'd made, it seems, already
A legend of himself before I came
To blink before the last of his first lightning.
Whatever there be, there'll be no more of that;
The coming on of his old monster Time
Has made him a still man; and he has dreams
Were fair to think on once, and all found hollow.
He knows how much of what men paint themselves
Would blister in the light of what they are;
He sees how much of what was great now shares

An eminence transformed and ordinary;
He knows too much of what the world has hushed
In others, to be loud now for himself;
He knows now at what height low-enemies
May reach his heart, and high friends let him fall;
But what not even such as he may know
Bedevils him the worst: his lark may sing
At heaven's gate how he will, and for as long
As joy may listen, but *he* sees no gate,
Save one whereat the spent clay waits a little
Before the churchyard has it, and the worm.
Not long ago, late in an afternoon,
I came on him unseen down Lambeth way,
And on my life I was afear'd of him:
He gloomed and mumbled like a soul from Tophet,
His hands behind him and his head bent solemn.
"What is it now," said I,—"another woman?"
That made him sorry for me, and he smiled.
"No, Ben," he mused; "it's Nothing. It's all Nothing.
We come, we go; and when we're done, we're done.
Spiders and flies—we're mostly one or t'other—
We come, we go; and when we're done, we're done."
"By God, you sing that song as if you knew it!"
Said I, by way of cheering him; "what ails ye?"
"I think I must have come down here to think,"
Says he to that, and pulls his little beard;
"Your fly will serve as well as anybody,
And what's his hour? He flies, and flies, and flies,
And in his fly's mind has a brave appearance;
And then your spider gets him in her net,
And eats him out, and hangs him up to dry.
That's Nature, the kind mother of us all.
And then your slattern housemaid swings her broom,
And where's your spider? And that's Nature, also.
It's Nature, and it's Nothing. It's all Nothing.

28

BEN JONSON ENTERTAINS A MAN FROM STRATFORD

It's all a world where bugs and emperors
Go singularly back to the same dust,
Each in his time; and the old, ordered stars *Good*
That sang together, Ben, will sing the same
Old stave to-morrow."

　　　　　　　　　When he talks like that,
There's nothing for a human man to do
But lead him to some grateful nook like this
Where we be now, and there to make him drink.
He'll drink, for love of me, and then be sick; *drink sickens him*
A sad sign always in a man of parts,
And always very ominous. The great
Should be as large-in liquor as in love,—
And our great friend is not so large in either:
One disaffects him, and the other fails him;
Whatso he drinks that has an antic in it,
He's wondering what's to pay in his insides;
And while his eyes are on the Cyprian
He's fribbling all the time with that damned House.
We laugh here at his thrift, but after all
It may be thrift that saves him from the devil;
God gave it, anyhow,—and we'll suppose
He knew the compound of his handiwork.
To-day the clouds are with him, but anon
He'll out of 'em enough to shake the tree *his works —*
Of life itself and bring down fruit unheard-of,— *extended met.*
And, throwing in the bruised and whole together,
Prepare a wine to make us drunk with wonder;
And if he live, there'll be a sunset spell
Thrown over him as over a glassed lake
That yesterday was all a black wild water.

God send he live to give us, if no more,
What now's a-rampage in him, and exhibit,

29

With a decent half-allegiance to the ages
An earnest of at least a casual eye
Turned once on what he owes to Gutenberg,
And to the fealty of more centuries
Than are as yet a picture in our vision.
"There's time enough,—I'll do it when I'm old,
And we're immortal men," he says to that;
And then he says to me, "Ben, what's 'immortal'?
Think you by any force of ordination
It may be nothing of a sort more noisy
Than a small oblivion of component ashes
That of a dream-addicted world was once
A moving atomy much like your friend here?"
Nothing will help that man. To make him laugh,
I said then he was a mad mountebank,—
And by the Lord I nearer made him cry.
I could have eat an eft then, on my knees,
Tail, claws, and all of him; for I had stung
The king of men, who had no sting for me.
And I had hurt him in his memories;
And I say now, as I shall say again,
I love the man this side idolatry.

He'll do it when he's old, he says. I wonder.
He may not be so ancient as all that.
For such as he, the thing that is to do
Will do itself,—but there's a reckoning;
The sessions that are now too much his own,
The roiling inward of a stilled outside,
The churning out of all those blood-fed lines,
The nights of many schemes and little sleep,
The full brain hammered hot with too much thinking,
The vexed heart over-worn with too much aching,—
This weary jangling of conjoined affairs
Made out of elements that have no end.

BEN JONSON ENTERTAINS A MAN FROM STRATFORD

And all confused at once, I understand,
Is not what makes a man to live forever.
O no, not now! He'll not be going now:
There'll be time yet for God knows what explosions
Before he goes. He'll stay awhile. Just wait:
Just wait a year or two for Cleopatra,
For she's to be a balsam and a comfort;
And that's not all a jape of mine now, either.
For granted once the old way of Apollo
Sings in a man, he may then, if he's able,
Strike unafraid whatever strings he will
Upon the last and wildest of new lyres;
Nor out of his new magic, though it hymn
The shrieks of dungeoned hell, shall he create
A madness or a gloom to shut quite out
A cleaving daylight, and a last great calm
Triumphant over shipwreck and all storms.
He might have given Aristotle creeps,
But surely would have given him his *katharsis.*

He'll not be going yet. There's too much yet
Unsung within the man. But when he goes,
I'd stake ye coin o' the realm his only care
For a phantom world he sounded and found wanting
Will be a portion here, a portion there,
Of this or that thing or some other thing
That has a patent and intrinsical
Equivalence in those egregious shillings.
And yet he knows, God help him! Tell me, now,
If ever there was anything let loose
On earth by gods or devils heretofore
Like this mad, careful, proud, indifferent Shakespeare!
Where was it, if it ever was? By heaven,
'Twas never yet in Rhodes or Pergamon—
In Thebes or Nineveh, a thing like this!

31

No thing like this was ever out of England;
And that he knows. I wonder if he cares.
Perhaps he does. . . . O Lord, that House in Stratford!

EROS TURANNOS

She fears him, and will always ask
  What fated her to choose him;
She meets in his engaging mask
  All reasons to refuse him;
But what she meets and what she fears
Are less than are the downward years,
Drawn slowly to the foamless weirs
  Of age, were she to lose him.

Between a blurred sagacity
  That once had power to sound him,
And Love, that will not let him be
  The Judas that she found him,
Her pride assuages her almost,
As if it were alone the cost.—
He sees that he will not be lost,
  And waits and looks around him.

A sense of ocean and old trees
  Envelops and allures him;
Tradition, touching all he sees,
  Beguiles and reassures him;
And all her doubts of what he says
Are dimmed with what she knows of days—
Till even prejudice delays
  And fades, and she secures him.

The falling leaf inaugurates
  The reign of her confusion;

32

OLD TRAILS

The pounding wave reverberates
  The dirge of her illusion;
And home, where passion lived and died,
Becomes a place where she can hide,
While all the town and harbor side
  Vibrate with her seclusion.

We tell you, tapping on our brows,
  The story as it should be,—
As if the story of a house
  Were told, or ever could be;
We'll have no kindly veil between
Her visions and those we have seen,—
As if we guessed what hers have been,
  Or what they are or would be.

Meanwhile we do no harm; for they
  That with a god have striven,
Not hearing much of what we say,
  Take what the god has given;
Though like waves breaking it may be,
Or like a changed familiar tree,
Or like a stairway to the sea
  Where down the blind are driven.

OLD TRAILS

(WASHINGTON SQUARE)

I MET him, as one meets a ghost or two,
Between the gray Arch and the old Hotel.
"King Solomon was right, there's nothing new,"
Said he. "Behold a ruin who meant well."

33

He led me down familiar steps again,
Appealingly, and set me in a chair.
"My dreams have all come true to other men,"
Said he; "God lives, however, and why care?

"An hour among the ghosts will do no harm."
He laughed, and something glad within me sank.
I may have eyed him with a faint alarm,
For now his laugh was lost in what he drank.

"They chill things here with ice from hell," he said;
"I might have known it." And he made a face
That showed again how much of him was dead,
And how much was alive and out of place,

And out of reach. He knew as well as I
That all the words of wise men who are skilled
In using them are not much to defy
What comes when memory meets the unfulfilled.

What evil and infirm perversity
Had been at work with him to bring him back?
Never among the ghosts, assuredly,
Would he originate a new attack;

Never among the ghosts, or anywhere,
Till what was dead of him was put away,
Would he attain to his offended share
Of honor among others of his day.

"You ponder like an owl," he said at last;
"You always did, and here you have a cause.
For I'm a confirmation of the past,
A vengeance, and a flowering of what was.

34

OLD TRAILS

"Sorry? Of course you are, though you compress,
With even your most impenetrable fears,
A placid and a proper consciousness
Of anxious angels over my arrears.

"I see them there against me in a book
As large as hope, in ink that shines by night
Surely I see; but now I'd rather look
At you, and you are not a pleasant sight.

"Forbear, forgive. Ten years are on my soul,
And on my conscience. I've an incubus:
My one distinction, and a parlous toll
To glory; but hope lives on clamorous.

" 'Twas hope, though heaven I grant you knows of what—
The kind that blinks and rises when it falls,
Whether it sees a reason why or not—
That heard Broadway's hard-throated siren-calls;

" 'Twas hope that brought me through December storms,
To shores again where I'll not have to be
A lonely man with only foreign worms
To cheer him in his last obscurity.

"But what it was that hurried me down here
To be among the ghosts, I leave to you.
My thanks are yours, no less, for one thing clear:
Though you are silent, what you say is true.

"There may have been the devil in my feet,
For down I blundered, like a fugitive,
To find the old room in Eleventh Street.
God save us!—I came here again to live."

We rose at that, and all the ghosts rose then,
And followed us unseen to his old room.
No longer a good place for living men
We found it, and we shivered in the gloom.

The goods he took away from there were few,
And soon we found ourselves outside once more,
Where now the lamps along the Avenue
Bloomed white for miles above an iron floor.

"Now lead me to the newest of hotels,"
He said, "and let your spleen be undeceived:
This ruin is not myself, but some one else;
I haven't failed; I've merely not achieved."

Whether he knew or not, he laughed and dined
With more of an immune regardlessness
Of pits before him and of sands behind
Than many a child at forty would confess;

And after, when the bells in *Boris* rang
Their tumult at the Metropolitan,
He rocked himself, and I believe he sang.
"God lives," he crooned aloud, "and I'm the man!"

He was. And even though the creature spoiled
All prophecies, I cherish his acclaim.
Three weeks he fattened; and five years he toiled
In Yonkers,—and then sauntered into fame.

And he may go now to what streets he will—
Eleventh, or the last, and little care;
But he would find the old room very still
Of evenings, and the ghosts would all be there.

THE UNFORGIVEN

I doubt if he goes after them; I doubt
If many of them ever come to him.
His memories are like lamps, and they go out;
Or if they burn, they flicker and are dim.

A light of other gleams he has to-day
And adulations of applauding hosts;
A famous danger, but a safer way
Than growing old alone among the ghosts.

But we may still be glad that we were wrong:
He fooled us, and we'd shrivel to deny it;
Though sometimes when old echoes ring too long,
I wish the bells in *Boris* would be quiet.

THE UNFORGIVEN

WHEN he, who is the unforgiven,
Beheld her first, he found her fair:
No promise ever dreamt in heaven
Could then have lured him anywhere
That would have been away from there;
And all his wits had lightly striven,
Foiled with her voice, and eyes, and hair.

There's nothing in the saints and sages
To meet the shafts her glances had,
Or such as hers have had for ages
To blind a man till he be glad,
And humble him till he be mad.
The story would have many pages,
And would be neither good nor bad.

And, having followed, you would find him
Where properly the play begins;

But look for no red light behind him—
No fumes of many-colored sins,
Fanned high by screaming violins.
God knows what good it was to blind him,
Or whether man or woman wins.

And by the same eternal token,
Who knows just how it will all end?—
This drama of hard words unspoken,
This fireside farce, without a friend
Or enemy to comprehend
What augurs when two lives are broken,
And fear finds nothing left to mend.

He stares in vain for what awaits him,
And sees in Love a coin to toss;
He smiles, and her cold hush berates him
Beneath his hard half of the cross;
They wonder why it ever was;
And she, the unforgiving, hates him
More for her lack than for her loss.

He feeds with pride his indecision,
And shrinks from what will not occur,
Bequeathing with infirm derision
His ashes to the days that were,
Before she made him prisoner;
And labors to retrieve the vision
That he must once have had of her.

He waits, and there awaits an ending,
And he knows neither what nor when;
But no magicians are attending
To make him see as he saw then,
And he will never find again

38

THEOPHILUS

The face that once had been the rending
Of all his purpose among men.

He blames her not, nor does he chide her,
And she has nothing new to say;
If he were Bluebeard he could hide her,
But that's not written in the play,
And there will be no change to-day;
Although, to the serene outsider,
There still would seem to be a way.

THEOPHILUS

By what serene malevolence of names
Had you the gift of yours, Theophilus?
Not even a smeared young Cyclops at his games
Would have you long,—and you are one of us.

Told of your deeds I shudder for your dreams
And they, no doubt, are few and innocent.
Meanwhile, I marvel; for in you, it seems,
Heredity outshines environment.

What lingering bit of Belial, unforeseen,
Survives and amplifies itself in you?
What manner of devilry has ever been
That your obliquity may never do?

Humility befits a father's eyes,
But not a friend of us would have him weep.
Admiring everything that lives and dies,
Theophilus, we like you best asleep.

Sleep—sleep; and let us find another man
To lend another name less hazardous:
Caligula, maybe, or Caliban,
Or Cain,—but surely not Theophilus.

VETERAN SIRENS

THE ghost of Ninon would be sorry now
To laugh at them, were she to see them here,
So brave and so alert for learning how
To fence with reason for another year.

Age offers a far comelier diadem
Than theirs; but anguish has no eye for grace,
When time's malicious mercy cautions them
To think a while of number and of space.

The burning hope, the worn expectancy,
The martyred humor, and the maimed allure,
Cry out for time to end his levity,
And age to soften its investiture;

But they, though others fade and are still fair,
Defy their fairness and are unsubdued;
Although they suffer, they may not forswear
The patient ardor of the unpursued.

Poor flesh, to fight the calendar so long;
Poor vanity, so quaint and yet so brave;
Poor folly, so deceived and yet so strong,
So far from Ninon and so near the grave.

SIEGE PERILOUS

Long warned of many terrors more severe
To scorch him than hell's engines could awaken,
He scanned again, too far to be so near,
The fearful seat no man had ever taken.

So many other men with older eyes
Than his to see with older sight behind them
Had known so long their one way to be wise,—
Was any other thing to do than mind them?

So many a blasting parallel had seared
Confusion on his faith,—could he but wonder
If he were mad and right, or if he feared
God's fury told in shafted flame and thunder?

There fell one day upon his eyes a light
Ethereal, and he heard no more men speaking;
He saw their shaken heads, but no long sight
Was his but for the end that he went seeking.

The end he sought was not the end; the crown
He won shall unto many still be given.
Moreover, there was reason here to frown:
No fury thundered, no flame fell from heaven.

ANOTHER DARK LADY

Think not, because I wonder where you fled,
That I would lift a pin to see you there;
You may, for me, be prowling anywhere,
So long as you show not your little head:

41

No dark and evil story of the dead
Would leave you less pernicious or less fair—
Not even Lilith, with her famous hair;
And Lilith was the devil, I have read.

I cannot hate you, for I loved you then.
The woods were golden then. There was a road
Through beeches; and I said their smooth feet showed
Like yours. Truth must have heard me from afar,
For I shall never have to learn again
That yours are cloven as no beech's are.

THE VOICE OF AGE

She'd look upon us, if she could,
As hard as Rhadamanthus would;
Yet one may see,—who sees her face,
Her crown of silver and of lace,
Her mystical serene address
Of age alloyed with loveliness,—
That she would not annihilate
The frailest of things animate.

She has opinions of our ways,
And if we're not all mad, she says,—
If our ways are not wholly worse
Than others, for not being hers,—
There might somehow be found a few
Less insane things for us to do,
And we might have a little heed
Of what Belshazzar couldn't read.

She feels, with all our furniture,
Room yet for something more secure

42

Than our self-kindled aureoles
To guide our poor forgotten souls;
But when we have explained that grace
Dwells now in doing for the race,
She nods—as if she were relieved;
Almost as if she were deceived.

She frowns at much of what she hears,
And shakes her head, and has her fears;
Though none may know, by any chance,
What rose-leaf ashes of romance
Are faintly stirred by later days
That would be well enough, she says,
If only people were more wise,
And grown-up children used their eyes.

THE DARK HOUSE

WHERE a faint light shines alone,
Dwells a Demon I have known.
Most of you had better say
"The Dark House," and go your way.
Do not wonder if I stay.

For I know the Demon's eyes,
And their lure that never dies.
Banish all your fond alarms,
For I know the foiling charms
Of her eyes and of her arms,

And I know that in one room
Burns a lamp as in a tomb;
And I see the shadow glide,
Back and forth, of one denied
Power to find himself outside.

43

There he is who is my friend,
Damned, he fancies, to the end—
Vanquished, ever since a door
Closed, he thought, for evermore
On the life that was before.

And the friend who knows him best
Sees him as he sees the rest
Who are striving to be wise
While a Demon's arms and eyes
Hold them as a web would flies.

All the words of all the world,
Aimed together and then hurled,
Would be stiller in his ears
Than a closing of still shears
On a thread made out of years.

But there lives another sound,
More compelling, more profound;
There's a music, so it seems,
That assuages and redeems,
More than reason, more than dreams.

There's a music yet unheard
By the creature of the word,
Though it matters little more
Than a wave-wash on a shore—
Till a Demon shuts a door.

So, if he be very still
With his Demon, and one will,
Murmurs of it may be blown
To my friend who is alone
In a room that I have known.

THE POOR RELATION

After that from everywhere
Singing life will find him there;
Then the door will open wide,
And my friend, again outside,
Will be living, having died.

THE POOR RELATION

note from hymns

No longer torn by what she knows
And sees within the eyes of others,
Her doubts are when the daylight goes,
Her fears are for the few she bothers.
She tells them it is wholly wrong
Of her to stay alive so long;
And when she smiles her forehead shows
A crinkle that had been her mother's.

Beneath her beauty, blanched with pain,
And wistful yet for being cheated,
A child would seem to ask again
A question many times repeated;
But no rebellion has betrayed
Her wonder at what she has paid
For memories that have no stain,
For triumph born to be defeated.

To those who come for what she was—
The few left who know where to find her—
She clings, for they are all she has;
And she may smile when they remind her,
As heretofore, of what they know
Of roses that are still to blow
By ways where not so much as grass
Remains of what she sees behind her.

45

They stay a while, and having done
What penance or the past requires,
They go, and leave her there alone
To count her chimneys and her spires.
Her lip shakes when they go away,
And yet she would not have them stay;
She knows as well as anyone
That Pity, having played, soon tires.

But one friend always reappears,
A good ghost, not to be forsaken;
Whereat she laughs and has no fears
Of what a ghost may reawaken,
But welcomes, while she wears and mends
The poor relation's odds and ends,
Her truant from a tomb of years—
Her power of youth so early taken.

Poor laugh, more slender than her song
It seems; and there are none to hear it
With even the stopped ears of the strong
For breaking heart or broken spirit.
The friends who clamored for her place,
And would have scratched her for her face,
Have lost her laughter for so long
That none would care enough to fear it.

None live who need fear anything
From her, whose losses are their pleasure;
The plover with a wounded wing
Stays not the flight that others measure;
So there she waits, and while she lives,
And death forgets, and faith forgives,
Her memories go foraging
For bits of childhood song they treasure.

THE BURNING BOOK

And like a giant harp that hums
On always, and is always blending
The coming of what never comes
With what has past and had an ending,
The City trembles, throbs, and pounds
Outside, and through a thousand sounds
The small intolerable drums
Of Time are like slow drops descending.

Bereft enough to shame a sage
And given little to long sighing,
With no illusion to assuage
The lonely changelessness of dying,—
Unsought, unthought-of, and unheard,
She sings and watches like a bird,
Safe in a comfortable cage
From which there will be no more flying.

THE BURNING BOOK

Or the Contented Metaphysician

To the lore of no manner of men
    Would his vision have yielded
When he found what will never again
    From his vision be shielded,—
Though he paid with as much of his life
    As a nun could have given,
And to-night would have been as a knife,
    Devil-drawn, devil-driven.

For to-night, with his flame-weary eyes
    On the work he is doing,
He considers the tinder that flies
    And the quick flame pursuing.

47

In the leaves that are crinkled and curled
    Are his ashes of glory,
And what once were an end of the world
    Is an end of a story.

But he smiles, for no more shall his days
    Be a toil and a calling
For a way to make others to gaze
    On God's face without falling.
He has come to the end of his words,
    And alone he rejoices
In the choiring that silence affords
    Of ineffable voices.

To a realm that his words may not reach
    He may lead none to find him;
An adept, and with nothing to teach,
    He leaves nothing behind him.
For the rest, he will have his release,
    And his embers, attended
By the large and unclamoring peace
    Of a dream that is ended.

FRAGMENT

FAINT white pillars that seem to fade
As you look from here are the first one sees
Of his house where it hides and dies in a shade
Of beeches and oaks and hickory trees.
Now many a man, given woods like these,
And a house like that, and the Briony gold,
Would have said, "There are still some gods to please,
And houses are built without hands, we're told."

LISETTE AND EILEEN

There are the pillars, and all gone gray.
Briony's hair went white. You may see
Where the garden was if you come this way.
That sun-dial scared him, he said to me;
"Sooner or later they strike," said he,
And he never got that from the books he read.
Others are flourishing, worse than he,
But he knew too much for the life he led.

And who knows all knows everything
That a patient ghost at last retrieves;
There's more to be known of his harvesting
When Time the thresher unbinds the sheaves;
And there's more to be heard than a wind that grieves
For Briony now in this ageless oak,
Driving the first of its withered leaves
Over the stones where the fountain broke.

LISETTE AND EILEEN

"When he was here alive, Eileen,
  There was a word you might have said;
So never mind what I have been,
  Or anything,—for you are dead.

"And after this when I am there
  Where he is, you'll be dying still.
Your eyes are dead, and your black hair,—
  The rest of you be what it will.

"'Twas all to save him? Never mind,
  Eileen. You saved him. You are strong.
I'd hardly wonder if your kind
  Paid everything, for you live long.

49

"You last, I mean. That's what I mean.
I mean you last as long as lies.
You might have said that word, Eileen,—
And you might have your hair and eyes.

"And what you see might be Lisette,
Instead of this that has no name.
Your silence—I can feel it yet,
Alive and in me, like a flame.

"Where might I be with him to-day,
Could he have known before he heard?
But no—your silence had its way,
Without a weapon or a word.

"Because a word was never told,
I'm going as a worn toy goes.
And you are dead; and you'll be old;
And I forgive you, I suppose.

"I'll soon be changing as all do,
To something we have always been;
And you'll be old. . . . He liked you, too,
I might have killed you then, Eileen.

"I think he liked as much of you
As had a reason to be seen,—
As much as God made black and blue.
He liked your hair and eyes, Eileen."

LLEWELLYN AND THE TREE

Could he have made Priscilla share
    The paradise that he had planned,
Llewellyn would have loved his wife
    As well as any in the land.

LLEWELLYN AND THE TREE

Could he have made Priscilla cease
  To goad him for what God left out,
Llewellyn would have been as mild
  As any we have read about.

Could all have been as all was not,
  Llewellyn would have had no story;
He would have stayed a quiet man
  And gone his quiet way to glory.

But howsoever mild he was
  Priscilla was implacable;
And whatsoever timid hopes
  He built—she found them, and they fell.

And this went on, with intervals
  Of labored harmony between
Resounding discords, till at last
  Llewellyn turned—as will be seen.

Priscilla, warmer than her name,
  And shriller than the sound of saws,
Pursued Llewellyn once too far,
  Not knowing quite the man he was.

The more she said, the fiercer clung
  The stinging garment of his wrath;
And this was all before the day
  When Time tossed roses in his path.

Before the roses ever came
  Llewellyn had already risen.
The roses may have ruined him,
  They may have kept him out of prison.

And she who brought them, being Fate,
  Made roses do the work of spears,—
Though many made no more of her
  Than civet, coral, rouge, and years.

You ask us what Llewellyn saw,
  But why ask what may not be given?
To some will come a time when change
  Itself is beauty, if not heaven.

One afternoon Priscilla spoke,
  And her shrill history was done;
At any rate, she never spoke
  Like that again to anyone.

One gold October afternoon
  Great fury smote the silent air;
And then Llewellyn leapt and fled
  Like one with hornets in his hair.

Llewellyn left us, and he said
  Forever, leaving few to doubt him;
And so, through frost and clicking leaves,
  The Tilbury way went on without him.

And slowly, through the Tilbury mist,
  The stillness of October gold
Went out like beauty from a face.
  Priscilla watched it, and grew old.

He fled, still clutching in his flight
  The roses that had been his fall;
The Scarlet One, as you surmise,
  Fled with him, coral, rouge, and all.

LLEWELLYN AND THE TREE

Priscilla, waiting, saw the change
  Of twenty slow October moons;
And then she vanished, in her turn
  To be forgotten, like old tunes.

So they were gone—all three of them,
  I should have said, and said no more,
Had not a face once on Broadway
  Been one that I had seen before.

The face and hands and hair were old,
  But neither time nor penury
Could quench within Llewellyn's eyes
  The shine of his one victory.

The roses, faded and gone by,
  Left ruin where they once had reigned;
But on the wreck, as on old shells,
  The color of the rose remained.

His fictive merchandise I bought
  For him to keep and show again,
Then led him slowly from the crush
  Of his cold-shouldered fellow men.

"And so, Llewellyn," I began—
  "Not so," he said; "not so at all:
I've tried the world, and found it good,
  For more than twenty years this fall.

"And what the world has left of me
  Will go now in a little while."
And what the world had left of him
  Was partly an unholy guile.

53

"That I have paid for being calm
  Is what you see, if you have eyes;
For let a man be calm too long,
  He pays for much before he dies.

"Be calm when you are growing old
  And you have nothing else to do;
Pour not the wine of life too thin
  If water means the death of you.

"You say I might have learned at home
  The truth in season to be strong?
Not so; I took the wine of life
  Too thin, and I was calm too long.

"Like others who are strong too late,
  For me there was no going back;
For I had found another speed,
  And I was on the other track.

"God knows how far I might have gone
  Or what there might have been to see;
But my speed had a sudden end,
  And here you have the end of me."

The end or not, it may be now
  But little farther from the truth
To say those worn satiric eyes
  Had something of immortal youth.

He may among the millions here
  Be one; or he may, quite as well,
Be gone to find again the Tree
  Of Knowledge, out of which he fell.

BEWICK FINZER

He may be near us, dreaming yet
　Of unrepented rouge and coral;
Or in a grave without a name
　May be as far off as a moral.

BEWICK FINZER

TIME was when his half million drew
　The breath of six per cent;
But soon the worm of what-was-not
　Fed hard on his content;
And something crumbled in his brain
　When his half million went.

Time passed, and filled along with his
　The place of many more;
Time came, and hardly one of us
　Had cirdence to restore,
From what appeared one day, the man
　Whom we had known before.

The broken voice, the withered neck,
　The coat worn out with care,
The cleanliness of indigence,
　The brilliance of despair,
The fond imponderable dreams
　Of affluence,—all were there.

Poor Finzer, with his dreams and schemes,
　Fares hard now in the race,
With heart and eye that have a task
　When he looks in the face
Of one who might so easily
　Have been in Finzer's place.

He comes unfailing for the loan
　We give and then forget;
He comes, and probably for years
　Will he be coming yet,—
Familiar as an old mistake,
　And futile as regret.

BOKARDO

Well, Bokardo, here we are;
　Make yourself at home.
Look around—you haven't far
　To look—and why be dumb?
Not the place that used to be,
Not so many things to see;
But there's room for you and me.
　And you—you've come.

Talk a little; or, if not,
　Show me with a sign
Why it was that you forgot
　What was yours and mine.
Friends, I gather, are small things
In an age when coins are kings;
Even at that, one hardly flings
　Friends before swine.

Rather strong? I knew as much,
　For it made you speak.
No offense to swine, as such,
　But why this hide-and-seek?
You have something on your side,
And you wish you might have died,
So you tell me. And you tried
　One night last week?

56

BOKARDO

You tried hard? And even then
  Found a time to pause?
When you try as hard again,
  You'll have another cause.
When you find yourself at odds
With all dreamers of all gods,
You may smite yourself with rods—
  But not the laws.

Though they seem to show a spite
  Rather devilish,
They move on as with a might
  Stronger than your wish.
Still, however strong they be,
They bide man's authority:
Xerxes, when he flogged the sea,
  May've scared a fish.

It's a comfort, if you like,
  To keep honor warm,
But as often as you strike
  The laws, you do no harm.
To the laws, I mean. To you—
That's another point of view,
One you may as well indue
  With some alarm.

Not the most heroic face
  To present, I grant;
Nor will you insure disgrace
  By fearing what you want.
Freedom has a world of sides,
And if reason once derides
Courage, then your courage hides
  A deal of cant.

57

Learn a little to forget
    Life was once a feast;
You aren't fit for dying yet,
    So don't be a beast.
Few men with a mind will say,
Thinking twice, that they can pay
Half their debts of yesterday,
    Or be released.

There's a debt now on your mind
    More than any gold?
And there's nothing you can find
    Out there in the cold?
Only—what's his name?—Remorse?
And Death riding on his horse?
Well, be glad there's nothing worse
    Than you have told.

Leave Remorse to warm his hands
    Outside in the rain.
As for Death, he understands,
    And he will come again.
Therefore, till your wits are clear,
Flourish and be quiet—here.
But a devil at each ear
    Will be a strain?

Past a doubt they will indeed,
    More than you have earned.
I say that because you need
    Ablution, being burned?
Well, if you must have it so,
Your last flight went rather low.
Better say you had to know
    What you have learned.

BOKARDO

[handwritten: past is evil accept / override it.]

And that's over. Here you are,
  Battered by the past.
Time will have his little scar,
  But the wound won't last.
Nor shall harrowing surprise
Find a world without its eyes
If a star fades when the skies
  Are overcast.

God knows there are lives enough,
  Crushed, and too far gone
Longer to make sermons of,
  And those we leave alone.
Others, if they will, may rend
The worn patience of a friend
Who, though smiling, sees the end,
  With nothing done.

But your fervor to be free
  Fled the faith it scorned;
Death demands a decency
  Of you, and you are warned.
But for all we give we get
Mostly blows? Don't be upset;
You, Bokardo, are not yet
  Consumed or mourned.

There'll be falling into view
  Much to rearrange;
And there'll be a time for you
  To marvel at the change.
They that have the least to fear
Question hardest what is here;
When long-hidden skies are clear,
  The stars look strange

59

THE MAN AGAINST THE SKY

BETWEEN me and the sunset, like a dome
Against the glory of a world on fire,
Now burned a sudden hill,
Bleak, round, and high, by flame-lit height made higher,
With nothing on it for the flame to kill
Save one who moved and was alone up there
To loom before the chaos and the glare
As if he were the last god going home
Unto his last desire.

Dark, marvelous, and inscrutable he moved on
Till down the fiery distance he was gone,
Like one of those eternal, remote things
That range across a man's imaginings
When a sure music fills him and he knows
What he may say thereafter to few men,—
The touch of ages having wrought
An echo and a glimpse of what he thought
A phantom or a legend until then;
For whether lighted over ways that save,
Or lured from all repose,
If he go on too far to find a grave,
Mostly alone he goes.

Even he, who stood where I had found him,
On high with fire all round him,
Who moved along the molten west,
And over the round hill's crest
That seemed half ready with him to go down,
Flame-bitten and flame-cleft,
As if there were to be no last thing left
Of a nameless unimaginable town,—

THE MAN AGAINST THE SKY

Even he who climbed and vanished may have taken
Down to the perils of a depth not known,
From death defended though by men forsaken,
The bread that every man must eat alone;
He may have walked while others hardly dared
Look on to see him stand where many fell;
And upward out of that, as out of hell,
He may have sung and striven
To mount where more of him shall yet be given,
Bereft of all retreat,
To sevenfold heat,—
As on a day when three in Dura shared
The furnace, and were spared
For glory by that king of Babylon
Who made himself so great that God, who heard,
Covered him with long feathers, like a bird.

Again, he may have gone down easily,
By comfortable altitudes, and found,
As always, underneath him solid ground
Whereon to be sufficient and to stand
Possessed already of the promised land,
Far stretched and fair to see:
A good sight, verily,
And one to make the eyes of her who bore him
Shine glad with hidden tears.
Why question of his ease of who before him,
In one place or another where they left
Their names as far behind them as their bones,
And yet by dint of slaughter toil and theft,
And shrewdly sharpened stones,
Carved hard the way for his ascendency
Through deserts of lost years?
Why trouble him now who sees and hears
No more than what his innocence requires,

61

And therefore to no other height aspires
Than one at which he neither quails nor tires?
He may do more by seeing what he sees
Than others eager for iniquities;
He may, by seeing all things for the best,
Incite futurity to do the rest.

Or with an even likelihood,
He may have met with atrabilious eyes
The fires of time on equal terms and passed
Indifferently down, until at last
His only kind of grandeur would have been,
Apparently, in being seen.
He may have had for evil or for good
No argument; he may have had no care
For what without himself went anywhere
To failure or to glory, and least of all
For such a stale, flamboyant miracle;
He may have been the prophet of an art
Immovable to old idolatries;
He may have been a player without a part,
Annoyed that even the sun should have the skies
For such a flaming way to advertise;
He may have been a painter sick at heart
With Nature's toiling for a new surprise;
He may have been a cynic, who now, for all
Of anything divine that his effete
Negation may have tasted,
Saw truth in his own image, rather small,
Forbore to fever the ephemeral,
Found any barren height a good retreat
From any swarming street,
And in the sun saw power superbly wasted:
And when the primitive old-fashioned stars
Came out again to shine on joys and wars

THE MAN AGAINST THE SKY

More primitive, and all arrayed for doom,
He may have proved a world a sorry thing
In his imagining,
And life a lighted highway to the tomb.

Or, mounting with infirm unsearching tread,
His hopes to chaos led,
He may have stumbled up there from the past,
And with an aching strangeness viewed the last
Abysmal conflagration of his dreams,—
A flame where nothing seems
To burn but flame itself, by nothing fed;
And while it all went out,
Not even the faint anodyne of doubt
May then have eased a painful going down
From pictured heights of power and lost renown,
Revealed at length to his outlived endeavor
Remote and unapproachable forever;
And at his heart there may have gnawed
Sick memories of a dead faith foiled and flawed
And long dishonored by the living death
Assigned alike by chance
To brutes and hierophants;
And anguish fallen on those he loved around him
May once have dealt the last blow to confound him,
And so have left him as death leaves a child,
Who sees it all too near;
And he who knows no young way to forget
May struggle to the tomb unreconciled.
Whatever suns may rise or set
There may be nothing kinder for him here
Than shafts and agonies;
And under these
He may cry out and stay on horribly;
Or, seeing in death too small a thing to fear,

He may go forward like a stoic Roman
Where pangs and terrors in his pathway lie,—
Or, seizing the swift logic of a woman,
Curse God and die.

Or maybe there, like many another one
Who might have stood aloft and looked ahead,
Black-drawn against wild red,
He may have built, unawed by fiery gules
That in him no commotion stirred,
A living reason out of molecules
Why molecules occurred,
And one for smiling when he might have sighed
Had he seen far enough,
And in the same inevitable stuff
Discovered an odd reason too for pride
In being what he must have been by laws
Infrangible and for no kind of cause.
Deterred by no confusion or surprise
He may have seen with his mechanic eyes
A world without a meaning, and had room,
Alone amid magnificence and doom,
To build himself an airy monument
That should, or fail him in his vague intent,
Outlast an accidental universe—
To call it nothing worse—
Or, by the burrowing guile
Of Time disintegrated and effaced,
Like once-remembered mighty trees go down
To ruin, of which by man may now be traced
No part sufficient even to be rotten,
And in the book of things that are forgotten
Is entered as a thing not quite worth while.
He may have been so great
That satraps would have shivered at his frown,

THE MAN AGAINST THE SKY

And all he prized alive may rule a state
No larger than a grave that holds a clown;
He may have been a master of his fate,
And of his atoms,—ready as another
In his emergence to exonerate
His father and his mother;
He may have been a captain of a host,
Self-eloquent and ripe for prodigies,
Doomed here to swell by dangerous degrees,
And then give up the ghost.
Nahum's great grasshoppers were such as these,
Sun-scattered and soon lost.

Whatever the dark road he may have taken,
This man who stood on high
And faced alone the sky,
Whatever drove or lured or guided him,—
A vision answering a faith unshaken,
An easy trust assumed of easy trials,
A sick negation born of weak denials,
A crazed abhorrence of an old condition,
A blind attendance on a brief ambition,—
Whatever stayed him or derided him,
His way was even as ours;
And we, with all our wounds and all our powers,
Must each await alone at his own height
Another darkness or another light;
And there, of our poor self dominion reft,
If inference and reason shun
Hell, Heaven, and Oblivion,
May thwarted will (perforce precarious,
But for our conservation better thus)
Have no misgiving left
Of doing yet what here we leave undone?
Or if unto the last of these we cleave,

Believing or protesting we believe
In such an idle and ephemeral
Florescence of the diabolical,—
If, robbed of two fond old enormities,
Our being had no onward auguries,
What then were this great love of ours to say
For launching other lives to voyage again
A little farther into time and pain,
A little faster in a futile chase
For a kingdom and a power and a Race
That would have still in sight
A manifest end of ashes and eternal night?
Is this the music of the toys we shake
So loud,—as if there might be no mistake
Somewhere in our indomitable will?
Are we no greater than the noise we make
Along one blind atomic pilgrimage
Whereon by crass chance billeted we go
Because our brains and bones and cartilage
Will have it so?
If this we say, then let us all be still
About our share in it, and live and die
More quietly thereby.

Where was he going, this man against the sky?
You know not, nor do I.
But this we know, if we know anything:
That we may laugh and fight and sing
And of our transience here make offering
To an orient Word that will not be erased,
Or, save in incommunicable gleams
Too permanent for dreams,
Be found or known.
No tonic and ambitious irritant
Of increase or of want

THE MAN AGAINST THE SKY

Has made an otherwise insensate waste
Of ages overthrown
A ruthless, veiled, implacable foretaste
Of other ages that are still to be
Depleted and rewarded variously
Because a few, by fate's economy,
Shall seem to move the world the way it goes;
No soft evangel of equality,
Safe-cradled in a communal repose
That huddles into death and may at last
Be covered well with equatorial snows—
And all for what, the devil only knows—
Will aggregate an inkling to confirm
The credit of a sage or of a worm,
Or tell us why one man in five
Should have a care to stay alive
While in his heart he feels no violence
Laid on his humor and intelligence
When infant Science makes a pleasant face
And waves again that hollow toy, the Race;
No planetary trap where souls are wrought
For nothing but the sake of being caught
And sent again to nothing will attune
Itself to any key of any reason
Why man should hunger through another season
To find out why 'twere better late than soon
To go away and let the sun and moon
And all the silly stars illuminate
A place for creeping things,
And those that root and trumpet and have wings
And herd and ruminate,
Or dive and flash and poise in rivers and seas,
Or by their loyal tails in lofty trees
Hang screeching lewd victorious derision
Of man's immortal vision.

Shall we, because Eternity records
Too vast an answer for the time-born words
We spell, whereof so many are dead that once
In our capricious lexicons
Were so alive and final, hear no more
The Word itself, the living word
That none alive has ever heard
Or ever spelt,
And few have ever felt
Without the fears and old surrenderings
And terrors that began
When Death let fall a feather from his wings
And humbled the first man?
Because the weight of our humility,
Wherefrom we gain
A little wisdom and much pain,
Falls here too sore and there too tedious,
Are we in anguish or complacency,
Not looking far enough ahead
To see by what mad couriers we are led
Along the roads of the ridiculous,
To pity ourselves and laugh at faith
And while we curse life bear it?
And if we see the soul's dead end in death,
Are we to fear it?
What folly is here that has not yet a name
Unless we say outright that we are liars?
What have we seen beyond our sunset fires
That lights again the way by which we came?
Why pay we such a price, and one we give
So clamoringly, for each racked empty day
That leads one more last human hope away,
As quiet fiends would lead past our crazed eyes
Our children to an unseen sacrifice?
If after all that we have lived and thought,

THE MAN AGAINST THE SKY

All comes to Nought,—
If there be nothing after Now,
And we be nothing anyhow,
And we know that,—why live?
'Twere sure but weaklings' vain distress
To suffer dungeons where so many doors
Will open on the cold eternal shores
That look sheer down
To the dark tideless floods of Nothingness
Where all who know may drown.

THE CHILDREN OF THE NIGHT

(1890-1897)

To the Memory of
My Father and Mother

JOHN EVERELDOWN

"WHERE are you going to-night, to-night,—
   Where are you going, John Evereldown?
There's never the sign of a star in sight,
   Nor a lamp that's nearer than Tilbury Town.
Why do you stare as a dead man might?
Where are you pointing away from the light?
And where are you going to-night, to-night,—
   Where are you going, John Evereldown?"

"Right through the forest, where none can see,
   There's where I'm going, to Tilbury Town.
The men are asleep,—or awake, may be,—
   But the women are calling John Evereldown.
Ever and ever they call for me,
And while they call can a man be free?
So right through the forest, where none can see,
   There's where I'm going, to Tilbury Town."

"But why are you going so late, so late,—
   Why are you going, John Evereldown?
Though the road be smooth and the way be straight,
   There are two long leagues to Tilbury Town.
Come in by the fire, old man, and wait!
Why do you chatter out there by the gate?
And why are you going so late, so late,—
   Why are you going, John Evereldown?"

"I follow the women wherever they call,—
That's why I'm going to Tilbury Town.
God knows if I pray to be done with it all,
But God is no friend to John Evereldown.
So the clouds may come and the rain may fall,
The shadows may creep and the dead men crawl,—
But I follow the women wherever they call,
And that's why I'm going to Tilbury Town."

LUKE HAVERGAL

Go to the western gate, Luke Havergal,
There where the vines cling crimson on the wall,
And in the twilight wait for what will come.
The leaves will whisper there of her, and some,
Like flying words, will strike you as they fall;
But go, and if you listen she will call.
Go to the western gate, Luke Havergal—
Luke Havergal.

No, there is not a dawn in eastern skies
To rift the fiery night that's in your eyes;
But there, where western glooms are gathering,
The dark will end the dark, if anything:
God slays Himself with every leaf that flies,
And hell is more than half of paradise.
No, there is not a dawn in eastern skies—
In eastern skies.

Out of a grave I come to tell you this,
Out of a grave I come to quench the kiss
That flames upon your forehead with a glow
That blinds you to the way that you must go.

74

Yes, there is yet one way to where she is,
Bitter, but one that faith may never miss.
Out of a grave I come to tell you this—
To tell you this.

There is the western gate, Luke Havergal,
There are the crimson leaves upon the wall.
Go, for the winds are tearing them away,—
Nor think to riddle the dead words they say,
Nor any more to feel them as they fall;
But go, and if you trust her she will call.
There is the western gate, Luke Havergal—
Luke Havergal.

THREE QUATRAINS

I

As long as Fame's imperious music rings
   Will poets mock it with crowned words august;
And haggard men will clamber to be kings
   As long as Glory weighs itself in dust.

II

Drink to the splendor of the unfulfilled,
   Nor shudder for the revels that are done:
The wines that flushed Lucullus are all spilled,
   The strings that Nero fingered are all gone.

III

We cannot crown ourselves with everything,
   Nor can we coax the Fates for us to quarrel:

No matter what we are, or what we sing,
　Time finds a withered leaf in every laurel

AN OLD STORY

STRANGE that I did not know him then,
　That friend of mine!
I did not even show him then
　One friendly sign;

But cursed him for the ways he had
　To make me see
My envy of the praise he had
　For praising me.

I would have rid the earth of him
　Once, in my pride. . . .
I never knew the worth of him
　Until he died.

BALLADE BY THE FIRE

SLOWLY I smoke and hug my knee,
　The while a witless masquerade
Of things that only children see
　Floats in a mist of light and shade:
　They pass, a flimsy cavalcade,
And with a weak, remindful glow,
　The falling embers break and fade,
As one by one the phantoms go.

Then, with a melancholy glee
  To think where once my fancy strayed,
I muse on what the years may be
  Whose coming tales are all unsaid,
  Till tongs and shovel, snugly laid
Within their shadowed niches, grow
  By grim degrees to pick and spade,
As one by one the phantoms go.

But then, what though the mystic Three
  Around me ply their merry trade?—
And Charon soon may carry me
  Across the gloomy Stygian glade?—
  Be up, my soul; nor be afraid
Of what some unborn year may show;
  But mind your human debts are paid,
As one by one the phantoms go.

ENVOY

Life is the game that must be played:
  This truth at least, good friends, we know;
So live and laugh, nor be dismayed
  As one by one the phantoms go.

BALLADE OF BROKEN FLUTES

(To A. T. Schumann)

In dreams I crossed a barren land,
  A land of ruin, far away;
Around me hung on every hand
  A deathful stillness of decay;
  And silent, as in bleak dismay

77

That song should thus forsaken be,
  On that forgotten ground there lay
The broken flutes of Arcady.

The forest that was all so grand
  When pipes and tabors had their sway
Stood leafless now, a ghostly band
  Of skeletons in cold array.
  A lonely surge of ancient spray
Told of an unforgetful sea,
  But iron blows had hushed for aye
The broken flutes of Arcady.

No more by summer breezes fanned,
  The place was desolate and gray;
But still my dream was to command
  New life into that shrunken clay.
  I tried it. And you scan to-day,
With uncommiserating glee,
  The songs of one who strove to play
The broken flutes of Arcady.

ENVOY

So, Rock, I join the common fray,
  To fight where Mammon may decree;
And leave, to crumble as they may,
  The broken flutes of Arcady.

HER EYES

Up from the street and the crowds that went,
  Morning and midnight, to and fro,
Still was the room where his days he spent,
  And the stars were bleak, and the nights were slow.

78

HER EYES

Year after year, with his dream shut fast,
 He suffered and strove till his eyes were dim,
For the love that his brushes had earned at last,
 And the whole world rang with the praise of him.

But he cloaked his triumph, and searched, instead,
 Till his cheeks were sere and his hairs were gray.
"There are women enough, God knows," he said . . .
 "There are stars enough—when the sun's away."

Then he went back to the same still room
 That had held his dream in the long ago,
When he buried his days in a nameless tomb,
 And the stars were bleak, and the nights were slow.

And a passionate humor seized him there—
 Seized him and held him until there grew
Like life on his canvas, glowing and fair,
 A perilous face—and an angel's too.

Angel and maiden, and all in one,—
 All but the eyes. They were there, but yet
They seemed somehow like a soul half done.
 What was the matter? Did God forget? . . .

But he wrought them at last with a skill so sure
 That her eyes were the eyes of a deathless woman,—
With a gleam of heaven to make them pure,
 And a glimmer of hell to make them human.

God never forgets.—And he worships her
 There in that same still room of his,
For his wife, and his constant arbiter
 Of the world that was and the world that is.

79

And he wonders yet what her love could be
To punish him after that strife so grim;
But the longer he lives with her eyes to see,
The plainer it all comes back to him.

TWO MEN

THERE be two men of all mankind
    That I should like to know about;
But search and question where I will,
    I cannot ever find them out.

Melchizedek, he praised the Lord,
    And gave some wine to Abraham;
But who can tell what else he did
    Must be more learned than I am.

Ucalegon, he lost his house
    When Agamemnon came to Troy;
But who can tell me who he was—
    I'll pray the gods to give him joy.

There be two men of all mankind
    That I'm forever thinking on:
They chase me everywhere I go,—
    Melchizedek, Ucalegon.

VILLANELLE OF CHANGE

SINCE Persia fell at Marathon,
    The yellow years have gathered fast:
Long centuries have come and gone.

THE HOUSE ON THE HILL

And yet (they say) the place will don
  A phantom fury of the past,
Since Persia fell at Marathon;

And as of old, when Helicon
  Trembled and swayed with rapture vast
(Long centuries have come and gone),

This ancient plain, when night comes on,
  Shakes to a ghostly battle-blast,
Since Persia fell at Marathon.

But into soundless Acheron
  The glory of Greek shame was cast:
Long centuries have come and gone,

The suns of Hellas have all shone,
  The first has fallen to the last:—
Since Persia fell at Marathon,
Long centuries have come and gone.

THE HOUSE ON THE HILL

They are all gone away,
  The House is shut and still,
There is nothing more to say.

Through broken walls and gray
  The winds blow bleak and shrill:
They are all gone away.

Nor is there one to-day
  To speak them good or ill:
There is nothing more to say.

81

Why is it then we stray
  Around the sunken sill?
They are all gone away,

And our poor fancy-play
  For them is wasted skill:
There is nothing more to say.

There is ruin and decay
  In the House on the Hill:
They are all gone away,
There is nothing more to say.

RICHARD CORY

Whenever Richard Cory went down town,
We people on the pavement looked at him:
He was a gentleman from sole to crown,
Clean favored, and imperially slim.

And he was always quietly arrayed,
And he was always human when he talked;
But still he fluttered pulses when he said,
"Good-morning," and he glittered when he walked.

And he was rich—yes, richer than a king—
And admirably schooled in every grace:
In fine, we thought that he was everything
To make us wish that we were in his place.

So on we worked, and waited for the light,
And went without the meat, and cursed the bread;
And Richard Cory, one calm summer night,
Went home and put a bullet through his head.

DEAR FRIENDS

BOSTON

My northern pines are good enough for me,
But there's a town my memory uprears—
A town that always like a friend appears,
And always in the sunrise by the sea.
And over it, somehow, there seems to be
A downward flash of something new and fierce,
That ever strives to clear, but never clears
The dimness of a charmed antiquity.

CALVARY

Friendless and faint, with martyred steps and slow
Faint for the flesh, but for the spirit free,
Stung by the mob that came to see the show,
The Master toiled along to Calvary;
We gibed him, as he went, with houndish glee,
Till his dimned eyes for us did overflow;
We cursed his vengeless hands thrice wretchedly,—
And this was nineteen hundred years ago.

But after nineteen hundred years the shame
Still clings, and we have not made good the loss
That outraged faith has entered in his name.
Ah, when shall come love's courage to be strong!
Tell me, O Lord—tell me, O Lord, how long
Are we to keep Christ writhing on the cross!

DEAR FRIENDS

Dear friends, reproach me not for what I do,
Nor counsel me, nor pity me; nor say
That I am wearing half my life away
For bubble-work that only fools pursue.

83

And if my bubbles be too small for you,
Blow bigger then your own: the games we play
To fill the frittered minutes of a day,
Good glasses are to read the spirit through.

And whoso reads may get him some shrewd skill;
And some unprofitable scorn resign,
To praise the very thing that he deplores;
So, friends (dear friends), remember, if you will,
The shame I win for singing is all mine,
The gold I miss for dreaming is all yours.

THE STORY OF THE ASHES AND THE FLAME

No matter why, nor whence, nor when she came,
There was her place. No matter what men said,
No matter what she was; living or dead,
Faithful or not, he loved her all the same.
The story was as old as human shame,
But ever since that lonely night she fled,
With books to blind him, he had only read
The story of the ashes and the flame.

There she was always coming pretty soon
To fool him back, with penitent scared eyes
That had in them the laughter of the moon
For baffled lovers, and to make him think—
Before she gave him time enough to wink—
Her kisses were the keys to Paradise.

AMARYLLIS

ONCE, when I wandered in the woods alone,
An old man tottered up to me and said,
"Come, friend, and see the grave that I have made
For Amaryllis." There was in the tone

84

THE PITY OF THE LEAVES

Of his complaint such quaver and such moan
That I took pity on him and obeyed,
And long stood looking where his hands had laid
An ancient woman, shrunk to skin and bone.

Far out beyond the forest I could hear
The calling of loud progress, and the bold
Incessant scream of commerce ringing clear;
But though the trumpets of the world were glad,
It made me lonely and it made me sad
To think that Amaryllis had grown old.

ZOLA

BECAUSE he puts the compromising chart
Of hell before your eyes, you are afraid;
Because he counts the price that you have paid
For innocence, and counts it from the start,
You loathe him. But he sees the human heart
Of God meanwhile, and in His hand was weighed
Your squeamish and emasculate crusade
Against the grim dominion of his art.

Never until we conquer the uncouth
Connivings of our shamed indifference
(We call it Christian faith) are we to scan
The racked and shrieking hideousness of Truth
To find, in hate's polluted self-defence
Throbbing, the pulse, the divine heart of man.

THE PITY OF THE LEAVES

VENGEFUL across the cold November moors,
Loud with ancestral shame there came the bleak
Sad wind that shrieked, and answered with a shriek,
Reverberant through lonely corridors.

The old man heard it; and he heard, perforce,
Words out of lips that were no more to speak—
Words of the past that shook the old man's cheek
Like dead, remembered footsteps on old floors.

And then there were the leaves that plagued him so!
The brown, thin leaves that on the stones outside
Skipped with a freezing whisper. Now and then
They stopped, and stayed there—just to let him know
How dead they were, but if the old man cried,
They fluttered off like withered souls of men.

AARON STARK

WITHAL a meagre man was Aaron Stark,
Cursed and unkempt, shrewd, shrivelled, and morose.
A miser was he, with a miser's nose,
And eyes like little dollars in the dark.
His thin, pinched mouth was nothing but a mark;
And when he spoke there came like sullen blows
Through scattered fangs a few snarled words and close,
As if a cur were chary of its bark.

Glad for the murmur of his hard renown,
Year after year he shambled through the town,
A loveless exile moving with a staff;
And oftentimes there crept into his ears
A sound of alien pity, touched with tears,—
And then (and only then) did Aaron laugh.

THE GARDEN

THERE is a fenceless garden overgrown
With buds and blossoms and all sorts of leaves;
And once, among the roses and the sheaves,
The Gardener and I were there alone.

CHARLES CARVILLE'S EYES

He led me to the plot where I had thrown
The fennel of my days on wasted ground,
And in that riot of sad weeds I found
The fruitage of a life that was my own.

My life! Ah, yes, there was my life, indeed!
And there were all the lives of humankind;
And they were like a book that I could read,
Whose every leaf, miraculously signed,
Outrolled itself from Thought's eternal seed.
Love-rooted in God's garden of the mind.

CLIFF KLINGENHAGEN

CLIFF KLINGENHAGEN had me in to dine
With him one day; and after soup and meat,
And all the other things there were to eat,
Cliff took two glasses and filled one with wine
And one with wormwood. Then, without a sign
For me to choose at all, he took the draught
Of bitterness himself, and lightly quaffed
It off, and said the other one was mine.

And when I asked him what the deuce he meant
By doing that, he only looked at me
And smiled, and said it was a way of his.
And though I know the fellow, I have spent
Long time a-wondering when I shall be
As happy as Cliff Klingenhagen is.

CHARLES CARVILLE'S EYES

A MELANCHOLY face Charles Carville had,
But not so melancholy as it seemed,
When once you knew him, for his mouth redeemed
His insufficient eyes, forever sad:

In them there was no life-glimpse, good or bad,
Nor joy nor passion in them ever gleamed;
His mouth was all of him that ever beamed;
His eyes were sorry, but his mouth was glad.

He never was a fellow that said much,
And half of what he did say was not heard
By many of us: we were out of touch
With all his whims and all his theories
Till he was dead, so those blank eyes of his
Might speak them. Then we heard them, **every word.**

THE DEAD VILLAGE

HERE there is death. But even here, they say,
Here where the dull sun shines this afternoon
As desolate as ever the dead moon
Did glimmer on dead Sardis, men were gay;
And there were little children here to play,
With small soft hands that once did keep in tune
The strings that stretch from heaven, till too soon
The change came, and the music passed away.

Now there is nothing but the ghosts of things,—
No life, no love, no children, and no men;
And over the forgotten place there clings
The strange and unrememberable light
That is in dreams. The music failed, and then
God frowned, and shut the village from His sight.

TWO SONNETS

materialism
& idealism (say) (Kaplan)

I

Just as I wonder at the twofold screen
Of twisted innocence that you would plait
For eyes that uncourageously await
The coming of a kingdom that has been,
So do I wonder what God's love can mean
To you that all so strangely estimate
The purpose and the consequent estate
Of one short shuddering step to the Unseen.

No, I have not your backward faith to shrink
Lone-faring from the doorway of God's home
To find Him in the names of buried men;
Nor your ingenious recreance to think
We cherish, in the life that is to come,
The scattered features of dead friends again.

II

Never until our souls are strong enough
To plunge into the crater of the Scheme—
Triumphant in the flash there to redeem
Love's handsel and forevermore to slough,
Like cerements at a played-out masque, the rough
And reptile skins of us whereon we set
The stigma of scared years—are we to get
Where atoms and the ages are one stuff.

Nor ever shall we know the cursed waste
Of life in the beneficence divine
Of starlight and of sunlight and soul-shine
That we have squandered in sin's frail distress,
Till we have drunk, and trembled at the taste,
The mead of Thought's prophetic endlessness.

THE CLERKS

I DID not think that I should find them there
When I came back again; but there they stood,
As in the days they dreamed of when young blood
Was in their cheeks and women called them fair.
Be sure, they met me with an ancient air,—
And yes, there was a shop-worn brotherhood
About them; but the men were just as good,
And just as human as they ever were.

And you that ache so much to be sublime.
And you that feed yourselves with your descent,
What comes of all your visions and your fears?
Poets and kings are but the clerks of Time,
Tiering the same dull webs of discontent,
Clipping the same sad alnage of the years.

FLEMING HELPHENSTINE

AT first I thought there was a superfine
Persuasion in his face; but the free glow
That filled it when he stopped and cried, "Hollo!"
Shone joyously, and so I let it shine.
He said his name was Fleming Helphenstine,
But be that as it may;—I only know
He talked of this and that and So-and-So,
And laughed and chaffed like any friend of mine.

But soon, with a queer, quick frown, he looked at me,
And I looked hard at him; and there we gazed
In a strained way that made us cringe and wince:
Then, with a wordless clogged apology
That sounded half confused and half amazed,
He dodged,—and I have never seen him since.

HORACE TO LEUCONOE

THOMAS HOOD

THE man who cloaked his bitterness within
This winding-sheet of puns and pleasantries,
God never gave to look with common eyes
Upon a world of anguish and of sin:
His brother was the branded man of Lynn;
And there are woven with his jollities
The nameless and eternal tragedies
That render hope and hopelessness akin.

We laugh, and crown him; but anon we feel
A still chord sorrow-swept,—a weird unrest;
And thin dim shadows home to midnight steal,
As if the very ghost of mirth were dead—
As if the joys of time to dreams had fled,
Or sailed away with Ines to the West.

HORACE TO LEUCONOË

I PRAY you not, Leuconoë, to pore
With unpermitted eyes on what may be
Appointed by the gods for you and me,
Nor on Chaldean figures any more.
'T were infinitely better to implore
The present only:—whether Jove decree
More winters yet to come, or whether he
Make even this, whose hard, wave-eaten shore
Shatters the Tuscan seas to-day, the last—
Be wise withal, and rack your wine, nor fill
Your bosom with large hopes; for while I sing,
The envious close of time is narrowing;—
So seize the day, or ever it be past,
And let the morrow come for what it will.

REUBEN BRIGHT

BECAUSE he was a butcher and thereby
Did earn an honest living (and did right),
I would not have you think that Reuben Bright
Was any more a brute than you or I;
For when they told him that his wife must die,
He stared at them, and shook with grief and fright,
And cried like a great baby half that night,
And made the women cry to see him cry.

And after she was dead, and he had paid
The singers and the sexton and the rest,
He packed a lot of things that she had made
Most mournfully away in an old chest
Of hers, and put some chopped-up cedar boughs
In with them, and tore down the slaughter house.

THE ALTAR

ALONE, remote, nor witting where I went,
I found an altar builded in a dream—
A fiery place, whereof there was a gleam
So swift, so searching, and so eloquent
Of upward promise, that love's murmur, blent
With sorrow's warning, gave but a supreme
Unending impulse to that human stream
Whose flood was all for the flame's fury bent.

Alas! I said,—the world is in the wrong.
But the same quenchless fever of unrest
That thrilled the foremost of that martyred throng
Thrilled me, and I awoke . . . and was the same
Bewildered insect plunging for the flame
That burns, and must burn somehow for the best.

SONNET

THE TAVERN

WHENEVER I go by there nowadays
And look at the rank weeds and the strange grass,
The torn blue curtains and the broken glass,
I seem to be afraid of the old place;
And something stiffens up and down my face,
For all the world as if I saw the ghost
Of old Ham Amory, the murdered host,
With his dead eyes turned on me all aglaze.

The Tavern has a story, but no man
Can tell us what it is. We only know
That once long after midnight, years ago,
A stranger galloped up from Tilbury Town,
Who brushed, and scared, and all but overran
That skirt-crazed reprobate, John Evereldown.

SONNET

OH for a poet—for a beacon bright
To rift this changless glimmer of dead gray;
To spirit back the Muses, long astray,
And flush Parnassus with a newer light;
To put these little sonnet-men to flight
Who fashion, in a shrewd mechanic way,
Songs without souls, that flicker for a day,
To vanish in irrevocable night.

What does it mean, this barren age of ours?
Here are the men, the women, and the flowers,
The seasons, and the sunset, as before.
What does it mean? Shall there not one arise
To wrench one banner from the western skies,
And mark it with his name forevermore?

GEORGE CRABBE

GIVE him the darkest inch your shelf allows,
Hide him in lonely garrets, if you will,—
But his hard, human pulse is throbbing still
With the sure strength that fearless truth endows.
In spite of all fine science disavows,
Of his plain excellence and stubborn skill
There yet remains what fashion cannot kill,
Though years have thinned the laurel from his brows.

Whether or not we read him, we can feel
From time to time the vigor of his name
Against us like a finger for the shame
And emptiness of what our souls reveal
In books that are as altars where we kneel
To consecrate the flicker, not the flame.

CREDO

I CANNOT find my way: there is no star
In all the shrouded heavens anywhere;
And there is not a whisper in the air
Of any living voice but one so far
That I can hear it only as a bar
Of lost, imperial music, played when fair
And angel fingers wove, and unaware,
Dead leaves to garlands where no roses are.

No, there is not a glimmer, nor a call,
For one that welcomes, welcomes when he fears,
The black and awful chaos of the night;
For through it all—above, beyond it all—
I know the far-sent message of the years,
I feel the coming glory of the Light.

94

SONNET

ON THE NIGHT OF A FRIEND'S WEDDING

If ever I am old, and all alone,
I shall have killed one grief, at any rate;
For then, thank God, I shall not have to wait
Much longer for the sheaves that I have sown.
The devil only knows what I have done,
But here I am, and here are six or eight
Good friends, who most ingenuously prate
About my songs to such and such a one.

But everything is all askew to-night,—
As if the time were come, or almost come,
For their untenanted mirage of me
To lose itself and crumble out of sight,
Like a tall ship that floats above the foam
A little while, and then breaks utterly.

SONNET

The master and the slave go hand in hand,
Though touch be lost. The poet is a slave,
And there be kings do sorrowfully crave
The joyance that a scullion may command.
But, ah, the sonnet-slave must understand
The mission of his bondage, or the grave
May clasp his bones, or ever he shall save
The perfect word that is the poet's wand.

The sonnet is a crown, whereof the rhymes
Are for Thought's purest gold the jewel-stones;
But shapes and echoes that are never done
Will haunt the workshop, as regret sometimes
Will bring with human yearning to sad thrones
The crash of battles that are never won.

95

VERLAINE

Why do you dig like long-clawed scavengers
To touch the covered corpse of him that fled
The uplands for the fens, and rioted
Like a sick satyr with doom's worshippers?
Come! let the grass grow there; and leave his verse
To tell the story of the life he led.
Let the man go: let the dead flesh be dead,
And let the worms be its biographers.

Song sloughs away the sin to find redress
In art's complete remembrance: nothing clings
For long but laurel to the stricken brow
That felt the Muse's finger; nothing less
Than hell's fulfilment of the end of things
Can blot the star that shines on Paris now.

SONNET

When we can all so excellently give
The measure of love's wisdom with a blow,—
Why can we not in turn receive it so,
And end this murmur for the life we live?
And when we do so frantically strive
To win strange faith, why do we shun to know
That in love's elemental over-glow
God's wholeness gleams with light superlative?

Oh, brother men, if you have eyes at all,
Look at a branch, a bird, a child, a rose,
Or anything God ever made that grows,—
Nor let the smallest vision of it slip,
Till you may read, as on Belshazzar's wall,
The glory of eternal partnership.

96

THE CHORUS OF OLD MEN IN "ÆGEUS"

SUPREMACY

THERE is a drear and lonely tract of hell
From all the common gloom removed afar:
A flat, sad land it is, where shadows are,
Whose lorn estate my verse may never tell.
I walked among them and I knew them well:
Men I had slandered on life's little star
For churls and sluggards; and I knew the scar
Upon their brows of woe ineffable.

But as I went majestic on my way,
Into the dark they vanished, one by one,
Till, with a shaft of God's eternal day,
The dream of all my glory was undone,—
And, with a fool's importunate dismay,
I heard the dead men singing in the sun.

THE CHORUS OF OLD MEN IN "ÆGEUS"

YE gods that have a home beyond the world,
Ye that have eyes for all man's agony,
Ye that have seen this woe that we have seen,—
Look with a just regard,
And with an even grace,
Here on the shattered corpse of a shattered king,
Here on a suffering world where men grow old
And wander like sad shadows till, at last,
Out of the flare of life,
Out of the whirl of years,
Into the mist they go,
Into the mist of death.

97

O shades of you that loved him long before
The cruel threads of that black sail were spun,
May loyal arms and ancient welcomings
Receive him once again
Who now no longer moves
Here in this flickering dance of changing days,
Where a battle is lost and won for a withered wreath,
And the black master Death is over all
To chill with his approach,
To level with his touch,
The reigning strength of youth,
The fluttered heart of age.

Woe for the fateful day when Delphi's word was lost—
Woe for the loveless prince of Æthra's line!
Woe for a father's tears and the curse of a king's release—
Woe for the wings of pride and the shafts of doom!
And thou, the saddest wind
That ever blew from Crete,
Sing the fell tidings back to that thrice unhappy ship!—
Sing to the western flame,
Sing to the dying foam.
A dirge for the sundered years and a dirge for the years to be!

Better his end had been as the end of a cloudless day,
Bright, by the word of Zeus, with a golden star,
Wrought of a golden fame, and flung to the central sky,
To gleam on a stormless tomb for evermore:—
Whether or not there fell
To the touch of an alien hand
The sheen of his purple robe and the shine of his diadem,
Better his end had been
To die as an old man dies,—
But the fates are ever the fates, and a crown is ever a crown

THE WILDERNESS

Come away! come away! there's a frost along the marshes,
And a frozen wind that skims the shoal where it shakes the
dead black water;
There's a moan across the lowland and a wailing through the
woodland
Of a dirge that sings to send us back to the arms of those that
love us.
There is nothing left but ashes now where the crimson chills of
autumn
Put off the summer's languor with a touch that made us glad
For the glory that is gone from us, with a flight we cannot
follow,
To the slopes of other valleys and the sounds of other shores.

Come away! come away! you can hear them calling, calling,
Calling us to come to them, and roam no more.
Over there beyond the ridges and the land that lies between us,
There's an old song calling us to come!

Come away! come away!—for the scenes we leave behind us
Are barren for the lights of home and a flame that's young
forever;
And the lonely trees around us creak the warning of the night-
wind,
That love and all the dreams of love are away beyond the
mountains.
The songs that call for us to-night, they have called for men
before us,
And the winds that blow the message, they have blown ten
thousand years;
But this will end our wander-time, for we know the joy that
waits us
In the strangeness of home-coming, and a woman's waiting
eyes.

99

Come away! come away! there is nothing now to cheer us—
Nothing now to comfort us, but love's road home:—
Over there beyond the darkness there's a window gleams to
*   greet us,*
And a warm hearth waits for us within.

Come away! come away!—or the roving-fiend will hold us,
And make us all to dwell with him to the end of human faring:
There are no men yet may leave him when his hands are
    clutched upon them,
There are none will own his enmity, there are none will call him
    brother.
So we'll be up and on the way, and the less we boast the better
For the freedom that God gave us and the dread we do not
    know:—
The frost that skips the willow-leaf will again be back to
    blight it,
And the doom we cannot fly from is the doom we do not see.

Come away! come away! there are dead men all around us—
Frozen men that mock us with a wild, hard laugh
That shrieks and sinks and whimpers in the shrill November
*   rushes,*
And the long fall wind on the lake.

OCTAVES

I

We thrill too strangely at the master's touch;
We shrink too sadly from the larger self
Which for its own completeness agitates
And undetermines us; we do not feel—
We dare not feel it yet—the splendid shame
Of uncreated failure; we forget,

The while we groan, that God's accomplishment
Is always and unfailingly at hand.

II

TUMULTUOUSLY void of a clean scheme
Whereon to build, whereof to formulate,
The legion life that riots in mankind
Goes ever plunging upward, up and down,
Most like some crazy regiment at arms,
Undisciplined of aught but Ignorance,
And ever led resourcelessly along
To brainless carnage by drunk trumpeters.

III

To me the groaning of world-worshippers
Rings like a lonely music played in hell
By one with art enough to cleave the walls
Of heaven with his cadence, but without
The wisdom or the will to comprehend
The strangeness of his own perversity,
And all without the courage to deny
The profit and the pride of his defeat.

IV

WHILE we are drilled in error, we are lost
Alike to truth and usefulness. We think
We are great warriors now, and we can brag
Like Titans; but the world is growing young,
And we, the fools of time, are growing with it:—
We do not fight to-day, we only die;
We are too proud of death, and too ashamed
Of God, to know enough to be alive.

V

THERE is one battle-field whereon we fall
Triumphant and unconquered; but, alas!
We are too fleshly fearful of ourselves
To fight there till our days are whirled and blurred
By sorrow, and the ministering wheels
Of anguish take us eastward, where the clouds
Of human gloom are lost against the gleam
That shines on Thought's impenetrable mail.

VI

WHEN we shall hear no more the cradle-songs
Of ages—when the timeless hymns of Love
Defeat them and outsound them—we shall know
The rapture of that large release which all
Right science comprehends; and we shall read,
With unoppressed and unoffended eyes,
That record of All-Soul whereon God writes
In everlasting runes the truth of Him.

VII

THE guerdon of new childhood is repose:—
Once he has read the primer of right thought,
A man may claim between two smithy strokes
Beatitude enough to realize
God's parallel completeness in the vague
And incommensurable excellence
That equitably uncreates itself
And makes a whirlwind of the Universe.

VIII

THERE is no loneliness:—no matter where
We go, nor whence we come, nor what good friends

OCTAVES

Forsake us in the seeming, we are all
At one with a complete companionship;
And though forlornly joyless be the ways
We travel, the compensate spirit-gleams
Of Wisdom shaft the darkness here and there,
Like scattered lamps in unfrequented streets.

IX

WHEN one that you and I had all but sworn
To be the purest thing God ever made
Bewilders us until at last it seems
An angel has come back restigmatized,—
Faith wavers, and we wonder what there is
On earth to make us faithful any more,
But never are quite wise enough to know
The wisdom that is in that wonderment.

X

WHERE does a dead man go?—The dead man dies;
But the free life that would no longer feed
On fagots of outburned and shattered flesh
Wakes to a thrilled invisible advance,
Unchained (or fettered else) of memory;
And when the dead man goes it seems to me
'T were better for us all to do away
With weeping, and be glad that he is gone.

XI

STILL through the dusk of dead, blank-legended,
And unremunerative years we search
To get where life begins, and still we groan
Because we do not find the living spark

Where no spark ever was; and thus we die,
Still searching, like poor old astronomers
Who totter off to bed and go to sleep,
To dream of untriangulated stars.

XII

WITH conscious eyes not yet sincere enough
To pierce the glimmered cloud that fluctuates
Between me and the glorifying light
That screens itself with knowledge, I discern
The searching rays of wisdom that reach through
The mist of shame's infirm credulity,
And infinitely wonder if hard words
Like mine have any message for the dead.

XIII

I GRANT you friendship is a royal thing,
But none shall ever know that royalty
For what it is till he has realized
His best friend in himself. 'T is then, perforce,
That man's unfettered faith indemnifies
Of its own conscious freedom the old shame,
And love's revealed infinitude supplants
Of its own wealth and wisdom the old scorn.

XIV

THOUGH the sick beast infect us, we are fraught
Forever with indissoluble Truth,
Wherein redress reveals itself divine,
Transitional, transcendent. Grief and loss,
Disease and desolation, are the dreams
Of wasted excellence; and every dream

Has in it something of an ageless fact
That flouts deformity and laughs at years.

XV

WE lack the courage to be where we are:—
We love too much to travel on old roads,
To triumph on old fields; we love too much
To consecrate the magic of dead things,
And yieldingly to linger by long walls
Of ruin, where the ruinous moonlight
That sheds a lying glory on old stones
Befriends us with a wizard's enmity.

XVI

SOMETHING as one with eyes that look below
The battle-smoke to glimpse the foeman's charge,
We through the dust of downward years may scan
The onslaught that awaits this idiot world
Where blood pays blood for nothing, and where life
Pays life to madness, till at last the ports
Of gilded helplessness be battered through
By the still crash of salvatory steel.

XVII

To you that sit with Sorrow like chained slaves,
And wonder if the night will ever come,
I would say this: The night will never come,
And sorrow is not always. But my words
Are not enough; your eyes are not enough;
The soul itself must insulate the Real,
Or ever you do cherish in this life—
In this life or in any life—repose.

XVIII

LIKE a white wall whereon forever breaks
Unsatisfied the tumult of green seas,
Man's unconjectured godliness rebukes
With its imperial silence the lost waves
Of insufficient grief. This mortal surge
That beats against us now is nothing else
Than plangent ignorance. Truth neither shakes
Nor wavers; but the world shakes, and we shriek.

XIX

NOR jewelled phrase nor mere mellifluous rhyme
Reverberates aright, or ever shall,
One cadence of that infinite plain-song
Which is itself all music. Stronger notes
Than any that have ever touched the world
Must ring to tell it—ring like hammer-blows,
Right-echoed of a chime primordial,
On anvils, in the gleaming of God's forge.

XX

THE prophet of dead words defeats himself:
Whoever would acknowledge and include
The foregleam and the glory of the real,
Must work with something else than pen and ink
And painful preparation: he must work
With unseen implements that have no names,
And he must win withal, to do that work.
Good fortitude, clean wisdom, and strong skill.

XXI

To curse the chilled insistence of the dawn
Because the free gleam lingers; to defraud

TWO QUATRAINS

The constant opportunity that lives
Unchallenged in all sorrow; to forget
For this large prodigality of gold
That larger generosity of thought,—
These are the fleshly clogs of human greed,
The fundamental blunders of mankind.

XXII

FOREBODINGS are the fiends of Recreance;
The master of the moment, the clean seer
Of ages, too securely scans what is,
Ever to be appalled at what is not;
He sees beyond the groaning borough lines
Of Hell, God's highways gleaming, and he knows
That Love's complete communion is the end
Of anguish to the liberated man.

XXIII

HERE by the windy docks I stand alone,
But yet companioned. There the vessel goes,
And there my friend goes with it; but the wake
That melts and ebbs between that friend and me
Love's earnest is of Life's all-purposeful
And all-triumphant sailing, when the ships
Of Wisdom loose their fretful chains and swing
Forever from the crumbled wharves of Time.

TWO QUATRAINS

I

As eons of incalculable strife
Are in the vision of one moment caught,
So are the common, concrete things of life
Divinely shadowed on the walls of Thought.

II

WE shriek to live, but no man ever lives
Till he has rid the ghost of human breath;
We dream to die, but no man ever dies
Till he has quit the road that runs to death.

THE TORRENT

I FOUND a torrent falling in a glen
Where the sun's light shone silvered and leaf-split;
The boom, the foam, and the mad flash of it
All made a magic symphony; but when
I thought upon the coming of hard men
To cut those patriarchal trees away,
And turn to gold the silver of that spray,
I shuddered. Yet a gladness now and then
Did wake me to myself till I was glad
In earnest, and was welcoming the time
For screaming saws to sound above the chime
Of idle waters, and for me to know
The jealous visionings that I had had
Were steps to the great place where trees and torrents go.

L'ENVOI

Now in a thought, now in a shadowed word,
Now in a voice that thrills eternity,
Ever there comes an onward phrase to me
Of some transcendent music I have heard;
No piteous thing by soft hands dulcimered,
No trumpet crash of blood-sick victory,
But a glad strain of some vast harmony
That no brief mortal touch has ever stirred.

L'ENVOI

There is no music in the world like this,
No character wherewith to set it down,
No kind of instrument to make it sing.
No kind of instrument? Ah, yes, there is;
And after time and place are overthrown,
God's touch will keep its one chord quivering.

CAPTAIN CRAIG, ETC.

(1902)

To the Memory of
John Hays Gardiner

CAPTAIN CRAIG

I

I DOUBT if ten men in all Tilbury Town
Had ever shaken hands with Captain Craig,
Or called him by his name, or looked at him
So curiously, or so concernedly,
As they had looked at ashes; but a few—
Say five or six of us—had found somehow
The spark in him, and we had fanned it there,
Choked under, like a jest in Holy Writ,
By Tilbury prudence. He had lived his life
And in his way had shared, with all mankind,
Inveterate leave to fashion of himself,
By some resplendent metamorphosis,
Whatever he was not. And after time,
When it had come sufficiently to pass
That he was going patch-clad through the streets,
Weak, dizzy, chilled, and half starved, he had laid
Some nerveless fingers on a prudent sleeve,
And told the sleeve, in furtive confidence,
Just how it was: "My name is Captain Craig,"
He said, "and I must eat." The sleeve moved on,
And after it moved others—one or two;
For Captain Craig, before the day was done,
Got back to the scant refuge of his bed
And shivered into it without a curse—
Without a murmur even. He was cold,

And old, and hungry; but the worst of it
Was a forlorn familiar consciousness
That he had failed again. There was a time
When he had fancied, if worst came to worst,
And he could do no more, that he might ask
Of whom he would. But once had been enough,
And soon there would be nothing more to ask.
He was himself, and he had lost the speed
He started with, and he was left behind.
There was no mystery, no tragedy;
And if they found him lying on his back
Stone dead there some sharp morning, as they might,—
Well, once upon a time there was a man—
Es war einmal ein König, if it pleased him.
And he was right: there were no men to blame:
There was just a false note in the Tilbury tune—
A note that able-bodied men might sound
Hosannas on while Captain Craig lay quiet.
They might have made him sing by feeding him
Till he should march again, but probably
Such yielding would have jeopardized the rhythm;
They found it more melodious to shout
Right on, with unmolested adoration,
To keep the tune as it had always been,
To trust in God, and let the Captain starve.

He must have understood that afterwards—
When we had laid some fuel to the spark
Of him, and oxidized it—for he laughed
Out loud and long at us to feel it burn,
And then, for gratitude, made game of us:
"You are the resurrection and the life,"
He said, "and I the hymn the Brahmin sings;
O Fuscus! and we'll go no more a-roving."

114

CAPTAIN CRAIG

We were not quite accoutred for a blast
Of any lettered nonchalance like that,
And some of us—the five or six of us
Who found him out—were singularly struck.
But soon there came assurance of his lips,
Like phrases out of some sweet instrument
Man's hand had never fitted, that he felt
"No penitential shame for what had come,
No virtuous regret for what had been,—
But rather a joy to find it in his life
To be an outcast usher of the soul
For such as had good courage of the Sun
To pattern Love." The Captain had one chair;
And on the bottom of it, like a king,
For longer time than I dare chronicle,
Sat with an ancient ease and eulogized
His opportunity. My friends got out,
Like brokers out of Arcady; but I—
May be for fascination of the thing,
Or may be for the larger humor of it—
Stayed listening, unwearied and unstung.
When they were gone the Captain's tuneful ooze
Of rhetoric took on a change; he smiled
At me and then continued, earnestly:
"Your friends have had enough of it; but you,
For a motive hardly vindicated yet
By prudence or by conscience, have remained;
And that is very good, for I have things
To tell you: things that are not words alone—
Which are the ghosts of things—but something firmer.
"First, would I have you know, for every gift
Or sacrifice, there are—or there may be—
Two kinds of gratitude: the sudden kind
We feel for what we take, the larger kind
We feel for what we give. Once we have learned

As much as this, we know the truth has been
Told over to the world a thousand times;—
But we have had no ears to listen yet
For more than fragments of it: we have heard
A murmur now and then, an echo here
And there, and we have made great music of it;
And we have made innumerable books
To please the Unknown God. Time throws away
Dead thousands of them, but the God that knows
No death denies not one: the books all count,
The songs all count; and yet God's music has
No modes, his language has no adjectives."

"You may be right, you may be wrong," said I;
"But what has this that you are saying now—
This nineteenth-century Nirvana-talk—
To do with you and me?" The Captain raised
His hand and held it westward, where a patched
And unwashed attic-window filtered in
What barren light could reach us, and then said,
With a suave, complacent resonance: "There shines
The sun. Behold it. We go round and round,
And wisdom comes to us with every whirl
We count throughout the circuit. We may say
The child is born, the boy becomes a man,
The man does this and that, and the man goes,—
But having said it we have not said much,
Not very much. Do I fancy, or you think,
That it will be the end of anything
When I am gone? There was a soldier once
Who fought one fight and in that fight fell dead.
Sad friends went after, and they brought him home
And had a brass band at his funeral,
As you should have at mine; and after that
A few remembered him. But he was dead,

They said, and they should have their friend no more.—
However, there was once a starveling child—
A ragged-vested little incubus,
Born to be cuffed and frighted out of all
Capacity for childhood's happiness—
Who started out one day, quite suddenly,
To drown himself. He ran away from home,
Across the clover-fields and through the woods,
And waited on a rock above a stream,
Just like a kingfisher. He might have dived,
Or jumped, or he might not; but anyhow,
There came along a man who looked at him
With such an unexpected friendliness,
And talked with him in such a common way,
That life grew marvelously different:
What he had lately known for sullen trunks
And branches, and a world of tedious leaves,
Was all transmuted; a faint forest wind
That once had made the loneliest of all
Sad sounds on earth, made now the rarest music;
And water that had called him once to death
Now seemed a flowing glory. And that man,
Born to go down a soldier, did this thing.
Not much to do? Not very much, I grant you:
Good occupation for a sonneteer,
Or for a clown, or for a clergyman,
But small work for a soldier. By the way,
When you are weary sometimes of your own
Utility, I wonder if you find
Occasional great comfort pondering
What power a man has in him to put forth?
'Of all the many marvelous things that are,
Nothing is there more marvelous than man,'
Said Sophocles; and he lived long ago;
'And earth, unending ancient of the gods

117

He furrows; and the ploughs go back and forth,
Turning the broken mould, year after year.' . . .

"I turned a little furrow of my own
Once on a time, and everybody laughed—
As I laughed afterwards; and I doubt not
The First Intelligence, which we have drawn
In our competitive humility
As if it went forever on two legs,
Had some diversion of it: I believe
God's humor is the music of the spheres—
But even as we draft omnipotence
Itself to our own image, we pervert
The courage of an infinite ideal
To finite resignation. You have made
The cement of your churches out of tears
And ashes, and the fabric will not stand:
The shifted walls that you have coaxed and shored
So long with unavailing compromise
Will crumble down to dust and blow away,
And younger dust will follow after them;
Though not the faintest or the farthest whirled
First atom of the least that ever flew
Shall be by man defrauded of the touch
God thrilled it with to make a dream for man
When Science was unborn. And after time,
When we have earned our spiritual ears,
And art's commiseration of the truth
No longer glorifies the singing beast,
Or venerates the clinquant charlatan,—
Then shall at last come ringing through the sun,
Through time, through flesh, a music that is true.
For wisdom is that music, and all joy
That wisdom:—you may counterfeit, you think,
The burden of it in a thousand ways;

But as the bitterness that loads your tears
Makes Dead Sea swimming easy, so the gloom,
The penance, and the woeful pride you keep,
Make bitterness your buoyance of the world.
And at the fairest and the frenziedest
Alike of your God-fearing festivals,
You so compound the truth to pamper fear
That in the doubtful surfeit of your faith
You clamor for the food that shadows eat.
You call it rapture or deliverance,—
Passion or exaltation, or what most
The moment needs, but your faint-heartedness
Lives in it yet: you quiver and you clutch
For something larger, something unfulfilled,
Some wiser kind of joy that you shall have
Never, until you learn to laugh with God."
And with a calm Socratic patronage,
At once half sombre and half humorous,
The Captain reverently twirled his thumbs
And fixed his eyes on something far away;
Then, with a gradual gaze, conclusive, shrewd,
And at the moment unendurable
For sheer beneficence, he looked at me.

"But the brass band?" I said, not quite at ease
With altruism yet.—He made a sort
Of reminiscent little inward noise,
Midway between a chuckle and a laugh,
And that was all his answer: not a word
Of explanation or suggestion came
From those tight-smiling lips. And when I left,
I wondered, as I trod the creaking snow
And had the world-wide air to breathe again,—
Though I had seen the tremor of his mouth
And honored the endurance of his hand—

Whether or not, securely closeted
Up there in the stived haven of his den,
The man sat laughing at me; and I felt
My teeth grind hard together with a quaint
Revulsion—as I recognize it now—
Not only for my Captain, but as well
For every smug-faced failure on God's earth;
Albeit I could swear, at the same time,
That there were tears in the old fellow's eyes.
I question if in tremors or in tears
There be more guidance to man's worthiness
Than—well, say in his prayers. But oftentimes
It humors us to think that we possess
By some divine adjustment of our own
Particular shrewd cells, or something else,
What others, for untutored sympathy,
Go spirit-fishing more than half their lives
To catch—like cheerful sinners to catch faith;
And I have not a doubt but I assumed
Some egotistic attribute like this
When, cautiously, next morning I reduced
The fretful qualms of my novitiate,
For most part, to an undigested pride.
Only, I live convinced that I regret
This enterprise no more than I regret
My life; and I am glad that I was born.

That evening, at "The Chrysalis," I found
The faces of my comrades all suffused
With what I chose then to denominate
Superfluous good feeling. In return,
They loaded me with titles of odd form
And unexemplified significance,
Like "Bellows-mender to Prince Æolus,"

CAPTAIN CRAIG

"Pipe-filler to the Hoboscholiast,"
"Bread-fruit for the Non-Doing," with one more
That I remember, and a dozen more
That I forget. I may have been disturbed,
I do not say that I was not annoyed,
But something of the same serenity
That fortified me later made me feel
For their skin-pricking arrows not so much
Of pain as of a vigorous defect
In this world's archery. I might have tried,
With a flat facetiousness, to demonstrate
What they had only snapped at and thereby
Made out of my best evidence no more
Than comfortable food for their conceit;
But patient wisdom frowned on argument,
With a side nod for silence, and I smoked
A series of incurable dry pipes
While Morgan fiddled, with obnoxious care,
Things that I wished he wouldn't. Killigrew,
Drowsed with a fond abstraction, like an ass,
Lay blinking at me while he grinned and made
Remarks. The learned Plunket made remarks.

It may have been for smoke that I cursed cats
That night, but I have rather to believe
As I lay turning, twisting, listening,
And wondering, between great sleepless yawns,
What possible satisfaction those dead leaves
Could find in sending shadows to my room
And swinging them like black rags on a line,
That I, with a forlorn clear-headedness
Was ekeing out probation. I had sinned
In fearing to believe what I believed,
And I was paying for it.—Whimsical,
You think,—factitious; but "there is no luck,

No fate, no fortune for us, but the old
Unswerving and inviolable price
Gets paid: God sells himself eternally,
But never gives a crust," my friend had said;
And while I watched those leaves, and heard those cats,
And with half mad minuteness analyzed
The Captain's attitude and then my own,
I felt at length as one who throws himself
Down restless on a couch when clouds are dark,
And shuts his eyes to find, when he wakes up
And opens them again, what seems at first
An unfamiliar sunlight in his room
And in his life—as if the child in him
Had laughed and let him see; and then I knew
Some prowling superfluity of child
In me had found the child in Captain Craig
And let the sunlight reach him. While I slept,
My thought reshaped itself to friendly dreams,
And in the morning it was with me still.

Through March and shifting April to the time
When winter first becomes a memory
My friend the Captain—to my other friend's
Incredulous regret that such as he
Should ever get the talons of his talk
So fixed in my unfledged credulity—
Kept up the peroration of his life,
Not yielding at a threshold, nor, I think,
Too often on the stairs. He made me laugh
Sometimes, and then again he made me weep
Almost; for I had insufficiency
Enough in me to make me know the truth
Within the jest, and I could feel it there
As well as if it were the folded note
I felt between my fingers. I had said

CAPTAIN CRAIG

Before that I should have to go away
And leave him for the season; and his eyes
Had shone with well-becoming interest
At that intelligence. There was no mist
In them that I remember; but I marked
An unmistakable self-questioning
And a reticence of unassumed regret.
The two together made anxiety—
Not selfishness, I ventured. I should see
No more of him for six or seven months,
And I was there to tell him as I might
What humorous provision we had made
For keeping him locked up in Tilbury Town.
That finished—with a few more commonplace
Prosaics on the certified event
Of my return to find him young again—
I left him neither vexed, I thought, with us,
Nor over much at odds with destiny.
At any rate, save always for a look
That I had seen too often to mistake
Or to forget, he gave no other sign.

That train began to move; and as it moved,
I felt a comfortable sudden change
All over and inside. Partly it seemed
As if the strings of me had all at once
Gone down a tone or two; and even though
It made me scowl to think so trivial
A touch had owned the strength to tighten them,
It made me laugh to think that I was free.
But free from what—when I began to turn
The question round—was more than I could say:
I was no longer vexed with Killigrew,
Nor more was I possessed with Captain Craig;
But I was eased of some restraint, I thought,

123

Not qualified by those amenities,
And I should have to search the matter down;
For I was young, and I was very keen.
So I began to smoke a bad cigar
That Plunket, in his love, had given me
The night before; and as I smoked I watched
The flying mirrors for a mile or so,
Till to the changing glimpse, now sharp, now faint,
They gave me of the woodland over west,
A gleam of long-forgotten strenuous years
Came back, when we were Red Men on the trail,
With Morgan for the big chief Wocky-Bocky;
And yawning out of that I set myself
To face again the loud monotonous ride
That lay before me like a vista drawn
Of bag-racks to the fabled end of things.

II

YET that ride had an end, as all rides have;
And the days coming after took the road
That all days take,—though never one of them
Went by but I got some good thought of it
For Captain Craig. Not that I pitied him,
Or nursed a mordant hunger for his presence;
But what I thought (what Killigrew still thinks)
An irremediable cheerfulness
Was in him and about the name of him,
And I fancy that it may be most of all
For cheer in them that I have saved his letters.
I like to think of him, and how he looked—
Or should have looked—in his renewed estate,
Composing them. They may be dreariness
Unspeakable to you that never saw
The Captain; but to five or six of us

CAPTAIN CRAIG

Who knew him they are not so bad as that.
It may be we have smiled not always where
The text itself would seem to indicate
Responsive titillation on our part,—
Yet having smiled at all we have done well,
Knowing that we have touched the ghost of him.
He tells me that he thinks of nothing now
That he would rather do than be himself,
Wisely alive. So let us heed this man:—

"The world that has been old is young again.
The touch that faltered clings; and this is May.
So think of your decrepit pensioner
As one who cherishes the living light,
Forgetful of dead shadows. He may gloat,
And he may not have power in his arms
To make the young world move; but he has eyes
And ears, and he can read the sun. Therefore
Think first of him as one who vegetates
In tune with all the children who laugh best
And longest through the sunshine, though far off
Their laughter, and unheard; for 't is the child,
O friend, that with his laugh redeems the man.
Time steals the infant, but the child he leaves;
And we, we fighters over of old wars—
We men, we shearers of the Golden Fleece—
Were brutes without him,—brutes to tear the scars
Of one another's wounds and weep in them,
And then cry out on God that he should flaunt
For life such anguish and flesh-wretchedness.
But let the brute go roaring his own way:
We do not need him, and he loves us not.

"I cannot think of anything to-day
That I would rather do than be myself,

Primevally alive, and have the sun
Shine into me; for on a day like this,
When chaff-parts of a man's adversities
Are blown by quick spring breezes out of him—
When even a flicker of wind that wakes no more
Than a tuft of grass, or a few young yellow leaves,
Comes like the falling of a prophet's breath
On altar-flames rekindled of crushed embers,—
Then do I feel, now do I feel, within me
No dreariness, no grief, no discontent,
No twinge of human envy. But I beg
That you forego credentials of the past
For these illuminations of the present,
Or better still, to give the shadow justice,
You let me tell you something: I have yearned
In many another season for these days,
And having them with God's own pageantry
To make me glad for them,—yes, I have cursed
The sunlight and the breezes and the leaves
To think of men on stretchers or on beds,
Or on foul floors, things without shapes or names,
Made human with paralysis and rags;
Or some poor devil on a battle-field,
Left undiscovered and without the strength
To drag a maggot from his clotted mouth;
Or women working where a man would fall—
Flat-breasted miracles of cheerfulness
Made neuter by the work that no man counts
Until it waits undone; children thrown out
To feed their veins and souls on offal . . . Yes,
I have had half a mind to blow my brains out
Sometimes; and I have gone from door to door,
Ragged myself, trying to do something—
Crazy, I hope.—But what has this to do
With Spring? Because one half of humankind

Lives here in hell, shall not the other half
Do any more than just for conscience' sake
Be miserable? Is this the way for us
To lead these creatures up to find the light,—
Or to be drawn down surely to the dark
Again? Which is it? What does the child say?

"But let us not make riot for the child
Untaught, nor let us hold that we may read
The sun but through the shadows; nor, again,
Be we forgetful ever that we keep
The shadows on their side. For evidence,
I might go back a little to the days
When I had hounds and credit, and grave friends
To borrow my books and set wet glasses on them,
And other friends of all sorts, grave and gay,
Of whom one woman and one man stand out
From all the rest, this morning. The man said
One day, as we were riding, 'Now, you see,
There goes a woman cursed with happiness:
Beauty and wealth, health, horses,—everything
That she could ask, or we could ask, is hers,
Except an inward eye for the dim fact
Of what this dark world is. The cleverness
God gave her—or the devil—cautions her
That she must keep the china cup of life
Filled somehow, and she fills it—runs it over—
Claps her white hands while some one does the sopping
With fingers made, she thinks, for just that purpose,
Giggles and eats and reads and goes to church,
Makes pretty little penitential prayers,
And has an eighteen-carat crucifix
Wrapped up in chamois-skin. She gives enough,
You say; but what is giving like hers worth?

What is a gift without the soul to guide it?
"Poor dears, and they have cancers?—Oh!" she says;
And away she works at that new altar-cloth
For the Reverend Hieronymus Mackintosh—
Third person, Jerry. "Jerry," she says, "can say
Such lovely things, and make life seem so sweet!"
Jerry can drink, also.—And there she goes,
Like a whirlwind through an orchard in the springtime—
Throwing herself away as if she thought
The world and the whole planetary circus
Were a flourish of apple-blossoms. Look at her!
And here is this infernal world of ours—
And hers, if only she might find it out—
Starving and shrieking, sickening, suppurating,
Whirling to God knows where . . . But look at her!'

"And after that it came about somehow,
Almost as if the Fates were killing time,
That she, the spendthrift of a thousand joys,
Rode in her turn with me, and in her turn
Made observations: 'Now there goes a man,'
She said, 'who feeds his very soul on poison:
No matter what he does, or where he looks,
He finds unhappiness; or, if he fails
To find it, he creates it, and then hugs it:
Pygmalion again for all the world—
Pygmalion gone wrong. You know I think
If when that precious animal was young,
His mother, or some watchful aunt of his,
Had spanked him with *Pendennis* and *Don Juan*,
And given him the *Lady of the Lake*,
Or *Cord and Creese,* or almost anything,
There might have been a tonic for him? Listen:
When he was possibly nineteen years old

CAPTAIN CRAIG

He came to me and said, "I understand
You are in love"—yes, that is what he said,—
"But never mind, it won't last very long;
It never does; we all get over it.
We have this clinging nature, for you see
The Great Bear shook himself once on a time
And the world is one of many that let go."
And yet the creature lives, and there you see him·
And he would have this life no fairer thing
Than a certain time for numerous marionettes
To do the Dance of Death. Give him a rose,
And he will tell you it is very sweet,
But only for a day. Most wonderful!
Show him a child, or anything that laughs,
And he begins at once to crunch his wormwood
And then runs on with his "realities."
What does he know about realities,
Who sees the truth of things almost as well
As Nero saw the Northern Lights? Good gracious!
Can't you do something with him? Call him something—
Call him a type, and that will make him cry:
One of those not at all unusual,
Prophetic, would-be-Delphic manger-snappers
That always get replaced when they are gone;
Or one of those impenetrable men,
Who seem to carry branded on their foreheads,
"We are abstruse, but not quite so abstruse
As possibly the good Lord may have wished;"
One of those men who never quite confess
That Washington was great;—the kind of man
That everybody knows and always will,—
Shrewd, critical, facetious, insincere,
And for the most part harmless, I'm afraid.
But even then, you might be doing well
To tell him something.'—And I said I would.

"So in one afternoon you see we have
The child in absence—or, to say the least,
In ominous defect,—and in excess
Commensurate, likewise. Now the question is,
Not which was right and which was wrong, for each,
By virtue of one-sidedness, was both;
But rather—to my mind, as heretofore—
Is it better to be blinded by the lights,
Or by the shadows? By the lights, you say?
The shadows are all devils, and the lights
Gleam guiding and eternal? Very good;
But while you say so do not quite forget
That sunshine has a devil of its own,
And one that we, for the great craft of him,
But vaguely recognize. The marvel is
That this persuasive and especial devil,
By grace of his extreme transparency,
Precludes all common vision of him; yet
There is one way to glimpse him and a way,
As I believe, to test him,—granted once
That we have ousted prejudice, which means
That we have made magnanimous advance
Through self-acquaintance. Not an easy thing
For some of us; impossible, may be,
For most of us: the woman and the man
I cited, for example, would have wrought
The most intractable conglomerate
Of everything, if they had set themselves
To analyze themselves and not each other;
If only for the sake of self-respect.
They would have come to no place but the same
Wherefrom they started; one would have lived awhile
In paradise without defending it,
And one in hell without enjoying it;
And each had been dissuaded neither more

Nor less thereafter. There are such on earth
As might have been composed primarily
For mortal warning: he was one of them,
And she—the devil makes us hesitate.
'T is easy to read words writ well with ink
That makes a good black mark on smooth white paper;
But words are done sometimes with other ink
Whereof the smooth white paper gives no sign
Till science brings it out; and here we come
To knowledge, and the way to test a devil.

"To most of us, you say, and you say well,
This demon of the sunlight is a stranger;
But if you break the sunlight of yourself,
Project it, and observe the quaint shades of it,
I have a shrewd suspicion you may find
That even as a name lives unrevealed
In ink that waits an agent, so it is
The devil—or this devil—hides himself
To all the diagnoses we have made
Save one. The quest of him is hard enough—
As hard as truth; but once we seem to know
That his compound obsequiousness prevails
Unferreted within us, we may find
That sympathy, which aureoles itself
To superfluity from you and me,
May stand against the soul for five or six
Persistent and indubitable streaks
Of irritating brilliance, out of which
A man may read, if he have knowledge in him,
Proportionate attest of ignorance,
Hypocrisy, good-heartedness, conceit,
Indifference,—by which a man may learn
That even courage may not make him glad
For laughter when that laughter is itself

The tribute of recriminating groans.
Nor are the shapes of obsolescent creeds
Much longer to flit near enough to make
Men glad for living in a world like this;
For wisdom, courage, knowledge, and the faith
Which has the soul and is the soul of reason—
These are the world's achievers. And the child—
The child that is the saviour of all ages,
The prophet and the poet, the crown-bearer,
Must yet with Love's unhonored fortitude,
Survive to cherish and attain for us
The candor and the generosity,
By leave of which we smile if we bring back
The first revealing flash that wakened us
When wisdom like a shaft of dungeon-light
Came searching down to find us.

"Halfway back

I made a mild allusion to the Fates,
Not knowing then that ever I should have
Dream-visions of them, painted on the air,—
Clotho, Lachesis, Atropos. Faint-hued
They seem, but with a faintness never fading,
Unblurred by gloom, unshattered by the sun,
Still with eternal color, colorless,
They move and they remain. The while I write
These very words I see them,—Atropos,
Lachesis, Clotho; and the last is laughing.
When Clotho laughs, Atropos rattles her shears;
But Clotho keeps on laughing just the same.
Some time when I have dreamed that Atropos
Has laughed, I'll tell you how the colors change—
The colors that are changeless, colorless."

CAPTAIN CRAIG

I fear I may have answered Captain Craig's
Epistle Number One with what he chose,
Good-humoredly but anxiously, to take
For something that was not all reverence;
From Number Two it would have seemed almost
As if the flanges of the old man's faith
Had slipped the treacherous rails of my allegiance,
Leaving him by the roadside, humorously
Upset, with nothing more convivial
To do than be facetious and austere:—

"If you decry *Don César de Bazan,*
There is an imperfection in your vitals.
Flamboyant and old-fashioned? Overdone?
Romantico-robustious?—Dear young man,
There are fifteen thousand ways to be one-sided,
And I have indicated two of them
Already. Now you bait me with a third—
As if it were a spider with nine legs;
But what it is that you would have me do,
What fatherly wrath you most anticipate,
I lack the needed impulse to discern;
Though I who shape no songs of any sort,
I who have made no music, thrilled no canvas,—
I who have added nothing to the world
The world would reckon save long-squandered wit—
Might with half-pardonable reverence
Beguile my faith, maybe, to the forlorn
Extent of some sequestered murmuring
Anent the vanities. No doubt I should,
If mine were the one life that I have lived;
But with a few good glimpses I have had
Of heaven through the little holes in hell,
I can half understand what price it is
The poet pays, at one time and another,

133

For those indemnifying interludes
That are to be the kernel in what lives
To shrine him when the new-born men come singing

"So do I comprehend what I have read
From even the squeezed items of account
Which I have to my credit in that book
Whereof the leaves are ages and the text
Eternity. What do I care to-day
For pages that have nothing? I have lived,
And I have died, and I have lived again;
And I am very comfortable. Yes,
Though I look back through barren years enough
To make me seem—as I transmute myself
In downward retrospect from what I am—
As unproductive and as unconvinced
Of living bread and the soul's eternal draught
As a frog on a Passover-cake in a streamless desert,—
Still do I trust the light that I have earned,
And having earned, received. You shake your head,
But do not say that you will shake it off.

"Meanwhile I have the flowers and the grass,
My brothers here the trees, and all July
To make me joyous. Why do you shake your head?
Why do you laugh?—because you are so young?
Do you think if you laugh hard enough the truth
Will go to sleep? Do you think of any couch
Made soft enough to put the truth to sleep?
Do you think there are no proper comedies
But yours that have the fashion? For example,
Do you think that I forget, or shall forget,
One friendless, fat, fantastic nondescript
Who knew the ways of laughter on low roads,—
A vagabond, a drunkard, and a sponge,

134

CAPTAIN CRAIG

But always a free creature with a soul?
I bring him back, though not without misgivings,
And caution you to damn him sparingly.

"Count Pretzel von Würzburger, the Obscene
(The beggar may have had another name,
But no man to my knowledge ever knew it)
Was a poet and a skeptic and a critic,
And in his own mad manner a musician:
He found an old piano in a bar-room,
And it was his career—three nights a week,
From ten o'clock till twelve—to make it rattle;
And then, when I was just far down enough
To sit and watch him with his long straight hair,
And pity him, and think he looked like Liszt,
I might have glorified a musical
Steam-engine, or a xylophone. The Count
Played half of everything and 'improvised'
The rest: he told me once that he was born
With a genius in him that 'prohibited
Complete fidelity,' and that his art
'Confessed vagaries,' therefore. But I made
Kind reckoning of his vagaries then:
I had the whole great pathos of the man
To purify me, and all sorts of music
To give me spiritual nourishment
And cerebral athletics; for the Count
Played indiscriminately—with an *f,*
And with incurable presto—cradle-songs
And carnivals, spring-songs and funeral marches,
The Marseillaise and Schubert's Serenade—
And always in a way to make me think
Procrustes had the germ of music in him.
And when this interesting reprobate
Began to talk—then there were more vagaries:

135

He made a reeking fetich of all filth,
Apparently; but there was yet revealed
About him, through his words and on his flesh,
That ostracizing nimbus of a soul's
Abject, apologetic purity—
That phosphorescence of sincerity—
Which indicates the curse and the salvation
Of a life wherein starved art may never perish.

"One evening I remember clearliest
Of all that I passed with him. Having wrought,
With his nerve-ploughing ingenuity,
The *Träumerei* into a Titan's nightmare,
The man sat down across the table from me
And all at once was ominously decent.
' "The more we measure what is ours to use," '
He said then, wiping his froth-plastered mouth
With the inside of his hand, ' "the less we groan
For what the gods refuse." I've had that sleeved
A decade for you. Now but one more stein,
And I shall be prevailed upon to read
The only sonnet I have ever made;
And after that, if you propitiate
Gambrinus, I shall play you that Andante
As the world has never heard it played before.'
So saying, he produced a piece of paper,
Unfolded it, and read, 'SONNET UNIQUE
DE PRETZEL VON WURZBURGER, DIT L'OBSCÉNE:—

" 'Carmichael had a kind of joke-disease,
And he had queer things fastened on his wall.
There are three green china frogs that I recall
More potently than anything, for these
Three frogs have demonstrated, by degrees,
What curse was on the man to make him fall:

136

CAPTAIN CRAIG

'They are not ordinary frogs at all,
They are the Frogs of Aristophanes."

" 'God! how he laughed whenever he said that;
And how we caught from one another's eyes
The flash of what a tongue could never tell!
We always laughed at him, no matter what
The joke was worth. But when a man's brain dies,
We are not always glad . . . Poor Carmichael!'

" 'I am a sowbug and a necrophile,'
Said Pretzel, 'and the gods are growing old;
The stars are singing *Golden hair to gray,*
Green leaf to yellow leaf,—or chlorophyl
To xanthophyl, to be more scientific,—
So speed me one more stein. You may believe
That I'm a mendicant, but I am not:
For though it look to you that I go begging,
The truth is I go giving—giving all
My strength and all my personality,
My wisdom and experience—all myself,
To make it final—for your preservation;
Though I be not the one thing or the other,
Though I strike between the sunset and the dawn,
Though I be cliff-rubbed wreckage on the shoals
Of Circumstance,—doubt not that I comprise,
Far more than my appearance. Here he comes;
Now drink to good old Pretzel! Drink down Pretzel!
Quousque tandem, Pretzel, and O Lord,
How long! But let regret go hang: the good
Die first, and of the poor did many cease
To be. Beethoven after Wordsworth. *Prosit!*
There were geniuses among the trilobites,
And I suspect that I was one of them.'

"How much of him was earnest and how much
Fantastic, I know not; nor do I need
Profounder knowledge to exonerate
The squalor or the folly of a man
Than consciousness—though even the crude laugh
Of indigent Priapus follow it—
That I get good of him. And if you like him,
Then some time in the future, past a doubt,
You'll have him in a book, make metres of him,—
To the great delight of Mr. Killigrew,
And the grief of all your kinsmen. Christian shame
And self-confuted Orientalism
For the more sagacious of them; vulture-tracks
Of my Promethean bile for the rest of them;
And that will be a joke. There's nothing quite
So funny as a joke that's lost on earth
And laughed at by the gods. Your devil knows it.

"I come to like your Mr. Killigrew,
And I rejoice that you speak well of him.
The sprouts of human blossoming are in him,
And useful eyes—if he will open them;
But one thing ails the man. He smiles too much.
He comes to see me once or twice a week,
And I must tell him that he smiles too much.
If I were Socrates, it would be simple."

———

Epistle Number Three was longer coming.
I waited for it, even worried for it—
Though Killigrew, and of his own free will,
Had written reassuring little scraps
From time to time, and I had valued them
The more for being his. "The Sage," he said.

138

"From all that I can see, is doing well—
I should say very well. Three meals a day,
Siestas, and innumerable pipes—
Not to the tune of water on the stones,
But rather to the tune of his own Ego,
Which seems to be about the same as God.
But I was always weak in metaphysics,
And pray therefore that you be lenient.
I'm going to be married in December,
And I have made a poem that will scan—
So Plunket says. You said the other wouldn't:

> "*Augustus Plunket, Ph.D.,*
>   *And oh, the Bishop's daughter;*
> *A very learned man was he*
>   *And in twelve weeks he got her;*

> *And oh, she was as fair to see*
> *As pippins on the pippin tree . . .*
> *Tu, tui, tibi, te,—chubs in the mill water.*

"Connotative, succinct, and erudite;
Three dots to boot. Now goodman Killigrew
May wind an epic one of these glad years,
And after that who knoweth but the Lord—
The Lord of Hosts who is the King of Glory?"

Still, when the Captain's own words were before me
I seemed to read from them, or into them,
The protest of a mortuary joy
Not all substantiating Killigrew's
Off-hand assurance. The man's face came back
The while I read them, and that look again,
Which I had seen so often, came back with it.

I do not know that I can say just why,
But I felt the feathery touch of something wrong:—

"Since last I wrote—and I fear weeks have gone
Too far for me to leave my gratitude
Unuttered for its own acknowledgment—
I have won, without the magic of Amphion
Without the songs of Orpheus or Apollo,
The frank regard—and with it, if you like,
The fledged respect—of three quick-footed friends.
('Nothing is there more marvelous than man,'
Said Sophocles; and I say after him:
'He traps and captures, all-inventive one,
The light birds and the creatures of the wold,
And in his nets the fishes of the sea.')
Once they were pictures, painted on the air,
Faint with eternal color, colorless,—
But now they are not pictures, they are fowls.

"At first they stood aloof and cocked their small,
Smooth, prudent heads at me and made as if,
With a cryptic idiotic melancholy,
To look authoritative and sagacious;
But when I tossed a piece of apple to them,
They scattered back with a discord of short squawks
And then came forward with a craftiness
That made me think of Eden. Atropos
Came first, and having grabbed the morsel up,
Ran flapping far away and out of sight,
With Clotho and Lachesis hard after her;
But finally the three fared all alike,
And next day I persuaded them with corn.
In a week they came and had it from my fingers
And looked up at me while I pinched their bills
And made them sneeze. Count Pretzel's Carmichael

Had said they were not ordinary birds
At all,—and they are not: they are the Fates,
Foredoomed of their own insufficiency
To be assimilated.—Do not think,
Because in my contented isolation
It suits me at this time to be jocose,
That I am nailing reason to the cross,
Or that I set the bauble and the bells
Above the crucible; for I do nought,
Say nought, but with an ancient levity
That is the forbear of all earnestness.

"The cross, I said.—I had a dream last night:
A dream not like to any other dream
That I remember. I was all alone,
Sitting as I do now beneath a tree,
But looking not, as I am looking now,
Against the sunlight. There was neither sun
Nor moon, nor do I think of any stars;
Yet there was light, and there were cedar trees,
And there were sycamores. I lay at rest,
Or should have seemed at rest, within a trough
Between two giant roots. A weariness
Was on me, and I would have gone to sleep,
But I had not the courage. If I slept,
I feared that I should never wake again;
And if I did not sleep I should go mad,
And with my own dull tools, which I had used
With wretched skill so long, hack out my life.
And while I lay there, tortured out of death,
Faint waves of cold, as if the dead were breathing,
Came over me and through me; and I felt
Quick fearful tears of anguish on my face
And in my throat. But soon, and in the distance,
Concealed, importunate, there was a sound

Of coming steps,—and I was not afraid;
No, I was not afraid then, I was glad;
For I could feel, with every thought, the Man,
The Mystery, the Child, a footfall nearer.
Then, when he stood before me, there was no
Surprise, there was no questioning: I knew him,
As I had known him always; and he smiled.
'Why are you here?' he asked; and reaching down,
He took up my dull blades and rubbed his thumb
Across the edges of them and then smiled
Once more.—'I was a carpenter,' I said,
'But there was nothing in the world to do.'—
'Nothing?' said he.—'No, nothing,' I replied.—
'But are you sure,' he asked, 'that you have skill?
And are you sure that you have learned your trade?
No, you are not.'—He looked at me and laughed
As he said that; but I did not laugh then,
Although I might have laughed.—'They are dull,' said he;
'They were not very sharp if they were ground;
But they are what you have, and they will earn
What you have not. So take them as they are,
Grind them and clean them, put new handles to them,
And then go learn your trade in Nazareth.
Only be sure that you find Nazareth'—
'But if I starve—what then?' said I.—He smiled.

"Now I call that as curious a dream
As ever Meleager's mother had,—
Æneas, Alcibiades, or Jacob.
I'll not except the scientist who dreamed
That he was Adam and that he was Eve
At the same time; or yet that other man
Who dreamed that he was Æschylus, reborn
To clutch, combine, compensate, and adjust
The plunging and unfathomable chorus

Wherein we catch, like a bacchanale through thunder,
The chanting of the new Eumenides,
Implacable, renascent, farcical,
Triumphant, and American. He did it,
But did it in a dream. When he awoke
One phrase of it remained; one verse of it
Went singing through the remnant of his life
Like a bag-pipe through a mad-house.—He died young,
And if I ponder the small history
That I have gleaned of him by scattered roads,
The more do I rejoice that he died young.
That measure would have chased him all his days,
Defeated him, deposed him, wasted him,
And shrewdly ruined him—though in that ruin
There would have lived, as always it has lived,
In ruin as in failure, the supreme
Fulfilment unexpressed, the rhythm of God
That beats unheard through songs of shattered men
Who dream but cannot sound it.—He declined,
From all that I have ever learned of him,
With absolute good-humor. No complaint,
No groaning at the burden which is light,
No brain-waste of impatience—'Never mind,'
He whispered, 'for I might have written Odes.'

"Speaking of odes now makes me think of ballads.
Your admirable Mr. Killigrew
Has latterly committed what he calls
A Ballad of London—London 'Town,' of course—
And he has wished that I pass judgment on it.
He says there is a 'generosity'
About it, and a 'sympathetic insight;'
And there are strong lines in it, so he says.
But who am I that he should make of me
A judge? You are his friend, and you know best

The measure of his jingle. I am old,
And you are young. Be sure, I may go back
To squeak for you the tunes of yesterday
On my old fiddle—or what's left of it—
And give you as I'm able a young sound;
But all the while I do it I remain
One of Apollo's pensioners (and yours),
An usher in the Palace of the Sun,
A candidate for mattocks and trombones
(The brass-band will be indispensable),
A patron of high science, but no critic.
So I shall have to tell him, I suppose,
That I read nothing now but Wordsworth, Pope,
Lucretius, Robert Burns, and William Shakespeare.
Now this is Mr. Killigrew's performance:

" 'Say, do you go to London Town,
    You with the golden feather?'—
'And if I go to London Town
    With my golden feather?'—
'These autumn roads are bright and brown,
The season wears a russet crown;
And if you go to London Town,
    We'll go down together.'

"I cannot say for certain, but I think
The brown bright nightingale was half assuaged
Before your Mr. Killigrew was born.
If I have erred in my chronology,
No matter,—for the feathered man sings now:

" 'Yes, I go to London Town'
    (Merrily waved the feather),
'And if you go to London Town,
    Yes, we'll go together.'

So in the autumn bright and brown,
Just as the year began to frown,
All the way to London Town
 Rode the two together.

"*'I go to marry a fair maid'*
 (Lightly swung the feather)—
'Pardie, a true and loyal maid'
 (Oh, the swinging feather!)—
'For us the wedding gold is weighed,
For us the feast will soon be laid;
We'll make a gallant show,' he said,—
 'She and I together.'

"The feathered man may do a thousand things,
And all go smiling; but the feathered man
May do too much. Now mark how he continues:

"*'And you—you go to London Town?'*
 (Breezes waved the feather)—
'Yes, I go to London Town.'
 (Ah, the stinging feather!)—
'Why do you go, my merry blade?
Like me, to marry a fair maid?'—
'Why do I go? . . . God knows,' he said;
 And on they rode together.

"Now you have read·it through, and you know best
What worth it has. We fellows with gray hair
Who march with sticks to music that is gray
Judge not your vanguard fifing. You are one
To judge; and you will tell me what you think.
Barring the Town, the Fair Maid, and the Feather,
The dialogue and those parentheses,

145

You cherish it, undoubtedly. 'Pardie!'
You call it, with a few conservative
Allowances, an excellent small thing
For patient inexperience to do:
Derivative, you say,—still rather pretty.
But what is wrong with Mr. Killigrew?
Is he in love, or has he read Rossetti?—
Forgive me! I am old and garrulous . . .
When are you coming back to Tilbury Town?

III

I FOUND the old man sitting in his bed,
Propped up and uncomplaining. On a chair
Beside him was a dreary bowl of broth,
A magazine, some glasses, and a pipe.
"I do not light it nowadays," he said,
"But keep it for an antique influence
That it exerts, an aura that it sheds—
Like hautboys, or Provence. You understand:
The charred memorial defeats us yet,
But think you not for always. We are young,
And we are friends of time. Time that made smoke
Will drive away the smoke, and we shall know
The work that we are doing. We shall build
With embers of all shrines one pyramid,
And we shall have the most resplendent flame
From earth to heaven, as the old words go,
And we shall need no smoke . . . Why don't you laugh!

I gazed into those calm, half-lighted eyes
And smiled at them with grim obedience.
He told me that I did it very well,
But added that I should undoubtedly
Do better in the future: "There is nothing,"

146

He said, "so beneficial in a sick-room
As a well-bred spontaneity of manner.
Your sympathetic scowl obtrudes itself,
And is indeed surprising. After death,
Were you to take it with you to your coffin
An unimaginative man might think
That you had lost your life in worrying
To find out what it was that worried you.
The ways of unimaginative men
Are singularly fierce . . . Why do you stand?
Sit here and watch me while I take this soup
The doctor likes it, therefore it is good.

"The man who wrote the decalogue," pursued
The Captain, having swallowed four or five
Heroic spoonfuls of his lukewarm broth,
"Forgot the doctors. And I think sometimes
The man of Galilee (or, if you choose,
The men who made the sayings of the man)
Like Buddha, and the others who have seen,
Was to men's loss the Poet—though it be
The Poet only of him we revere,
The Poet we remember. We have put
The prose of him so far away from us,
The fear of him so crudely over us,
That I have wondered—wondered."—Cautiously,
But yet as one were cautious in a dream,
He set the bowl down on the chair again,
Crossed his thin fingers, looked me in the face,
And looking smiled a little. "Go away,"
He said at last, "and let me go to sleep.
I told you I should eat, but I shall not.
To-morrow I shall eat; and I shall read
Some clauses of a jocund instrument
That I have been preparing here of late

147

For you and for the rest, assuredly.
'Attend the testament of Captain Craig:
Good citizens, good fathers and your sons,
Good mothers and your daughters.' I should say so.
Now go away and let me go to sleep."

I stood before him and held out my hand,
He took it, pressed it; and I felt again
The sick soft closing on it. He would not
Let go, but lay there, looking up to me
With eyes that had a sheen of water on them
And a faint wet spark within them. So he clung,
Tenaciously, with fingers icy warm,
And eyes too full to keep the sheen unbroken.
I looked at him. The fingers closed hard once,
And then fell down.—I should have left him then.

But when we found him the next afternoon,
My first thought was that he had made his eyes
Miraculously smaller. They were sharp
And hard and dry, and the spark in them was dry.
For a glance it all but seemed as if the man
Had artfully forsworn the brimming gaze
Of yesterday, and with a wizard strength
Inveigled in, reduced, and vitalized
The straw-shine of October; and had that
Been truth, we should have humored him no less,
Albeit he had fooled us,—for he said
That we had made him glad by coming to him.
And he was glad: the manner of his words
Revealed the source of them; and the gray smile
Which lingered like a twilight on his face
Told of its own slow fading that it held
The promise of the sun. Cadaverous,
God knows it was; and we knew it was honest.

148

"So you have come to hear the old man read
To you from his last will and testament:
Well, it will not be long—not very long—
So listen." He brought out from underneath
His pillow a new manuscript, and said,
"You have done well to come and hear me read
My testament. There are men in the world
Who say of me, if they remember me,
That I am poor;—and I believe the ways
Of certain men who never find things out
Are stranger than the way Lord Bacon wrote
Leviticus, and *Faust."* He fixed his eyes
Abstractedly on something far from us,
And with a look that I remembered well
Gazed hard the while we waited. But at length
He found himself and soon began to chant,
With a fitful shift at thin sonorousness
The jocund instrument; and had he been
Definitively parceling to us
All Kimberley and half of Ballarat,
The lordly quaver of his poor old words
Could not have been the more magniloquent.
No promise of dead carbon or of gold,
However, flashed in ambush to corrupt us:

"I, Captain Craig, abhorred iconoclast,
Sage-errant, favored of the Mysteries,
And self-reputed humorist at large,
Do now, confessed of my world-worshiping,
Time-questioning, sun-fearing, and heart-yielding,
Approve and unreservedly devise
To you and your assigns for evermore,
God's universe and yours. If I had won
What first I sought, I might have made you beam
By giving less; but now I make you laugh

149

By giving more than what had made you beam,
And it is well. No man has ever done
The deed of humor that God promises,
But now and then we know tragedians
Reform, and in denial too divine
For sacrifice, too firm for ecstasy,
Record in letters, or in books they write,
What fragment of God's humor they have caught,
What earnest of its rhythm; and I believe
That I, in having somewhat recognized
The formal measure of it, have endured
The discord of infirmity no less
Through fortune than by failure. What men lose,
Man gains; and what man gains reports itself
In losses we but vaguely deprecate,
So they be not for us;—and this is right,
Except that when the devil in the sun
Misguides us we go darkly where the shine
Misleads us, and we know not what we see:
We know not if we climb or if we fall;
And if we fly, we know not where we fly.

"And here do I insert an urging clause
For climbers and up-fliers of all sorts,
Cliff-climbers and high-fliers: Phaethon,
Bellerophon, and Icarus did each
Go gloriously up, and each in turn
Did famously come down—as you have read
In poems and elsewhere; but other men
Have mounted where no fame has followed them,
And we have had no sight, no news of them,
And we have heard no crash. The crash may count,
Undoubtedly, and earth be fairer for it;
Yet none save creatures out of harmony
Have ever, in their fealty to the flesh,

150

Made crashing an ideal. It is the flesh
That ails us, for the spirit knows no qualm,
No failure, no down-falling: so climb high,
And having set your steps regard not much
The downward laughter clinging at your feet,
Nor overmuch the warning; only know,
As well as you know dawn from lantern-light,
That far above you, for you, and within you,
There burns and shines and lives, unwavering
And always yours, the truth. Take on yourself
But your sincerity, and you take on
Good promise for all climbing: fly for truth,
And hell shall have no storm to crush your flight,
No laughter to vex down your loyalty.

"I think you may be smiling at me now—
And if I make you smile, so much the better;
For I would have you know that I rejoice
Always to see the thing that I would see—
The righteous thing, the wise thing. I rejoice
Always to think that any thought of mine,
Or any word or any deed of mine,
May grant sufficient of what fortifies
Good feeling and the courage of calm joy
To make the joke worth while. Contrariwise,
When I review some faces I have known—
Sad faces, hungry faces—and reflect
On thoughts I might have moulded, human words
I might have said, straightway it saddens me
To feel perforce that had I not been mute
And actionless, I might have made them bright
Somehow, though only for the moment. Yes,
Howbeit I may confess the vanities,
It saddens me; and sadness, of all things
Miscounted wisdom, and the most of all

When warmed with old illusions and regrets,
I mark the selfishest, and on like lines
The shrewdest. For your sadness makes you climb
With dragging footsteps, and it makes you groan;
It hinders you when most you would be free,
And there are many days it wearies you
Beyond the toil itself. And if the load
It lays on you may not be shaken off
Till you have known what now you do not know—
Meanwhile you climb; and he climbs best who sees
Above him truth burn faithfulest, and feels
Within him truth burn purest. Climb or fail,
One road remains and one firm guidance always;
One way that shall be taken, climb or fall.

"But 'falling, falling, falling.' There's your song,
The cradle-song that sings you to the grave.
What is it your bewildered poet says?—

" 'The toiling ocean thunders of unrest
And aching desolation; the still sea
Paints but an outward calm that mocks itself
To the final and irrefragable sleep
That owns no shifting fury; and the shoals
Of ages are but records of regret
Where Time, the sun's arch-phantom, writes on sand
The prelude of his ancient nothingness.'

" 'T is easy to compound a dirge like that,
And it is easy too to be deceived
And alienated by the fleshless note
Of half-world yearning in it; but the truth
To which we all are tending,—charlatans
And architects alike, artificers
In tinsel as in gold, evangelists

Of ruin and redemption, all alike,—
The truth we seek and equally the truth
We do not seek, but yet may not escape,
Was never found alone through flesh contempt
Or through flesh reverence. Look east and west
And we may read the story: where the light
Shone first the shade now darkens; where the shade
Clung first, the light fights westward—though the shade
Still feeds, and there is yet the Orient.

"But there is this to be remembered always:
Whatever be the altitude you reach,
You do not rise alone; nor do you fall
But you drag others down to more or less
Than your preferred abasement. God forbid
That ever I should preach, and in my zeal
Forget that I was born an humorist;
But now, for once, before I go away,
I beg of you to be magnanimous
A moment, while I speak to please myself:

"Though I have heard it variously sung
That even in the fury and the clash
Of battles, and the closer fights of men
When silence gives the knowing world no sign,
One flower there is, though crushed and cursed it be,
Keeps rooted through all tumult and all scorn,—
Still do I find, when I look sharply down,
There's yet another flower that grows well
And has the most unconscionable roots
Of any weed on earth. Perennial
It grows, and has the name of Selfishness;
No doubt you call it Love. In either case,
You propagate it with a diligence
That hardly were outmeasured had its leaf

The very juice in it of that famed herb
Which gave back breath to Glaucus; and I know
That in the twilight, after the day's work,
You take your little children in your arms,
Or lead them by their credulous frail hands
Benignly out and through the garden-gate
And show them there the things that you have raised;
Not everything, perchance, but always one
Miraculously rooted flower plot
Which is your pride, their pattern. Socrates,
Could he be with you there at such a time,
Would have some unsolicited shrewd words
To say that you might hearken to; but I
Say nothing, for I am not Socrates.—
So much, good friends, for flowers; and I thank you.

"There was a poet once who would have roared
Away the world and had an end of stars.
Where was he when I quoted him?—oh, yes:
'T is easy for a man to link loud words
With woeful pomp and unschooled emphasis
And add one thundered contribution more
To the dirges of all-hollowness, I said;
But here again I find the question set
Before me, after turning books on books
And looking soulward through man after man,
If there indeed be more determining
Play-service in remotely sounding down
The world's one-sidedness. If I judge right,
Your pounding protestations, echoing
Their burden of unfraught futility,
Surge back to mute forgetfulness at last
And have a kind of sunny, sullen end,
Like any cold north storm.—But there are few
Still seas that have no life to profit them,

CAPTAIN CRAIG

And even in such currents of the mind
As have no tide-rush in them, but are drowsed,
Crude thoughts may dart in armor and upspring
With waking sound, when all is dim with peace,
Like sturgeons in the twilight out of Lethe;
And though they be discordant, hard, grotesque,
And all unwelcome to the lethargy
That you think means repose, you know as well
As if your names were shouted when they leap,
And when they leap you listen.—Ah! friends, friends,
There are these things we do not like to know:
They trouble us, they make us hesitate,
They touch us, and we try to put them off.
We banish one another and then say
That we are left alone: the midnight leaf
That rattles where it hangs above the snow—
Gaunt, fluttering, forlorn—scarcely may seem
So cold in all its palsied loneliness
As we, we frozen brothers, who have yet
Profoundly and severely to find out
That there is more of unpermitted love
In most men's reticence than most men think.

"Once, when I made it out fond-headedness
To say that we should ever be apprised
Of our deserts and their emolument
At all but in the specious way of words,
The wisdom of a warm thought woke within me
And I could read the sun. Then did I turn
My long-defeated face full to the world,
And through the clouded warfare of it all
Discern the light. Through dusk that hindered it,
I found the truth, and for the first whole time
Knew then that we were climbing. Not as one
Who mounts along with his experience

155

Bound on him like an Old Man of the Sea—
Not as a moral pedant who drags chains
Of his unearned ideals after him
And always to the lead-like thud they make
Attunes a cold inhospitable chant
Of All Things Easy to the Non-Attached,—
But as a man, a scarred man among men,
I knew it, and I felt the strings of thought
Between us to pull tight the while I strove;
And if a curse came ringing now and then
To my defended ears, how could I know
The light that burned above me and within me,
And at the same time put on cap-and-bells
For such as yet were groping?"

                                    Killigrew
Made there as if to stifle a small cough.
I might have kicked him, but regret forbade
The subtle admonition; and indeed
When afterwards I reprimanded him,
The fellow never knew quite what I meant.
I may have been unjust.—The Captain read
Right on, without a chuckle or a pause,
As if he had heard nothing:

                              "How, forsooth,
Shall any man, by curses or by groans,
Or by the laugh-jarred stillness of all hell,
Be so drawn down to servitude again
That on some backward level of lost laws
And undivined relations, he may know
No longer Love's imperative resource,
Firm once and his, well treasured then, but now
Too fondly thrown away? And if there come
But once on all his journey, singing down

156

To find him, the gold-throated forward call,
What way but one, what but the forward way,
Shall after that call guide him? When his ears
Have earned an inward skill to methodize
The clash of all crossed voices and all noises,
How shall he grope to be confused again,
As he has been, by discord? When his eyes
Have read the book of wisdom in the sun,
And after dark deciphered it on earth,
How shall he turn them back to scan some huge
Blood-lettered protest of bewildered men
That hunger while he feeds where they would starve
And all absurdly perish?"

                    Killigrew
Looked hard for a subtle object on the wall,
And, having found it, sighed. The Captain paused:
If he grew tedious, most assuredly
Did he crave pardon of us; he had feared
Beforehand that he might be wearisome,
But there was not much more of it, he said,—
No more than just enough. And we rejoiced
That he should look so kindly on us then.
("Commend me to a dying man's grimace
For absolute humor, always," Killigrew
Maintains; but I know better.)

                    "Work for them,
You tell me? Work the folly out of them?
Go back to them and teach them how to climb,
While you teach caterpillars how to fly?
You tell me that Alnaschar is a fool
Because he dreams? And what is this you ask?
I make him wise? I teach him to be still?
While you go polishing the Pyramids,

157

I hold Alnaschar's feet? And while you have
The ghost of Memnon's image all day singing,
I sit with aching arms and hardly catch
A few spilled echoes of the song of songs—
The song that I should have as utterly
For mine as other men should once have had
The sweetest a glad shepherd ever trilled
In Sharon, long ago? Is this the way
For me to do good climbing any more
Than Phaethon's? Do you think the golden tone
Of that far-singing call you all have heard
Means any more for you than you should be
Wise-heartedly, glad-heartedly yourselves?
Do this, there is no more for you to do;
And you have no dread left, no shame, no scorn.
And while you have your wisdom and your gold,
Songs calling, and the Princess in your arms,
Remember, if you like, from time to time,
Down yonder where the clouded millions go,
Your bloody-knuckled scullions are not slaves,
Your children of Alnaschar are not fools.

"Nor are they quite so foreign or far down
As you may think to see them. What you take
To be the cursedest mean thing that crawls
On earth is nearer to you than you know:
You may not ever crush him but you lose,
You may not ever shield him but you gain—
As he, with all his crookedness, gains with you.
Your preaching and your teaching, your achieving,
Your lifting up and your discovering,
Are more than often—more than you have dreamed—
The world-refracted evidence of what
Your dream denies. You cannot hide yourselves
In any multitude or solitude,

158

CAPTAIN CRAIG

Or mask yourselves in any studied guise
Of hardness or of old humility,
But soon by some discriminating man—
Some humorist at large, like Socrates—
You get yourselves found out.—Now I should be
Found out without an effort. For example:
When I go riding, trimmed and shaved again,
Consistent, adequate, respectable,—
Some citizen, for curiosity,
Will ask of a good neighbor, 'What is this?'—
'It is the funeral of Captain Craig,'
Will be the neighbor's word.—'And who, good man
Was Captain Craig?'—'He was an humorist;
And we are told that there is nothing more
For any man alive to say of him.'—
'There is nothing very strange in that,' says A;
'But the brass band? What has he done to be
Blown through like this by cornets and trombones?
And here you have this incompatible dirge—
Where are the jokes in that?'—Then B should say:
'Maintained his humor: nothing more or less.
The story goes that on the day before
He died—some say a week, but that's a trifle—
He said, with a subdued facetiousness,
"Play Handel, not Chopin; assuredly not
Chopin." '—He was indeed an humorist."

He made the paper fall down at arm's length;
And with a tension of half-quizzical
Benignity that made it hard for us,
He looked up—first at Morgan, then at me—
Almost, I thought, as if his eyes would ask
If we were satisfied; and as he looked,
The tremor of an old heart's weariness
Was on his mouth. He gazed at each of us,

159

But spoke no further word that afternoon.
He put away the paper, closed his eyes,
And went to sleep with his lips flickering;
And after that we left him.—At midnight
Plunket and I looked in; but he still slept,
And everything was going as it should.
The watchman yawned, rattled his newspaper,
And wondered what it was that ailed his lamp.

Next day we found the Captain wide awake,
Propped up, and searching dimly with a spoon
Through another dreary dish of chicken-broth,
Which he raised up to me, at my approach,
So fervently and so unconsciously,
That one could only laugh. He looked again
At each of us, and as he looked he frowned;
And there was something in that frown of his
That none of us had ever seen before.
"Kind friends," he said, "be sure that I rejoice
To know that you have come to visit me;
Be sure I speak with undisguised words
And earnest, when I say that I rejoice."—
"But what the devil!" whispered Killigrew.
I kicked him, for I thought I understood.
The old man's eyes had glimmered wearily
At first, but now they glittered like to those
Of a glad fish. "Beyond a doubt," said he,
"My dream this morning was more singular
Than any other I have ever known.
Give me that I might live ten thousand years,
And all those years do nothing but have dreams,
I doubt me much if any one of them
Could be so quaint or so fantastical,
So pregnant, as a dream of mine this morning.
You may not think it any more than odd;

CAPTAIN CRAIG

You may not feel—you cannot wholly feel—
How droll it was:—I dreamed that I found Hamlet—
Found him at work, drenched with an angry sweat,
Predestined, he declared with emphasis,
To root out a large weed on Lethe wharf;
And after I had watched him for some time,
I laughed at him and told him that no root
Would ever come the while he talked like that:
The power was not in him, I explained,
For such compound accomplishment. He glared
At me, of course,—next moment laughed at me,
And finally laughed with me. I was right,
And we had eisel on the strength of it:—
'They tell me that this water is not good,'
Said Hamlet, and you should have seen him smile
Conceited? Pelion and Ossa?—pah . . .

"But anon comes in a crocodile. We stepped
Adroitly down upon the back of him,
And away we went to an undiscovered country—
A fertile place, but in more ways than one
So like the region we had started from,
That Hamlet straightway found another weed
And there began to tug. I laughed again,
Till he cried out on me and on my mirth,
Protesting all he knew: 'The Fates,' he said,
'Have ordered it that I shall have these roots.'
But all at once a dreadful hunger seized him,
And it was then we killed the crocodile—
Killed him and ate him. Washed with eisel down
That luckless reptile was, to the last morsel;
And there we were with flag-fens all around us,—
And there was Hamlet, at his task again,
Ridiculous. And while I watched his work,
The drollest of all changes came to pass.

161

The weed had snapped off just above the root,
Not warning him, and I was left alone.
The bubbles rose, and I laughed heartily
To think of him; I laughed when I woke up;
And when my soup came in I laughed again;
I think I may have laughed a little—no?—
Not when you came? . . . Why do you look like that?
You don't believe me? Crocodiles—why not?
Who knows what he has eaten in his life?
Who knows but I have eaten Atropos? . . .
'Briar and oak for a soldier's crown,' you say?
Provence? Oh, no . . . Had I been Socrates,
Count Pretzel would have been the King of Spain."

Now of all casual things we might have said
To make the matter smooth at such a time,
There may have been a few that we had found
Sufficient. Recollection fails, however,
To say that we said anything. We looked.
Had he been Carmichael, we might have stood
Like faithful hypocrites and laughed at him;
But the Captain was not Carmichael at all,
For the Captain had no frogs: he had the sun.
So there we waited, hungry for the word,—
Tormented, unsophisticated, stretched—
Till, with a drawl, to save us, Killigrew
Good-humoredly spoke out. The Captain fixed
His eyes on him with some severity.

"That was a funny dream, beyond a doubt,"
Said Killigrew;—"too funny to be laughed at;
Too humorous, we mean."—"Too humorous?"
The Captain answered; "I approve of that.
Proceed."—We were not glad for Killigrew.
'Well," he went on, "'t was only this. You see

162

CAPTAIN CRAIG

My dream this morning was a droll one too:
I dreamed that a sad man was in my room,
Sitting, as I do now, beside the bed.
I questioned him, but he made no reply,—
Said not a word, but sang."—"Said not a word,
But sang," the Captain echoed. "Very good.
Now tell me what it was the sad man sang."
"Now that," said Killigrew, constrainedly,
And with a laugh that might have been left out,
"Is why I know it must have been a dream.
But there he was, and I lay in the bed
Like you; and I could see him just as well
As you see my right hand. And for the songs
He sang to me—there's where the dream part comes."

"You don't remember them?" the Captain said,
With a weary little chuckle; "very well,
I might have guessed it. Never mind your dream,
But let me go to sleep."—For a moment then
There was a frown on Killigrew's good face,
And then there was a smile. "Not quite," said he;
"The songs that he sang first were sorrowful,
And they were stranger than the man himself—
And he was very strange; but I found out,
Through all the gloom of him and of his music,
That a—say, well, say mystic cheerfulness,
Pervaded him; for slowly, as he sang,
There came a change, and I began to know
The method of it all. Song after song
Was ended; and when I had listened there
For hours—I mean for dream-hours—hearing him,
And always glad that I was hearing him,
There came another change—a great one. Tears
Rolled out at last like bullets from his eyes,
And I could hear them fall down on the floor

163

Like shoes; and they were always marking time
For the song that he was singing. I have lost
The greater number of his verses now,
But there are some, like these, that I remember:

> *" 'Ten men from Zanzibar,*
> *Black as iron hammers are,*
> *Riding on a cable-car*
> *Down to Crowley's theatre.'* . . .

"Ten men?" the Captain interrupted there—
"Ten men, my Euthyphron? That is beautiful.
But never mind, I wish to go to sleep:
Tell Cebes that I wish to go to sleep. . . .
O ye of little faith, your golden plumes
Are like to drag . . . par-dee!"—We may have smiled
In after days to think how Killigrew
Had sacrificed himself to fight that silence,
But we were grateful to him, none the less;
And if we smiled, that may have been the reason.
But the good Captain for a long time then
Said nothing: he lay quiet—fast asleep,
For all that we could see. We waited there
Till each of us, I fancy, must have made
The paper on the wall begin to squirm,
And then got up to leave. My friends went out,
And I was going, when the old man cried:
"You leave me now—now it has come to this?
What have I done to make you go? Come back!
Come back!"

There was a quaver in his cry
That we shall not forget—reproachful, kind,
Indignant, piteous. It seemed as one
Marooned on treacherous tide-feeding sand

164

CAPTAIN CRAIG

Were darkly calling over the still straits
Between him and irrevocable shores
Where now there was no lamp to fade for him,
No call to give him answer. We were there
Before him, but his eyes were not much turned
On us; nor was it very much to us
That he began to speak the broken words,
The scattered words, that he had left in him.

"So it has come to this? And what is this?
Death, do you call it? Death? And what is death?
Why do you look like that at me again?
Why do you shrink your brows and shut your lips?
If it be fear, then I can do no more
Than hope for all of you that you may find
Your promise of the sun; if it be grief
You feel, to think that this old face of mine
May never look at you and laugh again,
Then tell me why it is that you have gone
So long with me, and followed me so far,
And had me to believe you took my words
For more than ever misers did their gold?"

He listened, but his eyes were far from us—
Too far to make us turn to Killigrew,
Or search the futile shelves of our own thoughts
For golden-labeled insincerities
To make placebos of. The marrowy sense
Of slow November rain that splashed against
The shingles and the glass reminded us
That we had brought umbrellas. He continued:
"Oh, can it be that I, too credulous,
Have made myself believe that you believe
Yourselves to be the men that you are not?
I prove and I prize well your friendliness,

165

But I would have that your last look at me
Be not like this; for I would scan to-day
Strong thoughts on all your faces—no regret,
No still commiseration—oh, not that!—
No doubt, no fear. A man may be as brave
As Ajax in the fury of his arms,
And in the midmost warfare of his thoughts
Be frail as Paris . . . For the love, therefore,
That brothered us when we stood back that day
From Delium—the love that holds us now
More than it held us at Amphipolis—
Forget you not that he who in his work
Would mount from these low roads of measured shame
To tread the leagueless highway must fling first
And fling forevermore beyond his reach
The shackles of a slave who doubts the sun.
There is no servitude so fraudulent
As of a sun-shut mind; for 't is the mind
That makes you craven or invincible,
Diseased or puissant. The mind will pay
Ten thousand fold and be the richer then
To grant new service; but the world pays hard,
And accurately sickens till in years
The dole has eked its end and there is left
What all of you are noting on all days
In these Athenian streets, where squandered men
Drag ruins of half-warriors to the grave—
Or to Hippocrates."

His head fell back,
And he lay still with wearied eyes half-closed.
We waited, but a few faint words yet stayed:
"Kind friends," he said, "friends I have known so long,
Though I have jested with you in time past,
Though I have stung your pride with epithets

CAPTAIN CRAIG

Not all forbearing,—still, when I am gone,
Say Socrates wrought always for the best
And for the wisest end . . . Give me the cup!
The truth is yours, God's universe is yours . . .
Good-by . . . good citizens . . . give me the cup" . . .
Again we waited; and this time we knew
Those lips of his that would not flicker down
Had yet some fettered message for us there.
We waited, and we watched him. All at once,
With a faint flash, the clouded eyes grew clear,
And then we knew the man was coming back.
We watched him, and I listened. The man smiled
And looked about him—not regretfully,
Not anxiously; and when at last he spoke,
Before the long drowse came to give him peace,
One word was all he said. "Trombones," he said.

That evening, at "The Chrysalis" again,
We smoked and looked at one another's eyes,
And we were glad. The world had scattered ways
For us to take, we knew; but for the time
That one snug room where big beech logs roared smooth
Defiance to the cold rough rain outside
Sufficed. There were no scattered ways for us
That we could see just then, and we were glad:
We were glad to be on earth, and we rejoiced
No less for Captain Craig that he was gone.
We might, for his dead benefit, have run
The gamut of all human weaknesses
And uttered after-platitudes enough—
Wrecked on his own abstractions, and all such—
To drive away Gambrinus and the bead
From Bernard's ale; and I suppose we might
Have praised, accordingly, the Lord of Hosts

For letting us believe that we were not
The least and idlest of His handiwork.

So Plunket, who had knowledge of all sorts,
Yet hardly ever spoke, began to plink
O tu, Palermo!—quaintly, with his nails,—
On Morgan's fiddle, and at once got seized,
As if he were some small thing, by the neck.
Then the consummate Morgan, having told
Explicitly what hardship might accrue
To Plunket if he did that any more,
Made roaring chords and acrobatic runs—
And then, with his kind eyes on Killigrew,
Struck up the schoolgirls' march in *Lohengrin,*
So Killigrew might smile and stretch himself
And have to light his pipe. When that was done
We knew that Morgan, by the looks of him,
Was in the mood for almost anything
From Bach to Offenbach; and of all times
That he has ever played, that one somehow—
That evening of the day the Captain died—
Stands out like one great verse of a good song,
One strain that sings itself beyond the rest
For magic and a glamour that it has.

The ways have scattered for us, and all things
Have changed; and we have wisdom, I doubt not,
More fit for the world's work than we had then;
But neither parted roads nor cent per cent
May starve quite out the child that lives in us—
The Child that is the Man, the Mystery,
The Phœnix of the World. So, now and then,
That evening of the day the Captain died
Returns to us; and there comes always with it
The storm, the warm restraint, the fellowship,

ISAAC AND ARCHIBALD

The friendship and the firelight, and the fiddle.
So too there comes a day that followed it—
A windy, dreary day with a cold white shine,
Which only gummed the tumbled frozen ruts
That made us ache. The road was hard and long,
But we had what we knew to comfort us,
And we had the large humor of the thing
To make it advantageous; for men stopped
And eyed us on that road from time to time,
And on that road the children followed us;
And all along that road the Tilbury Band
Blared indiscreetly the Dead March in Saul.

ISAAC AND ARCHIBALD

(To Mrs. Henry Richards)

Isaac and Archibald were two old men.
I knew them, and I may have laughed at them
A little; but I must have honored them
For they were old, and they were good to me.

I do not think of either of them now,
Without remembering, infallibly,
A journey that I made one afternoon
With Isaac to find out what Archibald
Was doing with his oats. It was high time
Those oats were cut, said Isaac; and he feared
That Archibald—well, he could never feel
Quite sure of Archibald. Accordingly
The good old man invited me—that is,
Permitted me—to go along with him;
And I, with a small boy's adhesiveness
To competent old age, got up and went.

I do not know that I cared overmuch
For Archibald's or anybody's oats,
But Archibald was quite another thing,
And Isaac yet another; and the world
Was wide, and there was gladness everywhere.
We walked together down the River Road
With all the warmth and wonder of the land
Around us, and the wayside flash of leaves,—
And Isaac said the day was glorious;
But somewhere at the end of the first mile
I found that I was figuring to find
How long those ancient legs of his would keep
The pace that he had set for them. The sun
Was hot, and I was ready to sweat blood;
But Isaac, for aught I could make of him,
Was cool to his hat-band. So I said then
With a dry gasp of affable despair,
Something about the scorching days we have
In August without knowing it sometimes;
But Isaac said the day was like a dream,
And praised the Lord, and talked about the breeze.
I made a fair confession of the breeze,
And crowded casually on his thought
The nearness of a profitable nook
That I could see. First I was half inclined
To caution him that he was growing old,
But something that was not compassion soon
Made plain the folly of all subterfuge.
Isaac was old, but not so old as that.

So I proposed, without an overture,
That we be seated in the shade a while,
And Isaac made no murmur. Soon the talk
Was turned on Archibald, and I began
To feel some premonitions of a kind

ISAAC AND ARCHIBALD

That only childhood knows; for the old man
Had looked at me and clutched me with his eye,
And asked if I had ever noticed things.
I told him that I could not think of them,
And I knew then, by the frown that left his face
Unsatisfied, that I had injured him.
"My good young friend," he said, "you cannot feel
What I have seen so long. You have the eyes—
Oh, yes—but you have not the other things:
The sight within that never will deceive,
You do not know—you have no right to know;
The twilight warning of experience,
The singular idea of loneliness,—
These are not yours. But they have long been mine,
And they have shown me now for seven years
That Archibald is changing. It is not
So much that he should come to his last hand,
And leave the game, and go the old way down;
But I have known him in and out so long,
And I have seen so much of good in him
That other men have shared and have not seen,
And I have gone so far through thick and thin,
Through cold and fire with him, that now it brings
To this old heart of mine an ache that you
Have not yet lived enough to know about.
But even unto you, and your boy's faith,
Your freedom, and your untried confidence,
A time will come to find out what it means
To know that you are losing what was yours,
To know that you are being left behind;
And then the long contempt of innocence—
God bless you, boy!—don't think the worse of it
Because an old man chatters in the shade—
Will all be like a story you have read
In childhood and remembered for the pictures.

And when the best friend of your life goes **down,**
When first you know in him the slackening
That comes, and coming always tells the end,—
Now in a common word that would have passed
Uncaught from any other lips than his,
Now in some trivial act of every day,
Done as he might have done it all along
But for a twinging little difference   .
That nips you like a squirrel's teeth—oh, yes,
Then you will understand it well enough.
But oftener it comes in other ways;
It comes without your knowing when it comes;
You know that he is changing, and you know
That he is going—just as I know now
That Archibald is going, and that I
Am staying. . . . Look at me, my boy,
And when the time shall come for you to see
That I must follow after him, try then
To think of me, to bring me back again,
Just as I was to-day. Think of the place
Where we are sitting now, and think of me—
Think of old Isaac as you knew him then,
When you set out with him in August once
To see old Archibald."—The words come back
Almost as Isaac must have uttered them.
And there comes with them a dry memory
Of something in my throat that would not move.

If you had asked me then to tell just why
I made so much of Isaac and the things
He said, I should have gone far for an answer;
For I knew it was not sorrow that I felt,
Whatever I may have wished it, or tried then
To make myself believe. My mouth was full
Of words, and they would have been comforting

ISAAC AND ARCHIBALD

To Isaac, spite of my twelve years, I think;
But there was not in me the willingness
To speak them out.   Therefore I watched the ground;
And I was wondering what made the Lord
Create a thing so nervous as an ant,
When Isaac, with commendable unrest,
Ordained that we should take the road again—
For it was yet three miles to Archibald's,
And one to the first pump.   I felt relieved
All over when the old man told me that;
I felt that he had stilled a fear of mine
That those extremities of heat and cold
Which he had long gone through with Archibald
Had made the man impervious to both;
But Isaac had a desert somewhere in him,
And at the pump he thanked God for all things
That He had put on earth for men to drink,
And he drank well,—so well that I proposed
That we go slowly lest I learn too soon
The bitterness of being left behind,
And all those other things.   That was a joke
To Isaac, and it pleased him very much;
And that pleased me—for I was twelve years old.

At the end of an hour's walking after that
The cottage of old Archibald appeared.
Little and white and high on a smooth round hill
It stood, with hackmatacks and apple-trees
Before it, and a big barn-roof beyond;
And over the place—trees, houses, fields and all—
Hovered an air of still simplicity
And a fragrance of old summers—the old style
That lives the while it passes.   I dare say
That I was lightly conscious of all this
When Isaac, of a sudden, stopped himself,

173

And for the long first quarter of a minute
Gazed with incredulous eyes, forgetful quite
Of breezes and of me and of all else
Under the scorching sun but a smooth-cut field,
Faint yellow in the distance. I was young,
But there were a few things that I could see,
And this was one of them.—"Well, well!" said he;
And "Archibald will be surprised, I think,"
Said I. But all my childhood subtlety
Was lost on Isaac, for he strode along
Like something out of Homer—powerful
And awful on the wayside, so I thought.
Also I thought how good it was to be
So near the end of my short-legged endeavor
To keep the pace with Isaac for five miles.

Hardly had we turned in from the main road
When Archibald, with one hand on his back
And the other clutching his huge-headed cane,
Came limping down to meet us.—"Well! well! well!"
Said he; and then he looked at my red face,
All streaked with dust and sweat, and shook my hand,
And said it must have been a right smart walk
That we had had that day from Tilbury Town.—
"Magnificent," said Isaac; and he told
About the beautiful west wind there was
Which cooled and clarified the atmosphere.
"You must have made it with your legs, I guess,"
Said Archibald; and Isaac humored him
With one of those infrequent smiles of his
Which he kept in reserve, apparently,
For Archibald alone. "But why," said he,
"Should Providence have cider in the world
If not for such an afternoon as this?"
And Archibald, with a soft light in his eyes,

ISAAC AND ARCHIBALD

Replied that if he chose to go down cellar,
There he would find eight barrels—one of which
Was newly tapped, he said, and to his taste
An honor to the fruit. Isaac approved
Most heartily of that, and guided us
Forthwith, as if his venerable feet
Were measuring the turf in his own door-yard,
Straight to the open rollway. Down we went,
Out of the fiery sunshine to the gloom,
Grateful and half sepulchral, where we found
The barrels, like eight potent sentinels,
Close ranged along the wall. From one of them
A bright pine spile stuck out alluringly,
And on the black flat stone, just under it,
Glimmered a late-spilled proof that Archibald
Had spoken from unfeigned experience.
There was a fluted antique water-glass
Close by, and in it, prisoned, or at rest,
There was a cricket, of the brown soft sort
That feeds on darkness. Isaac turned him out,
And touched him with his thumb to make him jump,
And then composedly pulled out the plug
With such a practised hand that scarce a drop
Did even touch his fingers. Then he drank
And smacked his lips with a slow patronage
And looked along the line of barrels there
With a pride that may have been forgetfulness
That they were Archibald's and not his own.
"I never twist a spigot nowadays,"
He said, and raised the glass up to the light,
"But I thank God for orchards." And that glass
Was filled repeatedly for the same hand
Before I thought it worth while to discern
Again that I was young, and that old age,
With all his woes, had some advantages.

"Now, Archibald," said Isaac, when we stood
Outside again, "I have it in my mind
That I shall take a sort of little walk—
To stretch my legs and see what you are doing.
You stay and rest your back and tell the boy
A story: Tell him all about the time
In Stafford's cabin forty years ago,
When four of us were snowed up for ten days
With only one dried haddock. Tell him all
About it, and be wary of your back.
Now I will go along."—I looked up then
At Archibald, and as I looked I saw
Just how his nostrils widened once or twice
And then grew narrow. I can hear to-day
The way the old man chuckled to himself—
Not wholesomely, not wholly to convince
Another of his mirth,—as I can hear
The lonely sigh that followed.—But at length
He said: "The orchard now's the place for us;
We may find something like an apple there,
And we shall have the shade, at any rate."
So there we went and there we laid ourselves
Where the sun could not reach us; and I champed
A dozen of worm-blighted astrakhans
While Archibald said nothing—merely told
The tale of Stafford's cabin, which was good,
Though "master chilly"—after his own phrase—
Even for a day like that. But other thoughts
Were moving in his mind, imperative,
And writhing to be spoken: I could see
The glimmer of them in a glance or two,
Cautious, or else unconscious, that he gave
Over his shoulder: . . . "Stafford and the rest—
But that's an old song now, and Archibald
And Isaac are old men. Remember, boy,

176

ISAAC AND ARCHIBALD

That we are old. Whatever we have gained,
Or lost, or thrown away, we are old men.
You look before you and we look behind,
And we are playing life out in the shadow—
But that's not all of it. The sunshine lights
A good road yet before us if we look,
And we are doing that when least we know it;
For both of us are children of the sun,
Like you, and like the weed there at your feet.
The shadow calls us, and it frightens us—
We think; but there's a light behind the stars
And we old fellows who have dared to live,
We see it—and we see the other things,
The other things . . . Yes, I have seen it come
These eight years, and these ten years, and I know
Now that it cannot be for very long
That Isaac will be Isaac. You have seen—
Young as you are, you must have seen the strange
Uncomfortable habit of the man?
He'll take my nerves and tie them in a knot
Sometimes, and that's not Isaac. I know that—
And I know what it is: I get it here
A little, in my knees, and Isaac—here."
The old man shook his head regretfully
And laid his knuckles three times on his forehead.
"That's what it is: Isaac is not quite right.
You see it, but you don't know what it means:
The thousand little differences—no,
You do not know them, and it's well you don't;
You'll know them soon enough—God bless you, boy!—
You'll know them, but not all of them—not all.
So think of them as little as you can:
There's nothing in them for you, or for me—
But I am old and I must think of them;
I'm in the shadow, but I don't forget

The light, my boy,—the light behind the stars.
Remember that: remember that I said it;
And when the time that you think far away
Shall come for you to say it—say it, boy;
Let there be no confusion or distrust
In you, no snarling of a life half lived,
Nor any cursing over broken things
That your complaint has been the ruin of.
Live to see clearly and the light will come
To you, and as you need it.—But there, there,
I'm going it again, as Isaac says,
And I'll stop now before you go to sleep.—
Only be sure that you growl cautiously,
And always where the shadow may not reach you."

Never shall I forget, long as I live,
The quaint thin crack in Archibald's voice,
The lonely twinkle in his little eyes,
Or the way it made me feel to be with him.
I know I lay and looked for a long time
Down through the orchard and across the road,
Across the river and the sun-scorched hills
That ceased in a blue forest, where the world
Ceased with it. Now and then my fancy caught
A flying glimpse of a good life beyond—
Something of ships and sunlight, streets and singing,
Troy falling, and the ages coming back,
And ages coming forward: Archibald
And Isaac were good fellows in old clothes,
And Agamemnon was a friend of mine;
Ulysses coming home again to shoot
With bows and feathered arrows made another,
And all was as it should be. I was young.

So I lay dreaming of what things I would,
Calm and incorrigibly satisfied

ISAAC AND ARCHIBALD

With apples and romance and ignorance,
And the still smoke from Archibald's clay pipe.
There was a stillness over everything,
As if the spirit of heat had laid its hand
Upon the world and hushed it; and I felt
Within the mightiness of the white sun
That smote the land around us and wrought out
A fragrance from the trees, a vital warmth
And fullness for the time that was to come,
And a glory for the world beyond the forest.
The present and the future and the past,
Isaac and Archibald, the burning bush,
The Trojans and the walls of Jericho,
Were beautifully fused; and all went well
Till Archibald began to fret for Isaac
And said it was a master day for sunstroke.
That was enough to make a mummy smile,
I thought; and I remained hilarious,
In face of all precedence and respect,
Till Isaac (who had come to us unheard)
Found he had no tobacco, looked at me
Peculiarly, and asked of Archibald
What ailed the boy to make him chirrup so.
From that he told us what a blessed world
The Lord had given us.—"But, Archibald,"
He added, with a sweet severity
That made me think of peach-skins and goose-flesh,
"I'm half afraid you cut those oats of yours
A day or two before they were well set."
"They were set well enough," said Archibald,—
And I remarked the process of his nose
Before the words came out. "But never mind
Your neighbor's oats: you stay here in the shade
And rest yourself while I go find the cards.
We'll have a little game of seven-up

And let the boy keep count."—"We'll have the game,
Assuredly," said Isaac; "and I think
That I will have a drop of cider, also."

They marched away together towards the house
And left me to my childish ruminations
Upon the ways of men. I followed them
Down cellar with my fancy, and then left them
For a fairer vision of all things at once
That was anon to be destroyed again
By the sound of voices and of heavy feet—
One of the sounds of life that I remember,
Though I forget so many that rang first
As if they were thrown down to me from Sinai.

So I remember, even to this day,
Just how they sounded, how they placed themselves,
And how the game went on while I made marks
And crossed them out, and meanwhile made some Trojans.
Likewise I made Ulysses, after Isaac,
And a little after Flaxman. Archibald
Was injured when he found himself left out,
But he had no heroics, and I said so:
I told him that his white beard was too long
And too straight down to be like things in Homer.
"Quite so," said Isaac.—"Low," said Archibald;
And he threw down a deuce with a deep grin
That showed his yellow teeth and made me happy.
So they played on till a bell rang from the door,
And Archibald said, "Supper."—After that
The old men smoked while I sat watching them
And wondered with all comfort what might come
To me, and what might never come to me;
And when the time came for the long walk home
With Isaac in the twilight, I could see

THE RETURN OF MORGAN AND FINGAL

The forest and the sunset and the sky-line,
No matter where it was that I was looking:
The flame beyond the boundary, the music,
The foam and the white ships, and two old men
Were things that would not leave me.—And that **night**
There came to me a dream—a shining one,
With two old angels in it. They had wings,
And they were sitting where a silver light
Suffused them, face to face. The wings of one
Began to palpitate as I approached,
But I was yet unseen when a dry voice
Cried thinly, with unpatronizing triumph,
"I've got you, Isaac; high, low, jack, and the game."

Isaac and Archibald have gone their way
To the silence of the loved and well-forgotten.
I knew them, and I may have laughed at them;
But there's a laughing that has honor in it,
And I have no regret for light words now.
Rather I think sometimes they may have made
Their sport of me;—but they would not do that,
They were too old for that. They were old men,
And I may laugh at them because I knew them.

THE RETURN OF MORGAN AND FINGAL

AND there we were together again—
    Together again, we three:
Morgan, Fingal, fiddle, and all,
    They had come for the night with me.

The spirit of joy was in Morgan's wrist,
    There were songs in Fingal's throat;
And secure outside, for the spray to **drench,**
    Was a tossed and empty boat.

181

And there were the pipes, and there was the punch,
  And somewhere were twelve years;
So it came, in the manner of things unsought,
  That a quick knock vexed our ears.

The night wind hovered and shrieked and snarled,
  And I heard Fingal swear;
Then I opened the door—but I found no more
  Than a chalk-skinned woman there.

I looked, and at last, "What is it?" I said—
  "What is it that we can do?"
But never a word could I get from her
  But "You—you three—it is you!"

Now the sense of a crazy speech like that
  Was more than a man could make;
So I said, "But we—we are what, we three?"
  And I saw the creature shake.

"Be quick!" she cried, "for I left her dead—
  And I was afraid to come;
But you, you three—God made it be—
  Will ferry the dead girl home.

"Be quick! be quick!—but listen to that
  Who is that makes it?—hark!"
But I heard no more than a knocking splash
  And a wind that shook the dark.

"It is only the wind that blows," I said,
  "And the boat that rocks outside."
And I watched her there, and I pitied her there—
  "Be quick! be quick!" she cried.

THE RETURN OF MORGAN AND FINGAL

She cried so loud that her voice went in
　　To find where my two friends were;
So Morgan came, and Fingal came,
　　And out we went with her.

'T was a lonely way for a man to take
　　And a fearsome way for three;
And over the water, and all day long,
　　They had come for the night with me.

But the girl was dead, as the woman had said,
　　And the best we could see to do
Was to lay her aboard. The north wind roared,
　　And into the night we flew.

Four of us living and one for a ghost,
　　Furrowing crest and swell,
Through the surge and the dark, for that faint far spark,
　　We ploughed with Azrael.

Three of us ruffled and one gone mad,
　　Crashing to south we went;
And three of us there were too spattered to care
　　What this late sailing meant.

So down we steered and along we tore
　　Through the flash of the midnight foam:
Silent enough to be ghosts on guard.
　　We ferried the dead girl home.

We ferried her down to the voiceless wharf,
　　And we carried her up to the light;
And we left the two to the father there,
　　Who counted the coals that night.

Then back we steered through the foam again,
  But our thoughts were fast and few;
And all we did was to crowd the surge
  And to measure the life we knew;—

Till at last we came where a dancing gleam
  Skipped out to us, we three,—
And the dark wet mooring pointed home
  Like a finger from the sea.

Then out we pushed the teetering skiff
  And in we drew to the stairs;
And up we went, each man content
  With a life that fed no cares.

Fingers were cold and feet were cold,
  And the tide was cold and rough;
But the light was warm, and the room was warm,
  And the world was good enough.

And there were the pipes, and there was the punch,
  More shrewd than Satan's tears:
Fingal had fashioned it, all by himself,
  With a craft that comes of years.

And there we were together again—
  Together again, we three:
Morgan, Fingal, fiddle, and all,
  They were there for the night with me.

AUNT IMOGEN

Aunt Imogen was coming, and therefore
The children—Jane, Sylvester, and Young George—
Were eyes and ears; for there was only one
Aunt Imogen to them in the whole world,

AUNT IMOGEN

And she was in it only for four weeks
In fifty-two. But those great bites of time
Made all September a Queen's Festival;
And they would strive, informally, to make
The most of them.—The mother understood,
And wisely stepped away. Aunt Imogen
Was there for only one month in the year,
While she, the mother,—she was always there;
And that was what made all the difference.
She knew it must be so, for Jane had once
Expounded it to her so learnedly
That she had looked away from the child's eyes
And thought; and she had thought of many things.

There was a demonstration every time
Aunt Imogen appeared, and there was more
Than one this time. And she was at a loss
Just how to name the meaning of it all:
It puzzled her to think that she could be
So much to any crazy thing alive—
Even to her sister's little savages
Who knew no better than to be themselves;
But in the midst of her glad wonderment
She found herself besieged and overcome
By two tight arms and one tumultuous head.
And therewith half bewildered and half pained
By the joy she felt and by the sudden love
That proved itself in childhood's honest noise.
Jane, by the wings of sex, had reached her first;
And while she strangled her, approvingly,
Sylvester thumped his drum and Young George howled.
But finally, when all was rectified.
And she had stilled the clamor of Young George
By giving him a long ride on her shoulders,
They went together into the old room

That looked across the fields; and Imogen
Gazed out with a girl's gladness in her eyes,
Happy to know that she was back once more
Where there were those who knew her, and at last
Had gloriously got away again
From cabs and clattered asphalt for a while;
And there she sat and talked and looked and laughed
And made the mother and the children laugh.
Aunt Imogen made everybody laugh.

There was the feminine paradox—that she
Who had so little sunshine for herself
Should have so much for others. How it was
That she could make, and feel for making it,
So much of joy for them, and all along
Be covering, like a scar, and while she smiled,
That hungering incompleteness and regret—
That passionate ache for something of her own,
For something of herself—she never knew.
She knew that she could seem to make them all
Believe there was no other part of her
Than her persistent happiness; but the why
And how she did not know. Still none of them
Could have a thought that she was living down—
Almost as if regret were criminal,
So proud it was and yet so profitless—
The penance of a dream, and that was good.
Her sister Jane—the mother of little Jane,
Sylvester, and Young George—might make herself
Believe she knew, for she—well, she was Jane.

Young George, however, did not yield himself
To nourish the false hunger of a ghost
That made no good return. He saw too much:
The accumulated wisdom of his years

AUNT IMOGEN

Had so conclusively made plain to him
The permanent profusion of a world
Where everybody might have everything
To do, and almost everything to eat,
That he was jubilantly satisfied
And all unthwarted by adversity.
Young George knew things. The world, he had found out,
Was a good place, and life was a good game—
Particularly when Aunt Imogen
Was in it. And one day it came to pass—
One rainy day when she was holding him
And rocking him—that he, in his own right,
Took it upon himself to tell her so;
And something in his way of telling it—
The language, or the tone, or something else—
Gripped like insidious fingers on her throat,
And then went foraging as if to make
A plaything of her heart. Such undeserved
And unsophisticated confidence
Went mercilessly home; and had she sat
Before a looking glass, the deeps of it
Could not have shown more clearly to her then
Than one thought-mirrored little glimpse had shown,
The pang that wrenched her face and filled her eyes
With anguish and intolerable mist.
The blow that she had vaguely thrust aside
Like fright so many times had found her now:
Clean-thrust and final it had come to her
From a child's lips at last, as it had come
Never before, and as it might be felt
Never again. Some grief, like some delight,
Stings hard but once: to custom after that
The rapture or the pain submits itself,
And we are wiser than we were before.
And Imogen was wiser; though at first

Her dream-defeating wisdom was indeed
A thankless heritage: there was no sweet,
No bitter now; nor was there anything
To make a daily meaning for her life—
Till truth, like Harlequin, leapt out somehow
From ambush and threw sudden savor to it—
But the blank taste of time. There were no dreams,
No phantoms in her future any more:
One clinching revelation of what was
One by-flash of irrevocable chance,
Had acridly but honestly foretold
The mystical fulfilment of a life
That might have once . . . But that was all gone by:
There was no need of reaching back for that:
The triumph was not hers: there was no love
Save borrowed love: there was no might have been.

But there was yet Young George—and he had gone
Conveniently to sleep, like a good boy;
And there was yet Sylvester with his drum,
And there was frowzle-headed little Jane;
And there was Jane the sister, and the mother,—
Her sister, and the mother of them all.
They were not hers, not even one of them:
She was not born to be so much as that,
For she was born to be Aunt Imogen.
Now she could see the truth and look at it;
Now she could make stars out where once had palled
A future's emptiness; now she could share
With others—ah, the others!—to the end
The largess of a woman who could smile;
Now it was hers to dance the folly down,
And all the murmuring; now it was hers
To be Aunt Imogen.—So, when Young George
Woke up and blinked at her with his big eyes,

And smiled to see the way she blinked at him,
'T was only in old concord with the stars
That she took hold of him and held him close,
Close to herself, and crushed him till he laughed.

THE KLONDIKE

NEVER mind the day we left, or the day the women clung **to us;**
All we need now is the last way they looked at us.
Never mind the twelve men there amid the cheering—
Twelve men or one man, 't will soon be all the same;
For this is what we know: we are five men together,
Five left o' twelve men to find the golden river.

Far we came to find it out, but the place was here for **all of us;**
Far, far we came, and here we have the last of us.
We that were the front men, we that would be early,
We that had the faith, and the triumph in our eyes:
We that had the wrong road, twelve men together,—
Singing when the devil sang to find the golden river.

Say the gleam was not for us, but never say we doubted **it;**
Say the wrong road was right before we followed it.
We that were the front men, fit for all forage,—
Say that while we dwindle we are front men still;
For this is what we know to-night: we're starving here **together—**
Starving on the wrong road to find the golden river.

Wrong, we say, but wait a little: hear him in the corner **there;**
He knows more than we, and he'll tell us if we listen **there—**
He that fought the snow-sleep less than all the others
Stays awhile yet, and he knows where he stays:
Foot and hand a frozen clout, brain a freezing feather,
Still he's here to talk with us and to' the golden river.

"Flow," he says, "and flow along, but you cannot flow away
    from us;
All the world's ice will never keep you far from us;
Every man that heeds your call takes the way that leads him—
The one way that's his way, and lives his own life:
Starve or laugh, the game goes on, and on goes the river;
Gold or no, they go their way—twelve men together.

"Twelve," he says, "who sold their shame for a lure you call too
    fair for them—
You that laugh and flow to the same word that urges them:
Twelve who left the old town shining in the sunset,
Left the weary street and the small safe days:
Twelve who knew but one way out, wide the way or narrow:
Twelve who took the frozen chance and laid their lives on yellow.

"Flow by night and flow by day, nor ever once be seen by them;
Flow, freeze, and flow, till time shall hide the bones of them;
Laugh and wash their names away, leave them all forgotten,
Leave the old town to crumble where it sleeps;
Leave it there as they have left it, shining in the valley,—
Leave the town to crumble down and let the women marry.

"Twelve of us or five," he says, "we know the night is on us now:
Five while we last, and we may as well be thinking now:
Thinking each his own thought, knowing, when the light comes,
Five left or none left, the game will not be lost.
Crouch or sleep, we go the way, the last way together:
Five or none, the game goes on, and on goes the river.

"For after all that we have done and all that we have failed
    to do,
Life will be life and a world will have its work to do:
Every man who follows us will heed in his own fashion
The calling and the warning and the friends who do not know:

Each will hold an icy knife to punish his heart's lover,
And each will go the frozen way to find the golden river."

There you hear him, all he says, and the last we'll ever get from
 him.
Now he wants to sleep, and that will be the best for him.
Let him have his own way—no, you needn't shake him—
Your own turn will come, so let the man sleep.
For this is what we know: we are stalled here together—
Hands and feet and hearts of us, to find the golden river.

And there's a quicker way than sleep? . . . Never mind the
 looks of him:
All he needs now is a finger on the eyes of him.
You there on the left hand, reach a little over—
Shut the stars away, or he'll see them all night:
He'll see them all night and he'll see them all to-morrow,
Crawling down the frozen sky, cold and hard and yellow.

Won't you move an inch or two—to keep the stars away from
 him?
—No, he won't move, and there's no need of asking him.
Never mind the twelve men, never mind the women;
Three while we last, we'll let them all go;
And we'll hold our thoughts north while we starve here together,
Looking each his own way to find the golden river.

THE GROWTH OF "LORRAINE"

I

WHILE I stood listening, discreetly dumb,
Lorraine was having the last word with me:
"I know," she said, "I know it, but you see
Some creatures are born fortunate, and some

Are born to be found out and overcome,—
Born to be slaves, to let the rest go free;
And if I'm one of them (and I must be)
You may as well forget me and go home.

"You tell me not to say these things, I know,
But I should never try to be content:
I've gone too far; the life would be too slow.
Some could have done it—some girls have the stuff;
But I can't do it: I don't know enough.
I'm going to the devil."—And she went.

II

I DID not half believe her when she said
That I should never hear from her again;
Nor when I found a letter from Lorraine,
Was I surprised or grieved at what I read:
"Dear friend, when you find this, I shall be dead.
You are too far away to make me stop.
They say that one drop—think of it, one drop!—
Will be enough,—but I'll take five instead.

"You do not frown because I call you friend,
For I would have you glad that I still keep
Your memory, and even at the end—
Impenitent, sick, shattered—cannot curse
The love that flings, for better or for worse,
This worn-out, cast-out flesh of mine to sleep."

THE SAGE

FOREGUARDED and unfevered and serene,
Back to the perilous gates of Truth he went—
Back to fierce wisdom and the Orient,
To the Dawn that is, that shall be, and has been:

ERASMUS

Previsioned of the madness and the mean,
He stood where Asia, crowned with ravishment,
The curtain of Love's inner shrine had rent,
And after had gone scarred by the Unseen.

There at his touch there was a treasure chest,
And in it was a gleam, but not of gold;
And on it, like a flame, these words were scrolled:
"I keep the mintage of Eternity.
Who comes to take one coin may take the rest,
And all may come—but not without the key."

ERASMUS

WHEN he protested, not too solemnly,
That for a world's achieving maintenance
The crust of overdone divinity
Lacked aliment, they called it recreance;
And when he chose through his own glass to scan
Sick Europe, and reduced, unyieldingly,
The monk within the cassock to the man
Within the monk, they called it heresy.

And when he made so perilously bold
As to be scattered forth in black and white,
Good fathers looked askance at him and rolled
Their inward eyes in anguish and affright;
There were some of them did shake at what was told,
And they shook best who knew that he was right.

THE WOMAN AND THE WIFE

I—THE EXPLANATION

"You thought we knew," she said, "but we were wrong.
This we can say, the rest we do not say;
Nor do I let you throw yourself away
Because you love me. Let us both be strong,
And we shall find in sorrow, before long,
Only the price Love ruled that we should pay:
The dark is at the end of every day,
And silence is the end of every song.

"You ask me for one proof that I speak right,
But I can answer only what I know;
You look for just one lie to make black white,
But I can tell you only what is true—
God never made me for the wife of you.
This we can say,—believe me! . . . Tell me so!"

II—THE ANNIVERSARY

"Give me the truth, whatever it may be.
You thought we knew, now tell me what you miss:
You are the one to tell me what it is—
You are a man, and you have married me.
What is it worth to-night that you can see
More marriage in the dream of one dead kiss
Than in a thousand years of life like this?
Passion has turned the lock, Pride keeps the key.

"Whatever I have said or left unsaid,
Whatever I have done or left undone,—
Tell me. Tell me the truth. . . . Are you afraid?
Do you think that Love was ever fed with lies
But hunger lived thereafter in his eyes?
Do you ask me to take moonlight for the sun?"

THE BOOK OF ANNANDALE

I

PARTLY to think, more to be left alone,
George Annandale said something to his friends—
A word or two, brusque, but yet smoothed enough
To suit their funeral gaze—and went upstairs;
And there, in the one room that he could call
His own, he found a sort of meaningless
Annoyance in the mute familiar things
That filled it; for the grate's monotonous gleam
Was not the gleam that he had known before,
The books were not the books that used to be,
The place was not the place. There was a lack
Of something; and the certitude of death
Itself, as with a furtive questioning,
Hovered, and he could not yet understand.
He knew that she was gone—there was no need
Of any argued proof to tell him that,
For they had buried her that afternoon,
Under the leaves and snow; and still there was
A doubt, a pitiless doubt, a plunging doubt,
That struck him, and upstartled when it struck,
The vision, the old thought in him. There was
A lack, and one that wrenched him; but it was
Not that—not that. There was a present sense
Of something indeterminably near—
The soul-clutch of a prescient emptiness
That would not be foreboding. And if not,
What then?—or was it anything at all?
Yes, it was something—it was everything—
But what was everything? or anything?

195

Tired of time, bewildered, he sat down;
But in his chair he kept on wondering
That he should feel so desolately strange
And yet—for all he knew that he had lost
More of the world than most men ever win—
So curiously calm. And he was left
Unanswered and unsatisfied: there came
No clearer meaning to him than had come
Before; the old abstraction was the best
That he could find, the farthest he could go;
To that was no beginning and no end—
No end that he could reach. So he must learn
To live the surest and the largest life
Attainable in him, would he divine
The meaning of the dream and of the words
That he had written, without knowing why,
On sheets that he had bound up like a book
And covered with red leather. There it was—
There in his desk, the record he had made,
The spiritual plaything of his life:
There were the words no eyes had ever seen
Save his; there were the words that were not made
For glory or for gold. The pretty wife
Whom he had loved and lost had not so much
As heard of them. They were not made for her.
His love had been so much the life of her,
And hers had been so much the life of him,
That any wayward phrasing on his part
Would have had no moment. Neither had lived enough
To know the book, albeit one of them
Had grown enough to write it. There it was,
However, though he knew not why it was:
There was the book, but it was not for her,
For she was dead. And yet, there was the book

Thus would his fancy circle out and out,
And out and in again, till he would make
As if with a large freedom to crush down
Those under-thoughts. He covered with his hands
His tired eyes, and waited: he could hear—
Or partly feel and hear, mechanically—
The sound of talk, with now and then the steps
And skirts of some one scudding on the stairs,
Forgetful of the nerveless funeral feet
That she had brought with her; and more than once
There came to him a call as of a voice—
A voice of love returning—but not hers.
Whose he knew not, nor dreamed; nor did he know,
Nor did he dream, in his blurred loneliness
Of thought, what all the rest might think of him.

For it had come at last, and she was gone
With all the vanished women of old time,—
And she was never coming back again.
Yes, they had buried her that afternoon,
Under the frozen leaves and the cold earth,
Under the leaves and snow. The flickering week,
The sharp and certain day, and the long drowse
Were over, and the man was left alone.
He knew the loss—therefore it puzzled him
That he should sit so long there as he did,
And bring the whole thing back—the love, the trust,
The pallor, the poor face, and the faint way
She last had looked at him—and yet not weep,
Or even choose to look about the room
To see how sad it was; and once or twice
He winked and pinched his eyes against the flame
And hoped there might be tears. But hope was all,
And all to him was nothing: he was lost.
And yet he was not lost: he was astray—

Out of his life and in another life;
And in the stillness of this other life
He wondered and he drowsed. He wondered when
It was, and wondered if it ever was
On earth that he had known the other face—
The searching face, the eloquent, strange face—
That with a sightless beauty looked at him
And with a speechless promise uttered words
That were not the world's words, or any kind
That he had known before. What was it, then?
What was it held him—fascinated him?
Why should he not be human? He could sigh,
And he could even groan,—but what of that?
There was no grief left in him. Was he glad?

Yet how could he be glad, or reconciled,
Or anything but wretched and undone?
How could he be so frigid and inert—
So like a man with water in his veins
Where blood had been a little while before?
How could he sit shut in there like a snail?
What ailed him? What was on him? Was he glad?
Over and over again the question came,
Unanswered and unchanged,—and there he was.
But what in heaven's name did it all mean?
If he had lived as other men had lived,
If home had ever shown itself to be
The counterfeit that others had called home,
Then to this undivined resource of his
There were some key; but now . . . Philosophy?
Yes, he could reason in a kind of way
That he was glad for Miriam's release—
Much as he might be glad to see his friends
Laid out around him with their grave-clothes on,
And this life done for them; but something else

There was that foundered reason, overwhelmed it,
And with a chilled, intuitive rebuff
Beat back the self-cajoling sophistries
That his half-tutored thought would half-project.

What was it, then? Had he become transformed
And hardened through long watches and long grief
Into a loveless, feelingless dead thing
That brooded like a man, breathed like a man,—
Did everything but ache? And was a day
To come some time when feeling should return
Forever to drive off that other face—
The lineless, indistinguishable face—
That once had thrilled itself between his own
And hers there on the pillow,—and again
Between him and the coffin-lid had flashed
Like fate before it closed,—and at the last
Had come, as it should seem, to stay with him,
Bidden or not? He were a stranger then,
Foredrowsed awhile by some deceiving draught
Of poppied anguish, to the covert grief
And the stark loneliness that waited him,
And for the time were cursedly endowed
With a dull trust that shammed indifference
To knowing there would be no touch again
Of her small hand on his, no silencing
Of her quick lips on his, no feminine
Completeness and love-fragrance in the house,
No sound of some one singing any more,
No smoothing of slow fingers on his hair,
No shimmer of pink slippers on brown tiles.

But there was nothing, nothing, in all that:
He had not fooled himself so much as that;
He might be dreaming or he might be sick,

199

But not like that. There was no place for fear,
No reason for remorse. There was the book
That he had made, though. . . . It might be the book;
Perhaps he might find something in the book;
But no, there could be nothing there at all—
He knew it word for word; but what it meant—
He was not sure that he had written it
For what it meant; and he was not quite sure
That he had written it;—more likely it
Was all a paper ghost. . . . But the dead wife
Was real: he knew all that, for he had been
To see them bury her; and he had seen
The flowers and the snow and the stripped limbs
Of trees; and he had heard the preacher pray;
And he was back again, and he was glad.
Was he a brute? No, he was not a brute:
He was a man—like any other man:
He had loved and married his wife Miriam,
They had lived a little while in paradise
And she was gone; and that was all of it.

But no, not all of it—not all of it:
There was the book again; something in that
Pursued him, overpowered him, put out
The futile strength of all his whys and wheres,
And left him unintelligibly numb—
Too numb to care for anything but rest.
It must have been a curious kind of book
That he had made it: it was a drowsy book
At any rate. The very thought of it
Was like the taste of some impossible drink—
A taste that had no taste, but for all that
Had mixed with it a strange thought-cordial,
So potent that it somehow killed in him
The ultimate need of doubting any more—

Of asking any more. Did he but live
The life that he must live, there were no more
To seek.—The rest of it was on the way.

Still there was nothing, nothing, in all this—
Nothing that he cared now to reconcile
With reason or with sorrow. All he knew
For certain was that he was tired out:
His flesh was heavy and his blood beat small;
Something supreme had been wrenched out of him
As if to make vague room for something else.
He had been through too much. Yes, he would stay
There where he was and rest.—And there he stayed;
The daylight became twilight, and he stayed;
The flame and the face faded, and he slept.
And they had buried her that afternoon,
Under the tight-screwed lid of a long box,
Under the earth, under the leaves and snow.

II

Look where she would, feed conscience how she might,
There was but one way now for Damaris—
One straight way that was hers, hers to defend,
At hand, imperious. But the nearness of it,
The flesh-bewildering simplicity,
And the plain strangeness of it, thrilled again
That wretched little quivering single string
Which yielded not, but held her to the place
Where now for five triumphant years had slept
The flameless dust of Argan.—He was gone,
The good man she had married long ago;
And she had lived, and living she had learned,
And surely there was nothing to regret:
Much happiness had been for each of them,

And they had been like lovers to the last:
And after that, and long, long after that,
Her tears had washed out more of widowed grief
Than smiles had ever told of other joy.—
But could she, looking back, find anything
That should return to her in the new time,
And with relentless magic uncreate
This temple of new love where she had thrown
Dead sorrow on the altar of new life?
Only one thing, only one thread was left;
When she broke that, when reason snapped it off,
And once for all, baffled, the grave let go
The trivial hideous hold it had on her,—
Then she were free, free to be what she would,
Free to be what she was.—And yet she stayed,
Leashed, as it were, and with a cobweb strand,
Close to a tombstone—maybe to starve there.

But why to starve? And why stay there at all?
Why not make one good leap and then be done
Forever and at once with Argan's ghost
And all such outworn churchyard servitude?
For it was Argan's ghost that held the string,
And her sick fancy that held Argan's ghost—
Held it and pitied it. She laughed, almost,
There for the moment; but her strained eyes filled
With tears, and she was angry for those tears—
Angry at first, then proud, then sorry for them.
So she grew calm; and after a vain chase
For thoughts more vain, she questioned of herself
What measure of primeval doubts and fears
Were still to be gone through that she might win
Persuasion of her strength and of herself
To be what she could see that she must be,
No matter where the ghost was.—And the more

She lived, the more she came to recognize
That something out of her thrilled ignorance
Was luminously, proudly being born,
And thereby proving, thought by forward thought,
The prowess of its image; and she learned
At length to look right on to the long days
Before her without fearing. She could watch
The coming course of them as if they were
No more than birds, that slowly, silently,
And irretrievably should wing themselves
Uncounted out of sight. And when he came
Again, she might be free—she would be free.
Else, when he looked at her she must look down,
Defeated, and malignly dispossessed
Of what was hers to prove and in the proving
Wisely to consecrate. And if the plague
Of that perverse defeat should come to be—
If at that sickening end she were to find
Herself to be the same poor prisoner
That he had found at first—then she must lose
All sight and sound of him, she must abjure
All possible thought of him: for he would go
So far and for so long from her that love—
Yes, even a love like his, exiled enough,
Might for another's touch be born again—
Born to be lost and starved for and not found;
Or, at the next, the second wretchedest,
It might go mutely flickering down and out,
And on some incomplete and piteous day,
Some perilous day to come, she might at last
Learn, with a noxious freedom, what it is
To be at peace with ghosts. Then were the blow
Thrice deadlier than any kind of death
Could ever be: to know that she had won
The truth too late—there were the dregs indeed

Of wisdom, and of love the final thrust
Unmerciful; and there where now did lie
So plain before her the straight radiance
Of what was her appointed way to take,
Were only the bleak ruts of an old road
That stretched ahead and faded and lay far
Through deserts of unconscionable years.

But vampire thoughts like these confessed the doubt
That love denied; and once, if never again,
They should be turned away. They might come back—
More craftily, perchance, they might come back—
And with a spirit-thirst insatiable
Finish the strength of her; but now, to-day
She would have none of them. She knew that love
Was true, that he was true, that she was true;
And should a death-bed snare that she had made
So long ago be stretched inexorably
Through all her life, only to be unspun
With her last breathing? And were bats and threads,
Accursedly devised with watered gules,
To be Love's heraldry? What were it worth
To live and to find out that life were life
But for an unrequited incubus
Of outlawed shame that would not be thrown down
Till she had thrown down fear and overcome
The woman that was yet so much of her
That she might yet go mad? What were it worth
To live, to linger, and to be condemned
In her submission to a common thought
That clogged itself and made of its first faith
Its last impediment? What augured it,
Now in this quick beginning of new life,
To clutch the sunlight and be feeling back,
Back with a scared fantastic fearfulness,

204

To touch, not knowing why, the vexed-up ghost
Of what was gone?

                   Yes, there was Argan's face,
Pallid and pinched and ruinously marked
With big pathetic bones; there were his eyes,
Quiet and large, fixed wistfully on hers;
And there, close-pressed again within her own,
Quivered his cold thin fingers. And, ah! yes,
There were the words, those dying words again,
And hers that answered when she promised him.
Promised him? . . . yes. And had she known the truth
Of what she felt that he should ask her that,
And had she known the love that was to be,
God knew that she could not have told him then.
But then she knew it not, nor thought of it;
There was no need of it; nor was there need
Of any problematical support
Whereto to cling while she convinced herself
That love's intuitive utility,
Inexorably merciful, had proved
That what was human was unpermanent
And what was flesh was ashes. She had told
Him then that she would love no other man,
That there was not another man on earth
Whom she could ever love, or who could make
So much as a love thought go through her brain;
And he had smiled. And just before he died
His lips had made as if to say something—
Something that passed unwhispered with his breath,
Out of her reach, out of all quest of it.
And then, could she have known enough to know
The meaning of her grief, the folly of it,
The faithlessness and the proud anguish of it,
There might be now no threads to punish her,

No vampire thoughts to suck the coward blood,
The life, the very soul of her.

                            Yes, Yes,
They might come back. . . . But why should they come back?
Why was it she had suffered? Why had she
Struggled and grown these years to demonstrate
That close without those hovering clouds of gloom
And through them here and there forever gleamed
The Light itself, the life, the love, the glory,
Which was of its own radiance good proof
That all the rest was darkness and blind sight?
And who was *she?* The woman she had known—
The woman she had petted and called "I"—
The woman she had pitied, and at last
Commiserated for the most abject
And persecuted of all womankind,—
Could it be she that had sought out the way
To measure and thereby to quench in her
The woman's fear—the fear of her not fearing?
A nervous little laugh that lost itself,
Like logic in a dream, fluttered her thoughts
An instant there that ever she should ask
What she might then have told so easily—
So easily that Annandale had frowned,
Had he been given wholly to be told
The truth of what had never been before
So passionately, so inevitably
Confessed.

               For she could see from where she sat
The sheets that he had bound up like a book
And covered with red leather; and her eyes
Could see between the pages of the book,
Though her eyes, like them, were closed. And she could read

As well as if she had them in her hand,
What he had written on them long ago,—
Six years ago, when he was waiting for her.
She might as well have said that she could see
The man himself, as once he would have looked
Had she been there to watch him while he wrote
Those words, and all for her. . . . For her whose face
Had flashed itself, prophetic and unseen,
But not unspirited, between the life
That would have been without her and the life
That he had gathered up like frozen roots
Out of a grave-clod lying at his feet,
Unconsciously, and as unconsciously
Transplanted and revived. He did not know
The kind of life that he had found, nor did
He doubt, not knowing it; but well he knew
That it was life—new life, and that the old
Might then with unimprisoned wings go free,
Onward and all along to its own light,
Through the appointed shadow.

                       While she gazed
Upon it there she felt within herself
The growing of a newer consciousness—
The pride of something fairer than her first
 Outclamoring of interdicted thought
Had ever quite foretold; and all at once
There quivered and requivered through her flesh,
Like music, like the sound of an old song,
Triumphant, love-remembered murmurings
Of what for passion's innocence had been
 Too mightily, too perilously hers,
Ever to be reclaimed and realized
Until to-day. To-day she could throw off
The burden that had held her down so long,

And she could stand upright, and she could see
The way to take, with eyes that had in them
No gleam but of the spirit. Day or night,
No matter; she could see what was to see—
All that had been till now shut out from her,
The service, the fulfillment, and the truth,
And thus the cruel wiseness of it all.

So Damaris, more like than anything
To one long prisoned in a twilight cave
With hovering bats for all companionship,
And after time set free to fight the sun,
Laughed out, so glad she was to recognize
The test of what had been, through all her folly,
The courage of her conscience; for she knew,
Now on a late-flushed autumn afternoon
That else had been too bodeful of dead things
To be endured with aught but the same old
Inert, self-contradicted martyrdom
Which she had known so long, that she could look
Right forward through the years, nor any more
Shrink with a cringing prescience to behold
The glitter of dead summer on the grass,
Or the brown-glimmered crimson of still trees
Across the intervale where flashed along,
Black-silvered, the cold river. She had found,
As if by some transcendent freakishness
Of reason, the glad life that she had sought
Where naught but obvious clouds could ever be—
Clouds to put out the sunlight from her eyes,
And to put out the love-light from her soul.
But they were gone—now they were all gone;
And with a whimsied pathos, like the mist
Of grief that clings to new-found happiness
Hard wrought, she might have pity for the small

Defeated quest of them that brushed her sight
Like flying lint—lint that had once been thread. . . .

Yes, like an anodyne, the voice of him,
There were the words that he had made for her,
For her alone. The more she thought of them
The more she lived them, and the more she knew
The life-grip and the pulse of warm strength in them.
They were the first and last of words to her,
And there was in them a far questioning
That had for long been variously at work,
Divinely and elusively at work,
With her, and with the grave that had been hers;
They were eternal words, and they diffused
A flame of meaning that men's lexicons
Had never kindled; they were choral words
That harmonized with love's enduring chords
Like wisdom with release; triumphant words
That rang like elemental orisons
Through ages out of ages; words that fed
Love's hunger in the spirit; words that smote;
Thrilled words that echoed, and barbed words that clung;—
And every one of them was like a friend
Whose obstinate fidelity, well tried,
Had found at last and irresistibly
The way to her close conscience, and thereby
Revealed the unsubstantial Nemesis
That she had clutched and shuddered at so long;
And every one of them was like a real
And ringing voice, clear toned and absolute,
But of a love-subdued authority
That uttered thrice the plain significance
Of what had else been generously vague
And indolently true. It may have been
The triumph and the magic of the soul,

Unspeakably revealed, that finally
Had reconciled the grim probationing
Of wisdom with unalterable faith,
But she could feel—not knowing what it was,
For the sheer freedom of it—a new joy
That humanized the latent wizardry
Of his prophetic voice and put for it
The man within the music.

                          So it came
To pass, like many a long-compelled emprise
That with its first accomplishment almost
Annihilates its own severity,
That she could find, whenever she might look,
The certified achievement of a love
That had endured, self-guarded and supreme,
To the glad end of all that wavering;
And she could see that now the flickering world
Of autumn was awake with sudden bloom,
New-born, perforce, of a slow bourgeoning.
And she had found what more than half had been
The grave-deluded, flesh-bewildered fear
Which men and women struggle to call faith.
To be the paid progression to an end
Whereat she knew the foresight and the strength
To glorify the gift of what was hers,
To vindicate the truth of what she was.
And had it come to her so suddenly?
There was a pity and a weariness
In asking that, and a great needlessness;
For now there were no wretched quivering strings
That held her to the churchyard any more:
There were no thoughts that flapped themselves like bats
Around her any more. The shield of love
Was clean, and she had paid enough to learn

How it had always been so. And the truth,
Like silence after some far victory,
Had come to her, and she had found it out
As if it were a vision, a thing born
So suddenly!—just as a flower is born,
Or as a world is born—so suddenly.

SAINTE-NITOUCHE

THOUGH not for common praise of him.
   Nor yet for pride or charity,
Still would I make to Vanderberg
   One tribute for his memory:

One honest warrant of a friend
   Who found with him that flesh was grass—
Who neither blamed him in defect
   Nor marveled how it came to pass;

Or why it ever was that he—
   That Vanderberg, of all good men,
Should lose himself to find himself,
   Straightway to lose himself again.

For we had buried Sainte-Nitouche,
   And he had said to me that night:
"Yes, we have laid her in the earth,
   But what of that?" And he was right.

And he had said: "We have a wife,
   We have a child, we have a church;
'T would be a scurrilous way out
   If we should leave them in the lurch.

211

"That's why I have you here with me
    To-night: you know a talk may take
The place of bromide, cyanide,
    Et cetera. For heaven's sake,

"Why do you look at me like that?
    What have I done to freeze you so?
Dear man, you see where friendship means
    A few things yet that you don't know;

"And you see partly why it is
    That I am glad for what is gone:
For Sainte-Nitouche and for the world
    In me that followed. What lives on—

"Well, here you have it: here at home—
    For even home will yet return.
You know the truth is on my side,
    And that will make the embers burn.

"I see them brighten while I speak,
    I see them flash,—and they are mine!
You do not know them, but I do:
    I know the way they used to shine.

"And I know more than I have told
    Of other life that is to be:
I shall have earned it when it comes,
    And when it comes I shall be free.

"Not as I was before she came,
    But farther on for having been
The servitor, the slave of her—
    The fool, you think. But there's your sin—

SAINTE-NITOUCHE

"Forgive me!—and your ignorance:
  Could you but have the vision here
That I have, you would understand
  As I do that all ways are clear

"For those who dare to follow them
  With earnest eyes and honest feet.
But Sainte-Nitouche has made the way
  For me, and I shall find it sweet.

"Sweet with a bitter sting left?—Yes,
  Bitter enough, God knows, at first;
But there are more steep ways than one
  To make the best look like the worst;

"And here is mine—the dark and hard,
  For me to follow, trust, and hold:
And worship, so that I may leave
  No broken story to be told.

"Therefore I welcome what may come,
  Glad for the days, the nights, the years."
An upward flash of ember-flame
  Revealed the gladness in his tears.

"You see them, but you know," said he,
  "Too much to be incredulous:
You know the day that makes us wise,
  The moment that makes fools of us.

"So I shall follow from now on
  The road that she has found for me:
The dark and starry way that leads
  Right upward, and eternally.

213

"Stumble at first? I may do that;
  And I may grope, and hate the night;
But there's a guidance for the man
  Who stumbles upward for the light,

"And I shall have it all from her,
  The foam-born child of innocence.
I feel you smiling while I speak,
  But that's of little consequence;

"For when we learn that we may find
  The truth where others miss the mark,
What is it worth for us to know
  That friends are smiling in the dark?

"Could we but share the lonely pride
  Of knowing, all would then be well;
But knowledge often writes itself
  In flaming words we cannot spell.

"And I, who have my work to do,
  Look forward; and I dare to see,
Far stretching and all mountainous,
  God's pathway through the gloom for me."

I found so little to say then
  That I said nothing.—"Say good-night,"
Said Vanderberg; "and when we meet
  To-morrow, tell me I was right.

"Forget the dozen other things
  That you have not the faith to say;
For now I know as well as you
  That you are glad to go away."

SAINTE-NITOUCHE

I could have blessed the man for that,
    And he could read me with a smile:
"You doubt," said he, "but if we live
    You'll know me in a little while."

He lived; and all as he foretold,
    I knew him—better than he thought:
My fancy did not wholly dig
    The pit where I believed him caught.

But yet he lived and laughed, and preached,
    And worked—as only players can:
He scoured the shrine that once was home
    And kept himself a clergyman.

The clockwork of his cold routine
    Put friends far off that once were near;
The five staccatos in his laugh
    Were too defensive and too clear;

The glacial sermons that he preached
    Were longer than they should have been;
And, like the man who fashioned them,
    The best were too divinely thin.

But still he lived, and moved, and had
    The sort of being that was his,
Till on a day the shrine of home
    For him was in the Mysteries:—

"My friend, there's one thing yet," said he,
    "And one that I have never shared
With any man that I have met;
    But you—you know me." And he stared

For a slow moment at me then
  With conscious eyes that had the gleam,
The shine, before the stroke:—"You know
  The ways of us, the way we dream:

"You know the glory we have won,
  You know the glamour we have lost;
You see me now, you look at me,—
  And yes, you pity me, almost;

"But never mind the pity—no,
  Confess the faith you can't conceal;
And if you frown, be not like one
  Of those who frown before they feel.

"For there is truth, and half truth,—yes,
  And there's a quarter truth, no doubt;
But mine was more than half. . . . You smile?
  You understand? You bear me out?

"You always knew that I was right—
  You are my friend—and I have tried
Your faith—your love."—The gleam grew small,
  The stroke was easy, and he died.

I saw the dim look change itself
  To one that never will be dim;
I saw the dead flesh to the grave,
  But that was not the last of him.

For what was his to live lives yet:
  Truth, quarter truth, death cannot reach;
Nor is it always what we know
  That we are fittest here to teach.

216

SAINTE-NITOUCHE

The fight goes on when fields are still,
  The triumph clings when arms are down;
The jewels of all coronets
  Are pebbles of the unseen crown;

The specious weight of loud reproof
  Sinks where a still conviction floats;
And on God's ocean after storm
  Time's wreckage is half pilot-boats;

And what wet faces wash to sight
  Thereafter feed the common moan:—
But Vanderberg no pilot had,
  Nor could have: he was all alone.

Unchallenged by the larger light
  The starry quest was his to make;
And of all ways that are for men,
  The starry way was his to take.

We grant him idle names enough
  To-day, but even while we frown
The fight goes on, the triumph clings,
  And there is yet the unseen crown

But was it his? Did Vanderberg
  Find half truth to be passion's thrall,
Or as we met him day by day,
  Was love triumphant, after all?

I do not know so much as that;
  I only know that he died right:
Saint Anthony nor Sainte-Nitouche
  Had ever smiled as he did—quite.

AS A WORLD WOULD HAVE IT

ALCESTIS

SHALL I never make him look at me again?
I look at him, I look my life at him,
I tell him all I know the way to tell,
    But there he stays the same.

Shall I never make him speak one word to me?
Shall I never make him say enough to show
My heart if he be glad? Be glad? . . . ah! God,
    Why did they bring me back?

I wonder, if I go to him again,
If I take him by those two cold hands again,
Shall I get one look of him at last, or feel
    One sign—or anything?

Or will he still sit there in the same way,
Without an answer for me from his lips,
Or from his eyes,—or even with a touch
    Of his hand on my hand? . . .

"Will you look down this once—look down at me?
Speak once—and if you never speak again,
Tell me enough—tell me enough to make
    Me know that you are glad!

"You are my King, and once my King would speak:
You were Admetus once, you loved me once:
Life was a dream of heaven for us once—
    And has the dream gone by?

218

AS A WORLD WOULD HAVE IT

"Do I cling to shadows when I call you Life?
Do you love me still, or are the shadows all?
Or is it I that love you in the grave,
    And you that mourn for me?

"If it be that, then do not mourn for me;
Be glad that I have loved you, and be King.
But if it be not that—if it be true . . .
    Tell me if it be true!"

Then with a choking answer the King spoke;
But never touched his hand on hers, or fixed
His eyes on hers, or on the face of her:
    "Yes, it is true," he said.

"You are alive, and you are with me now;
And you are reaching up to me that I—
That I may take you—I that am a King—
    I that was once a man."

So then she knew. She might have known before;
Truly, she thought, she must have known it long
Before: she must have known it when she came
    From that great sleep of hers.

She knew the truth, but not yet all of it:
He loved her, but he would not let his eyes
Prove that he loved her; and he would not hold
    His wife there in his arms.

So, like a slave, she waited at his knees,
And waited. She was not unhappy now.
She quivered, but she knew that he would speak
    Again—and he did speak.

And while she felt the tremor of his words,
He told her all there was for him to tell;
And then he turned his face to meet her face,
    That she might look at him.

She looked; and all her trust was in that look,
And all her faith was in it, and her love;
And when his answer to that look came back,
    It flashed back through his tears.

So then she put her arms around his neck,
And kissed him on his forehead and his lips;
And there she clung, fast in his arms again,
    Triumphant, with closed eyes.

At last, half whispering, she spoke once more:
"Why was it that you suffered for so long?
Why could you not believe me—trust in me?
    Was I so strange as that?

"We suffer when we do not understand;
And you have suffered—you that love me now—
Because you are a man. . . . There is one thing
    No man can understand.

"I would have given everything?—gone down
To Tartarus—to silence? Was it that?
I would have died? I would have let you live?—
    And was it very strange?"

THE CORRIDOR

It may have been the pride in me for aught
I know, or just a patronizing whim;
But call it freak or fancy, or what not,
I cannot hide that hungry face of him.

CORTEGE

I keep a scant half-dozen words he said,
And every now and then I lose his name;
He may be living or he may be dead,
But I must have him with me all the same.

I knew it, and I knew it all along,—
And felt it once or twice, or thought I did;
But only as a glad man feels a song
That sounds around a stranger's coffin lid.

I knew it, and he knew it, I believe,
But silence held us alien to the end;
And I have now no magic to retrieve
That year, to stop that hunger for a friend.

CORTÈGE

Four o'clock this afternoon,
Fifteen hundred miles away:
So it goes, the crazy tune,
So it pounds and hums all day

Four o'clock this afternoon,
Earth will hide them far away:
Best they go to go so soon,
Best for them the grave to-day.

Had she gone but half so soon,
Half the world had passed away.
Four o'clock this afternoon,
Best for them they go to-day.

Four o'clock this afternoon
Love will hide them deep, they say;
Love that made the grave so soon,
Fifteen hundred miles away.

221

Four o'clock this afternoon—
Ah, but they go slow to-day:
Slow to suit my crazy tune,
Past the need of all we say.

Best it came to come so soon,
Best for them they go to-day:
Four o'clock this afternoon,
Fifteen hundred miles away.

PARTNERSHIP

YES, you have it; I can see.
Beautiful? . . . Dear, look at me!
Look and let my shame confess
Triumph after weariness.
Beautiful? Ah, yes.

Lift it where the beams are bright;
Hold it where the western light,
Shining in above my bed,
Throws a glory on your head.
Now it is all said.

All there was for me to say
From the first until to-day.
Long denied and long deferred,
Now I say it in one word—
Now; and you have heard.

Life would have its way with us,
And I've called it glorious:
For I know the glory now
And I read it on your brow.
You have shown me how.

TWILIGHT SONG

I can feel your cheeks all wet,
But your eyes will not forget:
In the frown you cannot hide
I can read where faith and pride
Are not satisfied.

But the word was, two should live:
Two should suffer—and forgive:
By the steep and weary way,
For the glory of the clay,
Two should have their day.

We have toiled and we have wept
For the gift the gods have kept:
Clashing and unreconciled
When we might as well have smiled,
We have played the child.

But the clashing is all past,
And the gift is yours at last.
Lift it—hold it high again! . . .
Did I doubt you now and then?
Well, we are not men.

Never mind; we know the way,—
And I do not need to stay.
Let us have it well confessed:
You to triumph, I to rest.
That will be the best.

TWILIGHT SONG

THROUGH the shine, through the rain
We have shared the day's load;
To the old march again
We have tramped the long road;

We have laughed, we have cried,
And we've tossed the King's crown;
We have fought, we have died,
And we've trod the day down.
So it's lift the old song
Ere the night flies again,
Where the road leads along
Through the shine, through the rain.

Long ago, far away,
Came a sign from the skies;
And we feared then to pray
For the new sun to rise:
With the King there at hand,
Not a child stepped or stirred—
Where the light filled the land
And the light brought the word;
For we knew then the gleam
Though we feared then the day,
And the dawn smote the dream
Long ago, far away.

But the road leads us all,
For the King now is dead;
And we know, stand or fall,
We have shared the day's bread.
We may laugh down the dream,
For the dream breaks and flies;
And we trust now the gleam,
For the gleam never dies;—
So it's off now the load,
For we know the night's call,
And we know now the road
And the road leads us all.

VARIATIONS OF GREEK THEMES

Through the shine, through the rain,
We have wrought the day's quest;
To the old march again
We have earned the day's rest;
We have laughed, we have cried,
And we've heard the King's groans;
We have fought, we have died,
And we've burned the King's bones,
And we lift the old song
Ere the night flies again,
Where the road leads along
Through the shine, through the rain.

VARIATIONS OF GREEK THEMES

I

A HAPPY MAN

(*Carphyllides*)

WHEN these graven lines you see,
Traveler, do not pity me;
Though I be among the dead,
Let no mournful word be said.

Children that I leave behind,
And their children, all were kind;
Near to them and to my wife,
I was happy all my life.

My three sons I married right,
And their sons I rocked at night;
Death nor sorrow ever brought
Cause for one unhappy thought.

225

Now, and with no need of tears,
Here they leave me, full of years,—
Leave me to my quiet rest
In the region of the blest.

II

A MIGHTY RUNNER

(*Nicarchus*)

THE day when Charmus ran with five
In Arcady, as I'm alive,
He came in seventh.—"Five and one
Make seven, you say? It can't be done."—
Well, if you think it needs a note,
A friend in a fur overcoat
Ran with him, crying all the while,
"You'll beat 'em, Charmus, by a mile!"
And so he came in seventh.
Therefore, good Zoilus, you see
The thing is plain as plain can be;
And with four more for company,
He would have been eleventh.

III

THE RAVEN

(*Nicarchus*)

THE gloom of death is on the raven's wing,
  The song of death is in the raven's cries:
But when Demophilus begins to sing,
  The raven dies.

IV

EUTYCHIDES

(*Lucilius*)

EUTYCHIDES, who wrote the songs,
Is going down where he belongs.
O you unhappy ones, beware:
Eutychides will soon be there!
For he is coming with twelve lyres,
And with more than twice twelve quires
Of the stuff that he has done
In the world from which he's gone.
Ah, now must you know death indeed,
For he is coming with all speed;
And with Eutychides in Hell,
Where's a poor tortured soul to dwell?

V

DORICHA

(*Posidippus*)

So now the very bones of you are gone
Where they were dust and ashes long ago;
And there was the last ribbon you tied on
To bind your hair, and that is dust also;
And somewhere there is dust that was of old
A soft and scented garment that you wore—
The same that once till dawn did closely fold
You in with fair Charaxus, fair no more.

But Sappho, and the white leaves of her song,
Will make your name a word for all to learn,
And all to love thereafter, even while

227

It's but a name; and this will be as long
As there are distant ships that will return
Again to Naucratis and to the Nile.

VI

THE DUST OF TIMAS

(Sappho)

THIS dust was Timas; and they say
That almost on her wedding day
She found her bridal home to be
The dark house of Persephone.

And many maidens, knowing then
That she would not come back again,
Unbound their curls; and all in tears,
They cut them off with sharpened shears.

VII

ARETEMIAS

(Antipater of Sidon)

I'M sure I see it all now as it was,
When first you set your foot upon the shore
Where dim Cocytus flows for evermore,
And how it came to pass
That all those Dorian women who are there
In Hades, and still fair,
Came up to you, so young, and wept and smiled
When they beheld you and your little child.
And then, I'm sure, with tears upon your face
To be in that sad place,

228

You told of the two children you had borne,
And then of Euphron, whom you leave to mourn.
"One stays with him," you said,
"And this one I bring with me to the dead."

VIII

THE OLD STORY

(*Marcus Argentarius*)

LIKE many a one, when you had gold
Love met you smiling, we are told;
But now that all your gold is gone,
Love leaves you hungry and alone.

And women, who have called you more
Sweet names than ever were before,
Will ask another now to tell
What man you are and where you dwell.

Was ever anyone but you
So long in learning what is true?
Must you find only at the end
That who has nothing has no friend?

IX

TO-MORROW

(*Macedonius*)

TO-MORROW? Then your one word left is always now the same;
And that's a word that names a day that has no more a name.
To-morrow, I have learned at last, is all you have to give:

229

The rest will be another's now, as long as I may live.
You will see me in the evening?—And what evening has there
  been,
Since time began with women, but old age and wrinkled skin?

X

LAIS TO APHRODITE

(Plato)

WHEN I, poor Lais, with my crown
Of beauty could laugh Hellas down,
Young lovers crowded at my door,
Where now my lovers come no more.

So, Goddess, you will not refuse
A mirror that has now no use;
For what I was I cannot be,
And what I am I will not see.

XI

AN INSCRIPTION BY THE SEA

(Glaucus)

No dust have I to cover me,
  My grave no man may show;
My tomb is this unending sea,
  And I lie far below.
My fate, O stranger, was to drown;
And where it was the ship went down
  Is what the sea-birds know.

230

THE FIELD OF GLORY

WAR shook the land where Levi dwelt,
And fired the dismal wrath he felt,
That such a doom was ever wrought.
As his, to toil while others fought;
To toil, to dream—and still to dream,
With one day barren as another;
To consummate, as it would seem,
The dry despair of his old mother.

Far off one afternoon began
The sound of man destroying man;
And Levi, sick with nameless rage,
Condemned again his heritage,
And sighed for scars that might have come,
And would, if once he could have sundered
Those harsh, inhering claims of home
That held him while he cursed and wondered.

Another day, and then there came,
Rough, bloody, ribald, hungry, lame,
But yet themselves, to Levi's door,
Two remnants of the day before.
They laughed at him and what he sought;
They jeered him, and his painful acre;
But Levi knew that they had fought,
And left their manners to their Maker.

That night, for the grim widow's ears,
With hopes that hid themselves in fears,
He told of arms, and fiery deeds,
Whereat one leaps the while he reads,

231

And said he'd be no more a clown,
While others drew the breath of battle.—
The mother looked him up and down,
And laughed—a scant laugh with a rattle.

She told him what she found to tell,
And Levi listened, and heard well
Some admonitions of a voice
That left him no cause to rejoice.—
He sought a friend, and found the stars,
And prayed aloud that they should aid him;
But they said not a word of wars,
Or of a reason why God made him.

And who's of this or that estate
We do not wholly calculate,
When baffling shades that shift and cling
Are not without their glimmering;
When even Levi, tired of faith,
Beloved of none, forgot by many,
Dismissed as an inferior wraith,
Reborn may be as great as any.

MERLIN

(1917)

To George Burnham

MERLIN

I

"GAWAINE, GAWAINE, what look ye for to see,
So far beyond the faint edge of the world?
D'ye look to see the lady Vivian,
Pursued by divers ominous vile demons
That have another king more fierce than ours?
Or think ye that if ye look far enough
And hard enough into the feathery west
Ye'll have a glimmer of the Grail itself?
And if ye look for neither Grail nor lady,
What look ye for to see, Gawaine, Gawaine?"

So Dagonet, whom Arthur made a knight
Because he loved him as he laughed at him,
Intoned his idle presence on a day
To Gawaine, who had thought himself alone,
Had there been in him thought of anything
Save what was murmured now in Camelot
Of Merlin's hushed and all but unconfirmed
Appearance out of Brittany. It was heard
At first there was a ghost in Arthur's palace,
But soon among the scullions and anon
Among the knights a firmer credit held
All tongues from uttering what all glances told—
Though not for long. Gawaine, this afternoon,
Fearing he might say more to Lancelot

Of Merlin's rumor-laden resurrection
Than Lancelot would have an ear to cherish,
Had sauntered off with his imagination
To Merlin's Rock, where now there was no Merlin
To meditate upon a whispering town
Below him in the silence.—Once he said
To Gawaine: "You are young; and that being so,
Behold the shining city of our dreams
And of our King."—"Long live the King," said Gawaine.—
"Long live the King," said Merlin after him;
"Better for me that I shall not be King;
Wherefore I say again, Long live the King,
And add, God save him, also, and all kings—
All kings and queens. I speak in general.
Kings have I known that were but weary men
With no stout appetite for more than peace
That was not made for them."—"Nor were they made
For kings," Gawaine said, laughing.—"You are young,
Gawaine, and you may one day hold the world
Between your fingers, knowing not what it is
That you are holding. Better for you and me,
I think, that we shall not be kings."

                                            Gawaine,
Remembering Merlin's words of long ago,
Frowned as he thought, and having frowned again,
He smiled and threw an acorn at a lizard:
"There's more afoot and in the air to-day
Than what is good for Camelot. Merlin
May or may not know all, but he said well
To say to me that he would not be King.
Nor more would I be King." Far down he gazed
On Camelot, until he made of it
A phantom town of many stillnesses,

236

Not reared for men to dwell in, or for kings
To reign in, without omens and obscure
Familiars to bring terror to their days;
For though a knight, and one as hard at arms
As any, save the fate-begotten few
That all acknowledged or in envy loathed,
He felt a foreign sort of creeping up
And down him, as of moist things in the dark,—
When Dagonet, coming on him unawares,
Presuming on his title of Sir Fool,
Addressed him and crooned on till he was done:
"What look ye for to see, Gawaine, Gawaine?"

"Sir Dagonet, you best and wariest
Of all dishonest men, I look through Time,
For sight of what it is that is to be.
I look to see it, though I see it not.
I see a town down there that holds a king,
And over it I see a few small clouds—
Like feathers in the west, as you observe;
And I shall see no more this afternoon
Than what there is around us every day,
Unless you have a skill that I have not
To ferret the invisible for rats."

"If you see what's around us every day,
You need no other showing to go mad.
Remember that and take it home with you;
And say tonight, 'I had it of a fool—
With no immediate obliquity
For this one or for that one, or for me.'"
Gawaine, having risen, eyed the fool curiously:
"I'll not forget I had it of a knight,
Whose only folly is to fool himself;
And as for making other men to laugh,

And so forget their sins and selves a little,
There's no great folly there. So keep it up,
As long as you've a legend or a song,
And have whatever sport of us you like
Till havoc is the word and we fall howling.
For I've a guess there may not be so loud
A sound of laughing here in Camelot
When Merlin goes again to his gay grave
In Brittany. To mention lesser terrors,
Men say his beard is gone."

                              "Do men say that?"
A twitch of an impatient weariness
Played for a moment over the lean face
Of Dagonet, who reasoned inwardly:
"The friendly zeal of this inquiring knight
Will overtake his tact and leave it squealing,
One of these days."—Gawaine looked hard at him:
"If I be too familiar with a fool,
I'm on the way to be another fool,"
He mused, and owned a rueful qualm within him:
"Yes, Dagonet," he ventured, with a laugh,
"Men tell me that his beard has vanished wholly,
And that he shines now as the Lord's anointed,
And wears the valiance of an ageless youth
Crowned with a glory of eternal peace."

Dagonet, smiling strangely, shook his head:
"I grant your valiance of a kind of youth
To Merlin, but your crown of peace I question;
For, though I know no more than any churl
Who pinches any chambermaid soever
In the King's palace, I look not to Merlin
For peace, when out of his peculiar tomb
He comes again to Camelot. Time swings

238

MERLIN

A mighty scythe, and some day all your peace
Goes down before its edge like so much clover.
No, it is not for peace that Merlin comes,
Without a trumpet—and without a beard,
If what you say men say of him be true—
Nor yet for sudden war."

                                    Gawaine, for a moment,
Met then the ambiguous gaze of Dagonet,
And, making nothing of it, looked abroad
As if at something cheerful on all sides,
And back again to the fool's unasking eyes:
"Well, Dagonet, if Merlin would have peace,
Let Merlin stay away from Brittany,"
Said he, with admiration for the man
Whom Folly called a fool: "And we have known him;
We knew him once when he knew everything."

"He knew as much as God would let him know
Until he met the lady Vivian.
I tell you that, for the world knows all that;
Also it knows he told the King one day
That he was to be buried, and alive,
In Brittany; and that the King should see
The face of him no more. Then Merlin sailed
Away to Vivian in Broceliande,
Where now she crowns him and herself with flowers
And feeds him fruits and wines and many foods
Of many savors, and sweet ortolans.
Wise books of every lore of every land
Are there to fill his days, if he require them,
And there are players of all instruments—
Flutes, hautboys, drums, and viols; and she sings
To Merlin, till he trembles in her arms

239

And there forgets that any town alive
Had ever such a name as Camelot.
So Vivian holds him with her love, they say,
And he, who has no age, has not grown old.
I swear to nothing, but that's what they say.
That's being buried in Broceliande
For too much wisdom and clairvoyancy.
But you and all who live, Gawaine, have heard
This tale, or many like it, more than once;
And you must know that Love, when Love invites
Philosophy to play, plays high and wins,
Or low and loses. And you say to me,
'If Merlin would have peace, let Merlin stay
Away from Brittany.' Gawaine, you are young,
And Merlin's in his grave."

                        "Merlin said once
That I was young, and it's a joy for me
That I am here to listen while you say it.
Young or not young, if that be burial,
May I be buried long before I die.
I might be worse than young; I might be old."—
Dagonet answered, and without a smile:
"Somehow I fancy Merlin saying that;
A fancy—a mere fancy." Then he smiled:
"And such a doom as his may be for you,
Gawaine, should your untiring divination
Delve in the veiled eternal mysteries
Too far to be a pleasure for the Lord.
And when you stake your wisdom for a woman,
Compute the woman to be worth a grave,
As Merlin did, and say no more about it.
But Vivian, she played high. Oh, very high!
Flutes, hautboys, drums, and viols,—and her love.
Gawaine, farewell."

MERLIN

"Farewell, Sir Dagonet,
And may the devil take you presently."
He followed with a vexed and envious eye,
And with an arid laugh, Sir Dagonet's
Departure, till his gaunt obscurity
Was cloaked and lost amid the glimmering trees.
"Poor fool!" he murmured. "Or am I the fool?
With all my fast ascendency in arms,
That ominous clown is nearer to the King
Than I am—yet; and God knows what he knows,
And what his wits infer from what he sees
And feels and hears. I wonder what he knows
Of Lancelot, or what I might know now,
Could I have sunk myself to sound a fool
To springe a friend. . . . No, I like not this day.
There's a cloud coming over Camelot
Larger than any that is in the sky,—
Or Merlin would be still in Brittany,
With Vivian and the viols. It's all too strange."

And later, when descending to the city,
Through unavailing casements he could hear
The roaring of a mighty voice within,
Confirming fervidly his own conviction:
"It's all too strange, and half the world's half crazy!"—
He scowled: "Well, I agree with Lamorak."
He frowned, and passed: "And I like not this day."

II

Sir Lamorak, the man of oak and iron,
Had with him now, as a care-laden guest,
Sir Bedivere, a man whom Arthur loved
As he had loved no man save Lancelot.

241

Like one whose late-flown shaft of argument
Had glanced and fallen afield innocuously,
He turned upon his host a sudden eye
That met from Lamorak's an even shaft
Of native and unused authority;
And each man held the other till at length
Each turned away, shutting his heavy jaws
Again together, prisoning thus two tongues
That might forget and might not be forgiven.
Then Bedivere, to find a plain way out,
Said, "Lamorak, let us drink to some one here,
And end this dryness. Who shall it be—the King,
The Queen, or Lancelot?"—"Merlin," Lamorak growled:
And then there were more wrinkles round his eyes
Than Bedivere had said were possible.
"There's no refusal in me now for that,"
The guest replied; "so, 'Merlin' let it be.
We've not yet seen him, but if he be here,
And even if he should not be here, say 'Merlin.'"
They drank to the unseen from two new tankards,
And fell straightway to sighing for the past,
And what was yet before them. Silence laid
A cogent finger on the lips of each
Impatient veteran, whose hard hands lay clenched
And restless on his midriff, until words
Were stronger than strong Lamorak:

                                        "Bedivere,"

Began the solid host, "you may as well
Say now as at another time hereafter
That all your certainties have bruises on 'em,
And all your pestilent asseverations
Will never make a man a salamander—
Who's born, as we are told, so fire won't bite him,—
Or a slippery queen a nun who counts and burns

242

Herself to nothing with her beads and candles.
There's nature, and what's in us, to be sifted
Before we know ourselves, or any man
Or woman that God suffers to be born.
That's how I speak; and while you strain your mazard,
Like Father Jove, big with a new Minerva,
We'll say, to pass the time, that I speak well.
God's fish! The King had eyes; and Lancelot
Won't ride home to his mother, for she's dead.
The story is that Merlin warned the King
Of what's come now to pass; and I believe it
And Arthur, he being Arthur and a king,
Has made a more pernicious mess than one,
We're told, for being so great and amorous:
It's that unwholesome and inclement cub
Young Modred I'd see first in hell before
I'd hang too high the Queen or Lancelot;
The King, if one may say it, set the pace,
And we've two strapping bastards here to prove it.
Young Borre, he's well enough; but as for Modred,
I squirm as often as I look at him.
And there again did Merlin warn the King,
The story goes abroad; and I believe it."

Sir Bedivere, as one who caught no more
Than what he would of Lamorak's outpouring,
Inclined his grizzled head and closed his eyes
Before he sighed and rubbed his beard and spoke:
"For all I know to make it otherwise,
The Queen may be a nun some day or other;
I'd pray to God for such a thing to be,
If prayer for that were not a mockery.
We're late now for much praying, Lamorak,
When you and I can feel upon our faces
A wind that has been blowing over ruins

That we had said were castles and high towers—
Till Merlin, or the spirit of him, came
As the dead come in dreams. I saw the King
This morning, and I saw his face. Therefore,
I tell you, if a state shall have a king,
The king must have the state, and be the state;
Or then shall we have neither king nor state,
But bones and ashes, and high towers all fallen:
And we shall have, where late there was a kingdom,
A dusty wreck of what was once a glory—
A wilderness whereon to crouch and mourn
And moralize, or else to build once more
For something better or for something worse.
Therefore again, I say that Lancelot
Has wrought a potent wrong upon the King,
And all who serve and recognize the King,
And all who follow him and all who love him.
Whatever the stormy faults he may have had,
To look on him today is to forget them;
And if it be too late for sorrow now
To save him—for it was a broken man
I saw this morning, and a broken king—
The God who sets a day for desolation
Will not forsake him in Avilion,
Or whatsoever shadowy land there be
Where peace awaits him on its healing shores."

Sir Lamorak, shifting in his oaken chair,
Growled like a dog and shook himself like one:
"For the stone-chested, helmet-cracking knight
That you are known to be from Lyonnesse
To northward, Bedivere, you fol-de-rol
When days are rancid, and you fiddle-faddle
More like a woman than a man with hands
Fit for the smiting of a crazy giant

MERLIN

With armor an inch thick, as we all know
You are, when you're not sermonizing at us.
As for the King, I say the King, no doubt,
Is angry, sorry, and all sorts of things,
For Lancelot, and for his easy Queen,
Whom he took knowing she'd thrown sparks already
On that same piece of tinder, Lancelot,
Who fetched her with him from Leodogran
Because the King—God save poor human reason!—
Would prove to Merlin, who knew everything
Worth knowing in those days, that he was wrong.
I'll drink now and be quiet,—but, by God,
I'll have to tell you, Brother Bedivere,
Once more, to make you listen properly,
That crowns and orders, and high palaces,
And all the manifold ingredients
Of this good solid kingdom, where we sit
And spit now at each other with our eyes,
Will not go rolling down to hell just yet
Because a pretty woman is a fool.
And here's Kay coming with his fiddle face
As long now as two fiddles. Sit ye down,
Sir Man, and tell us everything you know
Of Merlin—or his ghost without a beard.
What mostly is it?"

               Sir Kay, the seneschal,
Sat wearily while he gazed upon the two:
"To you it mostly is, if I err not,
That what you hear of Merlin's coming back
Is nothing more or less than heavy truth.
But ask me nothing of the Queen, I say,
For I know nothing. All I know of her
Is what her eyes have told the silences
That now attend her; and that her estate

245

Is one for less complacent execration
Than quips and innuendoes of the city
Would augur for her sin—if there be sin—
Or for her name—if now she have a name.
And where, I say, is this to lead the King,
And after him, the kingdom and ourselves?
Here be we, three men of a certain strength
And some confessed intelligence, who know
That Merlin has come out of Brittany—
Out of his grave, as he would say it for us—
Because the King has now a desperation
More strong upon him than a woman's net
Was over Merlin—for now Merlin's here,
And two of us who knew him know how well
His wisdom, if he have it any longer,
Will by this hour have sounded and appraised
The grief and wrath and anguish of the King,
Requiring mercy and inspiring fear
Lest he forego the vigil now most urgent,
And leave unwatched a cranny where some worm
Or serpent may come in to speculate."

"I know your worm, and his worm's name is Modred—
Albeit the streets are not yet saying so,"
Said Lamorak, as he lowered his wrath and laughed
A sort of poisonous apology
To Kay: "And in the meantime, I'll be gyved!
Here's Bedivere a-wailing for the King,
And you, Kay, with a moist eye for the Queen.
I think I'll blow a horn for Lancelot;
For by my soul a man's in sorry case
When Guineveres are out with eyes to scorch him:
I'm not so ancient or so frozen certain
That I'd ride horses down to skeletons

If she were after me. Has Merlin seen him—
This Lancelot, this Queen-fed friend of ours?"

Kay answered sighing, with a lonely scowl:
"The picture that I conjure leaves him out;
The King and Merlin are this hour together,
And I can say no more; for I know nothing.
But how the King persuaded or beguiled
The stricken wizard from across the water
Outriddles my poor wits. It's all too strange."

"It's all too strange, and half the world's half crazy!"
Roared Lamorak, forgetting once again
The devastating carriage of his voice.
"Is the King sick?" he said, more quietly;
"Is he to let one damned scratch be enough
To paralyze the force that heretofore
Would operate a way through hell and iron,
And iron already slimy with his blood?
Is the King blind—with Modred watching him?
Does he forget the crown for Lancelot?
Does he forget that every woman mewing
Shall some day be a handful of small ashes?"

"You speak as one for whom the god of Love
Has yet a mighty trap in preparation.
We know you, Lamorak," said Bedivere:
"We know you for a short man, Lamorak,—
In deeds, if not in inches or in words;
But there are fens and heights and distances
That your capricious ranging has not yet
Essayed in this weird region of man's love.
Forgive me, Lamorak, but your words are words.
Your deeds are what they are; and ages hence
Will men remember your illustriousness,

247

If there be gratitude in history.
For me, I see the shadow of the end,
Wherein to serve King Arthur to the end,
And, if God have it so, to see the Grail
Before I die."

                       But Lamorak shook his head:
"See what you will, or what you may. For me,
I see no other than a stinking mess—
With Modred stirring it, and Agravaine
Spattering Camelot with as much of it
As he can throw. The Devil got somehow
Into God's workshop once upon a time,
And out of the red clay that he found there
He made a shape like Modred, and another
As like as eyes are to this Agravaine.
'I never made 'em,' said the good Lord God,
'But let 'em go, and see what comes of 'em.'
And that's what we're to do. As for the Grail,
I've never worried it, and so the Grail
Has never worried me."

                       Kay sighed. "I see
With Bedivere the coming of the end,"
He murmured; "for the King I saw today
Was not, nor shall he ever be again,
The King we knew. I say the King is dead;
The man is living, but the King is dead.
The wheel is broken."

                     "Faugh!" said Lamorak;
"There are no dead kings yet in Camelot;
But there is Modred who is hatching ruin,—
And when it hatches I may not be here.
There's Gawaine too, and he does not forget

MERLIN

My father, who killed his. King Arthur's house
Has more divisions in it than I like
In houses; and if Modred's aim be good
For backs like mine, I'm not long for the scene."

III

KING ARTHUR, as he paced a lonely floor
That rolled a muffled echo, as he fancied,
All through the palace and out through the world,
Might now have wondered hard, could he have heard
Sir Lamorak's apathetic disregard
Of what Fate's knocking made so manifest
And ominous to others near the King—
If any, indeed, were near him at this hour
Save Merlin, once the wisest of all men,
And weary Dagonet, whom he had made
A knight for love of him and his abused
Integrity. He might have wondered hard
And wondered much; and after wondering,
He might have summoned, with as little heart
As he had now for crowns, the fond, lost Merlin,
Whose Nemesis had made of him a slave,
A man of dalliance, and a sybarite.

"Men change in Brittany, Merlin," said the King;
And even his grief had strife to freeze again
A dreary smile for the transmuted seer
Now robed in heavy wealth of purple silk,
With frogs and foreign tassels. On his face,
Too smooth now for a wizard or a sage,
Lay written, for the King's remembering eyes,
A pathos of a lost authority
Long faded, and unconscionably gone;
And on the King's heart lay a sudden cold:

"I might as well have left him in his grave,
As he would say it, saying what was true,—
As death is true. This Merlin is not mine,
But Vivian's. My crown is less than hers,
And I am less than woman to this man."

Then Merlin, as one reading Arthur's words
On viewless tablets in the air before him:
"Now, Arthur, since you are a child of mine—
A foster-child, and that's a kind of child—
Be not from hearsay or despair too eager
To dash your meat with bitter seasoning,
So none that are more famished than yourself
Shall have what you refuse. For you are King,
And if you starve yourself, you starve the state;
And then by sundry looks and silences
Of those you loved, and by the lax regard
Of those you knew for fawning enemies,
You may learn soon that you are King no more,
But a slack, blasted, and sad-fronted man,
Made sadder with a crown. No other friend
Than I could say this to you, and say more;
And if you bid me say no more, so be it."

The King, who sat with folded arms, now bowed
His head and felt, unfought and all aflame
Like immanent hell-fire, the wretchedness
That only those who are to lead may feel—
And only they when they are maimed and worn
Too sore to covet without shuddering
The fixed impending eminence where death
Itself were victory, could they but lead
Unbitten by the serpents they had fed.
Turning, he spoke: "Merlin, you say the truth:
There is no man who could say more to me

250

Today, or say so much to me, and live.
But you are Merlin still, or part of him;
I did you wrong when I thought otherwise,
And I am sorry now. Say what you will.
We are alone, and I shall be alone
As long as Time shall hide a reason here
For me to stay in this infested world
Where I have sinned and erred and heeded not
Your counsel; and where you yourself—God save us!—
Have gone down smiling to the smaller life
That you and your incongruous laughter called
Your living grave. God save us all, Merlin,
When you, the seer, the founder, and the prophet,
May throw the gold of your immortal treasure
Back to the God that gave it, and then laugh
Because a woman has you in her arms . . .
Why do you sting me now with a small hive
Of words that are all poison? I do not ask
Much honey; but why poison me for nothing,
And with a venom that I know already
As I know crowns and wars? Why tell a king—
A poor, foiled, flouted, miserable king—
That if he lets rats eat his fingers off
He'll have no fingers to fight battles with?
I know as much as that, for I am still
A king—who thought himself a little less
Than God; a king who built him palaces
On sand and mud, and hears them crumbling now,
And sees them tottering, as he knew they must.
You are the man who made me to be King—
Therefore, say anything."

                              Merlin, stricken deep
With pity that was old, being born of old
Foreshadowings, made answer to the King:

"This coil of Lancelot and Guinevere
Is not for any mortal to undo,
Or to deny, or to make otherwise;
But your most violent years are on their way
To days, and to a sounding of loud hours
That are to strike for war. Let not the time
Between this hour and then be lost in fears,
Or told in obscurations and vain faith
In what has been your long security;
For should your force be slower then than hate,
And your regret be sharper than your sight,
And your remorse fall heavier than your sword,—
Then say farewell to Camelot, and the crown.
But say not you have lost, or failed in aught
Your golden horoscope of imperfection
Has held in starry words that I have read.
I see no farther now than I saw then,
For no man shall be given of everything
Together in one life; yet I may say
The time is imminent when he shall come
For whom I founded the Siege Perilous;
And he shall be too much a living part
Of what he brings, and what he burns away in,
To be for long a vexed inhabitant
Of this mad realm of stains and lower trials.
And here the ways of God again are mixed:
For this new knight who is to find the Grail
For you, and for the least who pray for you
In such lost coombs and hollows of the world
As you have never entered, is to be
The son of him you trusted—Lancelot,
Of all who ever jeopardized a throne
Sure the most evil-fated, saving one,
Your son, begotten, though you knew not then
Your leman was your sister, of Morgause;

For it is Modred now, not Lancelot,
Whose native hate plans your annihilation—
Though he may smile till he be sick, and swear
Allegiance to an unforgiven father
Until at last he shake an empty tongue
Talked out with too much lying—though his lies
Will have a truth to steer them. Trust him not,
For unto you the father, he the son
Is like enough to be the last of terrors—
If in a field of time that looms to you
Far larger than it is you fail to plant
And harvest the old seeds of what I say,
And so be nourished and adept again
For what may come to be. But Lancelot
Will have you first; and you need starve no more
For the Queen's love, the love that never was.
Your Queen is now your Kingdom, and hereafter
Let no man take it from you, or you die.
Let no man take it from you for a day;
For days are long when we are far from what
We love, and mischief's other name is distance.
Let .hat be all, for I can say no more;
Not even to Blaise the Hermit, were he living,
Could I say more than I have given you now
To hear; and he alone was my confessor."

The King arose and paced the floor again.
"I get gray comfort of dark words," he said;
"But tell me not that you can say no more:
You can, for I can hear you saying it.
Yet I'll not ask for more. I have enough—
Until my new knight comes to prove and find
The promise and the glory of the Grail,
Though I shall see no Grail. For I have built
On sand and mud, and I shall see no Grail."—

"Nor I," said Merlin. "Once I dreamed of it,
But I was buried. I shall see no Grail,
Nor would I have it otherwise. I saw
Too much, and that was never good for man.
The man who goes alone too far goes mad—
In one way or another. God knew best,
And he knows what is coming yet for me.
I do not ask. Like you, I have enough."

That night King Arthur's apprehension found
In Merlin an obscure and restive guest,
Whose only thought was on the hour of dawn,
When he should see the last of Camelot
And ride again for Brittany; and what words
Were said before the King was left alone
Were only darker for reiteration.
They parted, all provision made secure
For Merlin's early convoy to the coast,
And Arthur tramped the past. The loneliness
Of kings, around him like the unseen dead,
Lay everywhere; and he was loath to move,
As if in fear to meet with his cold hand
The touch of something colder. Then a whim,
Begotten of intolerable doubt,
Seized him and stung him until he was asking
If any longer lived among his knights
A man to trust as once he trusted all,
And Lancelot more than all. "And it is he
Who is to have me first," so Merlin says,—
"As if he had me not in hell already.
Lancelot! Lancelot!" He cursed the tears
That cooled his misery, and then he asked
Himself again if he had one to trust
Among his knights, till even Bedivere,
Tor. Bors, and Percival, rough Lamorak,

MERLIN

Griflet, and Gareth, and gay Gawaine, all
Were dubious knaves,—or they were like to be,
For cause to make them so; and he had made
Himself to be the cause. "God set me right,
Before this folly carry me on farther,"
He murmured; and he smiled unhappily,
Though fondly, as he thought: "Yes, there is one
Whom I may trust with even my soul's last shred;
And Dagonet will sing for me tonight
An old song, not too merry or too sad."

When Dagonet, having entered, stood before
The King as one affrighted, the King smiled:
"You think because I call for you so late
That I am angry, Dagonet? Why so?
Have you been saying what I say to you,
And telling men that you brought Merlin here?
No? So I fancied; and if you report
No syllable of anything I speak,
You will have no regrets, and I no anger.
What word of Merlin was abroad today?"

"Today have I heard no man save Gawaine,
And to him I said only what all men
Are saying to their neighbors. They believe
That you have Merlin here, and that his coming
Denotes no good. Gawaine was curious,
But ever mindful of your majesty.
He pressed me not, and we made light of it."

"Gawaine, I fear, makes light of everything,"
The King said, looking down. "Sometimes I wish
I had a full Round Table of Gawaines.
But that's a freak of midnight,—never mind it.
Sing me a song—one of those endless things
255

That Merlin liked of old, when men were younger
And there were more stars twinkling in the sky.
I see no stars that are alive tonight,
And I am not the king of sleep. So then,
Sing me an old song."

                              Dagonet's quick eye
Caught sorrow in the King's; and he knew more,
In a fool's way, than even the King himself
Of what was hovering over Camelot.
"O King," he said, "I cannot sing tonight.
If you command me I shall try to sing,
But I shall fail; for there are no songs now
In my old throat, or even in these poor strings
That I can hardly follow with my fingers.
Forgive me—kill me—but I cannot sing."
Dagonet fell down then on both his knees
And shook there while he clutched the King's cold hand
And wept for what he knew.

                              "There, Dagonet;
I shall not kill my knight, or make him sing.
No more; get up, and get you off to bed.
There'll be another time for you to sing,
So get you to your covers and sleep well."
Alone again, the King said, bitterly:
"Yes, I have one friend left, and they who know
As much of him as of themselves believe
That he's a fool. Poor Dagonet's a fool.
And if he be a fool, what else am I
Than one fool more to make the world complete?
'The love that never was!' . . . Fool, fool, fool, fool!"

The King was long awake. No covenant
With peace was his tonight; and he knew sleep

MERLIN

As he knew the cold eyes of Guinevere
That yesterday had stabbed him, having first
On Lancelot's name struck fire, and left him then
As now they left him—with a wounded heart,
A wounded pride, and a sickening pang worse yet
Of lost possession. He thought wearily
Of watchers by the dead, late wayfarers,
Rough-handed mariners on ships at sea,
Lone-yawning sentries, wastrels, and all others
Who might be saying somewhere to themselves,
"The King is now asleep in Camelot;
God save the King."—"God save the King, indeed,
If there be now a king to save," he said.
Then he saw giants rising in the dark,
Born horribly of memories and new fears
That in the gray-lit irony of dawn
Were partly to fade out and be forgotten;
And then there might be sleep, and for a time
There might again be peace. His head was hot
And throbbing; but the rest of him was cold,
As he lay staring hard where nothing stood,
And hearing what was not, even while he saw
And heard, like dust and thunder far away,
The coming confirmation of the words
Of him who saw so much and feared so little
Of all that was to be. No spoken doom
That ever chilled the last night of a felon
Prepared a dragging anguish more profound
And absolute than Arthur, in these hours,
Made out of darkness and of Merlin's words;
No tide that ever crashed on Lyonnesse
Drove echoes inland that were lonelier
For widowed ears among the fisher-folk,
Than for the King were memories tonight
Of old illusions that were dead for ever.

257

IV

THE tortured King—seeing Merlin wholly meshed
In his defection, even to indifference,
And all the while attended and exalted
By some unfathomable obscurity
Of divination, where the Grail, unseen,
Broke yet the darkness where a king saw nothing—
Feared now the lady Vivian more than Fate;
For now he knew that Modred, Lancelot,
The Queen, the King, the Kingdom, and the World,
Were less to Merlin, who had made him King,
Than one small woman in Broceliande.
Whereas the lady Vivian, seeing Merlin
Acclaimed and tempted and allured again
To service in his old magnificence,
Feared now King Arthur more than storms and robbers;
For Merlin, though he knew himself immune
To no least whispered little wish of hers
That might afflict his ear with ecstasy,
Had yet sufficient of his old command
Of all around him to invest an eye
With quiet lightning, and a spoken word
With easy thunder, so accomplishing
A profit and a pastime for himself—
And for the lady Vivian, when her guile
Outlived at intervals her graciousness;
And this equipment of uncertainty,
Which now had gone away with him to Britain
With Dagonet, so plagued her memory
That soon a phantom brood of goblin doubts
Inhabited his absence, which had else
Been empty waiting and a few brave fears,
And a few more, she knew, that were not brave,
Or long to be disowned, or manageable.

MERLIN

She thought of him as he had looked at her
When first he had acquainted her alarm
At sight of the King's letter with its import;
And she remembered now his very words:
"The King believes today as in his boyhood
That I am Fate," he said; and when they parted
She had not even asked him not to go;
She might as well, she thought, have bid the wind
Throw no more clouds across a lonely sky
Between her and the moon,—so great he seemed
In his oppressed solemnity, and she,
In her excess of wrong imagining,
So trivial in an hour, and, after all
A creature of a smaller consequence
Than kings to Merlin, who made kings and kingdoms
And had them as a father; and so she feared
King Arthur more than robbers while she waited
For Merlin's promise to fulfil itself,
And for the rest that was to follow after:
"He said he would come back, and so he will.
He will because he must, and he is Merlin,
The master of the world—or so he was;
And he is coming back again to me
Because he must and I am Vivian.
It's all as easy as two added numbers:
Some day I'll hear him ringing at the gate,
As he rang on that morning in the spring,
Ten years ago; and I shall have him then
For ever. He shall never go away
Though kings come walking on their hands and knees
To take him on their backs." When Merlin came,
She told him that, and laughed; and he said strangely:
"Be glad or sorry, but no kings are coming.
Not Arthur, surely; for now Arthur knows
That I am less than Fate."

Ten years ago
The King had heard, with unbelieving ears
At first, what Merlin said would be the last
Reiteration of his going down
To find a living grave in Brittany:
"Buried alive I told you I should be,
By love made little and by woman shorn,
Like Samson, of my glory; and the time
Is now at hand. I follow in the morning
Where I am led. I see behind me now
The last of crossways, and I see before me
A straight and final highway to the end
Of all my divination. You are King,
And in your kingdom I am what I was.
Wherever I have warned you, see as far
As I have seen; for I have shown the worst
There is to see. Require no more of me,
For I can be no more than what I was."
So, on the morrow, the King said farewell;
And he was never more to Merlin's eye
The King than at that hour; for Merlin knew
How much was going out of Arthur's life
With him, as he went southward to the sea.

Over the waves and into Brittany
Went Merlin, to Broceliande. Gay birds
Were singing high to greet him all along
A broad and sanded woodland avenue
That led him on forever, so he thought,
Until at last there was an end of it;
And at the end there was a gate of iron,
Wrought heavily and invidiously barred.
He pulled a cord that rang somewhere a bell
Of many echoes, and sat down to rest,
Outside the keeper's house, upon a bench

MERLIN

Of carven stone that might for centuries
Have waited there in silence to receive him.
The birds were singing still; leaves flashed and swung
Before him in the sunlight; a soft breeze
Made intermittent whisperings around him
Of love and fate and danger, and faint waves
Of many sweetly-stinging fragile odors
Broke lightly as they touched him; cherry-boughs
Above him snowed white petals down upon him,
And under their slow falling Merlin smiled
Contentedly, as one who contemplates
No longer fear, confusion, or regret,
May smile at ruin or at revelation.

A stately fellow with a forest air
Now hailed him from within, with searching words
And curious looks, till Merlin's glowing eye
Transfixed him and he flinched: "My compliments
And homage to the lady Vivian.
Say Merlin from King Arthur's Court is here,
A pilgrim and a stranger in appearance,
Though in effect her friend and humble servant.
Convey to her my speech as I have said it,
Without abbreviation or delay,
And so deserve my gratitude forever."
"But Merlin?" the man stammered; "Merlin? Merlin?"—
"One Merlin is enough. I know no other.
Now go you to the lady Vivian
And bring to me her word, for I am weary."
Still smiling at the cherry-blossoms falling
Down on him and around him in the sunlight,
He waited, never moving, never glancing
This way or that, until his messenger
Came jingling into vision, weighed with keys,
And inly shaken with much wondering

At this great wizard's coming unannounced
And unattended. When the way was open
The stately messenger, now bowing low
In reverence and awe, bade Merlin enter;
And Merlin, having entered, heard the gate
Clang back behind him; and he swore no gate
Like that had ever clanged in Camelot,
Or any other place if not in hell.
"I may be dead; and this good fellow here,
With all his keys," he thought, "may be the Devil,—
Though I were loath to say so, for the keys
Would make him rather more akin to Peter;
And that's fair reasoning for this fair weather."

"The lady Vivian says you are most welcome,"
Said now the stately-favored servitor,
"And are to follow me. She said, 'Say Merlin—
A pilgrim and a stranger in appearance,
Though in effect my friend and humble servant—
Is welcome for himself, and for the sound
Of his great name that echoes everywhere.' "—
"I like you and I like your memory,"
Said Merlin, curiously, "but not your gate.
Why forge for this elysian wilderness
A thing so vicious with unholy noise?"—
"There's a way out of every wilderness
For those who dare or care enough to find it,"
The guide said: and they moved along together,
Down shaded ways, through open ways with hedgerows.
And into shade again more deep than ever,
But edged anon with rays of broken sunshine
In which a fountain, raining crystal music,
Made faery magic of it through green leafage,
Till Merlin's eyes were dim with preparation
For sight now of the lady Vivian.

MERLIN

He saw at first a bit of living green
That might have been a part of all the green
Around the tinkling fountain where she gazed
Upon the circling pool as if her thoughts
Were not so much on Merlin—whose advance
Betrayed through his enormity of hair
The cheeks and eyes of youth—as on the fishes.
But soon she turned and found him, now alone,
And held him while her beauty and her grace
Made passing trash of empires, and his eyes
Told hers of what a splendid emptiness
Her tedious world had been without him in it
Whose love and service were to be her school,
Her triumph, and her history: "This is Merlin,"
She thought; "and I shall dream of him no more.
And he has come, he thinks, to frighten me
With beards and robes and his immortal fame;
Or is it I who think so? I know not.
I'm frightened, sure enough, but if I show it,
I'll be no more the Vivian for whose love
He tossed away his glory, or the Vivian
Who saw no man alive to make her love him
Till she saw Merlin once in Camelot,
And seeing him, saw no other. In an age
That has no plan for me that I can read
Without him, shall he tell me what I am,
And why I am, I wonder?" While she thought,
And feared the man whom her perverse negation
Must overcome somehow to soothe her fancy,
She smiled and welcomed him; and so they stood,
Each finding in the other's eyes a gleam
Of what eternity had hidden there.

"Are you always all in green, as you are now?"
Said Merlin, more employed with her complexion,

Where blood and olive made wild harmony
With eyes and wayward hair that were too dark
For peace if they were not subordinated;
"If so you are, then so you make yourself
A danger in a world of many dangers.
If I were young, God knows if I were safe
Concerning you in green, like a slim cedar,
As you are now, to say my life was mine:
Were you to say to me that I should end it,
Longevity for me were jeopardized.
Have you your green on always and all over?"

"Come here, and I will tell you about that,"
Said Vivian, leading Merlin with a laugh
To an arbored seat where they made opposites:
"If you are Merlin—and I know you are,
For I remember you in Camelot,—
You know that I am Vivian, as I am;
And if I go in green, why, let me go so,
And say at once why you have come to me
Cloaked over like a monk, and with a beard
As long as Jeremiah's. I don't like it.
I'll never like a man with hair like that
While I can feed a carp with little frogs.
I'm rather sure to hate you if you keep it,
And when I hate a man I poison him."

"You've never fed a carp with little frogs,"
Said Merlin; "I can see it in your eyes."—
"I might then, if I haven't," said the lady;
"For I'm a savage, and I love no man
As I have seen him yet. I'm here alone,
With some three hundred others, all of whom
Are ready, I dare say, to die for me;
I'm cruel and I'm cold, and I like snakes;

264

And some have said my mother was a fairy,
Though I believe it not."

                             "Why not believe it?"
Said Merlin; "I believe it. I believe
Also that you divine, as I had wished,
In my surviving ornament of office
A needless imposition on your wits,
If not yet on the scope of your regard.
Even so, you cannot say how old I am,
Or yet how young. I'm willing cheerfully
To fight, left-handed, Hell's three headed hound
If you but whistle him up from where he lives;
I'm cheerful and I'm fierce, and I've made kings;
And some have said my father was the Devil,
Though I believe it not. Whatever I am,
I have not lived in Time until to-day."
A moment's worth of wisdom there escaped him,
But Vivian seized it, and it was not lost.

Embroidering doom with many levities,
Till now the fountain's crystal silver, fading,
Became a splash and a mere chilliness,
They mocked their fate with easy pleasantries
That were too false and small to be forgotten,
And with ingenious insincerities
That had no repetition or revival.
At last the lady Vivian arose,
And with a crying of how late it was
Took Merlin's hand and led him like a child
Along a dusky way between tall cones
Of tight green cedars: "Am I like one of these?
You said I was, though I deny it wholly."—
"Very," said Merlin, to his bearded lips
Uplifting her small fingers.—"O, that hair?"

She moaned, as if in sorrow: "Must it be?
Must every prophet and important wizard
Be clouded so that nothing but his nose
And eyes, and intimations of his ears,
Are there to make us know him when we see him?
Praise heaven I'm not a prophet! Are you glad?"—

He did not say that he was glad or sorry;
For suddenly came flashing into vision
A thing that was a manor and a castle,
With walls and roofs that had a flaming sky
Behind them, like a sky that he remembered,
And one that had from his rock-sheltered haunt
Above the roofs of his forsaken city
Made flame as if all Camelot were on fire.
The glow brought with it a brief memory
Of Arthur as he left him, and the pain
That fought in Arthur's eyes for losing him,
And must have overflowed when he had vanished.
But now the eyes that looked hard into his
Were Vivian's, not the King's; and he could see,
Or so he thought, a shade of sorrow in them.
She took his two hands: "You are sad," she said.—
He smiled: "Your western lights bring memories
Of Camelot. We all have memories—
Prophets, and women who are like slim cedars;
But you are wrong to say that I am sad."—
"Would you go back to Camelot?" she asked,
Her fingers tightening. Merlin shook his head.
"Then listen while I tell you that I'm glad,"
She purred, as if assured that he would listen:
"At your first warning, much too long ago,
Of this quaint pilgrimage of yours to see
'The fairest and most orgulous of ladies'—
No language for a prophet, I am sure—

266

MERLIN

Said I, 'When this great Merlin comes to me,
My task and avocation for some time
Will be to make him willing, if I can,
To teach and feed me with an ounce of wisdom.'
For I have eaten to an empty shell,
After a weary feast of observation
Among the glories of a tinsel world
That had for me no glory till you came,
A life that is no life. Would you go back
To Camelot?"—Merlin shook his head again,
And the two smiled together in the sunset.

They moved along in silence to the door,
Where Merlin said: "Of your three hundred here
There is but one I know, and him I favor;
I mean the stately one who shakes the keys
Of that most evil sounding gate of yours,
Which has a clang as if it shut forever."—
"If there be need, I'll shut the gate myself,"
She said. "And you like Blaise? Then you shall have him.
He was not born to serve, but serve he must,
It seems, and be enamoured of my shadow.
He cherishes the taint of some high folly
That haunts him with a name he cannot know,
And I could fear his wits are paying for it.
Forgive his tongue, and humor it a little."—
"I knew another one whose name was Blaise,"
He said; and she said lightly, "Well, what of it?"—
"And he was nigh the learnedest of hermits;
His home was far away from everywhere.
And he was all alone there when he died."—
"Now be a pleasant Merlin," Vivian said,
Patting his arm, "and have no more of that;
For I'll not hear of dead men far away,
Or dead men anywhere this afternoon.

283

There'll be a trifle in the way of supper
This evening, but the dead shall not have any.
Blaise and this man will tell you all there is
For you to know. Then you'll know everything."
She laughed, and vanished like a humming-bird.

V

THE sun went down, and the dark after it
Starred Merlin's new abode with many a sconced
And many a moving candle, in whose light
The prisoned wizard, mirrored in amazement,
Saw fronting him a stranger, falcon-eyed,
Firm-featured, of a negligible age,
And fair enough to look upon, he fancied,
Though not a warrior born, nor more a courtier.
A native humor resting in his long
And solemn jaws now stirred, and Merlin smiled
To see himself in purple, touched with gold,
And fledged with snowy lace.—The careful Blaise,
Having drawn some time before from Merlin's wallet
The sable raiment of a royal scholar,
Had eyed it with a long mistrust and said:
"The lady Vivian would be vexed, I fear,
To meet you vested in these learned weeds
Of gravity and death; for she abhors
Mortality in all its hues and emblems—
Black wear, long argument, and all the cold
And solemn things that appertain to graves."—
And Merlin, listening, to himself had said,
"This fellow has a freedom, yet I like him;"
And then aloud: "I trust you. Deck me out,
However, with a temperate regard
For what your candid eye may find in me
Of inward coloring. Let them reap my beard,

MERLIN

Moreover, with a sort of reverence,
For I shall never look on it again.
And though your lady frown her face away
To think of me in black, for God's indulgence,
Array me not in scarlet or in yellow."—
And so it came to pass that Merlin sat
At ease in purple, even though his chin
Reproached him as he pinched it, and seemed yet
A little fearful of its nakedness.
He might have sat and scanned himself for ever
Had not the careful Blaise, regarding him,
Remarked again that in his proper judgment,
And on the valid word of his attendants,
No more was to be done. "Then do no more,"
Said Merlin, with a last look at his chin;
"Never do more when there's no more to do,
And you may shun thereby the bitter taste
Of many disillusions and regrets.
God's pity on us that our words have wings
And leave our deeds to crawl so far below them;
For we have all two heights, we men who dream,
Whether we lead or follow, rule or serve."—
"God's pity on us anyhow," Blaise answered,
"Or most of us. Meanwhile, I have to say,
As long as you are here, and I'm alive,
Your summons will assure the loyalty
Of all my diligence and expedition.
The gong that you hear singing in the distance
Was rung for your attention and your presence."—
"I wonder at this fellow, yet I like him,"
Said Merlin; and he rose to follow him.

The lady Vivian in a fragile sheath
Of crimson, dimmed and veiled ineffably
By the flame-shaken gloom wherein she sat,

269

And twinkled if she moved, heard Merlin coming,
And smiled as if to make herself believe
Her joy was all a triumph; yet her blood
Confessed a tingling of more wonderment
Than all her five and twenty worldly years
Of waiting for this triumph could remember;
And when she knew and felt the slower tread
Of his unseen advance among the shadows
To the small haven of uncertain light
That held her in it as a torch-lit shoal
Might hold a smooth red fish, her listening skin
Responded with a creeping underneath it,
And a crinkling that was incident alike
To darkness, love, and mice. When he was there,
She looked up at him in a whirl of mirth
And wonder, as in childhood she had gazed
Wide-eyed on royal mountebanks who made
So brief a shift of the impossible
That kings and queens would laugh and shake themselves;
Then rising slowly on her little feet,
Like a slim creature lifted, she thrust out
Her two small hands as if to push him back—
Whereon he seized them. "Go away," she said;
"I never saw you in my life before."—
"You say the truth," he answered; "when I met
Myself an hour ago, my words were yours.
God made the man you see for you to like,
If possible. If otherwise, turn down
These two prodigious and remorseless thumbs
And leave your lions to annihilate him."—

"I have no other lion than yourself,"
She said; "and since you cannot eat yourself,
Pray do a lonely woman, who is, you say,
More like a tree than any other thing

270

MERLIN

In your discrimination, the large honor
Of sharing with her a small kind of supper."—
"Yes, you are like a tree,--or like a flower;
More like a flower to-night." He bowed his head
And kissed the ten small fingers he was holding,
As calmly as if each had been a son;
Although his heart was leaping and his eyes
Had sight for nothing save a swimming crimson
Between two glimmering arms. "More like a flower
To-night," he said, as now he scanned again
The immemorial meaning of her face
And drew it nearer to his eyes. It seemed
A flower of wonder with a crimson stem
Came leaning slowly and regretfully
To meet his will—a flower of change and peril
That had a clinging blossom of warm olive
Half stifled with a tyranny of black,
And held the wayward fragrance of a rose
Made woman by delirious alchemy.
She raised her face and yoked his willing neck
With half her weight; and with hot lips that left
The world with only one philosophy
For Merlin or for Anaxagoras,
Called his to meet them and in one long hush
Of capture to surrender and make hers
The last of anything that might remain
Of what was now their beardless wizardry.
Then slowly she began to push herself
Away, and slowly Merlin let her go
As far from him as his outreaching hands
Could hold her fingers while his eyes had all
The beauty of the woodland and the world
Before him in the firelight, like a nymph
Of cities, or a queen a little weary
Of inland stillness and immortal trees.

271

"Are you to let me go again sometime,"
She said,—"before I starve to death, I wonder?
If not, I'll have to bite the lion's paws,
And make him roar. He cannot shake his mane,
For now the lion has no mane to shake;
The lion hardly knows himself without it,
And thinks he has no face, but there's a lady
Who says he had no face until he lost it.
So there we are. And there's a flute somewhere,
Playing a strange old tune. You know the words:
'The Lion and the Lady are both hungry.' "

Fatigue and hunger—tempered leisurely
With food that some devout magician's oven
Might after many failures have delivered,
And wine that had for decades in the dark
Of Merlin's grave been slowly quickening,
And with half-heard, dream-weaving interludes
Of distant flutes and viols, made more distant
By far, nostalgic hautboys blown from nowhere,—
Were tempered not so leisurely, may be,
With Vivian's inextinguishable eyes
Between two shining silver candlesticks
That lifted each a trembling flame to make
The rest of her a dusky loveliness
Against a bank of shadow. Merlin made,
As well as he was able while he ate,
A fair division of the fealty due
To food and beauty, albeit more times than one
Was he at odds with his urbanity
In honoring too long the grosser viand.
"The best invention in Broceliande
Has not been over-taxed in vain, I see,"
She told him, with her chin propped on her fingers
And her eyes flashing blindness into his:

272

MERLIN

"I put myself out cruelly to please you,
And you, for that, forget almost at once
The name and image of me altogether.
You needn't, for when all is analyzed,
It's only a bird-pie that you are eating."

"I know not what you call it," Merlin said;
"Nor more do I forget your name and image,
Though I do eat; and if I did not eat,
Your sending out of ships and caravans
To get whatever 'tis that's in this thing
Would be a sorrow for you all your days;
And my great love, which you have seen by now,
Might look to you a lie; and like as not
You'd actuate some sinewed mercenary
To carry me away to God knows where
And seal me in a fearsome hole to starve,
Because I made of this insidious picking
An idle circumstance. My dear fair lady—
And there is not another under heaven
So fair as you are as I see you now—
I cannot look at you too much and eat;
And I must eat, or be untimely ashes,
Whereon the light of your celestial gaze
Would fall, I fear me, for no longer time
Than on the solemn dust of Jeremiah—
Whose beard you likened once, in heathen jest,
To mine that now is no man's."

                                        "Are you sorry?"
Said Vivian, filling Merlin's empty goblet;
"If you are sorry for the loss of it,
Drink more of this and you may tell me lies
Enough to make me sure that you are glad;
But if your love is what you say it is,

Be never sorry that my love took off
That horrid hair to make your face at last
A human fact. Since I have had your name
To dream of and say over to myself,
The visitations of that awful beard
Have been a terror for my nights and days—
For twenty years. I've seen it like an ocean,
Blown seven ways at once and wrecking ships,
With men and women screaming for their lives;
I've seen it woven into shining ladders
That ran up out of sight and so to heaven,
All covered with white ghosts with hanging robes
Like folded wings,—and there were millions of them,
Climbing, climbing, climbing, all the time;
And all the time that I was watching them
I thought how far above me Merlin was,
And wondered always what his face was like.
But even then, as a child, I knew the day
Would come some time when I should see his face
And hear his voice, and have him in my house
Till he should care no more to stay in it,
And go away to found another kingdom."—
"Not that," he said; and, sighing, drank more wine;
"One kingdom for one Merlin is enough."—
"One Merlin for one Vivian is enough,"
She said. "If you care much, remember that;
But the Lord knows how many Vivians
One Merlin's entertaining eye might favor,
Indifferently well and all at once,
If they were all at hand. Praise heaven they're not."

"If they were in the world—praise heaven they're not—
And if one Merlin's entertaining eye
Saw two of them, there might be left him then
The sight of no eye to see anything—

274

Not even the Vivian who is everything,
She being Beauty, Beauty being She,
She being Vivian, and so on for ever."—
"I'm glad you don't see two of me," she said;
"For there's a whole world yet for you to eat
And drink and say to me before I know
The sort of creature that you see in me.
I'm withering for a little more attention,
But, being woman, I can wait. These cups
That you see coming are for the last there is
Of what my father gave to kings alone,
And far from always. You are more than kings
To me; therefore I give it all to you,
Imploring you to spâre no more of it
Than a small cockle-shell would hold for me
To pledge your love and mine in. Take the rest,
That I may see tonight the end of it.
I'll have no living remnant of the dead
Annoying me until it fades and sours
Of too long cherishing; for Time enjoys
The look that's on our faces when we scowl
On unexpected ruins, and thrift itself
May be a sort of slow unwholesome fire
That eats away to dust the life that feeds it.
You smile, I see, but I said what I said.
One hardly has to live a thousand years
To contemplate a lost economy;
So let us drink it while it's yet alive
And you and I are not untimely ashes.
My last words are your own, and I don't like 'em."—
A sudden laughter scattered from her eyes
A threatening wisdom. He smiled and let her laugh,
Then looked into the dark where there was nothing:
"There's more in this than I have seen," he thought,
"Though I shall see it."—"Drink," she said again;

"There's only this much in the world of it,
And I am near to giving all to you
Because you are so great and I so little."

With a long-kindling gaze that caught from hers
A laughing flame, and with a hand that shook
Like Arthur's kingdom, Merlin slowly raised
A golden cup that for a golden moment
Was twinned in air with hers; and Vivian,
Who smiled at him across their gleaming rims,
From eyes that made a fuel of the night
Surrounding her, shot glory over gold
At Merlin, while their cups touched and his trembled.
He drank, not knowing what, nor caring much
For kings who might have cared less for themselves,
He thought, had all the darkness and wild light
That fell together to make Vivian
Been there before them then to flower anew
Through sheathing crimson into candle-light
With each new leer of their loose, liquorish eyes.
Again he drank, and he cursed every king
Who might have touched her even in her cradle;
For what were kings to such as he, who made them
And saw them totter—for the world to see,
And heed, if the world would? He drank again,
And yet again—to make himself assured
No manner of king should have the last of it—
The cup that Vivian filled unfailingly
Until she poured for nothing. "At the end
Of this incomparable flowing gold,"
She prattled on to Merlin, who observed
Her solemnly, "I fear there may be specks."—
He sighed aloud, whereat she laughed at him
And pushed the golden cup a little nearer.
He scanned it with a sad anxiety,

And then her face likewise, and shook his head
As if at her concern for such a matter:
"Specks? What are specks? Are you afraid of them?"
He murmured slowly, with a drowsy tongue;
"There are specks everywhere. I fear them not.
If I were king in Camelot, I might
Fear more than specks. But now I fear them not.
You are too strange a lady to fear specks."

He stared a long time at the cup of gold
Before him but he drank no more. There came
Between him and the world a crumbling sky
Of black and crimson, with a crimson cloud
That held a far off town of many towers.
All swayed and shaken, till at last they fell,
And there was nothing but a crimson cloud
That crumbled into nothing, like the sky
That vanished with it, carrying away
The world, the woman, and all memory of them,
Until a slow light of another sky
Made gray an open casement, showing him
Faint shapes of an exotic furniture
That glimmered with a dim magnificence,
And letting in the sound of many birds
That were, as he lay there remembering,
The only occupation of his ears
Until it seemed they shared a fainter sound,
As if a sleeping child with a black head
Beside him drew the breath of innocence.

One shining afternoon around the fountain,
As on the shining day of his arrival,
The sunlight was alive with flying silver
That had for Merlin a more dazzling flash
Than jewels rained in dreams, and a richer sound

277

Than harps, and all the morning stars together,—
When jewels and harps and stars and everything
That flashed and sang and was not Vivian,
Seemed less than echoes of her least of words—
For she was coming. Suddenly, somewhere
Behind him, she was coming; that was all
He knew until she came and took his hand
And held it while she talked about the fishes.
When she looked up he thought a softer light
Was in her eyes than once he had found there;
And had there been left yet for dusky women
A beauty that was heretofore not hers,
He told himself he must have seen it then
Before him in the face at which he smiled
And trembled. "Many men have called me wise,"
He said, "but you are wiser than all wisdom
If you know what you are."—"I don't," she said;
"I know that you and I are here together;
I know that I have known for twenty years
That life would be almost a constant yawning
Until you came; and now that you are here,
I know that I am not to go away
Until you tell me that I'm hideous;
I know that I like fishes, ferns, and snakes,—
Maybe because I liked them when the world
Was young and you and I were salamanders;
I know, too, a cool place not far from here,
Where there are ferns that are like marching men
Who never march away. Come now and see them,
And do as they do—never march away.
When they are gone, some others, crisp and green,
Will have their place, but never march away."—
He smoothed her silky fingers, one by one:
"Some other Merlin, also, do you think,
Will have his place—and never march away?"—

278

MERLIN

Then Vivian laid a finger on his lips
And shook her head at him before she laughed:
"There is no other Merlin than yourself,
And you are never going to be old."

Oblivious of a world that made of him
A jest, a legend, and a long regret,
And with a more commanding wizardry
Than his to rule a kingdom where the king
Was Love and the queen Vivian, Merlin found
His queen without the blemish of a word
That was more rough than honey from her lips,
Or the first adumbration of a frown
To cloud the night-wild fire that in her eyes
Had yet a smoky friendliness of home,
And a foreknowing care for mighty trifles.
"There are miles and miles for you to wander in,"
She told him once: "Your prison yard is large,
And I would rather take my two ears off
And feed them to the fishes in the fountain
Than buzz like an incorrigible bee
For always around yours, and have you hate
The sound of me; for some day then, for certain,
Your philosophic rage would see in me
A bee in earnest, and your hand would smite
My life away. And what would you do then?
I know: for years and years you'd sit alone
Upon my grave, and be the grieving image
Of lean remorse, and suffer miserably;
And often, all day long, you'd only shake
Your celebrated head and all it holds,
Or beat it with your fist the while you groaned
Aloud and went on saying to yourself:
'Never should I have killed her, or believed
She was a bee that buzzed herself to death,

279

First having made me crazy, had there been
Judicious distance and wise absences
To keep the two of us inquisitive.' "—
"I fear you bow your unoffending head
Before a load that should be mine," said he;
"If so, you led me on by listening.
You should have shrieked and jumped, and then fled yelling;
That's the best way when a man talks too long.
God's pity on me if I love your feet
More now than I could ever love the face
Of any one of all those Vivians
You summoned out of nothing on the night
When I saw towers. I'll wander and amend."—
At that she flung the noose of her soft arms
Around his neck and kissed him instantly:
"You are the wisest man that ever was,
And I've a prayer to make: May all you say
To Vivian be a part of what you knew
Before the curse of her unquiet head
Was on your shoulder, as you have it now,
To punish you for knowing beyond knowledge.
You are the only one who sees enough
To make me see how far away I am
From all that I have seen and have not been;
You are the only thing there is alive
Between me as I am and as I was
When Merlin was a dream. You are to listen
When I say now to you that I'm alone.
Like you, I saw too much; and unlike you
I made no kingdom out of what I saw—
Or none save this one here that you must rule,
Believing you are ruled. I see too far
To rule myself. Time's way with you and me
Is our way, in that we are out of Time
And out of tune with Time. We have this place,

And you must hold us in it or we die.
Look at me now and say if what I say
Be folly or not; for my unquiet head
Is no conceit of mine. I had it first
When I was born; and I shall have it with me
Till my unquiet soul is on its way
To be, I hope, where souls are quieter.
So let the first and last activity
Of what you say so often is your love
Be always to remember that our lyres
Are not strung for Today. On you it falls
To keep them in accord here with each other,
For you have wisdom, I have only sight
For distant things—and you. And you are Merlin.
Poor wizard! Vivian is your punishment
For making kings of men who are not kings;
And you are mine, by the same reasoning,
For living out of Time and out of tune
With anything but you. No other man
Could make me say so much of what I know
As I say now to you. And you are Merlin!"

She looked up at him till his way was lost
Again in the familiar wilderness
Of night that love made for him in her eyes,
And there he wandered as he said he would;
He wandered also in his prison-yard,
And, when he found her coming after him,
Beguiled her with her own admonishing
And frowned upon her with a fierce reproof
That many a time in the old world outside
Had set the mark of silence on strong men—
Whereat she laughed, not always wholly sure,
Nor always wholly glad, that he who played
So lightly was the wizard of her dreams:

"No matter—if only Merlin keep the world
Away," she thought. "Our lyres have many strings,
But he must know them all, for he is Merlin."

And so for years, till ten of them were gone,—
Ten years, ten seasons, or ten flying ages—
Fate made Broceliande a paradise,
By none invaded, until Dagonet,
Like a discordant, awkward bird of doom,
Flew in with Arthur's message. For the King,
In sorrow cleaving to simplicity,
And having in his love a quick remembrance
Of Merlin's old affection for the fellow,
Had for this vain, reluctant enterprise
Appointed him—the knight who made men laugh,
And was a fool because he played the fool.

"The King believes today, as in his boyhood,
That I am Fate; and I can do no more
Than show again what in his heart he knows,"
Said Merlin to himself and Vivian:
"This time I go because I made him King,
Thereby to be a mirror for the world;
This time I go, but never after this,
For I can be no more than what I was,
And I can do no more than I have done."
He took her slowly in his arms and felt
Her body throbbing like a bird against him:
"This time I go; I go because I must."

And in the morning, when he rode away
With Dagonet and Blaise through the same gate
That once had clanged as if to shut for ever,
She had not even asked him not to go;
For it was then that in his lonely gaze

Of helpless love and sad authority
She found the gleam of his imprisoned power
That Fate withheld; and, pitying herself,
She pitied the fond Merlin she had changed,
And saw the Merlin who had changed the world.

VI

"No kings are coming on their hands and knees,
Nor yet on horses or in chariots,
To carry me away from you again,"
Said Merlin, winding around Vivian's ear
A shred of her black hair. "King Arthur knows
That I have done with kings, and that I speak
No more their crafty language. Once I knew it,
But now the only language I have left
Is one that I must never let you hear
Too long, or know too well. When towering deeds
Once done shall only out of dust and words
Be done again, the doer may then be wary
Lest in the complement of his new fabric
There be more words than dust."

      "Why tell me so?"
Said Vivian; and a singular thin laugh
Came after her thin question. "Do you think
That I'm so far away from history
That I require, even of the wisest man
Who ever said the wrong thing to a woman,
So large a light on what I know already—
When all I seek is here before me now
In your new eyes that you have brought for me
From Camelot? The eyes you took away
Were sad and old; and I could see in them
A Merlin who remembered all the kings

283

He ever saw, and wished himself, almost,
Away from Vivian, to make other kings,
And shake the world again in the old manner.
I saw myself no bigger than a beetle
For several days, and wondered if your love
Were large enough to make me any larger
When you came back. Am I a beetle still?"
She stood up on her toes and held her cheek
For some time against his, and let him go.

"I fear the time has come for me to wander
A little in my prison-yard," he said.—
"No, tell me everything that you have seen
And heard and done, and seen done, and heard done,
Since you deserted me. And tell me first
What the King thinks of me."—"The King believes
That you are almost what you are," he told her:
"The beauty of all ages that are vanished,
Reborn to be the wonder of one woman."—
"I knew he hated me. What else of him?"—
"And all that I have seen and heard and done,
Which is not much, would make a weary telling;
And all your part of it would be to sleep,
And dream that Merlin had his beard again."—
"Then tell me more about your good fool knight,
Sir Dagonet. If Blaise were not half-mad
Already with his pondering on the name
And shield of his unshielding nameless father,
I'd make a fool of him. I'd call him Ajax;
I'd have him shake his fist at thunder-storms,
And dance a jig as long as there was lightning,
And so till I forgot myself entirely.
Not even your love may do so much as that."—
"Thunder and lightning are no friends of mine,"
Said Merlin slowly, "more than they are yours;

284

MERLIN

They bring me nearer to the elements
From which I came than I care now to be."—
"You owe a service to those elements;
For by their service you outwitted age
And made the world a kingdom of your will."—
He touched her hand, smiling: "Whatever service
Of mine awaits them will not be forgotten,"
He said; and the smile faded on his face.—
"Now of all graceless and ungrateful wizards—"
But there she ceased, for she found in his eyes
The first of a new fear. "The wrong word rules
Today," she said; "and we'll have no more journeys."

Although he wandered rather more than ever
Since he had come again to Brittany
From Camelot, Merlin found eternally
Before him a new loneliness that made
Of garden, park, and woodland, all alike,
A desolation and a changelessness
Defying reason, without Vivian
Beside him, like a child with a black head,
Or moving on before him, or somewhere
So near him that, although he saw it not
With eyes, he felt the picture of her beauty
And shivered at the nearness of her being.
Without her now there was no past or future,
And a vague, soul-consuming premonition
He found the only tenant of the present;
He wondered, when she was away from him,
If his avenging injured intellect
Might shine with Arthur's kingdom a twin mirror,
Fate's plaything, for new ages without eyes
To see therein themselves and their declension.
Love made his hours a martyrdom without her;
The world was like an empty house without her.

Where Merlin was a prisoner of love
Confined within himself by too much freedom,
Repeating an unending exploration
Of many solitary silent rooms,
And only in a way remembering now
That once their very solitude and silence
Had by the magic of expectancy
Made sure what now he doubted—though his doubts,
Day after day, were founded on a shadow.

For now to Merlin, in his paradise,
Had come an unseen angel with a sword
Unseen, the touch of which was a long fear
For longer sorrow that had never come,
Yet might if he compelled it. He discovered,
One golden day in autumn as he wandered,
That he had made the radiance of two years
A misty twilight when he might as well
Have had no mist between him and the sun,
The sun being Vivian. On his coming then
To find her all in green against a wall
Of green and yellow leaves, and crumbling bread
For birds around the fountain while she sang
And the birds ate the bread, he told himself
That everything today was as it was
At first, and for a minute he believed it.
"I'd have you always all in green out here,"
He said, "if I had much to say about it."—
She clapped her crumbs away and laughed at him:
"I've covered up my bones with every color
That I can carry on them without screaming,
And you have liked them all—or made me think so."—
"I must have liked them if you thought I did,"
He answered, sighing; "but the sight of you

286

MERLIN

Today as on the day I saw you first,
All green, all wonderful" . . . He tore a leaf
To pieces with a melancholy care
That made her smile.—"Why pause at 'wonderful'?
You've hardly been yourself since you came back
From Camelot, where that unpleasant King
Said things that you have never said to me."—
He looked upon her with a worn reproach:
"The King said nothing that I keep from you."—
"What is it then?" she asked, imploringly;
"You man of moods and miracles, what is it?"—
He shook his head and tore another leaf:
"There is no need of asking what it is;
Whatever you or I may choose to name it,
The name of it is Fate, who played with me
And gave me eyes to read of the unwritten
More lines than I have read. I see no more
Today than yesterday, but I remember.
My ways are not the ways of other men;
My memories go forward. It was you
Who said that we were not in tune with Time;
It was not I who said it."—"But you knew it;
What matter then who said it?"—"It was you
Who said that Merlin was your punishment
For being in tune with him and not with Time—
With Time or with the world; and it was you
Who said you were alone, even here with Merlin;
It was not I who said it. It is I
Who tell you now my inmost thoughts." He laughed
As if at hidden pain around his heart,
But there was not much laughing in his eyes.
They walked, and for a season they were silent:
"I shall know what you mean by that," she said,
"When you have told me. Here's an oak you like,
And here's a place that fits me wondrous well

To sit in. You sit there. I've seen you there
Before; and I have spoiled your noble thoughts
By walking all my fingers up and down
Your countenance, as if they were the feet
Of a small animal with no great claws.
Tell me a story now about the world,
And the men in it, what they do in it,
And why it is they do it all so badly."—
"I've told you every story that I know,
Almost," he said.—"O, don't begin like that."—
"Well, once upon a time there was a King."—
"That has a more commendable address;
Go on, and tell me all about the King;
I'll bet the King had warts or carbuncles,
Or something wrong in his divine insides,
To make him wish that Adam had died young."

Merlin observed her slowly with a frown
Of saddened wonder. She laughed rather lightly,
And at his heart he felt again the sword
Whose touch was a long fear for longer sorrow.
"Well, once upon a time there was a king,"
He said again, but now in a dry voice
That wavered and betrayed a venturing.
He paused, and would have hesitated longer,
But something in him that was not himself
Compelled an utterance that his tongue obeyed,
As an unwilling child obeys a father
Who might be richer for obedience
If he obeyed the child: "There was a king
Who would have made his reign a monument
For kings and peoples of the waiting ages
To reverence and remember, and to this end
He coveted and won, with no ado
To make a story of, a neighbor queen

288

Who limed him with her smile and had of him,
In token of their sin, what he found soon
To be a sort of mongrel son and nephew—
And a most precious reptile in addition—
To ornament his court and carry arms,
And latterly to be the darker half
Of ruin. Also the king, who made of love
More than he made of life and death together,
Forgot the world and his example in it
For yet another woman—one of many—
And this one he made Queen, albeit he knew
That her unsworn allegiance to the knight
That he had loved the best of all his order
Must one day bring along the coming end
Of love and honor and of everything;
And with a kingdom builded on two pits
Of living sin,—so founded by the will
Of one wise counsellor who loved the king,
And loved the world and therefore made him king
To be a mirror for it,—the king reigned well
For certain years, awaiting a sure doom;
For certain years he waved across the world
A royal banner with a Dragon on it;
And men of every land fell worshipping
The Dragon as it were the living God,
And not the living sin."

       She rose at that,
And after a calm yawn, she looked at Merlin:
"Why all this new insistence upon sin?"
She said; "I wonder if I understand
This king of yours, with all his pits and dragons;
I know I do not like him." A thinner light
Was in her eyes than he had found in them
Since he became the willing prisoner

That she had made of him; and on her mouth
Lay now a colder line of irony
Than all his fears or nightmares could have drawn
Before today: "What reason do you know
For me to listen to this king of yours?
What reading has a man of woman's days,
Even though the man be Merlin and a prophet?"

"I know no call for you to love the king,"
Said Merlin, driven ruinously along
By the vindictive urging of his fate;
"I know no call for you to love the king,
Although you serve him, knowing not yet the king
You serve. There is no man, or any woman,
For whom the story of the living king
Is not the story of the living sin.
I thought my story was the common one,
For common recognition and regard."

"Then let us have no more of it," she said;
"For we are not so common, I believe,
That we need kings and pits and flags and dragons
To make us know that we have let the world
Go by us. Have you missed the world so much
That you must have it in with all its clots
And wounds and bristles on to make us happy—
Like Blaise, with shouts and horns and seven men
Triumphant with a most unlovely boar?
Is there no other story in the world
Than this one of a man that you made king
To be a moral for the speckled ages?
You said once long ago, if you remember,
'You are too strange a lady to fear specks';
And it was you, you said, who feared them not.
Why do you look at me as at a snake

290

MERLIN

All coiled to spring at you and strike you dead?
I am not going to spring at you, or bite you;
I'm going home. And you, if you are kind,
Will have no fear to wander for an hour.
I'm sure the time has come for you to wander;
And there may come a time for you to say
What most you think it is that we need here
To make of this Broceliande a refuge
Where two disheartened sinners may forget
A world that has today no place for them."

A melancholy wave of revelation
Broke over Merlin like a rising sea,
Long viewed unwillingly and long denied.
He saw what he had seen, but would not feel,
Till now the bitterness of what he felt
Was in his throat, and all the coldness of it
Was on him and around him like a flood
Of lonelier memories than he had said
Were memories, although he knew them now
For what they were—for what his eyes had seen,
For what his ears had heard and what his heart
Had felt, with him not knowing what it felt.
But now he knew that his cold angel's name
Was Change, and that a mightier will than his
Or Vivian's had ordained that he be there.
To Vivian he could not say anything
But words that had no more of hope in them
Than anguish had of peace: "I meant the world . . .
I meant the world," he groaned; "not you—not me."

Again the frozen line of irony
Was on her mouth. He looked up once at it.
And then away—too fearful of her eyes
To see what he could hear now in her laugh

That melted slowly into what she said,
Like snow in icy water: "This world of yours
Will surely be the end of us. And why not?
I'm overmuch afraid we're part of it,—
Or why do we build walls up all around us,
With gates of iron that make us think the day
Of judgment's coming when they clang behind us?
And yet you tell me that you fear no specks!
With you I never cared for them enough
To think of them. I was too strange a lady.
And your return is now a speckled king
And something that you call a living sin—
That's like an uninvited poor relation
Who comes without a welcome, rather late,
And on a foundered horse."

              "Specks? What are specks?"
He gazed at her in a forlorn wonderment
That made her say: "You said, 'I fear them not.'
'If I were king in Camelot,' you said,
'I might fear more than specks.' Have you forgotten?
Don't tell me, Merlin, you are growing old.
Why don't you make somehow a queen of me,
And give me half the world? I'd wager thrushes
That I should reign, with you to turn the wheel,
As well as any king that ever was.
The curse on me is that I cannot serve
A ruler who forgets that he is king."

In his bewildered misery Merlin then
Stared hard at Vivian's face, more like a slave
Who sought for common mercy than like Merlin:
"You speak a language that was never mine,
Or I have lost my wits. Why do you seize
The flimsiest of opportunities

MERLIN

To make of what I said another thing
Than love or reason could have let me say,
Or let me fancy? Why do you keep the truth
So far away from me, when all your gates
Will open at your word and let me go
To some place where no fear or weariness
Of yours need ever dwell? Why does a woman,
Made otherwise a miracle of love
And loveliness, and of immortal beauty,
Tear one word by the roots out of a thousand,
And worry it, and torture it, and shake it,
Like a small dog that has a rag to play with?
What coil of an ingenious destiny
Is this that makes of what I never meant
A meaning as remote as hell from heaven?"

"I don't know," Vivian said reluctantly,
And half as if in pain; "I'm going home.
I'm going home and leave you here to wander,
Pray take your kings and sins away somewhere
And bury them, and bury the Queen in also.
I know this king; he lives in Camelot,
And I shall never like him. There are specks
Almost all over him. Long live the king,
But not the king who lives in Camelot,
With Modred, Lancelot, and Guinevere—
And all four speckled like a merry nest
Of addled eggs together. You made him King
Because you loved the world and saw in him
From infancy a mirror for the millions.
The world will see itself in him, and then
The world will say its prayers and wash its face,
And build for some new king a new foundation.
Long live the King! . . . But now I apprehend
A time for me to shudder and grow old

And garrulous—and so become a fright
For Blaise to take out walking in warm weather—
Should I give way to long considering
Of worlds you may have lost while prisoned here
With me and my light mind. I contemplate
Another name for this forbidden place,
And one more fitting. Tell me, if you find it,
Some fitter name than Eden. We have had
A man and woman in it for some time,
And now, it seems, we have a Tree of Knowledge."
She looked up at the branches overhead
And shrugged her shoulders. Then she went away;
And what was left of Merlin's happiness,
Like a disloyal phantom, followed her.

He felt the sword of his cold angel thrust
And twisted in his heart, as if the end
Were coming next, but the cold angel passed
Invisibly and left him desolate,
With misty brow and eyes. "The man who sees
May see too far, and he may see too late
The path he takes unseen," he told himself
When he found thought again. "The man who sees
May go on seeing till the immortal flame
That lights and lures him folds him in its heart,
And leaves of what there was of him to die
An item of inhospitable dust
That love and hate alike must hide away;
Or there may still be charted for his feet
A dimmer faring, where the touch of time
Were like the passing of a twilight moth
From flower to flower into oblivion,
If there were not somewhere a barren end
Of moths and flowers, and glimmering far away
Beyond a desert where the flowerless days

294

MERLIN

Are told in slow defeats and agonies,
The guiding of a nameless light that once
Had made him see too much—and has by now
Revealed in death, to the undying child
Of Lancelot, the Grail. For this pure light
Has many rays to throw, for many men
To follow; and the wise are not all pure,
Nor are the pure all wise who follow it.
There are more rays than men. But let the man
Who saw too much, and was to drive himself
From paradise, play too lightly or too long
Among the moths and flowers, he finds at last
There is a dim way out; and he shall grope
Where pleasant shadows lead him to the plain
That has no shadow save his own behind him.
And there, with no complaint, nor much regret,
Shall he plod on, with death between him now
And the far light that guides him, till he falls
And has an empty thought of empty rest;
Then Fate will put a mattock in his hands
And lash him while he digs himself the grave
That is to be the pallet and the shroud
Of his poor blundering bones. The man who saw
Too much must have an eye to see at last
Where Fate has marked the clay; and he shall delve,
Although his hand may slacken, and his knees
May rock without a method as he toils;
For there's a delving that is to be done—
If not for God, for man. I see the light,
But I shall fall before I come to it;
For I am old. I was young yesterday.
Time's hand that I have held away so long
Grips hard now on my shoulder. Time has won.
Tomorrow I shall say to Vivian

That I am old and gaunt and garrulous,
And tell her one more story: I am old."

There were long hours for Merlin after that,
And much long wandering in his prison-yard,
Where now the progress of each heavy step
Confirmed a stillness of impending change
And imminent farewell. To Vivian's ear
There came for many days no other story
Than Merlin's iteration of his love
And his departure from Broceliande,
Where Merlin still remained. In Vivian's eye,
There was a quiet kindness, and at times
A smoky flash of incredulity
That faded into pain. Was this the Merlin—
This incarnation of idolatry
And all but supplicating deference—
This bowed and reverential contradiction
Of all her dreams and her realities—
Was this the Merlin who for years and years
Before she found him had so made her love him
That kings and princes, thrones and diadems,
And honorable men who drowned themselves
For love, were less to her than melon-shells?
Was this the Merlin whom her fate had sent
One spring day to come ringing at her gate,
Bewildering her love with happy terror
That later was to be all happiness?
Was this the Merlin who had made the world
Half over, and then left it with a laugh
To be the youngest, oldest, weirdest, gayest,
And wisest, and sometimes the foolishest
Of all the men of her consideration?
Was this the man who had made other men
As ordinary as arithmetic?

MERLIN

Was this man Merlin who came now so slowly
Towards the fountain where she stood again
In shimmering green? Trembling, he took her hands
And pressed them fondly, one upon the other,
Between his:

           "I was wrong that other day,
For I have one more story. I am old."
He waited like one hungry for the word
Not said; and she found in his eyes a light
As patient as a candle in a window
That looks upon the sea and is a mark
For ships that have gone down. "Tomorrow," he said;
"Tomorrow I shall go away again
To Camelot; and I shall see the King
Once more; and I may come to you again
Once more; and I shall go away again
For ever. There is now no more than that
For me to do; and I shall do no more.
I saw too much when I saw Camelot;
And I saw farther backward into Time,
And forward, than a man may see and live,
When I made Arthur king. I saw too far,
But not so far as this. Fate played with me
As I have played with Time; and Time, like me,
Being less than Fate, will have on me his vengeance.
On Fate there is no vengeance, even for God."
He drew her slowly into his embrace
And held her there, but when he kissed her lips
They were as cold as leaves and had no answer;
For Time had given him then, to prove his words,
A frozen moment of a woman's life.

When Merlin the next morning came again
In the same pilgrim robe that he had worn

While he sat waiting where the cherry-blossoms
Outside the gate fell on him and around him
Grief came to Vivian at the sight of him;
And like a flash of a swift ugly knife,
A blinding fear came with it. "Are you going?"
She said, more with her lips than with her voice;
And he said, "I am going. Blaise and I
Are going down together to the shore,
And Blaise is coming back. For this one day
Be good enough to spare him, for I like him.
I tell you now, as once I told the King,
That I can be no more than what I was,
And I can say no more than I have said.
Sometimes you told me that I spoke too long
And sent me off to wander. That was good.
I go now for another wandering,
And I pray God that all be well with you."

For long there was a whining in her ears
Of distant wheels departing. When it ceased,
She closed the gate again so quietly
That Merlin could have heard no sound of it.

VII

By Merlin's Rock, where Dagonet the fool
Was given through many a dying afternoon
To sit and meditate on human ways
And ways divine, Gawaine and Bedivere
Stood silent, gazing down on Camelot.
The two had risen and were going home:
"It hits me sore, Gawaine," said Bedivere,
"To think on all the tumult and affliction
Down there, and all the noise and preparation

298

That hums of coming death, and, if my fears
Be born of reason, of what's more than death.
Wherefore, I say to you again, Gawaine,—
To you—that this late hour is not too late
For you to change yourself and change the King:
For though the King may love me with a love
More tried, and older, and more sure, may be,
Than for another, for such a time as this
The friend who turns him to the world again
Shall have a tongue more gracious and an eye
More shrewd than mine. For such a time as this
The King must have a glamour to persuade him."

"The King shall have a glamour, and anon,"
Gawaine said, and he shot death from his eyes;
"If you were King, as Arthur is—or was—
And Lancelot had carried off your Queen,
And killed a score or so of your best knights—
Not mentioning my two brothers, whom he slew
Unarmored and unarmed—God save your wits!
Two stewards with skewers could have done as much,
And you and I might now be rotting for it."

"But Lancelot's men were crowded,—they were crushed;
And there was nothing for them but to strike
Or die, not seeing where they struck. Think you
They would have slain Gareth and Gaheris,
And Tor, and all those other friends of theirs?
God's mercy for the world he made, I say,
And for the blood that writes the story of it.
Gareth and Gaheris, Tor and Lamorak,—
All dead, with all the others that are dead!
These years have made me turn to Lamorak
For counsel—and now Lamorak is dead."

"Why do you fling those two names in my face?
'Twas Modred made an end of Lamorak,
Not I; and Lancelot now has done for Tor.
I'll urge no king on after Lancelot
For such a two as Tor and Lamorak:
Their father killed my father, and their friend
Was Lancelot, not I. I'll own my fault—
I'm living; and while I've a tongue can talk,
I'll say this to the King: 'Burn Lancelot
By inches till he give you back the Queen;
Then hang him—drown him—or do anything
To rid the world of him.' He killed my brothers,
And he was once my friend. Now damn the soul
Of him who killed my brothers! There you have me."

"You are a strong man, Gawaine, and your strength
Goes ill where foes are. You may cleave their limbs
And heads off, but you cannot damn their souls;
What you may do now is to save their souls,
And bodies too, and like enough your own.
Remember that King Arthur is a king,
And where there is a king there is a kingdom.
Is not the kingdom any more to you
Than one brief enemy? Would you see it fall
And the King with it, for one mortal hate
That burns out reason? Gawaine, you are king
Today. Another day may see no king
But Havoc, if you have no other word
For Arthur now than hate for Lancelot.
Is not the world as large as Lancelot?
Is Lancelot, because one woman's eyes
Are brighter when they look on him, to sluice
The world with angry blood? Poor flesh! Poor flesh!
And you, Gawaine,—are you so gaffed with hate
You cannot leave it and so plunge away

300

To stiller places and there see, for once,
What hangs on this pernicious expedition
The King in his insane forgetfulness
Would undertake—with you to drum him on?
Are you as mad as he and Lancelot
Made ravening into one man twice as mad
As either? Is the kingdom of the world,
Now rocking, to go down in sound and blood
And ashes and sick ruin, and for the sake
Of three men and a woman? If it be so,
God's mercy for the world he made, I say,—
And say again to Dagonet. Sir Fool,
Your throne is empty, and you may as well
Sit on it and be ruler of the world
From now till supper-time."

                                    Sir Dagonet,
Appearing, made reply to Bedivere's
Dry welcome with a famished look of pain,
On which he built a smile: "If I were King,
You, Bedivere, should be my counsellor;
And we should have no more wars over women.
I'll sit me down and meditate on that."
Gawaine, for all his anger, laughed a little,
And clapped the fool's lean shoulder; for he loved him
And was with Arthur when he made him knight.
Then Dagonet said on to Bedivere,
As if his tongue would make a jest of sorrow:
"Sometime I'll tell you what I might have done
Had I been Lancelot and you King Arthur—
Each having in himself the vicious essence
That now lives in the other and makes war.
When all men are like you and me, my lord,
When all are rational or rickety,
There may be no more war. But what's here now?

301

Lancelot loves the Queen, and he makes war
Of love; the King, being bitten to the soul
By love and hate that work in him together,
Makes war of madness; Gawaine hates Lancelot,
And he, to be in tune, makes war of hate;
Modred hates everything, yet he can see
With one damned illegitimate small eye
His father's crown, and with another like it
He sees the beauty of the Queen herself;
He needs the two for his ambitious pleasure,
And therefore he makes war of his ambition;
And somewhere in the middle of all this
There's a squeezed world that elbows for attention.
Poor Merlin, buried in Broceliande!
He must have had an academic eye
For woman when he founded Arthur's kingdom,
And in Broceliande he may be sorry.
Flutes, hautboys, drums, and viols. God be with him!
I'm glad they tell me there's another world,
For this one's a disease without a doctor."

"No, not so bad as that," said Bedivere;
The doctor, like ourselves, may now be learning;
And Merlin may have gauged his enterprise
Whatever the cost he may have paid for knowing.
We pass, but many are to follow us,
And what they build may stay; though I believe
Another age will have another Merlin,
Another Camelot, and another King.
Sir Dagonet, farewell."

              "Farewell, Sir Knight,
And you, Sir Knight: Gawaine, you have the world
Now in your fingers—an uncommon toy,
Albeit a small persuasion in the balance

With one man's hate. I'm glad you're not a fool,
For then you might be rickety, as I am,
And rational as Bedivere. Farewell.
I'll sit here and be king. God save the King!"

But Gawaine scowled and frowned and answered nothing
As he went slowly down with Bedivere
To Camelot, where Arthur's army waited
The King's word for the melancholy march
To Joyous Gard, where Lancelot hid the Queen
And armed his host, and there was now no joy,
As there was now no joy for Dagonet
While he sat brooding, with his wan cheek-bones
Hooked with his bony fingers: "Go, Gawaine,"
He mumbled: "Go your way, and drag the world
Along down with you. What's a world or so
To you if you can hide an ell of iron
Somewhere in Lancelot, and hear him wheeze
And sputter once or twice before he goes
Wherever the Queen sends him? There's a man
Who should have been a king, and would have been,
Had he been born so. So should I have been
A king, had I been born so, fool or no:
King Dagonet, or Dagonet the King;
King-Fool, Fool-King; 'twere not impossible.
I'll meditate on that and pray for Arthur,
Who made me all I am, except a fool.
Now he goes mad for love, as I might go
Had I been born a king and not a fool.
Today I think I'd rather be a fool;
Today the world is less than one scared woman—
Wherefore a field of waving men may soon
Be shorn by Time's indifferent scythe, because
The King is mad. The seeds of history
Are small, but given a few gouts of warm blood

303

For quickening, they sprout out wondrously
And have a leaping growth whereof no man
May shun such harvesting of change or death,
Or life, as may fall on him to be borne.
When I am still alive and rickety,
And Bedivere's alive and rational—
If he come out of this, and there's a doubt,—
The King, Gawaine, Modred, and Lancelot
May all be lying underneath a weight
Of bloody sheaves too heavy for their shoulders
All spent, and all dishonored, and all dead;
And if it come to be that this be so,
And it be true that Merlin saw the truth,
Such harvest were the best. Your fool sees not
So far as Merlin sees: yet if he saw
The truth—why then, such harvest were the best.
I'll pray for Arthur; I can do no more."

"Why not for Merlin? Or do you count him,
In this extreme, so foreign to salvation
That prayer would be a stranger to his name?"

Poor Dagonet, with terror shaking him,
Stood up and saw before him an old face
Made older with an inch of silver beard,
And faded eyes more eloquent of pain
And ruin than all the faded eyes of age
Till now had ever been, although in them
There was a mystic and intrinsic peace
Of one who sees where men of nearer sight
See nothing. On their way to Camelot,
Gawaine and Bedivere had passed him by,
With lax attention for the pilgrim cloak
They passed, and what it hid: yet Merlin saw

Their faces, and he saw the tale was true
That he had lately drawn from solemn strangers.

"Well, Dagonet, and by your leave," he said,
"I'll rest my lonely relics for a while
On this rock that was mine and now is yours.
I favor the succession; for you know
Far more than many doctors, though your doubt
Is your peculiar poison. I foresaw
Long since, and I have latterly been told
What moves in this commotion down below
To show men what it means. It means the end—
If men whose tongues had less to say to me
Than had their shoulders are adept enough
To know; and you may pray for me or not,
Sir Friend, Sir Dagonet."

                  "Sir fool, you mean,"
Dagonet said, and gazed on Merlin sadly:
"I'll never pray again for anything,
And last of all for this that you behold—
The smouldering faggot of unlovely bones
That God has given to me to call Myself.
When Merlin comes to Dagonet for prayer,
It is indeed the end."

                "And in the end
Are more beginnings, Dagonet, than men
Shall name or know today. It was the end
Of Arthur's insubstantial majesty
When to him and his knights the Grail foreshowed
The quest of life that was to be the death
Of many, and the slow discouraging
Of many more. Or do I err in this?"

305

"No," Dagonet replied; "there was a Light;
And Galahad, in the Siege Perilous,
Alone of all on whom it fell, was calm;
There was a Light wherein men saw themselves
In one another as they might become—
Or so they dreamed. There was a long to-do,
And Gawaine, of all forlorn ineligibles,
Rose up the first, and cried more lustily
Than any after him that he should find
The Grail, or die for it,—though he did neither;
For he came back as living and as fit
For new and old iniquity as ever.
Then Lancelot came back, and Bors came back,—
Like men who had seen more than men should see,
And still come back. They told of Percival
Who saw too much to make of this worn life
A long necessity, and of Galahad,
Who died and is alive. They all saw Something.
God knows the meaning or the end of it,
But they saw Something. And if I've an eye,
Small joy has the Queen been to Lancelot
Since he came back from seeing what he saw;
For though his passion hold him like hot claws,
He's neither in the world nor out of it.
Gawaine is king, though Arthur wears the crown;
And Gawaine's hate for Lancelot is the sword
That hangs by one of Merlin's fragile hairs
Above the world. Were you to see the King,
The frenzy that has overthrown his wisdom,
Instead of him and his upheaving empire,
Might have an end."

                              "I came to see the King,"
Said Merlin, like a man who labors hard
And long with an importunate confession.

MERLIN

"No, Dagonet, you cannot tell me why,
Although your tongue is eager with wild hope
To tell me more than I may tell myself
About myself. All this that was to be
Might show to man how vain it were to wreck
The world for self if it were all in vain.
When I began with Arthur I could see
In each bewildered man who dots the earth
A moment with his days a groping thought
Of an eternal will, strangely endowed
With merciful illusions whereby self
Becomes the will itself and each man swells
In fond accordance with his agency.
Now Arthur, Modred, Lancelot, and Gawaine
Are swollen thoughts of this eternal will
Which have no other way to find the way
That leads them on to their inheritance
Than by the time-infuriating flame
Of a wrecked empire, lighted by the torch
Of woman, who, together with the light
That Galahad found, is yet to light the world."

A wan smile crept across the weary face
Of Dagonet the fool: "If you knew that
Before your burial in Broceliande,
No wonder your eternal will accords
With all your dreams of what the world requires.
My master, I may say this unto you
Because I am a fool, and fear no man;
My fear is that I've been a groping thought
That never swelled enough. You say the torch
Of woman and the light that Galahad found
Are some day to illuminate the world?
I'll meditate on that. The world is done
For me; and I have been. to make men laugh,

307

A lean thing of no shape and many capers.
I made them laugh, and I could laugh anon
Myself to see them killing one another
Because a woman with corn-colored hair
Has pranked a man with horns. 'Twas but a flash
Of chance, and Lancelot, the other day
That saved this pleasing sinner from the fire
That she may spread for thousands. Were she now
The cinder the King willed, or were you now
To see the King, the fire might yet go out;
But the eternal will says otherwise.
So be it; I'll assemble certain gold
That I may say is mine and get myself
Away from this accurst unhappy court,
And in some quiet place where shepherd clowns
And cowherds may have more respondent ears
Than kings and kingdom-builders, I shall troll
Old men to easy graves and be a child
Again among the children of the earth.
I'll have no more kings, even though I loved
King Arthur, who is mad, as I could love
No other man save Merlin, who is dead."

"Not wholly dead, but old. Merlin is old."
The wizard shivered as he spoke, and stared
Away into the sunset where he saw
Once more, as through a cracked and cloudy glass,
A crumbling sky that held a crimson cloud
Wherein there was a town of many towers
All swayed and shaken, in a woman's hand
This time, till out of it there spilled and flashed
And tumbled, like loose jewels, town, towers, and walls,
And there was nothing but a crumbling sky
That made anon of black and red and ruin
A wild and final rain on Camelot.

MERLIN

He bowed, and pressed his eyes: "Now by my soul,
I have seen this before—all black and red—
Like that—like that—like Vivian—black and red;
Like Vivian, when her eyes looked into mine
Across the cups of gold. A flute was playing—
Then all was black and red."

                              Another smile
Crept over the wan face of Dagonet,
Who shivered in his turn. "The torch of woman,"
He muttered, "and the light that Galahad found,
Will some day save us all, as they saved Merlin.
Forgive my shivering wits, but I am cold,
And it will soon be dark. Will you go down
With me to see the King, or will you not?
If not, I go tomorrow to the shepherds.
The world is mad, and I'm a groping thought
Of your eternal will; the world and I
Are strangers, and I'll have no more of it—
Except you go with me to see the King."

"No, Dagonet, you cannot leave me now,"
Said Merlin, sadly. "You and I are old;
And, as you say, we fear no man. God knows
I would not have the love that once you had
For me be fear of me, for I am past
All fearing now. But Fate may send a fly
Sometimes, and he may sting us to the grave.
So driven to test our faith in what we see.
Are you, now I am coming to an end,
As Arthur's days are coming to an end,
To sting me like a fly? I do not ask
Of you to say that you see what I see,
Where you see nothing; nor do I require
Of any man more vision than is his;

309

Yet I could wish for you a larger part
For your last entrance here than this you play
Tonight of a sad insect stinging Merlin.
The more you sting, the more he pities you;
And you were never overfond of pity.
Had you been so, I doubt if Arthur's love,
Or Gawaine's, would have made of you a knight.
No, Dagonet, you cannot leave me now,
Nor would you if you could. You call yourself
A fool, because the world and you are strangers.
You are a proud man, Dagonet; you have suffered
What I alone have seen. You are no fool;
And surely you are not a fly to sting
My love to last regret. Believe or not
What I have seen, or what I say to you,
But say no more to me that I am dead
Because the King is mad, and you are old,
And I am older. In Broceliande
Time overtook me as I knew he must;
And I, with a fond overplus of words,
Had warned the lady Vivian already,
Before these wrinkles and this hesitancy
Inhibiting my joints oppressed her sight
With age and dissolution. She said once
That she was cold and cruel; but she meant
That she was warm and kind, and over-wise
For woman in a world where men see not
Beyond themselves. She saw beyond them all,
As I did; and she waited, as I did,
The coming of a day when cherry-blossoms
Were to fall down all over me like snow
In springtime. I was far from Camelot
That afternoon; and I am farther now
From her. I see no more for me to do
Than to leave her and Arthur and the world

310

Behind me, and to pray that all be well
With Vivian, whose unquiet heart is hungry
For what is not, and what shall never be
Without her, in a world that men are making,
Knowing not how, nor caring yet to know
How slowly and how grievously they do it,—
Though Vivian, in her golden shell of exile,
Knows now and cares, not knowing that she cares,
Nor caring that she knows. In time to be,
The like of her shall have another name
Than Vivian, and her laugh shall be a fire,
Not shining only to consume itself
With what it burns. She knows not yet the name
Of what she is, for now there is no name;
Some day there shall be. Time has many names,
Unwritten yet, for what we say is old
Because we are so young that it seems old.
And this is all a part of what I saw
Before you saw King Arthur. When we parted,
I told her I should see the King again,
And, having seen him, might go back again
To see her face once more. But I shall see
No more the lady Vivian. Let her love
What man she may, no other love than mine
Shall be an index of her memories.
I fear no man who may come after me,
And I see none. I see her, still in green,
Beside the fountain. I shall not go back.
We pay for going back; and all we get
Is one more needless ounce of weary wisdom
To bring away with us. If I come not,
The lady Vivian will remember me,
And say: 'I knew him when his heart was young,
Though I have lost him now. Time called him home,

And that was as it was; for much is lost
Between Broceliande and Camelot.'"

He stared away into the west again,
Where now no crimson cloud or phantom town
Deceived his eyes. Above a living town
There were gray clouds and ultimate suspense,
And a cold wind was coming. Dagonet,
Now crouched at Merlin's feet in his dejection,
Saw multiplying lights far down below,
Where lay the fevered streets. At length he felt
On his lean shoulder Merlin's tragic hand
And trembled, knowing that a few more days
Would see the last of Arthur and the first
Of Modred, whose dark patience had attained
To one precarious half of what he sought:
"And even the Queen herself may fall to him,"
Dagonet murmured.—"The Queen fall to Modred?
Is that your only fear tonight?" said Merlin;
"She may, but not for long."—"No, not my fear;
For I fear nothing. But I wish no fate
Like that for any woman the King loves,
Although she be the scourge and the end of him
That you saw coming, as I see it now."
Dagonet shook, but he would have no tears,
He swore, for any king, queen, knave, or wizard—
Albeit he was a stranger among those
Who laughed at him because he was a fool.
"You said the truth, I cannot leave you now,"
He stammered, and was angry for the tears
That mocked his will and choked him.

Merlin smiled,
Faintly, and for the moment: "Dagonet,
I need your word as one of Arthur's knights

312

MERLIN

That you will go on with me to the end
Of my short way, and say unto no man
Or woman that you found or saw me here.
No good would follow, for a doubt would live
Unstifled of my loyalty to him
Whose deeds are wrought for those who are to come;
And many who see not what I have seen,
Or what you see tonight, would prattle on
For ever, and their children after them,
Of what might once have been had I gone down
With you to Camelot to see the King.
I came to see the King,—but why see kings?
All this that was to be is what I saw
Before there was an Arthur to be king,
And so to be a mirror wherein men
May see themselves, and pause. If they see not,
Or if they do see and they ponder not,—
I saw; but I was neither Fate nor God.
I saw too much; and this would be the end,
Were there to be an end. I saw myself—
A sight no other man has ever seen;
And through the dark that lay beyond myself
I saw two fires that are to light the world."

On Dagonet the silent hand of Merlin
Weighed now as living iron that held him down
With a primeval power. Doubt, wonderment,
Impatience, and a self-accusing sorrow
Born of an ancient love, possessed and held him
Until his love was more than he could name,
And he was Merlin's fool, not Arthur's now:
"Say what you will, I say that I'm the fool
Of Merlin, King of Nowhere; which is Here.
With you for king and me for court, what else
Have we to sigh for but a place to sleep?

313

I know a tavern that will take us in;
And on the morrow I shall follow you
Until I die for you. And when I die . . ."—
"Well, Dagonet, the King is listening."—
And Dagonet answered, hearing in the words
Of Merlin a grave humor and a sound
Of graver pity, "I shall die a fool."
He heard what might have been a father's laugh,
Faintly behind him; and the living weight
Of Merlin's hand was lifted. They arose,
And, saying nothing, found a groping way
Down through the gloom together. Fiercer now,
The wind was like a flying animal
That beat the two of them incessantly
With icy wings, and bit them as they went.
The rock above them was an empty place
Where neither seer nor fool should view again
The stricken city. Colder blew the wind
Across the world, and on it heavier lay
The shadow and the burden of the night;
And there was darkness over Camelot.

THE TOWN DOWN THE RIVER

(1910)

To Theodore Roosevelt

THE MASTER *

(LINCOLN)

A FLYING word from here and there
Had sown the name at which we sneered,
But soon the name was everywhere,
To be reviled and then revered:
A presence to be loved and feared,
We cannot hide it, or deny
That we, the gentlemen who jeered,
May be forgotten by and by.

He came when days were perilous
And hearts of men were sore beguiled;
And having made his note of us,
He pondered and was reconciled.
Was ever master yet so mild
As he, and so untamable?
We doubted, even when he smiled,
Not knowing what he knew so well.

He knew that undeceiving fate
Would shame us whom he served unsought;
He knew that he must wince and wait—
The jest of those for whom he fought;

* Supposed to have been written not long after the Civil War.

317

He knew devoutly what he thought
Of us and of our ridicule;
He knew that we must all be taught
Like little children in a school.

We gave a glamour to the task
That he encountered and saw through,
But little of us did he ask,
And little did we ever do.
And what appears if we review
The season when we railed and chaffed?
It is the face of one who knew
That we were learning while we laughed.

The face that in our vision feels
Again the venom that we flung,
Transfigured to the world reveals
The vigilance to which we clung.
Shrewd, hallowed, harassed, and among
The mysteries that are untold,
The face we see was never young
Nor could it wholly have been old.

For he, to whom we had applied
Our shopman's test of age and worth,
Was elemental when he died,
As he was ancient at his birth:
The saddest among kings of earth,
Bowed with a galling crown, this man
Met rancor with a cryptic mirth,
Laconic—and Olympian.

The love, the grandeur, and the fame
Are bounded by the world alone;

318

The calm, the smouldering, and the flame
Of awful patience were his own:
With him they are forever flown
Past all our fond self-shadowings,
Wherewith we cumber the Unknown
As with inept, Icarian wings.

For we were not as other men:
'Twas ours to soar and his to see;
But we are coming down again,
And we shall come down pleasantly;
Nor shall we longer disagree
On what it is to be sublime,
But flourish in our perigee
And have one Titan at a time.

THE TOWN DOWN THE RIVER

I

SAID the Watcher by the Way
To the young and the unladen,
To the boy and to the maiden,
"God be with you both to-day.
First your song came ringing,
Now you come, you two,—
Knowing naught of what you do,
Or of what your dreams are bringing.

"O you children who go singing
To the Town down the River,
Where the millions cringe and shiver,
Tell me what you know to-day;
Tell me how far you are going,

319

Tell me how you find your way.
O you children who go dreaming,
Tell me what you dream to-day."

"He is old and we have heard him,"
Said the boy then to the maiden;
"He is old and heavy laden
With a load we throw away.
Care may come to find us,
Age may lay us low;
Still, we seek the light we know,
And the dead we leave behind us.

"Did he think that he would blind us
Into such a small believing
As to live without achieving,
When the lights have led so far?
Let him watch or let him wither,—
Shall he tell us where we are?
We know best who go together,
Downward, onward, and so far."

II

SAID the Watcher by the Way
To the fiery folk that hastened,
To the loud and the unchastened,
"You are strong, I see, to-day.
Strength and hope may lead you
To the journey's end,—
Each to be the other's friend
If the Town should fail to need you.

"And are ravens there to feed you
In the Town down the River,

Where the gift appalls the giver
And youth hardens day by day?
O you brave and you unshaken,
Are you truly on your way?
And are sirens in the River,
That you come so far to-day?"

"You are old, and we have listened,"
Said the voice of one who halted;
"You are sage and self-exalted,
But your way is not our way.
You that cannot aid us
Give us words to eat.
Be assured that they are sweet,
And that we are as God made us.

"Not in vain have you delayed us,
Though the River still be calling
Through the twilight that is falling
And the Town be still so far.
By the whirlwind of your wisdom
Leagues are lifted as leaves are;
But a king without a kingdom
Fails us, who have come so far."

III

SAID the Watcher by the Way
To the slower folk who stumbled,
To the weak and the world-humbled,
"Tell me how you fare to-day.
Some with ardor shaken,
All with honor scarred,
Do you falter, finding hard
The far chance that you have taken?

"Or, do you at length awaken
To an antic retribution,
Goading to a new confusion
The drugged hopes of yesterday?
O you poor mad men that hobble,
Will you not return, or stay?
Do you trust, you broken people,
To a dawn without the day?"

"You speak well of what you know not,"
Muttered one; and then a second:
"You have begged and you have beckoned,
But you see us on our way.
Who are you to scold us,
Knowing what we know?
Jeremiah, long ago,
Said as much as you have told us.

"As we are, then, you behold us:
Derelicts of all conditions,
Poets, rogues, and sick physicians,
Plodding forward from afar;
Forward now into the darkness
Where the men before us are;
Forward, onward, out of grayness,
To the light that shone so far."

IV

Said the Watcher by the Way
To some aged ones who lingered,
To the shrunken, the claw-fingered,
"So you come for me to-day."—
"Yes, to give you warning;
You are old," one said;

"You have old hairs on your head,
Fit for laurel, not for scorning.

"From the first of early morning
We have toiled along to find you;
We, as others, have maligned you,
But we need your scorn to-day.
By the light that we saw shining,
Let us not be lured alway;
Let us hear no River calling
When to-morrow is to-day."

"But your lanterns are unlighted
And the Town is far before you:
Let us hasten, I implore you,"
Said the Watcher by the Way.
"Long have I waited,
Longer have I known
That the Town would have its own,
And the call be for the fated.

"In the name of all created,
Let us hear no more, my brothers;
Are we older than all others?
Are the planets in our way?"—
"Hark," said one; "I hear the River,
Calling always, night and day."—
"Forward, then! The lights are shining,"
Said the Watcher by the Way.

AN ISLAND

(Saint Helena, 1821)

Take it away, and swallow it yourself.
Ha! Look you, there's a rat.

Last night there were a dozen on that shelf,
And two of them were living in my hat.
Look! Now he goes, but he'll come back—
Ha? But he will, I say . .
Il reviendra-z-à Pâques,
Ou à la Trinité . . .
Be very sure that he'll return again;
For said the Lord: Imprimis, we have rats,
And having rats, we have rain.—
So on the seventh day
He rested, and made Pain.
—Man, if you love the Lord, and if the Lord
Love liars, I will have you at your word
And swallow it. *Voilà.* Bah!

Where do I say it is
That I have lain so long?
Where do I count myself among the dead,
As once above the living and the strong?
And what is this that comes and goes,
Fades and swells and overflows,
Like music underneath and overhead?
What is it in me now that rings and roars
Like fever-laden wine?
What ruinous tavern-shine
Is this that lights me far from worlds and wars
And women that were mine?
Where do I say it is
That Time has made my bed?
What lowering outland hostelry is this
For one the stars have disinherited?

An island, I have said:
A peak, where fiery dreams and far desires
Are rained on, like old fires:

AN ISLAND

A vermin region by the stars abhorred,
Where falls the flaming word
By which I consecrate with unsuccess
An acreage of God's forgetfulness,
Left here above the foam and long ago
Made right for my duress;
Where soon the sea,
My foaming and long-clamoring enemy,
Will have within the cryptic, old embrace
Of her triumphant arms—a memory.
Why then, the place?
What forage of the sky or of the shore
Will make it any more,
To me, than my award of what was left
Of number, time, and space?

And what is on me now that I should heed
The durance or the silence or the scorn?
I was the gardener who had the seed
Which holds within its heart the food and fire
That gives to man a glimpse of his desire;
And I have tilled, indeed,
Much land, where men may say that I have planted
Unsparingly my corn—
For a world harvest-haunted
And for a world unborn.

Meanwhile, am I to view, as at a play,
Through smoke the funeral flames of yesterday,
And think them far away?
Am I to doubt and yet be given to know
That where my demon guides me, there I go?—
An island? Be it so.
For islands, after all is said and done,
Tell but a wilder game that was begun,

When Fate, the mistress of iniquities,
The mad Queen-spinner of all discrepancies,
Beguiled the dyers of the dawn that day,
And even in such a curst and sodden way
Made my three colors one.
—So be it, and the way be as of old:
So be the weary truth again retold
Of great kings overthrown
Because they would be kings, and lastly kings alone.
Fling to each dog his bone.

Flags that are vanished, flags that are soiled and furled,
Say what will be the word when I am gone:
What learned little acrid archive men
Will burrow to find me out and burrow again,—
But all for naught, unless
To find there was another Island. . . . Yes,
There are too many islands in this world,
There are too many rats, and there is too much rain.
So three things are made plain
Between the sea and sky:
Three separate parts of one thing, which is Pain . . .
Bah, what a way to die!—
To leave my Queen still spinning there on high,
Still wondering, I dare say,
To see me in this way . . .
Madame à sa tour monte
Si haut qu'elle peut monter—
Like one of our Commissioners . . . *ai! ai!*
Prometheus and the women have to cry,
But no, not I . . .
Faugh, what a way to die!

But who are these that come and go
Before me, shaking laurel as they pass?

AN ISLAND

Laurel, to make me know
For certain what they mean:
That now my Fate, my Queen,
Having found that she, by way of right reward,
Will after madness go remembering,
And laurel be as grass,—
Remembers the one thing
That she has left to bring.
The floor about me now is like a sward
Grown royally. Now it is like a sea
That heaves with laurel heavily,
Surrendering an outworn enmity
For what has come to be.

But not for you, returning with your curled
And haggish lips. And why are you alone?
Why do you stay when all the rest are gone?
Why do you bring those treacherous eyes that reek
With venom and hate the while you seek
To make me understand?—
Laurel from every land,
Laurel, but not the world?

Fury, or perjured Fate, or whatsoever,
Tell me the bloodshot word that is your name
And I will pledge remembrance of the same
That shall be crossed out never;
Whereby posterity
May know, being told, that you have come to me,
You and your tongueless train without a sound,
With covetous hands and eyes and laurel all around.
Foreshowing your endeavor
To mirror me the demon of my days,
To make me doubt him, loathe him, face to face.
Bowed with unwilling glory from the quest

That was ordained and manifest,
You shake it off and wish me joy of it?
Laurel from every place,
Laurel, but not the rest?
Such are the words in you that I divine,
Such are the words of men.
So be it, and what then?
Poor, tottering counterfeit,
Are you a thing to tell me what is mine?

Grant we the demon sees
An inch beyond the line,
What comes of mine and thine?
A thousand here and there may shriek and freeze,
Or they may starve in fine.
The Old Physician has a crimson cure
For such as these,
And ages after ages will endure
The minims of it that are victories.
The wreath may go from brow to brow,
The state may flourish, flame, and cease;
But through the fury and the flood somehow
The demons are acquainted and at ease,
And somewhat hard to please.
Mine, I believe, is laughing at me now
In his primordial way,
Quite as he laughed of old at Hannibal,
Or rather at Alexander, let us say.
Therefore, be what you may,
Time has no further need
Of you, or of your breed.
My demon, irretrievably astray,
Has ruined the last chorus of a play
That will, so he avers, be played again some day;
And you, poor glowering ghost,

328

AN ISLAND

Have staggered under laurel here to boast
Above me, dying, while you lean
In triumph awkward and unclean,
About some words of his that you have read?
Thing, do I not know them all?
He tells me how the storied leaves that fall
Are tramped on, being dead?
They are sometimes: with a storm foul enough
They are seized alive and they are blown far off
To mould on islands.—What else have you read?
He tells me that great kings look very small
When they are put to bed;
And this being said,
He tells me that the battles I have won
Are not my own,
But his—howbeit fame will yet atone
For all defect, and sheave the mystery:
The follies and the slaughters I have done
Are mine alone,
And so far History.
So be the tale again retold
And leaf by clinging leaf unrolled
Where I have written in the dawn,
With ink that fades anon,
Like Cæsar's, and the way be as of old.

Ho, is it you? I thought you were a ghost.
Is it time for you to poison me again?
Well, here's our friend the rain,—
Mironton, mironton, mirontaine . . .
Man, I could murder you almost,
You with your pills and toast.
Take it away and eat it, and shoot rats.
Ha! there he comes. Your rat will never fail,
My punctual assassin, to prevail—

While he has power to crawl,
Or teeth to gnaw withal—
Where kings are caged. Why has a king no cats?
You say that I'll achieve it if I try?
Swallow it?—No, not I . . .
God, what a way to die!

CALVERLY'S

WE go no more to Calverly's,
For there the lights are few and low;
And who are there to see by them,
Or what they see, we do not know.
Poor strangers of another tongue
May now creep in from anywhere,
And we, forgotten, be no more
Than twilight on a ruin there.

We two, the remnant. All the rest
Are cold and quiet. You nor I,
Nor fiddle now, nor flagon-lid,
May ring them back from where they lie.
No fame delays oblivion
For them, but something yet survives:
A record written fair, could we
But read the book of scattered lives.

There'll be a page for Leffingwell,
And one for Lingard, the Moon-calf;
And who knows what for Clavering,
Who died because he couldn't laugh?
Who knows or cares? No sign is here,
No face, no voice, no memory;

LEFFINGWELL

No Lingard with his eerie joy,
No Clavering, no Calverly.

We cannot have them here with us
To say where their light lives are gone,
Or if they be of other stuff
Than are the moons of Ilion.
So, be their place of one estate
With ashes, echoes, and old wars,—
Or ever we be of the night,
Or we be lost among the stars.

LEFFINGWELL

I—The Lure

No, no,—forget your Cricket and your Ant,
For I shall never set my name to theirs
That now bespeak the very sons and heirs
Incarnate of Queen Gossip and King Cant.
The case of Leffingwell is mixed, I grant,
And futile seems the burden that he bears;
But are we sounding his forlorn affairs
Who brand him parasite and sycophant?

I tell you, Leffingwell was more than these;
And if he prove a rather sorry knight,
What quiverings in the distance of what light
May not have lured him with high promises,
And then gone down?—He may have been deceived;
He may have lied,—he did; and he believed.

II—The Quickstep

THE dirge is over, the good work is done,
All as he would have had it, and we go;

And we who leave him say we do not know
How much is ended or how much begun.
So men have said before of many a one;
So men may say of us when Time shall throw
Such earth as may be needful to bestow
On you and me the covering hush we shun.

Well hated, better loved, he played and lost,
And left us; and we smile at his arrears;
And who are we to know what it all cost,
Or what we may have wrung from him, the buyer?
The pageant of his failure-laden years
Told ruin of high price. The place was higher.

III—Requiescat

We never knew the sorrow or the pain
Within him, for he seemed as one asleep—
Until he faced us with a dying leap,
And with a blast of paramount, profane,
And vehement valediction did explain
To each of us, in words that we shall keep,
Why we were not to wonder or to weep,
Or ever dare to wish him back again.

He may be now an amiable shade,
With merry fellow-phantoms unafraid
Around him—but we do not ask. We know
That he would rise and haunt us horribly,
And be with us o' nights of a certainty.
Did we not hear him when he told us so?

CLAVERING

I SAY no more for Clavering
  Than I should say of him who fails
To bring his wounded vessel home
  When reft of rudder and of sails;

I say no more than I should say
  Of any other one who sees
Too far for guidance of to-day,
  Too near for the eternities.

I think of him as I should think
  Of one who for scant wages played,
And faintly, a flawed instrument
  That fell while it was being made;

I think of him as one who fared,
  Unfaltering and undeceived,
Amid mirages of renown
  And urgings of the unachieved;

I think of him as one who gave
  To Lingard leave to be amused,
And listened with a patient grace
  That we, the wise ones, had refused;

I think of metres that he wrote
  For Cubit, the ophidian guest.
"What Lilith, or Dark Lady" . . . Well,
  Time swallows Cubit with the rest.

I think of last words that he said
  One midnight over Calverly:
"Good-by—good man." He was not good;
  So Clavering was wrong, you see.

I wonder what had come to pass
  Could he have borrowed for a spell
The fiery-frantic indolence
  That made a ghost of Leffingwell;

I wonder if he pitied us
  Who cautioned him till he was gray
To build his house with ours on earth
  And have an end of yesterday;

I wonder what it was we saw
  To make us think that we were strong;
I wonder if he saw too much,
  Or if he looked one way too long.

But when were thoughts or wonderings
  To ferret out the man within?
Why prate of what he seemed to be,
  And all that he might not have been?

He clung to phantoms and to friends,
  And never came to anything.
He left a wreath on Cubit's grave.
  I say no more for Clavering.

LINGARD AND THE STARS

THE table hurled itself, to our surprise,
At Lingard, and anon rapped eagerly:
"When earth is cold and there is no more sea,
There will be what was Lingard. Otherwise,
Why lure the race to ruin through the skies?
And why have Leffingwell, or Calverly?"—

PASA THALASSA THALASSA

"I wish the ghost would give his name," said he;
And searching gratitude was in his eyes.

He stood then by the window for a time,
And only after the last midnight chime
Smote the day dead did he say anything:
"Come out, my little one, the stars are bright;
Come out, you lælaps, and inhale the night."
And so he went away with Clavering.

PASA THALASSA THALASSA

"The sea is everywhere the sea."

I

GONE—faded out of the story, the sea-faring friend I remember?
Gone for a decade, they say: never a word or a sign.
Gone with his hard red face that only his laughter could wrinkle,
Down where men go to be still, by the old way of the sea.

Never again will he come, with rings in his ears like a pirate,
Back to be living and seen, here with his roses and vines;
Here where the tenants are shadows and echoes of years un·
    eventful,
Memory meets the event, told from afar by the sea.

Smoke that floated and rolled in the twilight away from the
    chimney
Floats and rolls no more. Wheeling and falling, instead,
Down with a twittering flash go the smooth and inscrutable
    swallows,
Down to the place made theirs by the cold work of the sea.

Roses have had their day, and the dusk is on yarrow and worm·
    wood—
Dusk that is over the grass, drenched with memorial dew;

335

Trellises lie like bones in a ruin that once was a garden,
Swallows have lingered and ceased, shadows and echoes are all.

II

WHERE is he lying to-night, as I turn away down to the valley,
Down where the lamps of men tell me the streets are alive?
Where shall I ask, and of whom, in the town or on land or on
  water,
News of a time and a place buried alike and with him?

Few now remain who may care, nor may they be wiser for
  caring,
Where or what manner the doom, whether by day or by night;
Whether in Indian deeps or on flood-laden fields of Atlantis,
Or by the roaring Horn, shrouded in silence he lies.

Few now remain who return by the weed-weary path to his
  cottage,
Drawn by the scene as it was—met by the chill and the change;
Few are alive who report, and few are alive who remember,
More of him now than a name carved somewhere on the sea.

"Where is he lying?" I ask, and the lights in the valley are
  nearer;
Down to the streets I go, down to the murmur of men.
Down to the roar of the sea in a ship may be well for another—
Down where he lies to-night, silent, and under the storms.

MOMUS

"WHERE'S the need of singing now?"—
Smooth your brow,
Momus, and be reconciled,
For King Kronos is a child—

UNCLE ANANIAS

Child and father,
Or god rather,
And all gods are wild.

"Who reads Byron any more?"—
Shut the door,
Momus, for I feel a draught;
Shut it quick, for some one laughed.—
"What's become of
Browning? Some of
Wordsworth lumbers like a raft?

"What are poets to find here?"—
Have no fear:
When the stars are shining blue
There will yet be left a few
Themes availing—
And these failing,
Momus, there'll be you.

UNCLE ANANIAS

His words were magic and his heart was true,
    And everywhere he wandered he was blessed.
Out of all ancient men my childhood knew
    I choose him and I mark him for the best.
Of all authoritative liars, too,
    I crown him loveliest.

How fondly I remember the delight
    That always glorified him in the spring;
The joyous courage and the benedight
    Profusion of his faith in everything!

He was a good old man, and it was right
  That he should have his fling.

And often, underneath the apple-trees,
  When we surprised him in the summer time,
With what superb magnificence and ease
  He sinned enough to make the day sublime!
And if he liked us there about his knees,
  Truly it was no crime.

All summer long we loved him for the same
  Perennial inspiration of his lies;
And when the russet wealth of autumn came,
  There flew but fairer visions to our eyes—
Multiple, tropical, winged with a feathery flame,
  Like birds of paradise.

So to the sheltered end of many a year
  He charmed the seasons out with pageantry
Wearing upon his forehead, with no fear,
  The laurel of approved iniquity.
And every child who knew him, far or near,
  Did love him faithfully.

THE WHIP

THE doubt you fought so long
The cynic net you cast,
The tyranny, the wrong,
The ruin, they are past;
And here you are at last,
Your blood no longer vexed.
The coffin has you fast,
The clod will have you next.

THE WHIP

But fear you not the clod,
Nor ever doubt the grave:
The roses and the sod
Will not forswear the wave.
The gift the river gave
Is now but theirs to cover:
The mistress and the slave
Are gone now, and the lover.

wife husband lover

You left the two to find
Their own way to the brink
Then—shall I call you blind?—
You chose to plunge and sink.
God knows the gall we drink
Is not the mead we cry for,
Nor was it, I should think—
For you—a thing to die for.

*in horserace
they were in
boat, it
sank
they swim to
shore*

Could we have done the same,
Had we been in your place?—
This funeral of your name
Throws no light on the case.
Could we have made the chase,
And felt then as you felt?—
But what's this on your face,
Blue, curious, like a welt?

2 boats

— he is hit in face

There were some ropes of sand
Recorded long ago,
But none, I understand,
Of water. Is it so?
And she—she struck the blow,
You but a neck behind. . .
You saw the river flow—
Still, shall I call you blind?

*— she hit him
to prevent him
getting to bank*

339

THE WHITE LIGHTS

(BROADWAY, 1906)

WHEN in from Delos came the gold
That held the dream of Pericles,
When first Athenian ears were told
The tumult of Euripides,
When men met Aristophanes,
Who fledged them with immortal quills—
Here, where the time knew none of these,
There were some islands and some hills.

When Rome went ravening to see
The sons of mothers end their days,
When Flaccus bade Leuconoë
To banish her Chaldean ways,
When first the pearled, alembic phrase
Of Maro into music ran—
Here there was neither blame nor praise
For Rome, or for the Mantuan.

When Avon, like a faery floor,
Lay freighted, for the eyes of One,
With gal'eons laden long before
By moonlit wharves in Avalon—
Here, where the white lights have begun
To seethe a way for something fair,
No prophet knew, from what was done,
That there was triumph in the air.

EXIT

FOR what we owe to other days,
Before we poisoned him with praise,

THE WISE BROTHERS

May we who shrank to find him weak
Remember that he cannot speak.

For envy that we may recall,
And for our faith before the fall,
May we who are alive be slow
To tell what we shall never know.

For penance he would not confess,
And for the fateful emptiness
Of early triumph undermined,
May we now venture to be kind.

LEONORA

THEY have made for Leonora this low dwelling in the ground,
And with cedar they have woven the four walls round.
Like a little dryad hiding she'll be wrapped all in green,
Better kept and longer valued than by ways that would have
        been.

They will come with many roses in the early afternoon,
They will come with pinks and lilies and with Leonora soon;
And as long as beauty's garments over beauty's limbs are thrown,
There'll be lilies that are liars, and the rose will have its own.

There will be a wondrous quiet in the house that they have made,
And to-night will be a darkness in the place where she'll be laid;
But the builders, looking forward into time, could only see
Darker nights for Leonora than to-night shall ever be.

THE WISE BROTHERS

FIRST VOICE

So long adrift, so fast aground,
What foam and ruin have we found—

We, the Wise Brothers?
Could heaven and earth be framed amiss,
That we should land in fine like this—
    We, and no others?

SECOND VOICE

Convoyed by what accursèd thing
Made we this evil reckoning—
    We, the Wise Brothers?
And if the failure be complete,
Why look we forward from defeat—
    We, and what others?

THIRD VOICE

Blown far from harbors once in sight,
May we not, going far, go right,—
    We, the Wise Brothers?
Companioned by the whirling spheres,
Have we no more than what appears—
    We, and all others?

BUT FOR THE GRACE OF GOD

"There, but for the grace of God, goes . . ."

THERE is a question that I ask,
    And ask again:
What hunger was half-hidden by the mask
    That he wore then?

There was a word for me to say
    That I said not;
And in the past there was another day
    That I forgot:

BUT FOR THE GRACE OF GOD

A dreary, cold, unwholesome day,
    Racked overhead,—
As if the world were turning the wrong way,
    And the sun dead:

A day that comes back well enough
    Now he is gone.
What then? Has memory no other stuff
    To seize upon?

Wherever he may wander now
    In his despair,
Would he be more contented in the slough
    If all were there?

And yet he brought a kind of light
    Into the room;
And when he left, a tinge of something bright
    Survived the gloom.

Why will he not be where he is,
    And not with me?
The hours that are my life are mine, not his,—
    Or used to be.

What numerous imps invisible
    Has he at hand,
Far-flying and forlorn as what they tell
    At his command?

What hold of weirdness or of worth
    Can he possess,
That he may speak from anywhere on earth
    His loneliness?

Shall I be caught and held again
    In the old net?—
He brought a sorry sunbeam with him then,
    But it beams yet.

FOR ARVIA

ON HER FIFTH BIRTHDAY

YOU Eyes, you large and all-inquiring Eyes,
That look so dubiously into me,
And are not satisfied with what you see,
Tell me the worst and let us have no lies:
Tell me the meaning of your scrutinies.
And of myself. Am I a Mystery?
Am I a Boojum—or just Company?
What do you say? What do you think, You Eyes?

You say not; but you think, beyond a doubt;
And you have the whole world to think about,
With very little time for little things.
So let it be; and let it all be fair—
For you, and for the rest who cannot share
Your gold of unrevealed awakenings.

THE SUNKEN CROWN

NOTHING will hold him longer—let him go;
Let him go down where others have gone down;
Little he cares whether we smile or frown,
Or if we know, or if we think we know.

344

SHADRACH O'LEARY

The call is on him for his overthrow,
Say we; so let him rise, or let him drown.
Poor fool! He plunges for the sunken crown,
And we—we wait for what the plunge may show.

Well, we are safe enough. Why linger, then?
The watery chance was his, not ours. Poor fool!
Poor truant, poor Narcissus out of school;
Poor jest of Ascalon; poor king of men.—
The crown, if he be wearing it, may cool
His arrogance, and he may sleep again.

DOCTOR OF BILLIARDS

Of all among the fallen from on high,
We count you last and leave you to regain
Your born dominion of a life made vain
By three spheres of insidious ivory.
You dwindle to the lesser tragedy—
Content, you say. We call, but you remain.
Nothing alive gone wrong could be so plain,
Or quite so blasted with absurdity.

You click away the kingdom that is yours,
And you click off your crown for cap and bells;
You smile, who are still master of the feast,
And for your smile we credit you the least;
But when your false, unhallowed laugh occurs,
We seem to think there may be something else.

SHADRACH O'LEARY

O'Leary was a poet—for a while:
He sang of many ladies frail and fair,

345

The rolling glory of their golden hair,
And emperors extinguished with a smile.
They foiled his years with many an ancient wile,
And if they limped, O'Leary didn't care:
He turned them loose and had them everywhere,
Undoing saints and senates with their guile.

But this was not the end. A year ago
I met him—and to meet was to admire:
Forgotten were the ladies and the lyre,
And the small, ink-fed Eros of his dream.
By questioning I found a man to know—
A failure spared, a Shadrach of the Gleam.

HOW ANNANDALE WENT OUT

"They called it Annandale—and I was there
To flourish, to find words, and to attend:
Liar, physician, hypocrite, and friend,
I watched him; and the sight was not so fair
As one or two that I have seen elsewhere:
An apparatus not for me to mend—
A wreck, with hell between him and the end,
Remained of Annandale; and I was there.

"I knew the ruin as I knew the man;
So put the two together, if you can,
Remembering the worst you know of me.
Now view yourself as I was, on the spot—
With a slight kind of engine. Do you see?
Like this . . . You wouldn't hang me? I thought not."

ALMA MATER

He knocked, and I beheld him at the door—
A vision for the gods to verify.

346

MINIVER CHEEVY

"What battered ancientry is this," thought I,
"And when, if ever, did we meet before?"
But ask him as I might, I got no more
For answer than a moaning and a cry:
Too late to parley, but in time to die,
He staggered, and lay shapeless on the floor.

When had I known him? And what brought him here?
Love, warning, malediction, hunger, fear?
Surely I never thwarted such as he?—
Again, what soiled obscurity was this:
Out of what scum, and up from what abyss,
Had they arrived—these rags of memory?

MINIVER CHEEVY

MINIVER CHEEVY, child of scorn,
  Grew lean while he assailed the seasons;
He wept that he was ever born,
  And he had reasons.

Miniver loved the days of old
  When swords were bright and steeds were prancing:
The vision of a warrior bold
  Would set him dancing.

Miniver sighed for what was not,
  And dreamed, and rested from his labors;
He dreamed of Thebes and Camelot,
  And Priam's neighbors.

Miniver mourned the ripe renown
  That made so many a name so fragrant;
He mourned Romance, now on the town,
  And Art, a vagrant.

Miniver loved the Medici,
    Albeit he had never seen one;
He would have sinned incessantly
    Could he have been one.

Miniver cursed the commonplace
    And eyed a khaki suit with loathing;
He missed the mediæval grace
    Of iron clothing.

Miniver scorned the gold he sought,
    But sore annoyed was he without it;
Miniver thought, and thought, and thought,
    And thought about it.

Miniver Cheevy, born too late,
    Scratched his head and kept on thinking;
Miniver coughed, and called it fate,
    And kept on drinking.

THE PILOT

From the Past and Unavailing
Out of cloudland we are steering:
After groping, after fearing,
Into starlight we come trailing,
And we find the stars are true.
Still, O comrade, what of you?
You are gone, but we are sailing,
And the old ways are all new.

For the Lost and Unreturning
We have drifted, we have waited;
Uncommanded and unrated,

VICKERY'S MOUNTAIN

We have tossed and wandered, yearning
For a charm that comes no more
From the old lights by the shore:
We have shamed ourselves in learning
What you knew so long before.

For the Breed of the Far-going
Who are strangers, and all brothers,
May forget no more than others
Who looked seaward with eyes flowing.
But are brothers to bewail
One who fought so foul a gale?
You have won beyond our knowing,
You are gone, but yet we sail.

VICKERY'S MOUNTAIN

Blue in the west the mountain stands,
  And through the long twilight
Vickery sits with folded hands,
  And Vickery's eyes are bright.

Bright, for he knows what no man else
  On earth as yet may know:
There's a golden word that he never tells,
  And a gift that he will not show.

He dreams of honor and wealth and fame,
  He smiles, and well he may;
For to Vickery once a sick man came
  Who did not go away.

The day before the day to be,
  "Vickery," said the guest,
"You know as you live what's left of me—
  And you shall know the rest.

349

"You know as you live that I have come
   To this we call the end.
No doubt you have found me troublesome,
   But you've also found a friend;

"For we shall give and you shall take
   The gold that is in view;
The mountain there and I shall make
   A golden man of you.

"And you shall leave a friend behind
   Who neither frets nor feels;
And you shall move among your kind
   With hundreds at your heels.

"Now this that I have written here
   Tells all that need be told;
So, Vickery, take the way that's clear.
   And be a man of gold."

Vickery turned his eyes again
   To the far mountain-side,
And wept a tear for worthy men
   Defeated and defied.

Since then a crafty score of years
   Have come, and they have gone;
But Vickery counts no lost arrears:
   He lingers and lives on.

Blue in the west the mountain stands,
   Familiar as a face.
Blue, but Vickery knows what sar ds
   Are golden at its base.

BON VOYAGE

He dreams and lives upon the day
  When he shall walk with kings.
Vickery smiles—and well he may.
  The life-caged linnet sings.

Vickery thinks the time will come
  To go. for what is his;
But hovering, unseen hands at home
  Will hold him where he is.

There's a golden word that he never tells
  And a gift that he will not show.
All to be given to some one else—
  And Vickery not to know.

BON VOYAGE

CHILD of a line accurst
  And old as Troy,
Bringer of best and worst
  In wild alloy—
Light, like a linnet first,
  He sang for joy.

Thrall to the gilded ease
  Of every day,
Mocker of all degrees
  And always gay,
Child of the Cyclades
  And of Broadway—

Laughing and half divine
  The boy began,
Drunk with a woodland wine
  Thessalian:
But there was rue to twine
  The pipes of Pan.

351

Therefore he skipped and flew
  The more along,
Vivid and always new
  And always wrong,
Knowing his only clew
  A siren song.

Careless of each and all
  He gave and spent:
Feast or a funeral
  He laughed and went,
Laughing to be so small
  In the event.

Told of his own deceit
  By many a tongue,
Flayed for his long defeat
  By being young,
Lured by the fateful sweet
  Of songs unsung—

Knowing it in his heart,
  But knowing not
The secret of an art
  That few forgot,
He played the twinkling part
  That was his lot.

And when the twinkle died,
  As twinkles do,
He pushed himself aside
  And out of view:
Out with the wind and tide,
  Before we knew.

THE COMPANION

LET him answer as he will,
Or be lightsome as he may,
Now nor after shall he say
Worn-out words enough to kill,
Or to lull down by their craft,
Doubt, that was born yesterday,
When he lied and when she laughed.

Let him find another name
For the starlight on the snow,
Let him teach her till she know
That all seasons are the same,
And all sheltered ways are fair,—
Still, wherever she may go,
Doubt will have a dwelling there.

ATHERTON'S GAMBIT

THE master played the bishop's pawn,
For jest, while Atherton looked on;
The master played this way and that,
And Atherton, amazed thereat,
Said "Now I have a thing in view
That will enlighten one or two,
And make a difference or so
In what it is they do not know."

The morning stars together sang
And forth a mighty music rang—

Not heard by many, save as told
Again through magic manifold
By such a few as have to play
For others, in the Master's way,
The music that the Master made
When all the morning stars obeyed.

Atherton played the bishop's pawn
While more than one or two looked on;
Atherton played this way and that,
And many a friend, amused thereat,
Went on about his business
Nor cared for Atherton the less;
A few stood longer by the game,
With Atherton to them the same.

The morning stars are singing still,
To crown, to challenge, and to kill;
And if perforce there falls a voice
On pious ears that have no choice
Except to urge an erring hand
To wreak its homage on the land,
Who of us that is worth his while
Will, if he listen, more than smile?

Who of us, being what he is,
May scoff at others' ecstasies?
However we may shine to-day,
More-shining ones are on the way;
And so it were not wholly well
To be at odds with Azrael,—
Nor were it kind of any one
To sing the end of Atherton.

TWO GARDENS IN LINNDALE

FOR A DEAD LADY

No more with overflowing light
Shall fill the eyes that now are faded,
Nor shall another's fringe with night
Their woman-hidden world as they did.
No more shall quiver down the days
The flowing wonder of her ways,
Whereof no language may requite
The shifting and the many-shaded.

The grace, divine, definitive,
Clings only as a faint forestalling;
The laugh that love could not forgive
Is hushed, and answers to no calling;
The forehead and the little ears
Have gone where Saturn keeps the years;
The breast where roses could not live
Has done with rising and with falling.

The beauty, shattered by the laws
That have creation in their keeping,
No longer trembles at applause,
Or over children that are sleeping;
And we who delve in beauty's lore
Know all that we have known before
Of what inexorable cause
Makes Time so vicious in his reaping.

TWO GARDENS IN LINNDALE

Two brothers, Oakes and Oliver,
Two gentle men as ever were,
Would roam no longer, but abide
In Linndale, where their fathers died,
And each would be a gardener.

355

"Now first we fence the garden through,
With this for me and that for you,"
Said Oliver.—"Divine!" said Oakes,
"And I, while I raise artichokes,
Will do what I was born to do."

"But this is not the soil, you know,"
Said Oliver, "to make them grow:
The parent of us, who is dead,
Compassionately shook his head
Once on a time and told me so."

"I hear you, gentle Oliver,"
Said Oakes, "and in your character
I find as fair a thing indeed
As ever bloomed and ran to seed
Since Adam was a gardener.

"Still, whatsoever I find there,
Forgive me if I do not share
The knowing gloom that you take on
Of one who doubted and is done:
For chemistry meets every prayer."

"Sometimes a rock will meet a plough,"
Said Oliver; "but anyhow
'Tis here we are, 'tis here we live,
With each to take and each to give:
There's no room for a quarrel now.

"I leave you in all gentleness
To science and a ripe success.
Now God be with you, brother Oakes,
With you and with your artichokes:
You have the vision, more or less."

TWO GARDENS IN LINNDALE

"By fate, that gives to me no choice,
I have the vision and the voice:
Dear Oliver, believe in me,
And we shall see what we shall see;
Henceforward let us both rejoice."

"But first, while we have joy to spare
We'll plant a little here and there;
And if you be not in the wrong,
We'll sing together such a song
As no man yet sings anywhere."

They planted and with fruitful eyes
Attended each his enterprise.
"Now days will come and days will go,
And many a way be found, we know,"
Said Oakes, "and we shall sing, likewise."

"The days will go, the years will go,
And many a song be sung, we know,"
Said Oliver; "and if there be
Good harvesting for you and me,
Who cares if we sing loud or low?"

They planted once, and twice, and thrice,
Like amateurs in paradise;
And every spring, fond, foiled, elate,
Said Oakes, "We are in tune with Fate:
One season longer will suffice."

Year after year 'twas all the same:
With none to envy, none to blame,
They lived along in innocence,
Nor ever once forgot the fence,
Till on a day the Stranger came.

He came to greet them where they were,
And he too was a Gardener:
He stood between these gentle men,
He stayed a little while, and then
The land was all for Oliver.

'Tis Oliver who tills alone
Two gardens that are now his own;
'Tis Oliver who sows and reaps
And listens, while the other sleeps,
For songs undreamed of and unknown.

'Tis he, the gentle anchorite,
Who listens for them day and night;
But most he hears them in the dawn,
When from his trees across the lawn
Birds ring the chorus of the light.

He cannot sing without the voice,
But he may worship and rejoice
For patience in him to remain,
The chosen heir of age and pain,
Instead of Oakes—who had no choice.

'Tis Oliver who sits beside
The other's grave at eventide,
And smokes, and wonders what new race
Will have two gardens, by God's grace,
In Linndale, where their fathers died.

And often, while he sits and smokes,
He sees the ghost of gentle Oakes
Uprooting, with a restless hand,
Soft, shadowy flowers in a land
Of asphodels and artichokes.

THE REVEALER

(ROOSEVELT)

He turned aside to see the carcase of the lion: and behold, there was a swarm of bees and honey in the carcase of the lion. . . . And the men of the city said unto him, What is sweeter than honey? and what is stronger than a lion?—*Judges*, 14.

THE palms of Mammon have disowned
The gift of our complacency;
The bells of ages have intoned
Again their rhythmic irony;
And from the shadow, suddenly,
'Mid echoes of decrepit rage,
The seer of our necessity
Confronts a Tyrian heritage.

Equipped with unobscured intent
He smiles with lions at the gate,
Acknowledging the compliment
Like one familiar with his fate;
The lions, having time to wait,
Perceive a small cloud in the skies,
Whereon they look, disconsolate,
With scared, reactionary eyes.

A shadow falls upon the land,—
They sniff, and they are like to roar;
For they will never understand
What they have never seen before.
They march in order to the door,
Not knowing the best thing to seek,
Nor caring if the gods restore
The lost composite of the Greek.

The shadow fades, the light arrives,
And ills that were concealed are seen;
The combs of long-defended hives
Now drip dishonored and unclean;
No Nazarite or Nazarene
Compels our questioning to prove
The difference that is between
Dead lions—or the sweet thereof.

But not for lions, live or dead,
Except as we are all as one,
Is he the world's accredited
Revealer of what we have done;
What You and I and Anderson
Are still to do is his reward;
If we go back when he is gone—
There is an Angel with a Sword.

He cannot close again the doors
That now are shattered for our sake;
He cannot answer for the floors
We crowd on, or for walls that shake;
He cannot wholly undertake
The cure of our immunity;
He cannot hold the stars, or make
Of seven years a century.

So Time will give us what we earn
Who flaunt the handful for the whole,
And leave us all that we may learn
Who read the surface for the soul;
And we'll be steering to the goal,
For we have said so to our sons:
When we who ride can pay the toll,
Time humors the far-seeing ones.

THE REVEALER

Down to our nose's very end
We see, and are invincible,—
Too vigilant to comprehend
The scope of what we cannot sell;
But while we seem to know as well
As we know dollars, or our skins,
The Titan may not always tell
Just where the boundary begins.

LANCELOT

(1920)

To Lewis M. Isaacs

LANCELOT *

I

GAWAINE, aware again of Lancelot
In the King's garden, coughed and followed him;
Whereat he turned and stood with folded arms
And weary-waiting eyes, cold and half-closed—
Hard eyes, where doubts at war with memories
Fanned a sad wrath. "Why frown upon a friend?
Few live that have too many," Gawaine said,
And wished unsaid, so thinly came the light
Between the narrowing lids at which he gazed.
"And who of us are they that name their friends?"
Lancelot said. "They live that have not any.
Why do they live, Gawaine? Ask why, and answer."

Two men of an elected eminence,
They stood for a time silent. Then Gawaine,
Acknowledging the ghost of what was gone,
Put out his hand: "Rather, I say, why ask?
If I be not the friend of Lancelot,
May I be nailed alive along the ground *~drawn wrong~*
And emmets eat me dead. If I be not
The friend of Lancelot, may I be fried
With other liars in the pans of hell.
What item otherwise of immolation
Your Darkness may invent, be it mine to endure
And yours to gloat on. For the time between,
Consider this thing you see that is my hand.
If once, it has been yours a thousand times;

* *Copyright, 1920, by Thomas Seltzer.*

365

Why not again? Gawaine has never lied
To Lancelot; and this, of all wrong days—
This day before the day when you go south
To God knows what accomplishment of exile—
Were surely an ill day for lies to find
An issue or a cause or an occasion.
King Ban your father and King Lot my father,
Were they alive, would shake their heads in sorrow
To see us as we are, and I shake mine
In wonder. Will you take my hand, or no?
Strong as I am, I do not hold it out
For ever and on air. You see—my hand."
Lancelot gave his hand there to Gawaine,
Who took it, held it, and then let it go,
Chagrined with its indifference.

               "Yes, Gawaine,
I go tomorrow, and I wish you well;
You and your brothers, Gareth, Gaheris,—
And Agravaine; yes, even Agravaine,
Whose tongue has told all Camelot and all Britain
More lies than yet have hatched of Modred's envy.
You say that you have never lied to me,
And I believe it so. Let it be so.
For now and always. Gawaine, I wish you well.
Tomorrow I go south, as Merlin went,
But not for Merlin's end. I go, Gawaine,
And leave you to your ways. There are ways left."

"There are three ways I know, three famous ways,
And all in Holy Writ." Gawaine said, smiling:
"The snake's way and the eagle's way are two,
And then we have a man's way with a maid—
Or with a woman who is not a maid.
Your late way is to send all women scudding,
To the last flash of the last cramoisy,

366

LANCELOT

While you go south to find the fires of God.
Since we came back again to Camelot
From our immortal Quest—I came back first—
No man has known you for the man you were
Before you saw whatever 't was you saw,
To make so little of kings and queens and friends
Thereafter. Modred? Agravaine? My brothers?
And what if they be brothers? What are brothers,
If they be not our friends, your friends and mine?
You turn away, and my words are no mark
On you affection or your memory?
So be it then, if so it is to be. *[handwritten: — father as in Merlin]*
God save you, Lancelot; for by Saint Stephen,
You are no more than man to save yourself."

"Gawaine, I do not say that you are wrong,
Or that you are ill-seasoned in your lightness;
You say that all you know is what you saw,
And on your own averment you saw nothing.
Your spoken word, Gawaine, I have not weighed
In those unhappy scales of inference
That have no beam but one made out of hates
And fears, and venomous conjecturings;
Your tongue is not the sword that urges me
Now out of Camelot. Two other swords *[handwritten: ? Agravaine & Modred]*
There are that are awake, and in their scabbards
Are parching for the blood of Lancelot.
Yet I go not away for fear of them,
But for a sharper care. You say the truth,
But not when you contend the fires of God
Are my one fear,—for there is one fear more.
Therefore I go. Gawaine, I wish you well."

"Well-wishing in a way is well enough;
So, in a way, is caution; so, in a way,

Are leeches, neatherds, and astrologers.
Lancelot, listen. Sit you down and listen:
You talk of swords and fears and banishment.
Two swords, you say; Modred and Agravaine,
You mean. Had you meant Gaheris and Gareth,
Or willed an evil on them, I should welcome
And hasten your farewell. But Agravaine
Hears little what I say; his ears are Modred's.
The King is Modred's father, and the Queen
A prepossession of Modred's lunacy.
So much for my two brothers whom you fear,
Not fearing for yourself. I say to you,
Fear not for anything—and so be wise
And amiable again as heretofore;
Let Modred have his humor, and Agravaine
His tongue. The two of them have done their worst,
And having done their worst, what have they done?
A whisper now and then, a chirrup or so
In corners,—and what else? Ask what, and answer."

Still with a frown that had no faith in it,
Lancelot, pitying Gawaine's lost endeavour
To make an evil jest of evidence,
Sat fronting him with a remote forbearance—
Whether for Gawaine blind or Gawaine false,
Or both, or neither, he could not say yet,
If ever; and to himself he said no more
Than he said now aloud: "What else, Gawaine?
What else, am I to say? Then ruin, I say;
Destruction, dissolution, desolation,
I say,—should I compound with jeopardy now.
For there are more than whispers here, Gawaine:
The way that we have gone so long together
Has underneath our feet, without our will,
Become a twofold faring. Yours, I trust,

368

May lead you always on, as it has led you,
To praise and to much joy. Mine, I believe,
Leads off to battles that are not yet fought,
And to the Light that once had blinded me.
When I came back from seeing what I saw,
I saw no place for me in Camelot.
There is no place for me in Camelot.
There is no place for me save where the Light
May lead me; and to that place I shall go.
Meanwhile I lay upon your soul no load
Of counsel or of empty admonition;
Only I ask of you, should strife arise
In Camelot, to remember, if you may,
That you've an ardor that outruns your reason,
Also a glamour that outshines your guile;
And you are a strange hater. I know that;
And I'm in fortune that you hate not me.
Yet while we have our sins to dream about,
Time has done worse for time than in our making,
Albeit there may be sundry falterings
And falls against us in the Book of Man."

"Praise Adam, you are mellowing at last!
I've always liked this world, and would so still;
And if it is your new Light leads you on
To such an admirable gait, for God's sake,
Follow it, follow it, follow it, Lancelot;
Follow it as you never followed glory.
Once I believed that I was on the way
That you call yours, but I came home again
To Camelot—and Camelot was right,
For the world knows its own that knows not you;
You are a thing too vaporous to be sharing
The carnal feast of life. You mow down men
Like elder-stems, and you leave women sighing

369

For one more sight of you; but they do wrong.
You are a man of mist, and have no shadow.
God save you, Lancelot. If I laugh at you,
I laugh in envy and in admiration."

The joyless evanescence of a smile,
Discovered on the face of Lancelot
By Gawaine's unrelenting vigilance,
Wavered, and with a sullen change went out;
And then there was the music of a woman
Laughing behind them, and a woman spoke:
"Gawaine, you said 'God save you, Lancelot.'
Why should He save him any more to-day
Than on another day? What has he done,
Gawaine, that God should save him?" Guinevere,
With many questions in her dark blue eyes
And one gay jewel in her golden hair,
Had come upon the two of them unseen,
Till now she was a russet apparition
At which the two arose—one with a dash
Of easy leisure in his courtliness,
One with a stately calm that might have pleased
The Queen of a strange land indifferently.
The firm incisive languor of her speech,
Heard once, was heard through battles. "Lancelot,
What have you done to-day that God should save you?
What has he done, Gawaine, that God should save him?
I grieve that you two pinks of chivalry
Should be so near me in my desolation,
And I, poor soul alone, know nothing of it.
What has he done, Gawaine?"

                                    With all her poise,
To Gawaine's undeceived urbanity
She was less queen than woman for the nonce,

LANCELOT

And in her eyes there was a flickering
Of a still fear that would not be veiled wholly
With any mask of mannered nonchalance.
"What has he done? Madam, attend your nephew;
And learn from him, in your incertitude,
That this inordinate man Lancelot,
This engine of renown, this hewer down daily
Of potent men by scores in our late warfare,
Has now inside his head a foreign fever
That urges him away to the last edge
Of everything, there to efface himself
In ecstasy, and so be done with us.
Hereafter, peradventure certain birds
Will perch in meditation on his bones,
Quite as if they were some poor sailor's bones,
Or felon's jettisoned, or fisherman's,
Or fowler's bones, or Mark of Cornwall's bones.
In fine, this flower of men that was our comrade
Shall be for us no more, from this day on,
Than a much remembered Frenchman far away.
Magnanimously I leave you now to prize
Your final sight of him; and leaving you,
I leave the sun to shine for him alone,
Whiles I grope on to gloom. Madam, farewell;
And you, contrarious Lancelot, farewell."

II

THE flash of oak leaves over Guinevere,
That afternoon, with the sun going down,
Made memories there for Lancelot, although
The woman who in silence looked at him
Now seemed his inventory of the world
That he must lose, or suffer to be lost
For love of her who sat there in the shade,

371

With oak leaves flashing in a golden light
Over her face and over her golden hair.
"Gawaine has all the graces, yet he knows;
He knows enough to be the end of us,
If so he would," she said. "He knows and laughs
And we are at the mercy of a man
Who, if the stars went out, would only laugh."
She looked away at a small swinging blossom,
And then she looked intently at her fingers,
While a frown gathered slowly round her eyes,
And wrinkled her white forehead.

        Lancelot,
Scarce knowing whether to himself he spoke
Or to the Queen, said emptily: "As for Gawaine,
My question is, if any curious hind
Or knight that is alive in Britain breathing,
Or prince, or king, knows more of us, or less,
Than Gawaine, in his gay complacency,
Knows or believes he knows. There's over much
Of knowing in this realm of many tongues,
Where deeds are less to those who tell of them
Than are the words they sow; and you and I
Are like to yield a granary of such words,
For God knows what next harvesting. Gawain
I fear no more than Gareth, or Colgrevance;
So far as it is his to be the friend
Of any man, so far is he my friend—
Till I have crossed him in some enterprise
Unlikely and unborn. So fear not Gawaine
But let your primal care be now for one
Whose name is yours."

      The Queen, with her blue eyes
Too bright for joy, still gazed on Lancelot,

         372

Who stared as if in angry malediction
Upon the shorn grass growing at his feet.
"Why do you speak as if the grass had ears
And I had none? What are you saying now,
So darkly to the grass, of knights and hinds?
Are you the Lancelot who rode, long since,
Away from me on that unearthly Quest,
Which left no man the same who followed it—
Or none save Gawaine, who came back so soon
That we had hardly missed him?" Faintly then
She smiled a little, more in her defence,
He knew, than for misprision of a man
Whom yet she feared: "Why do you set this day—
This golden day, when all are not so golden—
To tell me, with your eyes upon the ground,
That idle words have been for idle tongues
And ears a moment's idle entertainment?
Have I become, and all at once, a thing
So new to courts, and to the buzz they make,
That I should hear no murmur, see no sign?
Where malice and ambition dwell with envy,
They go the farthest who believe the least;
So let them,—while I ask of you again,
Why this day for all this? Was yesterday
A day of ouphes and omens? Was it Friday?
I don't remember. Days are all alike
When I have you to look on; when you go,
There are no days but hours. You might say now
What Gawaine said, and say it in our language."
The sharp light still was in her eyes, alive
And anxious with a reminiscent fear.

Lancelot, like a strong man stricken hard
With pain, looked up at her unhappily;
And slowly, on a low and final note,

Said: "Gawaine laughs alike at what he knows,
And at the loose convenience of his fancy;
He sees in others what his humor needs
To nourish it, and lives a merry life.
Sometimes a random shaft of his will hit
Nearer the mark than one a wise man aims
With infinite address and reservation;
So has it come to pass this afternoon."

Blood left the quivering cheeks of Guinevere
As color leaves a cloud; and where white was
Before, there was a ghostliness not white,
But gray; and over it her shining hair
Coiled heavily its mocking weight of gold.
The pride of her forlorn light-heartedness
Fled like a storm-blown feather; and her fear,
Possessing her, was all that she possessed.
She sought for Lancelot, but he seemed gone.
There was a strong man glowering in a chair
Before her, but he was not Lancelot,
Or he would look at her and say to her
That Gawaine's words were less than chaff in the wind—
A nonsense about exile, birds, and bones,
Born of an indolence of empty breath.
"Say what has come to pass this afternoon,"
She said, "or I shall hear you all my life,
Not hearing what it was you might have told."

He felt the trembling of her slow last words,
And his were trembling as he answered them:
"Why this day, why no other? So you ask,
And so must I in honor tell you more—
For what end, I have yet no braver guess
Than Modred has of immortality,
Or you of Gawaine. Could I have him alone

374

LANCELOT

Between me and the peace I cannot know,
My life were like the sound of golden bells
Over still fields at sunset, where no storm
Should ever blast the sky with fire again,
Or' thunder follow ruin for you and me,—
As like it will, if I for one more day,
Assume that I see not what I have seen,
See now, and shall see. There are no more lies
Left anywhere now for me to tell myself
That I have not already told myself,
And overtold, until today I seem
To taste them as I might the poisoned fruit
That Patrise had of Mador, and so died.
And that same apple of death was to be food
For Gawaine; but he left it and lives on,
To make his joy of living your confusion.
His life is his religion; he loves life
With such a manifold exuberance
That poison shuns him and seeks out a way
To wreak its evil upon innocence.
There may be chance in this, there may be law;
Be what there be, I do not fear Gawaine."

The Queen, with an indignant little foot,
Struck viciously the unoffending grass
And said: "Why not let Gawaine go his way?
I'll think of him no more, fear him no more,
And hear of him no more. I'll hear no more
Of any now save one who is, or was,
All men to me. And he said once to me
That he would say why this day, of all days,
Was more mysteriously felicitous
For solemn commination than another."
Again she smiled, but her blue eyes were telling
No more their story of old happiness.

"For me today is not as other days,"
He said, "because it is the first, I find,
That has empowered my will to say to you
What most it is that you must hear and heed.
When Arthur, with a faith unfortified,
Sent me alone, of all he might have sent,
That May-day to Leodogran your father,
I went away from him with a sore heart;
For in my heart I knew that I should fail
My King, who trusted me too far beyond
The mortal outpost of experience.
And this was after Merlin's admonition,
Which Arthur, in his passion, took for less
Than his inviolable majesty.
When I rode in between your father's guards
And heard his trumpets blown for my loud honor,
I sent my memory back to Camelot,
And said once to myself, 'God save the king!'
But the words tore my throat and were like blood
Upon my tongue. Then a great shout went up
From shining men around me everywhere;
And I remember more fair women's eyes
Than there are stars in autumn, all of them
Thrown on me for a glimpse of that high knight
Sir Lancelot—Sir Lancelot of the Lake.
I saw their faces and I saw not one
To sever a tendril of my integrity;
But I thought once again, to make myself
Believe a silent lie, 'God save the King' . . .
I saw your face, and there were no more kings."

The sharp light softened in the Queen's blue eyes,
And for a moment there was joy in them:
"Was I so menacing to the peace, I wonder,
Of anyone else alive? But why go back?

LANCELOT

I tell you that I fear Gawaine no more;
And if you fear him not, and I fear not
What you fear not, what have we then to fear?"
Fatigued a little with her reasoning,
She waited longer than a woman waits,
Without a cloudy sign, for Lancelot's
Unhurried answer: "Whether or not you fear,
Know always that I fear for me no stroke
Maturing for the joy of any knave
Who sees the world, with me alive in it, *Shab*
A place too crowded for the furtherance
Of his inflammatory preparations.
But Lot of Orkney had a wife, a dark one;
And rumor says no man who gazed at her,
Attentively, might say his prayers again
Without a penance or an absolution.
I know not about that; but the world knows
That Arthur prayed in vain once, if he prayed, *his sin*
Or we should have no Modred watching us.
Know then that what you fear to call my fear
Is all for you; and what is all for you
Is all for love, which were the same to me
As life—had I not seen what I have seen.
But first I am to tell you what I see,
And what I mean by fear. It is yourself
That I see now; and if I saw you only,
I might forego again all other service,
And leave to Time, who is Love's almoner,
The benefaction of what years or days
Remaining might be found unchronicled
For two that have not always watched or seen
The sands of gold that flow for golden hours.
If I saw you alone! But I know now
That you are never more to be alone.
The shape of one infernal foul attendant

377

Will be for ever prowling after you,
To leer at me like a damned thing whipped out
Of the last cave in hell. You know his name.
Over your shoulder I could see him now,
Adventuring his misbegotten patience
For one destroying word in the King's ear—
The word he cannot whisper there quite yet,
Not having it yet to say. If he should say it,
Then all this would be over, and our days
Of life, your days and mine, be over with it.
No day of mine that were to be for you
Your last, would light for me a longer span
Than for yourself; and there would be no twilight."

The Queen's implacable calm eyes betrayed
The doubt that had as yet for what he said
No healing answer: "If I fear no more
Gawaine, I fear your Modred even less.
Your fear, you say, is for an end outside
Your safety; and as much as that I grant you.
And I believe in your belief, moreover,
That some far-off unheard-of retribution
Hangs over Camelot, even as this oak-bough,
That I may almost reach, hangs overhead,
All dark now. Only a small time ago
The light was falling through it, and on me.
Another light, a longer time ago,
Was living in your eyes, and we were happy.
Yet there was Modred then as he is now,
As much a danger then as he is now,
And quite as much a nuisance. Let his eyes
Have all the darkness in them they may hold,
And there will be less left of it outside
For fear to grope and thrive in. Lancelot,
I say the dark is not what you fear most.

378

LANCELOT

There is a Light that you fear more today
Than all the darkness that has ever been;
Yet I doubt not that your Light will burn on
For some time yet without your ministration.
I'm glad for Modred,—though I hate his eyes,—
That he should hold me nearer to your thoughts
Than I should hold myself, I fear, without him;
I'm glad for Gawaine, also,—who, you tell me,
Misled my fancy with his joy of living."

Incredulous of her voice and of her lightness,
He saw now in the patience of her smile
A shining quiet of expectancy
That made as much of his determination
As he had made of giants and Sir Peris.
"But I have more to say than you have heard,"
He faltered—"though God knows what you have heard
Should be enough."

                    "I see it now," she said;
"I see it now as always women must
Who cannot hold what holds them any more.
If Modred's hate were now the only hazard—
The only shadow between you and me—
How long should I be saying all this to you,
Or you be listening? No, Lancelot,—no.
I knew it coming for a longer time
Than you fared for the Grail. You told yourself,
When first that wild light came to make men mad
Round Arthur's Table—as Gawaine told himself,
And many another tired man told himself—
That it was God, not something new, that called you.
Well, God was something new to most of them,
And so they went away. But you were changing
Long before you, or Bors, or Percival,

379

Or Galahad rode away—or poor Gawaine,
Who came back presently; and for a time
Before you went—albeit for no long time—
I may have made for your too loyal patience
A jealous exhibition of my folly—
All for those two Elaines; and one of them
Is dead, poor child, for you. How do you feel,
You men, when women die for you? They do,
Sometimes, you know. Not often, but sometimes."

Discomfiture, beginning with a scowl
And ending in a melancholy smile,
Crept over Lancelot's face the while he stared,
More like a child than like the man he was,
At Guinevere's demure serenity
Before him in the shadow, soon to change
Into the darkness of a darker night
Than yet had been since Arthur was a king.
"What seizure of an unrelated rambling
Do you suppose it was that had you then?"
He said; and with a frown that had no smile
Behind it, he sat brooding.

             The Queen laughed,
And looked at him again with lucent eyes
That had no sharpness in them; they were soft now,
And a blue light, made wet with happiness,
Distilled from pain into abandonment,
Shone out of them and held him while she smiled,
Although they trembled with a questioning
Of what his gloom foretold: "All that I saw
Was true, and I have paid for what I saw—
More than a man may know. Hear me, and listen:
You cannot put me or the truth aside,
With half-told words that I could only wish

380

LANCELOT

No man had said to me; not you, of all men.
If there were only Modred in the way,
Should I see now, from here and in this light,
So many furrows over your changed eyes?
Why do you fear for me when all my fears
Are for the needless burden you take on?
To put me far away, and your fears with me,
Were surely no long toil, had you the will
To say what you have known and I have known
Longer than I dare guess. Have little fear:
Never shall I become for you a curse
Laid on your conscience to be borne for ever;
Nor shall I be a weight for you to drag
On always after you, as a poor slave
Drags iron at his heels. Therefore, today,
These ominous reassurances of mine
Would seem to me to be a waste of life,
And more than life."

                    Lancelot's memory wandered
Into the blue and wistful distances
That her soft eyes unveiled. He knew their trick,
As he knew the great love that fostered it,
And the wild passionate fate that hid itself
In all the perilous calm of white and gold
That was her face and hair, and might as well
Have been of gold and marble for the world,
And for the King. Before he knew, she stood
Behind him with her warm hands on his cheeks,
And her lips on his lips; and though he heard
Not half of what she told, he heard enough
To make as much of it, or so it seemed,
As man was ever told, or should be told,
Or need be, until everything was told,
And all the mystic silence of the stars

Had nothing more to keep or to reveal.
"If there were only Modred in the way,"
She murmured, "would you come to me tonight?
The King goes to Carleon or Carlisle,
Or some place where there's hunting. Would you come,
If there were only Modred in the way?"
She felt his hand on hers and laid her cheek
Upon his forehead, where the furrows were:
"All these must go away, and so must I—
Before there are more shadows. You will come,
And you may tell me everything you must
That I must hear you tell me—if I must—
Of bones and horrors and of horrid waves
That break for ever on the world's last edge."

III

LANCELOT looked about him, but he saw
No Guinevere. The place where she had sat
Was now an empty chair that might have been
The shadowy throne of an abandoned world,
But for the living fragrance of a kiss
That he remembered, and a living voice
That hovered when he saw that she was gone.
There was too much remembering while he felt
Upon his cheek the warm sound of her words;
There was too much regret; there was too much
Remorse. Regret was there for what had gone,
Remorse for what had come. Yet there was time,
That had not wholly come. There was time enough
Between him and the night—as there were shoals
Enough, no doubt, that in the sea somewhere
Were not yet hidden by the drowning tide.
"So there is here between me and the dark
Some twilight left," he said. He sighed, and said

382

Again, "Time, tide, and twilight—and the dark;
And then, for me, the Light. But what for her?
I do not think of anything but life
That I may give to her by going now;
And if I look into her eyes again,
Or feel her breath upon my face again,
God knows if I may give so much as life;
Or if the durance of her loneliness
Would have it for the asking. What am I?
What have I seen that I must leave behind
So much of heaven and earth to burn itself
Away in white and gold, until in time
There shall be no more white and no more gold?
I cannot think of such a time as that;
I cannot—yet I must; for I am he
That shall have hastened it and hurried on
To dissolution all that wonderment—
That envy of all women who have said
She was a child of ice and ivory;
And of all men, save one. And who is he?
Who is this Lancelot that has betrayed
His King, and served him with a cankered honor?
Who is this Lancelot that sees the Light
And waits now in the shadow for the dark?
Who is this King, this Arthur, who believes
That what has been, and is, will be for ever,—
Who has no eye for what he will not see,
And will see nothing but what's passing here
In Camelot, which is passing? Why are we here?
What are we doing—kings, queens, Camelots,
And Lancelots? And what is this dim world
That I would leave, and cannot leave tonight
Because a Queen is in it and a King
Has gone away to some place where there's hunting—
Carleon or Carlisle! Who is this Queen,

This pale witch-wonder of white fire and gold,
This Guinevere that I brought back with me
From Cameliard for Arthur, who knew then
What Merlin told, as he forgets it now
And rides away from her—God watch the world!—
To some place where there's hunting! What are kings?
And how much longer are there to be kings?
When are the millions who are now like worms
To know that kings are worms, if they are worms?
When are the women who make toys of men
To know that they themselves are less than toys
When Time has laid upon their skins the touch
Of his all-shrivelling fingers? When are they
To know that men must have an end of them
When men have seen the Light and left the world
That I am leaving now. Yet, here I am,
And all because a king has gone a-hunting. . . .
Carleon or Carlisle!"

                          So Lancelot
Fed with a sullen rancor, which he knew
To be as false as he was to the King,
The passion and the fear that now in him
Were burning like two slow infernal fires
That only flight and exile far away
From Camelot should ever cool again.
"Yet here I am," he said,—"and here I am.
Time, tide, and twilight; and there is no twilight—
And there is not much time. But there's enough
To eat and drink in; and there may be time
For me to frame a jest or two to prove
How merry a man may be who sees the Light.
And I must get me up and go along,
Before the shadows blot out everything,
And leave me stumbling among skeletons.

God, what a rain of ashes falls on him
Who sees the new and cannot leave the old!"

He rose and looked away into the south
Where a gate was, by which he might go out,
Now, if he would, while Time was yet there with him—
Time that was tearing minutes out of life
While he stood shivering in his loneliness,
And while the silver lights of memory
Shone faintly on a far-off eastern shore
Where he had seen on earth for the last time
The triumph and the sadness in the face
Of Galahad, for whom the Light was waiting.
Now he could see the face of him again,
He fancied; and his flickering will adjured him
To follow it and be free. He followed it
Until it faded and there was no face,
And there was no more light. Yet there was time
That had not come, though he could hear it now
Like ruining feet of marching conquerors
That would be coming soon and were not men.
Forlornly and unwillingly he came back
To find the two dim chairs. In one of them
Was Guinevere, and on her phantom face
There fell a golden light that might have been
The changing gleam of an unchanging gold
That was her golden hair. He sprang to touch
The wonder of it, but she too was gone,
Like Galahad; he was alone again
With shadows, and one face that he still saw.
The world had no more faces now than one
That for a moment, with a flash of pain,
Had shown him what it is that may be seen
In embers that break slowly into dust,
Where for a time was fire. He saw it there

Before him, and he knew it was not good
That he should learn so late, and of this hour,
What men may leave behind them in the eyes
Of women who have nothing more to give,
And may not follow after. Once again
He gazed away to southward, but the face
Of Galahad was not there. He turned, and saw
Before him, in the distance, many lights
In Arthur's palace; for the dark had come
To Camelot, while Time had come and gone.

IV

Not having viewed Carleon or Carlisle,
The King came home to Camelot after midnight,
Feigning an ill not feigned; and his return
Brought Bedivere, and after him Gawaine,
To the King's inner chamber, where they waited
Through the grim light of dawn. Sir Bedivere,
By nature stern to see, though not so bleak
Within as to be frozen out of mercy,
Sat with arms crossed and with his head weighed low
In heavy meditation. Once or twice
His eyes were lifted for a careful glimpse
Of Gawaine at the window, where he stood
Twisting his fingers feverishly behind him,
Like one distinguishing indignantly,
For swift eclipse and for offence not his,
The towers and roofs and the sad majesty
Of Camelot in the dawn, for the last time.

Sir Bedivere, at last, with a long sigh
That said less of his pain than of his pity,
Addressed the younger knight who turned and heard
His elder, but with no large eagerness:

386

LANCELOT

"So it has come, Gawaine; and we are here.
I find when I see backward something farther,
By grace of time, than you are given to see—
Though you, past any doubt, see much that I
See not—I find that what the colder speech
Of reason most repeated says to us
Of what is in a way to come to us
Is like enough to come. And we are here.
Before the unseeing sun is here to mock us,
Or the King here to prove us, we are here.
We are the two, it seems, that are to make
Of words and of our presences a veil
Between him and the sight of what he does.
Little have I to say that I may tell him:
For what I know is what the city knows,
Not what it says,—for it says everything.
The city says the first of all who met
The sword of Lancelot was Colgrevance,
Who fell dead while he wept—a brave machine,
Cranked only for the rudiments of war.
But some of us are born to serve and shift,
And that's not well. The city says, also,
That you and Lancelot were in the garden,
Before the sun went down."

           "Yes," Gawaine groaned;
"Yes, we were there together in the garden,
Before the sun went down; and I conceive
A place among the possibilities
For me with other causes unforeseen
Of what may shake down soon to grief and ashes
This kingdom and this empire. Bedivere,
Could I have given a decent seriousness
To Lancelot while he said things to me
That pulled his heart half out of him by the roots.

And left him, I see now, half sick with pity
For my poor uselessness to serve a need
That I had never known, we might be now .
Asleep and easy in our beds at home,
And we might hear no murmurs after sunrise
Of what we are to hear. A few right words
Of mine, if said well, might have been enough.
That shall I never know. I shall know only
That it was I who laughed at Lancelot
When he said what lay heaviest on his heart.
By now he might be far away from here,
And farther from the world: But the Queen came;
The Queen came, and I left them there together;
And I laughed as I left them. After dark
I met with Modred and said what I could,
When I had heard him, to discourage him.
His mother was my mother. I told Bors,
And he told Lancelot; though as for that,
My story would have been the same as his,
And would have had the same acknowledgment:
'Thanks, but no matter'—or to that effect.
The Queen, of course, had fished him for his word,
And had it on the hook when she went home;
And after that, an army of red devils
Could not have held the man away from her.
And I'm to live as long as I'm to wonder
What might have been, had I not been—myself.
I heard him, and I laughed. Then the Queen came."

"Recriminations are not remedies,
Gawaine; and though you cast them at yourself,
And hurt yourself, you cannot end or swerve
The flowing of these minutes that leave hours
Behind us, as we leave our faded selves
And yesterdays. The surest-visioned of us

388

Are creatures of our dreams and inferences,
And though it look to us a few go far
For seeing far, the fewest and the farthest
Of all we know go not beyond themselves.
No, Gawaine, you are not the cause of this;
And I have many doubts if all you said,
Or in your lightness may have left unsaid,
Would have unarmed the Queen. The Queen was
    there."—
Gawaine looked up, and then looked down again:
"Good God, if I had only said—said something!"

"Say nothing now, Gawaine." Bedivere sighed,
And shook his head: "Morning is not in the west.
The sun is rising and the King is coming;
Now you may hear him in the corridor,
Like a sick landlord shuffling to the light
For one last look-out on his mortgaged hills.
But hills and valleys are not what he sees;
He sees with us the fire—the sign—the law.
The King that is the father of the law
Is weaker than his child, except he slay it.
Not long ago, Gawaine, I had a dream
Of a sword over kings, and of a world
Without them."—"Dreams, dreams."—"Hush, Gawaine."

                      King Arthur
Came slowly on till in the darkened entrance
He stared and shivered like a sleep-walker,
Brought suddenly awake where a cliff's edge
Is all he sees between another step
And his annihilation. Bedivere rose,
And Gawaine rose; and with instinctive arms
They partly guided, partly carried him,
To the King's chair.

"I thank you, gentlemen,
Though I am not so shaken, I dare say,
As you would have me. This is not the hour
When kings who do not sleep are at their best;
And had I slept this night that now is over,
No man should ever call me King again."
He pulled his heavy robe around him closer,
And laid upon his forehead a cold hand
That came down warm and wet. "You, Bedivere,
And you, Gawaine, are shaken with events
Incredible yesterday,—but kings are men.
Take off their crowns and tear away their colors
And let them see with my eyes what I see—
Yes, they are men, indeed! If there's a slave
In Britain with a reptile at his heart
Like mine that with his claws of ice and fire
Tears out of me the fevered roots of mercy,
Find him, and I will make a king of him!
And then, so that his happiness may swell
Tenfold, I'll sift the beauty of all courts
And capitals, to fetch the fairest woman
That evil has in hiding; after that,
That he may know the sovran one man living
To be his friend, I'll prune all chivalry
To one sure knight. In this wise our new king
Will have his queen to love, as I had mine,—
His friend that he may trust, as I had mine,—
And he will be as gay, if all goes well,
As I have been: as fortunate in his love,
And in his friend as fortunate—as I am!
And what am I? . . . And what are you—you two!
If you are men, why don't you say I'm dreaming?
I know men when I see them, I know daylight;
And I see now the gray shine of our dreams.
I tell you I'm asleep and in my bed! . . .

But no—no . . . I remember. You are men.
You are no dreams—but God, God, if you were!
If .I were strong enough to make you vanish
And have you back again with yesterday—
Before I lent myself to that false hunting,
Which yet may stalk the hours of many more
Than Lancelot's unhappy twelve who died,—
With a misguided Colgrevance to lead them,
And Agravaine to follow and fall next,—
Then should I know at last that I was King,
And I should then be King. But kings are men,
And I have gleaned enough these two years gone
To know that queens are women. Merlin told me:
'The love that never was.' Two years ago
He told me that: 'The love that never was!'
I saw—but I saw nothing. Like the bird
That hides his head, I made myself see nothing.
But yesterday I saw—and I saw fire.
I think I saw it first in Modred's eyes;
Yet he said only truth—and fire is right.
It is—it must be fire. The law says fire.
And I, the King who made the law, say fire!
What have I done—what folly have I said,
Since I came here, of dreaming? Dreaming? Ha!
I wonder if the Queen and Lancelot
Are dreaming! . . . Lancelot! Have they found him
    yet?
He slashed a way into the outer night—
Somewhere with Bors. We'll have him here anon,
And we shall feed him also to the fire.
There are too many faggots lying cold
That might as well be cleansing, for our good,
A few deferred infections of our state
That honor should no longer look upon.
Thank heaven, I man my drifting wits again!

Gawaine, your brothers, Gareth and Gaheris,
Are by our royal order there to see
And to report. They went unwillingly,
For they are new to law and young to justice;
But what they are to see will harden them
With wholesome admiration of a realm
Where treason's end is ashes. Ashes. Ashes!
Now this is better. I am King again.
Forget, I pray, my drowsy temporizing,
For I was not then properly awake. . . .
What? Hark! Whose crass insanity is that!
If I be King, go find the fellow and hang him
Who beats into the morning on that bell
Before there is a morning! This is dawn!
What! Bedivere? Gawaine? You shake your heads?
I tell you this is dawn! . . . What have I done?
What have I said so lately that I flinch
To think on! What have I sent those boys to see?
I'll put clouts on my eyes, and I'll not see it!
Her face, and hands, and little small white feet,
And all her shining hair and her warm body—
No—for the love of God, no!—it's alive!
She's all alive, and they are burning her—
The Queen—the love—the love that never was!
Gawaine! Bedivere! Gawaine!—Where is Gawaine!
Is he there in the shadow? Is he dead?
Are we all dead? Are we in hell?—Gawaine! . . .
I cannot see her now in the smoke. Her eyes
Are what I see—and her white body is burning!
She never did enough to make me see her
Like that—to make her look at me like that!
There's not room in the world for so much evil
As I see clamoring in her poor white face
For pity. Pity her, God! God! . . . Lancelot!"

V

GAWAINE, his body trembling and his heart
Pounding as if he were a boy in battle,
Sat crouched as far away from everything
As walls would give him distance. Bedivere
Stood like a man of stone with folded arms,
And wept in stony silence. The King moved
His pallid lips and uttered fitfully
Low fragments of a prayer that was half sad,
Half savage, and was ended in a crash
Of distant sound that anguish lifted near
To those who heard it. Gawaine sprang again
To the same casement where the towers and roofs
Had glimmered faintly a long hour ago,
But saw no terrors yet—though now he heard
A fiercer discord than allegiance rings
To rouse a mourning city: blows, groans, cries,
Loud iron struck on iron, horses trampling,
Death-yells and imprecations, and at last
A moaning silence. Then a murmuring
Of eager fearfulness, which had a note
Of exultation and astonishment,
Came nearer, till a tumult of hard feet
Filled the long corridor where late the King
Had made a softer progress.

                  "Well then, Lucan,"
The King said, urging an indignity
To qualify suspense: "For what arrears
Of grace are we in debt for this attention?
Why all this early stirring of our sentries,
And their somewhat unseasoned innovation,
To bring you at this unappointed hour?

Are we at war with someone or another,
Without our sanction or intelligence?
Are Lucius and the Romans here to greet us,
Or was it Lucius we saw dead?"

                                    Sir Lucan
Bowed humbly in amazed acknowledgment
Of his intrusion, meanwhile having scanned
What three grief-harrowed faces were revealing:
"Praise God, sir, there are tears in the King's eyes,
And in his friends'. Having regarded them,
And having ventured an abrupt appraisal
Of what I translate. . . ."

                        "Lucan," the King said,
"No matter what procedure or persuasion
Gave you an entrance—tell us what it is
That you have come to tell us, and no more.
There was a most uncivil sound abroad
Before you came. Who riots in the city?"

"Sir, will your patience with a clement ear,
Attend the confirmation of events,
I will, with all available precision,
Say what this morning has inaugurated.
No preface or prolonged exordium
Need aggravate the narrative, I venture.
The man of God, requiring of the Queen
A last assoiling prayer for her salvation,
Heard what none else did hear save God the Father.
Then a great hush descended on a scene
Where stronger men than I fell on their knees,
And wet with tears their mail of shining iron
That soon was to be cleft unconscionably
Beneath a blast of anguish as intense
And fabulous in ardor and effect

LANCELOT

As Jove's is in his lightning. To be short,
They led the Queen—and she went bravely to it,
Or so she was configured in the picture—
A brief way more; and we who did see that,
Believed we saw the last of all her sharing
In this conglomerate and perplexed existence.
But no—and here the prodigy comes in—
The penal flame had hardly bit the faggot,
When, like an onslaught out of Erebus,
There came a crash of horses, and a flash
Of axes, and a hewing down of heroes,
Not like to any in its harsh, profound,
Unholy, and uneven execution.
I felt the breath of one horse on my neck,
And of a sword that all but left a chasm
Where still, praise be to God, I have intact
A face, if not a fair one. I achieved
My flight, I trust, with honorable zeal,
Not having arms, or mail, or preservation
In any phase of necessary iron.
I found a refuge; and there saw the Queen,
All white, and in a swound of woe uplifted
By Lionel, while a dozen fought about him,
And Lancelot, who seized her while he struck,
And with his insane army galloped away,
Before the living, whom he left amazed,
Were sure they were alive among the dead.
Not even in the legendary mist
Of wars that none today may verify,
Did ever men annihilate their kind
With a more vicious inhumanity,
Or a more skilful frenzy. Lancelot
And all his heated adjuncts are by now
Too far, I fear, for such immediate
Reprisal as your majesty perchance . . ."

"O' God's name, Lucan," the King cried, "be still!"
He gripped with either sodden hand an arm
Of his unyielding chair, while his eyes blazed
In anger, wonder, and fierce hesitation.
Then with a sigh that may have told unheard
Of an unwilling gratitude, he gazed
Upon his friends who gazed again at him;
But neither King nor friend said anything
Until the King turned once more to Sir Lucan:
"Be still, or publish with a shorter tongue
The names of our companions who are dead.
Well, were you there? Or did you run so fast
That you were never there? You must have eyes,
Or you could not have run to find us here."

Then Lucan, with a melancholy glance
At Gawaine, who stood glaring his impatience,
Addressed again the King: "I will be short, sir;
Too brief to measure with finality
The scope of what I saw with indistinct
Amazement and incredulous concern.
Sir Tor, Sir Griflet, and Sir Aglovale
Are dead. Sir Gillimer, he is dead. Sir—Sir—
But should a living error be detailed
In my account, how should I meet your wrath
For such a false addition to your sorrow?"
He turned again to Gawaine, who shook now
As if the fear in him were more than fury.—
The King, observing Gawaine, beat his foot
In fearful hesitancy on the floor:
"No, Lucan; if so kind an error lives
In your dead record, you need have no fear.
My sorrow has already, in the weight
Of this you tell, too gross a task for that."

"Then I must offer you cold naked words,
Without the covering warmth of even one
Forlorn alternative," said Lucan, slowly:
"Sir Gareth, and Sir Gaheris—are dead."

The rage of a fulfilled expectancy,
Long tortured on a rack of endless moments,
Flashed out of Gawaine's overflowing eyes
While he flew forward, seizing Lucan's arms,
And hurled him while he held him.—"Stop, Gawaine,"
The King said grimly. "Now is no time for that.
If Lucan, in a too bewildered heat
Of observation or sad reckoning,
Has added life to death, our joy therefor
Will be the larger. You have lost yourself."

"More than myself it is that I have lost,"
Gawaine said, with a choking voice that faltered:
"Forgive me, Lucan; I was a little mad.
Gareth?—and Gaheris? Do you say their names,
And then say they are dead! They had no arms—
No armor. They were like you—and you live!
Why do you live when they are dead! You ran,
You say? Well, why were they not running—
If they ran only for a pike to die with?
I knew my brothers, and I know your tale
Is not all told. Gareth?—and Gaheris?
Would they stay there to die like silly children?
Did they believe the King would have them die
For nothing? There are dregs of reason, Lucan,
In lunacy itself. My brothers, Lucan,
Were murdered like two dogs. Who murdered them?"

Lucan looked helplessly at Bedivere,
The changeless man of stone, and then at Gawaine:

"I cannot use the word that you have used,
Though yours must have an answer. Your two brothers
Would not have squandered or destroyed themselves
In a vain show of action. I pronounce it,
If only for their known obedience
To the King's instant wish. Know then your brothers
Were caught and crowded, this way and then that,
With men and horses raging all around them;
And there were swords and axes everywhere
That heads of men were. Armored and unarmored,
They knew the iron alike. In so great press,
Discrimination would have had no pause
To name itself; and therefore Lancelot
Saw not—or seeing, he may have seen too late—
On whom his axes fell."

      "Why do you flood
The name of Lancelot with words enough
To drown him and his army—and his axes! . . .
His axes?—or his axe! Which, Lucan? Speak!
Speak, or by God you'll never speak again! . . .
Forgive me, Lucan; I was a little mad.
You, sir, forgive me; and you, Bedivere.
There are too many currents in this ocean
Where I'm adrift, and I see no land yet.
Men tell of a great whirlpool in the north
Where ships go round until the men aboard
Go dizzy, and are dizzy when they're drowning.
But whether I'm to drown or find the shore,
There is one thing—and only one thing now—
For me to know. . . . His axes? or his axe!
Say, Lucan, or I—O Lucan, speak—speak—speak!
Lucan, did Lancelot kill my two brothers?"

"I say again that in all human chance
He knew not upon whom his axe was falling."

LANCELOT

"So! Then it was his axe and not his axes.
It was his hell-begotten self that did it,
And it was not his men. Gareth! Gaheris!
You came too soon. There was no place for you
Where there was Lancelot. My folly it was,
Not yours, to take for true the inhuman glamour
Of his high-shining fame for that which most
Was not the man. The truth we see too late
Hides half its evil in our stupidity;
And we gape while we groan for what we learn.
An hour ago and I was all but eager
To mourn with Bedivere for grief I had
That I did not say something to this villain—
To this true, gracious, murderous friend of mine—
To comfort him and urge him out of this,
While I was half a fool and half believed
That he was going. Well, there is this to say:
The world that has him will not have him long.
You see how calm I am, now I have said it?
And you, sir, do you see how calm I am?
And it was I who told of shipwrecks—whirlpools—
Drowning! I must have been a little mad,
Not having occupation. Now I have one.
And I have now a tongue as many-phrased
As Lucan's. Gauge it, Lucan, if you will;
Or take my word. It's all one thing to me—
All one, all one! There's only one thing left . . .
Gareth and Gaheris! Gareth! . . . Lancelot!"

"Look, Bedivere," the King said: "look to Gawaine
Now lead him, you and Lucan, to a chair—
As you and Gawaine led me to this chair
Where I am sitting. We may all be led,
If there be coming on for Camelot
Another day like this. Now leave me here.

Alone with Gawaine. When a strong man goes
Like that, it makes him sick to see his friends
Around him. Leave us, and go now. Sometimes
I'll scarce remember that he's not my son,
So near he seems. I thank you, gentlemen."

The King, alone with Gawaine, who said nothing,
Had yet no heart for news of Lancelot
Or Guinevere. He saw them on their way
To Joyous Gard, where Tristram and Isolt
Had islanded of old their stolen love,
While Mark of Cornwall entertained a vengeance
Envisaging an ending of all that;
And he could see the two of them together
As Mark had seen Isolt there, and her knight,—
Though not, like Mark, with murder in his eyes.
He saw them as if they were there already,
And he were a lost thought long out of mind;
He saw them lying in each other's arms,
Oblivious of the living and the dead
They left in Camelot. Then he saw the dead
That lay so quiet outside the city walls,
And wept, and left the Queen to Lancelot—
Or would have left her, had the will been his
To leave or take; for now he could acknowledge
An inrush of a desolate thanksgiving
That she, with death around her, had not died.
The vision of a peace that humbled him,
And yet might save the world that he had won,
Came slowly into view like something soft
And ominous on all-fours, without a spirit
To make it stand upright. "Better be that,
Even that, than blood," he sighed, "if that be peace."
But looking down on Gawaine, who said nothing,
He shook his head: "The King has had his world,

And he shall have no peace. With Modred here,
And Agravaine with Gareth, who is dead
With Gaheris, Gawaine will have no peace.
Gawaine or Modred—Gawaine with his hate,
Or Modred with his anger for his birth,
And the black malady of his ambition—
Will make of my Round Table, where was drawn
The circle of a world, a thing of wreck
And yesterday—a furniture forgotten;
And I, who loved the world as Merlin did,
May lose it as he lost it, for a love
That was not peace, and therefore was not love."

VI

THE dark of Modred's hour not yet availing,
Gawaine it was who gave the King no peace;
Gawaine it was who goaded him and drove him
To Joyous Gard, where now for long his army,
Disheartened with unprofitable slaughter,
Fought for their weary King and wearily
Died fighting. Only Gawaine's hate it was
That held the King's knights and his warrior slaves
Close-hived in exile, dreaming of old scenes
Where Sorrow, and her demon sister Fear,
Now shared the dusty food of loneliness,
From Orkney to Cornwall. There was no peace,
Nor could there be, so Gawaine told the King,
And so the King in anguish told himself,
Until there was an end of one of them—
Of Gawaine or the King, or Lancelot,
Who might have had an end, as either knew,
Long since of Arthur and of Gawaine with him.
One evening in the moonlight Lancelot
And Bors, his kinsman, and the loyalest,

If least assured, of all who followed him,
Sat gazing from an ivy-cornered casement
In angry silence upon Arthur's horde,
Who in the silver distance, without sound,
Were dimly burying dead men. Sir Bors,
Reiterating vainly what was told
As wholesome hearing for unhearing ears,
Said now to Lancelot: "And though it be
For no more now than always, let me speak:
You have a pity for the King, you say,
That is not hate; and for Gawaine you have
A grief that is not hate. Pity and grief!
And the Queen all but shrieking out her soul
That morning when we snatched her from the faggots
That were already crackling when we came!
Why, Lancelot, if in you is an answer,
Have you so vast a charity for the King,
And so enlarged a grief for his gay nephew,
Whose tireless hate for you has only one
Disastrous appetite? You know for what—
For your slow blood. I knew you, Lancelot,
When all this would have been a merry fable
For smiling men to yawn at and forget,
As they forget their physic. Pity and grief
Are in your eyes. I see them well enough;
And I saw once with you, in a far land,
The glimmering of a Light that you saw nearer—
Too near for your salvation or advantage,
If you be what you seem. What I saw then
Made life a wilder mystery than ever,
And earth a new illusion. You, maybe,
Saw pity and grief. What I saw was a Gleam,
To fight for or to die for—till we know
Too much to fight or die. Tonight you turn
A page whereon your deeds are to engross

Inexorably their story of tomorrow;
And then tomorrow. How many of these tomorrows
Are coming to ask unanswered why this war
Was fought and fought for the vain sake of slaughter?
Why carve a compost of a multitude,
When only two, discriminately despatched,
Would sum the end of what you know is ending
And leave to you the scorch of no more blood
Upon your blistered soul? The Light you saw
Was not for this poor crumbling realm of Arthur,
Nor more for Rome; but for another state
That shall be neither Rome nor Camelot,
Nor one that we may name. Why longer, then,
Are you and Gawaine to anoint with war,
That even in hell would be superfluous,
A reign already dying, and ripe to die?
I leave you to your last interpretation
Of what may be the pleasure of your madness."

Meanwhile a mist was hiding the dim work
Of Arthur's men; and like another mist,
All gray, came Guinevere to Lancelot,
Whom Bors had left, not having had of him
The largess of a word. She laid her hands
Upon his hair, vexing him to brief speech:
"And you—are you like Bors?"

       "I may be so,"
She said; and she saw faintly where she gazed,
Like distant insects of a shadowy world,
Dim clusters here and there of shadowy men
Whose occupation was her long abhorrence:
"If he came here and went away again,
And all for nothing, I may be like Bors.
Be glad, at least, that I am not like Andred

Of Cornwall, who stood once behind a man
And slew him without saying he was there.
Not Arthur, I believe, nor yet Gawaine,
Would have done quite like that; though only God
May say what there's to come before this war
Shall have an end—unless you are to see,
As I have seen so long, a way to end it."

He frowned, and watched again the coming mist
That hid with a cold veil of augury
The stillness of an empire that was dying:
"And are you here to say that if I kill
Gawaine and Arthur we shall both be happy?"

"Is there still such a word as happiness?
I come to tell you nothing, Lancelot,
That folly and waste have not already told you.
Were you another man than Lancelot,
I might say folly and fear. But no,—no fear,
As I know fear, was yet composed and wrought,
By man, for your delay and your undoing.
God knows how cruelly and how truly now
You might say, that of all who breathe and suffer
There may be others who are not so near
To you as I am, and so might say better
What I say only with a tongue not apt
Or guarded for much argument. A woman,
As men have known since Adam heard the first
Of Eve's interpreting of how it was
In Paradise, may see but one side only—
Where maybe there are two, to say no more.
Yet here, for you and me, and so for all
Caught with us in this lamentable net,
I see but one deliverance: I see none,
Unless you cut for us a clean way out,

404

So rending these hate-woven webs of horror
Before they mesh the world. And if the world
Or Arthur's name be now a dying glory,
Why bleed it for the sparing of a man
Who hates you, and a King that hates himself?
If war be war—and I make only blood
Of your red writing—why dishonor Time
For torture longer drawn in your slow game
Of empty slaughter? Tomorrow it will be
The King's move, I suppose, and we shall have
One more magnificent waste of nameless pawns,
And of a few more knights. God, how you love
This game!—to make so loud a shambles of it,
When you have only twice to lift your finger
To signal peace, and give to this poor drenched
And clotted earth a time to heal itself.
Twice over I say to you, if war be war,
Why play with it? Why look a thousand ways
Away from what it is, only to find
A few stale memories left that would requite
Your tears with your destruction? Tears, I say,
For I have seen your tears; I see them now,
Although the moon is dimmer than it was
Before I came. I wonder if I dimmed it.
I wonder if I brought this fog here with me
To make you chillier even than you are
When I am not so near you. . . . Lancelot,
There must be glimmering yet somewhere within you
The last spark of a little willingness
To tell me why it is this war goes on.
Once I believed you told me everything;
And what you may have hidden was no matter,
For what you told was all I needed then.
But crumbs that are a festival for joy
Make a dry fare for sorrow; and the few

Spared words that were enough to nourish faith,
Are for our lonely fears a frugal poison.
So, Lancelot, if only to bring back
For once the ghost of a forgotten mercy,
Say now, even though you strike me to the floor
When you have said it, for what untold end
All this goes on. Am I not anything now?
Is Gawaine, who would feed you to wild swine,
And laugh to see them tear you, more than I am?
Is Arthur, at whose word I was dragged out
To wear for you the fiery crown itself
Of human torture, more to you than I am?
Am I, because you saw death touch me once,
Too gross a trifle to be longer prized?
Not many days ago, when you lay hurt
And aching on your bed, and I cried out
Aloud on heaven that I should bring you there,
You said you would have paid the price of hell
To save me that foul morning from the fire.
You paid enough: yet when you told me that,
With death going on outside the while you said it,
I heard the woman in me asking why.
Nor do I wholly find an answer now
In any shine of any far-off Light
You may have seen. Knowing the world, you know
How surely and how indifferently that Light
Shall burn through many a war that is to be,
To which this war were no more than a smear
On circumstance. The world has not begun.
The Light you saw was not the Light of Rome,
Or Time, though you seem battling here for time,
While you are still at war with Arthur's host
And Gawaine's hate. How many thousand men
Are going to their death before Gawaine
And Arthur go to theirs—and I to mine?"

LANCELOT

Lancelot, looking off into the fog,
In which his fancy found the watery light
Of a dissolving moon, sighed without hope
Of saying what the Queen would have him say:
"I fear, my lady, my fair nephew Bors,
Whose tongue affords a random wealth of sound,
May lately have been scattering on the air
For you a music less oracular
Than to your liking. . . . Say, then, you had split
The uncovered heads of two men with an axe,
Not knowing whose heads—if that's a palliation—
And seen their brains fly out and splash the ground
As they were common offal, and then learned
That you had butchered Gaheris and Gareth—
Gareth, who had for me a greater love
Than any that has ever trod the ways
Of a gross world that early would have crushed him,—
Even you, in your quick fever of dispatch,
Might hesitate before you drew the blood
Of him that was their brother, and my friend.
Yes, he was more my friend, was I to know,
Than I had said or guessed; for it was Gawaine
Who gave to Bors the word that might have saved us,
And Arthur's fading empire, for the time
Till Modred had in his dark wormy way
Crawled into light again with a new ruin
At work in that occult snake's brain of his.
And even in your prompt obliteration
Of Arthur from a changing world that rocks
Itself into a dizziness around him,
A moment of attendant reminiscence
Were possible, if not likely. Had he made
A knight of you, scrolling your name with his
Among the first of men—and in his love
Inveterately the first—and had you then

Betrayed his fame and honor to the dust
That now is choking him, you might in time—
You might, I say—to my degree succumb.
Forgive me, if my lean words are for yours
Too bare an answer, and ascribe to them
No tinge of allegation or reproach.
What I said once to you I said for ever—
That I would pay the price of hell to save you.
As for the Light, leave that for me alone;
Or leave as much of it as yet for me
May shine. Should I, through any unforeseen
Remote effect of awkwardness or chance,
Be done to death or durance by the King,
I leave some writing wherein I beseech
For you the clemency of afterthought.
Were I to die and he to see me dead,
My living prayer, surviving the cold hand
That wrote, would leave you in his larger prudence,
If I have known the King, free and secure
To bide the summoning of another King
More great than Arthur. But all this is language;
And I know more than words have yet the scope
To show of what's to come. Go now to rest;
And sleep, if there be sleep. There was a moon;
And now there is no sky where the moon was.
Sometimes I wonder if this be the world
We live in, or the world that lives in us."

The new day, with a cleansing crash of rain
That washed and sluiced the soiled and hoof-torn field
Of Joyous Gard, prepared for Lancelot
And his wet men the not unwelcome scene
Of a drenched emptiness without an army.
"Our friend the foe is given to dry fighting,"
Said Lionel, advancing with a shrug,

LANCELOT

To Lancelot, who saw beyond the rain.
And later Lionel said, "What fellows are they,
Who are so thirsty for their morning ride
That swimming horses would have hardly time
To eat before they swam? You, Lancelot,
If I see rather better than a blind man,
Are waiting on three pilgrims who must love you,
To voyage a flood like this. No friend have I,
To whisper not of three, on whom to count
For such a loyal wash. The King himself
Would entertain a kindly qualm or so,
Before he suffered such a burst of heaven
To splash even three musicians."

                         "Good Lionel,
I thank you, but you need afflict your fancy
No longer for my sake. For these who come,
If I be not immoderately deceived,
Are bearing with them the white flower of peace—
Which I could hope might never parch or wither,
Were I a stranger to this ravening world
Where we have mostly a few rags and tags
Between our skins and those that wrap the flesh
Of less familiar brutes we feed upon
That we may feed the more on one another."

"Well, now that we have had your morning grace
Before our morning meat, pray tell to me
The why and whence of this anomalous
Horse-riding offspring of the Fates. Who are they?"

"I do not read their features or their names;
But if I read the King, they are from Rome,
Spurred here by the King's prayer for no delay;

And I pray God aloud that I say true."
And after a long watching, neither speaking,
"You do," said Lionel; "for by my soul,
I see no other than my lord the Bishop,
Who does God's holy work in Rochester.
Since you are here, you may as well abide here,
While I go foraging."

                                 Now in the gateway,
The Bishop, who rode something heavily,
Was glad for rest though grim in his refusal
At once of entertainment or refection:
"What else you do, Sir Lancelot, receive me
As one among the honest when I say
That my voluminous thanks were less by cantos
Than my damp manner feels. Nay, hear my voice:
If once I'm off this royal animal,
How o' God's name shall I get on again?
Moreover, the King waits. With your accord,
Sir Lancelot, I'll dry my rainy face,
While you attend what's herein written down,
In language of portentous brevity,
For the King's gracious pleasure and for yours,
Whereof the burden is the word of Rome,
Requiring your deliverance of the Queen
Not more than seven days hence. The King returns
Anon to Camelot; and I go with him,
Praise God, if what he waits now is your will
To end an endless war. No recrudescence,
As you may soon remark, of what is past
Awaits the Queen, or any doubt soever
Of the King's mercy. Have you more to say
Than Rome has written, or do I perceive
Your tranquil acquiescence? Is it so?
Then be it so! Venite. Pax vobiscum."

LANCELOT

"To end an endless war with 'pax vobiscum'
Would seem a ready schedule for a bishop;
Would God that I might see the end of it!"
Lancelot, like a statue in the gateway,
Regarded with a qualified rejoicing
The fading out of his three visitors
Into the cold and swallowing wall of storm
Between him and the battle-wearied King
And the unwearying hatred of Gawaine.
To Bors his nephew, and to Lionel,
He glossed a tale of Roman intercession,
Knowing that for a time, and a long time,
The sweetest fare that he might lay before them
Would hold an evil taste of compromise.
To Guinevere, who questioned him at noon
Of what by then had made of Joyous Gard
A shaken hive of legend-heavy wonder,
He said what most it was the undying Devil,
Who ruled him when he might, would have him say:
"Your confident arrangement of the board
For this day's game was notably not to be;
Today was not for the King's move or mine,
But for the Bishop's; and the board is empty.
The words that I have waited for more days
Than are to now my tallage of gray hairs
Have come at last, and at last you are free.
So, for a time, there will be no more war;
And you are going home to Camelot."

"To Camelot?" . . .

                    "To Camelot." But his words
Were said for no queen's hearing. In his arms
He caught her when she fell; and in his arms
He carried her away. The word of Rome
Was in the rain. There was no other sound.

VII

All day the rain came down on Joyous Gard,
Where now there was no joy, and all that night
The rain came down. Shut in for none to find him
Where an unheeded log-fire fought the storm
With upward swords that flashed along the wall
Faint hieroglyphs of doom not his to read,
Lancelot found a refuge where at last
He might see nothing. Glad for sight of nothing,
He saw no more. Now and again he buried
A lonely thought among the coals and ashes
Outside the reaching flame and left it there,
Quite as he left outside in rainy graves
The sacrificial hundreds who had filled them.
"They died, Gawaine," he said, "and you live on,
You and the King, as if there were no dying;
And it was I, Gawaine, who let you live—
You and the King. For what more length of time,
I wonder, may there still be found on earth
Foot-room for four of us? We are too many
For one world, Gawaine; and there may be soon,
For one or other of us, a way out.
As men are listed, we are men for men
To fear; and I fear Modred more than any.
But even the ghost of Modred at the door—
The ghost I should have made him—would employ
For time as hard as this a louder knuckle,
Assuredly now, than that. And I would see
No mortal face till morning. . . . Well, are you well
Again? Are you as well again as ever?"

He led her slowly on with a cold show
Of care that was less heartening for the Queen

Than anger would have been, into the firelight,
And there he gave her cushions. "Are you warm?"
He said; and she said nothing. "Are you afraid?"
He said again; "are you still afraid of Gawaine?
As often as you think of him and hate him,
Remember too that he betrayed his brothers
To us that he might save us. Well, he saved us;
And Rome, whose name to you was never music,
Saves you again, with heaven alone may tell
What others who might have their time to sleep
In earth out there, with the rain falling on them,
And with no more to fear of wars tonight
Than you need fear of Gawaine or of Arthur.
The way before you is a safer way
For you to follow than when I was in it.
We children who forget the whips of Time,
To live within the hour, are slow to see
That all such hours are passing. They were past
When you came here with me."

                                    She looked away,
Seeming to read the firelight on the walls
Before she spoke: "When I came here with you,
And found those eyes of yours, I could have wished
And prayed it were the end of hours, and years.
What was it made you save me from the fire,
If only out of memories and forebodings
To build around my life another fire
Of slower faggots? If you had let me die,
Those other faggots would be ashes now,
And all of me that you have ever loved
Would be a few more ashes. If I read
The past as well as you have read the future
You need say nothing of ingratitude,
For I say only lies. My soul, of course,

It was you loved. You told me so yourself.
And that same precious blue-veined cream-white soul
Will soon be safer, if I understand you,
In Camelot, where the King is, than elsewhere
On earth. What more, in faith, have I to ask
Of earth or heaven than that! Although I fell
When you said Camelot, are you to know,
Surely, the stroke you gave me then was not
The measure itself of ecstasy? We women
Are such adept inveterates in our swooning
That we fall down for joy as easily
As we eat one another to show our love.
Even horses, seeing again their absent masters,
Have wept for joy; great dogs have died of it."
Having said as much as that, she frowned and held
Her small white hands out for the fire to warm them.
Forward she leaned, and forward her thoughts went—
To Camelot. But they were not there long,
Her thoughts; for soon she flashed her eyes again,
And he found in them what he wished were tears
Of angry sorrow for what she had said.
"What are you going to do with me?" she asked;
And all her old incisiveness came back,
With a new thrust of malice, which he felt
And feared. "What are you going to do with me?
What does a child do with a worn-out doll?
I was a child once; and I had a father.
He was a king; and, having royal ways,
He made a queen of me—King Arthur's queen.
And if that happened, once upon a time,
Why may it not as well be happening now
That I am not a queen? Was I a queen
When first you brought me here with one torn rag
To cover me? Was I overmuch a queen
When I sat up at last, and in a gear

LANCELOT

That would have made a bishop dance to Cardiff
To see me wearing it? Was I Queen then?"

"You were the Queen of Christendom," he said,
Not smiling at her, "whether now or not
You deem it an unchristian exercise
To vilipend the wearing of the vanished.
The women may have reasoned, insecurely,
That what one queen had worn would please another.
I left them to their ingenuities."

Once more he frowned away a threatening smile,
But soon forgot the memory of all smiling
While he gazed on the glimmering face and hair
Of Guinevere—the glory of white and gold
That had been his, and were, for taking of it,
Still his, to cloud, with an insidious gleam
Of earth, another that was not of earth,
And so to make of him a thing of night—
A moth between a window and a star,
Not wholly lured by one or led by the other.
The more he gazed upon her beauty there,
The longer was he living in two kingdoms,
Not owning in his heart the king of either,
And ruling not himself. There was an end
Of hours, he told her silent face again,
In silence. On the morning when his fury
Wrenched her from that foul fire in Camelot,
Where blood paid irretrievably the toll
Of her release, the whips of Time had fallen
Upon them both. All this to Guinevere
He told in silence and he told in vain.

Observing her ten fingers variously,
She sighed, as in equivocal assent,
"No two queens are alike."

                                    "Is that the flower
Of all your veiled invention?" Lancelot said,
Smiling at last: "If you say, saying all that,
You are not like Isolt—well, you are not.
Isolt was a physician, who cured men
Their wounds, and sent them rowelling for more;
Isolt was too dark, and too versatile;
She was too dark for Mark, if not for Tristram.
Forgive me; I was saying that to myself,
And not to make you shiver. No two queens—
Was that it?—are alike? A longer story
Might have a longer telling and tell less.
Your tale's as brief as Pelleas with his vengeance
On Gawaine, whom he swore that he would slay
At once for stealing of the lady Ettard."

"Treasure my scantling wits, if you enjoy them;
Wonder a little, too, that I conserve them
Through the eternal memory of one morning,
And in these years of days that are the death
Of men who die for me. I should have died.
I should have died for them."

                            "You are wrong," he said;
"They died because Gawaine went mad with hate
For loss of his two brothers and set the King
On fire with fear, the two of them believing
His fear was vengeance when it was in fact
A royal desperation. They died because
Your world, my world, and Arthur's world is dying,
As Merlin said it would. No blame is yours;
For it was I who led you from the King—
Or rather, to say truth, it was your glory
That led my love to lead you from the King—
By flowery ways, that always end somewhere,

To fire and fright and exile, and release.
And if you bid your memory now to blot
Your story from the book of what has been,
Your phantom happiness were a ghost indeed,
And I the least of weasels among men,—
Too false to manhood and your sacrifice
To merit a niche in hell. If that were so,
I'd swear there was no light for me to follow,
Save your eyes to the grave; and to the last
I might not know that all hours have an end;
I might be one of those who feed themselves
By grace of God, on hopes dryer than hay,
Enjoying not what they eat, yet always eating.
The Vision shattered, a man's love of living
Becomes at last a trap and a sad habit,
More like an ailing dotard's love of liquor
That ails him, than a man's right love of woman
Or of his God. There are men enough like that,
And I might come to that. Though I see far
Before me now, could I see, looking back,
A life that you could wish had not been lived,
I might be such a man. Could I believe
Our love was nothing mightier then than we were,
I might be such a man—a living dead man,
One of these days."

                        Guinevere looked at him,
And all that any woman has not said
Was in one look: "Why do you stab me now
With such a needless 'then'? If I am going—
And I suppose I am—are the words all lost
That men have said before to dogs and children
To make them go away? Why use a knife,
When there are words enough without your 'then'
To cut as deep as need be? What I ask you

Is never more to ask me if my life
Be one that I could wish had not been lived—
And that you never torture it again,
To make it bleed and ache as you do now,
Past all indulgence or necessity.
Were you to give a lonely child who loved you
One living thing to keep—a bird, may be—
Before you went away from her forever,
Would you, for surety not to be forgotten,
Maim it and leave it bleeding on her fingers?
And would you leave the child alone with it—
Alone, and too bewildered even to cry,
Till you were out of sight? Are you men never
To know what words are? Do you doubt sometimes
A Vision that lets you see so far away
That you forget so lightly who it was
You must have cared for once to be so kind—
Or seem so kind—when she, and for that only,
Had that been all, would throw down crowns and glories
To share with you the last part of the world?
And even the queen in me would hardly go
So far off as to vanish. If I were patched
And scrapped in what the sorriest fisher-wife
In Orkney might give mumbling to a beggar,
I doubt if oafs and yokels would annoy me
More than I willed they should. Am I so old
And dull, so lean and waning, or what not,
That you must hurry away to grasp and hoard
The small effect of time I might have stolen
From you and from a Light that where it lives
Must live for ever? Where does history tell you
The Lord himself would seem in so great haste
As you for your perfection? If our world—
Your world and mine and Arthur's, as you say—
Is going out now to make way for another,

Why not before it goes, and I go with it,
Have yet one morsel more of life together,
Before death sweeps the table and our few crumbs
Of love are a few last ashes on a fire
That cannot hurt your Vision, or burn long?
You cannot warm your lonely fingers at it
For a great waste of time when I am dead:
When I am dead you will be on your way,
With maybe not so much as one remembrance
Of all I was, to follow you and torment you.
Some word of Bors may once have given color
To some few that I said, but they were true—
Whether Bors told them first to me, or whether
I told them first to Bors. The Light you saw
Was not the Light of Rome; the word you had
Of Rome was not the word of God—though Rome
Has refuge for the weary and heavy-laden.
Were I to live too long I might seek Rome
Myself, and be the happier when I found it.
Meanwhile, am I to be no more to you
Than a moon-shadow of a lonely stranger
Somewhere in Camelot? And is there no region
In this poor fading world of Arthur's now
Where I may be again what I was once—
Before I die? Should I live to be old,
I shall have been long since too far away
For you to hate me then; and I shall know
How old I am by seeing it in your eyes."
Her misery told itself in a sad laugh,
And in a rueful twisting of her face
That only beauty's perilous privilege
Of injury would have yielded or suborned
As hope's infirm accessory while she prayed
Through Lancelot to heaven for Lancelot.
She looked away: "If I were God," she said,

419

"I should say, 'Let them be as they have been.
A few more years will heap no vast account
Against eternity, and all their love
Was what I gave them. They brought on the end
Of Arthur's empire, which I wrought through Merlin
For the world's knowing of what kings and queens
Are made for; but they knew not what they did—
Save as a price, and as a fear that love
Might end in fear. It need not end that way,
And they need fear no more for what I gave them;
For it was I who gave them to each other.'
If I were God, I should say that to you."
He saw tears quivering in her pleading eyes,
But through them she could see, with a wild hope,
That he was fighting. When he spoke, he smiled—
Much as he might have smiled at her, she thought,
Had she been Gawaine, Gawaine having given
To Lancelot, who yet would have him live,
An obscure wound that would not heal or kill.

"My life was living backward for the moment,"
He said, still burying in the coals and ashes
Thoughts that he would not think. His tongue was dry,
And each dry word he said was choking him
As he said on: "I cannot ask of you
That you be kind to me, but there's a kindness
That is your proper debt. Would you cajole
Your reason with a weary picturing
On walls or on vain air of what your fancy,
Like firelight, makes of nothing but itself?
Do you not see that I go from you only
Because you go from me?—because our path
Led where at last it had an end in havoc,
As long we knew it must—as Arthur too,
And Merlin knew it must?—as God knew it must?

LANCELOT

A power that I should not have said was mine—
That was not mine, and is not mine—avails me
Strangely tonight, although you are here with me;
And I see much in what has come to pass
That is to be. The Light that I have seen,
As you say true, is not the light of Rome,
Albeit the word of Rome that set you free
Was more than mine or the King's. To flout that word
Would sound the preparation of a terror
To which a late small war on our account
Were a king's pastime and a queen's annoyance;
And that, for the good fortune of a world
As yet not over-fortuned, may not be.
There may be war to come when you are gone,
For I doubt yet Gawaine; but Rome will hold you,
Hold you in Camelot. If there be more war,
No fire of mine shall feed it, nor shall you
Be with me to endure it. You are free;
And free, you are going home to Camelot.
There is no other way than one for you,
Nor is there more than one for me. We have lived,
And we shall die. I thank you for my life.
Forgive me if I say no more tonight."
He rose, half blind with pity that was no longer
The servant of his purpose or his will,
To grope away somewhere among the shadows
For wine to drench his throat and his dry tongue,
That had been saying he knew not what to her
For whom his life-devouring love was now
A scourge of mercy.

                Like a blue-eyed Medea
Of white and gold, broken with grief and fear
And fury that shook her speechless while she waited,
Yet left her calm enough for Lancelot

To see her without seeing, she stood up
To breathe and suffer. Fury could not live long,
With grief and fear like hers and love like hers,
When speech came back: "No other way now than one?
Free? Do you call me free? Do you mean by that
There was never woman alive freer to live
Than I am free to die? Do you call me free
Because you are driven so near to death yourself
With weariness of me, and the sight of me,
That you must use a crueller knife than ever,
And this time at my heart, for me to watch
Before you drive it home? For God's sake, drive it!
Drive it as often as you have the others,
And let the picture of each wound it makes
On me be shown to women and men for ever;
And the good few that know—let them reward you.
I hear them, in such low and pitying words
As only those who know, and are not many,
Are used to say: 'The good knight Lancelot
It was who drove the knife home to her heart,
Rather than drive her home to Camelot.'
Home! Free! Would you let me go there again—
To be at home?—be free? To be his wife?
To live in his arms always, and so hate him
That I could heap around him the same faggots
That you put out with blood? Go home, you say?
Home?—where I saw the black post waiting for me
That morning?—saw those good men die for me—
Gareth and Gaheris, Lamorak's brother Tor,
And all the rest? Are men to die for me
For ever? Is there water enough, do you think,
Between this place and that for me to drown in?"

"There is time enough, I think, between this hour
And some wise hour tomorrow, for you to sleep in.

422

LANCELOT

When you are safe again in Camelot,
The King will not molest you or pursue you;
The King will be a suave and chastened man.
In Camelot you shall have no more to dread
Than you shall hear then of this rain that roars
Tonight as if it would be roaring always.
I do not ask you to forgive the faggots,
Though I would have you do so for your peace.
Only the wise who know may do so much,
And they, as you say truly, are not many.
And I would say no more of this tonight."

"Then do not ask me for the one last thing
That I shall give to God! I thought I died
That morning. Why am I alive again,
To die again? Are you all done with me?
Is there no longer something left of me
That made you need me? Have I lost myself
So fast that what a mirror says I am
Is not what is, but only what was once?
Does half a year do that with us, I wonder,
Or do I still have something that was mine
That afternoon when I was in the sunset,
Under the oak, and you were looking at me?
Your look was not all sorrow for your going
To find the Light and leave me in the dark—
But I am the daughter of Leodogran,
And you are Lancelot,—and have a tongue
To say what I may not. . . . Why must I go
To Camelot when your kinsmen hold all France?
Why is there not some nook in some old house
Where I might hide myself—with you or not?
Is there no castle, or cabin, or cave in the woods?
Yes, I could love the bats and owls, in France,
A lifetime sooner than I could the King

423

That I shall see in Camelot, waiting there
For me to cringe and beg of him again
The dust of mercy, calling it holy bread.
I wronged him, but he bought me with a name
Too large for my king-father to relinquish—
Though I prayed him, and I prayed God aloud,
To spare that crown. I called it crown enough
To be my father's child—until you came.
And then there were no crowns or kings or fathers
Under the sky. I saw nothing but you.
And you would whip me back to bury myself
In Camelot, with a few slave maids and lackeys
To be my grovelling court; and even their faces
Would not hide half the story. Take me to France—
To France or Egypt,—anywhere else on earth
Than Camelot! Is there not room in France
For two more dots of mortals?—or for one?—
For me alone? Let Lionel go with me—
Or Bors. Let Bors go with me into France,
And leave me there. And when you think of me,
Say Guinevere is in France, where she is happy;
And you may say no more of her than that . . .
Why do you not say something to me now—
Before I go? Why do you look—and look?
Why do you frown as if you thought me mad?
I am not mad—but I shall soon be mad,
If I go back to Camelot where the King is.
Lancelot! . . . Is there nothing left of me?
Nothing of what you called your white and gold,
And made so much of? Has it all gone by?
He must have been a lonely God who made
Man in his image and then made only a woman!
Poor fool she was! Poor Queen! Poor Guinevere!
There were kings and bishops once, under her window
Like children, and all scrambling for a flower.

Time was!—God help me, what am I saying now!
Does a Queen's memory wither away to that?
Am I so dry as that? Am I a shell?
Have I become so cheap as this? . . . I wonder
Why the King cared!" She fell down on her knees
Crying, and held his knees with hungry fear.

Over his folded arms, as over the ledge
Of a storm-shaken parapet, he could see,
Below him, like a tumbling flood of gold,
The Queen's hair with a crumpled foam of white
Around it: "Do you ask, as a child would,
For France because it has a name? How long
Do you conceive the Queen of the Christian world
Would hide herself in France were she to go there?
How long should Rome require to find her there?
And how long, Rome or not, would such a flower
As you survive the unrooting and transplanting
That you commend so ingenuously tonight?
And if we shared your cave together, how long,
And in the joy of what obscure seclusion,
If I may say it, were Lancelot of the Lake
And Guinevere an unknown man and woman,
For no eye to see twice? There are ways to France,
But why pursue them for Rome's interdict,
And for a longer war? Your path is now
As open as mine is dark—or would be dark,
Without the Light that once had blinded me
To death, had I seen more. I shall see more,
And I shall not be blind. I pray, moreover,
That you be not so now. You are a Queen,
And you may be no other. You are too brave
And kind and fair for men to cheer with lies.
We cannot make one world of two, nor may we
Count one life more than one. Could we go back

To the old garden, we should not stay long;
The fruit that we should find would all be fallen,
And have the taste of earth."

                    When she looked up,
A tear fell on her forehead. "Take me away!"
She cried. "Why do you do this? Why do you say this?
If you are sorry for me, take me away
From Camelot! Send me away—drive me away—
Only away from there! The King is there—
And I may kill him if I see him there.
Take me away—take me away to France!
And if I cannot hide myself in France,
Then let me die in France!"

                        He shook his head,
Slowly, and raised her slowly in his arms,
Holding her there; and they stood long together.
And there was no sound then of anything,
Save a low moaning of a broken woman,
And the cold roaring down of that long rain.

All night the rain came down on Joyous Gard;
And all night, there before the crumbling embers
That faded into feathery death-like dust,
Lancelot sat and heard it. He saw not
The fire that died, but he heard rain that fell
On all those graves around him and those years
Behind him; and when dawn came, he was cold.
At last he rose, and for a time stood seeing
The place where she had been. She was not there;
He was not sure that she had ever been there;
He was not sure there was a Queen, or a King,
Or a world with kingdoms on it. He was cold.
He was not sure of anything but the Light—

The Light he saw not. "And I shall not see it,"
He thought, "so long as I kill men for Gawaine.
If I kill him, I may as well kill myself;
And I have killed his brothers." He tried to sleep,
But rain had washed the sleep out of his life,
And there was no more sleep. When he awoke,
He did not know that he had been asleep;
And the same rain was falling. At some strange hour
It ceased, and there was light. And seven days after,
With a cavalcade of silent men and women,
The Queen rode into Camelot, where the King was,
And Lancelot rode grimly at her side.

When he rode home again to Joyous Gard,
The storm in Gawaine's eyes and the King's word
Of banishment attended him. "Gawaine
Will give the King no peace," Lionel said;
And Lancelot said after him, "Therefore
The King will have no peace."—And so it was
That Lancelot, with many of Arthur's knights
That were not Arthur's now, sailed out one day
From Cardiff to Bayonne, where soon Gawaine,
The King, and the King's army followed them,
For longer sorrow and for longer war.

VIII

For longer war they came, and with a fury
That only Modred's opportunity,
Seized in the dark of Britain, could have hushed
And ended in a night. For Lancelot,
When he was hurried amazed out of his rest
Of a gray morning to the scarred gray wall
Of Benwick, where he slept and fought, and saw
Not yet the termination of a strife

That irked him out of utterance, found again
Before him a still plain without an army.
What the mist hid between him and the distance
He knew not, but a multitude of doubts
And hopes awoke in him, and one black fear,
At sight of a truce-waving messenger
In whose approach he read, as by the Light
Itself, the last of Arthur. The man reined
His horse outside the gate, and Lancelot,
Above him on the wall, with a sick heart,
Listened: "Sir Gawaine to Sir Lancelot
Sends greeting; and this with it, in his hand.
The King has raised the siege, and you in France
He counts no longer with his enemies.
His toil is now for Britain, and this war
With you, Sir Lancelot, is an old war,
If you will have it so."—"Bring the man in,"
Said Lancelot, "and see that he fares well."

All through the sunrise, and alone, he sat
With Gawaine's letter, looking toward the sea
That flowed somewhere between him and the land
That waited Arthur's coming, but not his.
"King Arthur's war with me is an old war,
If I will have it so," he pondered slowly;
"And Gawaine's hate for me is an old hate,
If I will have it so. But Gawaine's wound
Is not a wound that heals; and there is Modred—
Inevitable as ruin after flood.
The cloud that has been darkening Arthur's empire
May now have burst, with Arthur still in France,
Many hours away from Britain, and a world
Away from me. But I read this in my heart.
If in the blot of Modred's evil shadow,
Conjecture views a cloudier world than is,

So much the better, then, for clouds and worlds,
And kings. Gawaine says nothing yet of this,
But when he tells me nothing he tells all.
Now he is here, fordone and left behind,
Pursuant of his wish; and there are words
That he would say to me. Had I not struck him
Twice to the earth, unwillingly, for my life,
My best eye then, I fear, were best at work
On what he has not written. As it is,
If I go seek him now, and in good faith,
My faith may dig my grave. If so, then so.
If I know only with my eyes and ears,
I may as well not know."

                  Gawaine, having scanned
His words and sent them, found a way to sleep—
And sleeping, to forget. But he remembered
Quickly enough when he woke up to meet
With his the shining gaze of Lancelot
Above him in a shuttered morning gloom,
Seeming at first a darkness that had eyes.
Fear for a moment seized him, and his heart,
Long whipped and driven with fever, paused and flickered,
As like to fail too soon. Fearing to move,
He waited; fearing to speak, he waited; fearing
To see too clearly or too much, he waited;
For what, he wondered—even the while he knew
It was for Lancelot to say something.
And soon he did: "Gawaine, I thought at first
No man was here."

                  "No man was, till you came.
Sit down; and for the love of God who made you,
Say nothing to me now of my three brothers.
Gareth and Gaheris and Agravaine

429

Are gone; and I am going after them;
Of such is our election. When you gave
That ultimate knock on my revengeful head,
You did a piece of work."

                                  "May God forgive,"
Lancelot said, "I did it for my life,
Not yours."

                         "I know, but I was after yours;
Had I been Lancelot, and you Gawaine,
You might be dead."

                     "Had you been Lancelot,
And I Gawaine, my life had not been yours—
Not willingly. Your brothers are my debt
That I shall owe to sorrow and to God,
For whatsoever payment there may be.
What I have paid is not a little, Gawaine."

"Why leave me out? A brother more or less
Would hardly be the difference of a shaving.
My loose head would assure you, saying this,
That I have no more venom in me now
On their account than mine, which is not much.
There was a madness feeding on us all,
As we fed on the world. When the world sees,
The world will have in turn another madness;
And so, as I've a glimpse, *ad infinitum.*
But I'm not of the seers: Merlin it was
Who turned a sort of ominous early glimmer
On my profane young life. And after that
He falls himself, so far that he becomes
One of our most potential benefits—
Like Vivian, or the mortal end of Modred.

Why could you not have taken Modred also,
And had the five of us? You did your best,
We know, yet he's more poisonously alive
Than ever; and he's a brother, of a sort,
Or half of one, and you should not have missed him.
A gloomy curiosity was our Modred,
From his first intimation of existence.
God made him as He made the crocodile,
To prove He was omnipotent. Having done so,
And seeing then that Camelot, of all places
Ripe for annihilation, most required him,
He put him there at once, and there he grew.
And there the King would sit with him for hours,
Admiring Modred's growth; and all the time
His evil it was that grew, the King not seeing
In Modred the Almighty's instrument
Of a world's overthrow. You, Lancelot,
And I, have rendered each a contribution;
And your last hard attention on my skull
Might once have been a benison on the realm,
As I shall be, too late, when I'm laid out
With a clean shroud on—though I'd liefer stay
A while alive with you to see what's coming.
But I was not for that; I may have been
For something, but not that. The King, my uncle,
Has had for all his life so brave a diet
Of miracles, that his new fare before him
Of late has ailed him strangely; and of all
Who loved him once he needs you now the most—
Though he would not so much as whisper this
To me or to my shadow. He goes alone
To Britain, with an army brisk as lead,
To battle with his Modred for a throne
That waits, I fear, for Modred—should your France
Not have it otherwise. And the Queen's in this,

431

For Modred's game and prey. God save the Queen,
If not the King! I've always liked this world;
And I would a deal rather live in it
Than leave it in the middle of all this music.
If you are listening, give me some cold water."

Lancelot, seeing by now in dim detail
What little was around him to be seen,
Found what he sought and held a cooling cup
To Gawaine, who, with both hands clutching it,
Drank like a child. "I should have had that first,"
He said, with a loud breath, "before my tongue
Began to talk. What was it saying? Modred?
All through the growing pains of his ambition
I've watched him; and I might have this and that
To say about him, if my hours were days.
Well, if you love the King and hope to save him,
Remember his many infirmities of virtue—
Considering always what you have in Modred,
For ever unique in his iniquity.
My truth might have a prejudicial savor
To strangers, but we are not strangers now.
Though I have only one spoiled eye that sees,
I see in yours we are not strangers now.
I tell you, as I told you long ago—
When the Queen came to put my candles out
With her gold head and her propinquity—
That all your doubts that you had then of me,
When they were more than various imps and harpies
Of your inflamed invention, were sick doubts:
King Arthur was my uncle, as he is now;
But my Queen-aunt, who loved him something less
Than cats love rain, was not my only care.
Had all the women who came to Camelot
Been aunts of mine, I should have been, long since,

432

LANCELOT

The chilliest of all unwashed eremites
In a far land alone. For my dead brothers,
Though I would leave them where I go to them,
I read their story as I read my own,
And yours, and—were I given the eyes of God—
As I might yet read Modred's. For the Queen,
May she be safe in London where she's hiding
Now in the Tower. For the King, you only—-
And you but hardly—may deliver him yet
From that which Merlin's vision long ago,
If I made anything of Merlin's words,
Foretold of Arthur's end. And for ourselves,
And all who died for us, or now are dying
Like rats around us of their numerous wounds
And ills and evils, only this do I know—
And this you know: The world has paid enough
For Camelot. It is the world's turn now—
Or so it would be if the world were not
The world. 'Another Camelot,' Bedivere says;
'Another Camelot and another King'—
Whatever he means by that. With a lineal twist,
I might be king myself; and then, my lord,
Time would have sung my reign—I say not how.
Had I gone on with you, and seen with you
Your Gleam, and had some ray of it been mine,
I might be seeing more and saying less.
Meanwhile, I liked this world; and what was on
The Lord's mind when He made it is no matter.
Be lenient, Lancelot; I've a light head.
Merlin appraised it once when I was young,
Telling me then that I should have the world
To play with. Well, I've had it, and played with it;
And here I'm with you now where you have sent me
Neatly to bed, with a towel over one eye:
And we were two of the world's ornaments.

Praise all you are that Arthur was your King;
You might have had no Gleam had I been King,
Or had the Queen been like some queens I knew.
King Lot, my father—"

                             Lancelot laid a finger
On Gawaine's lips: "You are too tired for that."—
"Not yet," said Gawaine, "though I may be soon.
Think you that I forget this Modred's mother
Was mine as well as Modred's? When I meet
My mother's ghost, what shall I do—forgive?
When I'm a ghost, I'll forgive everything . . .
It makes me cold to think what a ghost knows.
Put out the bonfire burning in my head,
And light one at my feet. When the King thought
The Queen was in the flames, he called on you:
'God, God,' he said, and 'Lancelot.' I was there,
And so I heard him. That was a bad morning
For kings and queens, and there are to be worse.
Bedivere had a dream, once on a time:
'Another Camelot and another King,'
He says when he's awake; but when he dreams,
There are no kings. Tell Bedivere, some day,
That he saw best awake. Say to the King
That I saw nothing vaster than my shadow,
Until it was too late for me to see;
Say that I loved him well, but served him ill—
If you two meet again. Say to the Queen . . .
Say what you may say best. Remember me
To Pelleas, too, and tell him that his lady
Was a vain serpent. He was dying once
For love of her, and had me in his eye
For company along the dusky road
Before me now. But Pelleas lived, and married.
Lord God, how much we know!—What have I done?
434

Why do you scowl? Well, well,—so the earth clings
To sons of earth; and it will soon be clinging,
To this one son of earth you deprecate,
Closer than heretofore. I say too much,
Who should be thinking all a man may think
When he has no machine. I say too much—
Always. If I persuade the devil again
That I'm asleep, will you espouse the notion
For a small hour or so? I might be glad—
Not to be here alone." He gave his hand
Slowly, in hesitation. Lancelot shivered,
Knowing the chill of it. "Yes, you say too much,"
He told him, trying to smile: "Now go to sleep;
And if you may, forget what you forgive."

Lancelot, for slow hours that were as long
As leagues were to the King and his worn army,
Sat waiting,—though not long enough to know
From any word of Gawaine, who slept on,
That he was glad not to be there alone.—
"Peace to your soul, Gawaine," Lancelot said,
And would have closed his eyes. But they were closed.

IX

So Lancelot, with a world's weight upon him,
Went heavily to that heaviest of all toil,
Which of itself tells hard in the beginning
Of what the end shall be. He found an army
That would have razed all Britain, and found kings
For generals; and they all went to Dover,
Where the white cliffs were ghostlike in the dawn,
And after dawn were deathlike. For the word
Of the dead King's last battle chilled the sea
Before a sail was down; and all who came

With Lancelot heard soon from little men,
Who clambered overside with larger news,
How ill had fared the great.   Arthur was dead,
And Modred with him, each by the other slain;
And there was no knight left of all who fought
On Salisbury field save one, Sir Bedivere,
Of whom the tale was told that he had gone
Darkly away to some far hermitage,
To think and die.   There were tales told of a ship.

Anon, by further sounding of more men,
Each with a more delirious involution
Than his before him, he believed at last
The Queen was yet alive—if it were life
To draw now the Queen's breath, or to see Britain
With the Queen's eyes—and that she fared somewhere
To westward out of London, where the Tower
Had held her, as once Joyous Gard had held her,
For dolorous weeks and months a prisoner there,
With Modred not far off, his eyes afire
For her and for the King's avenging throne,
That neither King nor son should see again.
" 'The world had paid enough for Camelot,'
Gawaine said; and the Queen had paid enough,
God knows," said Lancelot.   He saw Bors again
And found him angry—angry with his tears,
And with his fate that was a reason for them:
"Could I have died with Modred on my soul,
And had the King lived on, then had I lived
On with him; and this played-out world of ours
Might not be for the dead."

                         "A played-out world,
Although that world be ours, had best be dead."
Said Lancelot: "There are worlds enough to follow.

436

LANCELOT

'Another Camelot and another King,'
Bedivere said. And where is Bedivere now?
And Camelot?"

                           "There is no Camelot,"
Bors answered. "Are we going back to France,
Or are we to tent here and feed our souls
On memories and on ruins till even our souls
Are dead? Or are we to set free for sport
An idle army for what comes of it?"

"Be idle till you hear from me again,
Or for a fortnight. Then, if you have no word,
Go back; and I may follow you alone,
In my own time, in my own way."

                           "Your way
Of late, I fear, has been too much your own;
But what has been, has been, and I say nothing.
For there is more than men at work in this;
And I have not your eyes to find the Light,
Here in the dark—though some day I may see it."

"We shall all see it, Bors," Lancelot said,
With his eyes on the earth. He said no more.
Then with a sad farewell, he rode away,
Somewhere into the west. He knew not where.

"We shall all see it, Bors," he said again.
Over and over he said it, still as he rode,
And rode, away to the west, he knew not where,
Until at last he smiled unhappily
At the vain sound of it. "Once I had gone
Where the Light guided me, but the Queen came,
And then there was no Light. We shall all see—"

He bit the words off short, snapping his teeth,
And rode on with his memories before him,
Before him and behind. They were a cloud
For no Light now to pierce. They were a cloud
Made out of what was gone; and what was gone
Had now another lure than once it had,
Before it went so far away from him —
To Camelot. And there was no Camelot now—
Now that no Queen was there, all white and gold,
Under an oaktree with another sunlight
Sifting itself in silence on her glory
Through the dark leaves above her where she sat,
Smiling at what she feared, and fearing least
What most there was to fear. Ages ago
That must have been; for a king's world had faded
Since then, and a king with it. Ages ago,
And yesterday, surely it must have been
That he had held her moaning in the firelight
And heard the roaring down of that long rain,
As if to wash away the walls that held them
Then for that hour together. Ages ago,
And always, it had been that he had seen her,
As now she was, floating along before him,
Too far to touch and too fair not to follow,
Even though to touch her were to die. He closed
His eyes, only to see what he had seen
When they were open; and he found it nearer,
Seeing nothing now but the still white and gold
In a wide field of sable, smiling at him,
But with a smile not hers until today—
A smile to drive no votary from the world
To find the Light. "She is not what it is
That I see now," he said: "No woman alive
And out of hell was ever like that to me.
What have I done to her since I have lost her?

438

LANCELOT

What have I done to change her? No, it is I—
I who have changed. She is not one who changes.
The Light came, and I did not follow it;
Then she came, knowing not what thing she did,
And she it was I followed. The gods play
Like that, sometimes; and when the gods are playing,
Great men are not so great as the great gods
Had led them once to dream. I see her now
Where now she is alone. We are all alone,
We that are left; and if I look too long
Into her eyes . . . I shall not look too long.
Yet look I must. Into the west, they say,
She went for refuge. I see nuns around her;
But she, with so much history tenanting
Her eyes, and all that gold over her eyes,
Were not yet, I should augur, one of them.
If I do ill to see her, then may God
Forgive me one more trespass. I would leave
The world and not the shadow of it behind me."

Time brought his weary search to a dusty end
One afternoon in Almesbury, where he left,
With a glad sigh, his horse in an innyard;
And while he ate his food and drank his wine,
Thrushes, indifferent in their loyalty
To Arthur dead and to Pan never dead,
Sang as if all were now as all had been.
Lancelot heard them till his thoughts came back
To freeze his heart again under the flood
Of all his icy fears. What should he find?
And what if he should not find anything?
"Words, after all," he said, "are only words;
And I have heard so many in these few days
That half my wits are sick."

439

                        He found the queen,
But she was not the Queen of white and gold
That he had seen before him for so long.
There was no gold; there was no gold anywhere.
The black hood, and the white face under it,
And the blue frightened eyes, were all he saw—
Until he saw more black, and then more white.
Black was a foreign foe to Guinevere;
And in the glimmering stillness where he found her
Now, it was death; and she Alcestis-like,
Had waited unaware for the one hand
Availing, so he thought, that would have torn
Off and away the last fell shred of doom
That was destroying and dishonoring
All the world held of beauty. His eyes burned
With a sad anger as he gazed at hers
That shone with a sad pity. "No," she said;
"You have not come for this. We are done with this.
For there are no queens here; there is a Mother.
The Queen that was is only a child now,
And you are strong. Remember you are strong,
And that your fingers hurt when they forget
How strong they are."

                        He let her go from him
And while he gazed around him, he frowned hard
And long at the cold walls: "Is this the end
Of Arthur's kingdom and of Camelot?"—
She told him with a motion of her shoulders
All that she knew of Camelot or of kingdoms;
And then said: "We are told of other States
Where there are palaces, if we should need them,
That are not made with hands. I thought you knew."

Dumb, like a man twice banished, Lancelot
Stood gazing down upon the cold stone floor;

And she, demurely, with a calm regard
That he met once and parried, stood apart,
Appraising him with eyes that were no longer
Those he had seen when first they had seen his.
They were kind eyes, but they were not the eyes
Of his desire; and they were not the eyes
That he had followed all the way from Dover.
"I feared the Light was leading you," she said,
"So far by now from any place like this
That I should have your memory, but no more.
Might not that way have been the wiser way?
There is no Arthur now, no Modred now,—
No Guinevere." She paused, and her voice wandered
Away from her own name: "There is nothing now
That I can see between you and the Light
That I have dimmed so long. If you forgive me,
And I believe you do—though I know all
That I have cost, when I was worth so little—
There is no hazard that I see between you
And all you sought so long, and would have found
Had I not always hindered you. Forgive me—
I could not let you go. God pity men
When women love too much—and women more."
He scowled and with an iron shrug he said:
"Yes, there is that between me and the light."
He glared at her black hood as if to seize it;
Their eyes met, and she smiled: "No, Lancelot;
We are going by two roads to the same end;
Or let us hope, at least, what knowledge hides,
And so believe it. We are going somewhere.
Why the new world is not for you and me,
I cannot say; but only one was ours.
I think we must have lived in our one world
All that earth had for us. You are good to me,
Coming to find me here for the last time:

For I should have been lonely many a night,
Not knowing if you cared. I do know now;
And there is not much else for me to know
That earth may tell me. I found in the Tower,
With Modred watching me, that all you said
That rainy night was true. There was time there
To find out everything. There were long days,
And there were nights that I should not have said
God would have made a woman to endure.
I wonder if a woman lives who knows
All she may do."

                      "I wonder if one woman
Knows one thing she may do," Lancelot said,
With a sad passion shining out of him
While he gazed on her beauty, palled with black
That hurt him like a sword. The full blue eyes
And the white face were there, and the red lips
Were there, but there was no gold anywhere.
"What have you done with your gold hair?" he said;
"I saw it shining all the way from Dover,
But here I do not see it. Shall I see it?"—
Faintly again she smiled: "Yes, you may see it
All the way back to Dover; but not here.
There's not much of it here, and what there is
Is not for you to see."

                        "Well, if not here,"
He said at last, in a low voice that shook,
"Is there no other place left in the world?"

"There is not even the world left, Lancelot,
For you and me."

                    "There is France left," he said.
His face flushed like a boy's, but he stood firm
As a peak in the sea and waited.

LANCELOT

                              "How many lives
Must a man have in one to make him happy?"
She asked, with a wan smile of recollection
That only made the black that was around
Her calm face more funereal: "Was it you,
Or was it Gawaine who said once to me,
'We cannot make one world of two, nor may we
Count one life more than one. Could we go back
To the old garden' . . . Was it you who said it,
Or was it Bors? He was always saying something.
It may have been Bors." She was not looking then
At Lancelot; she was looking at her fingers
In her old way, as to be sure again
How many of them she had.

                              He looked at her,
Without the power to smile, and for the time
Forgot that he was Lancelot: "Is it fair
For you to drag that back, out of its grave,
And hold it up like this for the small feast
Of a small pride?"

                        "Yes, fair enough for a woman,"
Guinevere said, not seeing his eyes. "How long
Do you conceive the Queen of the Christian world
Would hide herself in France . . ."

                          "Why do you pause?
I said it; I remember when I said it;
And it was not today. Why in the name
Of grief should we hide anywhere? Bells and banners
Are not for our occasion, but in France
There may be sights and silences more fair
Than pageants. There are seas of difference
Between this land and France, albeit to cross them

Were no immortal voyage, had you an eye
For France that you had once."

                     "I have no eye
Today for France, I shall have none tomorrow;
And you will have no eye for France tomorrow.
Fatigue and loneliness, and your poor dream
Of what I was, have led you to forget.
When you have had your time to think and see
A little more, then you will see as I do;
And if you see France, I shall not be there,
Save as a memory there. We are done, you and I,
With what we were. 'Could we go back again,
The fruit that we should find'—but you know best
What we should find. I am sorry for what I said;
But a light word, though it cut one we love,
May save ourselves the pain of a worse wound.
We are all women. When you see one woman—
When you see me—before you in your fancy,
See me all white and gold, as I was once.
I shall not harm you then; I shall not come
Between you and the Gleam that you must follow,
Whether you will or not. There is no place
For me but where I am; there is no place
For you save where it is that you are going.
If I knew everything as I know that,
I should know more than Merlin, who knew all,
And long ago, that we are to know now.
What more he knew he may not then have told
The King, or anyone,—maybe not even himself;
Though Vivian may know something by this time
That he has told her. Have you wished, I wonder,
That I was more like Vivian, or Isolt?
The dark ones are more devious and more famous,

And men fall down more numerously before them—
Although I think more men get up again,
And go away again, than away from us.
If I were dark, I might say otherwise.
Try to be glad, even if you are sorry,
That I was not born dark; for I was not.
For me there was no dark until it came
When the King came, and with his heavy shadow
Put out the sun that you made shine again
Before I was to die. So I forgive
The faggots; I can do no more than that—
For you, or God." She looked away from him
And in the casement saw the sunshine dying:
"The time that we have left will soon be gone;
When the bell rings, it rings for you to go,
But not for me to go. It rings for me
To stay—and pray. I, who have not prayed much,
May as well pray now. I have not what you have
To make me see, though I shall have, sometime,
A new light of my own. I saw in the Tower,
When all was darkest and I may have dreamed,
A light that gave to men the eyes of Time
To read themselves in silence. Then it faded,
And the men faded. I was there alone.
I shall not have what you have, or much else—
In this place. I shall see in other places
What is not here. I shall not be alone.
And I shall tell myself that you are seeing
All that I cannot see. For the time now,
What most I see is that I had no choice,
And that you came to me. How many years
Of purgatory shall I pay God for saying
This to you here?" Her words came slowly out,
And her mouth shook.

He took her two small hands
That were so pale and empty, and so cold:
"Poor child, I said too much and heard too little
Of what I said. But when I found you here,
So different, so alone, I would have given
My soul to be a chattel and a gage
For dicing fiends to play for, could so doing
Have brought one summer back."

"When they are gone,"
She said, with grateful sadness in her eyes,
"We do not bring them back, or buy them back,
Even with our souls. I see now it is best
We do not buy them back, even with our souls."

A slow and hollow bell began to sound
Somewhere above them, and the world became
For Lancelot one wan face—Guinevere's face.
"When the bell rings, it rings for you to go,"
She said; "and you are going . . . I am not.
Think of me always as I used to be,
All white and gold—for that was what you called me.
You may see gold again when you are gone;
And I shall not be there."—He drew her nearer
To kiss the quivering lips that were before him
For the last time. "No, not again," she said;
"I might forget that I am not alone . . .
I shall not see you in this world again,
But I am not alone. No, . . . not alone.
We have had all there was, and you were kind—
Even when you tried so hard once to be cruel.
I knew it then . . . or now I do. Good-bye."
He crushed her cold white hands and saw them falling
Away from him like flowers into a grave.

446

When she looked up to see him, he was gone;
And that was all she saw till she awoke
In her white cell, where the nuns carried her
With many tears and many whisperings.
"She was the Queen, and he was Lancelot,"
One said. "They were great lovers. It is not good
To know too much of love. We who love God
Alone are happiest. Is it not so, Mother?"—
"We who love God alone, my child, are safest,"
The Mother replied; "and we are not all safe
Until we are all dead. We watch, and pray."

Outside again, Lancelot heard the sound
Of reapers he had seen. With lighter tread
He walked away to them to see them nearer;
He walked and heard again the sound of thrushes
Far off. He saw below him, stilled with yellow,
A world that was not Arthur's, and he saw
The convent roof; and then he could see nothing
But a wan face and two dim lonely hands
That he had left behind. They were down there,
Somewhere, her poor white face and hands, alone.
"No man was ever alone like that," he thought,
Not knowing what last havoc pity and love
Had still to wreak on wisdom. Gradually,
In one long wave it whelmed him, and then broke—
Leaving him like a lone man on a reef,
Staring for what had been with him, but now
Was gone and was a white face under the sea,
Alive there, and alone—always alone.
He closed his eyes, and the white face was there,
But not the gold. The gold would not come back.
There were gold fields of corn that lay around him,
But they were not the gold of Guinevere—
Though men had once, for sake of saying words,

447

Prattled of corn about it. The still face
Was there, and the blue eyes that looked at him
Through all the stillness of all distances;
And he could see her lips, trying to say
Again, "I am not alone." And that was all
His life had said to him that he remembered
While he sat there with his hands over his eyes,
And his heart aching. When he rose again
The reapers had gone home. Over the land
Around him in the twilight there was rest.
There was rest everywhere; and there was none
That found his heart. "Why should I look for peace
When I have made the world a ruin of war?"
He muttered; and a Voice within him said:
"Where the Light falls, death falls; a world has died
For you, that a world may live. There is no peace.
Be glad no man or woman bears for ever
The burden of first days. There is no peace."

A word stronger than his willed him away
From Almesbury. All alone he rode that night,
Under the stars, led by the living Voice
That would not give him peace. Into the dark
He rode, but not for Dover. Under the stars,
Alone, all night he rode, out of a world
That was not his, or the King's; and in the night
He felt a burden lifted as he rode,
While he prayed he might bear it for the sake
Of a still face before him that was fading,
Away in a white loneliness. He made,
Once, with groping hand as if to touch it,
But a black branch of leaves was all he found.

Now the still face was dimmer than before,
And it was not so near him. He gazed hard,

But through his tears he could not see it now;
And when the tears were gone he could see only
That all he saw was fading, always fading;
And she was there alone. She was the world
That he was losing; and the world he sought
Was all a tale for those who had been living,
And had not lived. Once even he turned his horse,
And would have brought his army back with him
To make her free. They should be free together.
But the Voice within him said: "You are not free.
You have come to the world's end, and it is best
You are not free. Where the Light falls, death falls;
And in the darkness comes the Light." He turned
Again; and he rode on, under the stars,
Out of the world, into he knew not what,
Until a vision chilled him and he saw,
Now as in Camelot, long ago in the garden,
The face of Galahad who had seen and died,
And was alive, now in a mist of gold.
He rode on into the dark, under the stars,
And there were no more faces. There was nothing.
But always in the darkness he rode on,
Alone; and in the darkness came the Light.

THE THREE TAVERNS

(1920)

To
Thomas Sergeant Perry
and Lilla Cabot Perry

THE VALLEY OF THE SHADOW

THERE were faces to remember in the Valley of the Shadow,
There were faces unregarded, there were faces to forget;
There were fires of grief and fear that are a few forgotten ashes,
There were sparks of recognition that are not forgotten yet.
For at first, with an amazed and overwhelming indignation
At a measureless malfeasance that obscurely willed it thus,
They were lost and unacquainted—till they found themselves in
    others,
Who had groped as they were groping where dim ways were
    perilous.

There were lives that were as dark as are the fears and
    intuitions
Of a child who knows himself and is alone with what he knows;
There were pensioners of dreams and there were debtors of
    illusions,
All to fail before the triumph of a weed that only grows.
There were thirsting heirs of golden sieves that held not wine
    or water,
And had no names in traffic or more value there than toys:
There were blighted sons of wonder in the Valley of the Shadow,
Where they suffered and still wondered why their wonder made
    no noise.

There were slaves who dragged the shackles of a precedent
    unbroken,
Demonstrating the fulfilment of unalterable schemes,
Which had been, before the cradle, Time's inexorable tenants
Of what were now the dusty ruins of their father's dreams.

There were these, and there were many who had stumbled up
    to manhood,
Where they saw too late the road they should have taken
    long ago:
There were thwarted clerks and fiddlers in the Valley of the
    Shadow,
The commemorative wreckage of what others did not know.

And there were daughters older than the mothers who had
    borne them,
Being older in their wisdom, which is older than the earth;
And they were going forward only farther into darkness,
Unrelieved as were the blasting obligations of their birth;
And among them, giving always what was not for their pos-
    session,
There were maidens, very quiet, with no quiet in their eyes;
There were daughters of the silence in the Valley of the Shadow,
Each an isolated item in the family sacrifice.

There were creepers among catacombs where dull regrets were
    torches,
Giving light enough to show them what was there upon the
    shelves—
Where there was more for them to see than pleasure would
    remember
Of something that had been alive and once had been themselves.
There were some who stirred the ruins with a solid imprecation,
While as many fled repentance for the promise of despair:
There were drinkers of wrong waters in the Valley of the
    Shadow,
And all the sparkling ways were dust that once had led them
    there.

There were some who knew the steps of Age incredibly beside
    them,

And his fingers upon shoulders that had never felt the wheel;
And their last of empty trophies was a gilded cup of nothing,
Which a contemplating vagabond would not have come to steal.
Long and often had they figured for a larger valuation,
But the size of their addition was the balance of a doubt:
There were gentlemen of leisure in the Valley of the Shadow,
Not allured by retrospection, disenchanted, and played out.

And among the dark endurances of unavowed reprisals
There were silent eyes of envy that saw little but saw well;
And over beauty's aftermath of hazardous ambitions
There were tears for what had vanished as they vanished where
    they fell.
Not assured of what was theirs, and always hungry for the
    nameless,
There were some whose only passion was for Time who made
    them cold:
There were numerous fair women in the Valley of the Shadow,
Dreaming rather less of heaven than of hell when they were old.

Now and then, as if to scorn the common touch of common
    sorrow,
There were some who gave a few the distant pity of a smile;
And another cloaked a soul as with an ash of human embers,
Having covered thus a treasure that would last him for a while.
There were many by the presence of the many disaffected,
Whose exemption was included in the weight that others bore:
There were seekers after darkness in the Valley of the Shadow,
And they alone were there to find what they were looking for.

So they were, and so they are; and as they came are coming
    others,
And among them are the fearless and the meek and the unborn;
And a question that has held us heretofore without an answer
May abide without an answer until all have ceased to mourn.

For the children of the dark are more to name than are the
    wretched,
Or the broken, or the weary, or the baffled, or the shamed:
There are builders of new mansions in the Valley of the
    Shadow,
And among them are the dying and the blinded and the maimed.

THE WANDERING JEW

I saw by looking in his eyes
That they remembered everything;
And this was how I came to know
That he was here, still wandering.
For though the figure and the scene
Were never to be reconciled,
I knew the man as I had known
His image when I was a child.

With evidence at every turn,
I should have held it safe to guess
That all the newness of New York
Had nothing new in loneliness;
Yet here was one who might be Noah,
Or Nathan, or Abimelech,
Or Lamech, out of ages lost,—
Or, more than all, Melchizedek.

Assured that he was none of these,
I gave them back their names again,
To scan once more those endless eyes
Where all my questions ended then.
I found in them what they revealed
That I shall not live to forget,

456

And wondered if they found in mine
Compassion that I might regret.

Pity, I learned, was not the least
Of time's offending benefits
That had now for so long impugned
The conservation of his wits:
Rather it was that I should yield,
Alone, the fealty that presents
The tribute of a tempered ear
To an untempered eloquence.

Before I pondered long enough
On whence he came and who he was,
I trembled at his ringing wealth
Of manifold anathemas;
I wondered, while he seared the world,
What new defection ailed the race,
And if it mattered how remote
Our fathers were from such a place.

Before there was an hour for me
To contemplate with less concern
The crumbling realm awaiting us
Than his that was beyond return,
A dawning on the dust of years
Had shaped with an elusive light
Mirages of remembered scenes
That were no longer for the sight.

For now the gloom that hid the man
Became a daylight on his wrath,
And one wherein my fancy viewed
New lions ramping in his path.
The old were dead and had no fangs,

Wherefore he loved them—seeing not
They were the same that in their time
Had eaten everything they caught.

The world around him was a gift
Of anguish to his eyes and ears,
And one that he had long reviled
As fit for devils, not for seers.
Where, then, was there a place for him
That on this other side of death
Saw nothing good, as he had seen
No good come out of Nazareth?

Yet here there was a reticence,
And I believe his only one,
That hushed him as if he beheld
A Presence that would not be gone.
In such a silence he confessed
How much there was to be denied;
And he would look at me and live,
As others might have looked and died.

As if at last he knew again
That he had always known, his eyes
Were like to those of one who gazed
On those of One who never dies.
For such a moment he revealed
What life has in it to be lost;
And I could ask if what I saw,
Before me there, was man or ghost.

He may have died so many times
That all there was of him to see
Was pride, that kept itself alive
As too rebellious to be free;

NEIGHBORS

He may have told, when more than once
Humility seemed imminent,
How many a lonely time in vain
The Second Coming came and went.

Whether he still defies or not
The failure of an angry task
That relegates him out of time
To chaos, I can only ask.
But as I knew him, so he was;
And somewhere among men to-day
Those old, unyielding eyes may flash,
And flinch—and look the other way.

NEIGHBORS

As often as we thought of her,
    We thought of a gray life
That made a quaint economist
    Of a wolf-haunted wife;
We made the best of all she bore
    That was not ours to bear,
And honored her for wearing things
    That were not things to wear.

There was a distance in her look
    That made us look again;
And if she smiled, we might believe
    That we had looked in vain.
Rarely she came inside our doors,
    And had not long to stay;
And when she left, it seemed somehow
    That she was far away.

At last, when we had all forgot
    That all is here to change,
A shadow on the commonplace
    Was for a moment strange.
Yet there was nothing for surprise,
    Nor much that need be told:
Love, with its gift of pain, had given
    More than one heart could hold.

THE MILL

THE miller's wife had waited long,
    The tea was cold, the fire was dead;
And there might yet be nothing wrong
    In how he went and what he said:
"There are no millers any more,"
    Was all that she had heard him say;
And he had lingered at the door
    So long that it seemed yesterday.

Sick with a fear that had no form
    She knew that she was there at last;
And in the mill there was a warm
    And mealy fragrance of the past.
What else there was would only seem
    To say again what he had meant;
And what was hanging from a beam
    Would not have heeded where she went.

And if she thought it followed her,
    She may have reasoned in the dark
That one way of the few there were
    Would hide her and would leave no mark:

THE THREE TAVERNS

Black water, smooth above the weir
Like starry velvet in the night,
Though ruffled once, would soon appear
The same as ever to the sight.

THE DARK HILLS

DARK hills at evening in the west,
Where sunset hovers like a sound
Of golden horns that sang to rest
Old bones of warriors under ground,
Far now from all the bannered ways
Where flash the legions of the sun,
You fade—as if the last of days
Were fading, and all wars were done.

THE THREE TAVERNS

When the brethren heard of us, they came to meet us as far as
Appii Forum, and The Three Taverns.

(Acts xxviii, 15)

HERODION, Apelles, Amplias,
And Andronicus? Is it you I see—
At last? And is it you now that are gazing
As if in doubt of me? Was I not saying
That I should come to Rome? I did say that;
And I said furthermore that I should go
On westward, where the gateway of the world
Lets in the central sea. I did say that,
But I say only, now, that I am Paul—

461

COLLECTED POEMS

A prisoner of the Law, and of the Lord
A voice made free. If there be time enough
To live, I may have more to tell you then
Of western matters. I go now to Rome,
Where Cæsar waits for me, and I shall wait,
And Cæsar knows how long. In Cæsarea
There was a legend of Agrippa saying
In a light way to Festus, having heard
My deposition, that I might be free,
Had I stayed free of Cæsar; but the word
Of God would have it as you see it is—
And here I am. The cup that I shall drink
Is mine to drink—the moment or the place
Not mine to say. If it be now in Rome,
Be it now in Rome; and if your faith exceed
The shadow cast of hope, say not of me
Too surely or too soon that years and shipwreck,
And all the many deserts I have crossed
That are not named or regioned, have undone
Beyond the brevities of our mortal healing
The part of me that is the least of me.
You see an older man than he who fell
Prone to the earth when he was nigh Damascus,
Where the great light came down; yet I am he
That fell, and he that saw, and he that heard.
And I am here, at last; and if at last
I give myself to make another crumb
For this pernicious feast of time and men—
Well, I have seen too much of time and men
To fear the ravening of the wrath of either.

Yes, it is Paul you see—the Saul of Tarsus
That was a fiery Jew, and had men slain
For saying Something was beyond the Law,
And in ourselves. I fed my suffering soul

462

THE THREE TAVERNS

Upon the Law till I went famishing,
Not knowing that I starved. How should I know,
More then than any, that the food I had—
What else it may have been—was not for me?
My fathers and their fathers and their fathers
Had found it good, and said there was no other,
And I was of the line. When Stephen fell,
Among the stones that crushed his life away,
There was no place alive that I could see
For such a man. Why should a man be given
To live beyond the Law? So I said then,
As men say now to me. How then do I
Persist in living? Is that what you ask?
If so, let my appearance be for you
No living answer; for Time writes of death
On men before they die, and what you see
Is not the man. The man that you see not—
The man within the man—is most alive,
Though hatred would have ended, long ago,
The bane of his activities. I have lived,
Because the faith within me that is life
Endures to live, and shall, till soon or late,
Death, like a friend unseen, shall say to me
My toil is over and my work begun.

How often, and how many a time again,
Have I said I should be with you in Rome!
He who is always coming never comes,
Or comes too late, you may have told yourselves;
And I may tell you now that, after me,
Whether I stay for little or for long,
The wolves are coming. Have an eye for them,
And a more careful ear for their confusion
Than you need have much longer for the sound
Of what I tell you—should I live to say

463

More than I say to Cæsar. What I know
Is down for you to read in what is written;
And if I cloud a little with my own
Mortality the gleam that is immortal,
I do it only because I am I—
Being on earth and of it, in so far
As time flays yet the remnant. This you know;
And if I sting men, as I do sometimes,
With a sharp word that hurts, it is because
Man's habit is to feel before he sees;
And I am of a race that feels. Moreover,
The world is here for what is not yet here
For more than are a few; and even in Rome,
Where men are so enamored of the Cross
That fame has echoed, and increasingly,
The music of your love and of your faith
To foreign ears that are as far away
As Antioch and Haran, yet I wonder
How much of love you know, and if your faith
Be the shut fruit of words. If so, remember
Words are but shells unfilled. Jews have at least
A Law to make them sorry they were born
If they go long without it; and these Gentiles,
For the first time in shrieking history,
Have love and law together, if so they will,
For their defense and their immunity
In these last days. Rome, if I know the name,
Will have anon a crown of thorns and fire
Made ready for the wreathing of new masters,
Of whom we are appointed, you and I,—
And you are still to be when I am gone,
Should I go presently. Let the word fall
Meanwhile, upon the dragon-ridden field
Of circumstance, either to live or die;
Concerning which there is a parable,

464

THE THREE TAVERNS

Made easy for the comfort and attention
Of those who preach, fearing they preach in vain.
You are to plant, and then to plant again
Where you have gathered, gathering as you go;
For you are in the fields that are eternal,
And you have not the burden of the Lord
Upon your mortal shoulders. What you have
Is a light yoke, made lighter by the wearing,
Till it shall have the wonder and the weight
Of a clear jewel, shining with a light
Wherein the sun and all the fiery stars
May soon be fading. When Gamaliel said
That if they be of men these things are nothing
But if they be of God, they are for none
To overthrow, he spoke as a good Jew,
And one who stayed a Jew; and he said all.
And you know, by the temper of your faith,
How far the fire is in you that I felt
Before I knew Damascus. A word here,
Or there, or not there, or not anywhere,
Is not the Word that lives and is the life;
And you, therefore, need weary not yourselves
With jealous aches of others. If the world
Were not a world of aches and innovations,
Attainment would have no more joy of it.
There will be creeds and schisms, creeds in creeds,
And schisms in schisms; myriads will be done
To death because a farthing has two sides,
And is at last a farthing. Telling you this,
I, who bid men to live, appeal to Cæsar.
Once I had said the ways of God were dark,
Meaning by that the dark ways of the Law.
Such is the Glory of our tribulations;
For the Law kills the flesh that kills the Law,
And we are then alive. We have eyes then;

465

And we have then the Cross between two worlds--
To guide us, or to blind us for a time,
Till we have eyes indeed. The fire that smites
A few on highways, changing all at once,
Is not for all. The power that holds the world
Away from God that holds himself away—
Farther away than all your works and words
Are like to fly without the wings of faith—
Was not, nor ever shall be, a small hazard
Enlivening the ways of easy leisure
Or the cold road of knowledge. When our eyes
Have wisdom, we see more than we remember;
And the old world of our captivities
May then become a smitten glimpse of ruin,
Like one where vanished hewers have had their day
Of wrath on Lebanon. Before we see,
Meanwhile, we suffer; and I come to you,
At last, through many storms and through much night

Yet whatsoever I have undergone,
My keepers in this instance are not hard.
But for the chance of an ingratitude,
I might indeed be curious of their mercy,
And fearful of their leisure while I wait.
A few leagues out of Rome. Men go to Rome,
Not always to return—but not that now.
Meanwhile, I seem to think you look at me
With eyes that are at last more credulous
Of my identity. You remark in me
No sort of leaping giant, though some words
Of mine to you from Corinth may have leapt
A little through your eyes into your soul.
I trust they were alive, and are alive
Today; for there be none that shall indite
So much of nothing as the man of words

466

THE THREE TAVERNS

Who writes in the Lord's name for his name's sake
And has not in his blood the fire of time
To warm eternity. Let such a man—
If once the light is in him and endures—
5 Content himself to be the general man,
Set free to sift the decencies and thereby
To learn, except he be one set aside
For sorrow, more of pleasure than of pain;
Though if his light be not the light indeed,
10 But a brief shine that never really was,
And fails, leaving him worse than where he was,
Then shall he be of all men destitute.
And here were not an issue for much ink,
Or much offending faction among scribes.

15 The Kingdom is within us, we are told;
And when I say to you that we possess it,
In such a measure as faith makes it ours,
I say it with a sinner's privilege
Of having seen and heard, and seen again,
20 After a darkness; and if I affirm
To the last hour that faith affords alone
The Kingdom entrance and an entertainment,
I do not see myself as one who says
To man that he shall sit with folded hands
25 Against the Coming. If I be anything,
I move a driven agent among my kind,
Establishing by the faith of Abraham,
And by the grace of their necessities,
The clamoring word that is the word of life
30 Nearer than heretofore to the solution
Of their tomb-serving doubts. If I have loosed
A shaft of language that has flown sometimes
A little higher than the hearts and heads
Of nature's minions, it will yet be heard,

467

Like a new song that waits for distant ears.
I cannot be the man that I am not;
And while I own that earth is my affliction,
I am a man of earth, who says not all
To all alike. That were impossible.
Even as it were so that He should plant
A larger garden first. But you today
Are for the larger sowing; and your seed,
A little mixed, will have, as He foresaw,
The foreign harvest of a wider growth,
And one without an end. Many there are,
And are to be, that shall partake of it,
Though none may share it with an understanding
That is not his alone. We are all alone;
And yet we are all parcelled of one order—
Jew, Gentile, or barbarian in the dark
Of wildernesses that are not so much
As names yet in a book. And there are many,
Finding at last that words are not the Word,
And finding only that, will flourish aloft,
Like heads of captured Pharisees on pikes,
Our contradictions and discrepancies;
And there are many more will hang themselves
Upon the letter, seeing not in the Word
The friend of all who fail, and in their faith
A sword of excellence to cut them down.

As long as there are glasses that are dark—
And there are many—we see darkly through them;
All which have I conceded and set down
In words that have no shadow. What is dark
Is dark, and we may not say otherwise;
Yet what may be as dark as a lost fire
For one of us, may still be for another
A coming gleam across the gulf of ages,

468

shadow-light

THE THREE TAVERNS

And a way home from shipwreck to the shore;
And so, through pangs and ills and desperations,
There may be light for all. There shall be light.
As much as that, you know. You cannot say
This woman or that man will be the next
On whom it falls; you are not here for that.
Your ministration is to be for others
The firing of a rush that may for them
Be soon the fire itself. The few at first
Are fighting for the multitude at last;
Therefore remember what Gamaliel said
Before you, when the sick were lying down
In streets all night for Peter's passing shadow.
Fight, and say what you feel; say more than words.
Give men to know that even their days of earth
To come are more than ages that are gone.
Say what you feel, while you have time to say it.
Eternity will answer for itself,
Without your intercession; yet the way
For many is a long one, and as dark,
Meanwhile, as dreams of hell. See not your toil
Too much, and if I be away from you,
Think of me as a brother to yourselves,
Of many blemishes. Beware of stoics,
And give your left hand to grammarians;—
And when you seem, as many a time you may,
To have no other friend than hope, remember
That you are not the first, or yet the last.

The best of life, until we see beyond
The shadows of ourselves (and they are less
Than even the blindest of indignant eyes
Would have them) is in what we do not know.
Make, then, for all your fears a place to sleep
With all your faded sins; nor think yourselves

469

COLLECTED POEMS

advice Don't to bring up old sins!

Egregious and alone for your defects
Of youth and yesterday. I was young once;
And there's a question if you played the fool   *I was worse*
With a more fervid and inherent zeal
Than I have in my story to remember,
Or gave your necks to folly's conquering foot,
Or flung yourselves with an unstudied aim,
More frequently than I. Never mind that.
Man's little house of days will hold enough,
Sometimes, to make him wish it were not his,
But it will not hold all. Things that are dead
Are best without it, and they own their death
By virtue of their dying. Let them go,—
But think you not the world is ashes yet,
And you have all the fire. The world is here   *Vision many will*
Today, and it may not be gone tomorrow;   *go that so*
For there are millions, and there may be more,   *what*
To make in turn a various estimation   *we have*
Of its old ills and ashes, and the traps
Of its apparent wrath. Many with ears
That hear not yet, shall have ears given to them,
And then they shall hear strangely. Many with eyes
That are incredulous of the Mystery
Shall yet be driven to feel, and then to read   *lang and*
Where language has an end and is a veil,
Not woven of our words. Many that hate
Their kind are soon to know that without love   *love*
Their faith is but the perjured name of nothing.
I that have done some hating in my time   *from*
See now no time for hate; I that have left,   *wisdom*
Fading behind me like familiar lights
That are to shine no more for my returning,
Home, friends, and honors,—I that have lost all else
For wisdom, and the wealth of it, say now
To you that out of wisdom has come love,

Another look into future - and a heightened style

470

DEMOS

That measures and is of itself the measure
Of works and hope and faith. Your longest hours
Are not so long that you may torture them
And harass not yourselves; and the last days
Are on the way that you prepare for them,
And was prepared for you, here in a world
Where you have sinned and suffered, striven and seen.
If you be not so hot for counting them
Before they come that you consume yourselves,
Peace may attend you all in these last days—
And me, as well as you. Yes, even in Rome.

Well, I have talked and rested, though I fear
My rest has not been yours; in which event,
Forgive one who is only seven leagues
From Cæsar. When I told you I should come,
I did not see myself the criminal
You contemplate, for seeing beyond the Law
That which the Law saw not. But this, indeed,
Was good of you, and I shall not forget;
No, I shall not forget you came so far
To meet a man so dangerous. Well, farewell.
They come to tell me I am going now—
With them. I hope that we shall meet again,
But none may say what he shall find in Rome.

DEMOS

I

ALL you that are enamored of my name
  And least intent on what most I require,
    Beware; for my design and your desire,
Deplorably, are not as yet the same.

471

Beware, I say, the failure and the shame
    Of losing that for which you now aspire
    So blindly, and of hazarding entire
The gift that I was bringing when I came.

Give as I will, I cannot give you sight
    Whereby to see that with you there are some
    To lead you, and be led. But they are dumb
Before the wrangling and the shrill delight
    Of your deliverance that has not come,
And shall not, if I fail you—as I might.

II

So little have you seen of what awaits
    Your fevered glimpse of a democracy
    Confused and foiled with an equality
Not equal to the envy it creates,
That you see not how near you are the gates
    Of an old king who listens fearfully
    To you that are outside and are to be
The noisy lords of imminent estates.

Rather be then your prayer that you shall have
    Your kingdom undishonored. Having all,
    See not the great among you for the small,
But hear their silence; for the few shall save
    The many, or the many are to fall—
Still to be wrangling in a noisy grave.

THE FLYING DUTCHMAN

UNYIELDING in the pride of his defiance,
    Afloat with none to serve or to command,

TACT

Lord of himself at last, and all by Science,
  He seeks the Vanished Land.

Alone, by the one light of his one thought,
  He steers to find the shore from which we came,
Fearless of in what coil he may be caught
  On seas that have no name.

Into the night he sails; and after night
  There is a dawning, though there be no sun;
Wherefore, with nothing but himself in sight,
  Unsighted, he sails on.

At last there is a lifting of the cloud
  Between the flood before him and the sky;
And then—though he may curse the Power aloud
  That has no power to die—

He steers himself away from what is haunted
  By the old ghost of what has been before,—
Abandoning, as always, and undaunted,
  One fog-walled island more.

TACT

Observant of the way she told
  So much of what was true,
No vanity could long withhold
  Regard that was her due:
She spared him the familiar guile,
  So easily achieved,
That only made a man to smile
  And left him undeceived.

473

Aware that all imagining
  Of more than what she meant
Would urge an end of everything,
  He stayed; and when he went,
They parted with a merry word
  That was to him as light
As any that was ever heard
  Upon a starry night.

She smiled a little, knowing well
  That he would not remark
The ruins of a day that fell
  Around her in the dark:
He saw no ruins anywhere,
  Nor fancied there were scars
On anyone who lingered there,
  Alone below the stars.

ON THE WAY

(PHILADELPHIA, 1794)

NOTE.—The following imaginary dialogue between Alexander
Hamilton and Aaron Burr, which is not based upon any specific in-
cident in American history, may be supposed to have occurred a
few months previous to Hamilton's retirement from Washington's
Cabinet in 1795 and a few years before the political ingenuities of
Burr—who has been characterized, without much exaggeration, as
the inventor of American politics—began to be conspicuously for-
midable to the Federalists. These activities on the part of Burr
resulted, as the reader will remember, in the Burr-Jefferson tie
for the Presidency in 1800, and finally in the Burr-Hamilton duel
at Weehawken in 1804.

BURR

HAMILTON, if he rides you down, remember
That I was here to speak, and so to save

474

Your fabric from catastrophe. That's good;
For I perceive that you observe him also.
A President, a-riding of his horse,
May dust a General and be forgiven;
But why be dusted—when we're all alike,
All equal, and all happy? Here he comes—
And there he goes. And we, by your new patent,
Would seem to be two kings here by the wayside,
With our two hats off to his Excellency.
Why not his Majesty, and done with it?
Forgive me if I shook your meditation,
But you that weld our credit should have eyes
To see what's coming. Bury me first if *I* do.

HAMILTON

There's always in some pocket of your brain
A care for me; wherefore my gratitude
For your attention is commensurate
With your concern. Yes, Burr, we are two kings;
We are as royal as two ditch-diggers;
But owe me not your sceptre. These are the days
When first a few seem all; but if we live
We may again be seen to be the few
That we have always been. These are the days
When men forget the stars, and are forgotten.

BURR

But why forget them? They're the same that winked
Upon the world when Alcibiades
Cut off his dog's tail to induce distinction.
There are dogs yet, and Alcibiades
Is not forgotten.

HAMILTON

Yes, there are dogs enough,
God knows; and I can hear them in my dreams.

BURR

Never a doubt. But what you hear the most
Is your new music, something out of tune
With your intention. How in the name of Cain,
I seem to hear you ask, are men to dance,
When all men are musicians. Tell me that,
I hear you saying, and I'll tell you the name
Of Samson's mother. But why shroud yourself
Before the coffin comes? For all you know,
The tree that is to fall for your last house
Is now a sapling. You may have to wait
So long as to be sorry; though I doubt it,
For you are not at home in your new Eden
Where chilly whispers of a likely frost
Accumulate already in the air.
I think a touch of ermine, Hamilton,
Would be for you in your autumnal mood
A pleasant sort of warmth along the shoulders.

HAMILTON

If so it is you think, you may as well
Give over thinking. We are done with ermine.
What I fear most is not the multitude,
But those who are to loop it with a string
That has one end in France and one end here.
I'm not so fortified with observation
That I could swear that more than half a score
Among us who see lightning see that ruin
Is not the work of thunder. Since the world

Was ordered, there was never a long pause
For caution between doing and undoing.

BURR

Go on, sir; my attention is a trap
Set for the catching of all compliments
To Monticello, and all else abroad
That has a name or an identity.

HAMILTON

I leave to you the names—there are too many;
Yet one there is to sift and hold apart,
As now I see. There comes at last a glimmer
That is not always clouded, or too late.
But I was near and young, and had the reins
To play with while he manned a team so raw
That only God knows where the end had been
Of all that riding without Washington.
There was a nation in the man who passed us,
If there was not a world. I may have driven
Since then some restive horses, and alone,
And through a splashing of abundant mud;
But he who made the dust that sets you on
To coughing, made the road. Now it seems dry,
And in a measure safe.

BURR

　　　　　Here's a new tune
From Hamilton. Has your caution all at once,
And over night, grown till it wrecks the cradle?
I have forgotten what my father said
When I was born, but there's a rustling of it
Among my memories, and it makes a noise

About as loud as all that I have held
And fondled heretofore of your same caution.
But that's affairs, not feelings. If our friends
Guessed half we say of them, our enemies
Would itch in our friends' jackets. Howsoever,
The world is of a sudden on its head,
And all are spilled—unless you cling alone
With Washington. Ask Adams about that.

HAMILTON

We'll not ask Adams about anything.
We fish for lizards when we choose to ask
For what we know already is not coming,
And we must eat the answer. Where's the use
Of asking when this man says everything,
With all his tongues of silence?

BURR

I dare say.
I dare say, but I won't. One of those tongues
I'll borrow for the nonce. He'll never miss it.
We mean his Western Majesty, King George.

HAMILTON

I mean the man who rode by on his horse.
I'll beg of you the meed of your indulgence
If I should say this planet may have done
A deal of weary whirling when at last,
If ever, Time shall aggregate again
A majesty like his that has no name.

BURR

Then you concede his Majesty? That's good,
And what of yours? Here are two majesties.

ON THE WAY

Favor the Left a little, Hamilton,
Or you'll be floundering in the ditch that waits
For riders who forget where they are riding.
If we and France, as you anticipate,
Must eat each other, what Cæsar, if not yourself,
Do you see for the master of the feast?
There may be a place waiting on your head
For laurel thick as Nero's. You don't know.
I have not crossed your glory, though I might
If I saw thrones at auction.

HAMILTON

            Yes, you might.
If war is on the way, I shall be—here;
And I've no vision of your distant heels.

BURR

I see that I shall take an inference
To bed with me to-night to keep me warm.
I thank you, Hamilton, and I approve
Your fealty to the aggregated greatness
Of him you lean on while he leans on you.

HAMILTON

This easy phrasing is a game of yours
That you may win to lose. I beg your pardon,
But you that have the sight will not employ
The will to see with it. If you did so,
There might be fewer ditches dug for others
In your perspective; and there might be fewer
Contemporary motes of prejudice
Between you and the man who made the dust.
Call him a genius or a gentleman,

479

A prophet or a builder, or what not,
But hold your disposition off the balance,
And weigh him in the light. Once (I believe
I tell you nothing new to your surmise,
Or to the tongues of towns and villages)
I nourished with an adolescent fancy—
Surely forgivable to you, my friend—
An innocent and amiable conviction
That I was, by the grace of honest fortune,
A savior at his elbow through the war,
Where I might have observed, more than I did,
Patience and wholesome passion. I was there,
And for such honor I gave nothing worse
Than some advice at which he may have smiled.
I must have given a modicum besides,
Or the rough interval between those days
And these would never have made for me my friends,
Or enemies. I should be something somewhere—
I say not what—but I should not be here
If he had not been there. Possibly, too,
You might not—or that Quaker with his cane.

BURR

Possibly, too, I should. When the Almighty
Rides a white horse, I fancy we shall know it.

HAMILTON

It was a man, Burr, that was in my mind;
No god, or ghost, or demon—only a man:
A man whose occupation is the need
Of those who would not feel it if it bit them;
And one who shapes an age while he endures
The pin pricks of inferiorities;
A cautious man, because he is but one;

ON THE WAY

A lonely man, because he is a thousand.
No marvel you are slow to find in him
The genius that is one spark or is nothing:
His genius is a flame that he must hold
So far above the common heads of men
That they may view him only through the mist
Of their defect, and wonder what he is.
It seems to me the mystery that is in him
That makes him only more to me a man
Than any other I have ever known.

BURR

I grant you that his worship is a man.
I'm not so much at home with mysteries,
May be, as you—so leave him with his fire:
God knows that I shall never put it out.
He has not made a cripple of himself
In his pursuit of me, though I have heard
His condescension honors me with parts.
Parts make a whole, if we've enough of them;
And once I figured a sufficiency
To be at least an atom in the annals
Of your republic.   But I must have erred.

HAMILTON

You smile as if your spirit lived at ease
With error.   I should not have named it so,
Failing assent from you; nor, if I did,
Should I be so complacent in my skill
To comb the tangled language of the people
As to be sure of anything in these days.
Put that much in account with modesty.

BURR

What in the name of Ahab, Hamilton,
Have you, in the last region of your dreaming,
To do with "people"? You may be the devil
In your dead-reckoning of what reefs and shoals
Are waiting on the progress of our ship
Unless you steer it, but you'll find it irksome
Alone there in the stern; and some warm day
There'll be an inland music in the rigging,
And afterwards on deck. I'm not affined
Or favored overmuch at Monticello,
But there's a mighty swarming of new bees
About the premises, and all have wings.
If you hear something buzzing before long,
Be thoughtful how you strike, remembering also
There was a fellow Naboth had a vineyard,
And Ahab cut his hair off and went softly.

HAMILTON

I don't remember that he cut his hair off.

BURR

Somehow I rather fancy that he did.
If so, it's in the Book; and if not so,
He did the rest, and did it handsomely.

HAMILTON

Commend yourself to Ahab and his ways
If they inveigle you to emulation;
But where, if I may ask it, are you tending
With your invidious wielding of the Scriptures?
You call to mind an eminent archangel
Who fell to make him famous. Would you fall
So far as he, to be so far remembered?

482

ON THE WAY

BURR

Before I fall or rise, or am an angel,
I shall acquaint myself a little further
With our new land's new language, which is not—
Peace to your dreams—an idiom to your liking.
I'm wondering if a man may always know
How old a man may be at thirty-seven;
I wonder likewise if a prettier time
Could be decreed for a good man to vanish
Than about now for you, before you fade,
And even your friends are seeing that you have had
Your cup too full for longer mortal triumph.
Well, you have had enough, and had it young;
And the old wine is nearer to the lees
Than you are to the work that you are doing.

HAMILTON

When does this philological excursion
Into new lands and languages begin?

BURR

Anon—that is, already. Only Fortune
Gave me this afternoon the benefaction
Of your blue back, which I for love pursued,
And in pursuing may have saved your life—
Also the world a pounding piece of news:
Hamilton bites the dust of Washington,
Or rather of his horse. For you alone,
Or for your fame, I'd wish it might have been so.

HAMILTON

Not every man among us has a friend
So jealous for the other's fame. How long

Are you to diagnose the doubtful case
Of Demos—and what for? Have you a sword
For some new Damocles? If it's for me,
I have lost all official appetite,
And shall have faded, after January,
Into the law. I'm going to New York.

BURR

No matter where you are, one of these days
I shall come back to you and tell you something.
This Demos, I have heard, has in his wrist
A pulse that no two doctors have as yet
Counted and found the same, and in his mouth
A tongue that has the like alacrity
For saying or not for saying what most it is
That pullulates in his ignoble mind.
One of these days I shall appear again,
To tell you more of him and his opinions;
I shall not be so long out of your sight,
Or take myself so far, that I may not,
Like Alcibiades, come back again.
He went away to Phrygia, and fared ill.

HAMILTON

There's an example in Themistocles:
He went away to Persia, and fared well.

BURR

So? Must I go so far? And if so, why so?
I had not planned it so. Is this the road
I take? If so, farewell.

HAMILTON

Quite so. Farewell.

484

JOHN BROWN

THOUGH for your sake I would not have you now
So near to me tonight as now you are,
God knows how much a stranger to my heart
Was any cold word that I may have written;
And you, poor woman that I made my wife,
You have had more of loneliness, I fear,
Than I—though I have been the most alone,
Even when the most attended. So it was
God set the mark of his inscrutable
Necessity on one that was to grope,
And serve, and suffer, and withal be glad
For what was his, and is, and is to be,
When his old bones, that are a burden now,
Are saying what the man who carried them
Had not the power to say. Bones in a grave,
Cover them as they will with choking earth,
May shout the truth to men who put them there,
More than all orators. And so, my dear,
Since you have cheated wisdom for the sake
Of sorrow, let your sorrow be for you,
This last of nights before the last of days,
The lying ghost of what there is of me
That is the most alive. There is no death
For me in what they do. Their death it is
They should heed most when the sun comes again
To make them solemn. There are some I know
Whose eyes will hardly see their occupation,
For tears in them—and all for one old man;
For some of them will pity this old man,
Who took upon himself the work of God
Because he pitied millions. That will be
For them, I fancy, their compassionate

Best way of saying what is best in them
To say; for they can say no more than that,
And they can do no more than what the dawn
Of one more day shall give them light enough
To do. But there are many days to be,
And there are many men to give their blood,
As I gave mine for them. May they come soon!

May they come soon, I say. And when they come,
May all that I have said unheard be heard,
Proving at last, or maybe not—no matter—
What sort of madness was the part of me
That made me strike, whether I found the mark
Or missed it. Meanwhile, I've a strange content,
A patience, and a vast indifference
To what men say of me and what men fear
To say. There was a work to be begun,
And when the Voice, that I have heard so long,
Announced as in a thousand silences
An end of preparation, I began
The coming work of death which is to be,
That life may be. There is no other way
Than the old way of war for a new land
That will not know itself and is tonight
A stranger to itself, and to the world
A more prodigious upstart among states
Than I was among men, and so shall be
Till they are told and told, and told again;
For men are children, waiting to be told,
And most of them are children all their lives.
The good God in his wisdom had them so,
That now and then a madman or a seer
May shake them out of their complacency
And shame them into deeds. The major file
See only what their fathers may have seen,

Or may have said they saw when they saw nothing.
I do not say it matters what they saw.
Now and again to some lone soul or other
God speaks, and there is hanging to be done,—
As once there was a burning of our bodies
Alive, albeit our souls were sorry fuel.
But now the fires are few, and we are poised
Accordingly, for the state's benefit,
A few still minutes between heaven and earth.
The purpose is, when they have seen enough
Of what it is that they are not to see,
To pluck me as an unripe fruit of treason,
And then to fling me back to the same earth
Of which they are, as I suppose, the flower—
Not given to know the riper fruit that waits
For a more comprehensive harvesting.

Yes, may they come, and soon. Again I say,
May they come soon!—before too many of them
Shall be the bloody cost of our defection.
When hell waits on the dawn of a new state,
Better it were that hell should not wait long,—
Or so it is I see it who should see
As far or farther into time tonight
Than they who talk and tremble for me now,
Or wish me to those everlasting fires
That are for me no fear. Too many fires
Have sought me out and seared me to the bone—
Thereby, for all I know, to temper me
For what was mine to do. If I did ill
What I did well, let men say I was mad;
Or let my name for ever be a question
That will not sleep in history. What men say
I was will cool no cannon, dull no sword,
Invalidate no truth. Meanwhile, I was;

And the long train is lighted that shall burn,
Though floods of wrath may drench it, and hot feet
May stamp it for a slight time into smoke
That shall blaze up again with growing speed,
Until at last a fiery crash will come
To cleanse and shake a wounded hemisphere,
And heal it of a long malignity
That angry time discredits and disowns.

Tonight there are men saying many things;
And some who see life in the last of me
Will answer first the coming call to death;
For death is what is coming, and then life.
I do not say again for the dull sake
Of speech what you have heard me say before,
But rather for the sake of all I am,
And all God made of me. A man to die
As I do must have done some other work
Than man's alone. I was not after glory,
But there was glory with me, like a friend,
Throughout those crippling years when friends were few,
And fearful to be known by their own names
When mine was vilified for their approval.
Yet friends they are, and they did what was given
Their will to do; they could have done no more.
I was the one man mad enough, it seems,
To do my work; and now my work is over.
And you, my dear, are not to mourn for me,
Or for your sons, more than a soul should mourn
In Paradise, done with evil and with earth.
There is not much of earth in what remains
For you; and what there may be left of it
For your endurance you shall have at last
In peace, without the twinge of any fear
For my condition; for I shall be done

JOHN BROWN

With plans and actions that have heretofore
Made your days long and your nights ominous
With darkness and the many distances
That were between us. When the silence comes,
I shall in faith be nearer to you then
Than I am now in fact. What you see now
Is only the outside of an old man,
Older than years have made him. Let him die,
And let him be a thing for little grief.
There was a time for service and he served;
And there is no more time for anything
But a short gratefulness to those who gave
Their scared allegiance to an enterprise
That has the name of treason—which will serve
As well as any other for the present.
There are some deeds of men that have no names,
And mine may like as not be one of them.
I am not looking far for names tonight.
The King of Glory was without a name
Until men gave Him one; yet there He was,
Before we found Him and affronted Him
With numerous ingenuities of evil,
Of which one, with His aid, is to be swept
And washed out of the world with fire and blood.

Once I believed it might have come to pass
With a small cost of blood; but I was dreaming—
Dreaming that I believed. The Voice I heard
When I left you behind me in the north,—
To wait there and to wonder and grow old
Of loneliness,—told only what was best,
And with a saving vagueness, I should know
Till I knew more. And had I known even then—
After grim years of search and suffering,
So many of them to end as they began—

After my sickening doubts and estimations
Of plans abandoned and of new plans vain—
After a weary delving everywhere
For men with every virtue but the Vision—
Could I have known, I say, before I left you
That summer morning, all there was to know—
Even unto the last consuming word
That would have blasted every mortal answer
As lightning would annihilate a leaf,
I might have trembled on that summer morning;
I might have wavered; and I might have failed.

And there are many among men today
To say of me that I had best have wavered.
So has it been, so shall it always be,
For those of us who give ourselves to die
Before we are so parcelled and approved
As to be slaughtered by authority.
We do not make so much of what they say
As they of what our folly says of us;
They give us hardly time enough for that,
And thereby we gain much by losing little.
Few are alive to-day with less to lose
Than I who tell you this, or more to gain;
And whether I speak as one to be destroyed
For no good end outside his own destruction,
Time shall have more to say than men shall hear
Between now and the coming of that harvest
Which is to come. Before it comes, I go—
By the short road that mystery makes long
For man's endurance of accomplishment.
I shall have more to say when I am dead.

THE FALSE GODS

"WE are false and evanescent, and aware of our deceit,
From the straw that is our vitals to the clay that is our feet.
You may serve us if you must, and you shall have your wage
    of ashes,—
Though arrears due thereafter may be hard for you to meet.

"You may swear that we are solid, you may say that we are
    strong,
But we know that we are neither and we say that you are
    wrong;
You may find an easy worship in acclaiming our indulgence,
But your large admiration of us now is not for long.

"If your doom is to adore us with a doubt that's never still,
And you pray to see our faces—pray in earnest, and you will.
You may gaze at us and live, and live assured of our confusion:
For the False Gods are mortal, and are made for you to kill.

"And you may as well observe, while apprehensively at ease
With an Art that's inorganic and is anything you please,
That anon your newest ruin may lie crumbling unregarded,
Like an old shrine forgotten in a forest of new trees.

"Howsoever like no other be the mode you may employ,
There's an order in the ages for the ages to enjoy;
Though the temples you are shaping and the passions you are
    singing
Are a long way from Athens and a longer way from Troy.

"When we promise more than ever of what never shall arrive,
And you seem a little more than ordinarily alive,
Make a note that you are sure you understand our obligations—
For there's grief always auditing where two and two are five.

"There was this for us to say and there was this for you to
    know,
Though it humbles and it hurts us when we have to tell you so
If you doubt the only truth in all our perjured composition,
May the True Gods attend you and forget us when we go."

ARCHIBALD'S EXAMPLE

OLD ARCHIBALD, in his eternal chair,
Where trespassers, whatever their degree,
Were soon frowned out again, was looking off
Across the clover when he said to me:

"My green hill yonder, where the sun goes down
Without a scratch, was once inhabited
By trees that injured him—an evil trash
That made a cage, and held him while he bled.

"Gone fifty years, I see them as they were
Before they fell. They were a crooked lot
To spoil my sunset, and I saw no time
In fifty years for crooked things to rot.

"Trees, yes; but not a service or a joy
To God or man, for they were thieves of light.
So down they came. Nature and I looked on,
And we were glad when they were out of sight.

"Trees are like men, sometimes; and that being so,
So much for that." He twinkled in his chair,
And looked across the clover to the place
That he remembered when the trees were there.

LONDON BRIDGE

"Do I hear them? Yes, I hear the children singing—and what
    of it?
Have you come with eyes afire to find me now and ask me that?
If I were not their father and if you were not their mother,
We might believe they made a noise. . . . What are you—
    driving at!"

"Well, be glad that you can hear them, and be glad they are so
    near us,—
For I have heard the stars of heaven, and they were nearer still.
All within an hour it is that I have heard them calling,
And though I pray for them to cease, I know they never will;
For their music on my heart, though you may freeze it, will
    fall always,
Like summer snow that never melts upon a mountain-top.
Do you hear them? Do you hear them overhead—the children
    —singing?
Do you hear the children singing? . . . God, will you make
    them stop!"

"And what now in His holy name have you to do with moun-
    tains?
We're back to town again, my dear, and we've a dance tonight.
Frozen hearts and falling music? Snow and stars, and—what
    the devil!
Say it over to me slowly, and be sure you have it right."

"God knows if I be right or wrong in saying what I tell you,
Or if I know the meaning any more of what I say.
All I know is, it will kill me if I try to keep it hidden—
Well, I met him. . . . Yes, I met him, and I talked with him—
    today."

493

"You met him? Did you meet the ghost of someone you had
    poisoned,
Long ago, before I knew you for the woman that you are?
Take a chair; and don't begin your stories always in the
    middle.
Was he man, or was he demon? Anyhow, you've gone too far
To go back, and I'm your servant. I'm the lord, but you're
    the master.
Now go on with what you know, for I'm excited."

                                        "Do you mean—
Do you mean to make me try to think that you know less than
    I do?"

"I know that you foreshadow the beginning of a scene.
Pray be careful, and as accurate as if the doors of heaven
Were to swing or to stay bolted from now on for evermore."

"Do you conceive, with all your smooth contempt of every
    feeling,
Of hiding what you know and what you must have known
    before?
Is it worth a woman's torture to stand here and have you
    smiling,
With only your poor fetish of possession on your side?
No thing but one is wholly sure, and that's not one to scare
    me;
When I meet it I may say to God at last that I have tried.
And yet, for all I know, or all I dare believe, my trials
Henceforward will be more for you to bear than are your own;
And you must give me keys of yours to rooms I have not
    entered.
Do you see me on your threshold all my life, and there alone?
Will you tell me where you see me in your fancy—when it
    leads you
Far enough beyond the moment for a glance at the abyss?"

"Will you tell me what intrinsic and amazing sort of nonsense
You are crowding on the patience of the man who gives you—
    this?
Look around you and be sorry you're not living in an attic,
With a civet and a fish-net, and with you to pay the rent.
I say words that you can spell without the use of all your
    letters;
And I grant, if you insist, that I've a guess at what you
    meant."

"Have I told you, then, for nothing, that I met him? Are you
    trying
To be merry while you try to make me hate you?"

                                        "Think again,
My dear, before you tell me, in a language unbecoming
In a lady, what you plan to tell me next. If I complain,
If I seem an atom peevish at the preference you mention—
Or imply, to be precise—you may believe, or you may not,
That I'm a trifle more aware of what he wants than you are.
But I shouldn't throw that at you. Make believe that I forgot.
Make believe that he's a genius, if you like,—but in the
    meantime
Don't go back to rocking-horses. There, there, there, now."

                                    "Make believe!
When you see me standing helpless on a plank above a whirl-
    pool,
Do I drown, or do I hear you when you say it? Make believe?
How much more am I to say or do for you before I tell you
That I met him! What's to follow now may be for you to
    choose.
Do you hear me? Won't you listen? It's an easy thing to
    listen. . . ."

"And it's easy to be crazy when there's everything to lose."

"If at last you have a notion that I mean what I am saying,
Do I seem to tell you nothing when I tell you I shall try?
If you save me, and I lose him—I don't know—it won't much
matter.
I dare say that I've lied enough, but now I do not lie."

"Do you fancy me the one man who has waited and said
nothing
While a wife has dragged an old infatuation from a tomb?
Give the thing a little air and it will vanish into ashes.
There you are—piff! presto!"

"When I came into this room,
It seemed as if I saw the place, and you there at your table,
As you are now at this moment, for the last time in my life;
And I told myself before I came to find you, 'I shall tell him,
If I can, what I have learned of him since I became his wife.'
And if you say, as I've no doubt you will before I finish,
That you have tried unceasingly, with all your might and main,
To teach me, knowing more than I of what it was I needed,
Don't think, with all you may have thought, that you have tried
in vain;
For you have taught me more than hides in all the shelves of
knowledge
Of how little you found that's in me and was in me all along.
I believed, if I intruded nothing on you that I cared for,
I'd be half as much as horses,—and it seems that I was wrong;
I believed there was enough of earth in me, with all my
nonsense
Over things that made you sleepy, to keep something still
awake;
But you taught me soon to read my book, and God knows I
have read it—
Ages longer than an angel would have read it for your sake.
I have said that you must open other doors than I have entered

496

But I wondered while I said it if I might not be obscure.
Is there anything in all your pedigrees and inventories
With a value more elusive than a dollar's? Are you sure
That if I starve another year for you I shall be stronger
To endure another like it—and another—till I'm dead?"

"Has your tame cat sold a picture?—or more likely had a
   windfall?
Or for God's sake, what's broke loose? Have you a bee-hive
   in your head?
A little more of this from you will not be easy hearing
Do you know. that? Understand it, if you do; for if you
   won't. . . .
What the devil are you saying! Make believe you never said it,
And I'll say I never heard it. . . . Oh, you. . . . If you. . . ."

                              "If I don't?"

"There are men who say there's reason hidden somewhere in a
   woman,
But I doubt if God himself remembers where the key was
   hung."

"He may not; for they say that even God himself is growing.
I wonder if He makes believe that He is growing young;
I wonder if He makes believe that women who are giving
All they have in holy loathing to a stranger all their lives
Are the wise ones who build houses in the Bible. . . ."

                              "Stop—you devil!"

". . . Or that souls are any whiter when their bodies are called
   wives.
If a dollar's worth of gold will hoop the walls of hell together,
Why need heaven be such a ruin of a place that never was?

And if at last I lied my starving soul away to nothing,
Are you sure you might not miss it? Have you come to such
    a pass
That you would have me longer in your arms if you discovered
That I made you into someone else. . . . Oh! . . . Well, there
    are worse ways.
But why aim it at my feet—unless you fear you may be
    sorry. . . .
There are many days ahead of you."

                               "I do not see those days."

"I can see them. Granted even I am wrong, there are the
    children.
And are they to praise their father for his insight if we die?
Do you hear them? Do you hear them overhead—the children
    —singing?
Do you hear them? Do you hear the children?"

                        "Damn the children!"

                                 "Why?
What have *they* done? . . . Well, then,—do it. . . . Do it now,
    and have it over."

"Oh, you devil! . . . Oh, you. . . ."

                    "No, I'm not a devil, I'm a prophet—
One who sees the end already of so much that one end more
Would have now the small importance of one other small
    illusion,
Which in turn would have a welcome where the rest have gone
    before.
But if I were you, my fancy would look on a little farther
For the glimpse of a release that may be somewhere still in
    sight.

Furthermore, you must remember those two hundred invitations
For the dancing after dinner. We shall have to shine tonight.
We shall dance, and be as happy as a pair of merry spectres,
On the grave of all the lies that we shall never have to tell;
We shall dance among the ruins of the tomb of our endurance,
And I have not a doubt that we shall do it very well.
There!—I'm glad you've put it back; for I don't like it. Shut
the drawer now.
No—no—don't cancel anything. I'll dance until I drop.
I can't walk yet, but I'm going to. . . . Go away somewhere,
and leave me. . . .
Oh, you children! Oh, you children! . . . God, will they never
stop!"

TASKER NORCROSS

"WHETHER all towns and all who live in them—
So long as they be somewhere in this world
That we in our complacency call ours—
Are more or less the same, I leave to you.
I should say less. Whether or not, meanwhile,
We've all two legs—and as for that, we haven't—
There were three kinds of men where I was born:
The good, the not so good, and Tasker Norcross.
Now there are two kinds."

        "Meaning, as I divine,
Your friend is dead," I ventured.

            Ferguson,
Who talked himself at last out of the world
He censured, and is therefore silent now,
Agreed indifferently: "My friends are dead—
Or most of them."

             "Remember one that isn't."
I said, protesting. "Honor him for his ears;
Treasure him also for his understanding."
Ferguson sighed, and then talked on again:
"You have an overgrown alacrity
For saying nothing much and hearing less;
And I've a thankless wonder, at the start,
How much it is to you that I shall tell
What I have now to say of Tasker Norcross,
And how much to the air that is around you.
But given a patience that is not averse
To the slow tragedies of haunted men—
Horrors, in fact, if you've a skilful eye.
To know them at their firesides, or out walking,—"

"Horrors," I said, "are my necessity;
And I would have them, for their best effect,
Always out walking."

                   Ferguson frowned at me:
"The wisest of us are not those who laugh
Before they know. Most of us never know—
Or the long toil of our mortality
Would not be done. Most of us never know—
And there you have a reason to believe
In God, if you may have no other. Norcross,
Or so I gather of his infirmity,
Was given to know more than he should have known,
And only God knows why. See for yourself
An old house full of ghosts of ancestors.
Who did their best, or worst, and having done it,
Died honorably; and each with a distinction
That hardly would have been for him that had it,
Had honor failed him wholly as a friend.
Honor that is a friend begets a friend.

TASKER NORCROSS

Whether or not we love him, still we have him;
And we must live somehow by what we have,
Or then we die. If you say chemistry,
Then you must have your molecules in motion,
And in their right abundance. Failing either,
You have not long to dance. Failing a friend,
A genius, or a madness, or a faith
Larger than desperation, you are here
For as much longer than you like as may be.
Imagining now, by way of an example,
Myself a more or less remembered phantom—
Again, I should say less—how many times
A day should I come back to you? No answer.
Forgive me when I seem a little careless,
But we must have examples, or be lucid
Without them; and I question your adherence
To such an undramatic narrative
As this of mine, without the personal hook."

"A time is given in Ecclesiastes
For divers works," I told him. "Is there one
For saying nothing in return for nothing?
If not, there should be." I could feel his eyes
And they were like two cold inquiring points
Of a sharp metal. When I looked again,
To see them shine, the cold that I had felt
Was gone to make way for a smouldering
Of lonely fire that I, as I knew then,
Could never quench with kindness or with lies.
I should have done whatever there was to do
For Ferguson, yet I could not have mourned
In honesty for once around the clock
The loss of him, for my sake or for his,
Try as I might; nor would his ghost approve,
Had I the power and the unthinking will

501

To make him tread again without an aim
The road that was behind him—and without
The faith, or friend, or genius, or the madness
That he contended was imperative.

After a silence that had been too long,
"It may be quite as well we don't," he said;
"As well, I mean, that we don't always say it.
You know best what I mean, and I suppose
You might have said it better. What was that?
Incorrigible? Am I incorrigible?
Well, it's a word; and a word has its use,
Or, like a man, it will soon have a grave.
It's a good word enough. Incorrigible,
May be, for all I know, the word for Norcross.
See for yourself that house of his again
That he called home: An old house, painted white,
Square as a box, and chillier than a tomb
To look at or to live in. There were trees—
Too many of them, if such a thing may be—
Before it and around it. Down in front
There was a road, a railroad, and a river;
Then there were hills behind it, and more trees.
The thing would fairly stare at you through trees,
Like a pale inmate out of a barred window
With a green shade half down; and I dare say
People who passed have said: 'There's where he lives.
We know him, but we do not seem to know
That we remember any good of him,
Or any evil that is interesting.
There you have all we know and all we care.'
They might have said it in all sorts of ways;
And then, if they perceived a cat, they might
Or might not have remembered what they said.
The cat might have a personality—

TASKER NORCROSS

And maybe the same one the Lord left out
Of Tasker Norcross, who, for lack of it,
Saw the same sun go down year after year;
All which at last was my discovery.
And only mine, so far as evidence
Enlightens one more darkness. You have known
All round you, all your days, men who are nothing—
Nothing, I mean, so far as time tells yet
Of any other need it has of them
Than to make sextons hardy—but no less
Are to themselves incalculably something,
And therefore to be cherished. God, you see,
Being sorry for them in their fashioning,
Indemnified them with a quaint esteem
Of self, and with illusions long as life.
You know them well, and you have smiled at them;
And they, in their serenity, may have had
Their time to smile at you. Blessed are they
That see themselves for what they never were
Or were to be, and are, for their defect,
At ease with mirrors and the dim remarks
That pass their tranquil ears."

                              "Come, come," said I;
"There may be names in your compendium
That we are not yet all on fire for shouting.
Skin most of us of our mediocrity,
We should have nothing then that we could scratch.
The picture smarts. Cover it, if you please,
And do so rather gently. Now for Norcross."

Ferguson closed his eyes in resignation,
While a dead sigh came out of him. "Good God!"
He said, and said it only half aloud,
As if he knew no longer now, nor cared,

If one were there to listen: "Have I said nothing—
Nothing at all—of Norcross? Do you mean
To patronize him till his name becomes
A toy made out of letters? If a name
Is all you need, arrange an honest column
Of all the people you have ever known
That you have never liked. You'll have enough;
And you'll have mine, moreover. No, not yet.
If I assume too many privileges,
I pay, and I alone, for their assumption;
By which, if I assume a darker knowledge
Of Norcross than another, let the weight
Of my injustice aggravate the load
That is not on your shoulders. When I came
To know this fellow Norcross in his house,
I found him as I found him in the street—
No more, no less; indifferent, but no better.
'Worse' were not quite the word: he was not bad;
He was not . . . well, he was not anything.
Has your invention ever entertained
The picture of a dusty worm so dry
That even the early bird would shake his head
And fly on farther for another breakfast?"

"But why forget the fortune of the worm,"
I said, "if in the dryness you deplore
Salvation centred and endured? Your Norcross
May have been one for many to have envied."

"Salvation? Fortune? Would the worm say that?
He might; and therefore I dismiss the worm
With all dry things but one. Figures away,
Do you begin to see this man a little?
Do you begin to see him in the air,
With all the vacant horrors of his outline

504

For you to fill with more than it will hold?
If so, you needn't crown yourself at once
With epic laurel if you seem to fill it.
Horrors, I say, for in the fires and forks
Of a new hell—if one were not enough—
I doubt if a new horror would have held him
With a malignant ingenuity
More to be feared than his before he died.
You smile, as if in doubt. Well, smile again.
Now come into his house, along with me:
The four square sombre things that you see first
Around you are four walls that go as high
As to the ceiling. Norcross knew them well,
And he knew others like them. Fasten to that
With all the claws of your intelligence;
And hold the man before you in his house
As if he were a white rat in a box,
And one that knew himself to be no other.
I tell you twice that he knew all about it,
That you may not forget the worst of all
Our tragedies begin with what we know.
Could Norcross only not have known, I wonder
How many would have blessed and envied him!
Could he have had the usual eye for spots
On others, and for none upon himself,
I smile to ponder on the carriages
That might as well as not have clogged the town
In honor of his end. For there was gold,
You see, though all he needed was a little,
And what he gave said nothing of who gave it.
He would have given it all if in return
There might have been a more sufficient face
To greet him when he shaved. Though you insist
It is the dower, and always, of our degree
Not to be cursed with such invidious insight,

505

Remember that you stand, you and your fancy,
Now in his house; and since we are together,
See for yourself and tell me what you see.
Tell me the best you see. Make a slight noise
Of recognition when you find a book
That you would not as lief read upside down
As otherwise, for example. If there you fail,
Observe the walls and lead me to the place,
Where you are led. If there you meet a picture
That holds you near it for a longer time
Than you are sorry, you may call it yours,
And hang it in the dark of your remembrance,
Where Norcross never sees. How can he see
That has no eyes to see? And as for music,
He paid with empty wonder for the pangs
Of his infrequent forced endurance of it;
And having had no pleasure, paid no more
For needless immolation, or for the sight
Of those who heard what he was never to hear.
To see them listening was itself enough
To make him suffer; and to watch worn eyes,
On other days, of strangers who forgot
Their sorrows and their failures and themselves
Before a few mysterious odds and ends
Of marble carted from the Parthenon—
And all for seeing what he was never to see,
Because it was alive and he was dead—
Here was a wonder that was more profound
Than any that was in fiddles and brass horns.

"He knew, and in his knowledge there was death.
He knew there was a region all around him
That lay outside man's havoc and affairs,
And yet was not all hostile to their tumult,

Where poets would have served and honored him,
And saved him, had there been anything to save.
But there was nothing, and his tethered range
Was only a small desert. Kings of song
Are not for thrones in deserts. Towers of sound
And flowers of sense are but a waste of heaven
Where there is none to know them from the rocks
And sand-grass of his own monotony
That makes earth less than earth. He could see that,
And he could see no more. The captured light
That may have been or not, for all he cared,
The song that is in sculpture was not his,
But only, to his God-forgotten eyes,
One more immortal nonsense in a world
Where all was mortal, or had best be so,
And so be done with. 'Art,' he would have said,
'Is not life, and must therefore be a lie;'
And with a few profundities like that
He would have controverted and dismissed
The benefit of the Greeks. He had heard of them,
As he had heard of his aspiring soul—
Never to the perceptible advantage,
In his esteem, of either. 'Faith,' he said,
Or would have said if he had thought of it,
'Lives in the same house with Philosophy,
Where the two feed on scraps and are forlorn
As orphans after war. He could see stars,
On a clear night, but he had not an eye
To see beyond them. He could hear spoken words,
But had no ear for silence when alone.
He could eat food of which he knew the savor,
But had no palate for the Bread of Life,
That human desperation, to his thinking,
Made famous long ago, having no other.
Now do you see? Do you begin to see?"

I told him that I did begin to see;
And I was nearer than I should have been
To laughing at his malign inclusiveness,
When I considered that, with all our speed,
We are not laughing yet at funerals.
I see him now as I could see him then,
And I see now that it was good for me,
As it was good for him, that I was quiet;
For Time's eye was on Ferguson, and the shaft
Of its inquiring hesitancy had touched him,
Or so I chose to fancy more than once
Before he told of Norcross. When the word
Of his release (he would have called it so)
Made half an inch of news, there were no tears
That are recorded. Women there may have been
To wish him back, though I should say, not knowing,
The few there were to mourn were not for love,
And were not lovely. Nothing of them, at least,
Was in the meagre legend that I gathered
Years after, when a chance of travel took me
So near the region of his nativity
That a few miles of leisure brought me there;
For there I found a friendly citizen
Who led me to his house among the trees
That were above a railroad and a river.
Square as a box and chillier than a tomb
It was indeed, to look at or to live in—
All which had I been told. "Ferguson died,"
The stranger said, "and then there was an auction.
I live here, but I've never yet been warm.
Remember him? Yes, I remember him.
I knew him—as a man may know a tree—
For twenty years. He may have held himself
A little high when he was here, but now . . .
Yes, I remember Ferguson. Oh, yes."

SOUVENIR

Others, I found, remembered Ferguson,
But none of them had heard of Tasker Norcross.

A SONG AT SHANNON'S

Two men came out of Shannon's, having known
The faces of each other for as long
As they had listened there to an old song,
Sung thinly in a wastrel monotone
By some unhappy night-bird, who had flown
Too many times and with a wing too strong
To save himself, and so done heavy wrong
To more frail elements than his alone.

Slowly away they went, leaving behind
More light than was before them. Neither met
The other's eyes again or said a word.
Each to his loneliness or to his kind,
Went his own way, and with his own regret,
Not knowing what the other may have heard.

SOUVENIR

A vanished house that for an hour I knew
By some forgotten chance when I was young
Had once a glimmering window overhung
With honeysuckle wet with evening dew.
Along the path tall dusky dahlias grew,
And shadowy hydrangeas reached and swung
Ferociously; and over me, among
The moths and mysteries, a blurred bat flew.

Somewhere within there were dim presences
Of days that hovered and of years gone by.
I waited, and between their silences
There was an evanescent faded noise;
And though a child, I knew it was the voice
Of one whose occupation was to die.

DISCOVERY

WE told of him as one who should have soared
And seen for us the devastating light
Whereof there is not either day or night,
And shared with us the glamour of the Word
That fell once upon Amos to record
For men at ease in Zion, when the sight
Of ills obscured aggrieved him and the might
Of Hamath was a warning of the Lord.

Assured somehow that he would make us wise,
Our pleasure was to wait; and our surprise
Was hard when we confessed the dry return
Of his regret. For we were still to learn
That earth has not a school where we may go
For wisdom, or for more than we may know.

FIRELIGHT

TEN years together without yet a cloud,
They seek each other's eyes at intervals
Of gratefulness to firelight and four walls
For love's obliteration of the crowd.
Serenely and perennially endowed
And bowered as few may be, their joy recalls

INFERENTIAL

No snake, no sword; and over them there falls
The blessing of what neither says aloud.

Wiser for silence, they were not so glad
Were she to read the graven tale of lines
On the wan face of one somewhere alone;
Nor were they more content could he have had
Her thoughts a moment since of one who shines
Apart, and would be hers if he had known.

THE NEW TENANTS

THE day was here when it was his to know
How fared the barriers he had built between
His triumph and his enemies unseen,
For them to undermine and overthrow;
And it was his no longer to forego
The sight of them, insidious and serene,
Where they were delving always and had been
Left always to be vicious and to grow.

And there were the new tenants who had come,
By doors that were left open unawares,
Into his house, and were so much at home
There now that he would hardly have to guess,
By the slow guile of their vindictiveness,
What ultimate insolence would soon be theirs.

INFERENTIAL

ALTHOUGH I saw before me there the face
Of one whom I had honored among men
The least, and on regarding him again

511

Would not have had him in another place,
He fitted with an unfamiliar grace
The coffin where I could not see him then
As I had seen him and appraised him when
I deemed him unessential to the race.

For there was more of him than .what I saw.
And there was on me more than the old awe
That is the common genius of the dead.
I might as well have heard him: "Never mind;
If some of us were not so far behind,
The rest of us were not so far ahead."

THE RAT

As often as he let himself be seen
We pitied him, or scorned him, or deplored
The inscrutable profusion of the Lord
Who shaped as one of us a thing so mean—
Who made him human when he might have been
A rat, and so been wholly in accord
With any other creature we abhorred
As always useless and not always clean.

Now he is hiding all alone somewhere,
And in a final hole not ready then;
For now he is among those over there
Who are not coming back to us again.
And we who do the fiction of our share
Say less of rats and rather more of men.

Note - dispersion, overaweinting playfulness

RAHEL TO VARNHAGEN

NOTE.—Rahel Robert and Varnhagen von Ense were married, after many protestations on her part, in 1814. The marriage—so far as he was concerned at any rate—appears to have been satisfactory.

Now you have read them all; or if not all,
As many as in all conscience I should fancy
To be enough. There are no more of them—
Or none to burn your sleep, or to bring dreams
Of devils. If these are not sufficient, surely
You are a strange young man. I might live on
Alone, and for another forty years,
Or not quite forty,—are you happier now?—
Always to ask if there prevailed elsewhere
Another like yourself that would have held
These aged hands as long as you have held them,
Not once observing, for all I can see,
How they are like your mother's. Well, you have read
His letters now, and you have heard me say
That in them are the cinders of a passion
That was my life; and you have not yet broken
Your way out of my house, out of my sight,—
Into the street. You are a strange young man.
I know as much as that of you, for certain;
And I'm already praying, for your sake,
That you be not too strange. Too much of that
May lead you bye and bye through gloomy lanes
To a sad wilderness, where one may grope
Alone, and always, or until he feels
Ferocious and invisible animals
That wait for men and eat them in the dark.
Why do you sit there on the floor so long,
Smiling at me while I try to be solemn?

Do you not hear it said for your salvation,
When I say truth? Are you, at four and twenty,
So little deceived in us that you interpret
The humor of a woman to be noticed
As her choice between you and Acheron?
Are you so unscathed yet as to infer
That if a woman worries when a man,
Or a man-child, has wet shoes on his feet
She may as well commemorate with ashes
The last eclipse of her tranquillity?
If you look up at me and blink again,
I shall not have to make you tell me lies
To know the letters you have not been reading
I see now that I may have had for nothing
A most unpleasant shivering in my conscience
When I laid open for your contemplation
The wealth of my worn casket. If I did,
The fault was not yours wholly. Search again
This wreckage we may call for sport a face,
And you may chance upon the price of havoc
That I have paid for a few sorry stones
That shine and have no light—yet once were stars,
And sparkled on a crown. Little and weak
They seem; and they are cold, I fear, for you.
But they that once were fire for me may not
Be cold again for me until I die;
And only God knows if they may be then.
There is a love that ceases to be love
In being ourselves. How, then, are we to lose it?
You that are sure that you know everything
There is to know of love, answer me that.
Well? . . . You are not even interested.

Once on a far off time when I was young,
I felt with your assurance, and all through me,

514

RAHEL TO VARNHAGEN

That I had undergone the last and worst
Of love's inventions. There was a boy who brought
The sun with him and woke me up with it,
And that was every morning; every night
I tried to dream of him, but never could,
More than I might have seen in Adam's eyes
Their fond uncertainty when Eve began
The play that all her tireless progeny
Are not yet weary of. One scene of it
Was brief, but was eternal while it lasted;
And that was while I was the happiest
Of an imaginary six or seven,
Somewhere in history but not on earth,
For whom the sky had shaken and let stars
Rain down like diamonds. Then there were clouds,
And a sad end of diamonds; whereupon
Despair came, like a blast that would have brought
Tears to the eyes of all the bears in Finland,
And love was done. That was how much I knew.
Poor little wretch! I wonder where he is
This afternoon. Out of this rain, I hope.

At last, when I had seen so many days
Dressed all alike, and in their marching order,
Go by me that I would not always count them,
One stopped—shattering the whole file of Time,
Or so it seemed; and when I looked again,
There was a man. He struck once with his eyes,
And then there was a woman. I, who had come
To wisdom, or to vision, or what you like,
By the old hidden road that has no name,—
I, who was used to seeing without flying
So much that others fly from without seeing,
Still looked, and was afraid, and looked again.
And after that, when I had read the story

Told in his eyes, and felt within my heart
The bleeding wound of their necessity,
I knew the fear was his. If I had failed him
And flown away from him, I should have lost
Ingloriously my wings in scrambling back,
And found them arms again. If he had struck me
Not only with his eyes but with his hands,
I might have pitied him and hated love,
And then gone mad. I, who have been so strong—
Why don't you laugh?—might even have done all that.
I, who have learned so much, and said so much,
And had the commendations of the great
For one who rules herself—why don't you cry?—
And own a certain small authority
Among the blind, who see no more than ever,
But like my voice,—I would have tossed it all
To Tophet for one man; and he was jealous.
I would have wound a snake around my neck
And then have let it bite me till I died,
If my so doing would have made me sure
That one man might have lived; and he was jealous.
I would have driven these hands into a cage
That held a thousand scorpions, and crushed them,
If only by so poisonous a trial
I could have crushed his doubt. I would have wrung
My living blood with mediaeval engines
Out of my screaming flesh, if only that
Would have made one man sure. I would have paid
For him the tiresome price of body and soul,
And let the lash of a tongue-weary town
Fall as it might upon my blistered name;
And while it fell I could have laughed at it,
Knowing that he had found out finally
Where the wrong was. But there was evil in him
That would have made no more of his possession

516

RAHEL TO VARNHAGEN

Than confirmation of another fault;
And there was honor—if you call it honor
That hoods itself with doubt and wears a **crown**
Of lead that might as well be gold' and fire.
Give it as heavy or as light a name
As any there is that fits. I see myself
Without the power to swear to this or that
That I might be if he had been without it.
Whatever I might have been that I was not,
It only happened that it wasn't so.
Meanwhile, you might seem to be listening:
If you forget yourself and go to sleep,
My treasure, I shall not say this again.
Look up once more into my poor old face,
Where you see beauty, or the Lord knows **what,**
And say to me aloud what else there is
Than ruins in it that you most admire.

No, there was never anything like that;
Nature has never fastened such a mask
Of radiant and impenetrable merit
On any woman as you say there is
On this one. Not a mask? I thank you, **sir,**
But you see more with your determination,
I fear, than with your prudence or your conscience;
And you have never met me with my eyes
In all the mirrors I've made faces at.
No, I shall never call you strange again:
You are the young and inconvincible
Epitome of all bl:nd men since Adam.
May the blind lead the blind. if that be so?
And we shall need no mirrors? You are saying
What most I feared you might. But if the blind,
Or one of them, be not so fortunate
As to put out the eyes of recollection,

517

She might at last, without her meaning it,
Lead on the other, without his knowing it,
Until the two of them should lose themselves
Among dead craters in a lava-field
As empty as a desert on the moon.
I am not speaking in a theatre,
But in a room so real and so familiar
That sometimes I would wreck it. Then I pause,
Remembering there is a King in Weimar—
A monarch, and a poet, and a shepherd
Of all who are astray and are outside
The realm where they should rule. I think of him,
And save the furniture; I think of you,
And am forlorn, finding in you the one
To lavish aspirations and illusions
Upon a faded and forsaken house
Where love, being locked alone, was nigh to burning
House and himself together. Yes, you are strange,
To see in such an injured architecture
Room for new love to live in. Are you laughing?
No? Well, you are not crying, as you should be.
Tears, even if they told only gratitude
For your escape, and had no other story,
Were surely more becoming than a smile
For my unwomanly straightforwardness
In seeing for you, through my close gate of years
Your forty ways to freedom. Why do you smile?
And while I'm trembling at my faith in you
In giving you to read this book of danger
That only one man living might have written—
These letters, which have been a part of me
So long that you may read them all again
As often as you look into my face,
And hear them when I speak to you, and feel them
Whenever you have to touch me with your hand,—

RAHEL TO VARNHAGEN

Why are you so unwilling to be spared?
Why do you still believe in me? But no,
I'll find another way to ask you that.
I wonder if there is another way
That says it better, and means anything.
There is no other way that could be worse?
I was not asking you; it was myself
Alone that I was asking. Why do I dip
For lies, when there is nothing in my well
But shining truth, you say? How do you know?
Truth has a lonely life down where she lives;
And many a time, when she comes up to breathe,
She sinks before we seize her, and makes ripples.
Possibly you may know no more of me
Than a few ripples; and they may soon be gone,
Leaving you then with all my shining truth
Drowned in a shining water; and when you look
You may not see me there, but something else
That never was a woman—being yourself.
You say to me my truth is past all drowning,
And safe with you for ever? You know all that?
How do you know all that, and who has told you?
You know so much that I'm an atom frightened
Because you know so little. And what is this?
You know the luxury there is in haunting
The blasted thoroughfares of disillusion—
If that's your name for them—with only ghosts
For company? You know that when a woman
Is blessed, or cursed, with a divine impatience
(Another name of yours for a bad temper)
She must have one at hand on whom to wreak it
(That's what you mean, whatever the turn you give it),
Sure of a kindred sympathy, and thereby
Effect a mutual calm? You know that wisdom,
Given in vain to make a food for those

Who are without it, will be seen at last,
And even at last only by those who gave it,
As one or more of the forgotten crumbs
That others leave? You know that men's applause
And women's envy savor so much of dust
That I go hungry, having at home no fare
But the same changeless bread that I may swallow
Only with tears and prayers? Who told you that?
You know that if I read, and read alone,
Too many books that no men yet have written,
I may go blind, or worse? You know yourself,
Of all insistent and insidious creatures,
To be the one to save me, and to guard
For me their flaming language? And you know
That if I give much headway to the whim
That's in me never to be quite sure that even
Through all those years of storm and fire I waited
For this one rainy day, I may go on,
And on, and on alone, through smoke and ashes,
To a cold end? You know so dismal much
As that about me? . . . Well, I believe you do.

NIMMO

Since you remember Nimmo, and arrive
At such a false and florid and far drawn
Confusion of odd nonsense, I connive
No longer, though I may have led you on.

So much is told and heard and told again,
So many with his legend are engrossed,
That I, more sorry now than I was then,
May live on to be sorry for his ghost.

NIMMO

[handwritten marginalia: a painter who knew N. is talking]

You knew him, and you must have known his eyes,—
How deep they were, and what a velvet light
Came out of them when anger or surprise,
Or laughter, or Francesca, made them bright.

No, you will not forget such eyes, I think,—
And you say nothing of them. Very well.
I wonder if all history's worth a wink,
Sometimes, or if my tale be one to tell.

For they began to lose their velvet light;
Their fire grew dead without and small within;
And many of you deplored the needless fight
That somewhere in the dark there must have been.

All fights are needless, when they're not our own,
But Nimmo and Francesca never fought.
Remember that; and when you are alone,
Remember me—and think what I have thought.

Now, mind you, I say nothing of what was,
Or never was, or could or could not be:
Bring not suspicion's candle to the glass
That mirrors a friend's face to memory.

Of what you see, see all,—but see no more;
For what I show you here will not be there.
The devil has had his way with paint before,
And he's an artist,—and you needn't stare.

[handwritten marginalia: these conver- remarks – momentary – cop in Palette V. – and remembering evaluation]

There was a painter and he painted well:
He'd paint you Daniel in the lion's den,
Beelzebub, Elaine, or William Tell.
I'm coming back to Nimmo's eyes again.

521

The painter put the devil in those eyes,
Unless the devil did, and there he stayed;
And then the lady fled from paradise,
And there's your fact. The lady was afraid.

She must have been afraid, or may have been,
Of evil in their velvet all the while;
But sure as I'm a sinner with a skin,
I'll trust the man as long as he can smile.

I trust him who can smile and then may live
In my heart's house, where Nimmo is today.
God knows if I have more than men forgive
To tell him; but I played, and I shall pay.

I knew him then, and if I know him yet,
I know in him, defeated and estranged,
The calm of men forbidden to forget
The calm of women who have loved and changed.

But there are ways that are beyond our ways,
Or he would not be calm and she be mute,
As one by one their lost and empty days
Pass without even the warmth of a dispute.

God help us all when women think they see;
God save us when they do. I'm fair; but though
I know him only as he looks to me,
I know him,—and I tell Francesca so.

And what of Nimmo? Little would you ask
Of him, could you but see him as I can,
At his bewildered and unfruitful task
Of being what he was born to be—a man.

Bad line

PEACE ON EARTH

Better forget that I said anything
Of what your tortured memory may disclose;
I know him, and your worst remembering
Would count as much as nothing, I suppose.

Meanwhile, I trust him; and I know his way
Of trusting me, as always in his youth.
I'm painting here a better man, you say, clever
Than I, the painter; and you say the truth.

PEACE ON EARTH

He took a frayed hat from his head,
And "Peace on Earth" was what he said.
"A morsel out of what you're worth,
And there we have it: Peace on Earth.
Not much, although a little more
Than what there was on earth before
I'm as you see, I'm Ichabod,—
But never mind the ways I've trod;
I'm sober now, so help me God."

I could not pass the fellow by.
"Do you believe in God?" said I;
"And is there to be Peace on Earth?"

"Tonight we celebrate the birth,"
He said, "of One who died for men;
The Son of God, we say. What then?
Your God, or mine? I'd make you laugh
Were I to tell you even half
That I have learned of mine today
Where yours would hardly seem to stay.

523

Could He but follow in and out
Some anthropoids I know about,
The god to whom you may have prayed
Might see a world He never made."

"Your words are flowing full," said I;
"But yet they give me no reply;
Your fountain might as well be dry."

"A wiser One than you, my friend,
Would wait and hear me to the end;
And for his eyes a light would shine
Through this unpleasant shell of mine
That in your fancy makes of me
A Christmas curiosity.
All right, I might be worse than that;
And you might now be lying flat;
I might have done it from behind,
And taken what there was to find.
Don't worry, for I'm not that kind.
Do I believe in God? Is that
The price tonight of a new hat?
Has he commanded that his name
Be written everywhere the same?
Have all who live in every place
Identified his hidden face?
Who knows but he may like as well
My story as one you may tell?
And if he show me there be Peace
On Earth, as there be fields and trees
Outside a jail-yard, am I wrong
If now I sing him a new song?
Your world is in yourself, my friend,
For your endurance to the end;
And all the Peace there is on Earth

LATE SUMMER

Is faith in what your world is worth,
And saying, without any lies,
Your world could not be otherwise."

"One might say that and then be shot,"
I told him; and he said: "Why not?"
I ceased, and gave him rather more
Than he was counting of my store.
"And since I have it, thanks to you,
Don't ask me what I mean to do,"
Said he. "Believe that even I
Would rather tell the truth than lie—
On Christmas Eve. No matter why."

His unshaved, educated face,
His inextinguishable grace.
And his hard smile, are with me still,
Deplore the vision as I will;
For whatsoever he be at,
So droll a derelict as that
Should have at least another hat.

LATE SUMMER

(ALCAICS)

CONFUSED, he found her lavishing feminine
Gold upon clay, and found her inscrutable;
    And yet she smiled. Why, then, should horrors
Be as they were, without end, her playthings?

And why were dead years hungrily telling her
Lies of the dead, who told them again to her?
    If now she knew, there might be kindness
Clamoring yet where a faith lay stifled.

COLLECTED POEMS

A little faith in him, and the ruinous
Past would be for time to annihilate,
    And wash out, like a tide that washes
Out of the sand what a child has drawn there.

God, what a shining handful of happiness,
Made out of days and out of eternities,
    Were now the pulsing end of patience—
Could he but have what a ghost had stolen!

What was a man before him, or ten of them,
While he was here alive who could answer them,
    And in their teeth fling confirmations
Harder than agates against an egg-shell?

But now the man was dead, and would come again
Never, though she might honor ineffably
    The flimsy wraith of him she conjured
Out of a dream with his wand of absence.

And if the truth were now but a mummery,
Meriting pride's implacable irony,
    So much the worse for pride. Moreover,
Save her or fail, there was conscience always.

Meanwhile, a few misgivings of innocence,
Imploring to be sheltered and credited,
    Were not amiss when she revealed them.
Whether she struggled or not, he saw them.

Also, he saw that while she was hearing him
Her eyes had more and more of the past in them,
    And while he told what cautious honor
Told him was all he had best be sure of,

526

"The truth" - that is, the man isn't worth her memory.

LATE SUMMER

his hopes for her —

He wondered once or twice, inadvertently,
Where shifting winds were driving his argosies,
  Long anchored and as long unladen,
Over the foam for the golden chances.

— Jamesian

He:

"If men were not for killing so carelessly,
And women were for wiser endurances," —
  He said, "we might have yet a world here
Fitter for Truth to be seen abroad in;

foolishness as is Reality vs Truth

he thinks we have to see it

"If Truth were not so strange in her nakedness,
And we were less forbidden to look at it,
  We might not have to look." He stared then
Down at the sand where the tide threw forward

symbolism —
This is eg } how romantics learned from the 19th Cent?

his calm outwardly

Its cold, unconquered lines, that unceasingly
Foamed against hope, and fell. He was calm enough,
  Although he knew he might be silenced
Out of all calm; and the night was coming.

her speech

He cont:

"I climb for you the peak of his infamy
That you may choose your fall if you cling to it.
  No more for me unless you say more.
All you have left of a dream defends you:

ie he exposes it to her so that she'll know her fault if she stays with it. He can't do more

"The truth may be as evil an augury
As it was needful now for the two of us.
  We cannot have the dead between us.
Tell me to go, and I go."—She pondered:

ie the truth separates them

type of concentration

"What you believe is right for the two of us
Makes it as right that you are not one of us.
  If this be needful truth you tell me,
Spare me, and let me have lies hereafter."

note truth: the speaker & woman she refuses the dead & the woman

527

she chooses lies

She gazed away where shadows were covering
The whole cold ocean's healing indifference.
No ship was coming. When the darkness
Fell, she was there, and alone, still gazing.

AN EVANGELIST'S WIFE

"Why am I not myself these many days,
You ask? And have you nothing more to ask?
I do you wrong? I do not hear your praise
To God for giving you me to share your task?

"Jealous—of Her? Because her cheeks are pink,
And she has eyes? No, not if she had seven.
If you should only steal an hour to think,
Sometime, there might be less to be forgiven.

"No, you are never cruel. If once or twice
I found you so, I could applaud and sing.
Jealous of—What? You are not very wise.
Does not the good Book tell you anything?

"In David's time poor Michal had to go.
Jealous of God? Well, if you like it so."

THE OLD KING'S NEW JESTER

You that in vain would front the coming order
With eyes that meet forlornly what they must,
And only with a furtive recognition
See dust where there is dust,—
Be sure you like it always in your faces,

THE OLD KING'S NEW JESTER

Obscuring your best graces,
Blinding your speech and sight,
Before you seek again your dusty places
Where the old wrong seems right.

Longer ago than cave-men had their changes
Our fathers may have slain a son or two,
Discouraging a further dialectic
Regarding what was new;
And after their unstudied admonition
Occasional contrition
For their old-fashioned ways
May have reduced their doubts, and in addition
Softened their final days.

Farther away than feet shall ever travel
Are the vague towers of our unbuilded State;
But there are mightier things than we to lead us,
That will not let us wait.
And we go on with none to tell us whether
Or not we've each a tether
Determining how fast or far we go;
And it is well, since we must go together,
That we are not to know.

If the old wrong and all its injured glamour
Haunts you by day and gives your night no peace,
You may as well, agreeably and serenely,
Give the new wrong its lease;
For should you nourish a too fervid yearning
For what is not returning,
The vicious and unfused ingredient
May give you qualms—and one or two concerning
The last of your content.

LAZARUS

"No, Mary, there was nothing—not a word.
Nothing, and always nothing. Go again
Yourself, and he may listen—or at least
Look up at you, and let you see his eyes.
I might as well have been the sound of rain,
A wind among the cedars, or a bird;
Or nothing. Mary, make him look at you;
And even if he should say that we are nothing,
To know that you have heard him will be something.
And yet he loved us, and it was for love
The Master gave him back. Why did he wait
So long before he came? Why did he weep?
I thought he would be glad—and Lazarus—
To see us all again as he had left us—
All as it was, all as it was before."

Mary, who felt her sister's frightened arms
Like those of someone drowning who had seized her,
Fearing at last they were to fail and sink
Together in this fog-stricken sea of strangeness,
Fought sadly, with bereaved indignant eyes,
To find again the fading shores of home
That she had seen but now could see no longer
Now she could only gaze into the twilight,
And in the dimness know that he was there,
Like someone that was not. He who had been
Their brother, and was dead, now seemed alive
Only in death again—or worse than death;
For tombs at least, always until today,
Though sad were certain. There was nothing certain
For man or God in such a day as this;
For there they were alone, and there was he—

530

Alone; and somewhere out of Bethany,
The Master—who had come to them so late,
Only for love of them and then so slowly,
And was for their sake hunted now by men
Who feared Him as they feared no other prey—
For the world's sake was hidden. "Better the tomb
For Lazarus than life, if this be life,"
She thought; and then to Martha, "No, my dear,"
She said aloud; "not as it was before.
Nothing is ever as it was before,
Where Time has been. Here there is more than Time;
And we that are so lonely and so far
From home, since he is with us here again,
Are farther now from him and from ourselves
Than we are from the stars. He will not speak
Until the spirit that is in him speaks;
And we must wait for all we are to know,
Or even to learn that we are not to know.
Martha, we are too near to this for knowledge,
And that is why it is that we must wait.
Our friends are coming if we call for them,
And there are covers we'll put over him
To make him warmer. We are too young, perhaps,
To say that we know better what is best
Than he. We do not know how old he is.
If you remember what the Master said,
Try to believe that we need have no fear.
Let me, the selfish and the careless one,
Be housewife and a mother for tonight;
For I am not so fearful as you are,
And I was not so eager."

                              Martha sank
Down at her sister's feet and there sat watching
A flower that had a small familiar name

That was as old as memory, but was not
The name of what she saw now in its brief
And infinite mystery that so frightened her
That life became a terror. Tears again
Flooded her eyes and overflowed. "No, Mary,"
She murmured slowly, hating her own words
Before she heard them, "you are not so eager
To see our brother as we see him now;
Neither is he who gave him back to us.
I was to be the simple one, as always,
And this was all for me." She stared again
Over among the trees where Lazarus,
Who seemed to be a man who was not there,
Might have been one more shadow among shadows,
If she had not remembered. Then she felt
The cool calm hands of Mary on her face,
And shivered, wondering if such hands were real.

"The Master loved you as he loved us all,
Martha; and you are saying only things
That children say when they have had no sleep.
Try somehow now to rest a little while;
You know that I am here, and that our friends
Are coming if I call."

                              Martha at last
Arose, and went with Mary to the door,
Where they stood looking off at the same place,
And at the same shape that was always there
As if it would not ever move or speak,
And always would be there. "Mary, go now,
Before the dark that will be coming hides him.
I am afraid of him out there alone,
Unless I see him; and I have forgotten
What sleep is. Go now—make him look at you—

And I shall hear him if he stirs or whispers.
Go!—or I'll scream and bring all Bethany
To come and make him speak. Make him say once
That he is glad, and God may say the rest.
Though He say I shall sleep, and sleep for ever,
I shall not care for that . . . Go!"

                                    Mary, moving
Almost as if an angry child had pushed her,
Went forward a few steps; and having waited
As long as Martha's eyes would look at hers,
Went forward a few more, and a few more;
And so, until she came to Lazarus,
Who crouched with his face hidden in his hands,
Like one that had no face. Before she spoke,
Feeling her sister's eyes that were behind her
As if the door where Martha stood were now
As far from her as Egypt, Mary turned
Once more to see that she was there. Then, softly,
Fearing him not so much as wondering
What his first word might be, said, "Lazarus,
Forgive us if we seemed afraid of you;"
And having spoken, pitied her poor speech
That had so little seeming gladness in it,
So little comfort, and so little love.

There was no sign from him that he had heard,
Or that he knew that she was there, or cared
Whether she spoke to him again or died
There at his feet. "We love you, Lazarus,
And we are not afraid. The Master said
We need not be afraid. Will you not say
To me that you are glad? Look, Lazarus!
Look at my face, and see me. This is Mary."

533

She found his hands and held them. They were cool,
Like hers, but they were not so calm as hers.
Through the white robes in which his friends had wrapped him
When he had groped out of that awful sleep,
She felt him trembling and she was afraid.
At last he sighed; and she prayed hungrily
To God that she might hear again the voice
Of Lazarus, whose hands were giving her now
The recognition of a living pressure
That was almost a language. When he spoke,
Only one word that she had waited for
Came from his lips, and that word was her name.

"I heard them saying, Mary, that he wept
Before I woke." The words were low and shaken,
Yet Mary knew that he who uttered them
Was Lazarus; and that would be enough
Until there should be more . . . "Who made him come,
That he should weep for me? . . . Was it you, Mary?"
The questions held in his incredulous eyes
Were more than she would see. She looked away;
But she had felt them and should feel for ever,
She thought, their cold and lonely desperation
That had the bitterness of all cold things
That were not cruel. "I should have wept," he said,
"If I had been the Master. . . ."

                              Now she could feel
His hands above her hair—the same black hair
That once he made a jest of, praising it,
While Martha's busy eyes had left their work
To flash with laughing envy. Nothing of that
Was to be theirs again; and such a thought
Was like the flying by of a quick bird
Seen through a shadowy doorway in the twilight.

For now she felt his hands upon her head,
Like weights of kindness: "I forgive you, Mary. . . .
You did not know—Martha could not have known—
Only the Master knew. . . . Where is he now?
Yes, I remember. They came after him.
May the good God forgive him. . . . I forgive him.
I must; and I may know only from him
The burden of all this. . . Martha was here—
But I was not yet here. She was afraid. . . .
Why did he do it, Mary? Was it—you?
Was it for you? . . . Where are the friends I saw?
Yes, I remember. They all went away.
I made them go away. . . . Where is he now? . . .
What do I see down there? Do I see Martha—
Down by the door? . . . I must have time for this."

Lazarus looked about him fearfully,
And then again at Mary, who discovered
Awakening apprehension in his eyes,
And shivered at his feet. All she had feared
Was here; and only in the slow reproach
Of his forgiveness lived his gratitude.
Why had he asked if it was all for her
That he was here? And what had Martha meant?
Why had the Master waited? What was coming
To Lazarus, and to them, that had not come?
What had the Master seen before he came,
That he had come so late?

              "Where is he, Mary?"
Lazarus asked again. "Where did he go?"
Once more he gazed about him, and once more
At Mary for an answer. "Have they found him?
Or did he go away because he wished

Never to look into my eyes again? . . .
That, I could understand. . . . Where is he, Mary?"

"I do not know," she said. "Yet in my heart
I know that he is living, as you are living—
Living, and here. He is not far from us.
He will come back to us and find us all—
Lazarus, Martha, Mary—everything—
All as it was before. Martha said that.
And he said we were not to be afraid."
Lazarus closed his eyes while on his face
A tortured adumbration of a smile
Flickered an instant. "All as it was before,"
He murmured wearily. "Martha said that;
And he said you were not to be afraid . . .
Not you . . . Not you . . . Why should you be afraid?
Give all your little fears, and Martha's with them,
To me; and I will add them unto mine,
Like a few rain-drops to Gennesaret."

"If you had frightened me in other ways,
Not willing it," Mary said, "I should have known
You still for Lazarus. But who is this?
Tell me again that you are Lazarus;
And tell me if the Master gave to you
No sign of a new joy that shall be coming
To this house that he loved. Are you afraid?
Are you afraid, who have felt everything—
And seen . . . ?"

But Lazarus only shook his head,
Staring with his bewildered shining eyes
Hard into Mary's face. "I do not know,
Mary," he said, and after a long time,
"When I came back, I knew the Master's eyes

Were looking into mine. I looked at his,
And there was more in them than I could see.
At first I could see nothing but his eyes;
Nothing else anywhere was to be seen—
Only his eyes. And they looked into mine—
Long into mine, Mary, as if he knew."

Mary began to be afraid of words
As she had never been afraid before
Of loneliness or darkness, or of death,
But now she must have more of them or die:
"He cannot know that there is worse than death,"
She said. "And you . . ."

          "Yes, there is worse than death."
Said Lazarus; "and that was what he knew;
And that is what it was that I could see
This morning in his eyes. I was afraid,
But not as you are. There is worse than death,
Mary; and there is nothing that is good
For you in dying while you are still here.
Mary, never go back to that again.
You would not hear me if I told you more,
For I should say it only in a language
That you are not to learn by going back.
To be a child again is to go forward—
And that is much to know. Many grow old,
And fade, and go away, not knowing how much
That is to know. Mary, the night is coming,
And there will soon be darkness all around you.
Let us go down where Martha waits for us,
And let there be light shining in this house."

He rose, but Mary would not let him go:
"Martha, when she came back from here, said only

That she heard nothing. And have you no more
For Mary now than you had then for Martha?
Is Nothing, Lazarus, all you have for me?
Was Nothing all you found where you have been?
If that be so, what is there worse than that—
Or better—if that be so? And why should you,
With even our love, go the same dark road over?"

"I could not answer that, if that were so,"
Said Lazarus,—"not even if I were God.
Why should He care whether I came or stayed,
If that were so? Why should the Master weep—
For me, or for the world,—or save himself
Longer for nothing? And if that were so,
Why should a few years' more mortality
Make him a fugitive where flight were needless,
Had he but held his peace and given his nod
To an old Law that would be new as any?
I cannot say the answer to all that;
Though I may say that he is not afraid,
And that it is not for the joy there is
In serving an eternal Ignorance
Of our futility that he is here.
Is that what you and Martha mean by Nothing?
Is that what you are fearing? · If that be so,
There are more weeds than lentils in your garden.
And one whose weeds are laughing at his harvest
May as well have no garden; for not there
Shall he be gleaning the few bits and orts
Of life that are to save him. For my part,
I am again with you, here among shadows
That will not always be so dark as this;
Though now I see there's yet an evil in me
That made me let you be afraid of me.
No, I was not afraid—not even of life.

538

LAZARUS

I thought I was . . . I must have time for this;
And all the time there is will not be long.
I cannot tell you what the Master saw
This morning in my eyes. I do not know.
I cannot yet say how far I have gone,
Or why it is that I am here again,
Or where the old road leads. I do not know.
I know that when I did come back, I saw
His eyes again among the trees and faces—
Only his eyes; and they looked into mine—
Long into mine—long, long, as if he knew."

AVON'S HARVEST, ETC.

(1921)

To Seth Ellis Pope

AVON'S HARVEST

Fear, like a living fire that only death
Might one day cool, had now in Avon's eyes
Been witness for so long of an invasion
That made of a gay friend whom we had known
Almost a memory, wore no other name
As yet for us than fear. Another man
Than Avon might have given to us at least
A futile opportunity for words
We might regret. But Avon, since it happened,
Fed with his unrevealing reticence
The fire of death we saw that horribly
Consumed him while he crumbled and said nothing.

So many a time had I been on the edge,
And off again, of a foremeasured fall
Into the darkness and discomfiture
Of his oblique rebuff, that finally
My silence honored his, holding itself
Away from a gratuitous intrusion
That likely would have widened a new distance
Already wide enough, if not so new.
But there are seeming parallels in space
That may converge in time; and so it was
I walked with Avon, fought and pondered with him,
While he made out a case for So-and-so,
Or slaughtered What's-his-name in his old way,
With a new difference. Nothing in Avon lately

Was, or was ever again to be for us,
Like him that we remembered; and all the while
We saw that fire at work within his eyes
And had no glimpse of what was burning there.

So for a year it went; and so it went
For half another year—when, all at once,
At someone's tinkling afternoon at home
I saw that in the eyes of Avon's wife
The fire that I had met the day before
In his had found another living fuel.
To look at her and then to think of him,
And thereupon to contemplate the fall
Of a dim curtain over the dark end
Of a dark play, required of me no more
Clairvoyance than a man who cannot swim
Will exercise in seeing that his friend
Off shore will drown except he save himself.
To her I could say nothing, and to him
No more than tallied with a long belief
That I should only have it back again
For my chagrin to ruminate upon,
Ingloriously, for the still time it starved;
And that would be for me as long a time
As I remembered Avon—who is yet
Not quite forgotten. On the other hand,
For saying nothing I might have with me always
An injured and recriminating ghost
Of a dead friend. The more I pondered it
The more I knew there was not much to lose,
Albeit for one whose delving hitherto
Had been a forage of his own affairs,
The quest, however golden the reward,
Was irksome—and as Avon suddenly
And soon was driven to let me see, was needless.

It seemed an age ago that we were there
One evening in the room that in the days
When they could laugh he called the Library.
"He calls it that, you understand," she said,
"Because the dictionary always lives here.
He's not a man of books, yet he can read,
And write. He learned it all at school."—He smiled
And answered with a fervor that rang then
Superfluous: "Had I learned a little more
At school, it might have been as well for me."
And I remember now that he paused then,
Leaving a silence that one had to break.
But this was long ago, and there was now
No laughing in that house. We were alone
This time, and it was Avon's time to talk.

I waited, and anon became aware
That I was looking less at Avon's eyes
Than at the dictionary, like one asking
Already why we make so much of words
That have so little weight in the true balance.
"Your name is Resignation for an hour,"
He said; "and I'm a little sorry for you.
So be resigned. I shall not praise your work,
Or strive in any way to make you happy.
My purpose only is to make you know
How clearly I have known that you have known
There was a reason waited on your coming,
And, if it's in me to see clear enough,
To fish the reason out of a black well
Where you see only a dim sort of glimmer
That has for you no light."

                              "I see the well,"
I said, "but there's a doubt about the glimmer—

Say nothing of the light. I'm at your service;
And though you say that I shall not be happy,
I shall be if in some way I may serve.
To tell you fairly now that I know nothing
Is nothing more than fair."—"You know as much
As any man alive—save only one man,
If he's alive. Whether he lives or not
Is rather for time to answer than for me;
And that's a reason, or a part of one,
For your appearance here. You do not know him,
And even if you should pass him in the street
He might go by without your feeling him
Between you and the world. I cannot say
Whether he would, but I suppose he might."

"And I suppose you might, if urged," I said,
"Say in what water it is that we are fishing.
You that have reasons hidden in a well,
Not mentioning all your nameless friends that walk
The streets and are not either dead or living
For company, are surely, one would say
To be forgiven if you may seem distraught—
I mean distrait. I don't know what I mean.
I only know that I am at your service,
Always, yet with a special reservation
That you may deem eccentric. All the same
Unless your living dead man comes to life,
Or is less indiscriminately dead,
I shall go home."

                    "No, you will not go home,"
Said Avon; "or I beg that you will not."
So saying, he went slowly to the door
And turned the key. "Forgive me and my manners
But I would be alone with you this evening.

The key, as you observe, is in the lock;
And you may sit between me and the door,
Or where you will. You have my word of honor
That I would spare you the least injury
That might attend your presence here this evening."

"I thank you for your soothing introduction,
Avon," I said. "Go on. The Lord giveth,
The Lord taketh away. I trust myself
Always to you and to your courtesy.
Only remember that I cling somewhat
Affectionately to the old tradition."—
"I understand you and your part," said Avon;
"And I dare say it's well enough, tonight,
We play around the circumstance a little.
I've read of men that half way to the stake
Would have their little joke. It's well enough;
Rather a waste of time, but well enough."

I listened as I waited, and heard steps
Outside of one who paused and then went on;
And, having heard, I might as well have seen
The fear in his wife's eyes. He gazed away,
As I could see, in helpless thought of her,
And said to me: "Well, then, it was like this.
Some tales will have a deal of going back
In them before they are begun. But this one
Begins in the beginning—when he came.
I was a boy at school, sixteen years old,
And on my way, in all appearances,
To mark an even-tempered average
Among the major mediocrities
Who serve and earn with no especial noise
Or vast reward. I saw myself, even then,
A light for no high shining; and I feared

547

No boy or man—having, in truth, no cause.
I was enough a leader to be free,
And not enough a hero to be jealous.
Having eyes and ears, I knew that I was envied,
And as a proper sort of compensation
Had envy of my own for two or three—
But never felt, and surely never gave,
The wound of any more malevolence
Than decent youth, defeated for a day,
May take to bed with him and kill with sleep.
So, and so far, my days were going well,
And would have gone so, but for the black tiger
That many of us fancy is in waiting,
But waits for most of us in fancy only.
For me there was no fancy in his coming,
Though God knows I had never summoned him,
Or thought of him. To this day I'm adrift
And in the dark, out of all reckoning,
To find a reason why he ever was,
Or what was ailing Fate when he was born
On this alleged God-ordered earth of ours.
Now and again there comes one of his kind—
By chance, we say. I leave all that to you.
Whether it was an evil chance alone,
Or some invidious juggling of the stars,
Or some accrued arrears of ancestors
Who throve on debts that I was here to pay,
Or sins within me that I knew not of,
Or just a foretaste of what waits in hell
For those of us who cannot love a worm,—
Whatever it was, or whence or why it was,
One day there came a stranger to the school.
And having had one mordacious glimpse of him
That filled my eyes and was to fill my life,
I have known Peace only as one more word

Among the many others we say over
That have an airy credit of no meaning.
One of these days, if I were seeing many
To live, I might erect a cenotaph
To Job's wife. I assume that you remember;
If you forget, she's extant in your Bible."

Now this was not the language of a man
Whom I had known as Avon, and I winced
Hearing it—though I knew that in my heart
There was no visitation of surprise.
Unwelcome as it was, and off the key
Calamitously, it overlived a silence
That was itself a story and affirmed
A savage emphasis of honesty
That I would only gladly have attuned
If possible, to vinous innovation.
But his indifferent wassailing was always
Too far within the measure of excess
For that; and then there were those eyes of his.
Avon indeed had kept his word with me,
And there was not much yet to make me happy.

"So there we were," he said, "we two together,
Breathing one air. And how shall I go on
To say by what machinery the slow net
Of my fantastic and increasing hate
Was ever woven as it was around us?
I cannot answer; and you need not ask
What undulating reptile he was like,
For such a worm as I discerned in him
Was never yet on earth or in the ocean,
Or anywhere else than in my sense of him.
Had all I made of him been tangible,
The Lord must have invented long ago

549

Some private and unspeakable new monster
Equipped for such a thing's extermination;
Whereon the monster, seeing no other monster
Worth biting, would have died with his work done.
There's a humiliation in it now,
As there was then, and worse than there was then;
For then there was the boy to shoulder it
Without the sickening weight of added years
Galling him to the grave. Beware of hate
That has no other boundary than the grave
Made for it, or for ourselves. Beware, I say;
And I'm a sorry one, I fear, to say it,
Though for the moment we may let that go
And while I'm interrupting my own story
I'll ask of you the favor of a look
Into the street. I like it when it's empty.
There's only one man walking? Let him walk.
I wish to God that all men might walk always,
And so, being busy, love one another more."

"Avon," I said, now in my chair again,
"Although I may not be here to be happy,
If you are careless, I may have to laugh.
I have disliked a few men in my life,
But never to the scope of wishing them
To this particular pedestrian hell
Of your affection. I should not like that.
Forgive me, for this time it was your fault."

He drummed with all his fingers on his chair,
And, after a made smile of acquiescence,
Took up again the theme of his aversion,
Which now had flown along with him alone
For twenty years, like Io's evil insect,
To sting him when it would. The decencies

550

Forbade that I should look at him for ever,
Yet many a time I found myself ashamed
Of a long staring at him, and as often
Essayed the dictionary on the table,
Wondering if in its interior
There was an uncompanionable word
To say just what was creeping in my hair,
At which my scalp would shrink,—at which, again,
I would arouse myself with a vain scorn,
Remembering that all this was in New York—
As if that were somehow the banishing
For ever of all unseemly presences—
And listen to the story of my friend,
Who, as I feared, was not for me to save,
And, as I knew, knew also that I feared it.

"Humiliation," he began again,
"May be or not the best of all bad names
I might employ; and if you scent remorse,
There may be growing such a flower as that
In the unsightly garden where I planted,
Not knowing the seed or what was coming of it.
I've done much wondering if I planted it;
But our poor wonder, when it comes too late,
Fights with a lath, and one that solid fact
Breaks while it yawns and looks another way
For a less negligible adversary.
Away with wonder, then; though I'm at odds
With conscience, even tonight, for good assurance
That it was I, or chance and I together,
Did all that sowing. If I seem to you
To be a little bitten by the question,
Without a miracle it might be true;
The miracle is to me that I'm not eaten
Long since to death of it, and that you sit

With nothing more agreeable than a ghost.
If you had thought a while of that, you might,
Unhappily, not have come; and your not coming
Would have been desolation—not for you,
God save the mark!—for I would have you here.
I shall not be alone with you to listen;
And I should be far less alone tonight
With you away, make what you will of that.

"I said that we were going back to school,
And we may say that we are there—with him.
This fellow had no friend, and, as for that,
No sign of an apparent need of one,
Save always and alone—myself. He fixed
His heart and eyes on me, insufferably,—
And in a sort of Nemesis-like way,
Invincibly. Others who might have given
A welcome even to him, or I'll suppose so—
Adorning an unfortified assumption
With gold that might come off with afterthought—
Got never, if anything, more out of him
Than a word flung like refuse in their faces,
And rarely that. For God knows what good reason,
He lavished his whole altered arrogance
On me; and with an overweening skill,
Which had sometimes almost a cringing in it,
Found a few flaws in my tight mail of hate
And slowly pricked a poison into me
In which at first I failed at recognizing
An unfamiliar subtle sort of pity.
But so it was, and I believe he knew it;
Though even to dream it would have been absurd—
Until I knew it, and there was no need
Of dreaming. For the fellow's indolence.
And his malignant oily swarthiness

552

Housing a reptile blood that I could see
Beneath it, like hereditary venom
Out of old human swamps, hardly revealed
Itself the proper spawning-ground of pity.
But so it was. Pity, or something like it,
Was in the poison of his proximity;
For nothing else that I have any name for
Could have invaded and so mastered me
With a slow tolerance that eventually
Assumed a blind ascendency of custom
That saw not even itself. When I came in,
Often I'd find him strewn along my couch
Like an amorphous lizard with its clothes on,
Reading a book and waiting for its dinner.
His clothes were always odiously in order,
Yet I should not have thought of him as clean—
Not even if he had washed himself to death
Proving it. There was nothing right about him.
Then he would search, never quite satisfied,
Though always in a measure confident,
My eyes to find a welcome waiting in them,
Unwilling, as I see him now, to know
That it would never be there. Looking back,
I am not sure that he would not have died
For me, if I were drowning or on fire,
Or that I would not rather have let myself
Die twice than owe the debt of my survival
To him, though he had lost not even his clothes.
No, there was nothing right about that fellow;
And after twenty years to think of him
I should be quite as helpless now to serve him
As I was then. I mean—without my story.
Be patient, and you'll see just what I mean—
Which is to say, you won't. But you can listen,
And that's itself a large accomplishment

Uncrowned; and may be, at a time like this,
A mighty charity. It was in January
This evil genius came into our school,
And it was June when he went out of it—
If I may say that he was wholly out
Of any place that I was in thereafter.
But he was not yet gone. When we are told
By Fate to bear what we may never bear,
Fate waits a little while to see what happens;
And this time it was only for the season
Between the swift midwinter holidays
And the long progress into weeks and months
Of all the days that followed—with him there
To make them longer. I would have given an eye,
Before the summer came, to know for certain
That I should never be condemned again
To see him with the other; and all the while
There was a battle going on within me
Of hate that fought remorse—if you must have it—
Never to win, . . . never to win but once,
And having won, to lose disastrously,
And as it was to prove, interminably—
Or till an end of living may annul,
If so it be, the nameless obligation
That I have not the Christian revenue
In me to pay. A man who has no gold,
Or an equivalent, shall pay no gold
Until by chance or labor or contrivance
He makes it his to pay; and he that has
No kindlier commodity than hate,
Glossed with a pity that belies itself
In its negation and lacks alchemy
To fuse itself to—love, would you have me say?
I don't believe it. No, there is no such word.
If I say tolerance, there's no more to say.

And he who sickens even in saying that—
What coin of God has he to pay the toll
To peace on earth? Good will to men—oh, yes!
That's easy; and it means no more than sap,
Until we boil the water out of it
Over the fire of sacrifice. I'll do it;
And in a measurable way I've done it—
But not for him. What are you smiling at?
Well, so it went until a day in June.
We were together under an old elm,
Which now, I hope, is gone—though it's a crime
In me that I should have to wish the death
Of such a tree as that. There were no trees
Like those that grew at school—until he came.
We stood together under it that day,
When he, by some ungovernable chance,
All foreign to the former crafty care
That he had used never to cross my favor,
Told of a lie that stained a friend of mine
With a false blot that a few days washed off.
A trifle now, but a boy's honor then—
Which then was everything. There were some words
Between us, but I don't remember them.
All I remember is a bursting flood
Of half a year's accumulated hate,
And his incredulous eyes before I struck him.
He had gone once too far; and when he knew it,
He knew it was all over; and I struck him.
Pound for pound, he was the better brute;
But bulking in the way then of my fist
And all there was alive in me to drive it,
Three of him misbegotten into one
Would have gone down like him—and being larger,
Might have bled more, if that were necessary.
He came up soon; and if I live for ever,

The vengeance in his eyes, and a weird gleam
Of desolation—if I make you see it—
Will be before me as it is tonight.
I shall not ever know how long it was
I waited his attack that never came;
It might have been an instant or an hour
That I stood ready there, watching his eyes,
And the tears running out of them. They made
Me sick, those tears; for I knew, miserably,
They were not there for any pain he felt.
I do not think he felt the pain at all.
He felt the blow. . . . Oh, the whole thing was bad—
So bad that even the bleaching suns and rains
Of years that wash away to faded lines,
Or blot out wholly, the sharp wrongs and ills
Of youth, have had no cleansing agent in them
To dim the picture. I still see him going
Away from where I stood; and I shall see him
Longer, sometime, than I shall see the face
Of whosoever watches by the bed
On which I die—given I die that way.
I doubt if he could reason his advantage
In living any longer after that
Among the rest of us. The lad he slandered,
Or gave a negative immunity
No better than a stone he might have thrown
Behind him at his head, was of the few
I might have envied; and for that being known,
My fury became sudden history,
And I a sudden hero. But the crown
I wore was hot; and I would happily
Have hurled it, if I could, so far away
That over my last hissing glimpse of it
There might have closed an ocean. He went home
The next day, and the same unhappy chance

That first had fettered me and my aversion
To his unprofitable need of me
Brought us abruptly face to face again
Beside the carriage that had come for him.
We met, and for a moment we were still—
Together. But I was reading in his eyes
More than I read at college or at law
In years that followed. There was blankly nothing
For me to say, if not that I was sorry;
And that was more than hate would let me say—
Whatever the truth might be. At last he spoke,
And I could see the vengeance in his eyes,
And a cold sorrow—which, if I had seen
Much more of it, might yet have mastered me.
But I would see no more of it. 'Well, then,'
He said, 'have you thought yet of anything
Worth saying? If so, there's time. If you are silent,
I shall know where you are until you die.'
I can still hear him saying those words to me
Again, without a loss or an addition;
I know, for I have heard them ever since.
And there was in me not an answer for them
Save a new roiling silence. Once again
I met his look, and on his face I saw
There was a twisting in the swarthiness
That I had often sworn to be the cast
Of his ophidian mind. He had no soul.
There was to be no more of him—not then.
The carriage rolled away with him inside,
Leaving the two of us alive together
In the same hemisphere to hate each other.
I don't know now whether he's here alive,
Or whether he's here dead. But that, of course,
As you would say, is only a tired man's fancy.
You know that I have driven the wheels too fast

Of late, and all for gold I do not need.
When are we mortals to be sensible,
Paying no more for life than life is worth?
Better for us, no doubt, we do not know
How much we pay or what it is we buy."
He waited, gazing at me as if asking
The worth of what the universe had for sale
For one confessed remorse. Avon, I knew,
Had driven the wheels too fast, and not for gold.

"If you had given him then your hand," I said,
"And spoken, though it strangled you, the truth,
I should not have the melancholy honor
Of sitting here alone with you this evening.
If only you had shaken hands with him,
And said the truth, he would have gone his way,
And you your way. He might have wished you dead,
But he would not have made you miserable.
At least," I added, indefensibly,
"That's what I hope is true."

                      He pitied me,
But had the magnanimity not to say so.
"If only we had shaken hands," he said,
"And I had said the truth, we might have been
In half a moment rolling on the gravel.
If I had said the truth, I should have said
That never at any moment on the clock
Above us in the tower since his arrival
Had I been in a more proficient mood
To throttle him. If you had seen his eyes
As I did, and if you had seen his face
At work as I did, you might understand.
I was ashamed of it, as I am now,
But that's the prelude to another theme;

For now I'm saying only what had happened •
If I had taken his hand and said the truth.
The wise have cautioned us that where there's hate
There's also fear. The wise are right sometimes.
There may be now, but there was no fear then.
There was just hatred, hauled up out of hell
For me to writhe in; and I writhed in it."

I saw that he was writhing in it still;
But having a magnanimity myself,
I waited. There was nothing else to do
But wait, and to remember that his tale,
Though well along, as I divined it was,
Yet hovered among shadows and regrets
Of twenty years ago. When he began
Again to speak, I felt them coming nearer.

"Whenever your poet or your philosopher
Has nothing richer for us," he resumed,
"He burrows among remnants, like a mouse
In a waste-basket, and with much dry noise
Comes up again, having found Time at the bottom
And filled himself with its futility.
'Time is at once,' he says, to startle us,
'A poison for us, if we make it so,
And, if we make it so, an antidote
For the same poison that afflicted us.'
I'm witness to the poison, but the cure
Of my complaint is not, for me, in Time.
There may be doctors in eternity
To deal with it, but they are not here now.
There's no specific for my three diseases
That I could swallow, even if I should find it,
And I shall never find it here on earth."

559

"Mightn't it be as well, my friend," I said,
"For you to contemplate the uncompleted
With not such an infernal certainty?"

"And mightn't it be as well for you, my friend,"
Said Avon, "to be quiet while I go on?
When I am done, then you may talk all night—
Like a physician who can do no good,
But knows how soon another would have his fee
Were he to tell the truth. Your fee for this
Is in my gratitude and my affection;
And I'm not eager to be calling in
Another to take yours away from you,
Whatever it's worth. I like to think I know.
Well then, again. The carriage rolled away
With him inside; and so it might have gone
For ten years rolling on, with him still in it,
For all it was I saw of him. Sometimes
I heard of him, but only as one hears
Of leprosy in Boston or New York
And wishes it were somewhere else. He faded
Out of my scene—yet never quite out of it:
'I shall know where you are until you die,'
Were his last words; and they are the same words
That I received thereafter once a year,
Infallibly on my birthday, with no name;
Only a card, and the words printed on it.
No, I was never rid of him—not quite;
Although on shipboard, on my way from here
To Hamburg, I believe that I forgot him.
But once ashore, I should have been half ready
To meet him there, risen up out of the ground,
With hoofs and horns and tail and everything.
Believe me, there was nothing right about him,

Though it was not in Hamburg that I found him,
Later, in Rome, it was we found each other,
For the first time since we had been at school.
There was the same slow vengeance in his eyes
When he saw mine, and there was a vicious twist
On his amphibious face that might have been
On anything else a smile—rather like one
We look for on the stage than in the street.
I must have been a yard away from him
Yet as we passed I felt the touch of him
Like that of something soft in a dark room.
There's hardly need of saying that we said nothing,
Or that we gave each other an occasion
For more than our eyes uttered. He was gone
Before I knew it, like a solid phantom;
And his reality was for me some time
In its achievement—given that one's to be
Convinced that such an incubus at large
Was ever quite real. The season was upon us
When there are fitter regions in the world—
Though God knows he would have been safe enough—
Than Rome for strayed Americans to live in,
And when the whips of their itineraries
Hurry them north again. I took my time,
Since I was paying for it, and leisurely
Went where I would—though never again to move
Without him at my elbow or behind me.
My shadow of him, wherever I found myself,
Might horribly as well have been the man—
Although I should have been afraid of him
No more than of a large worm in a salad.
I should omit the salad, certainly,
And wish the worm elsewhere. And so he was,
In fact; yet as I go on to grow older,
I question if there's anywhere a fact

That isn't the malevolent existence
Of one man who is dead, or is not dead,
Or what the devil it is that he may be.
There must be, I suppose, a fact somewhere,
But I don't know it. I can only tell you
That later, when to all appearances
I stood outside a music-hall in London,
I felt him and then saw that he was there.
Yes, he was there, and had with him a woman
Who looked as if she didn't know. I'm sorry
To this day for that woman—who, no doubt,
Is doing well. Yes, there he was again;
There were his eyes and the same vengeance in them
That I had seen in Rome and twice before—
Not mentioning all the time, or most of it,
Between the day I struck him and that evening.
That was the worst show that I ever saw,
But you had better see it for yourself
Before you say so too. I went away,
Though not for any fear that I could feel
Of him or of his worst manipulations,
But only to be out of the same air
That made him stay alive in the same world
With all the gentlemen that were in irons
For uncommendable extravagances
That I should reckon slight compared with his
Offence of being. Distance would have made him
A moving fly-speck on the map of life,—
But he would not be distant, though his flesh
And bone might have been climbing Fujiyama
Or Chimborazo—with me there in London,
Or sitting here. My doom it was to see him,
Be where I might. That was ten years ago;
And having waited season after season
His always imminent evil recrudescence,

And all for nothing, I was waiting still,
When the *Titanic* touched a piece of ice
And we were for a moment where we are,
With nature laughing at us. When the noise
Had spent itself to names, his was among them;
And I will not insult you or myself
With a vain perjury. I was far from cold.
It seemed as for the first time in my life
I knew the blessedness of being warm;
And I remember that I had a drink,
Having assuredly no need of it.
Pity a fool for his credulity,
If so you must. But when I found his name
Among the dead, I trusted once the news;
And after that there were no messages
In ambush waiting for me on my birthday.
There was no vestige yet of any fear,
You understand—if that's why you are smiling."

I said that I had not so much as whispered
The name aloud of any fear soever,
And that I smiled at his unwonted plunge
Into the perilous pool of Dionysus.
"Well, if you are so easily diverted
As that," he said, drumming his chair again,
"You will be pleased, I think, with what is coming;
And though there be divisions and departures,
Imminent from now on, for your diversion
I'll do the best I can. More to the point,
I know a man who if his friends were like him
Would live in the woods all summer and all winter,
Leaving the town and its iniquities
To die of their own dust. But having his wits,
Henceforth he may conceivably avoid

The adventure unattended. Last October
He took me with him into the Maine woods,
Where, by the shore of a primeval lake,
With woods all round it, and a voyage away
From anything wearing clothes, he had reared somehow
A lodge, or camp, with a stone chimney in it,
And a wide fireplace to make men forget
Their sins who sat before it in the evening,
Hearing the wind outside among the trees
And the black water washing on the shore.
I never knew the meaning of October
Until I went with Asher to that place,
Which I shall not investigate again
Till I be taken there by other forces
Than are innate in my economy.
'You may not like it,' Asher said, 'but Asher
Knows what is good. So put your faith in Asher,
And come along with him.' He's an odd bird,
Yet I could wish for the world's decency
There might be more of him. And so it was
I found myself, at first incredulous,
Down there with Asher in the wilderness,
Alive at last with a new liberty
And with no sore to fester. He perceived
In me an altered favor of God's works,
And promptly took upon himself the credit,
Which, in a fashion, was as accurate
As one's interpretation of another
Is like to be. So for a frosty fortnight
We had the sunlight with us on the lake,
And the moon with us when the sun was down.
'God gave his adjutants a holiday,'
Asher assured me, 'when He made this place';
And I agreed with him that it was heaven,—
Till it was hell for me for then and after.

"There was a village miles away from us
Where now and then we paddled for the mail
And incidental small commodities
That perfect exile might require, and stayed
The night after the voyage with an antique
Survival of a broader world than ours
Whom Asher called The Admiral. This time,
A little out of sorts and out of tune
With paddling, I let Asher go alone,
Sure that his heart was happy. Then it was
That hell came. I sat gazing over there
Across the water, watching the sun's last fire
Above those gloomy and indifferent trees
That might have been a wall around the world,
When suddenly, like faces over the lake,
Out of the silence of that other shore
I was aware of hidden presences
That soon, no matter how many of them there were,
Would all be one. I could not look behind me,
Where I could hear that one of them was breathing,
For, if I did, those others over there
Might all see that at last I was afraid;
And I might hear them without seeing them,
Seeing that other one. You were not there;
And it is well for you that you don't know
What they are like when they should not be there.
And there were chilly doubts of whether or not
I should be seeing the rest that I should see
With eyes, or otherwise. I could not be sure;
And as for going over to find out,
All I may tell you now is that my fear
Was not the fear of dying, though I knew soon
That all the gold in all the sunken ships
That have gone down since Tyre would not have paid
For me the ferriage of myself alone

To that infernal shore. I was in hell,
Remember; and if you have never been there
You may as well not say how easy it is
To find the best way out. There may not be one.
Well, I was there; and I was there alone—
Alone for the first time since I was born;
And I was not alone. That's what it is
To be in hell. I hope you will not go there.
All through that slow, long, desolating twilight
Of incoherent certainties, I waited;
Never alone—never to be alone;
And while the night grew down upon me there,
I thought of old Prometheus in the story
That I had read at school, and saw mankind
All huddled into clusters in the dark,
Calling to God for light. There was a light
Coming for them, but there was none for me
Until a shapeless remnant of a moon
Rose after midnight over the black trees
Behind me. I should hardly have confessed
The heritage then of my identity
To my own shadow; for I was powerless there,
As I am here. Say what you like to say
To silence, but say none of it to me
Tonight. To say it now would do no good,
And you are here to listen. Beware of hate,
And listen. Beware of hate, remorse, and fear,
And listen. You are staring at the damned,
But yet you are no more the one than he
To say that it was he alone who planted
The flower of death now growing in his garden.
Was it enough, I wonder, that I struck him?
I shall say nothing. I shall have to wait
Until I see what's coming, if it comes,
When I'm a delver in another garden—

If such an one there be. If there be none,
All's well—and over. Rather a vain expense,
One might affirm—yet there is nothing lost.
Science be praised that there is nothing lost."

I'm glad the venom that was on his tongue
May not go down on paper; and I'm glad
No friend of mine alive, far as I know,
Has a tale waiting for me with an end
Like Avon's. There was here an interruption,
Though not a long one—only while we heard,
As we had heard before, the ghost of steps
Faintly outside. We knew that she was there
Again; and though it was a kindly folly,
I wished that Avon's wife would go to sleep.

"I was afraid, this time, but not of man—
Or man as you may figure him," he said.
"It was not anything my eyes had seen
That I could feel around me in the night,
There by that lake. If I had been alone,
There would have been the joy of being free
Which in imagination I had won
With unimaginable expiation—
But I was not alone. If you had seen me,
Waiting there for the dark and looking off
Over the gloom of that relentless water,
Which had the stillness of the end of things
That evening on it, I might well have made
For you the picture of the last man left
Where God, in his extinction of the rest,
Had overlooked him and forgotten him.
Yet I was not alone. Interminably
The minutes crawled along and over me,
Slow, cold, intangible, and invisible,

As if they had come up out of that water.
How long I sat there I shall never know,
For time was hidden out there in the black lake,
Which now I could see only as a glimpse
Of black light by the shore. There were no stars
To mention, and the moon was hours away
Behind me. There was nothing but myself,
And what was coming. On my breast I felt
The touch of death, and I should have died then.
I ruined good Asher's autumn as it was,
For he will never again go there alone,
If ever he goes at all. Nature did ill
To darken such a faith in her as his,
Though he will have it that I had the worst
Of her defection, and will hear no more
Apologies. If it had to be for someone,
I think it well for me it was for Asher.
I dwell on him, meaning that you may know him
Before your last horn blows. He has a name
That's like a tree, and therefore like himself—
By which I mean you find him where you leave him.
I saw him and The Admiral together
While I was in the dark, but they were far—
Far as around the world from where I was;
And they knew nothing of what I saw not
While I knew only I was not alone.
I made a fire to make the place alive,
And locked the door. But even the fire was dead,
And all the life there was was in the shadow
It made of me. My shadow was all of me;
The rest had had its day, and there was night
Remaining—only night, that's made for shadows,
Shadows and sleep and dreams, or dreams without it.
The fire went slowly down, and now the moon,
Or that late wreck of it, was coming up;

568

And though it was a martyr's work to move,
I must obey my shadow, and I did.
There were two beds built low against the wall,
And down on one of them, with all my clothes on,
Like a man getting into his own grave,
I lay—and waited. As the firelight sank,
The moonlight, which had partly been consumed
By the black trees, framed on the other wall
A glimmering window not far from the ground.
The coals were going, and only a few sparks
Were there to tell of them; and as they died
The window lightened, and I saw the trees.
They moved a little, but I could not move,
More than to turn my face the other way;
And then, if you must have it so, I slept.
We'll call it so—if sleep is your best name
For a sort of conscious, frozen catalepsy
Wherein a man sees all there is around him
As if it were not real, and he were not
Alive. You may call it anything you please
That made me powerless to move hand or foot,
Or to make any other living motion
Than after a long horror, without hope,
To turn my face again the other way.
Some force that was not mine opened my eyes,
And, as I knew it must be,—it was there."

Avon covered his eyes—whether to shut
The memory and the sight of it away,
Or to be sure that mine were for the moment
Not searching his with pity, is now no matter.
My glance at him was brief, turning itself
To the familiar pattern of his rug,
Wherein I may have sought a consolation—
As one may gaze in sorrow on a shell,

Or a small apple. So it had come, I thought;
And heard, no longer with a wonderment,
The faint recurring footsteps of his wife,
Who, knowing less than I knew, yet knew more.
Now I could read, I fancied, through the fear
That latterly was living in her eyes,
To the sure source of its authority.
But he went on, and I was there to listen:

"And though I saw it only as a blot
Between me and my life, it was enough
To make me know that he was watching there—
Waiting for me to move, or not to move,
Before he moved. Sick as I was with hate
Reborn, and chained with fear that was more than fear,
I would have gambled all there was to gain
Or lose in rising there from where I lay
And going out after it. 'Before the dawn,'
I reasoned, 'there will be a difference here.
Therefore it may as well be done outside.'
And then I found I was immovable,
As I had been before; and a dead sweat
Rolled out of me as I remembered him
When I had seen him leaving me at school.
'I shall know where you are until you die,'
Were the last words that I had heard him say;
And there he was. Now I could see his face,
And all the sad, malignant desperation
That was drawn on it after I had struck him,
And on my memory since that afternoon.
But all there was left now for me to do
Was to lie there and see him while he squeezed
His unclean outlines into the dim room,
And half erect inside, like a still beast
With a face partly man's, came slowly on

570

Along the floor to the bed where I lay,
And waited. There had been so much of waiting,
Through all those evil years before my respite—
Which now I knew and recognized at last
As only his more venomous preparation
For the vile end of a deceiving peace—
That I began to fancy there was on me
The stupor that explorers have alleged
As evidence of nature's final mercy
When tigers have them down upon the earth
And wild hot breath is heavy on their faces.
I could not feel his breath, but I could hear it;
Though fear had made an anvil of my heart
Where demons, for the joy of doing it,
Were sledging death down on it. And I saw
His eyes now, as they were, for the first time—
Aflame as they had never been before
With all their gathered vengeance gleaming in them,
And always that unconscionable sorrow
That would not die behind it. Then I caught
The shadowy glimpse of an uplifted arm,
And a moon-flash of metal. That was all. . . .

"When I believed I was alive again
I was with Asher and The Admiral,
Whom Asher had brought with him for a day
With nature. They had found me when they came;
And there was not much left of me to find.
I had not moved or known that I was there
Since I had seen his eyes and felt his breath;
And it was not for some uncertain hours
After they came that either would say how long
That might have been. It should have been much longer.
All you may add will be your own invention,
For I have told you all there is to tell.

571

Tomorrow I shall have another birthday,
And with it there may come another message—
Although I cannot see the need of it,
Or much more need of drowning, if that's all
Men drown for—when they drown. You know as much
As I know about that, though I've a right,
If not a reason, to be on my guard;
And only God knows what good that will do.
Now you may get some air. Good night!—and thank
    you."
He smiled, but I would rather he had not.

I wished that Avon's wife would go to sleep,
But whether she found sleep that night or not
I do not know. I was awake for hours,
Toiling in vain to let myself believe
That Avon's apparition was a dream,
And that he might have added, for romance,
The part that I had taken home with me
For reasons not in Avon's dictionary.
But each recurrent memory of his eyes,
And of the man himself that I had known
So long and well, made soon of all my toil
An evanescent and a vain evasion;
And it was half as in expectancy
That I obeyed the summons of his wife
A little before dawn, and was again
With Avon in the room where I had left him,
But not with the same Avon I had left.
The doctor, an august authority,
With eminence abroad as well as here,
Looked hard at me as if I were the doctor
And he the friend. "I have had eyes on Avon
For more than half a year," he said to me,
"And I have wondered often what it was

572

That I could see that I was not to see.
Though he was in the chair where you are looking,
I told his wife—I had to tell her something—
It was a nightmare and an aneurism;
And so, or partly so, I'll say it was.
The last without the first will be enough
For the newspapers and the undertaker;
Yet if we doctors were not all immune
From death, disease, and curiosity,
My diagnosis would be sorry for me.
He died, you know, because he was afraid—
And he had been afraid for a long time;
And we who knew him well would all agree
To fancy there was rather more than fear.
The door was locked inside—they broke it in
To find him—but she heard him when it came.
There are no signs of any visitors,
Or need of them. If I were not a child
Of science, I should say it was the devil.
I don't believe it was another woman,
And surely it was not another man."

MR. FLOOD'S PARTY

OLD Eben Flood, climbing alone one night
Over the hill between the town below
And the forsaken upland hermitage
That held as much as he should ever know
On earth again of home, paused warily.
The road was his with not a native near;
And Eben, having leisure, said aloud,
For no man else in Tilbury Town to hear:

"Well, Mr. Flood, we have the harvest moon
Again, and we may not have many more;
The bird is on the wing, the poet says,
And you and I have said it here before.
Drink to the bird." He raised up to the light
The jug that he had gone so far to fill,
And answered huskily: "Well, Mr. Flood,
Since you propose it, I believe I will."

Alone, as if enduring to the end
A valiant armor of scarred hopes outworn,
He stood there in the middle of the road
Like Roland's ghost winding a silent horn.
Below him, in the town among the trees,
Where friends of other days had honored him,
A phantom salutation of the dead
Rang thinly till old Eben's eyes were dim.

Then, as a mother lays her sleeping child
Down tenderly, fearing it may awake,
He set the jug down slowly at his feet
With trembling care, knowing that most things break;
And only when assured that on firm earth
It stood, as the uncertain lives of men
Assuredly did not, he paced away,
And with his hand extended paused again:

"Well, Mr. Flood, we have not met like this
In a long time; and many a change has come
To both of us, I fear, since last it was
We had a drop together. Welcome home!"
Convivially returning with himself,
Again he raised the jug up to the light;
And with an acquiescent quaver said:
"Well, Mr. Flood, if you insist, I might.

574

BEN TROVATO

"Only a very little, Mr. Flood—
For auld lang syne. No more, sir; that will do."
So, for the time, apparently it did,
And Eben evidently thought so too;
For soon amid the silver loneliness
Of night he lifted up his voice and sang,
Secure, with only two moons listening,
Until the whole harmonious landscape rang—

"For auld lang syne." The weary throat gave out,
The last word wavered, and the song was done.
He raised again the jug regretfully
And shook his head, and was again alone.
There was not much that was ahead of him,
And there was nothing in the town below—
Where strangers would have shut the many doors
That many friends had opened long ago.

BEN TROVATO

The deacon thought. "I know them," he began,
"And they are all you ever heard of them—
Allurable to no sure theorem,
The scorn or the humility of man.
You say 'Can I believe it?'—and I can;
And I'm unwilling even to condemn
The benefaction of a stratagem
Like hers—and I'm a Presbyterian.

"Though blind, with but a wandering hour to live,
He felt the other woman in the fur
That now the wife had on. Could she forgive
All that? Apparently. Her rings were gone,

575

Of course; and when he found that she had none,
He smiled—as he had never smiled at her."

THE TREE IN PAMELA'S GARDEN

PAMELA was too gentle to deceive
Her roses. "Let the men stay where they are,"
She said, "and if Apollo's avatar
Be one of them, I shall not have to grieve."
And so she made all Tilbury Town believe
She sighed a little more for the North Star
Than over men, and only in so far
As she was in a garden was like Eve.

Her neighbors—doing all that neighbors can
To make romance of reticence meanwhile—
Seeing that she had never loved a man,
Wished Pamela had a cat, or a small bird,
And only would have wondered at her smile
Could they have seen that she had overheard.

VAIN GRATUITIES

NEVER was there a man much uglier
In eyes of other women, or more grim:
"The Lord has filled her chalice to the brim,
So let us pray she's a philosopher,"
They said; and there was more they said of her—
Deeming it, after twenty years with him,
No wonder that she kept her figure slim
And always made you think of lavender.

But she, demure as ever, and as fair,
Almost, as they remembered her before
She found him, would have laughed had she been there;
And all they said would have been heard no more
Than foam that washes on an island shore
Where there are none to listen or to care.

JOB THE REJECTED

THEY met, and overwhelming her distrust
With penitence, he praised away her fear;
They married, and Job gave him half a year
To wreck the temple, as we knew he must.
He fumbled hungrily to readjust
A fallen altar, but the road was clear
By which it was her will to disappear
That evening when Job found him in the dust.

Job would have deprecated such a way
Of heaving fuel on a sacred fire,
Yet even the while we saw it going out,
Hardly was Job to find his hour to shout;
And Job was not, so far as we could say,
The confirmation of her soul's desire.

LOST ANCHORS

LIKE a dry fish flung inland far from shore,
There lived a sailor, warped and ocean-browned,
Who told of an old vessel, harbor-drowned
And out of mind a century before,

577

Where divers, on descending to explore
A legend that had lived its way around
The world of ships, in the dark hulk had found
Anchors, which had been seized and seen no more.

Improving a dry leisure to invest
Their misadventure with a manifest
Analogy that he may read who runs,
The sailor made it old as ocean grass—
Telling of much that once had come to pass
With him, whose mother should have had no sons.

RECALLED

LONG after there were none of them alive
About the place—where there is now no place
But a walled hole where fruitless vines embrace
Their parent skeletons that yet survive
In evil thorns—none of us could arrive
At a more cogent answer to their ways
Than one old Isaac in his latter days
Had humor or compassion to contrive.

I mentioned them, and Isaac shook his head:
"The Power that you call yours and I call mine
Extinguished in the last of them a line
That Satan would have disinherited.
When we are done with all but the Divine,
We die." And there was no more to be said.

MODERNITIES

SMALL knowledge have we that by knowledge met
May not some day be quaint as any told
In almagest or chronicle of old,

AFTERTHOUGHTS

Whereat we smile because we are as yet
The last—though not the last who may forget
What cleavings and abrasions manifold
Have marked an armor that was never scrolled
Before for human glory and regret.

With infinite unseen enemies in the way
We have encountered the intangible,
To vanquish where our fathers, who fought well,
Scarce had assumed endurance for a day;
Yet we shall have our darkness, even as they,
And there shall be another tale to tell.

AFTERTHOUGHTS

WE parted where the old gas-lamp still burned
Under the wayside maple and walked on,
Into the dark, as we had always done;
And I, no doubt, if he had not returned,
Might yet be unaware that he had earned
More than earth gives to many who have won
More than it has to give when they are gone—
As duly and indelibly I learned.

The sum of all that he came back to say
Was little then, and would be less today:
With him there were no Delphic heights to climb,
Yet his were somehow nearer the sublime.
He spoke, and went again by the old way—
Not knowing it would be for the last time.

CAPUT MORTUUM

Not even if with a wizard force I might
Have summoned whomsoever I would name,
Should anyone else have come than he who came,
Uncalled, to share with me my fire that night;
For though I should have said that all was right.
Or right enough, nothing had been the same
As when I found him there before the flame,
Always a welcome and a useful sight.

Unfailing and exuberant all the time,
Having no gold he paid with golden rhyme,
Of older coinage than his old defeat,
A debt that like himself was obsolete
In Art's long hazard, where no man may choose
Whether he play to win or toil to lose.

MONADNOCK THROUGH THE TREES

Before there was in Egypt any sound
Of those who reared a more prodigious means
For the self-heavy sleep of kings and queens
Than hitherto had mocked the most renowned,—
Unvisioned here and waiting to be found,
Alone, amid remote and older scenes,
You loomed above ancestral evergreens
Before there were the first of us around.

And when the last of us, if we know how,
See farther from ourselves than we do now,
Assured with other sight than heretofore

580

MANY ARE CALLED

That we have done our mortal best and worst,—
Your calm will be the same as when the first
Assyrians went howling south to war.

THE LONG RACE

Up the old hill to the old house again
Where fifty years ago the friend was young
Who should be waiting somewhere there among
Old things that least remembered most remain,
He toiled on with a pleasure that was pain
To think how soon asunder would be flung
The curtain half a century had hung
Between the two ambitions they had slain.

They dredged an hour for words, and then were done.
"Good-bye! . . . You have the same old weather-vane—
Your little horse that's always on the run."
And all the way down back to the next train,
Down the old hill to the old road again,
It seemed as if the little horse had won.

MANY ARE CALLED

The Lord Apollo, who has never died,
Still holds alone his immemorial reign,
Supreme in an impregnable domain
That with his magic he has fortified;
And though melodious multitudes have tried
In ecstasy, in anguish, and in vain,

581

With invocation sacred and profane
To lure him, even the loudest are outside.

Only at unconjectured intervals,
By will of him on whom no man may gaze,
By word of him whose law no man has read,
A questing light may rift the sullen walls,
To cling where mostly its infrequent rays
Fall golden on the patience of the dead.

REMBRANDT TO REMBRANDT

(AMSTERDAM, 1645)

AND there you are again, now as you are.
Observe yourself as you discern yourself
In your discredited ascendency;
Without your velvet or your feathers now,
Commend your new condition to your fate,
And your conviction to the sieves of time.
Meanwhile appraise yourself, Rembrandt van **Ryn**,
Now as you are—formerly more or less
Distinguished in the civil scenery,
And once a painter. There you are again,
Where you may see that you have on your shoulders
No lovelier burden for an ornament
Than one man's head that's yours. Praise be to God
That you have that; for you are like enough
To need it now, my friend, and from now on;
For there are shadows and obscurities
Immediate or impending on your view,
That may be worse than you have ever painted
For the bewildered and unhappy scorn

582

REMBRANDT TO REMBRANDT

Of injured Hollanders in Amsterdam
Who cannot find their fifty florins' worth
Of Holland face where you have hidden it
In your new golden shadow that excites them,
5 Or see that when the Lord made color and light
He made not one thing only, or believe
That shadows are not nothing. Saskia said,
Before she died, how they would swear at you,
And in commiseration at themselves.
10 She laughed a little, too, to think of them—
And then at me. . . . That was before she died.

And I could wonder, as I look at you,
There as I have you now, there as you are,
Or nearly so as any skill of mine
15 Has ever caught you in a bilious mirror,—
Yes, I could wonder long, and with a reason,
If all but everything achievable
In me were not achieved and lost already,
Like a fool's gold. But you there in the glass,
20 And you there on the canvas, have a sort
Of solemn doubt about it; and that's well
For Rembrandt and for Titus. All that's left
Of all that was is here; and all that's here
Is one man who remembers, and one child
25 Beginning to forget. One, two, and three,
The others died, and then—then Saskia died;
And then, so men believe, the painter died.
So men believe. So it all comes at once.
And here's a fellow painting in the dark,—
30 A loon who cannot see that he is dead
Before God lets him die. He paints away
At the impossible, so Holland has it,
For venom or for spite, or for defection,
Or else for God knows what. Well, if God knows,

34 ·   583.

And Rembrandt knows, it matters not so much
What Holland knows or cares. If Holland wants
Its heads all in a row, and all alike,
There's Franz to do them and to do them well—
Rat-catchers, archers, or apothecaries,
And one as like a rabbit as another.
Value received, and every Dutchman happy.
All's one to Franz, and to the rest of them,—
Their ways being theirs, are theirs.—But you, my friend,
If I have made you something as you are,
Will need those jaws and eyes and all the fight
And fire that's in them, and a little more,
To take you on and the world after you;
For now you fare alone, without the fashion
To sing you back and fling a flower or two
At your accusing feet. Poor Saskia saw
This coming that has come, and with a guile
Of kindliness that covered half her doubts
Would give me gold, and laugh . . . before she died.

And if I see the road that you are going,
You that are not so jaunty as aforetime,
God knows if she were not appointed well
To die. She might have wearied of it all
Before the worst was over, or begun.
A woman waiting on a man's avouch
Of the invisible, may not wait always
Without a word betweenwhiles, or a dash
Of poison on his faith. Yes, even she.
She might have come to see at last with others,
And then to say with others, who say more,
That you are groping on a phantom trail
Determining a dusky way to nowhere;
That errors unconfessed and obstinate
Have teemed and cankered in you for so long

584

That comes at last, and then, so it appears,
Only for you and me—and a few more,
Perchance, albeit their faces are not many
Among the ruins that are now around us.
5 That was a fall, my friend, we had together—
Or rather it was my house, mine alone,
That fell, leaving you safe. Be glad for that.
There's life in you that shall outlive my clay
That's for a time alive and will in time
10 Be nothing—but not yet. You that are there
Where I have painted you are safe enough,
Though I see dragons. Verily, that was a fall—
A dislocating fall, a blinding fall,
A fall indeed. But there are no bones broken;
15 And even the teeth and eyes that I make out
Among the shadows, intermittently,
Show not so firm in their accoutrement
Of terror-laden unreality
As you in your neglect of their performance,—
20 Though for their season we must humor them
For what they are: devils undoubtedly,
But not so perilous and implacable
In their undoing of poor human triumph
As easy fashion—or brief novelty
25 That ails even while it grows, and like sick fruit
Falls down anon to an indifferent earth
To break with inward rot. I say all this,
And I concede, in honor of your silence,
A waste of innocent facility
30 In tints of other colors than are mine.
I cannot paint with words, but there's a time
For most of us when words are all we have
To serve our stricken souls. And here you say,
"Be careful, or you may commit your soul
35 Soon to the very devil of your denial."

586

REMBRANDT TO REMBRANDT

I might have wagered on you to say that.
Knowing that I believe in you too surely
To spoil you with a kick or paint you over.

No, my good friend, Mynheer Rembrandt van Ryn—
5 Sometime a personage in Amsterdam,
But now not much—I shall not give myself
To be the sport of any dragon-spawn
Of Holland, or elsewhere. Holland was hell
Not long ago, and there were dragons then
10 More to be fought than any of these we see
That we may foster now. They are not real,
But not for that the less to be regarded;
For there are slimy tyrants born of nothing
That harden slowly into seeming life
15 And have the strength of madness. I confess,
Accordingly, the wisdom of your care
That I look out for them. Whether I would
Or not, I must; and here we are as one
With our necessity. For though you loom
20 A little harsh in your respect of time
And circumstance, and of ordained eclipse,
We know together of a golden flood
That with its overflow shall drown away
The dikes that held it; and we know thereby
25 That in its rising light there lives a fire
No devils that are lodging here in Holland
Shall put out wholly, or much agitate,
Except in unofficial preparation
They put out first the sun. It's well enough
30 To think of them; wherefore I thank you, sir,
Alike for your remembrance and attention.

But there are demons that are longer-lived
33 Than doubts that have a brief and evil term

603

COLLECTED POEMS

To congregate among the futile shards
And architraves of eminent collapse.
They are a many-favored family,
All told, with not a misbegotten dwarf
5 Among the rest that I can love so little
As one occult abortion in especial
Who perches on a picture (when it's done)
And says, "What of it, Rembrandt, if you do?"
This incubus would seem to be a sort
10 Of chorus, indicating, for our good,
The silence of the few friends that are left:
"What of it, Rembrandt, even if you know?"
It says again; "and you don't know for certain.
What if in fifty or a hundred years
15 They find you out? You may have gone meanwhile
So greatly to the dogs that you'll not care
Much what they find. If this be all you are—
This unaccountable aspiring insect—
You'll sleep as easy in oblivion
20 As any sacred monk or parricide;
And if, as you conceive, you are eternal,
Your soul may laugh, remembering (if a soul
Remembers) your befrenzied aspiration
To smear with certain ochres and some oil
25 A few more perishable ells of cloth,
And once or twice, to square your vanity,
Prove it was you alone that should achieve
A mortal eye—that may, no less, tomorrow
Show an immortal reason why today
30 Men see no more. And what's a mortal eye
More than a mortal herring, who has eyes
As well as you? Why not paint herrings, Rembrandt?
Or if not herrings, why not a split beef?
Perceive it only in its unalloyed
35 Integrity, and you may find in it

588

35

REMBRANDT TO REMBRANDT

A beautified accomplishment no less
Indigenous than one that appertains
To gentlemen and ladies eating it.
The same God planned and made you, beef and human;
5 And one, but for His whim, might be the other."

That's how he says it, Rembrandt, if you listen;
He says it, and he goes. And then, sometimes,
There comes another spirit in his place—
One with a more engaging argument,
10 And with a softer note for saying truth
Not soft. Whether it be the truth or not,
I name it so; for there's a string in me
Somewhere that answers—which is natural,
Since I am but a living instrument
15 Played on by powers that are invisible.
"You might go faster, if not quite so far,"
He says, "if in your vexed economy
There lived a faculty for saying yes
And meaning no, and then for doing neither;
20 But since Apollo sees it otherwise,
Your Dutchmen, who are swearing at you still
For your pernicious filching of their florins,
May likely curse you down their generation,
Not having understood there was no malice
25 Or grinning evil in a golden shadow
That shall outshine their slight identities
And hold their faces when their names are nothing.
But this, as you discern, or should by now
Surmise, for you is neither here nor there:
30 You made your picture as your demon willed it;
That's about all of that. Now make as many
As may be to be made,—for so you will,
Whatever the toll may be, and hold your light
So that you see, without so much to blind you

589

As even the cobweb-flash of a misgiving,
Assured and certain that if you see right
Others will have to see—albeit their seeing
Shall irk them out of their serenity
5 For such a time as umbrage may require.
But there are many reptiles in the night
That now is coming on, and they are hungry;
And there's a Rembrandt to be satisfied
Who never will be, howsoever much
10 He be assured of an ascendency
That has not yet a shadow's worth of sound
Where Holland has its ears. And what of that?
Have you the weary leisure or sick wit
That breeds of its indifference a false envy
15 That is the vermin on accomplishment?
Are you inaugurating your new service
With fasting for a food you would not eat?
You are the servant, Rembrandt, not the master,—
But you are not assigned with other slaves
20 That in their freedom are the most in fear.
One of the few that are so fortunate
As to be told their task and to be given
A skill to do it with a tool too keen
For timid safety, bow your elected head
25 Under the stars tonight, and whip your devils
Each to his nest in hell. Forget your days,
And so forgive the years that may not be
So many as to be more than you may need
For your particular consistency
30 In your peculiar folly. You are counting
Some fewer years than forty at your heels;
And they have not pursued your gait so fast
As your oblivion—which has beaten them,
And rides now on your neck like an old man
35 With iron shins and fingers. Let him ride

590

REMBRANDT TO REMBRANDT

(You haven't so much to say now about that),
And in a proper season let him run.
You may be dead then, even as you may now
Anticipate some other mortal strokes
5 Attending your felicity; and for that,
Oblivion heretofore has done some running
Away from graves, and will do more of it."

That's how it is your wiser spirit speaks,
Rembrandt. If you believe him, why complain?
10 If not, why paint? And why, in any event,
Look back for the old joy and the old roses,
Or the old fame? They are all gone together,
And Saskia with them; and with her left out,
They would avail no more now than one strand
15 Of Samson's hair wound round his little finger
Before the temple fell. Nor more are you
In any sudden danger to forget
That in Apollo's house there are no clocks
Or calendars to say for you in time
20 How far you are away from Amsterdam,
Or that the one same law that bids you see
Where now you see alone forbids in turn
Your light from Holland eyes till Holland ears
Are told of it; for that way, my good fellow,
25 Is one way more to death. If at the first
Of your long turning, which may still be longer
Than even your faith has measured it, you sigh
For distant welcome that may not be seen,
Or wayside shouting that will not be heard,
30 You may as well accommodate your greatness
To the convenience of an easy ditch,
And, anchored there with all your widowed gold,
Forget your darkness in the dark, and hear
34 No longer the cold wash of Holland scorn.

591

TRISTRAM

(1927)

To the Memory of
Edward Proby Fox

TRISTRAM

I

Isolt of the white hands, in Brittany,
Could see no longer northward anywhere
A picture more alive or less familiar
Than a blank ocean and the same white birds
Flying, and always flying, and still flying,
Yet never bringing any news of him
That she remembered, who had sailed away
The spring before—saying he would come back,
Although not saying when. Not one of them,
For all their flying, she thought, had heard the name
Of Tristram, or of him beside her there
That was the King, her father. The last ship
Was out of sight, and there was nothing now
For her to see before the night came down
Except her father's face. She looked at him
And found him smiling in the way she feared,
And loved the while she feared it. The King took
One of her small still hands in of his
That were so large and hard to be so kind,
And weighed a question, not for the first time:

"Why should it be that I must have a child
Whose eyes are wandering always to the north?
The north is a bad region full of wolves
And bears and hairy men that have no manners.
Why should her eyes be always on the north,

I wonder, when all's here that one requires
Of comfort, love, and of expediency?
You are not cheered, I see, or satisfied
Entirely by the sound of what I say.
You are too young, may be, to make yourself
A nest of comfort and expediency."

"I may be that," she said, and a quick flush
Made a pink forage of her laughing face,
At which he smiled again. "But not so young
As to be told for ever how young I am.
I have been growing for these eighteen years,
And waiting here, for one thing and another.
Besides, his manners are as good as yours,
And he's not half so hairy as you are,
Even though you be the King of Brittany,
Or the great Jove himself, and then my father."
With that she threw her arms around his neck,
Throbbing as if she were a child indeed.

"You are no heavier than a cat," said he,
"But otherwise you are somewhat like a tiger.
Relinquish your commendable affection
A little, and tell me why it is you dream
Of someone coming always from the north.
Are there no proper knights or princes else
Than one whose eyes, wherever they may be fixed,
Are surely not fixed hard on Brittany?
You are a sort of child, or many sorts,
Yet also are too high and too essential
To be much longer the quaint sport and food
Of shadowy fancies. For a time I've laughed
And let you dream, but I may not laugh always.
Because he praised you as a child one day,
And may have liked you as a child one day,

596

TRISTRAM

Why do you stare for ever into the north,
Over that water, where the good God placed
A land known only to your small white ears?"

"Only because the good God, I suppose,
Placed England somewhere north of Brittany—
Though not so far but one may come and go
As many a time as twice before he dies.
I know that's true, having been told about it.
I have been told so much about this world
That I have wondered why men stay in it.
I have been told of devils that are in it,
And some right here in Brittany. Griffon
Is one of them; and if he ever gets me,
I'll pray for the best way to kill myself."

King Howel held his daughter closer to him,
As if a buried and forgotten fear
Had come to life and was confronting him
With a new face. "Never you mind the devils,"
He said, "be they in Brittany or elsewhere.
They are for my attention, if need be.
You will affright me and amuse me less
By saying, if you are ready, how much longer
You are to starve yourself with your delusion
Of Tristram coming back. He may come back,
Or Mark, his uncle, who tonight is making
Another Isolt his queen—the dark Isolt,
Isolt of Ireland—may be coming back,
Though I'd as lief he would remain at home
In Cornwall, with his new queen—if he keeps her."

"And who is this far-off Isolt of Ireland?"
She said, like a thing waiting to be hurt:
"A creature that one hears of constantly,

597

And one that no man sees, or none to say so,
Must be unusual—if she be at all."

"The few men who have told of her to me
Have told of silence and of Irish pride,
Inhabiting too much beauty for one woman.
My eyes have never seen her; and as for beauty,
My eyes would rather look on yours, my child.
And as for Tristram coming back, what then—
One of these days? Any one may come back.
King Arthur may come back; and as for that,
Our Lord and Saviour may come back some time,
Though hardly all for you. Have you kept hid
Some promise or protestation heretofore,
That you may shape a thought into a reason
For making always of a distant wish
A dim belief? You are too old for that—
If it will make you happy to be told so.
You have been told so much." King Howel smiled,
And waited, holding her white hands in his.

"I have been told that Tristram will come back,"
She said; "and it was he who told me so.
Also I have this agate that he gave me;
And I believe his eyes."

                    "Believe his agate,"
The king said, "for as long as you may save it.
An agate's a fair plaything for a child,
Though not so boundless and immovable
In magnitude but that a child may lose it.
Since you esteem it such an acquisition,
Treasure it more securely, and believe it
As a bright piece of earth, and nothing more.
Believe his agate, and forget his eyes;

598

And go to bed. You are not young enough,
I see, to stay awake and entertain
Much longer your exaggerated fancies.
And if he should come back? Would you prepare
Upon the ruinous day of his departure
To drown yourself, and with yourself his agate?"

Isolt, now on a cushion at his feet,
Finding the King's hard knees a meagre pillow,
Sat upright, thinking. "No, I should not do that;
Though I should never trust another man
So far that I should go away with him.
King's daughters, I suppose, are bought and sold,
But you would not sell me."

          "You seize a question
As if it were an agate—or a fact,"
The King said, laughing at the calm gray eyes
That were so large in the small face before him.
"I might sell you, perhaps, at a fair bargain.
To play with an illustrious example,
If Modred were to overthrow King Arthur—
And there are prophets who see Arthur's end
In Modred, who's an able sort of reptile—
And come for you to go away with him,
And to be Queen of Britain, I might sell you,
Perhaps. You might say prayers that you be sold."

"I may say prayers that you be reasonable
And serious, and that you believe me so."
There was a light now in his daughter's eyes
Like none that he remembered having seen
In eyes before, whereat he paused and heard,
Not all amused. "He will come back," she said,
"And I shall wait. If he should not come back,

I shall have been but one poor woman more
Whose punishment for being born a woman
Was to believe and wait. You are my King,
My father, and of all men anywhere,
Save one, you are the world of men to me.
When I say this of him you must believe me,
As I believe his eyes. He will come back;
And what comes then I leave to him, and God."

Slowly the King arose, and with his hands
He lifted up Isolt, so frail, so light,
And yet, with all, mysteriously so strong.
He raised her patient face between his hands,
Observing it as if it were some white
And foreign flower, not certain in his garden
To thrive, nor like to die. Then with a vague
And wavering effect of shaking her
Affectionately back to his own world,
Which never would be hers, he smiled once more
And set her free. "You should have gone to bed
When first I told you. You had best go now,
And while you are still dreaming. In the morning
Your dreams, if you remember them, will all
Be less than one bird singing in a tree."

Isolt of the white hands, unchangeable,
Half childlike and half womanly, looked up
Into her father's eyes and shook her head,
Smiling, but less for joy than certainty:
"There's a bird then that I have never seen
In Brittany; and I have never heard him.
Good night, my father." She went slowly out,
Leaving him in the gloom.

                    "Good night, my child,
Good night," he said, scarce hearing his own voice

For crowded thoughts that were unseizable
And unforeseen within him. Like Isolt,
He stood now in the window looking north
Over the misty sea. A seven days' moon
Was in the sky, and there were a few stars
That had no fire. "I have no more a child,"
He thought, "and what she is I do not know.
It may be fancy and fantastic youth
That ails her now; it may be the sick touch
Of prophecy concealing disillusion.
If there were not inwoven so much power
And poise of sense with all her seeming folly,
I might assume a concord with her faith
As that of one elected soon to die.
But surely no infringement of the grave
In her conceits and her appearances
Encourages a fear that still is fear;
And what she is to know, I cannot say.
A changeling down from one of those white stars
Were more like her than like a child of mine."

Nothing in the cold glimmer of a moon
Over a still, cold ocean there before him
Would answer for him in the silent voice
Of time an idle question. So the King,
With only time for company, stood waiting
Alone there in the window, looking off
At the still sea between his eyes and England.

II

The moon that glimmered cold on Brittany
Glimmered as cold on Cornwall, where King Mark,
Only by kingly circumstance endowed
With friends enough to make a festival,

On this dim night had married and made Queen—
Of all fair women in the world by fate
The most forgotten in her loveliness
Till now—Isolt of Ireland, who had flamed
And fought so long with love that she called hate,
Inimical to Tristram for the stroke
That felled Morhaus her kinsman. Tristram, blind
With angry beauty, or in honor blind,
Or in obscure obedience unawakened,
Had given his insane promise to his uncle
Of intercession with the Irish King
And so drawn out of him a slow assent,
Not fathoming or distinguishing aright
Within himself a passion that was death,
Nor gauging with a timely recognition
The warfare of a woman's enmity
With love without love's name. He knew too late
How one word then would have made arras-rats
For her of all his uncles, and all kings
That he might serve with cloudy promises,
Not weighed until redeemed. Now there was time
For him to weigh them, and to weigh them well,
To the last scorching ounce of desperation,
Searing his wits and flesh like heated mail
Amidst the fiery downfall of a palace,
Where there was no one left except himself
To save, and no way out except through fire.
Partly to balk his rage, partly to curse
Unhindered an abject ineptitude
That like a drug had held him and withheld him
In seizing once from love's imperial garden
The flower of all things there, now Tristram leaned
Alone upon a parapet below
The lights of high Tintagel, where gay music
Had whipped him as a lash and driven him out

TRISTRAM

Into the misty night, which might have held
A premonition and a probing chill
For one more tranquil and less exigent,
And not so much on fire. Down through the gloom
He gazed at nothing, save a moving blur
Where foamed eternally on Cornish rocks
The moan of Cornish water; and he asked,
With a malignant inward voice of envy,
How many scarred cold things that once had laughed
And loved and wept and sung, and had been men,
Might have been knocked and washed indifferently
On that hard shore, and eaten gradually
By competent quick fishes and large crabs
And larger birds, not caring a wink which
Might be employed on their spent images,
No longer tortured there, if God was good,
By memories of the fools and royal pimps
That once unwittingly they might have been—
Like Tristram, who could wish himself as far
As they were from a wearing out of life
On a racked length of days. Now and again
A louder fanfare of malicious horns
Would sing down from the festival above him,
Smiting his angry face like a wet clout
That some invisible scullion might have swung,
Too shadowy and too agile to be seized
And flung down on those rocks. Now and again
Came over him a cold soul-retching wave
Of recognition past reality,
Recurrent, vile, and always culminating
In a forbidden vision thrice unholy
Of Mark, his uncle, like a man-shaped goat
Appraising with a small salacious eye,
And slowly forcing into his gaunt arms,
And all now in a few impossible hours

603

That were as possible as pain and death,
The shuddering unreal miracle of Isolt,
Which was as real as torture to the damned
In hell, or in Cornwall. Before long now
That music and that wordless murmuring
Of distant men and women, who divined
As much or little as they might, would cease;
The mocking lights above him would go out;
There would be silence; and the King would hold
Isolt—Isolt of the dark eyes—Isolt
Of the patrician passionate helplessness—
Isolt of the soft waving blue-black hair—
Isolt of Ireland—in his vicious arms
And crush the bloom of her resisting life
On his hot, watery mouth, and overcome
The protest of her suffering silk skin
With his crude senile claws. And it was he,
Tristram, the loud-accredited strong warrior,
Tristram, the loved of women, the harp-player,
Tristram, the learned Nimrod among hunters,
Tristram, the most obedient imbecile
And humble servant of King Mark his uncle,
Who had achieved all this. For lack of sight
And sense of self, and imperturbably,
He had achieved all this and might do more,
No doubt, if given the time. Whereat he cursed
Himself again, and his complacent years
Of easy blindness. Time had saved for him
The flower that he had not the wit to seize
And carry a few leagues across the water,
Till when he did so it was his no more,
And body and soul were sick to think of it.
Why should he not be sick? "Good God in heaven,"
He groaned aloud, "why should I not be sick!"—
"No God will answer you to say why not,"

604

Said one descending heavily but unheard,
And slowly, down the stairs. "And one like me,
Having seen more seasons out than you have seen,
Would say it was tonight your prime intention
To make yourself the sickest man in Cornwall."
Gouvernail frowned and shivered as he spoke,
And waited as a stranger waits in vain
Outside a door that none within will open.

"I may be that already," Tristram said,
"But I'm not cold. For I'm a seer tonight,
And consequently full of starry thoughts.
The stars are not so numerous as they were,
But there's a brotherly white moon up there,
Such as it is. Well, Gouvernail, what word
Has my illustrious and most amorous
And most imperious Uncle Mark prepared
For you to say to me that you come scowling
So far down here to say it? You are next
To nearest, not being my father, of all men
Of whom I am unworthy. What's the word?"

"Tristram, I left the King annoyed and anxious
On your account, and for the nonce not pleased."
"What most annoys my uncle, for the nonce?
God knows that I have done for him of late
More than an army, made of nephews only,
Shall ever be fools enough to do again.
When tired of feasting and of too much talk,
And too much wine and too much happy music,
May not his royal nephew have some air,
Even though his annoyed uncle be a king?
My father is a king, in Lyonesse;
And that's about as much as being a king
In Cornwall is—or one here now might say so."

605

"Forgive me, Tristram, but I'm old for this.
The King knows well what you have done for him,
And owns a gratitude beyond the gift
Of utterance for the service of your word.
But the King does not know, and cannot know,
Your purpose in an act ungenerous,
If not unseemly. What shall I say to him
If I go back to him alone? Tristram,
There are some treasured moments I remember
When you have made me loyal to you always
For saying good words of me, and with no care
Whether or not they came back to my ears.
Surely, if past attention and tuition
Are not forgotten, you will not forget
This present emptiness of my confusion.
If I go back alone, what shall I say?"

"Say to the King that if the King command
Implacably my presence, I will come.
But say as an addition that I'm sick,
And that another joyful hour with him
This night might have eventful influences.
Nothing could be more courteous, if said well,
Or more consistent with infirm allegiance.
Say to the King I'm sick. If he doubts that,
Or takes it ill, say to the King I'm drunk.
His comprehensions and remembrances
Will compass and envisage, peradventure,
The last deplorable profundity
Of my defection if you say, for me,
That in my joy my caution crept away
Like an unfaithful hound and went to sleep.
Gouvernail, you are cold."

Gouvernail sighed
And fixed an eye calm with experience,

And with affection kind, on Tristram, sadly.
"Yes, I am cold," he said. "Here at my heart
I feel a blasting chill. Will you not come
With me to see the King and Queen together?
Or must I mumble as I may to them,
Alone, this weary jest of your complaint?"

"God's love, have I not seen the two together!
And as for my complaint, mumble or not.
Mumble or shriek it; or, as you see fit,
Call for my harp and sing it." Tristram laid
His hands on Gouvernail's enduring shoulders
Which many a time had carried him for sport
In a far vanished childhood, and looked off
Where patient skill had made of shrubs and rocks
Together a wild garden half way down
To the dusk-hidden shore. "Believe my word,
My loyal and observing Gouvernail,"
He said, and met the older man's regard
With all that he could muster of a smile.
"Believe my word, and say what I have said,
Or something as much better as you may.
Believe my word no less that I am sick,
And that I'd feed a sick toad to my brother
If in my place he were not sick without it."

Gouvernail sighed, and with a deeper sigh
Looked off across the sea. "Tristram," he said,
"I can see no good coming out of this,
But I will give your message as I can,
And with as light misgiving as I may.
Yet where there is no love, too often I find
As perilous a constriction in our judgment
As where there is too much."

607

Tristram pursued

The mentor of his childhood and his youth
With no more words, and only made him
In the returning toil of his departure
A climbing silence that would soon be met
By sound and light, and by King Mark again,
And by Isolt again., Isolt of Ireland!
Isolt, so soon to be the bartered prey
Of an unholy sacrifice, by rites
Of Rome made holy. Tristram groaned and wept,
And heard once more the changeless moan below
Of an insensate ocean on those rocks
Whereon he had a mind to throw himself.
"My God! If I were dreaming this," he said,
"My sleep would be a penance for a year.
But I am neither dead nor dreaming now,
I'm living and awake. If this be life,
What a soul-healing difference death must be,
Being something else . . . Isolt! Isolt of Ireland!"

Gazing at emptiness for a long time
He looked away from life, and scarcely heard,
Coming down slowly towards him from above,
A troubling sound of cloth. "Good evening, sir.
Perhaps you do not know me, or remember
That once you gave a lady so much honor
As to acknowledge her obscure existence.
From late accounts you are not here to know
Your friends on this especial famous evening.
Why do you stay away from history
Like this? Kings are not married every night."

Perceiving there beside him a slim figure
Provisionally cloaked against the cold,
He bowed as in a weary deference

608

TRISTRAM

To childish fate. "Surely I know you, Madam;
You are among the creatures of distinction
Whose quality may be seen even in the dark.
You are Queen Morgan, a most famous lady,
And one that only kings in holy joy
Could ask or dream to be their messenger.
What new persuasion has the King conceived
Beyond this inspiration of your presence?"

"It is not dark," she said; "or not so dark
But that a woman sees—if she be careful
Not to fall down these memorable stairs
And break her necessary little neck
At Tristram's feet. And you might make of that
Only another small familiar triumph
Hardly worth sighing for. Well then, the King
Is vexed and vicious. Your man Gouvernail
Says you are sick with wine. Was that the best
That your two heads together could accomplish?
Will you not for the King's sake, or the Queen's,
Be more compliant, and not freeze to death?"

"Madam, say to the King that if the King
Command me, I will come. Having said that,
It would be gracious of you to be merry—
Malicious, if you must—and say, also,
You found in me a melancholy warning
For all who dim their wits obliviously.
Say it as delicately or as directly
As humors your imperial preference."

Queen Morgan, coming closer, put a small
And cat-like hand on Tristram: "In this world
Of lies, you lay a burden on my virtue
When you would teach me a new alphabet.

I'll turn my poor wits inside out, of course,
Telling an angry king how sick you are—
With wine or whatsoever. Though I shall know
The one right reason why you are not merry,
I'll never scatter it, not for the King's life—
Though I might for the Queen's. Isolt should live,
If only to be sorry she came here—
With you—away from Ireland to be married
To a man old enough to bury himself.
But kings are kings, and by contriving find
Ways over many walls. This being their fate,
It was a clever forethought of the Lord
That there should be a woman or two left
With even Isolt no longer possible.
A school of prudence would establish you
Among the many whose hearts have bled and healed."

"Madam, you are a woman and a queen ;
Wherefore a man, by force of courtesy,
Will hardly choose but listen. No doubt your words
Have a significance in their disguise;
Yet having none for me, they might be uttered
As well in a lost language found on ruins
As in our northern manner. If kings are kings
In your report, queens, I perceive, are queens,
And have their ways also."

                              "A sort of queen."
She laughed, showing her teeth and shining eyes,
And shrugged herself a little nearer to him,
Having not far to come: "But not the sort
That makes a noise where now there are so many.
If silly men pursue me and make songs
About me, it may be because they've heard
Some legend that I'm strange. I am not strange—
Not half so strange as you are."

TRISTRAM

Tristram saw
Before him a white neck and a white bosom
Beneath a fair and feline face whereon
Demure determination was engraved
As on a piece of moonlit living marble,
And could at once have smiled and sighed to see
So much premeditated danger wasted
On his despair and wrath. "Yes, you are strange,"
He said, "and a sagacious peril to men—
Wherefore they must pursue you and make songs.
You are an altogether perilous lady,
And you had best go back now to the King,
Saying that I'm not well. I would conserve
The few shreds left of my integrity
From your displeasure and for wiser vision.
Say to the King I feasted over much
In recognition of his happiness—
An error that apology too soon
Might qualify too late. Tell the King so,
And I am your obedient slave for ever."

A wry twist, all but imperceptible,
Disfigured for an instant her small mouth
Before she smiled and said: "We are the slaves,
Not you. Not even when most we are in power
Are women else than slaves to men they honor.
Men worthy of their reverence know this well,
And honor them sometimes to humor them.
We are their slaves and their impediments,
And there is much in us to be forgiven."

He drew the fringes of her cloak together,
Smiling as one who suffers to escape
Through silence to familiar misery.
"Madam, I fear that you are taking cold,"

611

He said. "Say to the King that I'm not well."
She laughed, and having mounted a few steps
Paused and looked down at him inscrutably:
" 'An error that apology too soon
May qualify too late?' Was it like that?
England is not so large as the wide sky
That holds the stars, and we may meet again.
Good night, Sir Tristram, Prince of Lyonesse."

III

Lost in a gulf of time where time was lost,
And heedless of a light queen's light last words
That were to be remembered, he saw now
Before him in the gloom a ghostly ship
Cleaving a way to Cornwall silently
From Ireland, with himself on board and one
That with her eyes told him intolerably
How little of his blind self a crowded youth,
With a sight error-flecked and pleasure-flawed,
Had made him see till on that silent voyage
There was no more to see than faith betrayed,
Or life disowned. The sorrow in his name
Came out, and he was Tristram, born for sorrow
Of an unguarded and forgotten mother,
Who may have seen as those who are to die
Are like to see. A king's son, he had given
Himself in honor unto another king
For gratitude, not knowing what he had given,
Or seeing what he had done. Now he could see,
And there was no need left of a ship's ghost,
Or ghost of anything else than life before him,
To make him feel, though he might not yet hear it,
The nearness of a doom that was descending
Upon him, and anon should hold him fast—

If he were not already held fast enough
To please the will of fate.

                    "Brangwaine!" he said,
Turning and trembling. For a softer voice
Than Morgan's now had spoken; a truer voice,
Which had not come alone to plead with him
In the King's name for courtesy.

                       "Sir Tristram! . . ."
Brangwaine began, and ended. Then she seized
His hands and held them quickly to her lips
In fealty that he felt was his for ever.
"Brangwaine, for this you make a friend of me
Until I die. If there were more for one
To say . . ." He said no more, for some one else
Than Brangwaine was above him on the stairs.
Coming down slowly and without a sound
She moved, and like a shadow saying nothing
Said nothing while she came. Isolt of Ireland,
With all her dark young majesty unshaken
By grief and shame and fear that made her shake
Till to go further would have been to fall,
Came nearer still to him and still said nothing,
Till terror born of passion became passion
Reborn of terror while his lips and hers
Put speech out like a flame put out by fire.
The music poured unheard, Brangwaine had vanished,
And there were these two in the world alone,
Under the cloudy light of a cold moon
That glimmered now as cold on Brittany
As on Cornwall.

                   Time was aware of them,
And would beat soon upon his empty bell

Release from such a fettered ecstasy
As fate would not endure. But until then
There was no room for time between their souls
And bodies, or between their silences,
Which were for them no less than heaven and hell,
Fused cruelly out of older silences
That once a word from either might have ended,
And so annihilated into life
Instead of death—could her pride then have spoken,
And his duped eyes have seen, before his oath
Was given to make them see. But silences
By time are slain, and death, or more than death,
May come when silence dies. At last Isolt
Released herself enough to look at him,
With a world burning for him in her eyes,
And two worlds crumbling for him in her words:
"What have I done to you, Tristram!" she said;
"What have you done to me! What have we done
To Fate, that she should hate us and destroy us,
Waiting for us to speak. What have we done
So false or foul as to be burned alive
And then be buried alive—as we shall be—
As I shall be!"

                    He gazed upon a face
Where all there was of beauty and of love
That was alive for him, and not for him,
Was his while it was there. "I shall have burned
And buried us both," he said. "Your pride would not
Have healed my blindness then, even had you prayed
For God to let you speak. When a man sues
The fairest of all women for her love,
He does not cleave the skull first of her kinsman
To mark himself a man. That was my way;
And it was not the wisest—if your eyes

Had any truth in them for a long time.
Your pride would not have let me tell them more—
Had you prayed God, I say."

        "I did do that,
Tristram, but he was then too far from heaven
To hear so little a thing as I was praying
For you on earth. You had not seen my eyes
Before you fought with Morhaus; and for that,
There was your side and ours. All history sings
Of two sides, and will do so till all men
Are quiet; and then there will be no men left,
Or women alive to hear them. It was long
Before I learned so little as that; and you
It was who taught me while I nursed and healed
Your wound, only to see you go away."

"And once having seen me go away from you,
You saw me coming back to you again,
Cheerful and healed, as Mark's ambassador.
Would God foresee such folly alive as that
In anything he had made, and still make more?
If so, his ways are darker than divines
Have drawn them for our best bewilderments.
Be it so or not, my share in this is clear.
I have prepared a way for us to take,
Because a king was not so much a devil
When I was young as not to be a friend,
An uncle, and an easy counsellor.
Later, when love was yet no more for me
Than a gay folly glancing everywhere
For triumph easier sometimes than defeat,
Having made sure that I was blind enough,
He sealed me with an oath to make you his
Before I had my eyes, or my heart woke

615

From pleasure in a dream of other faces
That now are nothing else than silly skulls
Covered with skin and hair. The right was his
To make of me a shining knight at arms,
By fortune maybe not the least adept
And emulous. But God! for seizing you,
And having you here tonight, and all his life
Having you here, by the blind means of me,
I could tear all the cords out of his neck
To make a rope, and hang the rest of him.
Isolt, forgive me! This is only sound
That I am making with a tongue gone mad
That you should be so near me as to hear me
Saying how far away you are to go
When you go back to him, driven by—me!
A fool may die with no great noise or loss;
And whether a fool should always live or not . . ."

Isolt, almost as with a frightened leap
Muffled his mouth with hers in a long kiss,
Blending in their catastrophe two fires
That made one fire. When she could look at him
Again, her tears, unwilling still to flow,
Made of her eyes two shining lakes of pain
With moonlight living in them; and she said,
"There is no time for you to tell me this;
And you are younger than time says you are,
Or you would not be losing it, saying over
All that I know too well, or for my sake
Giving yourself these names that are worth nothing.
It was our curse that you were not to see
Until you saw too late. No scourge of names
That you may lay for me upon yourself
Will have more consequence for me, or you,
Than beating with a leaf would have on horses;

So give yourself no more of them tonight.
The King says you are coming back with me.
How can you come? And how can you not come!
It will be cruel enough for me without you,
But with you there alive in the same walls
I shall be hardly worthy of life tonight
If I stay there alive—although I shall,
For this may not be all. This thing has come
For us, and you are not to see the end
Through any such fog of honor and self-hate
As you may seek to throw around yourself
For being yourself. Had you been someone else,
You might have been one like your cousin Andred,
Who looks at me as if he were a snake
That has heard something. Had you been someone else,
You might have been like Modred, or like Mark.
God—you like Mark! You might have been a slave.
We cannot say what either of us had been
Had we been something else. All we can say
Is that this thing has come to us tonight.
You can do nothing more unless you kill him.
And that would be the end of you and me.
Time on our side, this may not be the end."

"I might have been a slave, by you unseen,"
He answered, "and you still Isolt of Ireland,
To me unknown. That would have been for you
The better way. But that was not the way."

"No it was not," she said, trying to smile;
And weary then for trying, held him closer.
"But I can feel the hands of time on me,
And they will soon be tearing me away.
Tristram, say to me once before I go,
What you believe and what you see for us

Before you. Are you sure that a word given
Is always worth more than a world forsaken?
Who knows there may not be a lonely place
In heaven for souls that are ashamed and sorry
For fearing hell?"

                "It is not hell tonight,
Isolt," he said, "or any beyond the grave,
That I fear most for you or for myself.
Fate has adjusted and made sure of that
Where we are now—though we see not the end,
And time be on our side. Praise God for time,
And for such hope of what may come of it
As time like this may grant. I could be strong,
But to be over-strong now at this hour
Would only be destruction. The King's ways
Are not those of one man against another,
And you must live, and I must live—for you.
If there were not an army of guards below us
To bring you back to fruitless ignominy,
There would soon be an end of this offense
To God and the long insult of this marriage.
But to be twice a fool is not the least
Insane of ways to cure a first affliction.
God!—is it so—that you are going back
To be up there with him—with Mark—tonight?
Before you came, I had been staring down
On those eternal rocks and the white foam
Around them; and I thought how sound and long
A sleep would soon begin for us down there
If we were there together—before you came.
That was a fancy, born of circumstance,
And I was only visioning some such thing
As that. The moon may have been part of it.
I think there was a demon born with me

618

And in the malediction of my name,
And that his work is to make others suffer—
Which is the worst of burdens for a man
Whose death tonight were nothing, could the death
Of one be the best end of this for two."

"If that was to be said," Isolt replied,
"It will at least not have to be said over.
For since the death of one would only give
The other a twofold weight of wretchedness
To bear, why do you pour these frozen words
On one who cannot be so confident
As you that we may not be nearer life,
Even here tonight, than we are near to death?
I must know more than you have told me yet
Before I see, so clearly as you see it,
The sword that must for ever be between us.
Something in you was always in my father:
A darkness always was around my father,
Since my first eyes remembered him. He saw
Nothing, but he would see the shadow of it
Before he saw the color or shape it had,
Or where the sun was. Tristram, fair things yet
Will have a shadow black as night before them,
And soon will have a shadow black as night
Behind them. And all this may be a shadow,
Sometime, that we may live to see behind us—
Wishing that we had not been all so sure
Tonight that it was always to be night."

"Your father may have fancied where the sun was
When first he saw the shadow of King Mark
Coming with mine before me. You are brave
Tonight, my love. A bravery like yours now
Would be the summons for a mightier love

Than mine, if there were room for such a love
Among things hidden in the hearts of men.
Isolt! Isolt! . . ."

                   Out of her struggling eyes
There were tears flowing, and withheld in his,
Tears were a veil of pity and desperation
Through which he saw the dim face of Isolt
Before him like a phantom in a mist—
Till to be sure that she was not a phantom,
He clutched and held her fast against his heart,
And through the cloak she wore felt the warm life
Within her trembling to the life in him,
And to the sorrow and the passion there
That would be always there. "Isolt! Isolt!"
Was all the language there was left in him
And she was all that was left anywhere—
She that would soon be so much worse than gone
That if he must have seen her lying still,
Dead where she was, he could have said that fate
Was merciful at least to one of them.
He would have worn through life a living crown
Of death, for memory more to be desired
Than any furtive and forsworn desire,
Or shattered oath of his to serve a King,
His mother's brother, without wilful stain,
Was like to be with all else it might be.
So Tristram, in so far as there was reason
Left in him, would have reasoned—when Isolt
Drew his face down to hers with all her strength
Or so it seemed, and kissed his eyes and cheeks
And mouth until there was no reason left
In life but love—love that was not to be,
Save as a wrenching and a separation
Past reason or reprieve. If she forgot

For long enough to smile at him through tears,
He may have read it as a sign that God
Was watching her and all might yet be well;
And if he knew that all might not be well,
Some God might still be watching over her,
With no more power than theirs now against Rome,
Or the pernicious valor of sure ruin,
Or against fate, that like an unseen ogre
Made hungry sport of these two there alone
Above the moaning wash of Cornish water,
Cold upon Cornish rocks.

                              "No bravery, love,"
She said, "or surely none like mine, would hide,
Among things in my heart that are not hidden,
A love larger than all time and all places,
And stronger beyond knowledge than all numbers
Around us that can only make us dead
When they are done with us. Tristram, believe
That if I die my love will not be dead,
As I believe that yours will not be dead.
If in some after time your will may be
To slay it for the sake of a new face,
It will not die. Whatever you do to it,
It will not die. We cannot make it die,
We are not mighty enough to sentence love
Stronger than death to die, though we may die.
I do not think there is much love like ours
Here in this life, or that too much of it
Would make poor men and women who go alone
Into their graves without it more content,
Or more by common sorrow to be envied
Than they are now. This may be true, or not.
Perhaps I am not old enough to know—
Not having lived always, nor having seen

Much else than everything disorderly
Deformed to order into a small court,
Where love was most a lie. Might not the world,
If we could sift it into a small picture,
Be more like that than it would be like—this?
No, there is not much like this in the world—
And there may not be this!"

                              Tristram could see
Deep in the dark wet splendor of her eyes,
A terror that he knew was more for him
Than for herself. "You are still brave enough,"
He said, "and you might look to me for strength,
If I were a magician and a wizard,
To vanquish the invincible. Destruction
Of such a sort as one here among hundreds
Might wreak upon himself would be a pastime,
If ruin of him would make you free again
Without him."

                    "I would not be free without him,"
Isolt said, as if angry: "And you know
That I should not be free if I were free
Without him. Say no more about destruction
Till we see more, who are not yet destroyed.
O God, if only one of us had spoken—
When there was all that time!"

                          "You mean by that,
If only I had spoken," Tristram said;
And he could say no more till her quick lips
That clung to his again would let him speak.
"You mean, if only I had been awake
In paradise, instead of asleep there,
No jealous angel with a burning sword
Would have had power enough to drive me out,
Though God himself had sent him."

TRISTRAM

Isolt smiled,
As with a willing pity, and closed her eyes
To keep more tears from coming out of them;
And for a time nothing was to be heard
Except the pounding of two hearts in prison,
The torture of a doom-begotten music
Above them, and the wash of a cold foam
Below them on those cold eternal rocks
Where Tristram and Isolt had yesterday
Come to be wrecked together. When her eyes
Opened again, he saw there, watching him,
An aching light of memory; and his heart
Beat harder for remembering the same light
That he had seen before in the same eyes.

"Alone once in the moonlight on that ship,"
She said, still watching him and clinging warm
Against him, "I believed that you would speak,
For I could hear your silence like a song
Out of the sea. I stood by the ship's rail,
Looking away into the night, with only
You and the ocean and the moon and stars
There with me. I was not seeing where I looked,
For I had waited too long for your step
Behind me to care then if the ship sailed
Or sank, so long as one true word of yours
Went wheresoever the ship went with me.
If these eyes, that were looking off so far
Over the foam, found anything there that night
Worth looking at, they have forgotten it;
And if my ears heard even the waves that night,
Or if my cheeks felt even the wind that night,
They have forgotten waves and wind together,
Remembering only there was you somewhere
On the same ship where I was, all alone

623

As I was, and alive. When you did come,
At last, and were there with me, and still silent,
You had already made yourself in vain
The loyal counterfeit of someone else
That never was, and I hope never shall be,
To make me sure there was no love for me
To find in you, where love was all I found.
You had not quite the will or quite the wish,
Knowing King Mark, not to reveal yourself,
When revelation was no more the need
Of my far larger need than revelation.
There was enough revealed, but nothing told.
Since I dare say to you how sure I am
Of the one thing that's left me to be sure of,
Know me and love me as I was that night,
As I am now, and as I shall be always—
All yours; and all this means for you and me
Is no small care for you. If you had spoken
There on that ship what most was in your heart
To say—if you had held me close—like this—
If you had kissed me then—like this—I wonder
If there would have been kings and crowns enough
In Cornwall or in England or elsewhere
To make the crowns of all kings everywhere
Shine with a light that would have let me see
No king but you and no crown but our love.
Tristram, believe, whatever the rest may be,
This is all yours—for God to weigh at last,
And as he will. And if it be found wanting,
He will not find what's left so ordinary
As not to say of it, 'This was Isolt—
Isolt who was all love.' He made her so,
And some time he may tell her why it is
So many that are on earth are there to suffer.
I say this now, for time will not wait always,

And we shall not be here when we are old—
If time can see us old. I had not thought
Of that; and will not think of it again.
There must be women who are made for love,
And of it, and are mostly pride and fire
Without it. There would not be much else left
Of them without it than sold animals
That might as well be driven and eating grass
As weaving, riding, hunting, and being queens,
Or not being queens. But when two loves like ours
Wear down the wall of time dividing them,
Two oceans come together and flow over
Time and his evil work. It was too long,
That wall, but there is nothing left of it,
And there is only love where the wall was.
And while you love me you will not forget
That you are all there is in my life now
That I would live for longer. And since nothing
Is left to me but to be sure of nothing
That you have not been sure of and been told,
You can believe me, though you cannot save me.
No, there is only one way to do that. . . .
If I were sure this was to be the end,
I should make this the end . . . Tristram! Tristram!
With you in the same house!"

                              "Do not say that."
He shook, and held her face away from him,
Gazing upon it as a man condemned
To darkness might have gazed for the last time
At all there was of life that he should see
Before his eyes were blinded by white irons.
"Tell me to throw myself over this wall,
Down upon those dead rocks, and I will do it.
Tell me to fall down now upon the point

Of this too restive sword, and you will see
How brief a sting death has. Tell me to drink
Tonight the most efficient mortal poison,
And of all drink that may be poured tomorrow
None shall be poured for me. But do not say,
Or make me say, where I shall be tonight.
All I can say is, I shall not be here.
Something within me is too near to breaking,
And it is not my heart. That will not break,
Nor shall a madness that is in me now
Break time in two—time that is on our side.
Yet I would see as little of Mark tonight
As may be well for my forgetfulness.
That was the best for me to say to you,
And now it has been said. I shall not kill him."

She trembled in his arms, and with a cry
Of stricken love gave all there was of her
That she could give to him in one more kiss
In which the world was melted and was nothing
For them but love—until another cry,
From Brangwaine, all forgotten in the garden,
Made the world firm again. He leapt away,
Leaving Isolt bewildered and heart-sick
With fear for him, and for she knew not what,
And lastly for herself. But soon she felt
A noise that was like one of shadows fighting.
Then she saw Tristram, who was bringing with him
A choking load that he dragged after him;
And then she could see Brangwaine, white as death
Behind those two. And while she saw them there,
She could hear music from those walls above her,
And waves foaming on the cold rocks below.

When Tristram spoke, his words came hoarse and few.
"I knew the vermin I should find," he said,

And said no more. He muttered and hurled something
Away from him against the parapet,
Hearing the sound that a skull makes on stone;
And without looking one way or another,
He stood there for a time like a man struck
By doom to an ungovernable silence,
Breathing above the crumpled shape of Andred.

IV

Tristram, like one bereft of all attention,
Saw little and heard nothing until Isolt
Sprang with a gasp and held her lips to his
An instant, and looked once into his eyes
Before she whispered in his ears a name,
And sprang away from him. But this was not
Before King Mark had seen sufficiently
To find himself a shadow and Tristram
The substance of it in his Queen's cold eyes,
Which were as dark and dead to him as death
And had no answers in them.

                              "Gouvernail,"
The King said, after staring angrily
About him, "who is lying there at your feet?
Turn him, and let me see?"

                              "You know him, sir,"
Tristram replied, in tones of no address:
"The name of that you see down there is Andred;
And it is manifestly at your service."

"That was an unbecoming jest, I fear,
For you tonight, Tristram," answered the King.

627

"Do you not see what you have done to him?
Andred is bleeding."

            "I am glad of that, sir.
So long as there is less of that bad blood
In him, there will be so much less of Andred.
Wash him, and he will be as good as ever;
And that will be about as good as warts.
If I had been abrupt with him and drowned him,
I'd pity the sick fishes."   Tristram's words,
Coming he knew not whence, fell without life
As from a tongue without it.

              "Gouvernail,"
The King said, trembling in his desperation,
"The Queen and Brangwaine will go back with you.
Come down again with two men of the guard,
And when you come, take Andred through the garden."

"And through the little window he came out of,"
Said Tristram, in the way of one asleep.
Then, seeing the King as if for the first time,
He turned his head to see Isolt once more,
Vanishing, and to see for many a night
And day the last look in her frightened eyes.
But not inured yet fully to his doom,
He waited for the King to speak.

              "Tristram,"
He said, in words wherein his pride and fury
Together achieved almost an incoherence,
"My first right is to ask what Andred saw
That you should so mistreat him. Do not hide
Yourself in silence, for I saw enough."

Tristram's initial answer was a shrug
Of reckless hate before he spoke: "Well, sir,
If you have seen enough, what matters it
How little or much this thing here may have seen?
His reptile observation must have gathered
Far less than you prepared him to report.
There was not much to see that I remember."

"There was no preparation on my part,
And Andred's act was of a loyalty
As well intentioned as it was unsought
And unforeseen by me. I swear to this,
Tristram. Is there as much of truth in you
As that, or is there nothing you dare name
Left of you now that may survive an oath?"

"I know these kings' beginnings," Tristram said,
Too furious to be prudent, "and I know
The crafty clutch of their advantages
Over the small who cringe. And it appears
That a place waits for my apology
To fill for one thing left to thank God for."

"Tomorrow, if occasion shows itself,
Tristram, you may thank God you are alive.
Your plea for pardon has the taint of doubt
Upon it; yet I shall make a minute of it,
Here by the smudge of a sick lamp that smells
Of all I thought was honor."

                              Tristram saw
Confronting him two red and rheumy eyes,
Pouched in a face that nature had made comely,
And in appearance was indulgently
Ordained to wait on lust and wine and riot

For more years yet than leeches might foresee.
Meeting the crafty sadness always in them,
He found it more than sad and worse than crafty,
And saw that no commingled shame and rage
Like that which he could see in them tonight
Would go out soon. "Damn such a man," he thought;
And inward pain made sweat upon his forehead.
"I could almost believe that he believed
Himself, if I had never known him better.
Possession has a blade that will go deep
Unless I break it; and if I do that,
· I shall break with it everything. Isolt!
Isolt and honor are the swords he'll use,
Leaving me mine that I've sworn not to use.
Honor—from him? If he found Honor walking
Here in Cornwall, he would send men to name it,
And would arrest it as a trespasser.
How does one take a thrust that pierces two,
And still defend the other from destruction?"

"Well, Tristram, knight-at-arms and man of honor,"
Mark said, "what last assay have you for me
Of honor now? If you were not the son
Of my dead sister, I should be oppressed
To say how long the sight of you alive
Would be the living cross that my forbearance
Might have to bear. But no, not quite that, either.
I can at least expunge the sight of you
Henceforth from Cornwall, if you care to live."

"Nowhere among my fancies here tonight, sir,
Is there a wish to live and be a cross
Upon your shoulders. If you find a figure
More salient and germane to my condition,
I might then care to live. Your point of honor,

630

Reduced obscurely to a nothingness,
Would hardly be a solid resting-place,
Or a safe one, for me. Give me the choice
Of death, or of inflicting more than death,
I would not live from now until tomorrow.
All said, what have I done? What you have seen.
And if there's any man or Andred breathing
Who tells you lies of more than you have seen,
Give me his name, and he'll tell no more lies.
Andred is waking up; and if I've ears,
Here are those guards coming with Gouvernail.
Andred, if you were not my lizard-cousin,
You might not be awake."

      "I heard that, Tristram,"
Groaned a low voice. "I shall remember that.
I heard the Queen say, 'Tristram, I'm all yours—
All yours!' And then she kissed you till her mouth
Might have been part of yours. 'All yours! All yours!'
Let the King say if I'm a lizard now,
Or if I serve him well." He snarled and spat
At Tristram, who, forgetting, drew his sword,
And after staring at it in the moonlight
Replaced it slowly and reluctantly.

"I cannot kill a worm like that," he said.
"Yet a voice tells me I had better do so.
Take him away—or let the King say that.
This is no slave of mine."

        Gouvernail's men
Stood as if waiting for the moon to fall
Into the sea, but the King only nodded,
Like one bemused; and Andred, with an arm
Thrown over each of them, stumbled away.

The King gave one more nod, and Gouvernail
Like sorrow in the mould of a bowed man,
Went slowly after him.

                         Then the King said,
"Tristram, I cannot trust myself much longer,
With you before me, to be more than man."
His fury shook him into a long silence
That had an end in tears of helpless rage:
"Why have you come between me and my Queen,
Stealing her love as you might steal my gold!
Honor! Good God in heaven! Is this honor—
And after all that I have done for you?"

"Almost as much as buying her with gold,
Or its equivalent in peace, was honor.
And as for all that you have done for me,
There are some tenuous items on my side.
Did I not, fighting Morhaus in your name,
Rid Cornwall of a tribute that for years
Had sucked away the blood and life of Cornwall,
Like vampires feeding on it in the night?
And have I not in my blind gratitude
For kindness that would never have been yours
If it had cost you even a night's rest,
Brought you for Queen the fairest of all women?
If these two gifts, which are but two, were all,
What more, in the King's name, would the King ask?"

"The casuistries of youth will not go far
With me, Tristram. You brought to me a Queen,
Stealing her love while you were bringing her.
What weakness is it in me lets you live?"

"I beg your pardon, sir, and for one error.
Where there was never any love to steal,

632

No love was ever stolen. Honor—oh, yes!
If all the rituals, lies, and jigs and drinking
That make a marriage of an immolation—"

"By heaven, if you say one more word like that,"
The King cried, with his sword half out again,
"One of us will be left here!" Then he stopped,
As if a bat had flown against his ear
And whispered of the night. "But I will cease,
Mindful of who you are, with one more question.
You cast a cloud around the name of honor
As if the sight of it were none too sweet
In your remembrance. If it be not honor
That ails you now and makes a madman of you,
It may be there's a reptile with green eyes
Arrived for a long feeding on your heart—
Biting a bit, who knows?"

Tristram could see
In the King's eyes the light of a lewd smile
That angrily deformed his aging face
With an avenging triumph. "Is this your way
To make a madman of me? If it be so,
Before you take my reason, take my life.
But no—you cannot. You have taken that."
He drew his sword as if each gleaming inch
Had come in anguish out of his own flesh,
And would have given it for the King to keep—
Fearing himself, in his malevolence,
Longer to be its keeper. But the King,
Seizing his moment, gave Tristram no time
More than to show the trembling steel, and hear
The doom that he had felt and partly seen
With Isolt's hope to cheer him.

                                    "You have drawn
Your sword against the King, Tristram," he said.
"Now put it back. Your speech to me before
Was nearer your last than you are near to me—
Yet I'll not have your blood. I'll have your life,
Instead—since you are sure your life means only
One woman—and will keep it far from you;
So far that you shall hunger for it always.
When you go down those stairs for the last time,
And that time will be now, you leave Cornwall
Farther behind you than hell's way from heaven
Is told in leagues. And if the sight of you
Offends again my kingdom and infects it,
I swear by God you will be chained and burned.
And while you burn, her eyes will be held open
To watch your passion cooling in the flames.
Go!—and may all infernal fires attend you—
You and your nights and days, and all your dreams
Of her that you have not, and shall have never!"

"You know that for her sake, and for that only,
You are alive to say this," Tristram said;
And after one look upward at those lights
That soon would all be out, he swayed and trembled,
And slowly disappeared down the long stairs,
Passing the guards who knew him with a word
Of empty cheer, regardless of what thoughts
Of theirs were following him and his departure,
Which had no goal but the pursuing clutch
Of a mad retrospect.

                        He strode along
Until there was no moon but a white blur
Low in a blurred gray sky, and all those lights
That once had shone above him and Isolt,

634

And all that clamor of infernal joy
That once had shrilled above him and Isolt,
Were somewhere miles away among the ages
That he had walked and counted with his feet,
Which he believed, or dreamed that he believed,
Were taking him through hell to Camelot.
There he would send, or so again he dreamed,
A word to Lancelot or to Gawaine,
But what word he knew not. There was no word,
Save one, that he could seize and separate
Out of the burning fury and regret
That made a fire of all there was of him
That he could call himself. And when slow **rain**
Fell cold upon him as upon hot fuel,
It might as well have been a rain of oil
On faggots round some creature at a stake
For all the quenching there was in it then
Of a sick sweeping heat consuming him
With anguish of intolerable loss,
Which might be borne if it were only loss.
But there was with it, always and again,
A flame-lit picture of Isolt alone
With Mark, in his embrace, and with that **mouth**
Of his on hers, and that white body of hers
Unspeakably imprisoned in his arms
For nights and days and years. A time had been
When by the quick destruction of all else
And of himself, he might have spared Isolt
By leaving her alone for lonely pain
To prey on till she died and followed him
To whatsoever the dusk-hidden doors
Of death might hide for such a love as theirs;
And there was nothing there so foul, he thought—
So far as he could think—and out of reason,
As to be meted for a sin like theirs

That was not sin, but fate—which must itself
Be but a monstrous and unholy jest
Of sin stronger than fate, sin that had made
The world for love—so that the stars in heaven
Might laugh at it, and the moon hide from it,
And the rain fall on it, and a King's guile
And lust makes one more shuddering toy of it.
He would not see behind him, yet had eyes
That saw behind him and saw nowhere else.
Before him there was nothing left to see
But lines of rain that he could hardly see,
And shapes that had no shape along a road
That had no sodden end. So on he strode
Without a guiding end in sight or mind,
Save one, if there were such an end somewhere,
That suddenly might lead him off the world
To sink again into the mysteries
From which his love had come, to which his love
Would drag him back again with ropes of fire
Behind him in the rain at which he laughed,
As in his torture he might then have laughed
At heaven from hell. He had seen both tonight—
Two had seen both, and two for one were chosen,
Because a love that was to be fulfilled
Only in death, was for some crumbs of hope,
Which he had shared for mercy with Isolt,
Foredoomed to live—how or how long to live
With him, he knew not. If it lived with him
Tonight, it lived only as things asleep
In the same rain where he was not asleep
Were somewhere living, as tomorrow's light
Would prove they were. Tomorrow's light, he thought,
Might prove also that he was living once,
And that Isolt was living once where lamps
Were shining and where music dinned and shrieked

Above her, and cold waves foaming on rocks
Below her called and hushed and called again
To say where there was peace.

                      There was no peace
For Tristram until after two nights' walking,
And two days' ranging under dripping trees,
No care was left in him to range or walk,
Or to be found alive where finally,
Under an aged oak he cast himself,
Falling and lying as a man half dead
Might shape himself to die. Before he slept,
A shame came over him that he, Tristram,
A man stronger than men stronger than he,
Should now be weaker than a man unmade
By slow infirmity into a child
To be the sport of children. Then his rage
Put shame away and was again a madness,
And then a blank, wherein not even a name
That he remembered would stay long enough
For him to grasp it or to recognize it,
Before the ghost of what had been a name
Would vanish like a moonbeam on a tomb
When a cloud comes. Cloud after cloud came fast,
Obliterating before leaving clear
The word that he had lost. It was a name
Of someone far behind him in the gloom,
Where there were lights above, and music sounding
And the long wash of a cold sea below.
"Isolt!" He smiled as one who from a dream
Wakes to find he was dreaming and not dying,
And then he slept.

                When he awoke again,
It was to find around him, after fever,

A squalid box of woodland poverty,
In which he lay like a decrepit worm
Within an empty shell. Through a small square
Clear sunlight slanted, and there was outside
A scattered sound of life that fitfully
Twittered and shrilled. In time there was a tread
Of heavy steps, and soon a door was open;
Then in from somewhere silently there came
A yokel shape, unsightly and half-clad,
That shambled curiously but not unkindly
Towards the low sodden pallet where Tristram
Lay wondering where he was; and after him
Came one that he remembered with a leap
Of gladness in his heart.

                            "You—Gouvernail?"
He cried; and he fell back into a swoon
Of uselessness too deep for Gouvernail
To call him from by kindly word or touch
Till time was ready. In the afternoon,
Tristram, not asking what had come to pass,
Nor caring much, found himself in a cart,
Dimly aware of motion and low words
And of a dull security. He slept,
And half awoke, and slept again, till stones
Under the wheels and a familiar glimpse
Of unfamiliar walls around a court
Told of a journey done. That night he slept,
And in the morning woke to find himself
In a place strange to him. Whose place it was,
Or why he should be in it, was no matter.
There he could rest, and for a time forget.
So, for a time, he lost the name of life,
And of all else except Isolt. . . . "Isolt!"

TRISTRAM

That was the only name left in the world,
And that was only a name. "Isolt! Isolt!"

After an endless day of sleep and waking,
With Gouvernail adventuring in and out
Like an industrious and unquiet phantom,
He woke again with low light coming in
Through a red window. Now the room was dim,
But with a dimness that would let him see
That he was not alone. "Isolt!" he said,
And waited, knowing that it was not Isolt.

A crooning voice that had within its guile
A laughing ring of metal said, "Isolt?
Isolt is married. Are you young men never
To know that when a princess weds a king
The young man, if he be a wise young man,
Will never afford himself another fever,
And lie for days on a poor zany's rags,
For all the princesses in Christendom?
Gouvernail found you, I found Gouvernail,
And here you are, my lord. Forget Isolt,
And care a little for your royal self;
For you may be a king one of these days
And make some other young man as miserable
As Mark makes you. The world appears to be,
Though God knows why, just such a place as that.
Remember you are safe, and say your prayers.
For all you know of this life or the next,
You may be safer here than in your shroud.
Good night, Sir Tristram, Prince of Lyonesse."

Days after, vexed with doubt and indecision,
Queen Morgan, with her knight a captive now,
Sat gazing at him in a coming twilight,

Partly in anger, partly in weary triumph,
And more than all in a dark wonderment
Of what enchantment there was wanting in her
To keep this man so long out of her toll
Of willing remnants and of eager cinders,
Now scattered and forgotten save as names
To make her smile. If she sat smiling now,
It was not yet for contemplated havoc
Of this man's loyalty to a lost dream
Where she was nothing. She had made other men
Dream themselves dead for her, but not this man,
Who sat now glowering with a captive scorn
Before her, waiting grimly for a word
Of weariness or of anger or disdain
To set him free.

    "You are not sound enough,
My lord, for travel yet," she said. "I know,
For I have done more delving into life
And death than you, and into this mid-region
Between them, where you are, and where you sit
So cursed with loneliness and lethargy
That I could weep. Hard as this is for you,
It might be worse. You will go on your way,
While I sit knitting, withering and outworn,
With never a man that looks at me, save you,
So truthful as to tell me so." She laughed
At him again, and he heard metal laughing,
As he had heard it speaking, in her low
And stinging words.

    "You are not withering yet,"
He said; and his eyes ranged forgetfully
Over a studied feline slenderness
Where frugal silk was not frugality.

640

TRISTRAM

"I am too ill to see, in your account,
More than how safe I am with you." Isolt,
With her scared violet eyes and blue-black hair
Flew like a spirit driven from a star
Into that room and for a moment stayed
Before him. In his eyes he could feel tears
Of passion, desperation, and remorse,
Compounded with abysmal indignation
At a crude sullen hunger not deceived,
Born of a sloth enforced and of a scorn
Transformed malignly to a slow surrender.
His captor, when she saw them, came to him
And with a mocking croon of mother-comfort
Fondled him like a snake with two warm arms
And a warm mouth; and after long chagrin
Of long imprisonment, and long prisoned hate
For her that in his hatred of himself
He sought now like an animal, he made
No more acknowledgment of her cajoling
Than suddenly to rise without a word
And carry her off laughing in his arms,
Himself in hers half strangled.

                    Gouvernail,
As heretofore, found waiting him again
The same cold uncommunicating guards,
Past whom there was no word. Another day,
And still another and another day
Found them as mute in their obedience
As things made there of wood. Tristram, within
Meanwhile achieved a sorry composition
Of loyalty and circumstance. "Tomorrow,"
He said, "I must be out and on my way."
And Morgan only said, "Which way is that?"
And so on for a fortnight, when at last,

641

With anger in her eyes and injuries
Of his indifference envenoming
The venom in her passion and her pride,
She let him go—though not without a laugh
That followed him like steel piercing unseen
His flight away from her with Gouvernail.

"You leave me now," she said, "but Fate has eyes.
You are the only blind one who is here,
As you are still to see. I said before,
Britain is less than the whole firmament,
And we may meet again. Until we meet,
Farewell; and find somewhere a good physician
To draw the poison of a lost Isolt
Out of your sick young heart. Till he do so,
You may as well be rearing you a tomb
That else will hold you—presently. Farewell,
Farewell, Sir Tristram, Prince of Lyonesse,
The once redoubtable and undeceived,
Who now in his defeat would put Fate's eyes out.
Not yet, Sir Prince; and we may meet again."
She smiled; and a smile followed him long after
A sharp laugh was forgotten.

                                Gouvernail,
Riding along with Tristram silently
Till there was no glimpse left of Morgan's prison
Through the still trees behind them, sighed and said
"Where are we going, Tristram, and what next?"
And through the kindness of his weary grief
There glimmered in his eyes a loyal smile
Unseen by Tristram, though as well divined
As if revealed.

                "You are the last of men,
And so the last of friends now, Gouvernail,

For me to cleave to in extremities
Beyond the malefactions of this world.
You are apart and indispensable,
Holding me out of madness until doom,
Which I feel waiting now like death in the dark,
Shall follow me and strike, unrecognized,
For the last time. Away from that snake's nest
Behind me, it would be enough to know
It is behind me, were it not for knowledge
That in a serpent that is unsubdued
And spurned, a special venom will be waiting
Its time. And when the serpent is a woman,
Or a thin brained and thinner blooded Andred,
Infirm from birth with a malignant envy,
One may not with one thrust annihilate
The slow disease of evil eating in them
For one that never willed them any evil.
Twice have I heard in helpless recognition
A voice to bid me strike. I have not struck,
And shall not . . . For a time now, Gouvernail,
My memory sees a land where there is peace,
And a good king whose world is in his kingdom
And in his quaint possession of a child
Whose innocence may teach me to be wise
Till I be strong again. I see a face
That once was fond of me, and a white hand
Holding an agate that I left in it.
I see a friendliness of old assured
In Brittany. If anywhere there were peace
For me, it might be there—or for some time
Till I'm awake and am a man again."

"I was not saying all that to you, Tristram,"
Gouvernail answered, looking at his reins,
"But since you say it, I'll not fatigue my tongue

Gainsaying it for no good. Time is a casket
Wherein our days are covered certainties
That we lift out of it, one after one,
For what the day may tell. Your day of doom,
Tristram, may like as not be one for you
To smile at, could you see it where it waits,
Far down, I trust, with many a day between
That shall have gladness in it, and more light
Than this day has. When you are on the sea,
And there are white waves everywhere to catch
The sunlight and dance with it and be glad
The sea was made, you may be glad also.
Youth sees too far to see how near it is
To seeing farther. You are too blind today,
By dim necessity of circumstance,
More than to guess. Whether you take your crown
In Lyonesse or not, you will be king
Wherever you are. Many by chance are crowned
As kings that are born rather to be tinkers,
Or farmers, or philosophers, or farriers,
Or barbers, or almost anything under God
Than to be kings. Whether you will or not,
You are a king, Tristram, for you are one
Of the time-sifted few that leave the world,
When they are gone, not the same place it was.
Mark what you leave."

                               "There was a good man once,"
Said Tristram, "who fed sunshine to the blind
Until the blind went mad, and the good man
Died of his goodness, and died violently.
If untoward pleasantries are your affection,
Say this was in your casket and not mine.
There's a contentious kingdom in myself
For me to rule before I shall rule others.

TRISTRAM

If it is not too dark for me to fight
In there for my advantage and advancement,
And if my armor holds itself together
So long as not to be disintegrated
Before it breaks and I am broken with it,
There may be such a king as you foresee;
And failing him, I shall not fail my friend,
Who shall not be forgotten.   Gouvernail,
Be glad that you have no more darkness in you."

They rode along in silence, Gouvernail
Retasting an abridgement undeserved,
And undeserving of another venture,
Or so his unofficial ardor warned him,
Into a darkness and a namelessness
Wherein his worldly and well-meaning eyes
Had never sought a name for the unseen.

V

Griffon, the giant scourge of Brittany,
Threatened while Tristram was appraising it,
In his anticipation, all the peace
Awaiting him across the foaming waves
That were to wash, in Gouvernail's invention,
Time out of life.   And there King Howel's child,
Isolt of the white hands, living on hope,
Which in all seeming had itself alone
To live on, was for love and safety now
A prisoner in that castle by the sea
Where Tristram once, not thinking twice of it,
Had said that he would some day come again,
And more as a gay plaything than a pledge
Had left with her an agate which had been
For long her father's jest.   It was her heart,

Which she had taken out of her white bosom,
He said, and in the forest or in the sea
Would presently be lost and never found
Again—not even for Tristram when he came.
But when he came there was no time for talk
Of hearts and agates. Welcome and wonderment
Appeased, and the still whiteness of Isolt
Regarded once and then at once forgotten,
Tristram, like one athirst with wine before him,
Heard the King's talk of a marauding host
That neither force nor craft had yet subdued
Or more than scattered, like an obscene flock
Of rooks alert around a living quarry
That might not have a longer while to live
Than a few days would hold, or not so many.

"Praise be to God, I could almost have said
For your ill fortune, sir, and for your danger,"
Was Tristram's answer to the King's grim news.
"I have been groping slowly out of life
Into a slough of darkness and disuse—
A place too far from either for life or death
To share with me. Yes, I have had too much
Of what a fool, not knowing its right name,
Would call the joy of life. If that be joy,
Give me a draught out of your cup of trouble,
And let it be seen then what's left of me
To deal with your bad neighbor. For tonight,
Let me have rest before tomorrow's work,
Which may be early."

                              "Early and late, I fear,"
The King said, and eyed Tristram cautiously,
And with a melancholy questioning
Of much that was for him no more a question.

646

"If it be God that brings you here today,
I praise him in my thanks given to you,
Tristram, for this. Sleep, and forget tomorrow
Until tomorrow calls you. If ill comes
To you for this, I shall not wish to live—
But for my child. And if ill comes to her,
It will be death to live."

                "Tomorrow, sir,
These ills may be the dregs in empty cups
With all the bitterness drunk out of them.
No ill shall come to her till you and I
And all your men go down defending her;
And I can figure no such havoc as that.
I'm not a thousand men, or more than one,
Yet a new mind and eye, and a new arm
At work with yours, may not combine for ruin."

Uncertain afterwards in a foreseen
Achievement unachieved, Tristram rejoiced
At last when he saw Griffon at his feet
And saw the last of his pernicious minions
Dispatched or disappearing. And that night,
Having espied Isolt's forgotten harp,
He plucked and sang the shadow of himself,
To her his only self, unwittingly
Into the soul and fabric of her life,
Till death should find it there. So day by day
He fostered in his heart a tenderness
Unrecognized for more than a kind fear
For what imaginable small white pawn
Her candor and her flame-white loveliness
Could yet become for the cold game of kings,
Who might not always, if they would, play quite
Their game as others do.

Once by the shore
They lingered while a summer sun went down
Beyond the shining sea; and it was then
That sorrow's witchcraft, long at work in him,
Made pity out of sorrow, and of pity
Made the pale wine of love that is not love,
Yet steals from love a name. And while he felt
Within her candor and her artlessness
The still white fire of her necessity,
He asked in vain if this were the same fate
That for so long had played with him so darkly—
With him and with Isolt, Isolt of Ireland,
Isolt of the wild frightened violet eyes
That once had given him that last look of hers
Above the moaning call of those cold waves
On those cold Cornish rocks. This new Isolt,
This new and white Isolt, was nothing real
To him until he found her in his arms,
And, scarcely knowing how he found her there,
Kissed her and felt the sting of happy tears
On his bewildered lips. Her whiteness burned
Against him till he trembled with regret;
For hope so long unrealized real at last
To her, was perilously real to him.
He knew that while his life was in Cornwall,
Something of this white fire and loneliness
In Brittany must be his whereon to lavish
The comfort of kind lies while he should live.
There were some words that he would have been saying
When her eyes told him with a still reproof
That silence would say more; and Tristram wished
That silence might say all.

For a long time
They sat there, looking off across the water

TRISTRAM

Between them and Tintagel to the north,
Where Tristram saw himself chained to a stake
With flames around him and Isolt of Ireland
Held horribly to see. King Mark, he knew,
Would in his carnal rage cling to his word
And feast his eyes and hate insatiably
On his fulfilment of it—in itself
The least of Tristram's fear. It was her eyes,
Held open to behold him, that he saw,
More than it was himself, or any torture
That would be only torture worse than his
For her. He turned himself away from that,
And saw beside him two gray silent eyes
Searching in his with quaint solemnity
For some unspoken answer to a thought
Unspoken.

       "When I told my father first
That you would come, he only smiled at me,"
She said. "But I believe by saying always
That you were coming, he believed you would,
Just as I knew you would."

              "And why was that,
My child?" he asked, a captive once again
To her gray eyes and her white need of him;
"You might have told your father I was coming
Till the world's end, and I might not have come."

"You would have come, because I knew you would,"
She said, with a smile shaking on her lips
And fading in her eyes. "And you said that,
Because you knew, or because you knew nothing,
Or cared less than you know. Because you knew,
I like to fancy. It will do no harm."

649

"Were I so sure of that," he thought, "as you are,
There would be no infection of regret
In my remembrance of a usefulness
That Brittany will say was mine. Isolt
Of Brittany? Why were two names like that
Written for me by fate upon my heart
In red and white? Is this white fire of pity,
If pity it be, to burn deeper than love?"
Isolt of Ireland's dark wild eyes before him
In the moonlight, and that last look of hers,
Appeared in answer. Tristram gazed away
Into the north, and having seen enough,
He turned again to find the same gray light
In the same eyes that searched in his before
For an unspoken answer to a thought
Unspoken. They came silently away,
And Tristram sang again to her that night.

And he sang many a time to her thereafter
Songs of old warriors, and old songs of love
Triumphant over wars that were forgotten;
And many a time he found in her gray eyes,
And in the rose-white warmth of her attention,
Dominion of a sure necessity
Beyond experience and the need of reason,
Which had at first amused him and at last
Had made him wonder why there should be tears
In a man's eyes for such a mild white thing
That had so quaint a wisdom in its mildness,
Unless because he watched it going slowly
Its mild white way out of the world without him.
"Can she see farther into time, by chance,
Than I do?" he would ask, observing her:
"She might do so, and still see little farther
Than to the patient ends of her white fingers

650

That are so much alive, like all of her."
She found him smiling, but in her large eyes
There was no smile. There was a need of him
That made him cold, as if a ghost had risen
Before him with a wordless admonition
That he must go or stay. And many a time
He would have gone, if he had not perforce
As many a time remained to sing for her
Those old songs over, and as many a time
Found in her gaze that sure necessity
Which held him with a wisdom beyond thought,
Or with an innocence beyond all wisdom,
Until he sang one night for the last time
To the King's child. For she was his child now,
And for as long as there was life in him
Was his to cherish and to wonder at,
That he should have this white wise fiery thing
To call his wife.

            "Magicians might have done it"
He pondered once, alone, "but in so far
As I'm aware of them, there are none left
In Brittany so adept as to achieve it.
Stars may have done it." Then King Howel, pleased,
Though in his pleasure as incredulous
As if he were somehow a little injured,
Appearing out of silence from behind him,
Took Tristram's hands approvingly in his,
And said, "You have a child that was a woman
Before she was a child, and is today
Woman and child, and something not of either,
For you to keep or crush—without a sound
Of pain from her to tell you so. Beware
Somewhat of that, Tristram; and may you both
Be wise enough not to ask more of life

Than to be life, and fate." The last word fell
Like a last coin released unwillingly
By caution giving all. And while the King
Said what he said, Tristram was seeing only
A last look in two dark and frightened eyes
That always in the moonlight would be shining,
Alone above the sound of Cornish waves
That always in the moonlight would be breaking,
Cold upon Cornish rocks.

But occupation,
Like a neglected and insistent hound
Leaping upon his master's inattention,
Soon found him wearing on his younger shoulders
The yoke of a too mild and easy-trusting
And easy-futured king. He shaped and trained
An army that in time before would soon
Have made of Griffon a small anecdote
Hardly worth telling over after supper;
He built new ships and wharves, and razed old houses,
And so distressed a realm with renovation
Unsought and frowned on by slow denizens
For decades undisturbed, that many of them,
Viewing the visioned waste of a new hand,
Had wished him dead, or far from Brittany;
And for the flower of his activities,
He built a royal garden for Isolt
Of the white hands to bloom in, a white rose
Fairer than all fair roses in the world
Elsewhere—save one that was not white but dark,
Dark and love-red for ever, and not there,
Where the white rose was queen.

So for two years
She reigned and waited, and there in her garden

TRISTRAM

Let rumor's noise, like thunder heard far off,
Rumble itself to silence and as nigh
To nothing as might be. But near the end
Of a long afternoon, alone with him,
She sat there watching Tristram, who in turn,
Still mystified at having in his care
To keep or crush, even as her father said,
So brave and frail a flower, sat watching her
With eyes that always had at least been kind,
If they had not said always everything
She would have had them say. Staring at him,
Like someone suddenly afraid of life,
She chilled him slowly with a question: "Tristram,"
She said, "what should I do were you to die?"

"Are there no prettier notions in your head
Than that?" said he, and made a task of laughing.
"There are no mortal purposes in me
Today, yet I may say what you would do:
Were I to die, you would live on without me.
But I would rather sing you an old song
Than die, and even for you, this afternoon."

"Yes, presently you will sing me an old song,"
She said. "It was a wonder seized me then
And made me ask like that what I should do
Were you to die. Were you to tire of me,
And go away from me and stay some time,
I should not die, for then you would come back.
You came back once, and you would come again;
For you would learn at last you needed me
More than all other creatures. But if you died,
Then you would not come back. What should I do
If you should go away and never come back?
I see almost a shadow on you sometimes,

As if there were some fearful thing behind you,
Not to be felt or seen—while you are here."

"I can feel only the sun behind me now—
Which is a fearful thing if we consider it
Too long, or look too long into its face."
Saying that, he smiled at her, not happily,
But rather as one who has left something out,
And gazed away over a vine-hung wall,
And over the still ocean where one ship
Was coming slowly in.

                         "If I lost you
For a long time," she said, with her insistence,
"I should not cry for what had come between,
For I should have you here with me again.
I am not one who must have everything.
I was not fated to have everything.
One may be wise enough, not having all,
Still to be found among the fortunate."

She stood beside him now and felt his arm
Closing around her like an arm afraid.
"Little you know, my child," he thought, in anguish
A moment for the fear and innocence
That he was holding and was his to hold,
"What ashes of all this wisdom might be left you
After one blast of sick reality
To tell the wise what words are to the heart."
And then aloud: "There's a ship coming in
From somewhere north of us."

                         "There are no ships
From the north now that are worth looking at,"
She said; and he could feel her trembling warm
Against him till he felt her scorching him

With an unconscious and accusing fire.
"There was a time when I was always gazing
North for a ship, but nothing is there now;
Or ships are all alike that are there now."

"They are not all like this one," Tristram said,
More to himself than to the white Isolt
Arming herself with blindness against fate,
"For there are trumpets blowing, as if a king
Were coming—and there's a dragon on the sail.
One of King Arthur's barges—by the Lord
In heaven, it is!—comes here to Brittany,
And for a cause that lives outside my knowledge.
Were this the King, we should have known of him."

"What does it mean?" she whispered; and her words
Wavered as if a terror not yet revealed
Had flown already inland from that ship.

"God knows," he said, "but it will not be long
Before we shall all know." She followed him
Into her father's castle, where the new
Looked ancient now; and slowly, after silence,
He left her waiting there at the same window
Where she had waited for so long before,
When she was looking always to the north;
And having left her there, alone with wonder,
He went alone with wonder to the shore,
Where a gay ship was coming gaily in,
And saw descending from it soon, and gaily,
As always, Sir Gawaine from Camelot.

VI

Gawaine, in Cornwall once, having seen Isolt
Of Ireland with her pallid mask of pride,

Which may have been as easy a mask as any,
He thought, for prisoned love and scorn to wear,
Had found in her dark way of stateliness
Perfection providentially not his
To die for. He recalled a wish to die,
But only as men healed remember pain;
And here in Tristram's garden, far from Cornwall,
Gawaine, musing upon this white Isolt
Of Brittany, whose beauty had heretofore,
For him, lived rather as that of a white name
Than of a living princess, found himself
Again with a preoccupied perfection
To contemplate. The more he contemplated,
The more he arraigned fate and wondered why
Tristram should be at odds with banishment,
Or why Tristram should care who banished him,
Or for how long, or for what violet eyes
And Irish pride and blue-black Irish hair
Soever. He smiled with injured loyalty
For Tristram in a banishment like this,
With a whole world to shine in save Cornwall,
And Cornwall the whole world; and if he sighed,
He may have sighed apart, and harmlessly,
Perceiving in this Isolt a continence
Too sure for even a fool to ponder twice,
A little for himself. They faced each other
On a stone bench with vine-leaves over them,
And flowers too many for them to see before them,
And trees around them with birds singing in them,
And God's whole gift of summer given in vain
For one who could feel coming in her heart
A longer winter than any Breton sun
Should ever warm away, and with it coming,
Could laugh to hear Gawaine making her laugh.

TRISTRAM

"I have been seeing you for some hours," he said,
"And I appraise you as all wonderful.
The longer I observe and scrutinize you,
The less do I become a king of words
To bring them into action. They retreat
And hide themselves, leaving me as I may
To make the best of a disordered remnant,
Unworthy of allegiance to your face
And all the rest of you. You are supreme
In a deceit that says fragility
Where there is nothing fragile. You have eyes
That almost weep for grief, seeing from heaven
How trivial and how tragic a small place
This earth is, and so make a sort of heaven
Where they are seen. Your hair, if shorn and woven,
The which may God forbid, would then become
A nameless cloth of gold whiter than gold,
Imprisoning light captured from paradise.
Your small ears are two necessary leaves
Of living alabaster never of earth,
Whereof the flower that is your face is made,
And is a paradisal triumph also—
Along with your gray eyes and your gold hair
That is not gold. Only God knows, who made it,
What color it is exactly. I don't know.
The rest of you I dare not estimate,
Saving your hands and feet, which authorize
A period of some leisure for the Lord
On high for their ineffable execution.
Your low voice tells how bells of singing gold
Would sound through twilight over silent water.
Yourself is a celestial emanation
Compounded of a whiteness and a warmth
Not yet so near to heaven, or far from it,
As not to leave men wiser for their dreams

And distances in apprehending you.
Your signal imperfection, probably,
Is in your peril of having everything,
And thereby overwhelming with perfection
A man who sees so much of it at once,
And says no more of it than I am saying.
I shall begin today to praise the Lord,
I think, for sparing an unworthy heart
An early wound that once might not have healed.
If there lives in me more than should be told,
Not for the world's last oyster would I tell it
To the last ear alive, surely not yours."

"If you were one of the last two alive,
The other might make of you the last," she said,
Laughing. "You are not making love to me,
Gawaine, and if you were it wouldn't matter.
Your words, and even with edges a bit worn
By this time, will do service for years yet.
You will not find that you have dulled them much
On me, and you will have them with you always."

"I don't know now whether I am or not,"
Said he, "and say with you it wouldn't matter.
For Tristram, off his proper suavity,
Has fervor to slice whales; and I, from childhood,
Have always liked this world. No, I should say
That I was covering lightly under truth
A silent lie that may as well be silent;
For I can see more care than happiness
In those two same gray eyes that I was praising."

"Gawaine," she said, turning the same gray eyes
On his and holding them, with hers half laughing.
"Your fame is everywhere alike for lightness,

And I am glad that you have not my heart
To be a burden for you on too long
A journey, where you might find hearts of others
Not half so burdensome. Do you like that?
If you do not, say it was never said,
And listen as if my words were bells of gold,
Or what you will. You will be hanged some day
For saying things, and I shall not be there
To save you, saying how little you meant by them.
You may be lighter than even your enemies
Would see you in their little scales of envy,
Yet in your lightness, if I'm not a fool,
There lives a troubled wonder for a few
You care for. Now if two of them were here,
Would you say what was best, in your reflection,
And on your honor say no more of it,
For one of them alone here to believe
When Tristram goes with you to Camelot?
While he is there, King Arthur, it appears,
Will make of him a Knight of the Round Table—
All which would be illustrious and delightful
Enough for me, if that were to be all.
And though the world is in our confidence,
Your honor as a man will forget that;
And you will answer, wisely perhaps, or not,
One question, which in brief is only this:
What right name should an innocence like mine
Deserve, if I believed he would come back?"
She watched him with expectant eyes, wherefrom
The ghost of humor suddenly had vanished.

Gawaine, who felt a soreness at his heart
That he had seldom felt there for another
Before, and only briefly for himself,
Felt also a cloud coming in his eyes.

"I can see only one thing to believe,"
He said, believing almost he could see it,
"And that is, he will come—as he must come.
Why should he not come back again, for you?
Who in this world would not come back, for you!
God's life, dear lady, why should he not come back?"
He cried, and with a full sincerity
Whereat she closed her eyes and tried to speak,
Despairingly, with pale and weary lips
That would not speak until she made them speak.

"Gawaine," she said, "you are not fooling me;
And I should be a fool if hope remained
Within me that you might be. You know truth
As well as I do. He will not come back.
King Mark will kill him." For so long unspoken,
She had believed those words were tamed in her
Enough to be released and to return
To the same cage there in her aching heart
Where they had lived and fought since yesterday.
But when she felt them flying away from her,
And heard them crying irretrievably
Between her and Gawaine, and everywhere,
Tears followed them until she felt at last
The touch of Gawaine's lips on her cold fingers,
Kindly and light.

                    "No, Mark will hardly kill him,"
He told her. Breathing hard and hesitating,
He waited as a felon waits a whip,
And went on with a fluent desperation:
"Mark is in prison now—for forgery
Of the Pope's name, by force of which Tristram
Was to go forth to fight the Saracens,

660

And by safe inference to find a grave
Not far ahead. Impossible, if you like,
And awkward out of all ineptitude,
And clumsy beyond credence, yet the truth,
As the impossible so often is.
In his unwinking hate he saw Tristram
Too near for easy vengeance, and so blundered
Into the trap that has him. This was not
For me to tell, and it is not for you,
Upon your royal honor as a woman
Of honor more than royal to reveal.
Mercy compels me to forego my word
And to repeat the one right thing for you
In reason to believe. He will come back;
And you, if you are wise—and you are that
Beyond the warrant of your sheltered years—
Will find him wiser in his unworthiness,
And worthier of your wisdom and your love,
When this wild fire of what a man has not
Reveals at last, in embers all gone out,
That which he had, and has, and may have always,
To prize aright thereafter and to pray for.
Out of my right I talk to you like this,
And swear by heaven, since I have gone so far,
That your worst inference here is not my knowledge.
He may come back at once. If otherwise—well,
He will come back with a new vision in him
And a new estimation of God's choice.
I have told you what neither grief nor guile
Would of themselves alone have wrung from me.
The rest will be in you, you being yourself."

"Yes, you have thrown your offices away
And you have left your honor for me to keep,"
She said, and pressed his hands in gratitude.

"Here it will be as safe as in the sea.
I thank you, and believe you. Leave me here
Alone, to think; to think—and to believe."
She brushed her eyes and tried as if to smile,
But had no smile in answer. For Gawaine,
Infrequently in earnest, or sincere
To conscious inconvenience, was in love,
Or thought he was, and would enjoy alone,
Without a smile and as he might, the first
Familiar pangs of his renunciation.

He wandered slowly downward to the shore
Where he found Tristram, gazing at the ship
Which in the morning would be taking them
Together away from Brittany and Isolt
Of the white hands to England, where Tristram,
A knight only of Mark's investiture
Today, would there be one of the Round Table—
So long the symbol of a world in order,
Soon to be overthrown by love and fate
And loyalty forsworn. Had Gawaine then
Beheld a cloud that was not yet in sight,
There would have been more sorrow in his eyes
For time ahead of him than for time now,
Or for himself. But where he saw no cloud
That might not be dissolved, and so in time
Forgotten, there was no sorrow in his eyes
For time to come that would be longer coming,
To him, than for the few magnanimous days
Of his remembrance of enforced eclipse.

"Tristram," he said, "why in the name of God
Are you not looking at your garden now,
And why are you not in it with your wife?
662

TRISTRAM

I left her, after making love to her
With no progression of effect whatever,
More than to make her laugh at me, and then
To make her cry for you for going away.
I said you would be coming back at once,
And while I said it I heard pens in heaven
Scratching a doubtful evidence against me."

Tristram, in indecision between anger
Deserving no indulgence and surprise
Requiring less, scowled and laughed emptily:
"Gawaine, if you were anyone else alive
I might not always be at home to you,
Or to your bland particularities.
Why should a wedded exile hesitate
In his return to his own wife and garden?
I know the picture that your folly draws
Of woe that is awaiting me in Cornwall,
But we are going to Camelot, not to Cornwall.
King Mark, with all his wealth of hate for me,
Is not so rich and rotten and busy with it
As to be waiting everywhere at once
To see me coming. He waits most in Cornwall,
Preferring for mixed reasons of his own
Not frequently to shine far out of it."

"He may not be so rotten as some whose names
Have fallen from my deciduous memory,"
Gawaine said, with a shrug of helplessness,
"But all the same, with Mark and his resource
In England, your best way's away from there
As early and expeditiously as may be.
Mark's arm is not the only arm he uses;
My fear for you is not my only fear.
Fear for yourself in you may be as nothing,

Which is commendable and rather common
In Camelot, as fellows who read and write
Are not so rare there that we crown them for it.
But there's a fear more worthy than no fear,
And it may be the best inheritance
Of luckless ones with surer sight than yours,
And with perception more prophetical
Than yours. I say this hoping it will hurt,
But not offend. You see how lax I am
When I'm away from royal discipline,
And how forgetful of unspoken caution
I am when I'm afraid to be afraid.
I thrust my head into the lion's mouth,
And if my head comes off, it will have done,
For once if only once, the best it might.
I doubt if there's a man with eyes and ears
Who is more sadly and forlornly certain
Of what another's wisdom—born of weakness,
Like all born mortal attributes and errors—
Is like to leave behind it of itself
In you, when you have heard and hated it,
But all the same, Tristram, if I were you,
I'd sail away for Camelot tomorrow,
And there be made a Knight of the Round Table;
And then, being then a Knight of the Round Table,
I should come back. I should come back at once.
Now let the lion roar."

                    He laid his hands
On Tristram's iron shoulders, which he felt
Shaking under his touch, and with a smile
Of unreturned affection walked away
In silence to the ship. Tristram, alone,
Moved heavily along the lonely shore,
To seat himself alone upon a rock

TRISTRAM

Where long waves had been rolling in for ages,
And would be rolling when no man or woman
Should know or care to know whether or not
Two specks of life, in time so far forgotten
As in remembrance never to have been,
Were Tristram and Isolt—Isolt in Cornwall,
Isolt of the wild frightened violet eyes,
Isolt and her last look, Isolt of Ireland.
Alone, he saw the slanting waves roll in,
Each to its impotent annihilation
In a long wash of foam, until the sound
Become for him a warning and a torture,
Like a malign reproof reiterating
In vain its cold and only sound of doom.
Then he arose, with his eyes gazing still
Into the north, till with his face turned inland
He left the crested wash of those long waves
Behind him to fall always on that sand,
And to sound always that one word—"Isolt."

As if in undesigned obedience
To Gawaine's admonition, he went idly
And blindly back to the sun-flooded garden
Where sat the white Isolt whose name was not
The name those waves, unceasing and unheard,
Were sounding where they fell. Still as Gawaine
Had left her, Tristram found her. She looked up
With a wan light of welcome flashing sadly
To see him; and he knew that such a light
As that could shine for him only from eyes
Where tears had been before it. They were not
There now, and there was now no need of them
To make him ask, in a self-smiting rage
Of helpless pity, if such a love as hers
Might not unshared be nearer to God's need,

665

In His endurance of a blinder Fate,
Than a love shared asunder, but still shared,
By two for doom elected and withheld
Apart for time to play with. Once he had seen,
Imploring it, the light of a far wisdom
Tingeing with hope the night of time between,
But there was no light now. There might be peace,
Awaiting them where they were done with time—
Time for so long disowning both of them,
And slowly the soul first, saving the rest
To mock the soul—but there was no peace now.
When there was no time left for peace on earth,
After farewells and vestiges forgotten,
There might be time enough for peace somewhere;
But that was all far off, and in a darkness
Blacker than any night that ever veiled
A stormy chaos of the foaming leagues
That roared unseen between him and Cornwall.

All this was in his mind, as it was there
Always, if not thought always, when she spoke:
"Tristram, you are not angry or distressed
If I am not so happy here today
As you have seen me here before sometimes,
And may see me again. Tomorrow morning
If I am here, I shall be here alone.
I wonder for how long."

                              "For no day longer
Than I'm away," he said, and held her face
Between his hands. "Then, if you like, my child,
Your wonder may come after your surprise
That I should come so soon. There's no long voyage
From here to Camelot, and I've no long fear
King Arthur will engage himself for ever

In making me a Knight of the Round Table.
King Mark . . ."

              "And why do you mention him to me!"
She cried, forgetful of her long command
Of what she had concealed and stifled from him.
"I should have said King Mark was the last name
Of all, or all but one, that I should hear
From you today. Were there no better days!"

"King Mark says I'm a knight, but not King Arthur—
Not yet—was all that I was going to say;
And I am not saying that because I love him—
Only that you should hear the difference
From me, and have at least some joy of it.
I shall not feel Mark's sword upon my shoulder
Again until I feel the edge of it;
And that will not befall in Camelot,
Or wheresoever I shall carry with me
One of these arms that are not useless yet."

"And where do you plan next to carry them
To prove yourself a Knight of the Round Table?"
She said, and with a flame filling her eyes
As if a soul behind them were on fire.
"What next one among thieves, with Griffon gone,
Will be the nearest to your heart's desire?"

If her lip curled a little in asking that,
Tristram was looking down and did not see it.
"Where do I plan to carry my two arms
Away with me from Camelot, do you ask?
My purpose is to bring them here with me
To Brittany—both of them, God willing so.
You are not here with me, but in the past

This afternoon, and that's not well for you.
When I'm an exile, as you know I am,
Where would your fancy drive me, if not here?
All that was long ago."

                "So long ago,
Tristram, that you have lived for nothing else
Than for a long ago that follows you
To sleep, and has a life as long as yours.
Sometimes I wish that heaven had let you have her,
And given me back all that was left of you,
To teach and heal. I might be sure of that.
Or, to be sure of nothing, if only sure,
Would be a better way for both of us
Than to be here together as we have been
Since Gawaine came from Cornwall in that ship."

"From Cornwall? Are you dreaming when you say it?"
He questioned her as if he too were dreaming
That she had said it; and his heart was cold.
"From Cornwall? Did you not hear Gawaine saying
That he had come for me from Camelot?
Do you see Arthur, who loves Mark almost
As hard as I do, sending ships for me
From Cornwall? If you can see things like that,
You are seeing more of that which never was
Than will be needful where we need so much
Right seeing to see ourselves. If we see others,
Let us, for God's sake, see them where they are—
Not where they were. The past, or part of it,
Is dead—or we that would be living in it
Had best be dead. Why do you say to me
That Gawaine came from Cornwall in that ship?"

There was another gleam now in her eyes
Than yesterday had been imaginable

For Tristram, even had he been strangling her
In some imagined madness. "What?" she said;
"Did I say Cornwall? If I did, perhaps
It was because I thought the sound of it
Would make you happy. So far as I'm aware,
You have not heard that name in a long time.
Did I say Cornwall? If I did, forgive me.
I should have said that I said Camelot.
Not the same place at all."

                        Dimly alive
To knowledge of a naked heart before him,
For him to soothe and comfort with cold lies,
He knew that lies could have no cooling virtue,
Even though they might be falling on this heart
As fast and unregarded as rain falls
Upon an angry sea. Anger so new,
And unforetold, was hardly to be known
At first for what it was, or recognized
With more than silence. If he recognized it,
Before him in a garden full of sunshine,
He saw it as a shadow in the night
Between him and two dark and frightened eyes
And the last look that he had seen in them,
With music shrieking always in the moonlight
Above him, and below him the long sound
Of Cornish waves that would be sounding always,
Foaming on those cold rocks. For a long time
He saw not the white face accusing him,
And heard no sound that others might have heard
Where there was once a garden for Isolt—
Isolt of the white hands, who said no more
To him that afternoon. He left her there,
And like a man who was no longer there,
He stared over the wall, and over water

Where sunlight flashed upon a million waves,
Only to see through night, and through moonlight,
The coming after of a darker night
Than he could see, and of a longer night
Than there was time to fear. Assured of nothing,
He was too sure of all to tell more lies
In idle mercy to an angry woman
Whose unavailing alchemy of hope
No longer, or not now, found love in pity.

But with no more display of desolation
Than anyone's wife among a thousand wives
Might then have made, foreseeing nothing worse
Than to be left alone for no long time,
She met him without anger in the morning,
And in the morning said farewell to him,
With trumpets blowing and hundreds cheering him;
And from a moving shore she waved at him
One of her small white hands, and smiled at him,
That all should see her smiling when he sailed
Away from her for Camelot that morning.
Gawaine, recovered early from a wound
Within a soon-recuperating heart,
Waved a gay hat on board for two gray eyes
On shore; and as the ship went farther out,
The sound of trumpets blowing golden triumph
Rang faintly and more faintly as it went,
Farther and always farther, till no sound
Was heard, and there was nothing to be seen
But a ship sailing always to the north,
And slowly showing smaller to the sight.

She watched again from the same window now
Where she had watched and waited for so long
For the slow coming of another ship

670

That came at last. What other ship was coming,
And after what long time and change, if ever,
No seer or wizard of the future knew,
She thought, and Tristram least of all. Far off,
The ship was now a speck upon the water,
And soon, from where she was, would not be that,
And soon was not; and there was nothing left
That day, for her, in the world anywhere,
But white birds always flying, and still flying,
And always the white sunlight on the sea.

VII

Isolt alone with time, Isolt of Ireland,
So candid and exact in her abhorrence
Of Mark that she had driven him in defeat
To favors amiable if unillusioned,
Saw, with a silent love consuming her,
A silent hate inhibiting in Mark
A nature not so base as it was common,
And not so cruel as it was ruinous
To itself and all who thwarted it. Wherefore,
Tristram it was, Tristram alone, she knew,
That he would see alive in useless fire,
Thereafter to be haunted all his days
By vengeance unavenging. Where was vengeance
For the deforming wounds of difference
That fate had made and hate would only canker,
And death corrupt in him till he should die?
But this was not for Mark, and she said little
To Mark of more than must in ceremony
Be said, perforce, fearing him to misread
Her deprecating pity for his birthright
For the first meltings of renunciation,
Where there was none to melt.—"If I'm so fair,

671

Why then was all this comely merchandise
Not sold as colts are, in a market-place,"
She asked herself. "Then Tristram could have bought me
Whether he feared my love was hate or not,
And whether or not he killed my uncle Morhaus."
And there were days when she would make Brangwaine
Go over the bridge and into the woods with her
To cheer her while she thought.—"If I were Queen
In this forsaken land," Brangwaine said once,
"I'd give three bags of gold to three strong men,
And let them sew King Mark into a sack,
And let them sink him into the dark sea
On a dark night, and Andred after him.
So doing, I'd welcome Erebus, and so leave
This world a better place."—"If you sew Andred
Into a sack, I'll do the rest myself,
And give you more than your three bags of gold,"
Isolt said; and a penitential laugh
Tempered an outburst that was unrepeated—
Though for a year, and almost a year after,
Brangwaine had waited. But Isolt would laugh
For her no more. The fires of love and fear
Had slowly burned away so much of her
That all there was of her, she would have said,
Was only a long waiting for an end
Of waiting—till anon she found herself,
Still waiting, where a darkening eastern sea
Made waves that in their sound along the shore
Told of a doom that was no longer fear.

Incredulous after Lancelot's departure
From Joyous Gard, Tristram, alone there now,
With a magnificence and a mystery
More to be felt than seen among the shadows
Around him and behind him, saw the ocean

TRISTRAM

Before him from the window where he stood,
And seeing it heard the sound of Cornish foam
So far away that he must hear it always
On the world's end that was for him in Cornwall.
A forest-hidden sunset filled long clouds
Eastward over the sea with a last fire,
Dim fire far off, wherein Tristram beheld
Tintagel slowly smouldering in the west
To a last darkness, while on Cornish rocks
The moan of Cornish water foamed and ceased
And foamed again. Pale in a fiery light,
With her dark hair and her dark frightened eyes,
And their last look at him, Isolt of Ireland
Above him on the stairs, with only a wall
Waist-high between her and her last escape,
Stood watching there for him who was not there.
He could feel all those endless evening leagues
Of England foiling him and mocking him
From where it was too late for him to go,
And where, if he were there, coming so late,
There would be only darkness over death
To meet his coming while she stood alone
By the dark wall, with dark fire hiding her,
Waiting—for him. She would not be there long;
She must die there in that dark fire, or fall,
Throwing herself away on those cold rocks
Where there was peace, or she must come to him
Over those western leagues, mysteriously
Defeating time and place. She might do so
If she were dead, he thought, and were a ghost,
As even by now she might be, and her body,
Where love would leave so little of earth to burn,
Might even by now be burning. So, as a ghost
It was that she would have to come to him,
On little feet that he should feel were coming.

She would be dead, but there might be no pain
In that for him when the first death of knowing
That she was dead was ended, and he should know
She had found rest. She would come back to him
Sometimes, and touch him in the night so lightly
That he might see her between sleep and waking,
And see that last look in her eyes no more—
For it would not be there.

                    It was not there.
Woman or ghost, her last look in the moonlight
Was not in her eyes now. Softly, behind him,
The coming of her steps had made him turn
To see there was no fear in her eyes now;
And whether she had come to him from death,
Or through those dark and heavy velvet curtains,
She had come to him silent and alone,
And as the living come—living or not.
Whether it was a warm ghost he was holding,
Or a warm woman, or a dream of one,
With tear-filled eyes in a slow twilight shining
Upward and into his, only to leave him
With eyes defeated of all sight of her,
Was more than he dared now let fate reveal.
Whatever it was that he was holding there,
Woman or ghost or dream, was not afraid;
And the warm lips that pressed themselves again
On his, and held them there as if to die there,
Were not dead now. The rest might be illusion—
Camelot, Arthur, Guinevere, Gawaine,
Lancelot, and that voyage with Lancelot
To Joyous Gard, this castle by the sea—
The sea itself, and the clouds over it,
Like embers of a day that like a city
Far off somewhere in time was dying alone,

TRISTRAM

Slowly, in fire and silence—the fading light
Around them, and the shadowy room that held them—
All these,—if they were shadows, let them be so,
He thought. But let these two that were not shadows
Be as they were, and live—by time no more
Divided until time for them should cease.
They were not made for time as others were,
And time therefore would not be long for them
Wherein for love to learn that in their love,
Where fate was more than time and more than love,
Time never was, save in their fear of it—
Fearing, as one, to find themselves again
Intolerably as two that were not there.

Isolt, to see him, melted slowly from him,
Moving as if in motion, or in much thought,
All this might vanish and the world go with it.
Still in his arms, and sure that she was there,
She smiled at him as only joy made wise
By sorrow smiles at fear, as if a smile
Would teach him all there was for life to know,
Or not to know. Her dark and happy eyes
Had now a darkness in them that was light;
There was no longer any fear in them,
And there was no fear living on a face
That once, too fair for beauty to endure
Without the jealous graving of slow pain,
Was now, for knowledge born of all endurance,
Only beyond endurance beautiful
With a pale fire of love where shone together
Passion and comprehension beyond being
For any long time; and while she clung to him,
Each was a mirror for the other there
Till tears of vision and of understanding
Were like a mist of wisdom in their eyes,

Lest in each other they might see too soon
All that fate held for them when Guinevere,
In a caprice of singularity
Seizing on Mark's unsafe incarceration,
Made unrevealed a journey to Cornwall,
Convoyed by two attendant eminent leeches
Who found anon the other fairest woman
Alive no longer like to stay alive
Than a time-tortured and precarious heart,
Long wooed by death, might or might not protest.
All which being true, Guinevere gave herself
Humbly to God for telling him no lies;
And Lancelot gave his conscience to God also,
As he had given it once when he had felt
The world shake as he gave it. Stronger than God,
When all was done the god of love was fate,
Where all was love. And this was in a darkness
Where time was always dying and never dead,
And where God's face was never to be seen
To tell the few that were to lose the world
For love how much or little they lost for it,
Or paid with others' pain.

                    "Isolt! Isolt!"
He murmured, as if struggling to believe
That one name, and one face there in the twilight,
Might for a moment, or a moment longer,
Defeat oblivion. How could she be with him
When there were all those western leagues of twilight
Between him and Cornwall? She was not there
Until she spoke:

                    "Tristram!" was all she said;
And there was a whole woman in the sound
Of one word surely spoken. She was there,

Be Cornwall where it was or never was,
And England all a shadow on the sea
That was another shadow, and on time
That was one shadow more. If there was death
Descending on all this, and this was love,
Death then was only another shadow's name;
And there was no more fear in Tristram's heart
Of how she fared, and there was no more pain.
God must have made it so, if it was God—
Or death, if it was death. If it was fate,
There was a way to be made terribly
For more than time, yet one that each knew well,
And said well, silently, would not be long.
How long now mattered nothing, and what there was
Was all.

      "Tristram!" She said again his name,
And saying it she could feel against herself
The strength of him all trembling like a tower
Long shaken by long storms, in darkness far
From hers, where she had been alone with it
Too long for longer fear. But that was nothing,
For that was done, and they were done with time.
It was so plain that she could laugh to see it;
And almost laughing she looked up at him,
And said once more, "Tristram!"

                  She felt herself
Smothered and crushed in a forgetful strength
Like that of an incredulous blind giant,
Seizing amain on all there was of life
For him, and all that he had said was lost.
She waited, and he said, "Isolt! Isolt!"
He that had spoken always with a word
To spare, found hungrily that only one

Said all there was to say, till she drew more
From him and he found speech.

"There are no kings

Tonight," he told her, with at last a smile,
"To make for you another prison of this—
Or none like one in Cornwall. These two arms
Are prison enough to keep you safe in them
So long as they are mine."

"They are enough,

Tristram," she said. "All the poor kings and queens
Of time are nothing now. They are all gone
Where shadows go, after the sun goes down.
The last of them are far away from here,
And you and I are here alone together.
We are the kings and queens of everything;
And if we die, nothing can alter that,
Or say it was not so. Before we die,
Tell me how many lives ago it was
I left you in the moonlight on those stairs,
And went up to that music and those voices,
And for God's reason then did not go mad!
Tell me how old the world was when it died—
For I have been alone with time so long
That time and I are strangers. My heart knows
That I was there too long, but knows not yet
Why I was there, or why so many alive
Are as they are. They are not with me here.
They all went when the world went. You and I
Only are left, waiting alone for God—
Down here where the world was!"

Fire in her eyes

And twilight on her warm dark-waving hair

678

And on a warm white face too beautiful
To be seen twice alive and still be found
Alive and white and warm and the same face,
Compelled him with her pallid happiness
To see where life had been so long the fuel
Of love, that for a season he saw nothing,
Save a still woman somewhere in a moonlight,
Where there were stairs and lamps and a cold sound
That waves made long ago. Yet she was warm
There in his arms, and she was not the ghost
He feared she was, chilling him first with doubt.

"We are the last that are alive, Isolt,
Where the world was. Somewhere surrounding us
There are dim shapes of men with many names,
And there are women that are made of mist,
Who may have names and faces. If I see them,
They are too far away for you to see.
They all went when the world went. You are the world,
Isolt—you are the world!"

                "Whatever I am,
You are the last alive to make me listen
While you say that. You are the world, Tristram.
My worth is only what it is to you.
In Cornwall I was not appraised unduly,
Save as a queen to garnish, when essential,
A court where almost anything with a face
Would have been queen enough. And you know best
How much I was a queen. The best I know
Is all there is to know—that some command
In heaven, or some imperial whim of mercy
Brought Guinevere to Cornwall, and brought me
Here to this place that may be real sometime,
And to your arms that must be real indeed.

Let them be real! . . . O God, Tristram! Tristram!
Where are those blindfold years that we have lost
Because a blind king bought of a blind father
A child blinder than they? She might have drawn
A knife across her throat rather than go! . . .
But no—had she done that, she would have died;
And all her seeming needlessness alive
Would have been all it seemed. Oh, it would be
A fearful thing for me to close my eyes
Too long, and see too much that is behind me!
When they were open you might not be here.
Your arms that hold me now might not be yours,
But those of a strong monster and a stranger.
Make me believe again that you are here! . . .
Yes, you are here!"

     All her firm litheness melted
Into the sure surrender of a child
When she said that; and her dark eyes became
For a dim moment gray, and were like eyes
That he had left behind in Brittany.
Another moment, and they were dark again,
And there was no such place as Brittany.
Brittany must have died when the world died—
The world, and time. He had forgotten that,
Till he found now, insensibly almost,
How soft and warm and small so proud a queen
As this Isolt could be. Dimly deceived
By the dark surety of her stateliness
And by the dark indignity of distance,
His love may not have guessed how this Isolt
Of Ireland, with her pride that frightened kings,
Should one day so ineffably become
So like a darker child for him to break
Or save, with a word hushed or a word spoken;

And so his love may well never have seen
How surely it was fate that his love now
Should light with hers at the last fire of time
A flaming way to death. Fire in her eyes,
And sorrow in her smile, foretold unsaid
More than he saw.

                    "You are not sad that heaven
Should hide us here together, God knows how long,
And surely are not fearful," he said, smiling.
"Before there was a man or woman living,
It was all chronicled with nights and days
That we should find each other tonight like this.
There was no other way for love like ours
To be like this than always to have been.
Your love that I see looking into mine
Might have in it a shining of more knowledge
Than love needs to be wise; and love that's wise
Will not say all it means. Untimely words,
Where love and wisdom are not quarrelling,
Are good words not to say."

                         "If you see wisdom
Shining out of my eyes at you sometime,
Say it is yours, not mine. Untimely words
Are not for love, and are like frost on flowers
Where love is not for long. When we are done
With time, Tristram, nothing can be for long.
You would know that if you had been a woman
Alone in Cornwall since those lights went out,
And you went down those stairs. Sometime I'll ask
How far you wandered and what rainy end
There ever was to that unending night,
But now I shall not ask an answer more
Of you than this, or more of God than this;
For this is all—no matter for how long.

681

Do not forget, my love, that once Isolt
Said that; and wheresoever she may be then,
See her where she is now—alone with you,
And willing enough to be alone in heaven—
Or hell, if so it be—and let you live
Down here without her for a thousand years,
Were that the way of happiness for you,
Tristram. So long as fate itself may find
No refuge or concealment or escape
From heaven for me save in some harm for you
I shall not be unhappy after this."

"He that pays all for all is past all harm,"
He said: "I can forgive your thousand years,
And you are sorry for them. The one harm
Deserving a fantastic apprehension
Is one that surely cannot come tonight.
Only an army of infernal men—
And they would not be men—will find a way
Over these walls, or through them, to find me—
Or you, tonight. Untimely words again,
But only as a folly to match yours
In feigning harm for me. Dear God in heaven!
If one such reptile thought inhabited
A nature that was never mine before,
Some woman at hand should watch you properly
While I, like Judas, only running faster,
Might hang myself."

              He felt her body throbbing
As if it held a laugh buried alive,
And suddenly felt all his eloquence
Hushed with her lips. Like a wild wine her love
Went singing through him and all over him;
And like a warning her warm loveliness
Told him how far away it would all be

When it was warm no longer. For some time
He was a man rather by dread possessed
Than by possession, when he found again
That he was listening to the blended gold
And velvet that was always in her voice:

"Your meditations are far wanderers,
And you must have them all home before dark;
Or I shall find myself at work to learn
What's in me so to scatter them. Dear love,
If only you had more fear for yourself
You might, for caution, be my cause for less.
My cage is empty, and I'm out of it;
And you and I are in another cage—
A golden cage—together. Reason it is,
Not fear, that lets me know so much as that;
Also, the while you care not for yourself
Where shadows are, there are things always walking.
Meanwhile your fear for me has been a screen
Of distance between me and my destruction—
Mine, love, and yours. Fears are not always blind.
If love be blind, mine has been so for watching
Too long across an empty world for you;
And if it be myself now that is blind,
I may still hide myself somewhere alone—
Somewhere away from you. Whatever we are,
We are not so blind that we are not to know
The darkness when it comes, if it must come.
We are not children teasing little waves
To follow us along a solid shore.
I see a larger and a darker tide,
Somewhere, than one like that. But where and when,
I do not wish to see."

                              "If love that's blind,"
He said, holding her face and gazing at it,

683

"Sees only where a tide that's dark and large
May be somewhere sometime, love that has eyes
Will fix itself, and with a nearer wonder,
Upon Isolt—who is enough to see.
Isolt alone. All else that emulates
And envies her—black faggots in red flame,
A sunshine slanting into a dark forest,
A moonlight on white foam along black ledges,
Sunlight and rain, trees twinkling after rain,
Panthers and antelopes, children asleep—
All these are native elsewhere, and for now
Are not important. Love that has eyes to see
Sees now only Isolt. Isolt alone.
Isolt, and a few stars."

      "Were I the shadow
Of half so much as this that you are seeing
Of me, I should not be Isolt of Ireland,
Or any Isolt alive. All you can see
Of me is only what the Lord accomplished
When he made me for love. When he made you,
His love remembered that; and whether or not
His way was the most merciful, he knows—
Not we. Or was it fate, stronger than all?
A voice within me says that God, seeing all,
Was more compassionate than to let love see
Too far—loving his world too well for that.
We do not have to know—not yet. The flower
That will have withered from the world for ever
With us, will die sometime; and when it fades,
And dies, and goes, we shall have gone already,
And it will all be done. If I go first,
No fear of your forgetting shall attend me,
Leaving with you the mind and heart of love—
The love that knows what most it will remember.

TRISTRAM

If I lose you, I shall not have to wait—
Not long. There will be only one thing then
Worth waiting for. No, I shall not wait long . . .
I have said that. Now listen, while I say this:
My life to me is not a little thing;
It is a fearful and a lovely thing;
Only my love is more.''

                                 "God knows," he said,
"How far a man may be from his deserving
And yet be fated for the undeserved.
I might, were I the lord of your misgivings,
Be worthier of them for destroying them;
And even without the mightiness in me
For that, I'll tell you, for your contemplation,
Time is not life. For many, and many more,
Living is mostly for a time not dying—
But not for me. For me, a few more years
Of shows and slaughters, or the tinsel seat
Of a small throne, would not be life. Whatever
It is that fills life high and full, till fate
Itself may do no more, it is not time.
Years are not life.''

                            "I have not come so far
To learn," she said, and shook her head at him,
"What years are, for I know. Years are not life;
Years are the shells of life, and empty shells
When they hold only days, and days, and days.
God knows if I know that—so let it pass.
Let me forget; and let me ask you only
Not to forget that all your feats at arms,
Your glamour that is almost above envy,
Your strength and eminence and everything,
Leave me a woman still—a one-love woman,

Meaning a sort of ravenous one-child mother,
Whose one love pictures in her composition
Panthers and antelopes, children asleep,
And all sorts of engaging animals
That most resemble a much-disordered queen,
Her crown abandoned and her hair in peril,
And she herself a little deranged, no doubt,
With too much happiness. Whether he lives
Or dies for her, he tells her is no matter,
Wherefore she must obediently believe him.
All he would ask of her would be as easy
As hearing waves, washing the shore down there
For ever, and believing herself drowned.
In seeing so many of her, he might believe her
To be as many at once as drops of rain;
Perhaps a panther and a child asleep
At the same time."

               He saw dark laughter sparkling
Out of her eyes, but only until her face
Found his, and on his mouth a moving fire
Told him why there was death, and what lost song
Ulysses heard, and would have given his hands
And friends to follow and to die for. Slowly,
At last, the power of helplessness there was
In all that beauty of hers that was for him,
Breathing and burning there alone with him,
Until it was almost a part of him,
Suffused his passion with a tenderness
Attesting a sealed certainty not his
To cozen or wrench from fate, and one withheld
In waiting mercy from oblivious eyes—
His eyes and hers, that over darker water,
Where darker things than shadows would be coming,
Saw now no more than more stars in the sky.

TRISTRAM

He felt her throbbing softly in his arms,
And held her closer still—with half a fear
Returning that she might not be Isolt,
And might yet vanish where she sat with him,
Leaving him there alone, with only devils
Of hell supplanting her.

                   "Leave me the stars
A little longer," said Isolt. "In Cornwall,
So much alone there with them as I was,
One sees into their language and their story.
They must be more than fire; and if the stars
Are more than fire, what else is there for them
To be than love? I found all that myself;
For when a woman is left too much alone,
Sooner or later she begins to think;
And no man knows what then she may discover."

"Whether she be in Cornwall, or not there,
A woman driven to thinking of the stars
Too hard is in some danger," he said, sighing,
"Of being too much alone wherever she is."

Her face unseen, she smiled, hearing him sigh—
So much as if all patient chivalry
Were sighing with him. "One alone too long
In Cornwall has to think somewhat," she said,
"Or one may die. One may do worse than die.
If life that comes of love is more than death,
Love must be more than death and life together."

"Whether I know that life is more or not
Than death," he said, "I swear, with you for witness—
You and the stars—that love is more than either."

"If I should have to answer twice to that,
I should not let myself be here with you
Tonight, with all the darkness I see coming
On land and over water." Then she ceased,
And after waiting as one waits in vain
For distant voices that are silent, "Tell me!"
She cried, seizing him hard and gazing at him,
"Tell me if I should make you go away!
I'm not myself alone now, and the stars
All tell me so."

           He plucked her clinging hands
From his arms gently, and said, holding them,
"You cannot make me go away from you,
Isolt, for I believe, with you to tell me,
All your stars say. But never mind what they say
Of shadows coming. They are always coming—
Coming and going like all things but one.
Love is the only thing that in its being
Is what it seems to be. Glory and gold,
And all the rest, are weak and hollow staves
For even the poor to lean on. We know that—
We that have been so poor while grinning hinds
And shining wenches with all crowns to laugh at,
Have envied us, know that. Yet while you see
So many things written for you in starry fire,
Somehow you fear that I may lose my vision
Not seeing them. I shall not be losing it—
Not even in seeing beyond where you have seen.
Yes, I have seen your stars. You are the stars!
You are the stars when they all sing together.
You live, you speak, and you have not yet vanished.
You are Isolt—or I suppose you are!"

He was not sure of her not vanishing
Until he felt her tears, and her warm arms

688

Holding him with a sudden strength of love
That would have choked him had it not been love.
Each with unyielding lips refused the other
Language unasked; and their forgotten ears
Knew only as a murmur not remembered
A measured sea that always on the sand
Unseen below them, where time's only word
Was told in foam along a lonely shore,
Poured slowly its unceasing sound of doom—
Unceasing and unheard, and still unheard,
As with an imperceptible surrender
They moved and found each other's eyes again,
Burning away the night between their faces.

"Sometimes I fear that I shall fear for you
No more," she said; and to his ears her words
Were shaken music. "Why should I fear for you,
Or you for me, where nothing of earth is left,
Nothing of earth or time, that is worth fearing?
Sometimes I wonder if we are not like leaves
That have been blown by some warm wind of heaven
Far from the tree of life, still to be living
Here between life and death."

       "Why do those two
Vainglorious and abysmal little words
Pursue you and torment your soul?" said he.
"They are the serpents and uncertainties
That coil and rustle tonight among your fears,
Only because your fears have given to them
A shape without a substance. Life and death?
Do not believe your stars if they are saying
That any such words are in their language now.
Whenever they tell you they are made of love,
Believe it; and forget them when they tell you

Of this or that man's living a thousand years.
Why should he wish to live a thousand years?
Whether your stars are made of love or fire,
There is a love that will outshine the stars.
There will be love when there are no more stars.
Never mind what they say of darkness coming
That may come sometime, or what else they say
Of terrors hidden in words like life and death.
What do they mean? Never mind what they mean!
We have lived and we have died, and are alone
Where the world has no more a place for us,
Or time a fear for us, or death . . . Isolt!"
Her lips again had hushed him, and her name,
As when first he had found her in his arms,
Was all there was to say till he was saying
Muffled and husky words that groped and faltered,
Half silenced in a darkness of warm hair:
"Whatever it is that brings us here tonight,
Never believe—never believe again—
Your fear for me was more than love. Time lied,
If he said that. When we are done with time,
There is no time for fear. It was not fear—
It was love's other name. Say it was that!
Say to me it was only one of time's lies!
Whatever it was—never mind what it was!
There will be time enough for me to die.
Never mind death tonight. . . . Isolt! Isolt!"

VIII

Albeit the sun was high, the breath of morning
Was in the trees where Tristram stood alone
With happiness, watching a bright summer sea
That like a field of heaving steel and silver
Flashed there below him, and as harmlessly

690

As if an ocean had no darker work
To do than flash, and was to bear thereafter
No other freight than light. Joy sang in him
Till he could sing for joy, and would have done so,
Had not the lowly fear that humbles princes
Constrained him and so hindered him from giving
A little too much to those who served and feared him,
And willingly would listen; wherefore, turning
Away from the white music the waves made,
He lost himself again in a small forest,
Admiring the new miracle of the leaves,
And hearing, if one bird sang, as many as ten.
Now he could see once more the walls and towers
Of Joyous Gard over the tops of oaks
Before him; and while he stared at their appearance,
A cold familiar fear of the unreal
Seized him and held him fixed, like one awaiting
Some blast of magic that would shake them down
To dust, and all within them, and Isolt.
He saw the night-like hair and the white arms
And the wet-shining eyes that half asleep
Had laughed at him again before he left them,
Still shining and still sleepy; and for the while
He saw them, he saw neither towers nor walls;
And for a moment while he could see nothing,
He was not large enough to hold his heart.
But soon he smiled, seeing where nothing yet
Had crashed or vanished, or was like to fail him,
And moved along slowly around the place
To a green field that like a sea of land
Lay flecked and shadowed by the summer wind
That swept it, saying nothing of how soon
Or late the trampling feet of men and horses
Would make a sorry shambles of it all,
And for another queen. He wandered on,

And the green grass was music as he walked—
Until beyond it there were trees again,
And through them was the sea, still silver-white,
And flashing as before. Wherever he looked,
He saw dark eyes and hair and a white face
That was not white, but was the color of love;
Or that was near enough to being a name,
He thought—or might have thought, had he been thinking—
For that which had no name. To think at all
Would be a more perfidious insolence
To fate, he felt, than to forget the sun
That shone this morning down on Joyous Gard,
Where now there was all joy. He felt it shining,
And throughout time and space he felt it singing;
He felt and heard it moving on the grass
Behind him, and among the moving trees
Around him, and along the foaming shore,
And in the ocean where he splashed and swam
Like a triumphant and almighty fish,
Relinquishing the last concern of earth,
Save one that followed him. Below the waves
There were dark laughing eyes and faintly seen
Phantasmal flashings and white witcheries,
Like those of a dim nixie to be trusted
Never to drown him, or not willingly,
Nor to deceive him. For the time it takes
For joy to think of death and to forget it,
He thought of himself drowned. But when his head
Came up and above water, and he was blind
At first with many a shaft of laughing fire,
All shot from somewhere out of violet eyes,
He had thought long enough. Some day or other
He might think more of it, but for some time
He was to live not thinking of his end,
Or thinking of it he was not to live.

On shore again, he wished all mortal choice,
If choice there was, might come only to that.
Whatever it was that filled life high and full,
It was not time. So he had told Isolt
Under the stars; and so he told himself
Under the trees, and was believing it
With all his might and main. Something on him
Had fallen, in all appearance, that fell not
On men that for one reason or another
Were to fill life with time. He stretched his arms,
Laughing to be alive; and over his head
Leaves in the wind that gave them a gay voice
Flickered and ticked with laughter, saying to him,
"Tristram, it is for you to stay or go.
You will not go. If you leave all there is
That fate calls yours—one jewel of a lustre
More than of earth and of all else on earth,
Glowing in more than gold—the gods that live
In trees will tell the others, and there shall be
No place prepared in heaven or hell for one
Who failed in seeing until too late to see,
That for the sake of living it was his life
And all there was of life that he was leaving.
Probably you will not live very long
If you stay here; and the gods who live in trees
Care little how long man lives." He laughed again
To think of that, and heard the leaves and waves
Laughing to think of that. Like a man lost
In paradise, and before his time to die,
He wandered inland, much at ease with fate,
And in precarious content secure.

Security, the friendly mask of change
At which we smile, not seeing what smiles behind it,
For days and nights, and for more days and nights,

And so for more and more, was unmolested
Through a long vigil over Joyous Gard;
And no dark thunder coming from the west,
Or lightning, shook security, or seared it,
Or touched those walls and towers with even a flick
Significant of irruption or invasion.
He who had laughed at what the laughing trees
Had said, may have laughed well.

                           Summer was going,
When one day Tristram, having heard pleasantly
Isolt's half-hearted and by now less frequent
Reversion to the inveterate whether or not
Of her deserting him in time to save him,
Or of his vanishing, said, stroking her
As if she were some admirable cat,
"Whenever I set myself to count the pounds
Of beauty you have for your not having them,—
Through fear for me, perhaps,—I could affirm
That your disturbance has a virtue in it,
Which I had not foreseen. Were you too happy,
Your face might round itself like a full fruit,
And all those evanescent little planes
And changes that are like celestial traps
To catch and hold and lose the flying lights
And unseen shadows that make loveliness,
Might go—or rather might not be left the same;
Although if I saw you deformed and twisted,
You would still be the same."

                       "Dear child of thought,
Who forgets nothing if we give him time,"
She said, "if you saw me deformed and twisted,
You might sail back to Brittany so fast

694

That all the little fishes would be frightened.
Never persuade yourself that you believe
Or need believe, so boundlessly as that.
You will be happier if you leave to me
The love of someone else's imperfections.
I know—but never mind that. It will not come.
We are not for the fireside, or for old age
In any retreat of ancient stateliness.
If that were so, then this would not be so.
Yet when this fragment of your longer life
Has come and gone, it will have come and gone.
There is no doubt of that; and unseen years
May tell your memory more of me than love
May let you know today. After those years
In Cornwall, where my fire of life burned lower
Than you have ever known, I can say this.
Mine is a light that will go out sometime,
Tristram. I am not going to be old.
There is a little watchman in my heart
Who is always telling me what time it is.
I'll say this once to you, and never but once,
To tell you better why harm, for my poor sake,
Must not be yours. I could believe it best—
If I could say it—to say it was all over.
There is your world outside, all fame and banners,
And it was never mine to take from you.
You must not let me take your world away
From you, after all this. Love is not that.
Before you are much older, I suppose
You will go back to Brittany, where Isolt—
That other Isolt—will think, and some day know.
Women are not so bitter if once they know,
And if the other is dead. Now forget that,
And kiss me as if we were to live for ever.
Perhaps we shall, somewhere."

She smiled at him

And shivered, and they were silent for a while.
Then she said, "Do not say it. You'll only say
That if I lost my ears and had no hair,
And I had whelks and moles all over my face,
Your love would be the same as it is now—
So let's believe, and leave it. And if not that,
Your love would find new benefits and rewards
In losing all for me—while yet there's time
Not to lose all. If you think only of me,
You may forget how far a king's arm reaches,
And what reprisals he may buy with gold
And golden promises."

"May the kings all

Be damned," he said, "and their reprisals also.
If this that you have hidden from me so well
Hides truth within it—and may God say no!—
I shall have one more right, if more be needed,
Never to let you go while I'm alive.
Tell me you said it only to be sure
There was no truth in it."

She said no more,

And only smiled again, shaking her head,
While in her calm and shining eyes he found
Another last look; and it was not like one
That he had seen before and had remembered
Ever since that cold moonlight on those stairs,
And those cold waves below. But though the way
She looked at him this time, and all she told
So silently, and all she did not tell,
Was not forgotten, security remained
Unchanging, and a friendly sentinel;

696

And neither, as with a hush of understanding,
Save with unwilling eyes now and again,
Said more of shadows; and while autumn came,
Tristram would see no cloud, or a cloud coming,
Between them and the sun. Whether it rained
Or not, the sun was always shining there,
Or wheresoever the hour might find him riding,
Or sailing home with singing fishermen,
Or losing himself in forage of new scenes,
Alone, for the sheer joy of being alone
And seeing Isolt behind him with Brangwaine
And Gouvernail, and with almost a town
Of Lancelot's men and women to attend them.

Love must have wings to fly away from love,
And to fly back again. So Tristram's love,
And Tristram with it, flew, for the sake of flying,
Far as it would; and if he fared alone
Through mist and rain, there were two violet eyes
That made of mist and rain a pleasant fire,
Warming him as he went. If on the sea
That fell and rose interminably around him,
His manful avocation was to feign
Escape from blue-black waves of Irish hair,
There were no other waves worth mentioning.
And if allured by unfamiliar scenes
And distances, he found himself astray,
Or comfortably lost, there was no red
That any western sky might show so fair
Beyond the world as one that was still on it,
A red that mixed itself alive with white,
Never the same way twice. It mantled now
Fairer than phantom flame in a white face
That was itself a phantom, and yet so real
That seeing it fade and smile and fade again,

He trembled, wondering still and still assured
That not far off, and always waiting for him
In Joyous Gard, while he saw pictures of her
That were almost Isolt alive to see,
There was Isolt alive that he could feel
When his hands touched her, and find musical
When his heart listened. There were other women
Who murmured peradventure for men's ears
To hear, yet while his own were not engaged
Or implicated they were ghosts of women,
Dumb in a hell of men that had no ears,
For all they were to him—albeit his love
Of everything, where everything was Isolt,
Would not have had that so.

Having outwalked

His hours, he yielded to the setting sun,
And soon enhancing for the eyes of man
With gold of earth, and with his exaltation,
The distant gold of heaven, he borrowed a horse
For a journey, never alone, through falling shadows
And falling leaves. Back to the walls and towers
He went that now held heaven and all but God
To welcome him with wild and happy eyes
And dark hair waving over them, and a flame
Of red that in the firelight was immersed
In burning white, white fire and red together,
And her white arms to hold him while she asked
Where he had been, what insects he had seen,
And who was king of Salem. Leaves and flowers,
Wild roses for Isolt, encumbered him,
But were no bulk or burden as on he rode,
Singing, and seeing always in the firelight
He should find shining at his journey's end—
Isolt, always Isolt. She was not there,

698

He fancied, smiling; she had never been there,
Save in a dream of his; the towers and walls
Of Joyous Gard were only a dream of his;
But heaven had let him dream for a whole summer,
And he was dreaming still as he rode through
The silent gate, where there were silent men
Who looked at him as if he were a stranger,
Whose tongue was none of theirs. Troubled and vexed,
He felt the stillness of a difference
In their attention, as for some defect
Or lapse of his that he could not remember;
And saying a word about a stranger's horse,
He passed them on his way to the still door
Where joy so often entered and came out.
A wonted sense of welcome failing him,
He summoned it from the twilight on the stairs
And half began to sing with a dry throat
That held no song. He entered the same room
Where first Isolt had found him waiting for her,
And where, since then, he had so often found
Isolt, waiting for him. She was not there—
And that was strange. She was not always there,
But it was strange that she was not there now.
He stared about him, wondering that one room,
Holding so many things that he had seen,
And seen again, should hold at the same time
So much of silence. What had happened there?
Where were those arms, and the dark happy eyes,
Always half wet with joy at sight of him?
He made himself insist that he could smile
While helpless drops of fear came out of him,
And he asked of his heart that beat so hard
Why he should be afraid. It was no mark
In his experience to be found afraid,
But he could find no name warmer than fear

For the cold sickness that was in him now,
Although he named it only to disown it.
"A woman may not be always in one place,"
He thought, and said, "Isolt!" She was not there.
He saw the chimney, and saw no fire was there—
And that was strange. It was not always there,
But there or not there, it should be there now.
"And all fires are not lighted at one time,"
He thought, and said, "Isolt!" There was no sound
In this room, or the next room, or the next;
There was no sound anywhere in the whole house—
Except the pounding of his heart, which felt
To him as if it were the whole of him.
He was afraid, and done with all disowning,
And perilously was not afraid of that.
"Is not one here who dares to answer me?"
He muttered slowly, but he could not move—
Not even when he believed that he heard something
Alive behind the heavy velvet curtain
Where he had heard Isolt, so long ago
That now it seemed that she might never have come,
If now she were not gone. For a gasp of time
That only fooled him to a surer knowing
That this was not Isolt, he told himself
It was—like a man dying who lies to life
For the last empty joy of a last lie.
The sound he heard was not the mouse-like noise
That mice and women make. Be what it might,
He scarcely heard it; and not heeding it,
He stood alone with his hands hanging clenched,
More like a man of bronze than a man breathing,
Until he shook and would have swayed and fallen
Had he not stumbled heavily to a couch
That filled a corner filled already with shadows.
Sitting inert upon the edge of it,

He sent a searching gaze all over the room,
Seeing everything but the one thing he strove
To see; and last he stared upon the floor
Before him, where lay scattered some wild flowers,
Wild roses for Isolt, and saw them there
As if they were a thousand miles away.
Then he looked up again, turning his face
Enough to see in the same room with him,
Rigid and silent, like a friend ordained
To strike again a friend already stricken,
Gawaine from Camelot. Tristram arose,
Propping himself with pride and courtesy,
And stood there waiting for Gawaine to tell him
As much as he might tell.

                                "I have come too late."
He said; and then the look of Tristram vanquished
And routed the battalion of brave words
That he had mustered. "And for that I'm sorry.
Mark is abroad again, and has been free
For just how long the devil himself may know.
The Queen was by the shore, under some trees,
Where she would sit for hours alone sometimes,
Watching the ocean—or so Brangwaine says—
Alone and happy. Your wits will see the rest.
They carried her off with them in a small boat,
And now she's on a ship that sails to Cornwall.
I do not know a land that has a law
Whereby a man may follow a king's ship
For the king's wife, and have a form of welcome
Better than battle. You are not trimmed for that.
Forgive me—we did all we could. I am here,
And here too late. If I were you, I fancy,
I should tear one more leaf out of my book,
And let the next new page be its own story."

Each word of Gawaine's, falling like a blow
Dealt viciously by one unseen, fell slowly,
And with a not premeditated aim,
So accurate and unfailing in its proof
That when the last had fallen—without reply,
And without time to summon will or reason,
Tristram, the loud accredited strong warrior,
Tristram, the learned Nimrod among hunters,
Tristram, the loved of women, the harp-player,
Tristram, the doom of his prophetic mother,
Dropped like a log; and silent on the floor,
With wild flowers lying around him on the floor—
Wild roses for Isolt—lay like a log.

Gawaine, Brangwaine, and Gouvernail all waited
By the couch where they had laid him, but no words
Of any resigned allegiance to a fate
That ruled all men acknowledging its rewards,
And its ingratitudes and visitations,
Were on his tongue to say; and in his eyes
There was no kind of light that anyone there
Had seen in them before. After long time,
He stared at Brangwaine, and his lips moved once,
Trying to speak, but he said nothing then;
And he said nothing that was heard that night
By man or woman.

There was a week gone by
When Gawaine, less obscured at each day's end
In his confusions, and far less at home
Than ever, saw fit to feel that his return
Was urging him away. His presence there
Was no contagious good that he could see,
And he felt lonely and unnecessary.

702

There was no Tristram left that he remembered;
Brangwaine, whenever she saw him, did not see him;
And Gouvernail, to one who had always lived
For life, was only gloom looking for death,
And no right company for Gawaine. Brangwaine,
He learned, was going away with him tomorrow,
As far as Camelot, and he sighed to say so,
Seeing how fair she was. "Brangwaine, Gawaine, . . .
A deal of music in this world is wasted,"
He thought, "because a woman cries and kills it.
They've taken away Isolt, Tristram is mad,
Or dead, or God knows what's the name of it,
And all because a woman had eyes and ears,
And beauty enough to strike him dumb with it.
Why must a man, where there are loaves and fishes,
See only as far as one crumb on his table?
Why must he make one morsel of a lifetime?
Here is no place for me. If this be love,
May I live all alone out on a rock,
And starve out there with only the sea to drink,
And only myself to eat. If this be love,
May I wear blinkers always, or better yet,
Go blindfold through the perils of this world,
Which I have always liked, and so, God help me,
Be led to safety like a hooded horse
Through sparks and unseen fire. If this be love,
May I grow merry and old and amiable
On hate. I'll fix on someone who admires me,
And sting him, and then hate him all my days.
'Gawaine, Brangwaine,'—what else is that than song?
If I were a musician, and had leisure,
I'd surely some day make a tune of it.
'Brangwaine, Gawaine.' " He frowned upon events,
And sighed again that men were not alike.
" 'Gawaine, Brangwaine.' " Brangwaine was fair to see,

And life, while he could sing, was not very long,
And woe not his annoyed him.

Gawaine went
With all his men, and Brangwaine, the next day;
And Tristram, like a statue that was moving,
Still haunted Joyous Gard, where Gouvernail,
Disconsolate, and half scared out of sorrow,
Followed and feared, and waited for a sound
Of more than Yes or No. So for a month
He waited, hearing nothing of life without,
Barring a word from Camelot of Isolt
In Cornwall, and alive. He told Tristram,
And Tristram said, "Alive!" Saying no more,
He watched the waves with eyes where Gouvernail
Saw not what he would see in them. The light
That had been Tristram was gone out of them,
And Tristram was not there, even when he spoke,
Saying at last, "This is not good for you,
Gouvernail. You are not my friend for this.
Go back to Brittany and forget all this."
Gouvernail's ears were glad and his heart danced
To hear so many words, but long days passed
And went before he heard so many again.
Then came a letter which a stranger brought,
Who, seeing it held by Tristram, rode away,
Saying his work was done. With avid hands
And eyes half blind with hope, he tore it open,
To make whatever he would of words like these:

"Greeting, Sir Tristram, Prince of Lyonesse.
It was a joy to share with you a house
Where I was once. That was a pleasant house,
Say what you will of it; and it was pleasant
Of me to make you safe and comfortable,

Say what you will of that. This will be sent
For your distinguished and abused attention
From my domain, here in this land of Gore,
Which is my land, and is a pleasant land,
As you may say of it yourself sometime.
More to the salt and essence, there's a lady
Alive in Cornwall—or she was alive—
Who is alone and sore bestead, I fear me,
Amort for love of you. If you go soon—
Too soon you cannot go, if you would see her—
And are not burned alive, or flayed alive,
Or otherwise hindered or invalidated,
You may behold once more that Irish hair,
And those same Irish eyes that once engaged
And occupied you to your desperation.
I cannot answer on more authority
Than hope for your reception or return,
But you, being orgulous and full as an egg
Of fate, may find a way through fire and steel
To see that face again. Were I a man,
And were I thus apprised as to the lady,
I should anon be rowelling my good horse,
And on my way to Cornwall. Peace be with you,
And may no evil await or overtake you.
Farewell, Sir Tristram, Prince of Lyonesse."

Too sorely stricken already to feel stings,
Tristram, with Morgan's letter crushed and wrinkled,
Sat unresponsive, seeing, wherever he gazed,
Foam breaking, and dark stairs, and two dark eyes,
Frightened and wild again as when they left him
That night when he left them. When he would see
No more of them, he said to Gouvernail,
"Tomorrow I shall go for a far journey,
And may go farther still. So, Gouvernail,

705

Go back to Brittany and forget all this,
And tell them there that they were not forgotten.
Nothing that I can send or say to her
Will do much good. And if I lied to her,
She might remember me—only for that.
Tell her that I meant always to be kind—
And that's a little to tell. Say there was more
Than I was, or am yet, to be between us—
And that's a little to say to her. But say it.''—
"Sometime I will, Tristram, but not tomorrow.
Tomorrow I go with you, unless you kill me,"
Gouvernail said, "and that would be a little
For you to do. I have seen in and out,
And I'm as wise today as when my mother
Was glad because I cried that I was born.
Your mother was not, you say. Well, perhaps not."

IX

Against a parapet that overlooked
The sea, lying now like sound that was asleep,
King Mark sat gazing at Isolt's white face,
Mantled no more with red, and pale no longer
With life. The poor dominion that was his
Of her frail body was not revenge enough
To keep even hate alive, or to feed fury.
There was a needlessness about it now
That fury had not foreseen, and that foresight
Would never have forestalled. The sight of her,
Brought back to him a prisoner by his men
From Joyous Gard, and her first look at him,
Had given to death a smallness, and to life,
Ready for death, an uncomplaining triumph
Like nothing of his. There might be Tristram dead
By stealth, yet there would always be that face—

706

Isolt's white face. He saw it now, and said,
"I am not looking to you for much regard,
Though you might let your eyes, if not your tongue,
Say where I am. Do they know that I am here?
Why are you looking at the sea so long?"

"The sea was never so still as this before,"
She said. "It is like something after life,
And it is not like death. That ship out there
Is like two ships, and one of them a shadow.
When you came, I was asking if the shadow
Might not, if only we knew shadows better,
Be the real ship. I am not very well;
And lately I've had fancies. Do not mind them.
I have never seen the sea so still as this."

"Perhaps the sea is like ourselves," Mark said,
"And has as much to say of storms and calms
That shake or make it still, as we have power
To shake or to be still. I do not know.
I was just saying it for no harm or reason.
I shall do no more harm to either of you
Hereafter, and cannot do more to myself.
I should have lost my nature not to take you
Away from him—but now, having you here,
I'm not so sure of nature as once I was.
If it were fate for man here to be sure,
He might not stay so long. I do not know.
All I know now is that you sent for me,
And that I've told you all, or I believe so,
That you would hear me say. A month ago,
He might have stepped from folly to sure death,
Had his blind feet found Cornwall. But not now.
Your gates and doors are open. All I ask
Is that I shall not see him."

Isolt said then,
"There was a time when I should have told God
Himself that he had made you without mercy.
Forgive me that. For there was your side, always;
There were your ways, which are the ways of kings;
And there was blindness everywhere at first—
When there was all that time! You are kind now,
And I thank God that you are merciful."—
"When there is nothing left for us to lose,
There's no great mercy in our not losing it,"
He said. "God will not hear you if you thank him
Only for that. A weary spark of sense,
Or a dull feel of reason, is not mercy.
I have not changed. I'm only some days older
Than when they brought you back from there—brought you
And your white face together. You looked at me,
And I saw your white face."

She smiled at him,
And touched his hand with hers: "You are good to me.
Whatever you do, I shall not be here long.
Whatever you are, you have been good to me.
I shall not be afraid of you again—
No, nor of Andred. When he knows of this,
He will bow down to your authority
Like a small hungry dog and lick your fingers.
And all his insane hatred for Tristram,
And all his worse than insane love for me . . .
Poor loveless atom!"

"Andred?" Mark said, scowling,
And went on with a hoarse unhappy laugh:
"Morgan, when she was here, was playing with him
So much like a damned cat that I believed
His love, if you say love, was all for her.

708

TRISTRAM

I wondered that she wasted so much guile
Upon so little grace. The fellow is mad.
I should have seen that he was always mad.
We were all mad—that night. I should have seen.
I should have seen . . ." He rose and stalked along
Before the parapet, and back again;
Then, with a groan that savored of a snarl,
He cried, "God knows what else I should have seen!
Had I been made with eyes to read in the dark
All that was written there, I might have seen,
By straining them, some such effect as this.
How could I see where there was nothing shown
Or told for me to see? There was yourself,
But I believed that home was in your eyes,
Rather than hate, and that a crown to wear
Would outshine all your tears. Had I known early
All that I knew too late . . . I do not know.
I am not sure."

          "Whether you are or are not,"
She said, "you have been kind to me today.
You will not live, though you should live for ever,
To wish this kindness back. You might have given
Me nothing, and I should not have wondered more
Than I have wondered at your giving me this.
I should have suffered, and not thought it strange.
There was a cloud that covered us all, and now
You have been kind. If it was fate, we'll say
Bad fate was like bad weather. Oh, it is hard,
With such a stillness lying on everything
Today, to say that storms have ever been."

"There have been storms enough to sink us all,
And drown us. Yet we are still here afloat—

Here, or somewhere. Not even that ship you see
Will be there always."

     "And ships in their last port,"
She said, "have still a farther voyage to make,
Wherever it is they go. Were it not for love,
Poor life would be a ship not worth a launching.
Is it not true?"

    "I do not know," Mark said;
And for a long time stared upon the sea,
Which told him nothing.

     Isolt, watching him there,
And with a furtive sorrow in her heart
For one that was foredoomed to be himself,
Felt presently the coming of quick feet
Up the stone stairs within the walls behind her;
And turning where she lay, saw Brangwaine's fingers
Upon her lips, and saw more in her eyes
Than joy alone, or fear. Only one thing
Was there in life remaining to mean either;
And the wild red came back to Isolt's cheeks,
And to her throat.

    "He is waiting," Brangwaine said,
"And has the manner, if I may dare to say so,
Of one who should not wait."

     "Why should he wait?"
Mark answered, with a sullen glance at her;
And then, after one long unhappy look
At where Isolt was lying—or now half lying—
Went through the doorway and led Brangwaine with him,
Leaving Isolt alone to watch the sea

710

Until there was no sea, and she saw nothing—
Not even when she felt arms shaking that held her,
And his lips, after so long, on hers again,
And on her cheeks and eyes. When she could see,
She shrank a little away from him for love
And wonder, and then for love and, fear she drew
His face down to her heart and held it there
While her heart ached and it seemed right to die.
Searching his eyes to find him, she said only,
"I shall hear all you do not say to me,
Tristram. For you are only one man still,
Which is a thing that one man may forget.
You forget rest."

          "I shall remember it—
Sometime," he said. "When rest remembers me,
There will be time for that. I shall have rest."
Then he sat still, holding her hands as lightly
As if they were two leaves, and stared at her
Like a man back from death. "What has Mark done
That I should find his doors all open for me,
And see no swords, or fire? You have done this.
There is no other woman, and no man,
To do it. I can see now. The king of hell
Would not refuse, if your eyes asked him now,
To open the doors of hell."

          "They are all open,
Tristram, and I shall not go out of them—
Or I shall not go out as I came in.
They are the doors of heaven while you are here,
And shall be so when you are gone from here;
For I shall keep you here. Mark, I suppose,
Knew that. Mark has been good to me today—
So good that I might almost think him sorry

711

That he is Mark, and must be always Mark.
May we be sorry to be ourselves, I wonder?
I am not so, Tristram. You are not so.
Is there much then to sigh for?"

                    "I am not sighing
For that," he said, and kissed her thin white fingers.
"My love will tell you, if you need be told
At all, why sorrow comes with me . . . Isolt!
Isolt!"

      She smiled. "I am not afraid to die,
Tristram, if you are trying to think of that—
Or not to think of that. Why think of it?
My cup was running over; and having had all
That one life holds of joy, and in one summer,
Why should I be a miser crying to God
For more? There was a way for this to be,
And this must be the way. There was no other;
And I would have no other—not for myself.
Not now. Not now. It is for you, Tristram,
That I see this way best."

                "God knows," he said,
"How well my love, which is the best of me,
Knows what a gulf of trust and understanding
There is in yours, where I would drown and die
So gladly and so soon, could I, by going
That way, leave you behind me here, and happy.
I would be gone from you and be forgotten
Like waves in childhood or forgotten water,
If that were the way left to bring warm life
And warm joy back into these cheeks again,
And these eyes looking at me."

TRISTRAM

     The eyes smiled,
And the cheeks flushed with gladness; and Isolt
Said without sorrow, "I would not give two grains
Of sand to stay alive with you forgotten.
But I would give myself, or as much of me
As there is now, for God's word that my love
May not make yours a burden to be borne
Till you be weary of it. If we had seen,
If we had known—when there was all that time!
But no, there's nothing in that. We have known since then
All that we know today. Was it enough?
How shall we measure and weigh these lives of ours?
You said once that whatever it is that fills
Life up, and fills it full, it is not time.
You told my story when you said that to me,
But what of yours? Was it enough, Tristram?
Was it enough to fly so far away
From time that for a season time forgot us?
You said so, once. Was it too much to say?"

Her words had in their pleading an unwilling
And wistful intimation of things ended
That sorrow let escape. But he only smiled,
And pressed her asking hands. "It was enough,"
He said; "and I may tell you more than that,
Perhaps, when I am God, making new stars
To shine for you to see. They are more than fire,
You said; and they will tell you everything
That I may not say now."

     "It was enough!"
She murmured; and her words held happiness
Heard beyond earth, he thought. He turned his eyes
Away from hers that closed in weariness
And peace, to leave her smiling. Never before

713

Had such a stillness fallen on land or sea
That he remembered. Only one silent ship
Was moving, if it moved. He turned again
To the low couch before him and saw shining,
Under the darkness of her waving hair,
And with a pallid loveliness not pale
With life around them, the same violet eyes
Fixed upon his and with a calm that hurt him,
Telling him what they told, and holding more
Than it was good to tell. But they could smile
And lie for kindness; and she could tell him lies
While he for kindness listened:

                                   "You will go back
To Brittany after this, and there Isolt—
That other Isolt—" she said, "will, as time goes,
Fill up the strange and empty little place
That I may leave; and as time goes, and goes,
You may be king with her across the water;
Or, if you choose, you will be king, may be,
In your land, Lyonesse. I have never known
A man before with kingdoms at his feet,
Like scattered gold for him to leave or take,
And as he will. You will go back again
To Brittany; and when you are an old man,
You will remember this—this afternoon.
I am so sure of it that I'll not ask you
To tell me more about it." Her white fingers
Closed upon his, and her eyes closed again.

"I shall go back to Brittany, sometime,"
He said, "for whatsoever awaits me there.
There may be nothing. Women have changed before;
And more of them would be more fortunate,
For all I know, if more of them might change."

TRISTRAM

"I have seen many," she said, "like silent birds
Who could not fly with wings they thought were broken.
They were not broken, and the birds did fly.
I have seen wings that have been healed and mended,
Also. I have not seen many of them, perhaps.
Wings are but once for most of those who fly
Till they see time lying under them like a mist
That covers the earth. We have had wings and flown,
And one of us comes to earth again, and time,
Not to find much time left; and that is best
For her. One will have wings to fly again;
And that is best for him."

                    He looked across
The windless water and forgot what land
It was that lay beyond where he was looking.
He forgot everything, save all there was
For him, and turned again to see it there, lying
So silent, and unendurably so soon
Not to be there; to be so fair there now,
And then to vanish; to be so dark and white
And violet, and to die. And that was best,
She said; and she must know. He heard her saying
And saying again to him that it was best.
She would be saying it all his life to him,
To make him sure, leaving him and his wings
To fly wherever they would. "You do not say
How far I shall be flying, or for how long,"
He told her then, "and that's as well for me.
As for the best, I know no more of that
Than I see in your face and in your love
That looks at me. Love, it was far from here
And far from England and this inchmeal world
That our wings lifted us to let us fly
Where time forgot us. He waited for us here,

But his wings were too old to follow us.
We shall not go so far away from here
Again, till we go farther. It is enough
For me that you should ask if it was so,
And ask it with these eyes."

      "I would to God
That we might fly together away from here,
Like two birds over the sea," she murmured then,
And her words sang to him. "The sea was never
So still as it is now, and the wind never
So dead. It is like dying, and not like death.
No, do not say things now. This is not you,
Tristram. There was a mercy in fate for you
That later will be clear, when you see better
Than you need see today. Only remember
That all there was of me was always yours.
There was no more of me. Was it enough?
Tell me, was it enough? You said it was,
And I have still to ask. Women have ears
That will hold love as deserts will hold rain,
But you have told Isolt it was enough,
And she knows all there is. When first we met
In darkness, and were groping there together,
Not seeing ourselves—and there was all that time—
She was all yours. But time has died since then,
Time and the world, and she is always yours.
Pray God she be no burden. You that are still
To fly, pray God for that."

      He raised his eyes
And found hers waiting for them. "Time is not life—
For me," he said. "But your life was for you.
It was not mine to take away from you."
He went on wanderingly, and his words ached

716

Like slaves feeling a lash: "It was not mine.
I should have let you go away from there.
I should have made you go, or should have gone
Myself, leaving you there to tell yourself
It was your fear for me that frightened me,
And made me go."

     "If you should hear my ghost
Laughing at you sometime, you will know why,
Tristram," she said. And over her calm eyes
A smile of pity passed like a small cloud
Over two pools of violet in warm white,
Pallid with change and pain. "It was your life,
For mine was nothing alone. It was not time,
For you or me, when we were there together.
It was too much like always to be time.
If you said anything, love, you said it only
Because you are afraid to see me die—
Which is so little, now. There was no more;
And when I knew that I was here again,
I knew there was no more. . . . It was enough,
And it was all there was."

      Once more she drew him
Closer, and held him; and once more his head
Was lying upon her with her arms around it
As they would hold a child. She felt the strength
Of a man shaking in his helplessness,
And would not see it. Lying with eyes closed
And all her senses tired with pain and love,
And pity for love that was to die, she saw him
More as a thunder-stricken tower of life
Brought down by fire, than as a stricken man
Brought down by fate, and always to wear scars
That in his eyes and voice were changelessly

Revealed and hidden. There was another voice,
Telling of when there should be left for him
No place among the living any longer;
And there was peace and wisdom, saying to her,
It will be best then, when it is all done.
But her own peace and wisdom frightened her,
And she would see him only as he had been
Before. That was the best for her to see;
And it was best that each should see the other
Unseen, and as they were before the world
Was done with them, and for a little while,
In silence, to forget and to remember.
They did not see the ocean or the sky,
Or the one ship that moved, if it was moving,
Or the still leaves on trees. They did not see
The stairs where they had stood once in the moonlight,
Before the moon went out and Tristram went
From her to darkness, into time and rain,
Leaving her there with Mark and the cold sound
Of waves that foamed all night. They did not see
The silent shore below, or the black rocks,
Or the black shadow of fate that came unfelt,
Or, following it, like evil dressed as man,
A shape that crept and crawled along to Tristram,
And leapt upon him with a shining knife
That ceased to shine. After one cry to God,
And her last cry, she could hear Tristram, saying,
"If it was Andred—give him thanks—for me. . . .
It was not Mark. . . . Isolt!"

                           She heard no more.
There was no more for either of them to hear,
Or tell. It was all done. So there they lay,
And her white arms around his head still held him,
Closer than life. They did not hear the sound

Of Andred laughing, and they did not hear
The cry of Brangwaine, who had seen, too late,
Andred ascending stealthily alone,   .
Like death, and with death shining in his hand,
And in his eyes. They did not hear the steps
Of Mark, who followed, or of Gouvernail,
Who followed Mark.

           They were all silent there
While Mark, nearer the couch and watching it,
And all that there was on it, and half on it,
Was unaware of Andred at his knees,
Until he seized them and stared up at him
With unclean gleaming eyes. "Tell me, my lord
And master," he crooned, with fawning confidence,
"Tell me—and say if I have not done well!
See him—and say if I'm a lizard now!
See him, my master! Have I not done well?"

Mark, for a time withheld in angry wonder
At what he saw, and with accusing sorrow
For what he felt, said nothing and did nothing,
Till at the sight of Andred's upturned face
He reached and seized him, saying no word at all,
And like a still machine with hands began
Slowly to strangle him. Then, with a curse,
He flung him half alive upon the floor,
Where now, for the first time, a knife was lying,
All wet with Tristram's blood. He stared at it,
Almost as if his hands had left it there;
And having seen all he would of it, he flung it
Over the parapet and into the sea;
And where it fell, the faint sound of a splash
Far down was the one sound the sea had made
That afternoon. Only the ship had moved—

And was a smaller ship, farther away.
He watched it for a long time, silently,
And then stood watching Tristram and Isolt,
Who made no sound. "I do not know," he said,
And gazed away again from everything.

"No sea was ever so still as this before,"
Gouvernail said, at last; and while he spoke
His eyes were on the two that were together
Where they were lying as silent as the sea.
"They will not ask me why it is not strange
Of me to say so little."

        "No," Mark answered,
"Nothing was ever so still as this before. . . .
She said it was like something after life,
And it was not like death. She may have meant
To say to me it was like this; and this
Is peace."

        To make his wonder sure again
That they were there, he looked; and they were there.
And there was Andred, helpless on the floor,
Staring in a mad ecstasy of hope
At Mark, who scanned him with an absent hate
Of nature, and with a doubt—as he had looked
Sometimes at unreal creatures of the sea
Thrown ashore dead by storms. Saying unheard,
With lips that moved as in a tortured sleep,
Words that were only for the dead to hear,
He watched again as he had watched before
The two that were so still where they were lying,
And wondered if they listened—they were so still
Where they were lying. "I do not know," he said,
"What this is you have done. I am not sure . . ."

TRISTRAM

His words broke slowly of their own heaviness,
And were like words not spoken to be heard:
"I am not sure that you have not done well.
God knows what you have done. I do not know.
There was no more for them—and this is peace."

X

By the same parapet that overlooked
The same sea, lying like sound now that was dead,
Mark sat alone, watching an unknown ship
That without motion moved from hour to hour,
Farther away. There was no other thing
Anywhere that was not as fixed and still
As two that were now safe within the walls
Below him, and like two that were asleep.
"There was no more for them," he said again,
To himself, or to the ship, "and this is peace.
I should have never praise or thanks of them
If power were mine and I should waken them;
And what might once have been if I had known
Before—I do not know. So men will say
In darkness, after daylight that was darkness,
Till the world ends and there are no more kings
And men to say it. If I were the world's maker,
I should say fate was mightier than I was,
Who made these two that are so silent now,
And for an end like this. Nothing in this
Is love that I have found, nor is it in love
That shall find me. I shall know day from night
Until I die, but there are darknesses
That I am never to know, by day or night;
All which is one more weary thing to learn,
Always too late. There are some ills and evils
Awaiting us that God could not invent;

721

There are mistakes too monstrous for remorse
To fondle or to dally with, and failures
That only fate's worst fumbling in the dark
Could have arranged so well. And here once more
The scroll of my authority presents
Deficiency and dearth. I do not know
Whether these two that have torn life from time,
Like a death-laden flower out of the earth,
Have failed or won. Many have paid with more
Than death for no such flower. I do not know
How much there was of Morgan in this last
Unhappy work of Andred's, or if now
It matters—when such a sick misshapen grief
May with a motion of one feeble arm
Bring this to pass. There is too much in this
That intimates a more than random issue;
And this is peace—whatever it is for me.
Now it is done, it may be well for them,
And well for me when I have followed them.
I do not know."

                Alone he stood there, watching
The sea and its one ship, until the sea
Became a lonely darkness and the ship
Was gone, as a friend goes. The silent water
Was like another sky where silent stars
Might sleep for ever, and everywhere was peace.
It was a peace too heavy to be endured
Longer by one for whom no peace less heavy
Was coming on earth again. So Mark at last
Went sombrely within, where Gouvernail
And silence wearied him. Move as he might,
Silence was all he found—silence within,
Silence without, dark silence everywhere—
And peace.

And peace, that lay so heavy and dark
That night on Cornwall, lay as dark that night
On Brittany, where Isolt of the white hands
Sat watching, as Mark had watched, a silent sea
That was all stars and darkness. She was looking
With her gray eyes again, in her old way,
Into the north, and for she knew not what
Tonight. She was not looking for a ship,
And there was no ship coming. Yet there she sat,
And long into the night she sat there, looking
Away into the darkness to the north,
Where there was only darkness, and more stars.
No ship was coming that night to Brittany
From Cornwall. There was time enough for ships;
And when one came at last, with Gouvernail,
Alone, she had seen in him the end of waiting,
Before her father's eyes and his bowed head
Confirmed her sight and sense.

      King Howel paused,
Like one who shifts a grievous weight he carries,
Hoping always in vain to make it lighter,
And after gazing at the large gray eyes
In the wan face before him, would have spoken,
But no speech came. Dimly from where he was,
Through mist that filled his eyes, he pictured her
More as a white and lovely thing to kill
With words than as a woman who was waiting
For truth already told. "Isolt—my child!"
He faltered, and because he was her father,
His anguish for the blow that he was giving
Felt the blow first for her.

     "You are so kind
To me, my father," she said softly to him,

"That you will hold behind you now the knife
You bring with you, first having let me see it.
You are too kind. I said then to Gawaine
That he would not come back. Tristram is dead.
So—tell me all there is. I shall not die.
I have died too many times already for that.
I shall not ever die. Where was he, father?"
Her face was whiter and her large gray eyes
Glimmered with tears that waited.

                                        He told her then
A tale, by Gouvernail and himself twice-tempered,
Of Tristram on his way to Brittany,
Having seen that other Isolt, by Mark's reprieve,
Only once more before she was to die.
It was an insane sort of kinsman, Andred,
Not Mark, who slew him in a jealous hate;
All which was nebulously true enough
To serve, her father trusted, willing to leave
The rest of it unheard, whatever it was,
For time to bury and melt. With Tristram dead,
This child of his, with her gray eyes that saw
So much, seeing so far, might one day see
A reason to live without him—which, to him,
Her father, was not so hard as to conceive
A reason for man's once having and leaving her.
That night the King prayed heaven to make her see,
And in the morning found his child asleep—
After a night of tears and stifled words,
They told him. She had made almost no sound
That whole night; and for many a day to follow
She made almost no sound.

                              One afternoon
Her father found her by the sea, alone,

TRISTRAM

Where the cold waves that rolled along the sand
Were saying to her unceasingly, "Tristram—
Tristram." She heard them and was unaware
That they had uttered once another name
For Tristram's ears. She did not know of that,
More than a woman or man today may know
What women or men may hear when someone says
Familiar things forgotten, and did not see
Her father until she turned, hearing him speak:

"Two years ago it was that he came here
To make you his unhappy wife, my child,
Telling you then, and in a thousand ways,
Without the need of language, that his love
Was far from here. His willingness and my wish
Were more to save you then, so I believed,
Than to deceive you. You were not deceived;
And you are as far now from all deception,
Or living need of it. You are not going
On always with a ghost for company,
Until you die. If you do so, my way,
Which cannot be a long way now, may still
Be more than yours. If Tristram were alive,
You would be Tristram's queen, and the world's eyes
And mine would be content, seeing it so.
But he is dead, and you have dreamed too long,
Partly because your dream was partly true—
Which was the worst of all, but yet a dream.
Now it is time for those large solemn eyes
Of yours to open slowly, and to see
Before them, not behind. Tristram is dead,
And you are a king's daughter, fairer than fame
Has told—which are two seeds for you to plant
In your wise little head as in a garden,
Letting me see what grows. We pay for dreams

725

In waking out of them, and we forget
As much as needs forgetting. I'm not a king
With you; I am a father and a man—
A man not over wise or over foolish,
Who has not long to live, and has one child
To be his life when he is gone from here.
You will be Queen some day, if you will live,
My child, and all you are will shine for me.
You are my life, and I must live in you.
Kings that are marked with nothing else than honor
Are not remembered long."

                            "I shall be Queen
Of Here or There, may be—sometime," she said;
"And as for dreaming, you might hesitate
In shaking me too soon out of my sleep
In which I'm walking. Am I doing so ill
To dream a little, if dreams will help me now?
You are not educating me, my father,
When you would seize too soon, for my improvement,
All that I have. You are the dreamer now.
You are not playing today with the same child
Whose dream amused you once when you supposed
That she was learning wisdom at your knees.
Wisdom was never learned at any knees,
Not even a father's, and that father a king.
If I am wiser now than while I waited
For Tristram coming, knowing that he would come,
I may not wait so long for Tristram going,
For he will never go. I am not one
Who must have everything, yet I must have
My dreams if I must live, for they are mine.
Wisdom is not one word and then another,
Till words are like dry leaves under a tree;

TRISTRAM

Wisdom is like a dawn that comes up slowly
Out of an unknown ocean."

                    "And goes down
Sometimes," the king said, "into the same ocean.
You live still in the night, and are not ready
For the new dawn. When the dawn comes, my child,
You will forget. No, you will not forget,
But you will change. There are no mortal houses
That are so providently barred and fastened
As to keep change and death from coming in.
Tristram is dead, and change is at your door.
Two years have made you more than two years older,
And you must change."

                  "The dawn has come," she said,
"And wisdom will come with it. If it sinks
Away from me, and into night again—
Then I shall be alone, and I shall die.
But I shall never be all alone—not now;
And I shall know there was a fate more swift
Than yours or mine that hurried him farther on
Than we are yet. I would have been the world
And heaven to Tristram, and was nothing to him;
And that was why the night came down so dark
On me when Tristram died. But there was always
Attending him an almost visible doom
That I see now; and while he moved and looked
As one too mighty and too secure to die,
He was not mingled and equipped to live
Very long. It was not earth in him that burned
Itself to death; and she that died for him
Must have been more than earth. If he had lived,
He would have pitied me and smiled at me,
And he would always have been kind to me—

If he had lived; and I should not have known,
Not even when in his arms, how far away
He was from me. Now, when I cannot sleep,
Thinking of him, I shall know where he is."

King Howel shook his head. "Thank God, my child,
That I was wise enough never to thwart you
When you were never a child. If that was wisdom,
Say on my tomb that I was a wise man."
He laid his hands upon her sun-touched hair,
Which in Gawaine's appraisal had no color
That was a name, and saying no more to her
While he stood looking into her gray eyes
He smiled, like one with nothing else to do;
And with a backward glance unsatisfied,
He walked away.

    Isolt of the white hands,
Isolt with her gray eyes and her white face,
Still gazed across the water to the north
But not now for a ship. Were ships to come,
No fleet of them could hold a golden cargo
That would be worth one agate that was hers—
One toy that he had given her long ago,
And long ago forgotten. Yet there she gazed
Across the water, over the white waves,
Upon a castle that she had never seen,
And would not see, save as a phantom shape
Against a phantom sky. He had been there,
She thought, but not with her. He had died there,
But not for her. He had not thought of her,
Perhaps, and that was strange. He had been all,
And would be always all there was for her,
And he had not come back to her alive,
Not even to go again. It was like that

For women, sometimes, and might be so too often
For women like her. She hoped there were not many
Of them, or many of them to be, not knowing
More about that than about waves and foam,
And white birds everywhere, flying, and flying;
Alone, with her white face and her gray eyes,
She watched them there till even her thoughts were white,
And there was nothing alive but white birds flying,
Flying, and always flying, and still flying,
And the white sunlight flashing on the sea.

ROMAN BARTHOLOW

(1923)

To Percy Mackaye

ROMAN BARTHOLOW

I

WHERE now the morning light of a new spring
Fell warm on winter, patient in his grave,
And on a world not patient, Bartholow—
Like one above a dungeon where for years
Body and soul had fought futility
In vain for their deliverance—looked away
Over the falling lawn that was alive
And green again between him and the river.
Steel-blue below him, through a yellow dusk
Of trees, he saw the flowing gleam of water,
Whereon his fancy limned the mirrored face
Of spring, too blind again with her own beauty
To measure man's advantage,—though he might
This morning have addressed a votive shout,
Affirming his emergence, to the Power
That filled him as light fills a buried room
When earth is lifted and the sun comes in.
He would have raised an altar now to spring,
And one to God; and one more to the friend
Who, coming strangely out of the unknown
To find him here in his ancestral prison,
Had brought with him release. Never before
Would he have said that any friend alive
Had magic to make light so gross a weight
As long had held him frozen out of sense
And hearing of all save a dead negation

That would not let him die. When Gabrielle,
Serving a triple need, so fondly sought
And rarely found, of beauty, mind and fire,
Had failed him—where was life, and what was left?
So Bartholow had asked himself in vain,
And many a time again without an answer;
While she, in her discreet bewilderment,
Had known him only as a furniture
That was alive and tiresome, he supposed,
And only rather bravely to be cherished,
Like a mute fretful changeling, for the soul,
At last insurgent in him, she knew not.
"Our souls are foreign in us till our fears
Attest them and they clamor to be known
And owned; they are our slayers and our saviours,
And we more slain than saved." So Bartholow
Had reasoned once; and so, for all he knew
Might have abandoned reason to the ruin
Of all the joy regained that was within him
And in the morning light that was around him,
And over this old ivied house of stone,
Built years ago by one whose glowering faith
In gold on earth and hope of it in heaven
Hung where the shadows of a century
Had favored his ancestral eminence.

Penn-Raven, on his first observing him
Dim-featured on the wall, had said at last,
Slowly, "If there is much of him in you,
Your soul had better never been aroused.
Now show me your grandmother, if you please,
And then your mother. Never mind the rest,
For you are not the son of any father."
Bartholow, delving then where memory
Found love at odds with umbrage, had essayed

ROMAN BARTHOLOW

A patent laugh. "But you are right," he said;
"My father was to me a mighty stranger—
Fearsome, but always on the side of right
As he discerned it. There were some collisions
Between us, and a few sparks, though no fire
That ever burned enough to make a scar.
For the most part he let me go my way;
And when the way was hard, I made it so.
We'll say that many are better and some worse
Than I was then." Penn-Raven, being a stranger
In those days, had said little; Bartholow
Said not much more. Each knew the other's heart,
Or so he fancied, and had found it right.
Later Penn-Raven, having found the soul
In Bartholow that ailed him, had with ease
Ineffable healed it—having wrought meanwhile
More than his indeterminate attention
Saw waiting for his pains. More than a year
A neighbor, and of late, unwillingly,
A resident saviour domiciled, he had lived
More as an over-lord than as a guest,
Entreating always, always amiably,
A day not far off on the calendar
To mark the festival of his departure.
There would be always locusts and wild honey
Enough somewhere. So that for gratitude,
Bartholow loved him almost as a novice
Loves God, though not remembering there are faces
On which one may not wholly look and live.

But now, with all this morning light upon him
He looked about him with a life renewed
Upon a world renewed, and gave himself
Less to remembering an obscure monition
Than to confessing an assured renascence,—

735

Albeit his whim was once or twice to fancy
That if he stamped upon the footworn flags
Beneath him, he should hear a sullen ring
Of buried emptiness, like that wherein
His endless and indignant yesterdays
Had held him. He was holding a long breath
Of living air, for joy of having it,
When suddenly a footfall and a voice
Summoned his eyes agreeably to the sight
Of one whose garment of mortality,
Fashioned unhandsomely of misfit patchwork,
Was made for him to wear, not asking why.
Bartholow, smiling, looked him up and down
Aware that in his gaze was no encroaching
On more than wilful incongruity,
Flaunting a more pernicious taste in frenzy
Than order would elect. Soiled heavy shoes
Laced half way to the knee, were to the purpose;
The rest was all a chequered inflammation
Of myriad hues that had, like those on Joseph,
No capturable names. A fishing basket
Hung weighted from one shoulder, and a rod,
Held with a flexile and immaculate hand
Lay wrapped across the other; and underneath
A shapeless variegated sort of cap
There was a face made more for comedy
Than for the pain that comedy concealed,
Socratic, unforgettable, grotesque,
Inscrutable, and alone. Bartholow gave
His hand in greeting to this apparition,
Who searched him in his turn as if in doubt.
"Good morning, sir, my name is Umfraville;
But I'll eat fire and smoke if I know yours.
I make it at a venture sixty days
Or more ago that I found hereabouts

ROMAN BARTHOLOW

A restive and unpleasant lord of acres
Who had unhappily no joy of me
Or pleasure of himself. So, naturally,
I vanished, knowing there were dogs about,
And weapons. He was wan and rather dour
To look on, and his eyes were like two lamps
Preparing to go out. The name of him
Was Roman Bartholow—somewhat a scholar,
Somewhat a farmer in a parlor way,
And something of a delver in the dark,
Hoping to find there his immortal soul.
He never said it in so many words,
But that's the esoteric upshot of it.
I knew him once when even the sight of him
Was anodyne for sorrow or disaster,
And when his feet had wings. He wore a look
In those days more or less akin to yours
To-day, but you are not the man. Where is he
And who is this who does me now the honor
Of giving me his honorable hand?
O *saepe mecum*, here be trout for breakfast,
If you expound. If not, away we go,
The fishes and the fisherman together,
Never again for you to contemplate.
Meanwhile, appraise them; and if they invoke
Approval, pay for them as heretofore;
For I have brought with me an evil thirst
That barks away from water."

                           Bartholow,
With cordial and explicit gratitude,
Obeyed; and when the empty creel returned,
More followed on a tray. "No, not for me,"
He said. "The morning is itself enough—
For me."

"Then by my soul," said Umfraville,
"You have found yours. No doubt, some day or other,
I shall find mine but not by fishing for it.
Once I believed that I had found my soul,
But therein I was wrong and only bilious.
We cannot harvest evidence unseen
As we do carrots, and we cannot buy it;
Nor may we take it from the open hand
Of love or friendship, merely wishing it.
Otherwise, maybe we should not be here,
Toiling so mortal hard, or not so hard,
To stay a little longer. You and I,
As I conceive, are not among the toilers—
Though God send I may give you no offense
Or give my tongue a too familiar motion;
For you are on the broad and open road
Where all your friends and enemies are with you,
Impinging on your equanimity
Each in his way, and you in turn observing
How much of easy death in life there is
Where life is easy. I, who have neither friend—
Save you—nor enemy worth mentioning,
Go as I will, or as I must, by ways
Not on the map; and that's as well for me.
By which you mark that I'll be serious
When instigated by a miracle.
In brief, what lost elixir have you swallowed,
And when am I to know the taste of it?"
Bartholow saw the spirit on the tray
Diminishing, and answered, "I've a doubt
If your interior machinery
Has need of an elixir more remote
Than you have here. For you there is no age.
Another forty years will find you young,
Still eating Greek and Latin, and, as now,

Still fishing—not for man or for your soul,
But for the only joy there is for you
That lives in water. There's a difference
In one who lives to see himself behind him,
And after a few years of living death
Sees a new self before him, as I do.
There was a friend who came to make it so,
And one that if I gave him all I own
Would leave me rich in wealth unpayable.
How much of all this do you understand?''

''I understand a fraction more of it,
Maybe, than you have told; for I'm a reader,
And there are books that walk. I know your friend,
Though only as a motion on the landscape,
Out of my world. If he has made you over,
If he has raised the veil and given you eyes
To see what's going on where I see nothing,
Well, I say peace be with him, and with you.
I am not worthy of your mysteries—
If you remember all that a man should
Of Aristophanes.''

                        ''Which I do not,''
Bartholow said, smiling. ''But you are worthy
Of all the mysteries of earth and heaven
That your content may cry for. Casually,
What surety have you that your world and his
Are all so different as you see them now?
How is it, if you know the gentleman
Only outside, you are so sure of him?''

''I may have known a gentleman or so,
Or so I tell myself,'' said Umfraville,
''But I should look a little at my shoes,
Or maybe at the stars, before I tossed

A name too soon to one that raised the veil,
Merely because he raised it. Being myself
A nondescript, I take upon myself
A more ingenuous right of utterance
Than tongues of others ordinarily
Might sanction or employ. What matters it,
When there be some of God's elect who make
A warfare of a sirloin? Observation
Might, with a misconceived authority,
Fill hell with saints, and set the devil on high
To frustrate the archangels. What's it all
To me, one way or other? Born with a face
That on a bullfrog would ensure for life
The lucubrations of a celibate,
I ask, in God's name, what's it all to me?
I see that you are noticing my raiment,
And murmuring, *Kyrie eleison,*—
Greek for What Next. I notice it myself.
I must have color without, if none within;
Though never of a hue so violent
As to fill fish with terror when I seek
Their innocent and iridescent lives
Whereon we lower than the angels feed.
Now I'll go home again across the river,
While yet your Caledonian poison plays
And sings within me, not unpleasantly;
And if perchance in some unlikely future
You find yourself astray and in the dark,
And the veil down again, and if you ask
What fellow it was one morning in the spring
Who said that of all men he found in you
Alone a friend, and would, were it feasible,
Pay with an arm to prove his loyalty,—
I'll tell you, truly as I know this hand
Of yours that I am holding now in mine,

The appointed words that are for you to say:
Say it was one who laughed when others laughed
And thereby kept a sorry craft afloat
That else had foundered or been strangely missing;
Say it was nature's inadvertency
Confessed in one on whom there were few men,
And fewer women, to look humanly,
And one that only dogs could ever love;
Say it was one who lived again the past
In books, where there were none to laugh at him,
And where—to him, at least—a world was kind
That is no more a world. More frugally,
Say it was Umfraville, the fisherman."

Bartholow, still retaining the warm hand
In his, met now the flushed impossible face
Before him with a sorrow at his heart
And a smile on his lips: "I will say all
You tell me, or as much as I remember.
You hardly ask of me that I shall call you
All the quaint names that you have called yourself.
Out of another mouth you might resent them
And ask what their involved irrelevance
Might intimate. All the same, I'll not forget
The name that's yours. Be sure of that. Good-bye!
One of these days I'll find myself across
The river, at your door—if you invite me—
And weigh the tonnage of my ignorance
Upon your classic scales."

                The visitor
Made answer only with a warmer clasp
And a long gaze of misty gratefulness.
Then he went slowly on his way alone,

As he went everywhere, and out of sight—
Leaving his friend reborn to breathe again,
Insatiably, the morning of new life.

II

At last, having inhaled the morning air
Until it made him ache with renovation,
He gazed again below him at the river
Where now another face was dimly mirrored.
The learned fisherman, who knew books and brooks
Alike, surely had not the face of spring,
Yet for the moment his uncouth regard
Supplanted nature; and while Bartholow
Stood watching the cool water through the trees,
An airy caricature of loneliness
Hovered a while between him and all else.
Then, with a sigh for such a piece of life
So doomed and irremediably defeated,
He walked away over the footworn flags
And over the long driveway of new gravel,
Circuitously through acres of young grass
To the old iron gate, set long ago
By the same ancestor in whom Penn-Raven
Saw for his host no lineal obligation.

By this time Bartholow pursued again
A phantom fisherman that was alive
Somewhere alone between him and the town,
And in his dim pursuit he found himself
Considering the oblique and infinite
Amend awaiting many before they leave
A world where fate, as for the sport of it,
Might once have reared invisible walls whereover
No crippled atomy should ever climb.

742

"Meanwhile," he thought, "it might be worse, and isn't;
He has a pittance, and so cannot starve;
And he wants little, having little need
Of more than he would use. That's how it is
We salve ourselves with our complacency,
And edge our morning appetite for trout,
Which others not so favored bring to us
Because they love us. And if that be so,
We'll honor them at least with our attention
To theirs. He must have caught me with his hook
This morning, for I feel a string that holds me.
In such a world as this no creature born
Should have to lose it for a face like that."
Still pondering, and with a rueful shrug
Of helplessness, he turned about and walked
The winding gravel to his house again
And entered it—first having filled himself
Gratefully with a final inhalation,
Like one forestalling a robust illusion
That after breakfast there would be no air.

Inside again, he smiled as he remembered
The startled fisherman's inquiring look
Of incredulity on his approach
With his moist offering, and went upstairs
To find if in a mirror there should live
Sufficient warrant of another's wonder;
And there, before the reassuring glass,
He found a face at least agreeable,
And surely not the blank and haggard mask
That he had seen so long there in the dark
Of his devouring fear and hopelessness,
When hope was a lost word and happiness
Not even a ghost that haunted him. He saw
Before him now a man of middle height,

COLLECTED POEMS

Shaped well for life and for the exercise
Of any task that he saw facing him—
Where, be it here confessed, he saw not any
That he might not approve in his own humor
To ponder or perform. A roundish head,
Of no ethereal or severe distinction,
Carried a face that would have passed unscanned
And unrecorded through the worldly gates
That his indifference left unvisited,
Save when his wife saw fit that he be seen
Where he saw little and remembered less.
He stood for a long time, incredulously
Intent upon the beaming duplicate
Of one who must have been, past any question,
The fond original of all he saw
To please him and to paint that happy smile
Of grateful recognition and thanksgiving;
And there he might have stayed, admiring life
In its revival, until eventide—
Had there not come, unsummoned, silently
Into the pleasant scene the mirrored grace
Of one whose laughter was no counterfeit,
And had no purpose that a man reborn
Might always in a moment wholly seize.

Gabrielle waited, laughing half aloud,
Most of her laughter coming from her eyes;
"Was ever such a morning admiration
Of anything so perfect or so happy?"
She spoke, and lingered, while he flushed a little
As he came forward slowly to the door
Where she was framed and her dark morning beauty
Was like an armor for the darts of time,
Where they fell yet for nothing and were lost
Against the magic of her slenderness.

744

ROMAN BARTHOLOW

All wrapped in garnet wool, still watching him,
And laughing with her sleepy-shining eyes,
"Was it Apollo, or Antinous,
You met there in the looking-glass?" she said.
"My classic gentlemen have lost their names,
But they were monstrous handsome, all of them,
As I know you are not. I have him now—
Narcissus; and he liked himself so much
That he is now a little vegetable,
And nothing more. You might remember that.
If I had come but half an instant later,
I should have seen you dancing at yourself.
I'm certain of it."

                He came farther forward,
And laying his warm hands upon her shoulders
Looked hungrily into her laughing eyes,
Which looked away as if the sun had hurt them.
"My soul was dancing here for joy already,
Before you came," he told her; "even as once
A king in Israel danced with all his might
Before an ark. His wife, who didn't like it,
Saw him and laughed. You might remember that.
David was not infallibly a pattern,
Yet he had notions that were sound enough
Concerning wives who laugh. He sent them off
To brood alone on their discrepancies,—
And they were sorry then they ever laughed
At David when he danced." He drew her fondly
And slowly nearer, holding up her face
To gaze upon: "You might remember that."

"And you might let me go; for I'm no more
Than half awake and only partly dry.
You might go down and look at your grandfather.

745

If you are not a spider, go away—
For I'm not up. For heaven's sake—!''

                                        He crushed
The fragrant elements of mingled wool
And beauty in his arms and pressed with his
A cool silk mouth, which made a quick escape,
Leaving an ear—to which he told unheard
The story of his life intensively.

"I know," she answered, in a purring voice
That had somewhere a muffled hardness in it;
"And you have heard me saying without end
That I'm as glad as you that you are born
Again; for both of us were nearly gone.
With half another of those years behind us,
We should have been two moving skeletons
With just enough meat on us to scare people
Whenever we should move. I know some things,
But I'm an ignoramus of the soul,
As you two men have noticed. I've a soul,
I hope, yet I'm not sure." She looked up slowly,
And tapped his cheeks with her pink finger-tips.
"You may be seeming, in a sleepy way,
To think you do not know, or care," he said;
"But you are thinking harder of your breakfast,
And that's a normal thought. The weight your soul
Is bearing now in its obscurity
Is more that you are hungry than uncertain."

She nodded. "And I hope there's more than porridge,
For I'm as hungry as that one-eyed person
Who lived with others like him in a cave."

"The ravens have attended to all that;
And we are of the fortunate this morning,
In that we shall not starve."

                              "You mean your Raven?
"What has the Raven found for us to eat?"

"No, quite another bird. A worthy one,
Though quite another, of another plumage.
Good-bye. Remember David, and repent."

He left her and went singing down the stairs,
Where presently, when she conceived herself
Secure for matutinal panegyric,
She found him scowling in the library
Over some pages that she could not read.
"What in the world are you at now, so early,"
She questioned him, "and why do you scowl so?"

He felt a flitting pressure of her lips
Upon his hair, and looked up gratefully:
"I'm at the oldest of all occupations,
Looking for something that I cannot find—
Buried alive this time in an old play.
Listen: *Einai me tōn sōn axion*
Mustēriōn. What do you make of that?"

"No more than music. Has it any meaning?
If I could read it I should not need you
For music in the morning. It sings well,
But you must ruin it all for my poor wits."

" 'Let me be worthy of your mysteries,'
Approximately, is the ruin of it
That your poor wits require. Do you believe me

Worthy of yours—your mysteries?" He gazed
Into her languid eyes inquiringly
And laughed as if in answer.

                    "I believe
That you are always foolish in the morning,"
She said. "Shall we be waiting for the Raven,
Or shall we be at breakfast when he comes
In all his weird magnificence to greet us?
We shall not have to wait. I hear him croaking.
Never in all my quiet life before
Was there a morning when I heard so much
Man-music in it. He says, *Chi mi frena* . . .
And how is one to know?"

                         The minstrel checked
The flow of his irrelevant aubade
Before the doorway of the library:
"Good morning! If you heard my song, forgive me.
Like the ordained, I sing because I must.
You two should not have waited." He came in,
Fixing on each in turn a violet eye
That smouldered, with a darker fire behind
Which kindled with an intermittent flame
A nameless light whereon but few could look
Long without flinching—Bartholow being one
Who could; which may have been, or not, a part
Of his revival into a new being
Like and unlike the old. As he surveyed
Penn-Raven coming in, the eyes he met,
Softening with a slow unconsciousness,
Took on a sheen of innocence no player
Might own among his arts. No subterfuge,
Or sleeping evil or apparent scorn
Was in their changing power. The square face

748

And heavy forehead were for more men's envy
Than a soft mouth, where lips that were too full
Were for the cautious like a false addition
To be deplored. The nose was large and right;
And, as men stand, Penn-Raven would have stood
Firmer to see than many who had more
Of earth to stand on. It was in his eyes
That most of him was latent or revealed
Unto the eyes of others who could find him.
And there were few who could—Bartholow being,
For price of larger sight, one who could not.
"This morning there are mysteries abroad,"
Said Gabrielle; "and even at this table
I'm warned of one awaiting us. I guess
What's coming only as I read a name
That's not yet written. Well, here it is. Be careful."

Penn-Raven's eyes, already luminous
With admiration, were now flashing on her
The shine of a new interest. "Mysteries,"
He said, "when out of place are injudicious;
But here, if I see truly, I see trout."

"Why not? You look at them for all the world
As if you were the devil's child who caught them."

"How do you know it was the devil's child
Who caught them?" Bartholow said, indulgently.
"I'll say it was a sad and learned man
Who caught them—leaving you and our friend here
To comfort him with your imagined thanks.
He has imagination."

                              "Not too much,
I hope," she murmured, with a faint recoil;

"That is, if he's the same unhappy monster
That once, a year ago, brought you a gift
Like this, and his face with it. For I've seen him
Here in this house; and he has looked at me.
Pfah! Take it away, for I'm not hungry."

Bartholow frowned. "If you had ridden your fancy
Around the last immeasurable orbit
Of the last satellite of the last sun,
You and your fancy could have trundled home
No sort of wilder trash than you imply
When you say that."

              She broke a roll and laughed:
"Surely an avalanche of words like yours
Would crush the morning appetite of lions.
I like the man who said that all who talk
Through breakfast should have poison in their coffee.
Hereafter I'll have mine in bed again."

"By which you mean," Penn-Raven said, removing
A spinal column from the pink-white flesh
Before him on the plate, "you fear the Greeks,
Et dona ferentes. Contrariwise, I wish
There might be more of them. Hush, my dear sir,
Or she may change her mind." He munched amain
The delicate fresh viand in his mouth,
Beaming on Bartholow and Gabrielle
With childish eyes that were as innocent
As those of a large house-dog meditating.

"I know a lady who, as I remember,
Has chattered well at breakfast before now,"
Bartholow said. He struck away the tail
Of a large trout with a malingering fork,

And eyed the rest of it indifferently.
"My notion was to hear you purr a little
Over a mild surprise; and all you do
Is to make faces and be disappointing.
I'm glad that in the past no vanity
Has ever told me that I understood
Your ways and cerebrations, for I don't.
What in the name of all trout that are speckled
Has a man's face to do with eating them?
And why, because he did your face the honor—
An easy one, I grant—of looking at it,
Must you be seeing in him only a satyr?
I will assure you now that all you saw
Was his affliction in the difference,
And a soul groping in its loneliness."

"I think the Raven wants another fish.
Let him have mine; for mine is beautiful,
Even in death," she said.

                    Penn-Raven turned,
And after an involuntary frown
That had a question in it, the keen eyes
Put off again their sharpness. Then he said,
"Hush, hush, my children. If you mean to fight,
I'll take the fishes off into a corner
And eat them all myself. What man accurst
Is he who has in his inheritance
A face that shatters happiness like yours?
If he be one that I have passed in town
Sometimes, he has a face to frighten Hogarth,
But never one to keep him long away
From such a fare as this. Dear sir, and madam,
I cannot on the fringe of decency
Consume alone the sum of everything;

Wherefore, if only out of loving-kindness,
Bartholow, eat that fish.''

       ''I beg your pardon,''
He said, and that was nearly all he said
While he essayed without enthusiasm
The far-sought evidence of Umfraville's
Ill timed remembrance. Gabrielle, insisting,
Gave hers to her expostulating guest.
''They may be large, but they're not numerous,''
She said, ''and I should weep to see them wasted.''

''One's ignorance would not envisage you
As overmuch at home among the weeping,''
He told her, and his eyes changed while he smiled
And studied her like one strangely in earnest.
''Not freely at the table, or not often;
Though I can weep as well as anyone
When I've a mind to.''

      ''And when you've a mind to,''
Bartholow said, ''you can be rational.
I'd say this morning you had lost your wits,
Only I know you haven't; though God knows
I've given you leave to lose a few of them
During some years of mine that we'll forget,
Or say that we forget, now they are gone.
On unforeseen occasions when you turn
Your bee loose in that comely skull of yours,
I may be critical, while underneath
I'm all humility and admiration.''

''As I,'' she said, ''am all acknowledgment.
Now everything is as it was before,
And we are quite the same as yesterday.

ROMAN BARTHOLOW

The Raven sees it, and his feathers all
Are smooth again. We startled him somewhat.''

''The Raven has no comment or complaint,''
The guest assured her, ''and he has no part
In your engaging fits and ebullitions,—
Although the face of one unlovely stranger
Would hardly seem enough—but I refrain.
I say no more. Both you and your good man
Are still intact; and there are birds outside
That sing mellifluously in the trees,
And the sun shines on everything. What more
Are we to ask, or likely to receive?
With your agreement I'll dismiss myself
And leave you to bind up your wounds alone.
My call is for a smoke along the river—
Your proof that I'm a creature still of earth,
Fit yet for no Nirvana. Peace be with you.''

He went, and Gabrielle soon followed him
As far as to the door, where she surveyed
With tired and indolent indifference
The green beginning of another summer.
Bartholow, coming after, looked once more
Below him at the budding yellow trees
That soon would be a fence of emerald,
Obscuring all beyond except a far
Familiar stillness of eternal hills.

''If we are to believe we have a river,
We must apply the cruel axe, I fancy.
Rivers and trees are an old harmony,
And we, who are not old, may quite as well
Enjoy as lose it.''

Gabrielle smiled at him
Impassively. "And we may quite as well
Enjoy as lose each other, I dare say,
And with each other lose all our bad acting.
How in the world should we go on without it?
This morning, before breakfast, you did well—
So very well, to say the truth about it,
That I had anguish to keep up with you;
And I did hardly that, though I did something.
We know each other just enough, my dear,
To be a little sorry for ourselves,
And so a little careful. Get an axe,
And let the river and the world look in
Upon us and our joy. I'll sit and watch
The deed, imagining that you are Gladstone."

He shook his head and smiled, as if the smile
Hurt him: "I cannot wonder, or not fairly,
At anything you say, though I may ask
Whether or not through all that time behind me
When I was lost in hell, you were like this.
If so you were, praise God I never knew it.
You tell me I was acting when a mirror
Made sure this morning I was here again,
And here alive? I should not name it so.
And were it even so—and you know better—
Is there not hid somewhere, for some of us
To find, a mystery that we may name
The joy of being? You have heard of it."

"Yes, I have read about it in a book;
And once I knew it. That was long ago.
Assuming, then, your face was not a fiction,
And I'm aware enough that it was not,
How much of *me* was there in all that rapture?"

ROMAN BARTHOLOW

"You might have seen by looking in my eyes,
But your eyes only laughed and looked away
Whenever they met mine. Are mine so dimmed
That they may see in yours no more concern
For my escape than a laugh says they do?
There are more comical occurrences
Than coming out of death to life again.
I know the old house of our other love
Is only a poor ruin falling now
To dust, which if we stir it only chokes us.
My way would be to wreck the remnant of it,
And let the fire of our intelligence
Burn down to honest earth the residue.
Then over the few ashes we may find,
My way would be to let new vision build
With new love a new house. Am I a fool,
Saying this, or am I no more than peculiar?"

He waited, armored against all surprise
When only a thin smile was her first answer.
"You are an angel, and, for all I know,
A carpenter—but how are you to build
This house, and out of what? New love? New vision?
Where do we buy these things? I'm not assured
That you will build this house."

                        "Never alone,
God knows. Yet if you cared enough to try,
There might be still an unforeseen adventure
Awaiting you and your indifference.
With all so new around you, possibly
You might be sorry when your memory told you,
If so it ever should, why there are now
No more of us than you and I together."

"And have you not the Raven? Without him,
What else might you not be without this morning?
And what would you be doing now all alone—
With only me? And what would you be seeing?
I'm sure that you would not be standing here,
Or seeing here such a pretty fire of ruins.
I told you all about the skeletons
That we should be by this time without him.
Would any children take the place of him?
Would you exchange for them the miracle
Of your release, rebirth, or what-you-call-it?
I'm almost wholly certain you would not.
Let me be stricken only with a face
A little harder for your contemplation,
And I'll see new love running like a hero
Out of a haunted tomb."

                              He bit his lips
Indignantly and slowly walked away—
Into the hall and back again: "If this
That you are saying had yourself in it,
If I had never known you and your eyes
Without your mask, I might assuredly
Believe, and with a reason, that somewhere
Among your forbears in forgotten ages
There was a colder fish than any swimming
To-day in any ocean."

                              "And if you,"
She said, "should go on so ferociously,
I might believe, and with a reason also,
That you have in you more of your grandfather
Than you or I supposed. If you pursue
These revelations of my lineage,

756

Your words will haunt me like that creature's face,
And I'll be surely scared.'' She glanced at him
With a quick flash of insecurity,
And added, ''I am half afraid already;
Not of your friend, or of your grandfather,
But of this queer new house that you are building
Of timber out of trees that never grew.
For even a phantom house, if made unwisely,
May fall down on us and hurt horribly.
I know enough of houses to say that,
For I have built them.''

        ''You have never built
The house that I see rising in the light
Around me now,'' he said, and fixed his words
With a taut smile of courage.

        ''Nor have you,''
She told him slowly, gazing at the river.
'If you attempt it, you are to find out,
I fear, that you are not the carpenter
That your spring fiction makes of you this morning.
I know that in your eyes I'm not abhorrent,
As you know that in mine you are no more so;
I know the world has yet for us an envy,
Observing us in our felicity,
And I know the world's envy cannot last.
If you believe that I should go away,
No clubs or whips or tears or indirections
Will be required of your sincerity,
And I shall ask of you no gold. Forgive me!''
His only answer was a broken smile,
Until at last, after a shrug, he spoke:
'I'll go so far this time as to forgive you,

Although for no deserving qualities
Of afterthought, my dear, in your defection.
I think we see a little better now
The work of those black years when I was blind.
You suffered, and were dismally alone,
But why, for God's sake, have it out of me
In your sad acrobatics of new language.
If there's to be the ceremonial
Of your forgiving of each empty day
That I have made for you unwillingly,
Your task is hard; and even when you are old,
And I am in my grave, your withered zeal
Will have its occupation to the end.
If we are to do nothing but remember,
I'd say with you that you had better go,
And I go after you, and after us
The world—or all that most of it remembers."

"You mentioned, I believe," she said, amused
Indifferently, "a tongue that you defined
As my new language, and there you surprised me;
For mine is older than the Jebusites,
While yours came yesterday. You understand it—
You and your new-born wisdom, but I can't;
And there's where our disaster, like a rat,
Lives hidden in our walls. In your new house
There would be certainly another like him.
You know it, yet you cannot make yourself
Believe your knowledge; and I'm only asking,
In my poor only way, if this be wisdom.
If your illumination will be honest,
You'll see in this the shadow of a color
Of that which is not altogether true.
A sudden ugliness on me, my dear,
Would make it all so comprehensible!"

Bartholow threw his hands up hopelessly:
"What is it? Would you have me on my knees?
Or why do you insist on this invention?"

"By no means. You would not believe yourself
More there than on your feet. Nor should I like
Your unfamiliar picture of submission:
The whip-hand, though it flourish over us
Only a lash of fancy, has effect.
I see the Raven coming up the hill."

They scanned each other's eyes, but hers were fixed
Not long on his before they flinched again
And looked away from him. He gazed at her
As at a stranger in a sanctuary,
Then past her at the trees along the river
Until her silence told him she was moving.
"I understand," he said; and his words followed
Her slow unguided steps. "I understand;
I am not worthy of your mysteries."

III

Barring an amateur alacrity
In woodmanship, Bartholow found himself
Content with earthy toil well done by those
Who found in him an easy overseer,
Though not an eyeless one. "You manage others
More than yourself," Penn-Raven told him once,
While yet the demons held him; "for those devils
Had coiled a snare for you so cunningly
That long before your knowledge they had caught you;
And after that their evil diligence
Was only by degrees to weave around
Your being, with invisible tight threads

759

A thing that, were it not so mortal close,
Would be more like a shroud than you imagine.''
But now the shroud, or name it as he would,
Was gone; and in the freedom of his arms
He felt the call of action. "Get your axe,"
His wife had said, and laughed. He thought of that;
Yet in it there was nothing humorous
While he was there alone; nor, when Penn-Raven,
Approaching, was apprised of her advice,
Was there in his abetting indolence
An overplus of wholesome comedy.
All comedy had faded for the nonce;
And even as nature mostly rubbed along
Without it, so might he, or for a morning.
"There are more axes in the world than one,"
He told his guest; "and there are several trees."

Penn-Raven shook his head and found a chair.
"My vision of your toiling in the distance
Will do for one of you and me together,"
He said. "The sound of your vicarious axe
Will do the rest. I shall be happy here,
Knowing that you are strong and on your feet,
And therefore, in a measure, like Antæus,
Who, I believe, was not above the soil
In his activities. Because your soul
Has found itself and is at last alive,
Never believe that you have not a body.
Lose that, and off your soul will go again
Into the dungeon where it was I found you,
And you will go there with it. Get your axe;
And I'll sit here, saying that you are Gladstone."

Bartholow sighed and answered wearily,
"I wonder if you know how many flies

760

Are on the roof; or maybe you don't hear them.
If not, why am I hearing the same name
Twice in a morning in the same connection?''

''Coincidence, my friend; coincidence—
And fame. If you are truly celebrated,
Your great toe is immortal. Get your axe,
And let us have a more sufficient view
Of your inspiring river. I like rivers
Better than oceans, for we see both sides.
An ocean is for ever asking questions
And writing them aloud along the shore.
Rivers are not monotonous.''

     ''They may be—
Sometimes,'' Bartholow answered. ''If you see
Too far down into them, they may be worse.
I have seen more in this one, in time past,
Than I wish ever to see out of it,
While time endures. But that's all over now.''
He smiled, and with an effort brought a laugh
Up from somewhere within him, while Penn-Raven,
Like a ripe artist sure of his achievement,
Surveyed his living work affectionately,
And with a questioning of whether man
Or God were to be garlanded.

      Far down
Below him he heard soon, luxuriously
Approving it, the sound of Bartholow's
Industrious axe—with intermittent gaps
Of silence, after which no clearing crash
Had altered yet the scene. A woman's face
Without the falling down of any tree
Before she came, was adequate for that.

761

He rose, and having found another chair
For Gabrielle, who sat with folded hands
And listened like one hearing something else
Than axes. "He's alive again," he said;
"Or we should hear no music of that nature
Now on the morning air."

                            She closed her eyes,
As if in his originality
All thought had foundered, and then opened them
As with an interest. "He will cut one down,"
She told him, in an odd domestic way
That he found somehow more disquieting
In her than scorn or satire would have been.
"He'll cut one down," she said again, more slowly,
"And then come up for Cyrus. I can see him
As well as if I saw him. His arms ache,
And he's already wishing that he hadn't."

"I doubt if you need worry or be sorry
For any long time over that," he said,
Smiling away a frown whereat she laughed
As she had laughed before at Bartholow.
"A little seasoning will do his arms
And all the rest of him a year of good
Without it; for he's not long out of prison,
As he would say; and even a prison like his,
Without a purpose or alternative,
Is not the place where a sick soul, alone,
Makes even a giant stronger than he was
Before the door closed on him in the dark.
And he, be it said for his felicity
And his longevity, was not a giant,
Even before there was a darkness for him.
I said 'alone,' because you said it first.

ROMAN BARTHOLOW

When you saw no more reason to be silent
Where silence would have been, or so it was
You made me believe, as false to fate,
If that were possible, as to yourself.
Otherwise there had been two silences
About the place—or three, remembering yours."

He saw the gradual tension of her lips
Relaxing, as if words they first had held
Imprisoned were no longer fighting her;
"Mine was a silence, then, to be remembered.
Thank you for that. Thank you for telling me,
Although you were so near forgetting it,
That I may have a silence too that counts.
God knows how drearily I counted it,
If you do not—you men. When I was little,
I'm told that I would howl astonishingly
When there was nothing but myself and silence
To entertain me; and as I stare back
Into some nearer years that now, thank heaven—
And you—are ended, I am ready enough
To say I may have been, when I was forming,
Quite as inadequate for my destiny
As many, I fear, have pardonably inferred
Since then. If you had come a season later
I shiver to think what noises out of me
There might have been, even here—though I'm a child
No longer. It was coming to be creepy,
With only my remembrance of a man
I married once, before he lost himself,
Moving about the house for company—
Nor often moving. He would sit for hours
Trying to make believe that he was reading,
While all he read, as he has told me since,
Was in a language where the words were gone

763

Like stars under a cloud. Sometimes he feared
The cloud would melt and he should see the words.
To see them, or to fear them without seeing,
Was equally to be alone in hell,
He said,—to be alone without the pleasure
Of even the damned as a companionship;
Though all the time, and once I told him so,
He had forgotten me; for I was there.
There were three years of that, and then . . ."

"Well, what?"

Penn-Raven said. "Or was your pause to mean
That I shall tell you? How am I to know?
Once I believed I knew—not long ago
In time, but longer in eternity,
Which is not time. I wonder if you know
Just where the difference is between the two
Or if there be one—or one more abysmal
Than say between a long year and a short one,
A false one and a real one? Once I believed
I knew more than I know—or so it seems.
If you are still alone, where shall I say
That I am? Will you look at me and answer?
I am not asking much in saying that,
For I am asking only everything—
Which in our coin of words may more than often
Weigh less than little. If you made me rich
With a false gold that one may count as real
Only in deams, you cannot have it back,
For now it is all gone. There's no need now
Even to look for it. Will you look at me?"

"Assuredly," she said, obeying him
With languid and reluctant eyes half shut
Against the fire in his. "Is that enough?"

ROMAN BARTHOLOW

"No," he said slowly, as her flinching gaze
Looked off uneasily into the distance;
"No, not if you are asking for the truth;
And even if you do ask it, who am I
That I should venture now to say for you
A thing that you know best, or should know best,
Without a man's tuition or assistance?
I think of only one thing I may say,
And one that will add little to your store,
Where you fling everything indifferently
Into the dark and leave it unappraised.
You see there's hanging somewhere between heaven
And earth, where heaven is earth and earth is heaven,
A region where no argument avails.
We stay, or go. I do not say it matters—
When we are dead."

                    "You've said we never die,"
She answered,—"and almost as if you knew it;
But there I've always had my little doubt.
You may for every other mortal question
Be the one man alive with the last answer,
Yet I am no more sad than I am happy
For cleaving to at least one ignorance
Where even the smallest of us are as great
As are the giants. There's one democracy
Where I'm at home to all; and there's no other."

"My theme was farther from democracy
Than your illusions are from your evasions."
There was a darker fire now in his eyes
Than hers had fire to meet; and though she smiled
She felt the searing of his inquisition
Like white iron on her soul. "All I may say
Might well be wished unsaid, or better so.

Say we are whirling amid spheres of reason,
Our floating out of one into another
May prove a sorry voyage if we forego
The plain way to the shore of our departure;
Say we are less than our pursuing forces,
We may be stricken early in our flight,
And after an obscure awakening
May find ourselves elsewhere no further on
In our escape from our discrepancies
Than here among them; and we may not all,
Even there, be sure we see how vain it was
To cloud them with illusions and evasions
Like yours. And if there burrow among others
Many who see no more than you are seeing
In your disheartened hunger for escape,
I might say there was vision in their blindness—
If I saw more than truth.''

                ''What more is there
Than truth for you to see,'' said Gabrielle,
Her lips grown tight again, ''in all your spheres?
If truth be all it is that we are after,
What more is there before us when we have it?
I'm not so much a tenant of the spheres
As you are—and I don't much iike 'escape';
I'd hardly say it was the only word,
Considering all there are, for you to fling
So freely at me—now. There may be others
More to the purpose. I shall not know men,
Though I live on till all humanity
Be dry bones at my feet, and the world frozen.''

The bitterness of his anticipation
Was in her speech, and it remained alive,
Surviving utterance to her brittle smile;

And it was of a savor to endure
As long with him as were the strokes he heard
Of an unconscious and relentless axe,
Below him and unseen. He counted them
As if he were the tree on which they fell,
Feeling them as apparently the tree did;
Though in their stubborn echo there was yet,
For him who listened where his injured wonder
Saw fronting him the grave of more than life,
A thrill wherein he shared ingenuously
The salvage of another's resurrection.

IV

Early one silent evening in July,
Faintly aware of roses and syringas,
And of a steely glimpse of quiet water
Through boding trees below him in the light
Of a huge moon above the distant hills,
Penn-Raven paced alone over the flags
That were a floor outside the ivied house
Where he had been too long—unwillingly
At first, as he believed, and latterly
Without the will to go. "All this will end,"
He thought, in the old way of all who think
Too little and too late; "and when all this
Is ended, the same moon will shine again
As it shines now, and over the same river.
The river and the moonlight and the trees,
When I am gone will be as when I came—
The same, all but the trees. A few of them,
And eminently one, will not be here."
A fragile smile upon a solid face
Told of a sharp remembrance.

                              Bartholow,
Coming unheard out of a silent house,
And all unconscious then of one so near him,
Gazed over the calm shine of broken water
And upward, at the sky over the hill,
And at the moon. "God!" he said, half aloud;
"God, what it is to be alive again!
I hope there is at least one other man
Somewhere on earth who knows."

                              The fragile smile,
Unseen behind him, suddenly was a laugh—
Though not, if Bartholow had measured it,
Quite that of an imaginary colleague
Sharing a new born rapture like his own
Of living in a new world after dying
In one that was no more. "Let both of us
Hope there is one at least," Penn-Raven said,
Out of a shadow; "and there may be two.
Somewhere among the world's invisible millions
There may be two—or three. And if I may,
I'll ask if your eccentric preparation
For gliding off alone into the silence—
First having praised the Lord, and properly—
Has any crude significance. Your stick
Would hardly crush an enemy's cranium,
You are no virtuoso in your fists,
And I can see no violence in your eyes,—
For which, may peace attend you."

                              "I am going,"
Bartholow said, "for the new joy of moving.
It was a nine days' wonder for nine days,
And after ninety is a wonder still.
Don't ask, I pray, if I'm in any doubt

768

ROMAN BARTHOLOW

Of whence it came, or if I'm small enough
To figure in a dream of idiocy
That if I should assign to you for ever
All that I have, or may have, to call mine,
I should pay half of one forlorn per cent
Of all I owe to you. Remember that;
And when I walk away from you alone,
Leaving you here behind me uninvited,
Say 'There goes one so glad to be himself
That he deserts the friend who made him so.'
And that will tell you all; or if not all,
More than enough. There comes along an hour
When we find even our saviours in the way,
And we are best alone. My darkest urging
To-night is for a walk along the river.
We see it better than once on a time."

"We do," Penn-Raven answered absently;
And added instantly, "We do, indeed.
It was a memorable tree, my lord,
That you brought down for us that sunny morning;
And you, craving your grace, were some time at it.
I'll hardly see the falling of one like it
Before I'm off again for other regions.
God knows you've paid in hospitality
Your fee a thousand fold, and then a thousand—
If you persuade your eccentricity
Still to believe there ever was a fee.
Transform your ledger, leaving your red lines
And digits on my side; for I'm in debt
Immeasurably to you; and have been so
For gain past all our counting. Where's the use
Of counting when you know that I shall pay
In gold about the time I pay in blood?
My one defense of my persistence here

769

Is in yourselves and your unleavable
Domain—and, since your triumph, in your river.
It was a tree indeed that you brought down.
When I'm away, I shall still hear that axe.''

"No, no,—some other evening, when it rains,''
Bartholow answered, lightly, "we'll attend
To these obscure details of your departure;
By which I mean that I'll do anything
But urge a man to stay. If you agree,
We'll wait until it rains.''

             "I may do that,''
Penn-Raven said. "I may, or I may not;
For even a friend may ride his best friend's patience
Until it founders like a worn out horse.
With your connivance I'll not wait for that.
By which I mean, you are a patient host;
Though ever since the downfall of that tree,
There's been a burden on you. I have seen it,
And I have borne it with you, saying nothing.
There may or may be not for me a moment
When I shall ask you sometime to believe
Tradition less than life, and shipwreck worse
Than anchorage in time—though pride may twitch
A while at your composure. If I'm wrong,
And two to one I am, being no prophet
Of more than your continued usefulness,
You may forgive an honest awkwardness,
Praising your fate that I'm not here much longer
To brush your kingly velvet the wrong way,
Having done something once to make it smoother.
Meanwhile, the event of my still being here
When you return from your noctambulism
Is clamped with all the probabilities.

My eyes are always on the probable.
Poor in all else, I'm rich in my conceit
Of seeing that if I say too much at once
Your prayer will be for rain before to-morrow."

Bartholow, startled into indecision,
Answered him with a lightness like to that
Of a weight raised with an unwonted ease:
"To say that I've no glimpse of what you see
Would be a waste of blindness, and a lie;
Yet I conceive you wrong. When I come back,
If in the mood I will say more of this;
And if not now, surely that rainy night
I mentioned, soon or later, will occur,
When I may have to hold you here to listen,
If only for an evening—which, I trust,
Will not come on too soon; for when you go,
You will be taking more away with you
Than I may look to find again elsewhere,
Though I should wander always after it.
Remember that; and let your memory
Be sure you keep it warm till I return.
Where should I be by now if a friend's fancy
Had never sent you here as a last hope
That you might cure the lame and make him walk?
Well, he can walk. Observe him." Saying that,
He stepped along the gravel jauntily,
Leaving a friend for whom at least the sky
Was all a confirmation of no rain.
"In what the devil does he 'conceive' me wrong?"
Penn-Raven thought. "And in what am I right,
If not in saving while it may be saved
All there is left, if there be anything left,
For him? I'm witness to futilities,
And I believe he knows it, that may wreck him

Before he sees that he is on the rocks
That he'll not say are waiting where a dark
And silent water that lies over them
Inveigles him along to immolation.
I cannot see before him with his eyes,
And would not if I could—come what may come.''

He sat for a time watching, lazily,
The moonshine on the water through the trees,
Wondering when he might again, if ever,
Revisit, save in a wan memory,
This glimmering scene of all that he had lost
Before he knew that he had never found it.
It was an easy fancy to be seeing
Himself there as a ghost alone outside
A lighted ruin where he knew there lived
Another ghost, and one that had of late
Said little for his ears. After a time,
Assured and reassured that he had felt
The dying of his last uncertainties,
An anguish born of battling recollections,
And of an evening-hidden host of odors
Thrown on him by leaf-shielded moon-black blossoms,
Choked him and held him for as long as death.
Then he went calmly into his friend's house
And laid his thick lips closely upon those
Of his friend's wife, who, toiling with a book,
Was reading wearily of deeds remote
From all abrupt and amorous interventions.
Before she noticed him or said a word,
She pushed away his head, and with a cry
Stifled insensibly into a gasp
Of anger mixed with a remembered fear,
She stared away from him and at a window—
Where there was nothing more that was in sight

Than a few clumsy moths indignantly
Refusing to be free.

     "Were you afraid?"
He said. And from his question Gabrielle
Could isolate combined regret, reproach,
Pride, misery and farewell. "Were you afraid—
Afraid of me? Or was it mostly anger?
I should have said it was a little late
To be afraid, though only the Lord knows
What women are afraid of, or what not.
Of course I beg your pardon, for I feared
That if I waited for it I should lose it."

She sat with her eyes fixed upon the window,
But not as if she saw it any longer;
And when she turned them finally on him
He chose to see more fear than anger in them.
"I'll tell you one thing women are afraid of,"
She said. "They are afraid of being seen
In arms of other men than 'ave a right
To hold them. If I'm rather vague about it,
Or if in your opinion I'm eccentric,
Forgive me. Yes, I was a moment frightened."
"Not of those foolish moths outside the screen,
I hope. Having outworn their metaphors,
Now they are wearing out their silly wings.
They are the same as always, and no wiser."

"I never told you, but a week ago
You heard him, and you must remember him.
I felt the presence of eyes looking at us
Through the same window, but you let me go
Before I was afraid, and that was all—
Till I heard someone shuffling at the door.

It was that awful beast who brought the fish,
And I stood facing him. I saw his eyes
That night, and I have seen them ever since.
He brought a book, and said his wretched name
Was Umfraville; and then he went away.
I fancy we have had him here before
Of evenings—though by chance, or providence,
I have not had to see him. Now there's one
Dark mystery the less in a dark world—
If you remember such a thing as breakfast,
And my not eating it.''

      ''I do,'' he said.
''I do; but there are memories more intense,
As there are disillusions more enduring,
And revelations that are more destroying,
Than all your portraitures and premonitions
Of this ill-favored bookworm may inflict
On me and my departure. When I go,
I shall have brought one man to life again,
And in so doing shall have lost all else
Than life, and more than life. You question that,
And with a reasoning unimpeachable;
For none may lose what he has not to lose,
Or find again what never has been his.
I say this only for the barren gain
Of saying it; though as you see me now,
Knowing that I had better never more
Be near you, nor say more to you hereafter,
Or you to me, my dream denies my knowledge.''

Slowly she clutched and held with angry fingers
The book that she was reading when he came,
And looked away until in her cold eyes,
Now meeting his again, he felt a gleam

Of bitter patience and of resignation.
"If I have more to give than I have given,"
She said, glancing away from him a little,
"Many would say to you it is my life.
And if I cannot say so, and say truly,
You may as well know why—though I've a guess
That somewhere in your tragic suavity
I may have missed a murmur on your part,
Or lost a warning, that I may as well
Say nothing. Are you sure that you know why?"

"I am not sure that I know anything,"
Penn-Raven said, "except that I was blind;
And that my one illusion of defence
Was gone before my plunging trust in it
Would let me see that I was blind. Belief
Is easy where the wish is to believe,
Or so it has been said,—and I believed.
If in your reason for not saying something
You see an end that's worth a journey there,
Go on; and as I may, I'll follow you.
I see but one end, and I don't see that."

"Whatever the worth, or lack of it, be now,"
She said, with a sharp languor that had claws,
"You may as well sit down. If you stand up,
You may be seen by someone else outside.
If that unhappy monster comes again
He'll wonder what you mean by glowering at me
As if I were a serpent in a garden.
That was a fleeting pleasantry of mine
At which you might have smiled. My reason, then,
For saying that my life is not the most
That I have not yet given to you, is this—

And it is only this: My life is less
To me to-night than I may give a stranger
Out of my purse, to keep him warm and fed
Till he forgets me. If my life would save him,
And make him happy till he died in peace,
I'm not so sure to-night he mightn't have it,
If he could have it quickly. You may say,
And safely, that I'm shooting a new arrow
At a new target without hitting it—
If so you like,—yet I've a childish wish
That you remember me when you are gone
As one who at a pinch remembered others,
And did a little good. Your tragedies,
Your revelations and your disillusions,
Are blows that with a struggle I dare say
One might survive. Are you the only one
Who has had revelations, disillusions,
Tragedies? When you came you found me sick
To desperation with all three. The rest
I take upon myself. Call me all names
There are that are not complimentary,
But never tell me that I cast on you
The burden or the blame. It was all one—
Or so I thought it was—and I was here,
Prowling about eternally alone,
And always in the dark. It was all dark
Until you came from nowhere with a lamp;
And if I read more by the light of it
Than once I fancied I should ever read,
You do not hear me saying I was blind.
I am no blinder now than I was then;
And I've a notion, when the worst is over,
You'll find your way along with no great anguish.
Men have incurred more woe for sterner trials
Than you for yours, and they have suffered less."

ROMAN BARTHOLOW

He saw that while she spoke her lips were shaking,
And in the poise of her dry monotone
He felt a quiver of weak scorn that failed;
And while he studied her unhappy eyes,
In which a mist was imminent, he smiled,
Impassively, as a physician might
At a brave invalid's improvisations,
And shook his head: "Your life is less, you say,
To you than a vague benefit bestowed
On those who for your purpose, one infers,
Might throw the needless baggage of their names
Into the rivers of annihilation—
As you, in turn, might throw into your river
As many nameless pebbles. And the rest
You take upon yourself indifferently.
What if it happens you have not so much
As fate has, in the way of a last word,
To say of what it is that you may take
So lightly, and upon yourself alone?
There are some burdens that are borne alone,
And there are some that settle heavily,
Grinding as hard, and harder, upon those
Who mimic the oblivious and immune.
We are all players to our necessities,
But here to-night there is no need of playing;
And when I go away from here to-morrow,
Out of your sight and back again to nowhere,
Leaving you free to count your store again,
You may discover there is more in you
Left yet for living than you say there is."

"You qualify the picture with a tinge
Of your own color, as you always do,
And always did," she said, evading him.
"Women are more proficient, we are told,

777

In these accomplishments than men. No matter;
I drew at least an outline. If you fail
To like it, or to see the merit of it,
I'm without art and without interest
Enough to make another for you now.''

He shook his head again at her, and sighed.
"You'll go no farther on the wings of that
Than a few dusty flutterings may take you
Along the ground. And if I say just why,
Candor may soon be driving both of us
Into a rough and unfamiliar region
So near that you may think it more remote
From where you are than childhood or the grave.
When there, I'll only hope a glimpse of truth
May not surprise you, or dishearten you
Beyond endurance. When you said before
That all was dark when I came here to you,
You saw beyond the frontier, but not far;
And you were not there long enough to say
That when I came there were two darknesses,
And one the darker for the light you made.
At first you found only a stranger here;
And on approaching and observing him
As well as an enforced and endless groping
After the shine of almost any light
But yours would let you think that you had seen him,
You thought him an obscure adventurer,
No doubt,—if not a charlatan, or worse—
Until you knew that he was innocent
Of all contrivance or black stratagem,
Which would have been concealed about as well
From you as would your river from the moon;
And then you knew, as you must know to-night,

ROMAN BARTHOLOW

That he had found in you all he had sought,
Past hope of any finding. All was wreck
Around you; and he saw no other light,
In or about the place, than your pale fire,
Fading and all but lost. And then it was
He found in him that had you as a wife
One he could see that was for you no longer
More than another stranger in a cave—
Indifferent there to you and to your guidance,
If that would be its name. So many changes
Have altered you since then, that all I know
For certain is that if you know yourself,
You know too much for your tranquillity.''

"If I am such a cold chameleon
As that,'' she said, hiding a furtive yawn,
"Your warmth—or I've a notion so—is wasted.
You cannot make a lizard any warmer
By catching it and saying it's a lizard.
Moreover, I'm an atom less acquainted
Than you appear to be with all these changes.
I wonder if by some capricious chance
They may be rather yours than mine—these changes;
For surely you are not as you were then,
More than the Roman Bartholow I married
Is now as he was when you came to him.
You made him over, but I'm asking yet,
How such an awkward mingling of the soul
And body as there is in your medicine
Had virtue to restore him. All the same,
I would not have you think me credulous,
Incurably, for I know as well as you
That his illumination cannot last.
I know it, for I know it never does.''

Before she finished there was in his eyes
The gloomy coming of a stormy scowl,
Where now the pride of a sure faith impeached
Told of a disillusion more profound,
At first, than one of love that was unshared—
And lately, with a false and frozen lightness,
Unsought and unacknowledged. "If you care,"
He said, distinctly, moistening his thick lips,
"Enough about yourself to see to-night
The face of someone in your looking-glass
That you have seen there frequently before,
You may as well begin your banishing
At once of these inept irrelevancies.
If science tells you it was not the soul
That ailed him when I came, why not believe it?
And why, seeing him here alive again
Do you insist that he shall not be here?
These demons of insistence, if encouraged,
May serve you well; for you are not yet old.
Time is alive with opportunities,
And you are here to seize them, if you will."

"Do you mean anything when you say that,"
She asked, "or are you only saying it?"
Her lips were shaking and her cheeks were pale,
And in her eyes there was an anger flashing,
At which he only smiled and shook his head
Once more without an answer. "Are you laughing,"
She said,—"or what, for God's sake, are you doing?
Is this the converse of a woman scorned,
Or are you saying that if I insist,
On heaven knows what, I shall be killing someone?
I may, if I'm annoyed, begin with you—
Though doubtless I shall not. You wouldn't feel it."

780

ROMAN BARTHOLOW

He drew his lips in tightly, while his eyes
Revealed again to Gabrielle's cold chagrin
Their calm primeval sheen of innocence
That always had bewildered and accused her.
"Nothing on earth, my child," he said, serenely;
"Nothing, unless to mention generally
That we are all at work on one another
Not knowing how or when, nor, as a rule,
Much caring. If you find you do not care,
You may as well, or better, not be working;
But while you are alive you might regard
A good man's resurrection as no loss
To those who need him in a world where few
Are like him in his coming usefulness.
Whether you do or not, expel forever
All unavailing thought of prodigies
Or miracles I may have exercised.
There is a field for them, or their appearance,
Though I have never gleaned or wandered in it;
There's also an unfailing fountain head
Of power and peace; and if but once we prove
The benefit of its immortal taste,
Our living thirst will have a living drink—
Dilute it or offend it as we may
With trashy draughts of easy consequence,
Mingled with reason."

                              Gabrielle flung herself
Forward a little, and with cynic triumph,
And with a grateful venom in her voice,
Struck at him like a snake: "Like me, for instance—
Mingled with reason. We'll remember that,
Always. If we forget and leave that out,
The fires of heaven will make an end of us,
And on the instant. What you really mean
Is not that we may fool ourselves for ever,

781

But rather, 'there's a way that seemeth right,
But the end whereof are the ways of death.' I fancy
The men who made the Proverbs knew as much
About this mingling of our drink as you do.
If I see disapproval in your eyes,
Why do you spare my feelings with a club
When you could hurt me less with a sharp knife?
And if there's anything you've not yet said
For my well-being and advantage, say it;
Only, be sure you mingle it with reason.''

"If you compound these incongruities
For your amusement,'' he said, acridly,
"I cannot answer for your joy of them.
You will remember them when I am gone,
To-morrow, and will not be glad for them;
And you will see, to-morrow or sometime,
How far the reckless whims of weariness
Are from a love that you have never known,
And have not yet in you the power to know.
Once in a life, they tell us, and once only,
So great a thing as a great love may come—
To crown us, or to mark us with a scar
No craft or custom shall obliterate;
All which may well be true, or partly true,
Or not be true. For you it doesn't matter,
So long as you're at ease with circumstance
And have your eminence of admiration.
Now you are not at ease with anything,
And are as far into the dark again
As when the stranger came. Had he been wiser,
Your beauty and your nearness and your burden
Might not have overwhelmed his loyalty,
Or, for a time, blotted out everything
There was for him but you—and was not you;

ROMAN BARTHOLOW

Though he believed it was until one day
The fire that he had let you build for him
Upon his altar suddenly went out,
And there was in his temple only smoke
And darkness. It was then for the first time
That he heard your ghost laughing in the darkness,
As he should always have been hearing it—
And would, had he been wiser. You were dead
Before he came, and that's the way it was
That he could hear your ghost. Your sacrifice,
Given as he sees now that it was given,
Is his to pay, not yours. If you have eyes,
You see what he has paid—or he pays twice
In your not seeing. You knew that in his love
You had, whether or not you cared for knowing,
More than a few in any thousand men
May lay upon the altar of one woman;
And, haunting an old ruin as you were then,
You reasoned that another ruin or two
Would not much matter, and in any event
Would be a change. And that was your grand passion."

Gabrielle, staring at him in slow anger,
Saw in his eyes a gleam of mystic hardness;
And then she saw the book that she was holding.
"You make an awful noise over the dead,
At any rate," she said, and said it sharply.
"If I'm to listen to much more of it,
I'll soon be tearing leaves out of this book
And eating them. Is this what we shall hear
In our emancipation from now on?
You've given the pendulum a swing that's fit
To break the wheels; and you have struck me with it.
Forgive me if I seem a little stunned,
Or if my words go wrong, or I say less

783

Than I might say. If life were more to me,
I might say more of an immortal passion
That only one pure mortal in a million,
Or so I understand, may give a woman—
While she gives nothing. There's a rat somewhere
In your most holy temple. I can hear him.''

A sudden fear that anger had released
Within her was now fighting with her heart,
And there was nothing in the room around her
That she had ever seen as now she saw it.
Over the floor before her she could fancy
A chair and a man in it coming nearer,
While in the molten wonder of his eyes,
That were no fancy, she could only watch
The burning of a sad fanatic fire
That she had never seen in them before,
And one she knew that she was not to see
In a man's eyes again. She saw it burning
Until she saw no more; and while he spoke,
Although her eyes were covered with her fingers,
She felt the fire in his, and saw it burning.

''If you have heard what you have heard,'' he said,
''For what it was I told you, I may toss
The tinsel of your insincerity
Where soon the dust of time will cover it;
But if you heard no more than your perverse
Evasions of it willed that you should hear,
Your life may well be less to you indeed
Than one or other of those easy trifles
That you may fling to those you call your poor.
Who are the rich to you, and who the poor?
You have brought one man nearer to the shreds
Of living death than you may bring another,

784

And there is yet yourself. You are still here,
And if your dream is to live on with him,
No house that you and he may build together
Will stand long on a lie; and if you choose
To tell him all, there will not be a house
For you to build. Let the worst be the worst—
Though I hope not—well, then, it matters not,
Or not this time. You are yourself—no other—
And we that are ourselves are all or nothing;
And if life, as I view it, has a reason,
Death is among the least of little things.
If there's within you, and I hope there is,
A power to rend the shell you cannot see
That in your loneliness has grown around you,
And yet may crush you, make of it all you may.
For, if there be within you no such power,
If there be only what you say there is,
You are too beautiful to be alive.''

V

When he had watched her there for a time longer
With the same eyes, he left her where she was
And vanished heavily. She could see him going,
Although she saw him not; and she could see
His eyes, although they were no longer there
For her to see. To know that she was burned,
There was no need to touch the fire again
That burned her; and she knew there was no cure
In asking why. ''Why, then,'' she asked herself,
''Did I sit here before him for so long,
Like a vain martyr willing to be tortured?''
And that was her one question till another
Came slowly out of silence, like a face
Out of a shadow, coming cruelly

And bringing with it only the same answer.
If there was any other to be found,
It was her task, and hers alone, to find it.
There might be one, if she looked hard enough
Into herself to see; for it was there,
And only there, she knew, that she might read it—
If there it was. Others had found elsewhere
Their answer, but their fortune was not hers;
For she had not their vision for the dark,
And had not their invisible clue to follow.

She gazed about the room with frightened eyes,
In a child's way, as if in a child's hope
That what she sought might yet be found where search
Repeated yielded nothing but the same
Dark empty places. Weary at last of that,
Her questioning deserted the dim walls
And corners, and the silence of the floor,
For the cold shining surface of a table,
Whereon were scattered things of common use,
That lay as they had lain there before clouds
Had wrapt her days with night and stifled them
Till day was night within her and around her.
They had outlived it all, and were the same
As they had been when all was unrevealed
That was to come before it was revealed,
And as they would be still, there or somewhere,
When Bartholow and Gabrielle were names
That none remembered. What was it all for,
Unless, indeed, as her inquisitor
Had said before he vanished,—for a reason?
If he said right, why were so few to know
That reason, or to know there was a reason,
Or to believe they knew? To think of him,
And still to see him there as she had seen him

ROMAN BARTHOLOW

Only an age of minutes past, and still
To endure the nameless calm and virulence
Of his invective, and his blasting eyes,
Renewed in her an undulating rage
That slowly rose until it broke and fell
Vainly upon a wreck that long had been
Adrift and empty, and worth no more wrecking.
Already it had broken many times;
And if again, or many times again,
What of it? There would be no more next time
For it to fall upon than there was now.
The fire that smote so deep had smitten less
Than he supposed, for there was less to smite;
And the waves coming after were no more
Than waves at midnight on an empty ocean.
So—let them come, she thought; and then considered
Bartholow for a while, who had not come.
He had seen much in his illumination—
Failing a better name for the unknown—
That she, having a soul that had no eyes,
If she had any, had not been born to see;
And he had suffered hard. She knew all that,
If she knew nothing else. And if a man
Had suffered much to see, had not a woman
Suffered as much not seeing? Gabrielle,
Recalling how the sunshine wakened her
Upon the morning of her wedding day,
Remembered that she went to sleep again;
And now she wondered, in a misty way,
What might have come to pass if they had given
Themselves back to each other before chains
They might have broken then, or broken since,
Had held them, and so given back all those years
That now could not be given. For they were gone,
Those years with him; and what was coming now

She did not know. There was a way to know
And one that made her lips quiver again
Unwillingly, and brought, for the first time,
Tears to her eyes to-night. Her eyes were hot
With too much gazing into a dark fire
Before its angry devastation came
To waste itself on what was left of her
And leave it scorched; and while her tears ran down
Over her face they were not washing off,
She knew, the scars that were for Bartholow
To see and read—if he still cared enough,
Once having seen them there when he came back,
More than to see them there. In such a thought
There was a prowling hope that smothered fear,
And there was a quick fear that strangled hope.
But now it was not fear, and was not hope,
That weakly would have stretched the severed ends
Of worldliness together; for the strands
That once were soft were sodden now, and frayed
Beyond all tying. And if they were tied,
The knot would always be a knot.

                                    Once more
Her search went creeping over rugs and walls
And into corners, where, among the shadows,
Nothing that was the shadow of an answer
Was there that she had overlooked. Her eyes,
At last refusing to stare any longer
At always the same vacant shapes and patterns,
Grew blind again with tears of weariness
And weary pain; and she could feel once more
Their flowing fire. If she could be afraid,
Then pity, when Bartholow came back, might wring
From fear somehow an answer; and if then
She told him, out of pity might rise hope,

And out of hope might rise that house of his.
Employing hope, they might begin to build it,
Knowing that it would not last very long,
And yet when it was there, and they were in it,
Would be a sort of house the while it lasted—
Although there were some phantom rats in it
Already, and more coming. "God, what a house
That house will be!" she thought; and though new tears
Were flowing hot out of her eyes again,
She laughed—until her fancy was a mirror
Wherein she recognized herself and hated
All that she saw. She felt her body shaking,
Partly in anger, partly in desolation,
But rather more in a despairing wonder
At all this unintelligible waste
That was her life and should not have been so.
There was no great persuasion she could find
In any text or pretext or lost warning
For all who seize on comfort without love;
There were too many who had seized and held it,
Giving romance no more ascendency
Than honor might allow, and so, in time,
Gone their allotted and unspotted ways
Into their tombs, with no interrogations
After their unoffending epitaphs.
And so she would have gone, had all gone well,
And had the destinies been rational,
Instead of casting her into this pit
Where there was only darkness and a scrap
Of night above that was another darkness.
And so she would have gone, she said again,
Had all gone well. There was no doubt of it,
She said, had all gone well; and said it over,
Until at last those four cold heavy words
Were like the slow, incessant falling down

Of four hot hammers on a brain that ached
Like the bruised body of a beaten child,
Until again a freezing clutch of triumph—
One she had felt a thousand times before
And had as frequently before put off—
Drew her, it seemed, away from under them.
"Well, when he comes, he comes; and after that,
What matters it what comes?" Here was a question,
If there was not another in the world,
That she might answer.

                While she answered it
She heard the crunching of his coming feet
Along the gravel, and then on the stones
She heard them coming; and she heard them now
Inside the silent house. Into the room
They came, and there they waited. "So?" he said;
"So near asleep as that, and all alone?
Where is the Raven?"

                She looked up at his face,
Measuring in her mind a change on hers
That was by now beyond all artifice
To conquer or conceal. Bartholow frowned
On Gabrielle, or so she believed then,
With a confirming flash of accusation
That she had long awaited, and sometimes,
Like one too long condemned without a charge
And then forgotten, more than half wished to see.
But she had never found it until now;
Yet now she found it, and was not yet sure
Where most his wound would be. "The Raven talked
So long," she said, with an unreal precision
That pierced him as he listened, "that I . . ."

ROMAN BARTHOLOW

"Yes?"
Bartholow said, encouragingly. "He talked
So long that you . . ."

"Yes," Gabrielle said slowly;
"He talked so long to me that I dismissed him—
Or let him go. At any rate, he went.
I think he must have gone down by the river,
Unless you met him on the upper road."
The flatness of her saying more like that
Failed in her throat. The rest was a dry cough.

He waited, standing there as he had stood
When he came in, and as he might have stood
Had he been clay upon an armature
Instead of injured flesh and hidden bones.
"I have not seen him on the upper road,
Or any road. What have you two been saying
To make a death's head of you in an hour?
I'm not a man to make wild elephants
Of mice and squirrels, yet if you have leisure,
I'll stay at home a while till I know more.
Since my return back to the world again,
I may have been too much away from here—
Too much in the woods, maybe. If I sit down,
The picture of us here alone together
Will be more homelike and more sociable.
It will be like old times."

In the same chair,
And with a nonchalance more devastating
After Penn-Raven's tyrannous reproach,
Bartholow, like a new inquisitor,
Had now the other's place. His eyes were bright
With healthy calm, and in them Gabrielle

Saw yet no veiled combustion, or a sign
Of any conflagration that was coming.
Rather in their cool gaze there was a quiet
That was almost content—or might have been,
Could they have been less cool. They were not cold,
But they might soon become so, and so freeze
All her indifference to a slow death,
Leaving the rest of her that was alive
To grope alone for lost obscurities.

"From all this wreckage that he left behind,
One might—without imagining unduly—
Build evidence of a storm," he said at length,
With a selective accent and a poise
Too sure for certainty. "Why should a storm
Be falling on us now, and with a sky
That is all moon and stars and quietness?
I'm sure that no injurious elements
Have been at work outside; yet in this room,
Or rather on your face, there are the marks
Of an uncommon crash. Have you been trying,
By any chance, to build yourself a house
With me away, and after a new plan
That I might not approve? If you do so,
Your private architecture may collapse
With a worse fall than you foresaw for mine
One rare spring morning. Are you more adept
Than all those ancient forces that are able
To wear down even the strongest of our houses?
Sometimes I'd say it was a miracle
Of God that holds the best of them together
While we, with our peculiar properties,
Not yet appraised, are moving into them.
I wonder why so many of them stand—
Or if they would so long without the props

Of caution that should be invisible.
I wonder why so many of them last—
Or if they do. All this, of course you see,
Is merely my ephemeral speculation.
Only of late have just a few queer flashes
Been sharp enough to make me see them twice—
Once with eyes open, once having closed them tight.
The wise, I fancy, are those who may see nothing
Where there is nothing they would see. Moreover,
I'll owe you an immense apology;
And there's a friend to whom I'll owe another,
Being already his ungracious debtor
For all but everything. If this goes on,
I'll see myself insolvent. And how then
Shall we build houses?''

                                                  "There will be no houses,''
Gabrielle said, scarce knowing when she said it;
"Or none, I mean, that we shall build together.
I might have told you so without your asking;
And once I did so, nearly. But you heard
Only what you would hear. Never mind me,
But build it all alone, or with another
Who will not shake it down over your head,
And over hers. Perhaps if I had known
More than I did, and felt less than I did,
That all was gone and there was nothing coming,
I might have gone before it was all gone.
Before you knew me, it was your conceit
To praise me, saying that I had a mind.
But I should have had more than I did have,
Or less. Either provision might have saved us—
Or me, I mean; for now I can see nothing
Before me, or behind me. It's all gone.
I should have lived in velvet ignorance,

With one to share it and to keep it smooth,
And with a mind that never would have burrowed
As yours did into me to find so little.
I wish you had found less and found it sooner,—
Or more, and only found it. But you failed
In finding either; and that's all of it.
So—why build houses? Other men have built them,
Though often, if not always, I dare say,
In a new place, with new material,—
Ready at hand, or soon to come along
When the old vanishes. *Les morts vont vite*—
Or *Vive la reine;* or one without the other.
The queen may come, or not. How shall I know?"
Bartholow, having driven as he believed
Or fancied he believed, a vicious bolt
At a veiled emblem of uncertainty,
And one that only sorrow and remorse
Together might withdraw, saw Gabrielle
Before him as an unreal mockery
That pride and faith and his infatuation
Had once made real. Now there was nothing real,
Now there was only pride; though for a time
There was a multitude of other names
That gathered slowly into a dark swarm
Where pride was only one. He felt their wings
And stings, and while they battened on his pain,
Sat watching Gabrielle until he knew
That she knew more than he of what was gone,
And so had known before there was a friend
To save him and to filch her from his arms.
Whether or not he prized her any more
Than would a Sultan of another language,
And with no mind for blood, prize what a thief
That was a friend had stolen and made his,
The damnable reiterate possessive

Strangled him to an insincerity
That while it numbed him was indifference.
"If she was only that, they're all the same—
Or would be so," he thought; "and all that beauty
Is now no more than a few living cinders,
And ashes that yet live." He cursed at once
Himself and his avenging fatuousness
For saying a thing like that, even in silence,
And bowed his head. "Good God!" he said aloud;
And that was all he said for a long time.
Gabrielle heard the moths outside the screen,
Still angry at their freedom, while she faced
A freedom hardly worth another anger
That she felt rising in her at herself,
For being herself. Penn-Raven's anodyne
Of cold assurance after his attack
Had healed her as a dash of icy water
Might heal in her the deep devouring wound
That years had made for minutes to make deeper;
And if in such a wound there was no fear,
More than a weariness of too much pain,
There was no fear left anywhere worth feeling.
He would have told her there was none, she thought
And shivered when she thought of him alive.
Bartholow, knowing only the unknown,
And sharing only the unsharable,
Would have his day; and when his night should come
He would be free and in the dark again,
Without her for a burden to be lost
In being borne. So now she felt the cold
Of his accusing and inscrutable eyes
With only a blank sorrow for the past,
And with a chilly calm for what was yet
Impending and assured. There was no hope
Worth delving after in the frozen poise

That held her shifting glance now and again,
But never shifted in its iciness;
And there was neither grief nor wrath betrayed
Where either would have been, by now, to her
An arid and infirm extravagance.

"Why do you tell me now that other men
Have built of their insolvency new houses?
What are all houses that all other men
Have built, or may build, worth to me to-night,
Now that I see no house? May all go well
With those who are to build and live in them;
But I would rather hear no more of them
While I see mine, or one that in my dream
Would have been mine, ruined and in the dust
Of other dreams. The time we throw away
On dreams we know that our intelligence
Would laugh at and disown, the devil reckons,
Knowing that we may count so much the less
Against him, having known they were all dreams.
Well, we had better know them and be dead,
Or be alive and leave them dead behind us.
I am not going to die of this, you see,
And you need have no fear that I shall hurt you.
I could not if I would. You are not worth . . .
But, no, I was not saying that. I'm sorry.
We'll blot that much away with a black line,
And then forget it. You are too beautiful
To hurt; and you have hurt yourself enough.
You were not made for this; and now you know it—
And why it was that I should know no more
Than to believe in dreams that were for me
Nearer to credence than realities
Were then, or are to-night. You were not made
To throw yourself at the first thing you caught

In your first web. You are not like the spider.
She lets a prey too strong break as he will
Her net and fly away from her again.
You should have done so. You are not equipped
With any self-indemnifying genius,
Or any sort of communal cheap armour
Or any legend, or effete tradition,
Or native evil, to do otherwise.
He would have flown away if you had let him,
Or I know nothing of him—or of you.
Never until one morning in the spring. . . ."

"When there were trout for breakfast. Yes, I know,"
She added, sharply. "I remember them,
And I remember too, the devil's eyes
A week before in that man Umfraville.
If you must lend the devil your books to read,
Why must he bring them back when you are gone?"

"I cannot answer you when you ask that,"
He said, with half a question in his voice,
"For I am not the ruler of his kingdom.
Never until one morning in the spring,
As I was saying, did even a flicker of this
Go by my sight, almost to be forgotten
While it was going. Why should I have kept it
Before me, as you say that you have kept
The visage of a learned fisherman?
Would it have been so strange if in my folly
I should have called myself remorseful names,
And then forgotten wholly? If I know you
As once I knew you, I should hardly say so."
"You know so much of me," Gabrielle said,
With a dry languor that for Bartholow

Was like a tune that he had heard somewhere
Before, played raspingly on flattened strings,
"That I'll add nothing to your golden hoard
Of wisdom. I should only blemish it.
I'll keep the few poor farthings of my knowledge
Where they belong. You are too wise already
To let me, if I would,—and I would not—
Say even another word about that house;
And that would be in you, all by itself
A very necessary part of wisdom;
And there's one other item I commend
In your appraisal of my destitution.
I was not made for this. When you said that,
You said the best of all that was worth saying,
For which I thank you. I was not made for this.
I was a plant prepared for other soil
Than yours on which I fell; and so I've shrunk.
I'd best have withered."

                        Bartholow felt once more
The shaking of her voice before it ceased,
And Gabrielle believed that his eyes changed
As if at last the ice in them were melting—
Or more as if he wished that it might melt.
She felt them searching her with a sad wonder,
That would not yet believe, or, if believing,
Would not relinquish a forsworn indulgence
Of a wrecked hope that viewed incredulously
The wreck with which it sank. If he had said
Aloud, instead of saying with his eyes
That his hard pity had become for him—
As well she knew it had—a reliquary
For a few lonely memories left of habit,
He would have told her no more than she heard.

ROMAN BARTHOLOW

"No, there is no long reason that I follow,"
He said, "for any longer talk of houses
That might be good for you and me to live in.
Not that it matters now, except for you.
You are not destitute, and you may build
Yourself another house, one of these days,—
One that will be away from trees and rivers,
And nearer the world's music. I was wrong
To shut you up in such a place as this,
And it was wrong of you to let me do it—
Though God knows I was far from saying so
Till you, telling me nothing, told enough
For me to hear. I heard you in the woods,
And sometimes in the moonlight by the river,
Telling yourself that you had better stayed
Nearer to your familiar streets and scenes,
As all believed you would—until you smiled,
And there was jealousy in Ascalon.
You had no right to be so beautiful,
Or I to be so blind. When I did see,
My sight was only darkness. It was wrong,
And sadly wrong, for me to go so far
Into that darkness and to take you with me,
Though I saw not where I was taking you,
Nor more where I was going. It was dark. . . .
No. I should hardly say there was a reason
For you and me to talk of houses now.
Your doubt that morning when I told of one
That I was building, as you prophesied,
More out of nothing than of anything,
Was founded more to last than any house
That you and I may build of sand on sand—
Like children I have seen down by the river.
After one tide there would be no more houses;
Only the sand again the same as ever,

The same as it is now there in the moonlight;
And as for that, the same as it is here.
There is no need of going to the river,
Either for sand or moonshine. We have both,
Here on high ground, and we have nothing else;
And when we know that we have only sand
And moonshine for a fabric, why say more
Of houses?"

     "I shall say no more of them,"
She said, and the same shaking of her lips
Came back and held her silent while she bit them
Into a short and insecure subjection
That gave her speech again: "It is not good
To say the same thing always, or to look
Too long at nothing, as we are looking now.
If I were someone else, I might see more,
For then there might be more. If I were you,
I might regain myself, as you have done,
And so persuade myself that I was going,
Like you, by endless roads into a region
Where there should be no sand. I spare your moonshine,
For it may not be that. If I were wiser,
I might yet live to make myself all over,
And make you to forget me as I was
When we were here together in the darkness,
In all that I should be. This episode,
Although it fills your eyes with ice to-night
Instead of execration and hell fire,
Is only a short part of a long story
That would have been about the same without it,
And had the same conclusion. If I were lighter,
I might rise out of this and fly away
On wings a little worse for a blind singeing.
But you were right—I was not made for this;

800

And I was made no more, so it appears,
For that. I'm always asking why it was
That I was made. Assuredly not for you.
But why should I be tiresome, or assume
That you care, now, whether I am or not?
I'm only saying I shall soon be gone
Away from here, and you will soon be free.
As you have said, you are not going to die.
Far from it, I surmise. If I saw death
As a worse thing than your deliverance,
Awaiting you some day, from everything
Alive that was a trailing shred of me,
I'd wish to live—almost; and wholly wish it
If we could read and speak in the same language,
In the same world. You might remember that."

In the familiar turn of her last words
There was a momentary wistfulness
That pierced him as he listened, and unrolled,
In a slow gleam that faded, the long picture
Of his complacent years before the clouds
Of truth covered the light and put it out,
For a long time. "I shall remember that,"
He said, and looked into her lonely eyes
Calmly, without a vestige left in his
Of hope or hesitation. He had striven
So long to keep them cold that he foresaw
The melting down of his inclemency
Into misleading tears if he heard more
Like that. "O yes, I shall remember it,
And with it things you may not have remembered,
And some you do not know. My debt to you,
Although it may be vague, is measureless;
And the worst part of all that I am paying
Is my regret that you should have paid more.

Without you, I should not be as I am;
And as I am, or rather as we are now,
I see somewhere the progress of all roads,
Even those that in appearance have no end,
And the continuance of all works undone.
Here in this coil of our complexities
One may as well not say where roads have ends,
Or how far they are going in the darkness,
Or where we may be driven, or drive others.
Those who are led may lead, and those who lead
May follow. In the darkness all is dark.
Which, too, is vague enough.''

                                              ''Not in the least,''
She said, pinching her lips together slowly
Before she spoke. ''I see no vagueness there;
Though I could see a waste of mercy there—
But for a stranger waste of more than that,
And old as women. Some of us are changing.
But those who change the most will not change much,
And will not have to. And it's well for them
They are not all like me—and well for you;
For then you might be lonely when I'm gone.
No, I have not forgot what you were saying,
Nor could you in a lifetime be more lucid.
I am the bridge, then, over which you pass,
Here in the dark, to find a lighted way
To a new region where I cannot follow,
And where there is not either sand or moonshine,
And a new sun shines always. Well, that's something.
It may be all it was that I was worth.
'You are not worth—' you said; and then you stopped.
And I shall never know, unless you tell me,
Just what it was that I was ever worth.
Not much—or so I fear . . . Good night.''

ROMAN BARTHOLOW

She rose,

And would have said no more, had he not spoken:
"I'm sorry that my tongue let loose those words,
For now I may as well as not be sorry.
With or without a cause for saying them,
They were no part of me. If you forget them,
You will have less to burden you, and less
To bear away with you. I was born here,
But I shall not die here."

"They're better loose

And off your tongue," she said, "if they were on it,
Waiting to be let loose. If I forget them,
I shall forget so much that a few words
Like those will hardly be as audible
Hereafter as one insect in the grass,
Where now I seem to hear a million of them.
I wonder where they go when the cold comes.
Perhaps they go to heaven." Her lips moved
And would have smiled if they had not forgotten
What they were doing. She was nearer now
And she was looking at his eyes again,
To see for the last time if there was hidden
Within them anywhere a better reason
For her to linger than to go away.
Failing, she laid her hands upon his head
And touched his forehead with her shaking lips.
"You might remember that," she said, and left him.
Not sure that she knew why it was he trembled,
Yet sure enough that it was less for her
Than for the saviour-friend who had betrayed him,
She left him, and went slowly from the room,
And slowly to the stairs. When half way up,
She paused and saw him standing at the window,
Where the moths plunged and whirred eternally,

Torn by their own salvation. She passed on,
Slowly and softly, leaving him there alone
To watch the trees, the moonlight and the river,
And to see none of them. Now in her room,
She sat for a long time in a dim silence,
Watching alone, above him, in the moonlight,
The same world he was watching there below—
Save now she could see everything out there
So clearly that she would not look at it.

She stirred at last, and with a smaller light
Put out the world and sky; and she could see
All the mute things that once had been so much
A part of her that now they all had voices,
Each whispering of a stillness in the past,
Long faded, and of other stillnesses;
And she could feel, as if a ghost had come
Between her and her worn eyes in the mirror,
The fall of the first shadow she had thrown
So long before, and so unconsciously,
Over a man's illusions and his life,
And over hers. "Yes, we are all at work,"
She thought, recalling how another man
Had branded the words on her with his eyes,
"On one another—or we may be so;
And we are least alone with our regrets
When we are most apart—or may be so;"
And so on, like a wheel blown by the wind,
Accomplishing a futile revolution
Over and over, and unceasingly,
Until a dizzy respite frightened her
And she was on her feet. With a scared glance
At one familiar object and another
She waited for the pang of intercession
That would not seize her where she stood inert,

And for the promise of a braver way
Than her earth-weary vision recognized
As hers, where there was nothing beyond earth.
And earth, she knew, had failed in her to find,
In time, the only other way there was,
Which, lying without her knowledge or her sight,
Might as well not have been—and so had not.
She with her world behind her was alone,
And he with his before him was alone—
Past all pursuit. If she pursued him now,
He would look back at her as at a stranger,
And then be gone. Cold as it was, the road
Before her would be not so cold as that.
No preparation was awaiting her
That in a moment she had not achieved.
Anything dark thrown over a white face
To make it nothing would be equipage
Complete for such a brief and shadowy journey
As hers would be down there among the trees
And memories. Now the room was gloom again,
Until a slow gleam filled it. Through the window
She saw the moon and stars, and under them
The river through the trees, and the far hills
Beyond them. All was there as it had been,
And as it was to be. She felt herself
Drawn to the door, as if a kindly ghost
Were leading her and she must follow it
Where she was led. On through a silent house
That had been too long silent she went softly,
And down another stairway she went softly,
And through another door; and there she was.
Now she could see the moon and stars again
Over the silvered earth, where the night rang
With a small shrillness of a smaller world,
If not a less inexorable one,

Than hers had been; and after a few steps,
Made cautiously along the singing grass,
She saw the falling lawn that lay before her,
The shining path where she must not be seen,
The still trees in the moonlight, and the river.

VI

Finding himself alone there at the window,
Bartholow scarcely knew that he had risen,
Or moved; and though the scene outside was old,
Now it appeared as new, and like to nothing
Manifest there before. And for a time,
Nothing was all there was. There were the trees,
And there was all the rest; and yet the place
That he had known was gone. The silver gleam
That gave an outline to those unreal hills
Was more the moonlight of an empty stage,
Where all was over or would soon be so,
Than of a world where men and women lived
In houses they had made. Nothing was real
That he could see, and nothing had been real
That he remembered. Gabrielle, who had gone,
Was no more real to-night than was Penn-Raven,
Who had not come. "If he had never come,
All this would not have been," Bartholow thought;
And thought again: "If he had never come,
What would have been by now?" It was his turn
To search in vain to find a buried answer
Where search itself was blind. He found himself,
Now Gabrielle was gone and there remained
No face to wrench him, sick with a cold loathing
For a salvation bought with ignominy,
And for a saviour whose invidious fee
Was hospitality that he had steeped

And poisoned with unconscionable insult
Before it was flung back. Others had met
No doubt, with as oblique indignities,
And usuries unforeseen, yet none of them
Had wrought for him of their catastrophe
An armor that would gall him less to wear
Than would offense remembered to endure.
He was alone, as they had been alone
Before him, and as many a man unborn
Would some day be alone; and while he wondered
What sort of madness might awaken in him
If there were love as well as pride at work
To rouse it into being, his new-found soul
Trembled and ached with his offended clay,
Which rapidly was over-mastering
Its reigning spirit. He was glad for love
That love was gone, or if it was not gone,
Was far enough away now and behind him,
And was enough a shadow to remain one.
If there was anywhere awaiting him
A more sufficient love than hers had been,
He would not say that he might not again
Be waiting also; and he would not say
How much or little his exacting passion
For heaven and earth together might then deserve.
But while he heard feet pounding in the distance
There was no time for these inanities
Over an unconjectured feminine
Now less than Arethusa to the purpose;
And while he saw Penn-Raven's heavy shape
Coming along intolerably nearer,
There was no room left in him for abstractions
In which a new abhorrence had no part.
With Gabrielle before him, fabricating
Of her self-weariness and self-contempt

Her stoic swan-song of inconsequence,
Penn-Raven, though he could not be far off,
Was not so tangibly a thing alive,
Or one that was anon to be disposed of,—
As clearly now he was who came in singing,
Non ti scordar di me.

               "Not all by chance,
My friend," he said, when he saw Bartholow;
"Not all by chance; I sing because I must.
And, as it were, intuitively in tune,
Sometimes, with the occasion. Farewell's the word.
With your expressed assurance of no urging,
I shall not wait for rain before I go.
The wiser part of me—if such a part
Wins your magnanimous acknowledgment—
Tells me at last that now my hour is near,
And that for certain I shall soon be gone.
In fine, to-morrow morning. All my goods
Will fill a more minute receptacle,
I fear, than I shall when they carry me
To my last lodging; and if half an hour
Be less than I require to strap my chattels,
Whip me away and say to all who ask,
'I never knew this man. He came to me
From nowhere, and you see him going back.'
Bartholow, I'm ineffably in debt
To you for ever. When you look at me,
I'll tell you more."

              "Go on," Bartholow said,
Not having yet possession of an impulse
More than to listen. He had not foreseen
A prelude in this key; and while it lasted
He could see nothing but a shadowy curtain,

Whereon there was a once-remembered scene
Drawn ominously and faintly on the cloth
Of night. A sickness of irresolution,
Or more of hesitation, overcame him—
Until he knew again that if he turned
His eyes too soon, deplorable destruction
Of one or other might attend his action;
While if he saw too long the meaningless
Conceit of moonlight and tranquillity
That humbled him, deplorable survival
Might by default ensue. "Go on," he said;
And as he said it he could feel himself
Inveigled nearer the abysmal verge
Of indecision, where below him lay
Unplumbed abasement. Though he might be mad,
Better be mad with pride alive in him,
He thought, than be an imbecile without it;
Or so it was that a vindictive remnant
Of hitherto subservient cave-man
Persuaded or enforced him to believe.
Meanwhile a furtive curiosity
Would soon be sated with Penn-Raven's lies.
"Go on," he said once more. "I can admire
This infinite ancestral view of mine
And hear unhindered with it all you say.
Surely we know each other well enough
Not always to be talking with our faces.
When we are in the dark we do not see
Each other's faces; yet we go on talking,
As if our faces were no more of us
Than unsuccessful ornaments of nature—
Better concealed, if we are to have friends.
If we must have them, or believe we must,
I'd recommend the putting out at once
Of all our eyes. Then we should have a world

Only a little darker than it is
To-night, and one less hazardous—may be.''

"You have an amiable inventiveness
Against your friends this evening, Bartholow,"
Penn-Raven answered. His uncertainty
Jarred a long silence like an oboe blown
By a strong novice with a reed too thin
For secure volume. "If you are in the dark—"
And there he paused. "If you are in the dark,
Let us have light. Let us have light at once,
But let us not at once put out our eyes;
For now it is we need them. Bartholow,
Your mask and its remote advantages
Are unbecoming and uncomfortable.
I can see that. Yet if it humors you
To wear the thing till you are weary of it,
Your native and superfluous privilege,
I grant you, is to wear it—if you will.
Indeed, I cannot easily remove it,
Not having, or I fear so, proper craft
Or safe intelligence to pluck it off
Without offense or pain. To-morrow morning,
As you have heard me say before, I vanish;
The time comes always for our vanishing;
And we who know best when the time has come
Are best remembered after we are gone.
I was already well apprised of this
Before you mentioned waiting for that rain,
Which may be long arriving, and then left me—
With something enigmatic in your words
And in your silky way of saying them.
If your way was a foil of courtesy
For mine of a somewhat abrupt assumption,
We may as well go back. When I surprised you—

810

ROMAN BARTHOLOW

For so I must have done—by suddenly
Confronting your impeccable composure
With my conjecture, I was seeing pictures,
And wishing then that you for your well-being
Might have been seeing a few of them also.
There were some names that I had for them then,
But now they are not worth your recollection.
Tradition, was it? Shipwreck? Anchorage?
Give once a name to a thing best without it,
You clip the wings and bell the neck of it;
And that which was itself, and self-secure,
Becomes imprisoned, crippled, false, and common.
The picture that you see now in the moonlight
Is not one that is waiting for a name;
And all the years there are for you to live,
Now you are born, are not for you to waste
In railing at unanswerable Fate,
Who has no ears. Setting it rather sharply,
You married the wrong woman—as a few,
By competent report, have done before you,
And will be doing always, or as long
As there are men and women to be married.
When time is older, men and women wiser,
Tradition less a tyrant, and shipwreck
No more a sacrament, we'll do all this
Better—or worse—but with a difference,
Undoubtedly. The way now for you two,—
Together, I mean—comes to a quiet end.
You see it, for this moonlight is not fog,
And pride is not an anchor that will hold you
Long from the rocks. The picture that I saw
Before you left was one of a bad storm,
With faces in it that I recognized—
As long as they were there; for presently
There were no faces, and there was no picture.

Not even the ship was there. It was all fancy,
And will be nothing worse if you steer well.
A voyage may have an end without a wreck,
As yours will have unless you make the moon
Your sun to sail by. You will not do that.''

Bartholow meanwhile, hearing of all this
No more than a few intermittent words
That flew at him as vainly as outside
The moths were plunging always at his window
Had been observing a sufficient wreck
Where neither ship nor sea was requisite
To make a picture with two faces in it.
He would not see it, see it though he must—
As he must know that one of them was now
In the same room with him. If once he turned
His eyes to see it, all to come then would come—
As the primeval in him willed it should,
Even as it willed anon that he should turn them,
And then himself. Slowly, inevitably,
And with a confidence unfortified
Except with an oblivious disregard
Of soiled regrets or mortal consequence,
He went a few steps forward, and then paused
With a few more to go. Now he could see
The solemn questioning in the other's eyes,
And in the living fire that he had found
So many a time behind them he could read
Composure worse than hate. ''Damn you, Penn-Raven,''
Bartholow said, securely and distinctly;
And, with a poise that was almost a leisure,
Came a step nearer. But he saw no change
In the white, heavy face, or the calm eyes,
Or the calm fire behind them. For an instant
A flinching sadness may have clouded them,

But only once, if then; and if at all,
It came and went unseen by Bartholow,
Who merely said once more, "Damn you, Penn-Raven."
Everything else that he had meant to say,
Or would have wished there might have been to say,
Was lost in a sick blur. Whether he struck
Before he leapt, or leapt before he struck,
He knew not. He did not know anything—
Until he felt Penn-Raven's heavy shape
Beneath him on the floor, and his thick neck
Luxuriously yielding to his fingers,
Which felt their way to death, or might have done so,
But for the shock of an abrupt upheaval
After which all was dark. When there was light
He saw, from the same chair where he had sat
With Gabrielle before him in another,
The sad eyes of his adversary gazing
Calmly and patiently down into his,
And felt the crushing of two iron hands
Upon his aching arms.

                "Well, Bartholow,"
Penn-Raven said, smiling unhappily,
"Your speed, if not your zeal, was unexpected;
And you have in you more of your grandfather
Than first one had imagined. You have done it,
And in a fashion done it rather well.
These aboriginal necessities
Of yours have had, we'll hope, an adequate
Eruption and release; and this achieved,
You're fit now for an action more serene
And for an energy more temperate.
Next time you are not likely to do more,
Or quite so much—unless, improbably,
I find that I have let you go too soon,

And with a faith too sure. So there you are,
With nothing broken in you but your pride,
Which happily will heal itself again—
Though I hope not the sooner for this onslaught;
For I can see in that no more to praise,
Or blame, than a familiar atavism,
By no means yours alone. If we consider
The many that have been alive to make us,
And are so many parts of each of us,
The qualified assent of our perception
Will hardly measure either up or down,
I fear, exclusively to our illusions.
Wherefor, if I exact of you your word
Of honor—and your word will be enough—
I'll trust you to be seated as you are,
And to extinguish all those hesitations
That linger in your eyes. Your desk, I think,
Is locked; and I would rather leave it so.
You do not want my death-wound on your soul,
Or my unpleasant carcass on your floor;
Yet having in my tangled heritage
A thread of elementary suspicion,
I see no instant reason to forget
That you have shown me, among other treasures,
A more pernicious and ingenious pop-gun
Than elsewhere I've admired. Now if your word
Of honor failed you, or if you forgot it,
And, so reduced, you made an end of me
By stealthy and unworthy agencies,
Your loss would not be mine; and your reward
Would be but one unwholesome smoky moment
Over the coarse and least implicit part
Of all that makes up me. Whether it die
To-night or half a century from to-night,
The rest of me may know so little of it

ROMAN BARTHOLOW

As maybe not to care. One or one more,
Or fewer, of its ephemeral extensions
Made shorter for your sake would hardly serve
To make you any happier than you are;
And you are not so happy as you will be
When all this other smoke that's choking you
Shall blow away and I shall be gone with it.
You may as well sit there where you are now
As walk about, though I shall not molest you
If walk about you must and will. That's wiser—
For you'll be none too agile or alert
For a time yet. I shall go presently,
And in the morning I shall go for ever—
Or naturally at once, if you insist;
Though I shall be inveterately beholden
To you and your attention if I stay
Around the clock again. All which implies,
I hope, a friendly reticence—and, I trust,
A humane brevity.''

                ''I have no means,''
Bartholow answered from his chair, ''to move you,
Or not without assistance or a scene
As long if not as noisy as the first;
And as your manner says you are not going
Without one or the other, you may stay—
That is if insult, given and received,
Is milk and honey for you, and the breath
Of life. If I had known you were a giant,
As well as a damned parasite and a thief,
I might have shot you and been sorry for it.
To pay so much as that for such a thing
As you would be to nurse the devil's blister.
I do not want your slaughter on my soul,
Or your unpleasant carcass on my floor.

As much as that, I heard; and that was true.
If there's an idiom that will undulate
Across your meditation less obscurely
Than mine, you might announce another cue
For me to follow; or, you might get out.''

Penn-Raven looked up slowly from the floor,
And with a frown of one annoyed and sorry
More than of one offended and dismissed,
Stared solemnly with his large violet eyes
At Bartholow, who found in them again
The same unfathomable innocence
That many a time before had made him smile
As with a kindly wonder. When he spoke,
His voice was that of a tragedian
Resuming after a subdued alarm
The lines of an unhappy narrative
Unfolding a mysterious history.
''All who have lived,'' he said, ''living at all,
Must have encountered incongruities
Tangled as yours are to your contemplation—
If not, as yours are, to be shaken soon,
Untangled, and untied. Your few last knots
That in your fever are to-night so many,
Are not so many; and you are only one.
Whereas, if there were any way to count them,
Those who are struggling with more knots than yours,
And worse, would make a nation. Bartholow,
There was a man once who believed himself
Nearer to God, and by the way of reason—
Where few may see, or seeing may dare to go—
Than all the martyrs by the way of faith.
Now, I am not so sure that he was there—
Though I believe it; and if I believe it,
For all my needs I know it. Yes, he was there;

And where he was, he is,—a little scarred
To-night, but nowhere else than where he was.
There is no going back from such a place—
Or not by the same road; yet there are pits
Along the way, and there are darknesses,
As on all other ways—only far deeper,
And, after an excess of blinding light,
Unconscionably darker. It is well
For him and his humility, I doubt not,
That all should be as obviously it is
Along that way; for he might otherwise find,
With restless and impetuous feet, like yours,
A darker path leading him back again
Where the old road that others had not seen
Might not be seen again, even by him;
And though it might be seen, might not be taken.
All the forgotten sights of infancy—
Which far outlives the cradle—though at first
A burden, would be no long time becoming
Endurable and as easy as before,
Putting out slowly the one sight that sees.
You are not there, and you are not to go there;
Though pride, that eminent adjunct of the devil,
May keep a dwindling sort of regency
Over the rule of your protesting wisdom,
For certain days. You are not going back,
Yet as one mortal to another mortal—
Each in appearance and unhappy proof
Still fallible—I'll imagine that you might.
You are still coiling your credulity
Around you like a snake that would be glad
If only you would let him go away
Before he has to bite you any more;
And that's not either love or bravery
In you, and the snake knows it. Let him go.

Love at its wildest has, if it be love,
A reticence and a sort of dignity
That passion, with pride always urging it
Along to the old wreck in the old storm,
Will not acknowledge or not unwillingly
Regard or recognize. Love, it is true,
May wear the stain of pride and still be love,
And on occasion irretrievably
Say more than should be told—and to no end
Than to sow fennel and regret where flowers
Too rare for the gratuity of a name
Were not to live . . . were not to live.'' He ceased,
And looked away as if he had forgotten
All he had said before so fluently;
And then he said, as with a slow remorse
That dragged a melancholy after it,
''Were not to be.''

                            Bartholow, still aware
That a few words of his if he should say them,
Or his departure without saying them,
Would soon enough accomplish an escape,
Sat waiting, an indignant and chagrined
Prisoner of his curiosity.
A vision of thick lips and violet eyes
Oppressed him, though the eyes were looking down
And the face mostly hidden by the hand
That covered them, till a more solemn pause
Than in the circumstances he could share
Galled him again to speech. ''Well, what's the matter?
There are no flowers now in your garden? Well,
You never told me that you had a garden.
You may, then, like an apt and able blackguard,
Have torn away on someone else's fence
The friendly cloak of lies that you have worn

So long over that shrunken soul of yours.
Easy mistakes are common in the dark,—
Notably so where there are friends together;
And you, with your cheap fennel and regret,
And your sweet compound of hypocrisy,
Are worse than common dirt. I like to say this;
And if your notion is to break my neck
For saying it, I'm not sure that I shall care.
When a man's last illusion, like a bubble
Covered with moonshine, breaks and goes to nothing,
And after that is rather less than nothing,
The bubble had then better be forgotten
And the poor fool who blew it be content
With knowing he was born to be a fool.
As we are born to be, apparently,
So are we; and it's well for most of us
We do not know too soon. We know too late.
Well, what's the matter? Has your spring of lies
Dried up—or is it almost full again?"
"Forgive me if I do not always listen,"
Penn-Raven answered. There was hesitation
More than uncertainty in his approach,
And there was disappointment and impatience
At first in his returning innocence,
Now master of his eyes and of the man
Who gazed unwillingly into their calm
And solemn fire. "Forgive me, Bartholow;
Your dreams have taken you so far from home
That I must wait for an awakening,
Or by degrees induce it. If I do,
You may be learning less reluctantly
How far you are from here, where there is nothing
To hold you any longer. For a time
There was a woman who was never here,
And it was your misguided quest of her,

Where she was not, that led you to the shadows,
And nearer to the tomb than either you
Or she, or rather your sad fiction of her,
Had wisdom to conceive. There was a man,
Also; and though far distant and unsought,
He was already on his way to save you,
Albeit he was untold and unaware
Of your disaster or your need of him.
Nothing between Arcturus and the earth
Is there more surely or insolubly
Than these things that are so. There was a man
On whom a light fell once, as once a light
Fell sharp on Saul—though it was not like that;
Or possibly it was. There are these things,
And they are so—until we give them names,
And harness them with words that have one meaning
For no two men; and likelier none at all
For one man—or one woman. Now and again
There may be one to pass on to another
A living torch that others cannot see—
And all should then be well; and would have been,
Even here and in this house, if in this man,
Who came because a will not his compelled him,
Fear and a fearful hope had faded out
Before there was a fire. There was no place
Under the stars, he thought, where love was more
Than love had always been: not everything,
Yet no small matter, even under the stars.
And there was in his armor, so he thought,
No rift—until he found there was no armor
Against a love that he had long abjured
As one that would be kinder for not coming.
Sure that his house that was not made with hands
Was built forever, he was too sure to see;
And you are not seeing so much to-night, I fear,

As your destructive and incensed endeavor
Never to see again is hiding from you.
Yet I see little in this that's ominous,
For your endeavor is only transitory,
And your destruction is less imminent
Than mine was lately in a way to be,
And would have been if like you I had heard
The call of our inferior forbears
To grievous action or infirm despair.
Not that I should have murdered anybody,
Or put myself away, and so undone
Deliriously my work not yet achieved,—
Although, not being beyond mortality,
I might abjectly have capitulated
As you did—not for pride, but worse than that:
I might have yielded, after disillusion,
To go the desolate way of doubt again.
There may be somewhere in forgotten song
A love like mine, though hardly quite another
In life, I fancy; for so it seems to me,
And so to me it is—or so it was.
Was, is, or may be always—let it fade;
Or if it will die sometime, let it die.
There are some ills that sooner will be dead
For our not vexing them with remedies;
And there are some that have their remedies
In their remedial evil. Let them fade;
And if they will die sometime, let them die.
Meanwhile our occupation is to live,
And somehow to be wiser for a woman
Who, as we thought, was here; and was not here.''

Bartholow's face, by this time slowly drawn
With anger and accumulating wonder
Into a tortured smile, suddenly fell

Into his hands; and his whole body shook
With a malevolent and indecent laughter
That ended in a sort of toiling moan,
Like that of a man strangling. "Oh, my God!"
He groaned, still shaking. But he said no more,
And only after a torn interval
Of revelation did his ears avouch
A furtive acquiescence and surrender.
Call himself what he might, his only choice
Was to be lashed with a fanatic whip
That left upon him now hardly a welt.
All this was for the moment understood,
Partly to be forgotten, partly scorned,
And wholly for a season to be crushed
And sunken, like a piece of yielding earth
Compelled inevitably and impossibly
To be a fulcrum for too many forces.

"Well, if you like it, laugh," Penn-Raven said:
And there was the same anxious innocence
In the large eyes that gazed on Bartholow,
Who now looked at him with a weary scorn
Whereon there yet remained a cloudy smear
Of his inclement mirth. "Yes, if you like it.
I cannot say I like the sound of it
And for your sake I'll hope no more of it
Is in you to be rankling a way out;
And there my fears are brief. You are not one
To steep a needless poison with another,
Bitter enough without it, and then swallow
The whole perfidious dose to no effect
Than to be sicker than you were before.
You are not one to fling yourself alive
Among wolves, hoping unworthily thereby
To be devoured at once without a fight

ROMAN BARTHOLOW

On your side to be free. You are not one,
Because a woman has with eyes not yours
Looked on a world not yours and now not hers,
To say that all worlds are as insubstantial
As a dream world of hers, or yours, or mine
May once have been. You are not one to flout
The power of all your services unseen
That soon you are to see, and are to give,
When really you conceive yourself alive.
You that have heretofore not seen or served
Are surely by some worthier subterfuge
Than this to fling the dust of one illusion
Over the chariot wheels of destiny
Into the eyes of truth. You are not one
To do all this because the flower you thought
Was love you found the fairest of all weeds
That ever bloomed alone where there were shadows.
For you it was no more than that; for me
It was *la bella donna assoluta;*
Though for itself, and in a proper garden,
It might not have been either; and for you
After a time, not much in any event.
You found it blooming in a lonely place
Where the sun touched it only to revive it
For new endurance of another day
That was like all before; and being yourself
A gardener more adept in admiration
Than in selection, brought it home with you,
And to a darker loneliness than ever,
And there it might have withered for the sun
That would have saved it, and so might have died;
But something of the weed was in it still,
And in its northern grace there was a taint.
Or may have been one, of a tropic languor.
We do not have to go so far as that

823

For the unseen survivals that are in us—
As your inimical activities
Have demonstrated. Put the surest of us
Too far beyond the boundaries of our nature,
And we shall be the last who are to say
Just what rebellions and indifferences
May thwart or poison us. We cannot know.
And if, like her, we see beyond ourselves
Nothing, what have we then within ourselves
Worth seeing or worth saving? She may live
To wither and to fade and be forgotten,
Or there may be awaiting her somewhere
On earth another garden far from here.
A miracle may reveal to her denial
Color and light that will not be denied;
And she may live to see. If such a garden
Be not awaiting her—well, you have heard:
She fades, and withers. Were she more a weed,
She might be all a weed. But she's not that—
Being flower and weed together, as we have seen.
Who shall say more of her? Not you, not I.
She may go soon—even here, before you know it.
Or she may not go soon. She may be old
Before she goes—though earth has little need
Of her allegiance to it. There is earth
Enough, and there will always be enough,
For you and me without her. She may go
So soon that you will hardly be aware
Of more than a weed sickled in the night
To shrivel in the sun; or, miracles yet,
And other gardens, may be still on earth
Awaiting her. I do not see them now,
Yet they may be. There are these things that are;
And here are we among them. Is it well,
Or is it ill, that we be where we are,—

ROMAN BARTHOLOW

Here, and among them? Be it well or ill,
Your doom now is to see, and see alone.
Whether she go to-morrow or to-night,
Or live on to fade out and be forgotten
Is now for you no matter—or for me.
I do not ask you for your gratitude,
Nor for your word that you are free. If that
Were branded with an iron across your forehead,
I should not read it any clearer there
Than on a living page that I see now
Before me in a volume that is you.
Your doom is to be free. The seed of truth
Is rooted in you, and the fruit is yours
For you to eat alone. You cannot share it,
Though you may give it, and a few thereby
May taste of it, and so not wholly starve.
Thank me or not, there is no other way;
And there is no road back for you to find.
And she . . . she is not either yours or mine.''

Bartholow, writhing, licked his lips and waited,
As if to leap again before he spoke.
But leaping, as he reasoned, would be folly,
And speech, if he remained, humiliation.
Yet there he must remain till he might rise
Of his own will and go away. The fear
Of death would not have held him as he was;
But there he was, and he was held. ''Go on,''
He said; ''I may as well have heard you out
Before you go out. When you go, you go;
And you are going soon.''

Penn-Raven frowned

As he had frowned before, as one annoyed
More than as one dismissed, and having sighed,

Said on: "She is not either yours or mine.
The ruins at last have crushed her; and she knows
At last that they were ruins before they fell.
And if she pushed a few of them away.
I am not sure that she has in her now
Power enough to lift the rest of them,
Or pride enough to care if they were lifted.
Negation is a careless architect,
Doomed always to be crushed or maimed somehow
In the undoing and the falling down
Of its own house. If a kind ignorance
Had shielded her from seeing how sure it was
To fall, it might have spared her the false toil
Of building in the dark. Her tragedy
Is knowing how hard it is to care so little
For all that is unknown, and heed so little
Of all that is unseen. She made herself
Believe she loved the world that wearied her
Until she left it and saw what it was,
Unwillingly, that she was not to see.
She learned of you on your awakening
What she was not to see, and she saw nothing.
To-day she will not let herself believe
She cares whether or not there's anything
Worth caring for. The soul in her is frozen,
Where yours was only sick. She plays with lies,
Knowing them to be lies, and humors them
The more because she is afraid of them
The most when they are friendly. But for knowledge,
Glowering always and invisibly
Before her like a shadowy sort of tiger,
She might assume a strength to raise herself
Again to look back at the chilly world
That you have taken from her; and if then
Should be the tiger's time to spring at her—

826

Well, there are wilder things awaiting us,
And worse, than tigers. But she knows her world
Too well to carry there a frozen soul
To warm at those false fires. She would go on
With you, if there were such a way for her,
But she would not be with you very long,
Or to more purpose than to know as much
Of you and of herself as now she knows
Too late—which is enough.''

                ''Yes, quite enough,''
Bartholow said. Deaf to the mystic fervor
That once had healed and liberated him
With its immortal implications,—now,
Like a betrayed apostate, he could hear
Nothing in speech or prophecy but sound.
And while he heard he wondered why it was
That he must listen when there was a door
But a few steps away, and a whole house,
Not mentioning a world, where he might hear
No more of this. ''Yes, it is quite enough—
Of her. There is no more for you to say
Of her, unless your pleasure be to say it
Here to yourself alone.''

                ''Your careful scorn
Is not unwarranted by circumstance,''
Penn-Raven answered. ''It will do no harm
To-night, and it will do no good to-morrow.
If you believe that all you found is lost,
And that you too are struggling among ruins,
You are not long for your belief. Your dawn
Is coming where a dark horizon hides it,
And where a new day comes with a new world.
The old that was a place for you to play in

Will be remembered as a man remembers
A field at school where many victories
Were lost in one defeat that was itself
A triumph over triumph—now disowned
In afterthought. You know as well as I
That you are the inheritor to-night
Of more than all the pottage or the gold
Of time would ever buy. You cannot lose it
By gift or sale or prodigality,
Nor any more by scorn. It is yours now,
And you must have it with you in all places,
Even as the wind must blow. I cannot say
All that I would, for you have ears to-night
Only for words; and when they are no more
Than language, our best words are mostly nothing.
The wiser way for you is to forget them
Until you cease to fear them. You have played
With life as if it were a golden toy,
Till you believe that you have shattered it.
To-morrow you will see that you have not.
In honor of your wish I'll say no more
Of her that I shall see no more. I failed
With her, as you did; and now she has failed.
To-morrow . . . but we'll say no more of her;
It is your wish.''

       ''For God's sake, go away!''
Bartholow rose, and would have gone himself,
Had not a subtle inspiration stayed him
While he prepared with a malignant zeal
One final insult. ''When you go,'' he said,
''And you are going soon, you may require
Assistance on your way out of my sight.
With your permission I'll arrange a means
To insure a swifter and a safer distance

Between us than your leisure might achieve
On your resource alone. A cheque will do it—
And there you have it. Do not hesitate,
For if you do your pantomime will only
Be one more lie; and you have lied enough
And stolen enough. Something in you is true,—
I know that; and I know that all the rest
Will be a small and rotten residue
For you to contemplate before you die.
If I were you, and were the parting guest,
I should not ask for more. You'll find this ample
For the removal of what you yourself
Denominate as your unpleasant carcass.
Take it, and now—get out of this!''

                      Penn-Raven,
Having observed the cheque attentively,
Stood holding it until with absent care
He folded it and put it in his pocket.
"Thank you," he said. "You are magnanimous,
Being so from birth. As your ferocity
Misled you but a little while ago,
Now in its turn your magnanimity
Prevails. There are small fellows everywhere
Who might not, as I do, dismiss the whim
You think your motive, and so be assured,
As I am, that you are not one of them.
Pity them, if you will, but never mind them,
Even while you serve them; for you are to serve
Henceforth as one may serve who is alive
Among so many that are not alive.
If they were yet alive, why should they play
So hard at living, leaving at the end
Only a few regrets for having played
No harder? There's a pathos here in this;

For all must yet be done by the unborn
And by the dead together before life
May know itself to be alive. The few
Who see, see this; and you are one of them,
Although to-night a cloud is hiding you
From your soul's eye. I do not ask of you
Your gratitude, or question any method
Your purpose entertains—though I may ask
Whether perchance obscure appearances
May or may not attend my too abrupt
Departure to the town, where we are known
Rather as friends, I fancy. There's a train
Away at midnight, but there's never sleep
For me on wheels and rails.''

                           Bartholow stared,
And then threw up his hands in helplessness.
''Damn you, and your obscure appearances!
Get out. I'll send your traps on after you,
Into the town, or back again to nowhere—
All as you may direct. And now—get out!''

Penn-Raven, hesitating, bowed his head,
Like one subdued by doubt. When he looked up
His eyes were those of an offended child
Wherein reproof and stricken innocence
Were seen through shining tears that were too much
For Bartholow's abused credulity.
Unwilling or unfit to trust himself
Again to speech, he said it in one look;
And then, turning his back upon his guest,
He moved away slowly towards the window
Where the same moths were flying at the screen
And there was the same moonlight. So he stood,
And so Penn-Raven stood, without a word,

Gazing at Bartholow regretfully,
And with no anger in his violet eyes.
His thick lips and his large white iron hands
Were trembling, but there was no fury in them
For Bartholow's attention had he seen them;
Although it may have been as well for both
That neither saw the other's face again
Until there was a crunch of rushing feet
Outside along the gravel, and anon
The sound of a slow knocking at the door.

VII

After this night, and yet another night,
There was a knocking on another door
Where none till now had ever come so early,
And few at any time, early or late;
Wherefore it was with mingled injuries
That Umfraville, the learned fisherman,
Like an unhappy turtle pushed his head
Slowly out of the cover that enclosed him,
Listening while his miscreated face
Became awake. There was another knocking
Hurried and hard, at which he growled and rose,
Yawning and inly cursing whatsoever
Untimely and unseemly visitant
The door might hide until he opened it.
He opened it, and there was Bartholow—
Pallid and changed, and calm.

                                        "I know your ways,"
He said at once, abruptly, while his eyes,
Pathetic with unwonted hesitancy
And a constrained humility, said more;
"I know your ways and hours, and therefore owe

Your patience my apologies. Forgive me,
For I have learned that you of all my friends,
Who are not half so many as they would seem,
Are the securest and the best worth having.
This have I learned of late, and rather strangely.
I could have said that you had told me so,
Across the river—almost when it happened.''

The learned hermit, gradually aware,
Though sleepily, of what his friend was saying,
Pushed wide the door, and Bartholow came in.
''I have been here alone and have heard nothing,''
Said Umfraville, who, robed in white and brown,
Was now more like a zebra than a scholar.
''So it has happened—has it? Wait a little,
And I'll hear more—or no. Your tongue is yours.
I knew you might be coming here sometime—
Like this—one of these days. Or I believed
I knew it. Being a student, I foresaw
The possible. Now for God's sake have a chair.''
With that, he stretched and yawned and disappeared,
Leaving his guest alone in a gray light
Where there was only books that few could read
In any light. Bartholow looked at them,
But they were all asleep and they said nothing
More than a mouldy whisper of the past.
After a mighty splashing, Umfraville
Appeared again arrayed in shopworn hues
Unsalable, at which another man
Than Bartholow this morning would have smiled.
''So it has happened,'' he began again.
''Well, I supposed it would; and longer since
Than I have seen you have I been supposing—
When I've had fancies. 'What's it all to me?'
I've asked myself; and yet, you being friendly—

832

ROMAN BARTHOLOW

Well, I've had fancies. While you found your soul,
I found your reason for the need of one;
Or so believed. I hope you have it with you;
For surely it would be a scurvy soul
To fail you now; that is, if what has happened
Is what apparently was happening.
There are the wise, and you are one of them,
Meanwhile, to know your friend and seek him out.
God made a sorry mess of his appearance,
But here he is, and as he is you have him.
Another man, we'll fancy, might have less
In having none soever to seek out;
But that's a fancy. Have they gone together,
Or has that bland and sainted scalawag,
Your saviour, gone with half your patrimony?
I warned you long ago that I'm a growth
Not loved in your clipped world; and I've a speech,
I fear, that may offend in friendliness
Till we've had some hot coffee. Even so,
You know that you have come to the right place
At the right time; and that's a deal of knowledge.
Before I let you talk I'll warm the works;
For mortal engines are inadequate
Except we give them fuel—by your leave.''

Bartholow, silent, sat abstractedly
Observing his uncouth and frog-like host
At some superfluous early occupation,
Which partly was a vague metallic noise
That he could hear, and partly a vain motion
That would some day be stopped like a mistake
That walked and fussed and fumbled and wore clothes
Too strange to cover life. He thought of that
Until he saw the world a spinning cinder,
Where neither fire nor pride would burn again,

833

Or be remembered. Then a steamful odor
Filled him, and he could hear a voice that said
Something about a cup that would not pass
Until he drank it . . .

                              "You have done well, so far,"
Said Umfraville at last. "You could not eat
Yet somehow you have eaten. You could not say
What most it was that you were here to say,
Yet somehow you have said as much of it
As need be said. You have done well, so far;
You have done well to tell me how she died,
But ill to tell me that you know not why.
You may say nothing, and within your right
Of silence have an end of my remarks
At any time when a word wearies you
Or scratches you, but you are not to say—
To me, at least—that you see mysteries
Among the reasons why she drowned herself.
You may say she was free to understand
That all was over, and that she was free
Thereafter to go flitting her own way
To whatsoever shades or lights or fires
There might be waiting and alluring her,
But surely you will do your tongue the honor
Not to pretend again that you believe it
When it says that to me—for I'm a student.
We readers of the dead are not so blind
That we see nothing that is not behind us."

Bartholow crossed his fingers, twisting them
In a confused uncertainty. "I believe
That I have told you everything but one thing,
Too near for telling. There's a warning humor

That waits even on the dead, and will protect them.
God knows that I would do no less for them—
For her, at least. Yet rather would I say it
Than be the creature of your inferences.
It is a common process, for that matter,
Whereby a change that once was unforeseen
Is born too late. When all was wrecked and ended,
I might, if I had been some other man,
Have had the remnant that was left of her
To cherish unto death. But how was that
To be, seeing I was no other man
Than he that is before you. There was talk,
On my side, of a new house we should build
Together—yet I knew the while I talked
That I was only talking; for I knew
There was no house to build. I'll not affront
The old funereal decencies by saying
More now than I have said. I don't forget
That she is lying cold there where I left her,
Or that when I go back there I shall find her.
There was a madness that was born with her,
And I am not her judge.''

      ''There may have been,''
Said Umfraville, ''a madness born with her—
Quite as you say. Quite as you say, indeed.
There is a madness born with all of us,
Possibly. There are signs enough of it.
No longer time ago than half a minute
I should have said again that I believed
You knew; but I believe now that you don't.
The poisoning inertia of our custom
Has had its way with many a man before,
And many a woman. She who died of it
That night, if so she died, was only one;

And you, who are alive in spite of it,
Are only one. Your saviour may have saved you,
But never fancy now that in your freedom
Your fee is paid. Your freedom is itself
Another poison, or may turn to one
If you consume too much of it. Your soul
May shrink, if you are too familiar with it,
To such offended and obscure concealment
That you may never end it in this life
Again—assuming always, or for now,
That you have found it. Something you have found,
I grant you, but a benison to beware
And to be wary of, and to respect
As you respect your senses—reasonably.
As for your friend, you've seen enough of him
In seeing him on his way out of your sight.
You have enough of him in his achievement.
If a true artist must go to the devil,
What's left of truth in him should keep the devil
Out of his art; whereas if your true seer
Must be a liar for variety,
He'll soon see double. And on the other hand,
Strange bottles hold God's wine, or we are told so.
And I believe old sayings, for I'm a student.
You have a choice of ambiguities."

Bartholow rose, and having risen, he smiled
A little with his lips at Umfraville.
"I should have hardly come to you," he said,
"For such an early douche of rudiments.
Illuminations are all dangerous
If we are too familiar with our fires,
You say; and though I might have drawn as much
As that from my own well, I'm not ungrateful.

836

ROMAN BARTHOLOW

I thank you, for I know you are my friend;
And I'll apologize eternally
For stirring you at such a vicious hour.
My coming is of itself an evidence
That I'm a trifle shaken, as you see."
"Only a trifle," said the fisherman;
"And a few rudiments will do no harm.
Sit down. Now as for these illuminations,
The world is always dark when they go out;
And yours would be the blackest of all worlds
Without your new-found light—well nigh as black
And unendurable as hers, may be.
You thought yourself alone; and all the time
The two of you were stifling there together,
Each having wrought so long upon the other
In silence that in speech you played with lies,
Fearing a thunderbolt if truth were spoken.
I question if you need reproach the past
For those indigenous injuries of custom;
And on the chance of trampling in the fields
Of more than my domain, which is not large,
I doubt if you need pity her for the end
She made. If my conviction tells as much
Of her eclipse as your renascence tells
Of yours, you cannot wish her for your sake,
And surely not for hers, with you again
On earth; for she was dead before she died."
"You mean then that I killed her? Is it so?"
Bartholow was a long time pondering
Before he spoke again. "It may be so.
Yet, when I left her there, could she have been
So peaceful? Have the dead a special kindness
For those who kill them? I can imagine so."
He scanned again the cold unanswering books
About him, and then gazed at Umfraville

Impassively: "You believe then that I killed her?
It may be so—though I should hardly say so."

The scholar clamped his jaws together slowly,
And sighed and shook his head before he spoke:
"Since neither of you knew what you were doing
When you were groping there alone together,
You will not add a cubit to your stature
Imagining you did this or you did that.
No doubt there are some extant vulgar cynics
Who'd say that she has won. I'm only saying
The race is over; and, to use your words,
I'm not the judge. I think, if I were you,
I'd be so facile as to leave all that
To custom, the arch-enemy of nature.
Nature is here apparently to suffer,
And we who are supreme in mercy, scope,
And vision, have never failed to do our part.
How many do the sweetest of our species
Conceive they may have killed, or worse than killed?
What wreckage have the gentlest of us left
Among those who have smiled and are forgotten?
What untold inward searing of the strong
Has been the jest of innocence and weakness?
What ugliness and emptiness of change
Has been the aftermath of silly triumph?
What stings of unforgetting recollection
Have been the wages of unworldly prudence?
How many a sickening wrench of hard belief
Has been the sport of a soft egotism?
What smeared ends of unfinished histories
Are in the chronicles of disillusion?
Having a face no man may gaze upon—
Saving an only friend who doesn't see it—
I may have made you fancy I see nothing;

And I'd be willing I should see no more,
Sometimes. There woke within me such a thought
As that when first I met your mendicant
Exotic soul-practitioner, Penn-Raven.
If it was he that saved you and redeemed you,
There was a great deal in you to be saved—
Or there was parlous little. Being your friend,
Also a student, it's an easy flight
To fancy there was much. You are soon to know,
For in the other event your light will fade
Before the crocuses are out again.
There is a voice that says it will not fade—
Though I'm not sure that one has need to hear it,
Or that it says your freedom, of itself,
May not be light enough. I cannot say
With your authority what it is that happens
When men that are themselves their prisoners
Go free again. I say, God help the women,
When they have only their own hearts to eat.
A man will eat another's and not know it,
And so conserve his own. So may a woman,
If she have one at hand that's appetizing,
And not so tough that she be weary of it.
Sometimes I have a robust apprehension
That if we were all honest cannibals,
And not such anthropophagous hypocrites,—
If we should feed on one another frankly,
And with no cloud of custom in the way
Of clarity and advancement,—we should climb
Higher than yet we are, with all the bones
Of all the weak beneath us. Never infer
From this that I approach the personal—
For I'm but an offscouring of the sphere
To which I am still clinging, for no reason
Except that I still cling. I've no illusion

That I have license to be personal
Beyond your problem—which is now not one
For you to pore on too remorsefully.
The more you make it visible, your position
Becomes a puzzlement and a devilment,
More than a desolation. In your heart
You are not sorry that your sybarite,
Your Ishmaelite, your omphalopsychite,
Or what the devil else he may have been,
Is on the road again to his next haven—
Which may, I trust, be far ahead of him.
Not even with his extortions are you sorry
That you are now alone, with no conceit
Or purpose to pursue him. Are you sure
That he is not still here?''

                              Bartholow gazed
Out through a dusty window at the river,
As if he had not heard. ''Yes, I am sure,''
He said, indifferently. ''He is not here.
He went away. But he would not have gone
If I had let him stay. He would have seen
Her face once more, he said. He did not see it.
He told me that obscure appearances
Would be remarked if he went suddenly;
But he went—suddenly. I did not see
Her face till yesterday. We brought her home,
And there she is. I have not slept since then.
I have not slept these two nights now; not since
Two men came in the moonlight to my door.
They saw it from that vessel anchored there.
They saw it in the moonlight. They could see
No other house than mine on the west side,
And they came there. I have not slept since then;

And I may not sleep yet—for a long time.
Why should I sleep, when you say that I killed her?''

"Suppose we say to that that I said nothing,"
Suggested Umfraville, deliberately.
"As I'm a scholar and a fisherman,
I have said nothing half so venomous
As half you say I've said. You are more racked
And clubbed, as I see now, than I believed;
So I forswear all ambiguities
And once again refer your case to custom.
You keep yourself so well within yourself
That you are likely to conceal your needs
When more than ever they should be revealed.
Your world's way, doubtless, and the way of custom.
But I'm a dweller of another world,
Where all my friends are shadows—who, if here,
Alive, would only wonder what they met
If they met me. My way among my kind—
If such a kind there be—is one that you
Alone, almost, of yours have had a wish
To contemplate. Therefore I call you friend,
And for reward offend you. For your saint,
Your saviour—I can only let him go,
And pray that he go far.''

                              "I'm not so racked
And clubbed that I need that,'' Bartholow said.
"When you berate yourself the most, your words
Contrive to fall on me; and when I feel them,
As now I do, undoubtedly I deserve them.
Yet I'm aware of an unconsciousness
Of their importance when this friend of mine,
Who saved me, and then made me wish him dead,
Inspires them. There is much you do not know

Of doors that are within us and are closed
Until one comes who has the key to them.
I have no proof that one to open them
Need be infallible. If he be sincere,
And have within himself the mastery . . .
I don't know. All I know is, it was done.
There were no mummeries, no miracles;
There was no degradation of the wits,
Or of the will; there was no name for it;
Yet something in me opened and the light
Came in. I could have given him all but life
For recompense. Also, I could have killed him,
Indifferently, while he was on the floor,
And I was at his throat.''

           ''Go on from there,''
Said Umfraville. ''Go on again from there!''
A griffin grinning into a smooth pool
Would have seen something like the face just then
That beamed on Bartholow, who dried his forehead
Mechanically with his handkerchief,
And sighed—and after, in a wan way, smiled.
''Go on from there, and—well, *aderitque Apollo;*
And he will give your language golden wings.
Your theme inveigles me,'' pursued the griffin.

''No I shall not go on again from there,''
Bartholow said, and frowned remorsefully.
''For long before I struck him I could see—
As I see now. And it was he who did it—
Who gave me sight. Was I blind when I struck him?
If I was blind a moment, I was blind.
He said that I was aboriginal,
But I'll say I was blind. I would have killed him,
Certainly. But I would not kill him now.

Nor would I wish him ill. We must all pay,
Somehow; and I believe that he has paid.
If he has not, he must. And as for her—
Your way for her may be as well as any.
If you say she was dead before she died,
She may have been so; and I may have killed her—
Before she died. I had not thought of that.
The way of custom is the way of death,
Or may be so, for some who follow it
Too far; and so it was I may have killed her.
I do not ask of you that you say now
Whether I did or not. You do not know.
She married without love; and when love came,
A life too late, I should have been a liar
To take it, or to say I treasured it;
For when it came at last, out of the ruins,
It was one remnant more among too many;
It was love only as a beauty scarred
Is beauty still. I could forgive the scar,
For that was nothing, and was far behind me;
But with him in the house I could not say so.
It was the smear on him that made me blind,
And made me strike. I do not know him yet.
Only, I know that I can see again,
With a new sight—and that he made me see.
Strange bottles, if you will."

         "Damnably strange—
And effervescent," grunted Umfraville.
The wine in this one blew the stopper out,
And yet the wine stays good. It's not the rule.
Well, you are out for knowledge, or for wisdom,
And wisdom has a driving way with rules.
Your wine may be the best; though for myself,
Give me the old elixir that you gave me

That morning when I brought the noble fish.
You do not know him yet? You never will.
So let him fade.''

       ''I cannot make him fade,
Though I could make him go.'' Bartholow felt
Again the sweat of effort on his forehead,
But otherwise, though more pallid, was himself,
And had himself in hand. ''Now I'll go home,''
He said. ''And I shall find her waiting there. .
No, he will not be there. And if he were——''

''He would amerce you for your negligence,
And you'd requite him with another cheque.
You must go farther for the mystery
Than that, if you're to find out where it lives.
Wherever he may be now, at your expense,
Whatever he may have done to you, or for you,
I seem to hear him laughing. I'm a sinner
To say it, but I say it for your safety,
Not for my satisfaction. As you know,
I have a speech that would be unbecoming
In anyone more inured and more at home
To the congealed amenities. I'm a student,
Wherefore I see him laughing. . . . What the devil?
What is it? What's the matter!''

       Bartholow breathed
A little harder and a little faster
But had no power to speak till finally
The tension broke within him and his head
Fell forward like a stone into his hands;
And there, while memory clutched and humbled him,
He moaned and choked and laughed. When he could speak,
His voice rocked with his body: ''No—you don't!

ROMAN BARTHOLOW

You do not hear him laughing—for he wept!
I told him his obscure appearances
Could not be too obscure—and then, he wept!
I said he was a blackguard—and he wept!
He got a thousand dollars to get out—
And then he wouldn't go until he wept. . . .
Damn him, he wept!'' He swayed there in his chair,
And all but out of it, laughing and moaning;
" 'I do not ask you for your gratitude,'
He said to me. He said that to me twice—
And then he wept! . . . And then they came to tell
What they had seen. They came up from the river—
In the moonlight . . . Strange bottles . . . Oh, my God!''

For a long time he sat there, trembling, shaking,
While Umfraville stood watching over him,
At first alarmed, at last assured. He waited,
Gravely and patiently, for another word
That would be slow, as he foresaw, to come;
But he still waited there, and still he waited,
With a fidelity inexhaustible
And a solemnity unchangeable,
Till questions that would not be answered yet
Glimmered at little in his doubtful eyes,
And over his amorphous countenance
There crept a slow and melancholy smile.

VIII

There was a wall of crimson all along
The river now; and Bartholow, gazing at it,
Knew in his heart it was for the last time
That he was seeing those trees, and the still water,
Which he had known from childhood. In his house,
Or one that all his life had been his house,

Nothing of his remained that would be there
To-morrow. In his heart nothing remained
But a recurrent ache when he remembered,
As now he must; for there would soon be sunset,
And he would soon be gone. He looked away
Over the falling lawn before him there
Where summer now lay buried and the first
Red leaves of autumn, flying silently,
Became a scattered silence on the grass.
He gazed, and saw the water through the rift
His axe had made that morning in the spring,
With Gabrielle watching him. That was long ago—
Too long, he told himself, to be seen there
Among so many pictures that were fading,
But were not yet invisible. No, not yet.
The frown of an unwelcome recollection
Wrinkled his face and changed it while he saw
The picture of a shipwreck on the air
Before him, and three faces. One was his,
That would be seen again; and one was hers,
That would not, surely, come back there again,
If even it might, to see or to be seen;
And there was one that he should see no more,
Living or dead, if life and death were kind.

Considering thus the scene that he had limned
Of cloudy and tempestuous memories,
He felt an echo sounding over floors
Of the old house—dismantled, empty, sold.
And waiting for new faces to come in
When he should go. "I shall be gone to-morrow,"
He thought; "and when this house where I was born
Has been here for another hundred years,
No doubt some unborn stranger will be gazing
As I am, at the river there below him,

846

ROMAN BARTHOLOW

With memories that may then be quite as cloudy
For him as mine have been for me to-day.
By then he may have lost as much as I
Lost once—or more, if there be more for one
To lose,—and he may then have found far less.
I wonder what a learned fisherman
Would say to that,'' he asked, as Umfraville,
After an exploration, came outside.
Tramping the flags with hard and heavy feet
He came to Bartholow as an animal,
Quaintly arrayed as man, might have approached
A master that he knew was leaving him.
There was a melancholy questioning
About him, and almost a dignity.
''They have left nothing that was made for me,
And that's as well,'' he said. ''The books you sent
Will be enough, and I shall not forget
The man who sent them. That's my way of saying
All that I cannot say. And you said something?''

''I wondered if another hundred years
May find another tenant in this house
With memories that will be no merrier then
For him than mine are now for me. That's fancy,
As you would say. Too much in order, surely,
To be imagination, I should say.''

''Merry is not your word this afternoon—
That's more what I should say,'' said Umfraville;
''Though I'll imagine a man somewhat merry,
Even in a tomb, alone there with his fathers,
If he be sure that one man, and one only,
Be not somewhere there with him. Your Penn-Raven,
Whether or not he's in your tomb, is not
Here in this house. At least, I didn't find him.

I'm wondering where three months have hidden him,
And how far off he is,—but I'm not asking.
If only we select our distances,
The world is of a comfortable size
For two to live in. What are you going to do,
If, as you may, sometime you come together,
And he weeps on your bosom for more gold?''

''We shall not come together,'' Bartholow said,
Smiling impassively. ''And if we should,
We shall agree upon our distances.
He has instructions, and he has a mind
That's apt and adequate for their absorption.
Yes, I believe him. Yes, and in his word.''

''He has a mind, and he has more than that,''
The scholar growled at length, unwillingly,
''If all you say is true; and your condition
Would argue rather more for you than lies.
He says you are yourself; and if your look
Be the certificate of your quality,
You are not far from where he says you are.
On your report he says enough to sink
A shipload of the uninitiated.
He says if in considering what we are
We ponder for a season on the many
Behind us who have made us what we are,
Our vanity will hardly have an eyelash
To cling with to the ridge of our achievement;
He tells you those who struggle with more knots
Than yours have ever been would be themselves
A commonwealth—and that's all true enough;
He tells you that some evils are themselves
Their proper remedies—and that may pass;
He says the fruit that he has given to you

848

ROMAN BARTHOLOW

Is one you may not share with other men—
Though you may give it, and those getting it
May thrive on it, not knowing the name of it,
Or whence it comes to them, or wherefore. Well,
I'm not so much at home there, but no matter.
He says that from now on you'll be alone,
Wherever you find yourself, and that you'll carry
Whatever it is you call it with you always,
Whether you will or not. He says, also,
There was a man, meaning himself—oh, damn him—
That was already on his way to save you,
Knowing no more, it seems, of your existence
Than you knew there was anywhere after you
A thing like him. And there you are. Joy! Joy!
If I were but a hand-step nearer bedlam,
I'd half believe the blackguard was half right."
"I called him once a blackguard—to his face,"
Bartholow said, reflecting; "and I met
With no denial. Yet I could wonder now
Just what the silence he commanded then
Was made of. Partly sorrow, I am sure,—
And I forgive your smiling; partly pain;
Partly compassionate bewilderment—
And I forgive your laughing. I should laugh,
Undoubtedly, or wish to, in your place;
If I were in your place, I'd be as blind
As you are, and as much to be forgiven.
Excused, I mean. If we're too soft with nature
In our forgivings, nature may laugh at us
As you were laughing then, and fling them back
Like vitriol in our faces. I'll excuse
Your mirth, my learned friend, but don't do that;
For now, to make it worse, you are too solemn—
As if you feared that you had wounded me.
You have not wounded me. Do you remember

That morning when I knocked you out of bed
So early—when I told you it had happened
And went somewhat to pieces at the end?
There was a time when I too should have laughed
At the mere whispered probability
Of such a scene awaiting anyone
Assisting at my drama. But you waited,
And in your wisdom never said a word,
Or laughed. You might as well have laughed at that
As at compassionate bewilderment—
Or what it was Penn-Raven may have felt
For me when he was told he was a blackguard,
Which, in the compound of his opposites,
I'll say to you he was. Now you look better.
If you have not forgotten such a morning,
You may remember that I mentioned then
Some doors within us that may not be opened
Till one may come who has the key to them.
When he has opened them and has made free
The life within that was a prisoner there,
How is a man who has a door in him
Still closed, like yours, to say what else he was
Than blackguard? Even though I say my doors
Are open, I'm not saying what else he was,
Or why it is that nature baits for men,
Between them and the pit, so many traps
To save them with a poisoned obligation.
Nature has ways, you say, not reasons. Well,
They lead us, if we find and follow them,
Strangely away from death."

                          "And into it—
As often, or as likely." Umfraville
Stared with a brooding melancholy scowl
Over the flaming trees and into time

Behind him, but he found so little there
That he soon looked again at Bartholow,
And with constrained inquiry. "Quite as often,"
He said, "or quite as likely. And for that,
If you've an urging in you, going forward,
To stray back by the phantom-ridden ways
Of memory—*tout' aniarotaton.*
Your steps are elsewhere. Pindar said all that,
You may remember,—*nessun maggior
Dolore*—long before there was a Dante.
You find it also in Cimmerian,
If you look far enough. But what's it all
To me? I'm asking—what's it all to me?
I'm only a dry mummy among books,
Except when I'm a-fishing or I'm drinking.
For me there's nothing wholly bad that's old,
And nothing good that's new since Porson type.
While time has a digamma left in it
For bait, I'll set my trap and catch myself.
Your traps and ways are yours; though as for poison,
Leaving him out, I pray that by this time
You see at last where custom was at work
Before he came. You fancied once I told you
That you had killed her,—which was nothing more
Than a politeness to Melpomene
On your part, and a negligence on mine.
My fault again," he added, having watched
A cloud across the face of Bartholow:
"I should have put more clothes upon my words;
"I should have said it without saying it;
I should have said, 'For God's sake, my good friend,
Relinquish all such dutiful self-damnation
As that. There were you two in the dark together,
And there her story ends.' The leaves you turn
Are blank; and where a story ends. it ends.

851

The author may have lost enthusiasm,
Or changed his mind, and so may write another—
But not upon those leaves. Books are my life,
And when there is no more of one, I know it.
'Let me be worthy of your mysteries'—
Or, at the least, of this one. Say to custom
All I have said to you, and then forget."

Bartholow, gazing at the open door,
Could half believe that he saw there the ghost
Of Gabrielle, going in and vanishing,
Slowly, as he had seen her when she left him,
That morning in the spring, when he had said
So much to her about a phantom house,
Which he knew as well then must always be
A phantom as he knew it was one now.
Before it was all gone the vision turned
Upon him the once unrevealing eyes
That now revealed so much; for he could see
All that he did not see when she was there,
A woman and alive. But he saw nothing
That would have been as happy in his house
Unbuilt as in her grave where she was lying.

He shook his head slowly at Umfraville.
"No, I shall not wear out the time that's left
In poring always over those blank leaves,"
He said; "and maybe they are not so blank
To me this afternoon as once they were.
There may be nothing on them for your eyes,
Which in their turn see much that might as well
Be blank for mine. I shall remember always
Your counsel, and should always value it,
Being yours, whether or not I followed it.
Your Custom, undeniably a giant,

Is not so monstrous that, if we had vision
To see ourselves before it was too late,
We might not overthrow him for another;
For we must have our giants, though the pride
Of our inferiority may insist
That we disguise them. There are more at work
On a forlorn disguise to fit the old
Than on a proper garment for the new.
New giants are at first intolerably
Not ours, and are uncoverably naked."—
"If you can see all that," said Umfraville,
"There are no pits of memory behind you
That you need waste a fear on, or a sigh.
Go out into your world and be a tailor,
But leave my world with me. I'll stay in it
With my familiar giants, who are dead,
And therefore do no harm."

      Bartholow smiled:
"About what time were they annihilated—
These harmless giants of yours? They are not dead,
My friend, though some of them are overthrown;
And even to-night, if you bestir yourself,
There may be time enough, and a way made,
For you to go with me—as far, at least,
As where your giants reigned." He looked again,
Affectionately, at an asking face
That hardly was a face, and read upon it
A loneliness of long deformity
That was the lonelier somehow for its learning.
"An hour or two on the Acropolis
Would let you see how far they are from dead."

The scholar shook his head: "They are not there;
And you are wronging them and wronging me,

Saying they are alive. They are all dead.
And I would have them so. No, I'll stay here.
Here I shall have my own Acropolis,
And have it as I will. If I were there,
All I should see would be the scraps and ashes
Of a lost world that I shall have intact,
And uninfested with modernities,
If I stay here. And if I went with you,
For God's sake what would you be doing with me?
Men would be saying soon to one another
That you were Satan, going to and fro
In the earth again and up and down in it,
With me along with you to scare away
The curious, who might otherwise be annoying.
No, no! There is a best place in the world
For me; and that's as far as possible
From your activities. You are going to live,
At last, that more may live. It is all true—
All as your prophet, damn him, said it was.
I see it now, but there was a long time
When I saw nothing but that meaty-faced,
Fanatic, esoteric head of his.
Nature, that has a deal to answer for,
Put something in him, inadvertently,
Prepared and graduated for the lymph
And essence of a worthier organism.
That's how it must have been. If you say not,
You say it on the same authority
That I say I'm a fairy of the hills.
No, no,—the place for me is over there
Across the river. There among my dead,
And only there, I'm properly alive.
So there I'll go, and with no more ado.
You dine to-night with friends who are concerned
That you have sold unwisely and too soon—

ROMAN BARTHOLOW

And then you go. You are the only friend
That I have left; and if that's not so bad
As a bad name to take away with you,
Shelve it among your memories. Good-bye!''

Bartholow pressed his hand and held it long
Before he let it go again. ''Good-bye!''
He said. ''We should have known each other better
If I had known myself. A word of yours
Will always find me—somewhere. You know best
Where you belong—whether among your dead,
Who are still with us, or among the living
Who are not yet alive.''

           The man of books
Answered him only with a lonely smile;
And then, among the slowly falling leaves,
He walked away and vanished gradually,
Like one who had not been. Yet he had been
For Bartholow the man who knew him best,
And loved him best,—acknowledging always one
That had betrayed and saved him. He was gone,
Also, and there was no more to be said
Of him; and there was no more to be paid,
Apparently, on either side. The sum
Of all that each had ever owed the other
Was covered, sealed, and cancelled in a grave,
Where lay a woman doomed never to live—
That he who had adored her and outgrown her
Might yet achieve. He sighed, and saw the ivy
Glimmering on the wall of the old house
Like an old garment over covered years,
Till his imagination made of it
The cover and the integument itself
Of the unseen. The tangled roots of wrong

Were drawing always out of hidden soil
The weird existence of a tangled vine
Too vaguely intertwisted and involved
For sanguine gardeners, who might only prune
Or train a few new branches. "Well, that's something,"
Gabrielle might have answered then, he fancied;
And she might then have smiled as wearily
As on that unforgotten unreal evening
When she had touched his forehead with her lips
Before she had gone silently upstairs,
And silently away. . . .

                He locked the door,
Aware that even the key to the old house
That had so long been his was his no longer,
And in the twilight went away from there.
Over the footworn flagstones and the gravel,
Under the trees and over the long road
Between him and the gate, he walked away,
Knowing that he had seen for the last time
The changeless outline of those eastern hills,
And all those changing trees that flamed along
A river that should flow for him no more.

DIONYSUS IN DOUBT

(1925)

To Craven Langstroth Betts

DIONYSUS IN DOUBT

From earth as far away
As night from day,
Or sleep from waking,
Somewhere a dawn like none
Before was breaking.
For long there was no sight or sound
Of any other one
Than I that was alive on that strange ground,
When surely and ineffably aware
That something else was there,
I turned and saw before me, ivy-crowned,
Flame-born of Zeus and of a burning mother,
One of the wasteful gods that will be found,
Though variously renowned,
Commensurable only with another.
And had he not been what he was—
Had he been one to live and have his day
Like us, who come and go away,—
My fancy might have made as if to see
Within his deathless eyes
A weariness, an incredulity,
And a benign surprise,
When over them would slowly pass,
Thinly and intermittently,
The filmy cloud of a cold augury.

"And what is this that we have here below?"
He said; whereat his eyes began to shine

As with a humor that was not for man
To fathom: "Will you tell me, if you can?
For you should know it well—
If not the story there may be to tell
Of a complacent yet impatient folk,
Anticipating and somewhat at ease
Already with millennial ecstasies
Of much too much at once. You know
All that, and—even so."
As if a languid shrug would say the rest,
And say it best,
He paused, inquiringly;
Then with a downward finger made me look
Till I made out to see
A place that was no other land than mine.
"How long must you be waiting for a sign—
All you down there?" said he.

Having no converse with a god before,
Humility forbore
Too brisk an estimate; whereat he smiled,
And partly frowned. "Where man remains a child,
The days are always longer than they are,
And there are more of them than are to be
As they have been. All which is true," said he,
"Of an inflexible and hasty nation
That sees already done
Rather too much that has not yet begun.
I mention them that are so confident
In their abrupt and arbitrary ways
Of capturing and harnessing salvation
With nets and ropes of words that never meant
Before so little as in these tiresome days
Of tireless legislation;
Also I marvel at a land like yours,

DIONYSUS IN DOUBT

Where predatory love
In freedom's name invades the last alcove;
And I foresee a reckoning, perforce,
That you, not eager to see far
From where your toys and trumpets are,
Make nothing of.

"Wherefore your freedom, given a time to pause,
Vindictively and unbecomingly
Becomes a prodigy for men to fear—
Or so she looks to me.
Appraising her from here,
I make of her an insecure delight
For man's prolonged abode,
And the wrong thing for him to meet at night
On a wrong road.
No wonder there are many of you perplexed
At her deceiving singularities,
And hazarding your fancy on the next
Of her oblique appearances;
Albeit as always you may only gape
And smile at her uncertain face and shape,
And thereby be indifferently amused—
Recovering too late your derelictions,
To find your tardy maledictions
All outlawed and refused.

"Freedom, familiar and at ease meanwhile
With your perennial smile,
Goes on with her old guile:
Having enjoined your conscience and your diet,
She spreads again her claws,
Preparatory, one infers,
From energy like hers,
For the infliction of more liberty;

And reckless of who reads them or desires them,
Regardless of who heeds them or requires them,
Fearful of someone left who might be quiet,
She clamps again her jaws
And makes a few more laws;
And you, you millions, or as many of you
As have not your herd-servitude in check,
Conspire somehow by law to wring the neck
Of nature, not seeing how large a neck it is
That your beneficent severities
Would humble and subdue—
To moronize a million for a few.
Oblivious of the many-venomed ways
Attendant on their failing who should fail,
By soporific tyranny misled
Into a spacious maze
Where vermin unsupposable are bred,
You may not see a sign of the snake's tail
Whereon you are to tread.''

With that he shook his head
As with a questioning, I thought,
Of his onslaught
Upon a fervid if inadequate
Insistence of an adolescent giant
To hang itself, if possible, defiant
Alike of too much weight
And of an ill-spun rope.
In weakness indirectly there was hope
For an unransomed kidnapped juvenile
Miscalled Democracy.
He met my divination with a smile
Of Heliconian serenity,
And soon resumed
His utterance as to one for faith entombed:

862

DIONYSUS IN DOUBT

"Yes, there is hope where you believe it is;
Also intelligence is hidden there—
Much as a tree's unguessed immensities
Are hidden in a seed.
But more than both
Of these that are so excellent,
And so long in arriving,
Hypocrisy, timidity, and sloth
Are there and are all thriving.
Yes, they are there indeed:
I see them and assay their qualities;
Not many of them are fair,
Nor any of them so rare
As to be known with more astonishment
Than are the most of man's idolatries,
Wherein you find him almost everywhere
Perniciously at prayer
For consummation and a furtherance
Of his benevolent ingrained repression
Of the next man's possession.
All which has no illusion, or surprise,
Or pleasure for my eyes.
If I withhold from yours the benefit
Of seeing with mine within and round about
Your region here below,
Whereto your steps will soon again be going—
Sometimes it may be better not to know
Than to be stoned for knowing."

Here my remonstrance with a smooth rebuff
Was laughed at once aside:
"All that is coming will come soon enough,"
He said, "and it will be no balm for pride;
And one forlorn prediction will achieve
No remedy or reprieve.

863

There are some fiery letters never learned
Till children who are reading them are burned
Before they are aware of any fire.
Remember that, all you that would aspire,
Unsinged and all alone,
To the unseen and the discredited,
And to the best for you unknown.
If I, meanwhile,
Appropriate the salvage of a smile,
You may take heart, and cease to look ahead.
Fatuities ripe for dying will be dead
Sometime, imaginably;
Wherefore, to be the more commendable
To my esteem, you may as well
Invent for me the best essential name
For him that with one hand puts out
The flame that warms a fluctuating brother,
And meritoriously with the other
Pours unpermitted oil upon his own.
Well, if you falter, give yourself no pain
To say aloud the undiscovered word
That I consign to silence and let be.
The gods will on occasion delve in vain
For nomenclature more profound
And more absurd,
Than gods have ever heard
For their assurance that a cube is round.
But your proficient idiom, not averse
To nonsense or a nullifying curse,
Will pray for you till you forget
That when a sphere is hammered square
All that was hammered is still there;
Also that Humbug is no less
Himself in his best dress.
I'm watching him, yet I see one that's worse

864

DIONYSUS IN DOUBT

For your concern than he:
Delinquent in two-fold apostasy,
This other's doings
Are like the tepid wooings
Of him who jilts the woman of his choice
Because another with a shrewder voice,
And with some innuendoes of a past,
Inveigles him until she has him fast,
Innocuous and amenable at last.

"Wherever the dissension or the danger
Or the distrust may be,
All you that for timidity
Or for expediency capitulate,
Are negative in yourselves and in the state;
Yet there are worse for you to see,
As everywhere you may remark:
Some animals, if you see them in a manger
And do not hear them bark,
Are silent not for any watch they keep,
Nor yet for love of whatso comes to feed,
But pleasantly and ineffectually
Are silent there because they are asleep.
There are too many sleepers in your land,
And in too many places
Defeat, indifference, and forsworn command
Are like a mask upon too many faces.
There are too many who stand
Erect and always amiable in error,
And always in accommodating terror
Before the glimmering imminence
Of too insistent a sincerity;
Too many are recommended not to see,
Or loudly to suggest,
That opulence, compromise, and lethargy

Together are not the bravest or the best
Among the imaginable remedies
For a young world's unrest;
Too many are not at all distressed
Or noticeably ill at ease
With nature's inner counsel when it means
That if a drowsy wisdom blinks and leans
Too much on legioned innocence
Armed only with a large mistake,
Something is due to shake;
Too many among you, having learned
Expediently how not to think,
Will close your mouths where I'm concerned—
Except to drink.''

Over his face once more
There passed a cloud that I had seen before;
But soon the frowning eyes were cleared,
And with another smile
Were fixed on mine a while:
''Sometimes I wonder what machine
Your innocence will employ,''
He said at length,
''When all are niched and ticketed and all
Are standardized and unexceptional,
To perpetrate complacency and joy
Of uniform size and strength;
Sometimes I ponder whether you have seen,
Or contemplated over much down there,
The treacherous way that you are now pursuing,
Or by just what immeasurable expense
Of unexplained omnipotence
You are to make it lead you anywhere
Than to the wonder of a sick despair
That waits upon a gullible undoing.

DIONYSUS IN DOUBT

So much of the insoluble
As that is not for me to tell.
For all I know,
An ultimate uniformity enthroned
May trim your vision very well;
And the poor cringing self, disowned,
May call it freedom and efficiency.
Others would somewhat rather call it hell,
And rather not be quite so free
To blend themselves with mediocrity.
How then your follies are to show
The vengeance they are now concealing,—
What your conformity may then resign
To perils more to fear than mine,—
How safe an average then may be decided
And what last prize divided,
Are manifestly not for my revealing.
If you are still too drowsy now to keep
The vigil of at least a glance
On that which reinforced intolerance
May next of yours be stealing,
From now to then you had all better sleep.

"In legend once there was a perfect bed,
Which your new freedom has inherited.
By virtue of much stretching and some cleaving,
All bound upon it were conformably
Certificated there for the receiving
Of its whole warmth and hospitality—
One man no longer than another
And every man thereby a brother.
If you misprize my word,
You may look down again from here to see
How eagerly the prisoners will agree
In liberty's illimitable name,

All to be made the same.
If proof inhibits your belief
My observation therein may have erred;
And there may still be no mistake
Of their disparities, or in the status
Of so gratuitous an apparatus
Among contrivances designed
To make men sorry for their kind,
Proving at last a laughter and a grief
To sting them like a snake.

"There are so many stories about snakes
In the perilous book of truth as it is written,
That all who will not read
Or in appearance will not heed—
Though dimly and unwillingly they must—
An inward venom of a slow mistrust,
May never tell you by a word or look
By what less pleasant serpent they are bitten
Than any in the book.
Happy as children eating worm-ripe fruit,
Praising the obvious for the absolute,
They see an end of that which has no end
Of their devising;
Wherefore their bitterness to behold in me,
Malignly and unwittingly,
A bounteous and retaliating friend
Is not surprising.
The gods have methods that are various,
Not always to themselves too clear;
And mine that may destroy you or defend you
Are gentle to those of Him that you revere
So blindly while they rend you,
Till mercifully and at last they end you—
If so they do.

DIONYSUS IN DOUBT

None of you have so long to wait
That you need be importunate,
Or too pestiferous,
In your confused assumptions of a state
Not yet prepared for you.
Better prepare the state that you possess
More to the focus of your sightlessness.
So doing, you may achieve to see,
With eyes not then afraid to look at me,
How even the blind, having resumed their senses,
May seize again their few lost evidences
Of an identity.
That which I said before I say again,
As unregarded and as much in vain
As then it was:
Some would have more things done
Today than are begun—
Things that will yet, in spite of the existence
Of an unformed and misapplied assistance,
Come properly to pass;
Though hardly, I should say, by the infliction
Of insult that is organized
Inordinately for the timid fiction
Of benefits no more prized
Than in observance to be seen from here
As if they were dishonored and despised.
Bad laws are like blind pilots authorized
To see not and to care not where they steer.''

All this to me was queer;
And on my tongue there was a tendency
To venture, graciously,
A syllable or an implication
That even a god might for a mortal ear,
Without immediate incineration

Of me and my interrogation,
Make his dark words more clear—
When dazzlingly, from all around,
There was a quiet lightning everywhere.
I heard what might have been the sound
Of silence burning in the air;
And there was no god there.

HAUNTED HOUSE

HERE was a place where none would ever come
For shelter, save as we did from the rain.
We saw no ghost, yet once outside again
Each wondered why the other should be dumb;
For we had fronted nothing worse than gloom
And ruin, and to our vision it was plain
Where thrift, outshivering fear, had let remain
Some chairs that were like skeletons of home.

There were no trackless footsteps on the floor
Above us, and there were no sounds elsewhere.
But there was more than sound; and there was more
Than just an axe that once was in the air
Between us and the chimney, long before
Our time. So townsmen said who found her there.

THE SHEAVES

WHERE long the shadows of the wind had rolled,
Green wheat was yielding to the change assigned;
And as by some vast magic undivined
The world was turning slowly into gold.

MAYA

Like nothing that was ever bought or sold
It waited there, the body and the mind;
And with a mighty meaning of a kind
That tells the more the more it is not told.

So in a land where all days are not fair,
Fair days went on till on another day
A thousand golden sheaves were lying there,
Shining and still, but not for long to stay—
As if a thousand girls with golden hair
Might rise from where they slept and go away.

KARMA

CHRISTMAS was in the air and all was well
With him, but for a few confusing flaws
In divers of God's images. Because
A friend of his would neither buy nor sell,
Was he to answer for the axe that fell?
He pondered; and the reason for it was,
Partly, a slowly freezing Santa Claus
Upon the corner, with his beard and bell.

Acknowledging an improvident surprise,
He magnified a fancy that he wished
The friend whom he had wrecked were here again.
Not sure of that, he found a compromise;
And from the fulness of his heart he fished
A dime for Jesus who had died for men.

MAYA

THROUGH an ascending emptiness of night,
Leaving the flesh and the complacent mind

Together in their sufficiency behind,
The soul of man went up to a far height;
And where those others would have had no sight
Or sense of else than terror for the blind,
Soul met the Will, and was again consigned
To the supreme illusion which is right.

"And what goes on up there," the Mind inquired,
"That I know not already to be true?"—
"More than enough, but not enough for you,"
Said the descending Soul: "Here in the dark,
Where you are least revealed when most admired,
You may still be the bellows and the spark."

AS IT LOOKED THEN

In a sick shade of spruce, moss-webbed, rock-fed,
Where, long unfollowed by sagacious man,
A scrub that once had been a pathway ran
Blindly from nowhere and to nowhere led,
One might as well have been among the dead
As half way there alive; so I began
Like a malingering pioneer to plan
A vain return—with one last look ahead.

And it was then that like a spoken word
Where there was none to speak, insensibly
A flash of blue that might have been a bird
Grew soon to the calm wonder of the sea—
Calm as a quiet sky that looked to be
Arching a world where nothing had occurred.

872

GENEVIEVE AND ALEXANDRA

SILVER STREET

HERE, if you will, your fancy may destroy
This house before you and see flaming down
To ashes and to mysteries the old town
Where Shakespeare was a lodger for Mountjoy;
Here played the mighty child who for his toy
Must have the world—king, wizard, sage and clown,
Queen, fiend and trollop—and with no more renown,
May be, than friends and envy might annoy.

And in this little grave-yard, if you will,
He stands again, as often long ago
He stood considering what it signified.
We may have doubted, or be doubting still—
But whether it be all so, or all not so,
One has to walk up Wood Street from Cheapside.

GENEVIEVE AND ALEXANDRA

GENEVIEVE

WHY look at me so much as if today
Were the last day on earth for both of us?
Not that I'm caring on my own account—

ALEXANDRA

Now for the love of heaven, dear Genevieve,
And for your love of me, and I'm your sister,
Say why it is that little tongue of yours,
Which God gave you to talk with and so tell

What evil it is that ails you, tells me nothing.
You sent for me as if the world were dying
All round you, quite as dogs do that are poisoned,
And here I am; and I'll be dying soon,
Of common ordinary desperation,
Unless you tell me more now in five minutes
Than I shall ferret for myself in ages.
Moreover, if you leave it all to me,
I'll make it a phenomenon so monstrous
That you may see me flying out of here
Like something scared.   What in the Lord's name is it?

GENEVIEVE

Poor child, have you no eyes?

ALEXANDRA

Two, Genevieve;
But they were never sharp enough to find
A way to make the man who married you
See more in me than in six hundred others.
I would have given half my fingers then
To make him look at me as if he saw me;
But it was you he saw, and you were frightened.
I wish the creature might have cared enough
To frighten me! But I was just a thing
With skirts and arms and legs and ears and hair,
Like all the rest he saw—till he saw you.
You know it, and I say it.   That's all over.

GENEVIEVE

My God, there's no beginning to some things,
Or I could speak.   For two weeks I have waited
For you to make it easy to be hard;

874

GENEVIEVE AND ALEXANDRA

And yet you tell me now that you have eyes!
Did you have eyes last night?

ALEXANDRA

I thought so.

GENEVIEVE

Yes?

ALEXANDRA

You are coming then to something, after all.
You may be coming, if one will only wait,
To what you mean. Surely you don't mean Her?

GENEVIEVE

I'll never look to you again for words
Where I find only silence.

ALEXANDRA

Now I see:
You counted on my old unpleasant way
Of saying to you what you say to the cat.
You've always been an angel, Genevieve;
I understand, and I'll be generous.
I'm old enough, the good Lord knows, who gave me
A feature or two fewer than I could use
Of beauty, and you more than you can use;
Or so it seems. The Lord's ways are past all
Our delving, and we've each of us a book
To read that has a leaf we'll not lay open.
It's an old game, and one Time plays with women
Who cannot meet the Lord half way. That's you,

875

My angel. There'll be something done about it;
For Time has had an eye even on you
These years together. Don't forget old sayings,
For they are true and they have not much mercy.

GENEVIEVE

And what's this you are saying of old sayings?
It's not the old I want now, but the new.
I've had enough that's old. I've had enough—
Year after year of it. Do I look old?

ALEXANDRA

Not yet; you needn't fret. But even at that,
There's time enough to tear the calendar
When days are dead.

GENEVIEVE

She's older than I am.

ALEXANDRA

She knows, my dear.

GENEVIEVE

She knows it, and he knows it!

ALEXANDRA

But that's not all he knows, or all she knows.

GENEVIEVE

What are you saying now?

876

GENEVIEVE AND ALEXANDRA

ALEXANDRA

Dear Genevieve,
I'm saying something new. Lord save us all,
I'm saying something new. You cried and crumpled
For me to do it, and you only ask,
'What are you saying now?' I'm saying this:
I'm saying there are men to take your gift
Of pride and ice and fear of being mortal,
And having it, to be happy all their days—
And others to do nothing of the sort;
I'm saying also that this man you married
Is not a cyclops or a cannibal
Who means to eat you pretty soon, even though
An alabaster shrine with now and then
A taper burning low, or going out,
Is not what he calls home, or good religion.
He calls it something else, and something worse.
I'm sorry, but he does.

GENEVIEVE

And you defend him.

ALEXANDRA

Defence and understanding, as I know them,
Are not of a necessity the same.

GENEVIEVE

How do you know so much?

ALEXANDRA

I don't know much;
I know a little. I wish you knew a little.

877

GENEVIEVE

I wish you knew a little more.

ALEXANDRA

You're crying.

GENEVIEVE

Well, if I am, what of it? I am not
The only woman who has ever cried.
I'm not the only woman, I dare say,
Who's in a cage, beating on iron bars
That even other women cannot see.

ALEXANDRA

Surely I see them—with a difference.

GENEVIEVE

How good of you to see them!

ALEXANDRA

Genevieve,
Be quiet until you know yourself again.
You tell of cages and of iron bars,
And there are bars, I grant you: bars enough,
But they are not of iron. Do you believe,
Because a man—a rather furry man
Who likes a woman with a dash of Eve
To liven her insensible perfection—
Looks now and then the other way, that you
Are cribbed in iron for the whole blessed length
Of all your silly days? Why won't you see,

GENEVIEVE AND ALEXANDRA

With all those eyes of yours that you don't use,
How little of what you have would be required
To send that other one to Jericho,
Or where you will? I wish I had your face!
If so, you might be free now as I am;
Free as a bird. O Lord, so free, so free!
I'll tell you what I'll do. Some day or other,
When I'm at home, I'm going to throw a brick
At that superb tall monstrous Ching-Chang vase
In the front room, which everyone admires.
There'll be a noise, and that will make a change.
You made a change, and all you get of it,
That I see, is a reason to be jealous.
Lord love us, you'll be jealous next of me,
Because your sacrificing spouse made out
Somehow to scratch my cheek with his hard whiskers
To honor my arrival. He might as well
Have done it with a broom, and I've a guess
Would rather.

GENEVIEVE

I can only say again
I wish you knew a little more.

ALEXANDRA

And I—
I wish you fancied less.

GENEVIEVE

Oh, is it fancy?

ALEXANDRA

Whatever it is, you make it what it is.
I know the man. He wants his house to live in.

He's not the sort who makes another man's
Romance a nightmare for the humor of it;
He's not one to be spinning webs of gold
As if he were a spider with an income;
He's what he is; and you that have him so,
I see, are in the best of ways to lose him.
But who am I, to talk of him? You made me,
And you'll remember that. Now that's all over.

GENEVIEVE

You pat me as you would a little dog.

ALEXANDRA

Of course.

GENEVIEVE

I wish you knew a little more.

ALEXANDRA

My darling, you have honored me three times
In wishing that identical sweet wish;
And if in all agreement with your text
I say as much myself and say it louder,
You'll treasure to my credit, when I'm dead,
One faint remembrance of humility.
Although I don't think you are listening,
I'm saying to you now that I'm an insect.
Lord, what a sigh!

GENEVIEVE

I hear you—all you say;
And what you say to me so easily
May be the end of wisdom, possibly.

880

GENEVIEVE AND ALEXANDRA

And I may change. I don't believe I shall,
Yet I may change—a little. I don't know.
It may be now that I don't care enough;
It may be too that I don't know enough—
To change. It may be that the few lights left
Around the shrine, as you say, may go out
Without my tending them or watching them.
It seems a jealous love is not enough
To bring at once to light, as I have seen it,
The farthest hidden of all mockeries
That home can hold and hide—until it comes.
Well, it has come. Oh, never mind me now!
Our tears are cheap, and men see few of them.
He doesn't know that I know.

ALEXANDRA

Genevieve,
Say something, if you only say you hate me.
Poor child, I cannot ask if you are right—
Or say that you are wrong, until I find
A gleam at least of meaning in all this.
Only, remember that of all small things
That have the most infernal power to grow,
Few may be larger than a few small words
That may not say themselves and be forgotten.
No more, then. I can live without an answer.
Indeed, I may be wrong; and it may be
That you are not my bogey-burdened sister.

GENEVIEVE

The farthest hidden things are still, my dear.
They make no noise. They creep from where they live
And strike us in the dark; and then we suffer.
And you my sister, of all women living,

Have made me know the truth of this I'm saying.
And you, as I'm a fool, know nothing more
Than what I've hardly said. Thank God for that.

ALEXANDRA

Why mock yourself with more unhappy names
Than sorrow shares with reason? Why not lay
For ever, with me to help you if I can,
The last of all the bogeys you have seen
Somewhere in awful corners that are dark
Because you make them so and keep them so?
You like the dark, may be. I don't. I hate it.
Now tell me what it is you've 'hardly said';
For I assure you that you've hardly said it.

GENEVIEVE

Oh yes, I said it; and you might have heard it.
You make a jest of love, and all it means.
I can bear that. The world has always done it,
The world has always borne it. Many men
And women have made laughter out of those
Who might as well have been in hell as here,
Alive and listening. When a love can hold
Its own with change no more, 'twere better then
For love to die. There might be then, perhaps,
If that were all, an easy death for love;
If not, then for the woman.

ALEXANDRA

If that were all?
You speak now as if that were not enough.

GENEVIEVE

It seems it isn't. There's another corner;
And in that corner there's another ghost.

882

GENEVIEVE AND ALEXANDRA

ALEXANDRA

What have I done? Have I done anything?

GENEVIEVE

Yes, you have made me see how poor I am;
How futile, and how far away I am
From what his hungry love and hungry mind
Thought I was giving when I gave myself.

ALEXANDRA

But when his eyes are on you, I can swear
That I see only kindness in his eyes.

GENEVIEVE

I'll send you home if you say that again.

ALEXANDRA

Be tranquil; I shall not say that again,
But tell me more about his hungry mind—
I understood the rest of it. Good Lord,
I never knew he had a hungry mind!

GENEVIEVE

He hasn't one when you are with him.

ALEXANDRA

What!

Genevieve

I say he hasn't one when you are with him.
You feed him. You can talk of what he knows
And cares about. Six years have been enough
To make what little mind I've ever had
A weariness too large for his endurance.
He knows how little I shall ever know;
He knows that in his measure I'm a fool.
And you say there's a—kindness in his eyes!
You tell me that! I'd rather be his dog.

Alexandra

What in the name of ruin, dear Genevieve,
Do you think you are doing now with words?

Genevieve

I'd rather be a by-word in the city,
And let him have his harem and be happy.

Alexandra

It's only your too generous invention,
I'm sure, that gives him one. I'm still about,
And I've a quick ear for iniquities.

Genevieve

To make up for an eye that's not so quick,
Most likely. You may talk yourself to sleep.
Assured that all the while I sit and listen
I shall see only kindness in his eyes.
I'd rather see him coming with a club
Than with his kindness. Though you may not like it,

GENEVIEVE AND ALEXANDRA

I know what I would rather do than see
Some of the things that you would have me see.

ALEXANDRA

I'd rather you would see him as he is—
Not as a nightmare that you may have had,
Once on a time, condemns and injures him.

GENEVIEVE

You would not have him injured for the world.
I thought so, but no matter what I thought.
I'd rather live in hovels and eat scraps,
And feed the pigs and all the wretched babies;
I'd rather steal my food from a blind man,
And give it back to him and starve to death;
I'd rather cut my feet off and eat poison;
I'd rather sit and skin myself alive
Than be a fool! I'd rather be a toad
Than live to see that—kindness in his eyes!

ALEXANDRA

Poor Genevieve! Don't think that you alone
Of womankind have had these little fancies.
You are not saying this—don't imagine it.
Your nerves are talking now, and they don't know
Or care what they are saying.

GENEVIEVE

Never mind that.
My needs are many, but I don't need that.

ALEXANDRA

Poor Genevieve!

GENEVIEVE

And don't say that again!

A MAN IN OUR TOWN

WE pitied him as one too much at ease
With Nemesis and impending indigence;
Also, as if by way of recompense,
We sought him always in extremities;
And while ways more like ours had more to please
Our common code than his improvidence,
There lurked alive in our experience
His homely genius for emergencies.

He was not one for men to marvel at,
And yet there was another neighborhood
When he was gone, and many a thrifty tear.
There was an increase in a man like that;
And though he be forgotten, it was good
For more than one of you that he was here.

EN PASSANT

I SHOULD have glanced and passed him, naturally,
But his designs and mine were opposite;
He spoke, and having temporized a bit,
He said that he was going to the sea:
"I've watched on highways for so long," said he,
"That I'll go down there to be sure of it."
And all at once his famished eyes were lit
With a wrong light—or so it was to me.

That evening there was talk along the shore
Of one who shot a stranger, saying first:
"You should have come when called. This afternoon
A gentleman unknown to me before,

NOT ALWAYS

"With deference always due to souls accurst,
Came out of his own grave—and not too soon."

NOT ALWAYS

I

In surety and obscurity twice mailed,
And first achieving with initial rout
A riddance of weak fear and weaker doubt,
He strove alone. But when too long assailed
By nothing, even a stronger might have quailed
As he did, and so might have gazed about
Where he could see the last light going out,
Almost as if the fire of God had failed.

And so it was till out of silence crept
Invisible avengers of a name
Unknown, like jungle-hidden jaguars.
But there were others coming who had kept
Their watch and word; and out of silence came
A song somewhat as of the morning stars.

NOT ALWAYS

II

There were long days when there was nothing said,
And there were longer nights where there was nought
But silence and recriminating thought
Between them like a field unharvested.
Antipathy was now their daily bread,
And pride the bitter drink they daily fought
To throw away. Release was all they sought
Of hope, colder than moonlight on the dead.

Wishing the other might at once be sure
And strong enough to shake the prison down,
Neither believed, although they strove together,
How long the stolid fabric would endure
That was a wall for them, and was to frown
And shine for them through many sorts of weather.

WHY HE WAS THERE

MUCH as he left it when he went from us
Here was the room again where he had been
So long that something of him should be seen,
Or felt—and so it was. Incredulous,
I turned about, loath to be greeted thus,
And there he was in his old chair, serene
As ever, and as laconic and as lean
As when he lived, and as cadaverous.

Calm as he was of old when we were young,
He sat there gazing at the pallid flame
Before him. "And how far will this go on?"
I thought. He felt the failure of my tongue,
And smiled: "I was not here until you came;
And I shall not be here when you are gone."

GLASS HOUSES

LEARN if you must, but do not come to me
For truth of what your pleasant neighbor says
Behind you of your looks or of your ways,
Or of your worth and virtue generally;

888

MORTMAIN

If he's a pleasure to you, let him be—
Being the same to him; and let your days
Be tranquil, having each the other's praise,
And each his own opinion peaceably.

Two others once did love each other well,
Yet not so well but that a pungent word
From each came stinging home to the wrong ears.
The rest would be an overflow to tell,
Surely; and you may slowly have inferred
That you may not be here a thousand years.

MORTMAIN

Avenel Gray at fifty had gray hair,
Gray eyes, and a gray cat—coincidence
Agreeable enough to be approved
And shared by all her neighbors; or by all
Save one, who had, in his abused esteem,
No share of it worth having. Avenel Gray
At fifty had the favor and the grace
Of thirty—the gray hair being only a jest
Of time, he reasoned, whereby the gray eyes
Were maybe twenty or maybe a thousand.
Never could he persuade himself to say
How old or young they were, or what was in them,
Or whether in the mind or in the heart
Of their possessor there had ever been,
Or ever should be, more than room enough
For the undying dead. All he could say
Would be that she was now to him a child,
A little frightened or a little vexed,
And now a sort of Miss Methuselah,

889

Adept and various in obscurity
And in omniscience rather terrible—
Until she smiled and was a child again,
Seeing with eyes that had no age in them
That his were growing older. Seneca Sprague
At fifty had hair grayer, such as it was,
Than Avenel's—an atoll, as it were,
Circling a smooth lagoon of indignation,
Whereunder were concealed no treacheries
Or monsters that were perilous to provoke.

Seneca sat one Sunday afternoon
With Avenel in her garden. There was peace
And languor in the air, but in his mind
There was not either—there was Avenel;
And where she was, and she was everywhere,
There was no peace for Seneca. So today
Should see the last of him in any garden
Where a sphynx-child, with gray eyes and gray hair,
Would be the only flower that he might wish
To pluck, wishing in vain. "I'm here again,"
Seneca said, "and I'm not here alone;
You may observe that I've a guest with me
This time, Time being the guest—scythe, glass, and all.
Time is a guest not given to a long waiting,
And, in so far as you may not have known it,
I'm Destiny. For more than twenty years
My search has been for an identity
Worth Time's acknowledgment; and heretofore
My search has been but a long faltering,
Paid with an unavailing gratitude
And unconfessed encouragement from you.
What is it in me that you like so much,
And love so little? I'm not so much a monkey
As many who have had their heart's desire,

MORTMAIN

And have it still. My perishable angel,
Since neither you nor I may live forever
Like this, I'll say the folly that has fooled us
Out of our lives was never mine, but yours.
There was an understanding long ago
Between the laws and atoms that your life
And mine together were to be a triumph;
But one contingency was overlooked,
And that was a complete one. All you love,
And all you dare to love, is far from here—
Too far for me to find where I am going."
"Going?" Avenel said. "Where are you going?"
There was a frightened wonder in her eyes,
Until she found a way for them to laugh:
"At first I thought you might be going to tell me
That you had found a new way to be old—
Maybe without remembering all the time
How gray we are. But when you soon began
To be so unfamiliar and ferocious—
Well, I began to wonder. I'm a woman."

Seneca sighed before he shook his head
At Avenel: "You say you are a woman,
And I suppose you are. If you are not,
I don't know what you are; and if you are,
I don't know what you mean.

                    "By what?" she said.
A faint bewildered flush covered her face,
While Seneca felt within her voice a note
As near to sharpness as a voice like hers
Might have in silent hiding. "What have I done
So terrible all at once that I'm a stranger?"

"You are no stranger than you always were,"
He said, "and you are not required to be so.

You are no stranger now than yesterday,
Or twenty years ago; or thirty years
Longer ago than that, when you were born—
You and your brother. I'm not here to scare you,
Or to pour any measure of reproach
Out of a surplus urn of chilly wisdom;
For watching you to find out whether or not
You shivered swallowing it would be no joy
For me. But since it has all come to this—
Which is the same as nothing, only worse,
I am not either wise or kind enough,
It seems, to go away from you in silence.
My wonder is today that I have been
So long in finding what there was to find,
Or rather in recognizing what I found
Long since and hid with incredulities
That years have worn away, leaving white bones
Before me in a desert. All those bones,
If strung together, would be a skeleton
That once upheld a living form of hope
For me to follow until at last it fell
Where there was only sand and emptiness.
For a long time there was not even a grave—
Hope having died there all alone, you see,
And in the dark. And you, being as you are,
Inseparable from your obsession—well,
I went so far last evening as to fancy,
Having no other counsellor than myself
To guide me, that you might be entertained,
If not instructed, hearing how far I wandered,
Following hope into an empty desert,
And what I found there. If we never know
What we have found, and are accordingly
Adrift upon the wreck of our invention,
We make our way as quietly to shore

MORTMAIN

As possible, and we say no more about it;
But if we know too well for our well-being
That what it is we know had best be shared
With one who knows too much of it already,
Even kindliness becomes, or may become,
A strangling and unwilling incubus.
A ghost would often help us if he could,
But being a ghost he can't. I may confuse
Regret with wisdom, but in going so far
As not impossibly to be annoying,
My wish is that you see the part you are
Of nature. When you find anomalies here
Among your flowers and are surprised at them,
Consider yourself and be surprised again;
For they and their potential oddities
Are all a part of nature. So are you,
Though you be not a part that nature favors,
And favoring, carries on. You are a monster;
A most adorable and essential monster.''

He watched her face and waited, but she gave him
Only a baffled glance before there fell
So great a silence there among the flowers
That even their fragrance had almost a sound;
And some that had no fragrance may have had,
He fancied, an accusing voice of color
Which her pale cheeks now answered with another;
Wherefore he gazed a while at tiger-lilies
Hollyhocks, dahlias, asters and hydrangeas—
The generals of an old anonymous host
That he knew only by their shapes and faces.
Beyond them he saw trees; and beyond them
A still blue summer sky where there were stars
In hiding, as there might somewhere be veiled
Eternal reasons why the tricks of time

Were played like this. Two insects on a leaf
Would fill about as much of nature's eye,
No doubt, as would a woman and a man
At odds with heritage. Yet there they sat,
A woman and a man, beyond the range
Of all deceit and all philosophy
To make them less or larger than they were.
The sun might only be a spark among
Superior stars, but one could not help that.

"If a grim God that watches each of us
In turn, like an old-fashioned schoolmaster,"
Seneca said, still gazing at the blue
Beyond the trees, "no longer satisfies,
Or tortures our credulity with harps
Or fires, who knows if there may not be laws
Harder for us to vanquish or evade
Than any tyrants? Rather, we know there are;
Or you would not be studying butterflies
While I'm encouraging Empedocles
In retrospect. He was a mountain-climber,
You may remember; and while I think of him,
I think if only there were more volcanoes,
More of us might be climbing to their craters
To find out what he found. You are sufficient,
You and your cumulative silences
Today, to make of his abysmal ashes
The dust of all our logic and our faith;
And since you can do that, you must have power
That you have never measured. Or, if you like,
A power too large for any measurement
Has done it for you, made you as you are,
And led me for the last time, possibly,
To bow before a phantom in your garden."
He smiled—until he saw tears in her eyes,

And then remarked, "Here comes a friend of yours.
Pyrrhus, you call him. Pyrrhus because he purrs."

"I found him reading Hamlet," Avenel said;
"By which I mean that I was reading Hamlet.
But he's an old cat now. And I'm another—
If you mean what you say, or seem to say.
If not, what in the world's name do you mean?"

He met the futile question with a question
Almost as futile and almost as old:
"Why have I been so long learning to read,
Or learning to be willing to believe
That I was learning? All that I had to do
Was to remember that your brother once
Was here, and is here still. Why have I waited—
Why have you made me wait—so long to say so?"
Although he said it kindly, and foresaw
That in his kindness would be pain, he said it—
More to the blue beyond the trees, perhaps,
Or to the stars that moved invisibly
To laws implacable and inviolable,
Than to the stricken ears of Avenel,
Who looked at him as if to speak. He waited,
Until it seemed that all the leaves and flowers,
The butterflies and the cat, were waiting also.

"Am I the only woman alive," she asked,
"Who has a brother she may not forget?
If you are here to be mysterious,
Ingenuousness like mine may disappoint you.
And there are women somewhere, certainly,
Riper for mysteries than I am yet.
You see me living always in one place,
And all alone."

                    "No, you are not alone,"
Seneca said: "I wish to God you were!
And I wish more that you had been so always,
That you might be so now. Your brother is here,
And yet he has not been here for ten years.
Though you've a skill to crowd your paradigms
Into a cage like that, and keep them there,
You may not yet be asking quite so much
Of others, for whom the present is not the past.
We are not all magicians; and Time himself
Who is already beckoning me away,
Would surely have been cut with his own scythe,
And long ago, if he had followed you
In all your caprioles and divagations.
You have deceived the present so demurely
That only few have been aware of it,
And you the least of all. You do not know
How much it was of you that was not you
That made me wait. And why I was so long
In seeing that it was never to be you,
Is not for you to tell me—for I know.
I was so long in seeing it was not you,
Because I would not see. I wonder, now,
If I should take you up and carry you off,
Like an addressable orang-outang,
You might forget the grave where half of you
Is buried alive, and where the rest of you,
Whatever you may believe it may be doing,
Is perilously employed." As if to save
His mistress the convention of an answer,
The cat jumped up into her lap and purred,
Folded his paws, and looked at Seneca
Suspiciously. "I might almost have done it,"
He said, "if insight and experience
Had not assured me it would do no good.

MORTMAIN

Don't be afraid. I have tried everything,
Only to be assured it was not you
That made me fail. If you were here alone,
You would not see the last of me so soon;
And even with you and the invisible
Together, maybe I might have seized you then
Just hard enough to leave you black and blue—
Not that you would have cared one way or other,
With him forever near you, and if unseen,
Always a refuge. No, I should not have hurt you.
It would have done no good—yet might perhaps
Have made me likelier to be going away
At the right time. Anyhow, damn the cat.''

Seneca looked at Avenel till she smiled,
And so let loose a tear that she had held
In each of her gray eyes. "I am too old,''
She said, "and too incorrigibly alone,
For you to laugh at me. You have been saying
More nonsense in an hour than I have heard
Before in forty years. Why do you do it?
Why do you talk like this of going away?
Where would you be, and what would you be doing?
You would be like a cat in a strange house—
Like Pyrrhus here in yours. I have not had
My years for nothing; and you are not so young
As to be quite so sure that I'm a child.
We are too old to be ridiculous,
And we've been friends too long.''

                                    "We have been friends
Too long,'' he said, "to be friends any longer.
And there you have the burden of a song
That I came here to sing this afternoon.
When I said friends you might have halted me,
For I meant neighbors.''

                        "I know what you meant,"
Avenel answered, gazing at the sky,
And then at Seneca. "The great question is,
What made me say it? You mention powers and laws,
As if you understood them. Am I stranger
Than powers and laws that make me as I am?"

"God knows you are no stranger than you are,
For which I praise Him," Seneca said, devoutly.
"I see no need of prayer to bring to pass
For me more prodigies or more difficulties.
I cry for them no longer when I know
That you are married to your brother's ghost,
Even as you were married to your brother—
Never contending or suspecting it,
Yet married all the same. You are alone,
But only in so far as to my eyes
The sight of your beloved is unseen.
Why should I come between you and your ghost,
Whose hand is always chilly on my shoulder,
Drawing me back whenever I go forward?
I should have been acclaimed stronger than he
Before he died, but he can twist me now,
And I resign my dream to his dominion.
And if by chance of an uncertain urge
Of weariness or pity you might essay
The stranglings of a twofold loyalty,
The depth and length and width of my estate,
Measured magnanimously, would be but that
Of half a grave. I'd best be rational,
I'm saying therefore to myself today,
And leave you quiet. I can originate
No reason larger than a leucocyte
Why you should not, since there two of you,
Be tranquil here together till the end."

MORTMAIN

"You would not tell me this if it were true,
And I, if it were true, should not believe it,"
Said Avenel, stroking slowly with cold hands
The cat's warm coat. "But I might still be vexed—
Yes, even with you; and that would be a pity.
It may be well for you to go away—
Or for a while—perhaps. I have not heard
Such an unpleasant nonsense anywhere
As this of yours. I like you, Seneca,
But not when you bring Time and Destiny,
As now you do, for company. When you come
Some other day, leave your two friends outside.
We have gone well without them for so long
That we shall hardly be tragedians now,
Not even if we may try; and we have been
Too long familiar with our differences
To quarrel—or to change."

        Avenel smiled
At Seneca with gray eyes wherein were drowned
Inquisitive injuries, and the gray cat yawned
At him as he departed with a sigh
That answered nothing. He went slowly home,
Imagining, as a fond improvisation,
That waves huger than Andes or Sierras
Would soon be overwhelming, as before,
A ship that would be sunk for the last time
With all on board, and far from Tilbury Town.

899

THE LAGGARDS

SCORNERS of earth, you that have one foot shod
With skyward wings, but are not flying yet,
You that observe no goal or station set
Between your groping and the towers of God
For which you languish, may it not be odd
And avaricious of you to forget
Your toll of an accumulating debt
For dusty leagues that you are still to plod?

But many have paid, you say, and paid again;
And having had worse than death are still alive,
Only to pay seven fold, and seven times seven.
They are many; and for cause not always plain,
They are the laggards among those who strive
On earth to raise the golden dust of heaven.

NEW ENGLAND

HERE where the wind is always north-north-east
And children learn to walk on frozen toes,
Wonder begets an envy of all those
Who boil elsewhere with such a lyric yeast
Of love that you will hear them at a feast
Where demons would appeal for some repose,
Still clamoring where the chalice overflows
And crying wildest who have drunk the least.

Passion is here a soilure of the wits,
We're told, and Love a cross for them to bear;
Joy shivers in the corner where she knits

BATTLE AFTER WAR

And Conscience always has the rocking-chair,
Cheerful as when she tortured into fits
The first cat that was ever killed by Care.

"IF THE LORD WOULD MAKE WINDOWS
IN HEAVEN"

SHE who had eyes but had not wherewithal
To see that he was doomed to his own way,
Dishonored his illusions day by day,
And year by year was more angelical.
Flaunting an injured instinct for the small,
She stifled always more than she would say;
Nursing a fear too futile to betray,
She sewed, and waited for the roof to fall.

A seer at home, she saw that his high lights
That were not shining, and were not afire,
Were such as never would be seen from there;
A saint abroad, she saw him on the heights,
And feared for him—who, if he went much higher,
Might one day not be seen from anywhere.

BATTLE AFTER WAR

OUT of a darkness, into a slow light
That was at first no light that had a name,
Like one thrust up from Erebus he came,
Groping alone, blind with remembered sight.
But there were not those faces in the night,
And all those eyes no longer were aflame
That once he feared and hated, being the same
As his that were the fuel of his fright.

901

He shone, for one so long among the lost,
Like a stout Roman after Pentecost:
"Terror will yield as much as we dare face
Ourselves in it, and it will yield no more,"
He said. And we see two now in his place,
Where there was room for only one before.

THE GARDEN OF THE NATIONS

(1923)

When we that are the bitten flower and fruit
Of time's achievement are undone between
The blight above, where blight has always been,
And the old worm of evil at the root,
We shall not have to crumble destitute
Of recompense, or measure our chagrin;
We shall be dead, and so shall not be seen
Amid the salvage of our disrepute.

And when we are all gone, shall mightier seeds
And scions of a warmer spring put forth
A bloom and fruitage of a larger worth
Than ours? God save the garden, if by chance,
Or by approved short sight, more numerous weeds
And weevils be the next inheritance!

REUNION

By some derision of wild circumstance
Not then our pleasure somehow to perceive,
Last night we fell together to achieve
A light eclipse of years. But the pale chance

902

A CHRISTMAS SONNET

Of youth resumed was lost. Time gave a glance
At each of us, and there was no reprieve;
And when there was at last a way to leave,
Farewell was a foreseen extravagance.

Tonight the west has yet a failing red,
While silence whispers of all things not here;
And round there where the fire was that is dead,
Dusk-hidden tenants that are chairs appear.
The same old stars will soon be overhead,
But not so friendly and not quite so near.

A CHRISTMAS SONNET

For One in Doubt

WHILE you that in your sorrow disavow
Service and hope, see love and brotherhood
Far off as ever, it will do no good
For you to wear his thorns upon your brow
For doubt of him. And should you question how
To serve him best, he might say, if he could,
"Whether or not the cross was made of wood
Whereon you nailed me, is no matter now."

Though other saviors have in older lore
A Legend, and for older gods have died—
Though death may wear the crown it always wore
And ignorance be still the sword of pride—
Something is here that was not here before,
And strangely has not yet been crucified.

DEMOS AND DIONYSUS

DIONYSUS

GOOD morning, Demos.

DEMOS

    I thought you were dead.

DIONYSUS

If you look too assuredly for death
To consummate your preference and desire,
Sometime you may endure, to your surprise
The pang of an especial disappointment.
Why such a fever of unfriendliness?
And why, again, so brief a courtesy?

DEMOS

There was no courtesy. Had I the power
To crown my will with its accomplishment,
The crowning would be brief enough, God knows.

DIONYSUS

And you would then be king.

DEMOS

    Say as you like,
Your words are of a measure with your works.

DIONYSUS

If you assume with me too large a license,
How do you know that you may not be seized

DEMOS AND DIONYSUS

With one of my more celebrated frenzies
And eat yourself alive? If you do that,
Who then shall be the king that shall inherit
The realm that is your envy and the dream
Of your immoderate magnificence?

DEMOS

There are to be no kings where I shall reign.

DIONYSUS

Not so? Then how are you to do your reigning?
I'm asking only as an eager child
Might ask as much of an impatient father.
We'll say a patient and unusual child,
Not listening always for a sudden answer.

DEMOS

Your days are as the pages of a book,
And one where Finis waits for no long reading.

DIONYSUS

You are somewhat irrelevant, and too hasty,
But that's to be forgiven of a king.
The king can do no wrong. As for my book
Where Finis waits, how far along are you
In reading it, and thereby in absorbing
The indemnifying gist of what it means?

DEMOS

I have read far enough to find in it
No sure indemnity save one of grief,
And one of death.

DIONYSUS

Nothing of life at all?

DEMOS

Nothing of life to me.

DIONYSUS

How came you then
So neutrally and unecstatically
At one time to be born?

DEMOS

I do not see
More than some words in that.

DIONYSUS

I know you don't,
The book of what you do not see, my friend,
Would have no Finis in it. Your dim faith—
Your faith in something somewhere out of nothing—
And your industrious malevolence
Against yourself and the divine escape
That makes a wine of water when it will—
Or not, if it will not—may soon or late
Consume your folly to a long fatigue,
And to an angry death. You measure me
By something in a flagon or a glass—
And we're away from that. Leaving aside
The lesser and the larger mysteries,
By what obscured immeasurable means
Are you to have in your attractive prison
The music of the world and of the stars
Without me, or to make of love and art
The better part—without me? Do you know?

906

DEMOS AND DIONYSUS

DEMOS

I do not see the prison.

DIONYSUS

But you will;
And having filled it you may blow it up
In the necessity of desperation.

DEMOS

I do not know your language; and far less
Do I concede with you in love and art
The better part.

DIONYSUS

And that you never will.

DEMOS

I hope not.

DIONYSUS

All your hope will come to pass,
If you achieve your way. You stamp your coin
Of words too small to compass their design,
Or to authenticate their currency.

DEMOS

Yet somehow they are current.

DIONYSUS

So they are;
And so are the uncounted flying seeds

907

Of death for you to breathe and eat and drink,
Never aware of their ascendency
Till you are down where they're devouring you
And you are groaning to be rid of them.

DEMOS

There are physicians.

DIONYSUS

There are not so many
That you may trust them for immunity
From your disease, or pay them for a cure
With your ingenious coin. Under your sway
They would all be as easily indisposed
As you are now, and at as blind a loss
To say what ailed them. Given release enough,
They might arrive, in a combined rebellion,
At some unethical unanimity
As to the poison most expedient
For the accomplishment of your transition,
But they would never cure you otherwise;
And they will never make you less the monster
That you would be, and may be—for a time.
There are futilities and enormities
That must be loved and honored and obeyed
Before they are found out. If you be one,
Or other, or both, as I believe you are,
God help the credulous and expectant slaves
Of your unconscionable supremacy.

DEMOS

They are expectant, certainly, and wisely;
My argument enfolds them and assures them.

908

DEMOS AND DIONYSUS

DIONYSUS

And obfuscates their proper sight of you.
In your forensic you are not unlike
The pleasant and efficient octopus,
Who inks the sea around him with a cloud
That hides his most essential devilishness,
Leaving his undulating tentacles
To writhe and shoot and strangle as they may.

DEMOS

By turning your two eyes to land again
You may regard some hundred million souls
Or more that are awaiting my tuition—
Where Reason and Equality, like strong twins,
Will soon be brother giants, overseeing
Incessantly the welfare of them all.
A little strangling will be good for them,
And they will have no courage to complain.

DIONYSUS

They will not have their souls by then. By then,
You and your twins—both illegitimate,
And the most credible liars ever conceived—
Will have reduced their souls to common fuel,
And their obedient selves to poor machines
That ultimately will disintegrate,
Leaving you outcast and discredited,
A king of ruins; though you are not yet worse
Than a malignant and a specious warning—
Albeit you may attain to your desire
If it be fate that you shall be the scourge
Of a slave-ridden state for long enough
To prove and alienate your demonship

909

Till you are done with. In the mixed meantime,
A thousand men, had they the will to speak,
Might shred your folly to its least of words
And thereby have the ruin less methodized
If not forestalled and thwarted. You may smile
Till you may be as far from recognition
As from a reason why a man should live,
But you will be no lovelier then for that
Than you are now. Why do you wet your lips
With your mendacious tongue, and rub your hands?

DEMOS

Why do I smile? Why do I rub my hands?
Because your thousand men will never speak.
I have you there, my master. Some will curse
Among themselves a little; some will grunt;
Others will shrug their unoffending shoulders
At my offensive name; others will stretch
Themselves, and in the refuge of a yawn
Will say they have enough to last their time
And that the future must attend itself—
As you foresee it will. They are all safe,
And comfortably gagged. They will not speak—
Or not more than a few—and fewer still
Will act; and those who do may do no more
Than a few shipwrecked generals on an island
Might do if they were all to draw their swords
At once, and then make faces and throw stones
At my perfidious and indifferent image.
I fear, my master, you are left behind.
One of these days, the world will be a hive—
The veritable asylum you deplore
So vainly now. Then every little bee
Will have his little task, and having done it,

DEMOS AND DIONYSUS

His time to play. So all will be in order,
And the souring hopes of individuals
To be some day themselves, though God knows how,
Will all be sweetened with synthetic honey.
The waste of excellence that you call art
Will be a thing remembered as a toy
Dug somewhere from forgotten history;
And this infirmity that you name love
Will be subdued to studious procreation.

DIONYSUS

Of what?

DEMOS

Why, of Reason and Equality.

DIONYSUS

Your twins again. With you for the king-bee,
And with an army of converted drones
Stinging your hive to order, as you say,
Where then would be the purpose or the need
Of any such hive? Were it not better now,
Beforehand, to forestall monotony
And servitude with one complete carouse,
Capped with a competent oblivion—
Or with a prayer at least for such an end?
If in the sorry picture that you flaunt
Before me as your ultimate panorama
Of an invertebrate futility
You see no reason to be sick at heart,—
I do. I see a reason to shed tears.
What will be left in your millennium
When self and soul are gone and all subdued
Insensibly?

DEMOS

Self and soul will not be missed,
Having been rather too much in the way,
And too long, for the good of the machine,
In which I see an end and a beginning.
Men have been playing heretofore too much
With feeling and with unprofitable fancy.

DIONYSUS

I see an end, but not yet the beginning.
Feeling and fancy? What do you know of them?

DEMOS

Enough to say that in the kingdom coming—
O yes, I shall be king—they shall be whipped
And rationed into reason. Where a few
That are peculiar would precede the many,
Measures are always waiting.

DIONYSUS

If there be not
A few that are peculiar in your world,
Your world will be a more peculiar place
Than all your nightmares have inhabited;
And howsoever you compel your zeal
To swallow your deceit, I'll apprehend
Their presence even in your machinery.
Something will break if they are not subdued.

DEMOS

They will be ground to death if they are there,
And in the way.

DEMOS AND DIONYSUS

Dionysus

And if the machine breaks
In breaking them, who patches the machine?
You and your amiable automatons
Will have no more the feeling or the fancy
To prove or guess what ails it.

Demos

     The machine,
Once running, will run always. As for you,
You will be driven off somewhere from the world,
And in some hell of exile and remembrance
Will see how it all goes, and how securely
The mechanistic hive subdues itself
To system and to order—and to Reason.

Dionysus

And to Equality. How do you know today
That I may not return again from hell—
Acceptably, perchance—and bring some honey?

Demos

Your sort of honey will have no taste then
For palates that are duly neutralized;
And all its evil sweet and stickiness
Will be a freight for you to ferry back
To the same place where you discovered it.

Dionysus

Why do you so invidiously insist
That I shall go so far—or that my honey

Is half so evil or so inimical
As that of your abject anticipation?

DEMOS

Abject? I do not wholly see it so.

DIONYSUS

It must have been the milder side of me
That held a lodging for so mild a word.
While I consider the compliant slaves
That you would have subdued to your machine,
I beg your mechanistic leave to shudder,
For your "subdued" pursues me.

DEMOS

As in due time
It will for certain seize you and arraign you
For what you are.

DIONYSUS

Would that it might do so!
Yet that's the one of all things onerous
And easy that will not be done for me.
Simplicity was not my father's name,
Nor was it ever mine; yet I'm unfeigned
To see, for those who may. My mother died
Because she would see God. I did not die.
Was it not strange that I should be twice born
For nothing, if I be what you make of me—
A lord of life that has no worthier fate
Than one of hell, with death and evil honey
For my companionship and consolation?

914

DEMOS AND DIONYSUS

DEMOS

I have not made of you a lord of life;
And as for recommending hell and honey,
There may be one for you without the other.
We shall have neither here.

DIONYSUS

I'm of a mind
To prophesy that you may have the one
And hunger for the other, till presently
You shall have both again, as you do now.
My way would not be yours; and my machine
Would have a more forbearing alternation
Attending a less dread beneficence.

DEMOS

What do you mean by that?

DIONYSUS

I mean as much
As an observing child might understand
Who grows to see between him and another
A living difference and an impetus
To breathe and be himself. I mean, also,
An increment of reason not like yours,
Which is the crucifixion of all reason,
But one that quickens in the seed of truth
And is the flower of truth—not always fair,
Yet always to be found if you will see it.
There *is* a Demos, and you know his name
By force of easy stealing; yet his face
Would be one of a melancholy stranger
To you if he saw yours. I know his face,

915

And why he keeps it hidden until the wreck
Of your invention shall betray itself
As a monstrosity beyond repair,
And only by slow toil to be removed.
I mean that all your frantic insolence
Of hate and of denatured eagerness
To build in air a solid monument
From the wrong end will end in a collapse,
With you beneath it bellowing for relief
Not interested or available.
I mean that of all noxious tyrannies
Potential in imaginable folly,
The tyrant of the most intolerable
And unenduring will obscure himself
With much the same suave and benevolent mask
As this that you are wearing now to cover
The guile you dare not show to your disciples.
I mean that your delirious clumsy leap
From reason to the folly you call reason
Will only make of you and of your dupes
A dislocated and unlovely mess
For undertakers, who are not yet born
To view the coming ruin that is to be
Their occupation and emolument—
If your delusion for a time prevail,
As like enough it will. I mean, also,
That after suffering time has had enough
Of you and of your sterile dispensation,
Some wholesome fire of thought and competence
Will make of what is left a cannistered
Memorial of unlovely orts and ashes,
To be a warning and a wonderment
Where you shall plot no more. I mean a world
Fit for a self-defending human race
To recognize, and finally to live in.

DEMOS AND DIONYSUS

DEMOS

I'll put the clamps on harder, just for that,
And let you see what Reason really is,
In fact and action. We have had too much
Of the insurgent individual
With his free fancy and free this and that,
And his ingenuous right to be himself.
What right has anyone now to be himself,
Since I am here to fix him in his place
And hold him there? And as for your fit world,
I'll have it all alike and of a piece—
Punctual, accurate, tamed and uniform,
And equal. Then romance and love and art
And ecstasy will be remembrances
Of man's young weakness on his way to reason.
When my world's once in order, you shall see.

DIONYSUS

I may, but God forbid the sight of it.
I'd rather stay in hell, which you imply
To be preparing for me.

DEMOS

               I approve
Unspeakably of such a preference
On your part. Go at once, for all I care,
And stay.

DIONYSUS

          I may go somewhere, for a while,
But I am one of those who have perforce
To live and to return. Should there be need
Of me, I may remain; and you may find

One day a merry welcome waiting you
In the same place where you say I belong:
Take off your mask and find another name,
Or I'll be sure you will. Good morning, Demos.

DEMOS

Good morning, Dionysus. Wait and see.

THE MAN WHO DIED TWICE

(1924)

To James Earle Fraser
and
Laura Gardin Fraser

THE MAN WHO DIED TWICE

If I had not walked aimlessly up town
That evening, and as aimlessly walked back,
My glance had not encountered then, if ever,
The caps and bonnets of a singing group
That loudly fought for souls, and was at first
No more than a familiar spot of sound
And color in a long familiar scene;
And even at that, if an oblique persuasion
Had not withheld me and inveigled me
To pause, I should have passed as others did,
Never to guess that while I might have touched him,
Fernando Nash was beating a bass drum
And shouting Hallelujah with a fervor
At which, as I remember, no man smiled.

Not having seen him for so many years,
And seeing him now almost as one not there
Save in remembrance or imagination,
I made of his identity, once achieved,
The ruin of a potential world-shaker—
For whom the world, which had for twenty years
Concealed him and reduced him, had not shaken.
Here were the features, and to some degree
The massive aggregate of the whole man,
Where former dominance and authority
Had now disintegrated, lapsed, and shrunken
To an inferior mystery that had yet
The presence in defeat. At a first view,

He looked a penitent Hercules, none too long
Out of a hospital. But seeing him nearer,
One read where manifest havoc must for years
Have been at work. What havoc, and what work,
I partly guessed; for I had known before
That he had always been, apart from being
All else he was, or rather along with it,
The marked of devils—who must have patiently
And slowly crucified, for subtle sport,
This foiled initiate who had seen and felt
Meanwhile the living fire that mortal doors
For most of us hold hidden. This I believe,
Though some, with more serenity than assurance,
May smile at my belief and wish me well.
Puzzled, I waited for a word with him;
And that was how I came to know all this
That I should not have known, so he averred,
But for a memory that survived in him
That I had never yelped at him with others,
Who feared him, and was not among the biters,
Who, in the years when he was dangerous
Had snapped at him until he disappeared
Into the refuge of remoter streets
And partly was forgiven. I was grateful—
Assuring him, as adroitly as I might,
That had he written me down among the biters,
I should have mourned his error. "Let them go;
They were so near forgotten," he said once,
Up there in his gaunt hall-room not long after,
"That memory now becomes a punishment
For nourishing their conceit with my contempt
As once I did. What music have they made
So different in futility since then
That one should hear of it? I make a music
That you can hear all up and down Broadway.

THE MAN WHO DIED TWICE

Glory to God! Mine are the drums of life—
After those other drums. I had it—once.
They knew I had it, and they hated me
For knowing just what they had. I had it—once!"
At that his eyes glowed and body shook,
And it was time to go. Fernando Nash,
I saw, would not be long in going farther.
The rough resentful egoist I had known
Was now a shell. The giant had been reduced;
And the old scorn that once had been his faith
Was now a sacrificial desperation.

A year before I found him in the street
Pounding a drum and shouting for the lost,
He had for a long time, from his account,
Inhabited the Valley of the Shadow—
A region where so many become so few
To know, that each man there believes himself
In his peculiar darkness more alone
Than any other. However that may have been,
Fernando Nash's darkness we may grant
Was dark enough, and as peculiar, surely,
As all those who had bitten him would have had it.
I was not one of them, though I fear now
That acquiescence was a larger part
Than he conceived in me of kindliness;
And I should not have thought him outwardly
Much given to soliciting, in those days,
Attention any softer than respect—
Which was not always, or by those who feared him,
Conferred without a sure and small alloy
Of hate, that made the giver and gift alike
A negligible mildew to Fernando,
In whose equipment of infirmities
A place that might have held a little envy

923

Was overfilled with scorn. Out of his realm,
And only with a tinkler's apprehension
Of what those unproved opuses of his
Were like to do when they began to sing,
There was no reason in eternity
For me to be distressed at his assurance
That they were all immortal. Who was I,
A hewer of wood, to say that they were not,
Or to be disaffected if they should be?
To-day I cannot tell you what was in them,
Nor shall to-morrow know; for they are now,
As ashes, mute as ashes. Whether he found
Their early glory to be going out,
Or whether in one last fury against fate
He made an end of them, as afterwards
He would have made an end of other relics,
I do not know. The most he ever told me
Later about them was that they were dead,
And how they died, and how much better it was
For them to be where dead things ought to be—
Adding at once, that I be not mistaken,
That he had known himself to be no liar
The while he praised them. It was not for them
That he fed scorn to envy in those days,
Nor out of them so much as out of him
That envy grew. "They knew I had it—once,"
He said; and with a scowl said it again,
Like a child trying twice the bitter taste
Of an unpalatable medicine;
"They knew I had it—once! Do you remember
What an upstanding Ajax I was then?
And what an eye I had? I scorched 'em with it.
I scared 'em; and they knew I was a giant.
I knew it, also; and if I had known
One other thing, I should have gone down then

THE MAN WHO DIED TWICE

Upon my knees for strength—I who believed
Myself to be secure. They knew a little,
But they knew nothing of what I know now.
A year before you found what's left of me,
That evening in the street, I should have said
My way was blank and ruinous to the end,
Bu there was more to be, Glory to God!
There was to be a more revealing end
Than that—an end that once had been for me
The bitterest end of all—and is not so.
For in the music I have heard since then
There are the drums of life. Glory to God!
I had it—once.''

               So much of him was gone,
That I would hear no more. All the way home,
The restive exultation in his eyes
And in his bearing, altered and subdued,
Was like that of a dead friend out of hell,
Humble, and hardly more than half assured
Of even his respite. There may have been a giant,
If he must have it so, but where was now
The man whom I remembered and was once
Fernando Nash? So much of him was gone,
That I should never learn, from what remained,
The story of the rest—or so I thought,
All the way home. But there was more concealed
Within the shell of him than I supposed—
More than I know to-day; though many a time
Thereafter I went back to him again,
Till I had heard enough to make me doubt
The use of doubting, for he had it—once.
I had known that, and then for years had lost him—
For all those years while he had crushed unripe
The grapes of heaven to make a wilder wine

Than earth gives even to giants who are to live
And still be giants. It may be well for men
That only few shall have the grapes of heaven
To crush. The grapes of heaven are golden grapes,
And golden dregs are the worst dregs of all—
Or so Fernando surely would have said
A year before.

     A year before I found him,
Pounding a drum and shouting to the street,
Fernando Nash heard clocks across the town
One midnight, and was forty-five years old;
And he was too far sundered from his faith
And his ambition, buried somewhere together
Behind him to go stumbling back for them,
Only to find a shadowy grave that held
So little and so much. The barren room—
The same in which I sought him a year later—
Was not much larger than the iron bed
On which he sat; and all there was of music
About the place was in a dusty box
Of orchestrations for the janitor,
And in the competent plain face of Bach,
Calm in achivement, looking down at him
Like an incurious Titan at a worm,
That once in adolescent insolence
Would have believed himself another Titan.
Fernando sat with his large heavy face
Held forward in his hands and cursed his works
Till malediction was a weariness,
And all his makeshift insolence a lie
That only cravens who had trained themselves
To fight and had not fought were silly enough
To fancy for the truth. No insolence
That he remembered would have been sufficient

926

THE MAN WHO DIED TWICE

Without additions and foreseen betrayals
To make of him this penitential emblem
Of that which he was not. When he had called
Himself a worm, another worm turned at once
Within his heart and bit him; and just then
The candid face of one that heretofore
Had been for him as near to the divine
As any might be, and through all had remained so,
Became as if alive there on the wall,
Transfigured into living recognition,
Wherein there was much wonder and some pity,
And more regret. The Titan, it would seem,
For the first time, and ruinously too late,
And only for a moment interested,
Saw what had happened and could do no more,
Having seen, than to recede ineffably
Aloft into the distance and the dark,
Until he was as high as a large star
That shines on death and life and death in life
Indifferently. Fernando Nash at length
Arose, leaving his bed for his one chair;
And under the sick gleam of one gas-flame,
That had for years to shadowy lodgers given
More noise than light, he sat before a glass
That was more like a round malevolent eye
Filmed with too many derelict reflections,
Appraising there a bleared and heavy face
Where sodden evil should have been a stranger.

"What are you doing here? And who are you?"
He mumbled, with a cloudy consciousness
Of having felt a ghostly blow in the face
From an unseemly mirrored visitor
That he had not invited. "And how long

Have you been on your way, do you suppose,
To come to this? If I remember you
As first you were anointed and ordained,
There was a daemon in you, not a devil,
Who told you then that when you heard those drums
Of death, it would be death to follow them.
You were to trust your daemon and to wait,
And wait, and still to wait. You had it—once.
You had it then—though you had not yet heard it,
Coming as it would have to come some time,
Blown down by choral horns out of a star
To quench those drums of death with singing fire
Unfelt by man before. You knew it then.
You felt it singing down out of the sky
When you were only a small boy at school;
And you knew then that it was all for you,
For you and for the world, that it was coming.
Where is it now? It may be coming yet,
For someone else, but you do not know that;
And that was not what you were meant to know.
O, you poor toad, why could you not have waited?
Why did you have to kill yourself like this?
Why did you let the devil's retinue
That was to be a part be everything,
And so defeat your daemon till your star
Should sing unheard for you whose ears were left
Only for drums and songs of your destroyers?
And now even they are gone—all but the drums.
You knew that if you waited, they, not you,
Should cease—that they should all be hushed at last
In that great golden choral fire of sound.
'Symphony Number Three. Fernando Nash.'
Five little words, like that, if you had waited,
Would be enough to-night, you flabby scallion,
To put you on the small roll of the mighty.

928

THE MAN WHO DIED TWICE

As for the other two, they're in a box
Under the bed; and they will soon be nowhere.
You do not have to mourn now over them,
For they were only ladders carrying you
Up to the half-way place from which you fell,
And should have fallen, since you were going to fall,
A little faster, and so broken at once
Your neck. Why could you not have fallen faster
And saved yourself all this? If you had given
The devil a sign to play those drums of death
Longer and louder at about that time,
You might be now a carrion more at ease
Than you are like to be till you make haste.
What else, in God's name, are you waiting for?
And where's the use? And while I'm asking that,
Where was the use of all your prentice-years
Wherein you toiled, while others only tinkled,
Till you were master of a new machine
That only your invention could have built
Or driven? You built it and you let it rust.
A fog of doubt that a small constant fire
Would have defeated had invisibly
And imperceptibly crept into it,
And made the miracle in it that was yours
A nameless toy for the first imbecile
To flout who found it—wherefore he'll not find it.
Presently Number One and Number Two
Will be beyond all finding. Number Three
Will not be farther from his eyes to-morrow;
And they'll all be as safe together then
As we should be if we had not been born.
The circle fills itself; and there you are
Inside it, where you can't crawl out of it.
It holds you like a rat in a round well,
Where he has only time and room to swim

929

In a ring until he disappears and drowns.
If it be true that rats abandon ships
That sail away to sink, praise be to rats!
If you were one, you'd never find another
For shipmate. He would know you for a fool,
And therefore dangerous. You're not even a rat;
For a good rat will wait for what is coming,
Whether it comes or not. You could not wait,
Knowing that it must come. You had it—once.
You had enough of it to make you know,
And were among the sceptred of the few
In having it. But where's your sceptre now?
You threw it away; and then went wallowing
After that other music, and those drums—
Assured by more than man's authority
That all you had not then was only waiting
To make of that which once was you a torch
Of sound and fire that was to flood the world
With wonder, and overwhelm those drums of death
To a last silence that should have no death.
That would have been somewhat the way of it,
You somewhat less than eminent dead fish,
If you had waited and had been content
To let those devils and those devil-women
Beat as they would your drums and dance and sing
And be invisible. You had followed them,
And seen and heard enough of them, God knows
Already. Your daemon had a lenience then,
And you had not the protest of a soul
Between you and your right to stay alive;
All which was as it was. But it was so
No longer when you knew it was not so,
And that one day a bush might bloom with fire
At any trivial hour of inattention,
Whereafter your employment would have been

930

THE MAN WHO DIED TWICE

A toil of joy for immortality.
Your drums of death, from which it all began,
Would then have been illusions most enduring
When most entirely and divinely dead;
And you, Fernando Nash, would now have been—
But who's alive to know that you're alive
To care? Look at that burned out face of yours,
You bloated greasy cinder, and say who.
Say who's to care, and then say, if you will,
Why anyone in a world where there's a cockroach,
Should care for you. You insufficient phoenix
That has to bake at last in his own ashes—
You kicked out, half-hatched bird of paradise
That had to die before you broke your shell,—
Who cares what you would be if you had flown?
A bird that men are never to see flying,
Or to hear singing, will not hold them long
Away from less ethereal captivations;
Just as a fabulous fish and almighty fish
That never swam to sight will hardly be
For long the unsighted end of their pursuit.
Why do you make then such a large ado
Over such undefended evidence?
You fat and unsubstantial jelly-fish,
That even your native ocean has disowned
And thrown ashore, why should men ask or care
What else you would have been if you had waited?
You crapulous and overgrown sick lump
Of failure and premeditated ruin,
What do you think you are—one of God's jokes?
You slunk away from him, still adequate
For his immortal service, and you failed him;
And you knew all the while what you were doing.
You damned yourself while you were still alive.
You bulk of nothing, what do you say to that?

You paramount whale of lust and drunkenness,
You thing that was, what do you say to that?''

No man so near to glory as he was once
Was ever, I fancied, quite so inglorious
As in his penance—which is here somewhat
Softened in deference to necessity—
Fernando Nash revealed himself to me
In passionate reminiscence a year later.·
Occasional strokes, at least, among the many
That I had counted must have registered
Luxurious and unmerited flagellation,
Wherein abasement was akin to pride,
If not a part of it. No man so mired
As he was in his narrative, I told him,
Could have such choral gold poured down from heaven
When he was young. But there he shook his head
In hopeless pity—not for the doomed, I saw,
But rather for the sanguine ordinary
That has no devil and so controls itself,
Having nothing in especial to control.

''Hewers of wood,'' I said, ''and drawers of water
Will always in their innocence be insisting
That your enamel of unrighteousness
Is too thick to be real.'' In his changed eyes,
Where the old fire was gone, there was almost
The coming of a smile: ''How do you know?''
He answered, asking. ''What have you done to know?
Where have you been that you should think you know?
Do you remember when I told you once
That every sleeve of genius hides a knife
That will, if necessary, carve a way
Through snakes and oxen? Most that I said then
Has gone with all the rest, but I keep this

932

THE MAN WHO DIED TWICE

As a memorial of my retribution.
I wonder if a notion has yet seized you
To bury the keenest sword you ever saw
For twenty years in mud, and then go back
To find what may be left of it. If not,
You need not. Save your curiosity
Two decades of unprofitable conjecture,
And look at me. Look at Fernando Nash,—
The heir-apparent of a throne that's ashes,
The king who lost his crown before he had it,
And saw it melt in hell.''

                       When he had ceased
I could almost have heard those drums of death
Pounding him on to a defeated grave,
Which, had I not by chance encountered him
Beating another drum for the Lord's glory
There in the street, would have been no man's grave,
Like that of one before him who still wears
The crown he could not lose. I thought of him,
Whose tomb was an obscure and stormy legend,
Sure of how little he had cared for that—
And how much less would this man here have cared
Whether he found a nameless grave, or no grave,
So long as he had left himself alive
Behind him in a world that would have loved him
Only the more for being out of it.
That long orchestral onslaught of redemption
Would have exonerated flesh and folly
And been his everlasting epitaph—
Which time would then have read as variously
As men are various in their ways and means
Of reading. That would have cancelled everything,
And all his earthly debts—or left him willing
To pay them peradventure as they might

Or must be paid. But they had run too long.
His birthright, signed away in fettered sloth
To the most ingenious and insatiable
Of usurers, had all vanished; and the more
He might have been a king, the more their greed
Would mock him and his tatters, and abase him;
And his vituperative temporizing
Over a soul in rags would mend no holes.
"But there's a crown that even the lowliest
May learn to wear," he said. "Glory to God!"
And his eyes glittered with an icy joy
That made me hope that he was wearing it.
"Of course we can't forget," he said in answer
To doubt that in my silence may have spoken;
"Yet there is much that we may leave behind,
And there is always more if we go on."

In marking after that the accuracy
Of his minute recount, I found it hard
Not to believe that he remembered all—
Save that which of itself was everything,
Or once had been so. There before the mirror,
That bitter midnight when he heard the clocks,
There was not much forgetting; and since then
Only one year was gone. Before that glass
He must have sat for more than a long hour,
Hurling the worst of his vocabulary
At his offending image. "Now you have learned
A part of what you are," he told his face,
"And you may say whatever occurs to you
As an addendum. You deficient swine,
Where do you see the best way out of it?
You are not crazy enough to cut your throat;
You are not solid enough to shoot yourself.
There's always water, but you don't like that;

THE MAN WHO DIED TWICE

And you're not sure enough of what might happen
If you should inadvertently have swallowed
A few small pills. But there's another way—
A longer and a more monotonous one,
Yet one that has no slight ascendency
Over the rest; for if you starve to death,
Maybe the God you've so industriously
Offended in most ways accessible
Will tell you something; and if you live again
You may attain to fewer discrepancies
In less within you that you may destroy.
That's a good way for you to meet your doubt,
And show at the same time a reverence
That's in you somewhere still.''   And I believe,
Though he may well then have believed in nothing
More real than a defective destiny,
That it was in him somewhere, as he said.
There was a fervor in his execration
That was not only drama; though I question
Whether I should have found him and his drum
That evening a year after, in the street,
If he had not gone farther, while he starved,
Into the valley—which had for twenty years
Already beguiled and held him. What had been
Without this uncompanioned expiation,
I do not know, and I might never have known.
The shape of one more foiled obscurity
Might some time as a cadaver have ensured
A massive and unusual exhibition
Of God's too fallible image—and no more.
Though some had wondered idly, and they might,
Why the defeated features of a giant
Should have been moulded so imperiously
To be the mask of frailty in oblivion,
None would have rated such a scrapped utensil

As more than common, or uncommon, waste;
None would have guessed what violent fire had once,
In such a cracked abandoned crucible,
Fused with inseparable obscure alloy
Celestial metal, which would else have been
The fabric of a seething instrument
That might have overflowed with other fire
Brought falling from ethereal distances.
It might, I say, cleaving inveterately
To my conviction that in this man's going
More went than when in Venice went the last
Authentic wizard, who in his house of sound
Hears not the siege of Time. Failing a way
To prove that one obscure evangelist,
Beating a drum and shouting for the Lord,
Not only might have been (to fill again
That weary sieve with wine) but was in fact
A giant among fewer than half your fingers
Of Jubal's clan, only his mark on me
Will now avail me for the confirmation
Of more, I fear, than the confirmable—
As he would have foretold. Reverting quaintly
And incompatibly with his arrogance
To the weak stings of his inferiors,
And even while dying, he smiled. "Poor souls," he said,
"That are born damned, although they may be feared
May be forgiven, though hated, and then hanged;
Whereas my early colleagues, had they known
How soon and surely I was to damn myself,
Not only would have ceased their fearing me,
But would have loved me—seeing that I was doomed.
That midnight—when I cursed myself so long—
Roundly and rightly, be it well understood—
There came a few revealing memories
That set me then to wondering just what soft

THE MAN WHO DIED TWICE

And anaesthetic language of affection
They would have brought for me if they had known
How far I was from all that formerly
Had for so long offended and oppressed them.
Poor children!—and they might all have been happy
If in the place of misapplied creation
A more discriminate wisdom had supplied
Discrimination—and some humility
Before God's few that are in spite of us
Surviving, somehow.'' And all this to me
Was not quite so irrelevant as to others
It may at first appear; for the same thought
Pursued me always in those other days
When I had harmonized ingeniously
Some brief and unoffending cerebration
Which, had it been one, would have been a song.
To some persuasion sharper than advice
I must have yielded slowly and at last
Let fall my lyre into the fearsome well
Of truth, hearing no protest from below;
Thereby surviving bitterness to indite
This tale of one who foundered in a slough
More fearsome, and lost there a mightier lyre.

He was not humble, this Fernando Nash;
Yet while he may have ministered on occasion
To a discreet humility in others,
I doubt if in the scorn he flung to us,
Mostly in silence, his preoccupation
Saw crumbs of any nurture less assuaging
Than wholesome and unfrosted honesty;
Albeit his arrogance may have merited
The few vindictive nippings that amazed
As much as they annoyed, and would have seemed
Allegiance, had their negligible venom

937

Been isolated from another virus,
Which later was to be a leprosy
Of self-contempt attending revelation.

When he had heard the last stroke of those clocks,
And called himself again the last hard name
That his abundant lexicon released,
He tore those two initial symphonies
Into as many pieces of oblivion
As he had reasons, or believed he had,
After those empty years, for their extinction.
"They were so 'temerarious' and 'exotic'
When they were written twenty years ago,"
He said, "that all who saw them laughed at them—
Not seeing with me that they would be to-day
About as temerarious and exotic
As Händel's hat. They were good harbingers,
But were they living they would not be mine;
They were not what it was that I was doing
The while I did them. Many, if they were theirs,
Would eat their ears for joy, but they're not theirs,
Or mine. Glory to God, they're nowhere now.
They were not mine; they were not yet the vintage;
Though I should have enjoyed, when I was young,
The taste of them. But they were not the wine
To fill my cup, and now it doesn't matter."

There was for some time an obscurity
For me in such a reasoning, but I learned,
And I have striven loyally to believe
That he did well—sure that he did not well
In going down those dark stairs again that night
For the beginning of a last debauch
That was to be a prelude, as he put it,
Wincing in reminiscence, for a fugue

938

THE MAN WHO DIED TWICE

Of ravening miseries and recriminations
Assembling in remorseful exposition
That was to be remorseless and infernal
Before they were devouring one another
In a malicious fantasy more infernal,
And richer in dissonance and involution
Than all his dreams together had heretofore
Aspired or dared to be. When half-way down
The second of those four forbidding stairways,
He heard those drums again, and on his face
He felt with more resentment than alarm
A touch of warning, like a chilly wind
Within a tomb. "You are too late," he said,
Holding his heavy jaws harder together;
"And you have come too many times before."
Then he went grimly down and out of doors,
And was alone there in a lonely street
That led where soon he might not be so lonely,
Or so severe in his particulars.

After three weeks that would have relegated
A village blacksmith or a stevedore
Of mortal average to a colder sleep
Than has a waking, he awoke one day
Late in the afternoon, miraculously
In bed again and wondering, as before,
How this time he had got there. Looking up,
He met the face of Bach upon the wall,
Who bowed at him, gravely but not unkindly;
And he, not yet alive to what was coming,
And not to be defective in attention
To a great master, bowed acknowledgment;
Whereat the salutations were repeated,
And there was a preparatory silence,
Heavy with strangeness and expectancy,

Which would have been a monitory dread—
But for the master's nod of satisfaction
And interest in the coming through a keyhole
Of a slow rat, equipped with evening dress,
Gold eye-glasses, and a conductor's wand,
Soon followed by a brisk and long procession
Of other rats, till more than seventy of them,
All dressed in black and white, and each of them
Accoutred with his chosen instrument,
Were ranged in order on the footworn carpet
That lay between Fernando and the door.
Having no chairs, they stood erect and ready,
And having made obeisance to the master
Upon the wall, who signified his pleasure,
And likewise to the man upon the bed,
They played with unforseen solemnity
The first chords of the first rat symphony
That human ears had heard. Baffled and scared,
Fernando looked at Bach, who nodded slowly,
And, as he fancied, somewhat ominously;
And still the music sounded, weird but firm,
And the more fearful as it forged along
To a dark and surging climax, which at length
Broke horribly into coarse and unclean laughter
That rose above a groaning of the damned;
And through it all there were those drums of death,
Which always had been haunting him from childhood.
Without a formal ending, or any sign
That there was ever to be an end, the rats
Danced madly to the long cacophony
They made, and they made faces at Fernando
The while they danced—till one of them, the leader,
Bowed mockingly, and vanished through the keyhole,
As he had come; and after him went others,
Each with a leering courtesy as he went,

THE MAN WHO DIED TWICE

Till more than seventy of them disappeared,
Leaving their auditor lying there alone
In a cold sweat, while his impassive master
Frowned, shook his head, and was again a picture.

Fernando Nash, deploring afterwards
This innovation of orchestral rats
As a most arbitrary intermezzo
Between the sordid prelude that was over
And the infernal fugue that was to come,
Smiled wearily, and shrugged his heavy shoulders,
Like one who would be glad to say no more,
Yet must relate the rest to somebody
Before he died. Somebody might believe him,
And it was I, who had not bitten him
(Achilles' heel was never to be cured),
Who might, if anyone might, believe him now,
And say to others that he was not mad
Through that incessant week of lonely torture
Which no food would have eased, and through the days
That followed while he starved indomitably,
With a cold hope that his long-punished heart
Would after time be still. Day after day,
And endless night following endless night,
There were those miseries and recriminations
Devouring one another but never dead,
Until one afternoon he lay remembering
The day when those unusual visitors
Had made a more unusual music for him,
And having made it mocked him and departed.
Again he looked up at the face of Bach,
Considering wearily, with a bleak regret
How far those features in their dusty frame
Were now from seeing that there was in this world
So frail a relic as Fernando Nash,

And how much farther still they were from caring,
With more than common care, could they have seen him.
Could they have seen him they would not have known
What fires had burned in that cadaverous ruin
Below them, or what hopes, or what remorse,
Or what regret. For a long time he lay
Aware of action hardly in a finger,
But with a coming wonder of surprise
For a new clearness which had late begun
To pierce forbidden chambers long obscured
Within him, and abandoned, being so dark
And empty that he would not enter them—
Fearful of what was not there to be found
Should he go there to see. They might be dark,
But folly that had made them so had kept them so,
Like an indulgent slayer who binds a wound
That he has washed with a lethargic poison,
And waits at ease with his malignity
For stagnant fury to accumulate
A mortal sloth within—and in so far
As that was in a manner merciful,
Though now it seemed there was to be an end
Of even that mercy. After grateful darkness,
There was to be the pain of seeing too clearly
More than a man so willing to see nothing
Should have to see.
                    Still motionless, he lay there
Laboring to persuade a lying hope
That this new clarity was the light that comes
Before the night comes, and would not last long—
Yet knowing that it was not. Like shining grain,
Long fouled and hidden by chaff and years of dust
In a dark place, and after many seasons
Winnowed and cleaned, with sunlight falling on it,
His wits were clear again. He had no power

THE MAN WHO DIED TWICE

To use them, and at first repudiated
The faintest wakening flicker of any wish
For use of any such power. But a short fight
Found his whole fragile armor of negation
So tattered that it fell away from him
Like time-worn kingly rags of self-delusion
At the rough touch of the inevitable—
Till he confessed a rueful willingness
To reason that with time and care this power
Would come, and coming might be used. He smiled
And closed his eyes, finding an awkward humor
In such an unforeseen enfranchisement
From such a long and thwarting servitude.
A calm that all his life had been a stranger
To the confusions that were born with him
Composed and overpowered him as he felt,
Enveloping and persuading body and brain
Together, a cool relief as if warm wings
Were in the air above him. So there he lay,
Without a motion or a wish to move,
And with a sense of having only to rise
And give his hands to life. A grateful shame
For all his insults to the Holy Ghost
That were forgiven was like an anodyne
Laid on a buried wound somewhere within him,
Deeper than surgeons go; and a vast joy,
Which broke and swept and covered him like a sea
Of innocence, leaving him eager as a child
That has outlived experience and remembers
Only the golden moment as it flows,
Told him in silence that was more than speech
That after passion, arrogance and ambition,
Doubt, fear, defeat, sorrow and desperation,
He had wrought out of martyrdom the peace
That passeth understanding. Still he lay there

Smiling to think how soon those burrowing teeth
Which he had felt within him for so long
Would cease their famished gnawing at his heart
Which after all the many prolonged assaults
It had 'survived was toiling loyally,
With only an uncertain fire to drive it;
And still he would not move.   There would be time
For all things in their order. He was hungry—
Hungry beyond a longer forced endurance,
But in this new unwillingness not to live,
No longer forced, there was a gratefulness
Of infinite freedom and humility,
After a bondage of indignant years
And evil sloth; and there was in this calm,
Which had unlooked for been so long in coming,
A balanced wealth of debts and benefits
Vaster than all ambition or achievement.
Hereafter it would be enough to serve,
And let the chosen shine.

               So there he lay,
Luxuriating vaguely on the moment
When he should rise and with a blessed effort
Go down those shadowy stairs again for food;
And if in his prevision of that moment
He had not lain so long awaiting it,
Those drums of death might opportunely then
Have stayed an hour the sound of their approach,
Throbbing as always, and intolerably,
Through stifling clouds of sound that hid, like smoke
Tumultuous and elusive melodies,
Now for so long imprisoned as no longer
To be released. Hearing them first, and faintly,
For once and for once only without flinching,
He smiled and sighed. Let others, if they must,

Hear them and follow them. He was at peace
With them for the first time in recollection,
And willingly for the future would remain so.
At last alive, it was enough to serve,
And so to be content where God should call him;
But there must be no haste. His fires were low,
And too much fuel might yet extinguish them.
At first he must be frugal with his coals,
If only for the peril of too much comfort
Given at once, and without more atonement.
So arrogant in his new humility
Was he becoming, and so chary was he
Of exultation, that to break his fast
With no excess of zeal he planned a fare
That would have saddened Simeon on his pillar;
And he might soon have been in search of it,
Had not another silence, like a blow
That somehow stunned him to clairvoyant awe,
Held him as if mysterious hands had bound him
With cords he could not see. Now he could hear
Those drums again, and they were coming nearer,
Still muffled within the same unyielding cloud
Of sound and fire, which had somewhere within it
A singing flame that he might not for long
Endure, should such a mocking hour as this
Be the one hour of all when after years
Of smouldering it should leap at him and scorch him.
He felt his fingers clutching hungrily
At nothing, as the fingers of one drowning
Would clutch at seaweed floating where he sank;
And he could feel the pounding of those drums
Like iron upon the fibre of his brain.
His feeble heart was leaping, and a cold
Invisible hand was heavy on his throat—
As if in mercy, if it need be so,

To strangle him there before he knew too soon
What he must know too late.

                        Now it was fear,
Not peace, that falling on him like a wave,
Covered and overwhelmed him; it was fear,
Not peace, that made him cold and left him trembling
After the cold had passed. The coming drums
Were like the vanguard of a Juggernaut
Approaching slowly through a rolling cloud
Of fiery sound that was anon to burst
And inundate him with an ecstasy
Of mad regret before those golden wheels
Behind should crush him. He could only wait,
Therefore, and in his helplessness be seared
With his own lightning. When the music leapt
Out of that fiery cloud and blinded him,
There would be recognition for a moment,
And then release. So his prophetic fancy,
Smiting him with deceit, foresaw the blow,
Not seeing what other shafts of doom and mercy
There are from which an injured God may choose
The one or many that in his exigence
His leisure may affect. Seldom it is
The mightier moments of necessity
That we can see are coming come to us
As we have seen them. Better or worse for us,
Anticipation waits upon surprise;
And though Fernando Nash in his exhaustion
Prayed now for that cold hand upon his throat
To close and have it over, no cold hand
Was there to close. Now there was nothing for him
But to lie still and hear those coming drums,
Muffled as always in a smoky cloud
Of burning sound that in a moment more

THE MAN WHO DIED TWICE

Would burst above him into flaming rain
That once he would have welcomed on his knees,
Unspeakably; and so he might have done
Could he have waited with his inner doors
Unbarred to the celestial messengers
Who may have come and gone a score of times,
Only to find again, and still again,
That he was absent on another journey
Into the dismal valley of the shadow
That was to be his home. But that was over.
They had not found him then. He had not waited.
Failing a willingness to be assured
That in so doing he would have left by now
The worst of a light burden far behind him
And found the rest to be Olympian gold,
He had impawned it all for mouldy pottage.

Telling me that, he sighed and shut his teeth,
And with a mortal smile shook his large head
At me before he went back to those drums.
They were not going to sound, as it appeared,
Their long approach for ever, but were soon
To cease, and only intermittently
Be heard again till choral gold came down
Out of a star to quench and vanquish them
With molten glory. Trembling there alone,
He knew that there would now be falling on him
The flaming rain he feared, or the one shaft
Of singing fire that he no longer feared—
At which that hand might close upon his throat
Till in oblivion there might then be peace;
And so at first there was—if there be peace
In the complete oblivion of achievement.
Instead of bursting as he prayed it might,
And ending him with one destroying blast

Of unendurable fulfilment, slowly
And imperceptibly that cloud of sound
Became a singing mist, which, having melted,
Revealed a fire that he had always felt,
But never known before. No lightning shaft
Of blinding and immediate dissolution
Was yet impending: there was only joy,
And a vast wonder that all this had been
So near him for so long. Smiling and still,
He listened gratefully. It had come at last;
And those far sent celestial messengers
That he had for so long a time denied
Had found him now. He had offended them,
He had insulted and forsaken them,
And he was not forsaken. They had come,
And in their coming had remembered only
That they were messengers, who like himself
Had now no choice; and they were telling him this
In the last language of mortality,
Which has no native barrier but the grave.
Now it was theirs to sing and his to wear
The glory, although there was a partnership
Somewhere that a surviving grace in him
Remembered; for though the star from which they came
Shone far within the dark infinity
That was himself, he had not made it shine—
Albeit he may have wrought more notably
Than might another for its extinguishment.

But there was time for not much more of that
Than a bewildered smile of acquiescence.
The quivering miracle of architecture
That was uprising lightly out of chaos,
And out of all the silence under time,
Was a gay temple where the Queen of Life

948

THE MAN WHO DIED TWICE

And her most loyal minions were protracting
Melodious and incessant festival
To the least lenient of divinities.
Joy, like an infinite wine, was everywhere.
Until it proved itself at last a languor,
Now less engrossed with festive pageantry
Than with an earth-born sensuous well-being
Which in the festive pageant was divine.
Of all the many of those who danced and sang
And celebrated, there was none to note
A silent entrance of the most abhorred
And oldest of all uninvited strangers—
A lean and slinking mute with a bassoon,
Who seized attention when a languid hush
Betrayed a perilous rift of weariness
Where pleasure was not joy, and blew a tune
Of hollow triumph on a chilly reed
From which all shrank. The tumult after that
Was an unprized expenditure of beauty
Awaiting doom. It was awaiting also
The faint approach of slow, infernal drums
That were not long in coming, bringing with them
A singing horde of demons, men and women,
Who filled the temple with offensive yells
And sang to flight the frightened worshippers.

Fearing to think, he lay as one secure
So long as he lay motionless. If he moved
It might be only to plunge down again
Into a more chaotic incoherence
And a more futile darkness than before.
There was no need of moving, and no need
Of asking; for he knew, as he had known
For years, unheard, that passionate regret
And searching lamentation of the banished,

Who in abandoned exile saw below them
The desecrated lights of a domain
Where they should walk no more. Inaudible
At first, he knew it only as a presence
Intangible, but he knew that it was there;
And as it went up slowly to the stars
Carrying all the sorrow of man with it,
He trembled that he should so long have been
So near to seizing immortality.
Well, here it was. And while he might have died
If it had ceased, he would have been as one
Who cared no more, having had everything,
Where there was no more caring. But he knew
That he was not yet dead, and that the rest
Would soon be coming. When the voices fell,
He knew that through them he should hear those drums
Again, but he was not afraid of them.
They were his drums, and the far sound of riot
Below there in the gloom was also his.
It was all his to give. "Poor fool," he thought;
"Praise God you are a fool, and call it yours."
And he lay tranquil through another silence.

Though he condemned the specious tyranny
Of illustrations and explicit schemes,
He kept in his creative charnel house
More pictures hidden of the dead and dying
Than men should see; and there were these among them,
Which he submitted once, reluctantly,
As to a loyal friend who would forgive them,
And then forget. Yet I remember now
That in the place of languid folly flown
To mourn apart, bereft of its illusions,
The desolation of its realities,
There woke amid the splendors that were lost

THE MAN WHO DIED TWICE

A frantic bacchanale of those usurpers,
Who in affronting life with evil rites
Of death, knew not themselves to be the dead—
In false authority mistaking riot
And scorn for power, and hell for paradise.
Intoxicated by their swift invasion
Whereafter conquest was an easy trifle,
And hating the magnificence they cursed,
Seeing not the beauty or the use of it,
They soiled with earthy feet the shining floor
Flinging the dregs of their debaucheries
From crystal cups against the gleaming walls
Of Life's immortal house. Too ignorant
Of where they were to be afraid to know,
They shrieked and sang in shrill delirium
With vicious ecstasy for louder drums—
Till, crowning insolence with infamy,
They must have wearied God—who, pitying them,
Smote with avenging trumpets into silence
All but those drums of death, which, played by Death
Himself, were beating sullenly alone.

They ceased, and after stillness in which time
And space, together perishing, were no more
To him than indecisions that were gone,
Far off there was a murmur and a stirring
Of liberation, and a marching hymn
Sang of a host returning. All the banished
Who had been driven from the house of life
To wander in the valley of the shadow
Were sounding as they came in chastened order
The praise of their deliverance and return.
A singing voice that gathered and ascended
Filled the vast dome above them till it glowed
With singing light that seemed at first eternal,

But was at first not so. There were those drums
Again, to frustrate with a last intrusion
The purifying and supreme festival
Of life that had returned and in its house
Was daring to be free. But freedom wavered
Out of the voices that were praising it;
And while it wavered, the lean hand of Death
Beat with a desperate malevolence,
More sinister in its evil emptiness
Than when that carnal chorus of the dead
With corybantic and infatuate glee
Had howled it out of hearing—till once more
There were those golden trumpets, and at last
There was that choral golden overflow
Of sound and fire, which he had always heard—
And had not heard before. Now it had come,
And had not gone. Nothing had gone that came.
All he had known and had not waited for
Was his; and having it, he could not wait now.
With blinding tears of praise and of exhaustion
Pouring out of his eyes and over his cheeks,
He groped and tottered into the dark hall,
Crying aloud to God, or man, or devil,
For paper—not for food. It may have been
The devil who heard him first and made of him,
For sport, the large and sprawling obstacle
They found there at the bottom of the stairs.

A fortnight after that, Fernando Nash
Lay contemplating with a special envy
A screen between him and another bed
That would anon be vacant. For some time,
So he had learned, the probabilities
Had seen for him a similar departure,
But seeing indifferently at the last hour

THE MAN WHO DIED TWICE

That some residual and peculiar service
Awaited the survival of as much
As was remaining of him to survive,
Had left him and abandoned him again
To life. The fire of personality,
Still glowing within him, drew mysteriously
From those assisting at his resurrection
A friendly patience, and a sort of wonder
That wore a laughing kindness. With a lesion
Like his there would be no more golden fire
Brought vainly by perennial messengers
For one that would no longer recognize them,
Or know that they had come. There were somewhere
Disfigured outlines of a glory spoiled
That hovered unrevealed and unremembered,
But they were like to those of blinding jewels
Wrought beyond earth to value beyond earth,
To be defaced and hammered valueless
By a sick idiot, and insanely sunk
In darker water than where ships go down
Hull-crushed at midnight. When he told me that,
He may have had a vision of himself
In his last, starless plunge. "Make a swift end
Of what I leave behind," he said to me.
"Burn me to ashes; and when that is done,
Take me somewhere to sea and let me sink,
And fear not for my soul. I have found that,
Though I have lost all else. All but those drums;
And they are but the last hope of the devil.
Mine are the drums of life—and they are mine.
You may not like them. All I ask of you
Is to believe me when I say to you
That what I had, I had. It was no dream
That followed me so long, and found me only
To make of me a child that should henceforth

953

Go into streets and beat the drums of life.
I make a joyful noise unto the Lord,
But I know it's a noise, and the Lord knows it—
Just as he knows that I have told to you
Only the truth, and that I had it—once.
Fool as I was and remnant as I am,
My prayer will be to you that you forget me,
If in your memory there survive a doubt
That I was less than you believed I was
Till I was chastened. For I swear to you
That as I knew the quality, not slight,
Of a young harvest that I would not save,
I know that in the fields where kings have been
Before me there was never found by them
A sheaf more golden than the grain I lost
When the Lord smote my field that afternoon.
I am not telling you this to salve a bruise,
For now the bruise is healed. I shall go lame
Because of it, but the Lord's ways are strange,
And I am not to suffer; and I believe
The reason for this is that I have not lied.
I have not lied to Him in praising Him,
Nor more to you in praising what He gave me
And in his wisdom took away again.
We cannot measure what the world has lost
Until we know the gauge the builders use
Who made it. All we know about the world
For certain is that it appears to be.
And in so far as I am sure of that
So am I sure that I was once as much
As you believed and others feared I was.
I have not drugged a clamoring vanity
With lies that for a little while may seem
To sweeten truth. There was no need of that;
And God knows now that there is less than ever.

THE MAN WHO DIED TWICE

Now I can beat my drum and let those drums
Of death pound as they will. Once, for an hour,
I lived; and for an hour my cup was full
With wine that not a hundred, if a score,
Have tasted that are told in history.
Having it unconfirmed, I might be mad
To-day if a wise God had not been kind,
And given me zeal to serve Him with a means
That you deplore and pardonably distrust.
The dower of ignorance is to distrust
All that it cannot feel, and to be rich
In that which it has not. I can be rich
In all that I have had, and richer still
In this that I have now. Glory to God!
Mine are the drums of life, and though I wait
For no more messengers—or for none save one,
Who will be coming soon—I had it, once.
Not more than once or twice, and hardly that,
In a same century will another have it,
To know what I have lost. You do not know.
I've made for you only a picture of it,
No worse or better than a hundred others
Might be of the same thing—all mostly trash.
But I have found far more than I have lost
And so shall not go mourning. God was good
To give my soul to me before I died
Entirely, and He was no more than just
In taking all the rest away from me.
I had it, and I knew it; and I failed Him.
I did not wait."

        "You could not wait," I told him.
"Instead of moulding you to suit the rules,
They made you mostly out of living brimstone,
And set you in a somewhat fiery world

955

Not to be burnt." But there he shook his head
And looked at me as he had looked before,
Like one who was a little sorry for me.
I had made several entrances already
With my determinism, and always failed.
He would have none of it. He was to blame,
And it was only right that he should lose
What he had won too late. "Why pity me?"
He asked, strangely, "You see that I'm content.
I shall not have to be here very long,
And there's not much that I may do for God
Except to praise Him. I shall not annoy you,
Or your misguided pity, with my evangel,
For you must have yours in another dress.
I shall not ask if you believe me wise
In this that I am doing. I do not care.
I'll only ask of you that you believe
What I have told you. For I had it—once."

To each his own credulity, I say,
And ask as much. Fernando Nash is dead;
And whether his allegiance to the Lord
With a bass drum was earnest of thanksgiving,
Confusion, penance, or the picturesque,
Is not the story. There was in the man,
With all his frailties and extravagances,
The caste of an inviolable distinction
That was to break and vanish only in fire
When other fires that had so long consumed him
Could find no more to burn; and there was in him
A giant's privacy of lone communion
With older giants who had made a music
Whereof the world was not impossibly
Not the last note; and there was in him always,
Unqualified by guile and unsubdued

THE MAN WHO DIED TWICE

By failure and remorse, or by redemption,
The grim nostalgic passion of the great
For glory all but theirs. And more than these,
There was the nameless and authentic seal
Of power and of ordained accomplishment—
Which may not be infallibly forthcoming,
Yet in this instance came. So I believe,
And shall, till admonition more disastrous
Than any that has yet imperilled it
Invalidates conviction. Though at first,
And many a time thereafter, my persuasion
May well have paused and halted, I believe
To-day that all he told me for the truth
Was true—as I believed him long ago
To be the giant of his acknowledgement.
Crippled or cursed or crucified, the giant
Was always there, and always will be there.
For reasons less concealed and more sufficient
Than words will ever make them, I believe him
To-day as I believed him while he died,
And while I sank his ashes in the sea.

CAVENDER'S HOUSE

(1929)

To the Memory of
William Vaughn Moody

CAVENDER'S HOUSE

I

INTO that house where no man went, he went
Alone; and in that house where day was night,
Midnight was like a darkness that had fingers.
He felt them holding him as if time's hands
Had found him; and he waited as one waits
Hooded for death, and with no fear to die.
It was not time and dying that frightened him,
Nor was it yet the night that was around him;
It was a darker night, and one within him,
That others not himself were not to know.
He stood by the same door that he had closed
Twelve years ago, and waited; and again
He closed the door, slowly and silently,
And was himself a part of darkness there,
There in his own dark house. Somewhere unseen
There would be chairs and things that he and she
Had sought and felt for, at one time or other,
When darkness was a part of every day
Before there was a light, and was no more.
A touch, and there was light, once on a time;
But now there must be no light in that house
Where no man went, or men, coming to see,
Would find him there; and he must not be there.
Though he must come from half way round the world,
He must not come to be found there tonight.
All by himself he was to find enough,

Attended by no man's discovery
Of him and his employment. Let the moon
Come in a little when he found the room
He sought, and he should see enough to know
The place that had compelled him for so long
To come so far, by the old law that hides
In whatsoever of design there is
In time and triumph.

There was triumph now
All round him where he sat with moonlight lying
Between him and a chair where once had been
A woman who had said less with her tongue
Than with her eyes, which had said nothing to him
That he would know. Triumph was everywhere;
He found the barren house alive with it,
But none of it was his. It was all hers,
The moonlight said, and he sighed hearing it.
He had not come for such a musty draught
Of lees to drink as that. He had come because
The world he wandered was a world too small
Where there was not that house. Some chemistry
Of fate, forestalling him, had long ago
Combined his coming with necessity,
Perhaps, if that would help. It would not help.
Nothing would help save one that was not there.
Nothing could help save one that he had left
Behind him, and had called him back again.

Why had she called him, if she was not there?
The moonlight, slowly giving a dim size
And shape to silence, had no more to show,
It seemed, than he saw now. All through the house
He could hear silence like a multitude
Of silences, and all apprised of him.

962

CAVENDER'S HOUSE

There was a silence that was watching him,
And there was one that listened like a spider,
Hearing his thoughts, and holding them to tell
To demons who would likely come for him
When they saw fit to come. They were there now,
Or might be; for a furtive unseen breathing
Was not the breath of man. If it was demons,
They may have called him with a woman's voice,
And this might be their triumph more than hers.
There was a fear in thinking over that,
But one conceived of doubt more than of terror.
He had engaged with all the doubts that were,
And had been thrown by them. He had been choked
By some of them, and sent afoot again
For new encounters. Fear was a breath of night,
When met by strangling doubt of what there was
Or certain to be feared. Let him know that,
And let him be a stranger once again
Among the millions, far from the old shadow,
And far from the old house. Let him be told
In answer to that one unanswered question,
And let the frenzied endless elements,
That gave him power to make of honest men
His honorable slaves, take him again
To their mysterious workshop and remould him
To something good or to no thing at all,
And let him then be dead. For he was tired
Of dying; he was tired of being so strong
As to be still alive and as a thing
Contrariously composed of opposites
Too firm to be deceived or reconciled;
And he was not yet told.

> At last he rose
And through the moonlit window looked away

Over still trees between him and a cliff
That ended his domain as death ends life.
There was no answer there, but still he looked
As if to find one. He was colder now,
And shivered as he turned again to see
Where moonlight filled a desolated hearth,
So many a time alive with fire that once
Had hummed a comfortable song of home,—
Which was a word that he might find in books,
By looking for it. There were new silences
And darknesses in the old house by now,
Surrounding and attending him, like eyes
He could not see; and there were noises too,
But none that mattered, since he could not hear
The sound of one not there. He sank himself
Again between the pillowy dusty arms
Of his old chair and looked hard at another,
Tonight as unforgiving as defeat
Without a reason. Had she called for him
To tell him nothing? Or what fever was it
That he had followed? Had he come so far
To find an empty chair? If more than that,
What else in heaven's name then was he to find?

Reft of its needless riches, the dead house
Was like a many-chambered cenotaph,
Each room a sepulchre with nothing in it
But stillness and the dark of memory.
There was no need of his exploring them
For surety that their least frequented nook
Would hold him welcomeless. Not even a nail
Would recognize him or be glad to see him.
The piece of moonlit floor between his feet
Would show him all there was, and hold his eyes
Till he saw less; for there were pictures on it,

CAVENDER'S HOUSE

Like shadows on black water in a well,
Darker than any well. He shut his eyes,
Only to see them nearer. Through his tears
He saw the pictures only multiplied
By sorrow, and remultiplied by doubt.
Let him be told and let him die, he said,
As he had said a thousand times before,
Always unanswered—an old vanity,
And half as rich in salvage as old ashes.
But there were pictures that would not be old,
Trespassing always in the way of peace,
And clearer for closed eyes—when, of a sudden,
They faded, and a sense of unseen light
Not moonlight filled him with a chilly warmth;
And it was long before he dared look up,
For doubt of what was there.

                          Why was it not
Miraculous and amazing to behold her
Before him in her chair, and in the room
As he remembered it?   All the old things
Were there again to see, and he was there;
So it was only right that she was there,
Being part of him. She was the part of him
That he had left behind and wandered from,
And wandering had starved for. She was there
Again as from a past that never was,
And it was not miraculous or amazing.
There were twelve years between them, yet he saw
No record in her face of any change,
Or stealthy work of time or of the world.
As he had seen her when he had believed her,
There she was now to see—fairer to see
Than anything else alive. She was alive,
Or there were surely to be seen or felt

A presence or an evidence of death
For him to recognize. She was not dead,
Or there would not be living in her eyes
The look that never told him anything
But what he told himself. Her pallid face,
Alive with light and darkness, change and shadow,
Was one that would be fair when it was haggard,
And one that would be still without an answer
Unless it answered now. He would not ask
As once he did, when as a man of wrath
He had brought down so heavily on himself
His tower of self that crushed and mangled him,
But leave to her alone, unhazarded,
Her proper native way of indirection,
Which was her only way. It was her time
To ask and answer now, or not to care.
There was an evil and an innocence
That were together nameless in her eyes,
And were a danger that he once had loved
And always had a little feared. Tonight,
If his remorse achieved humility,
They might reveal a reason, or show none
To be revealed, for longer fearing them,
Or fearing not to know. If it was fate
Or nature now that after weary years
He was to wait no more, she must have come
Forgiving him, and he must hold himself
In hope and silence. If he was to learn
Too late for nature, it was not too late
To learn; although it was too late for envy
Of others who had married safer faces,
And were asleep and were not wanderers.
She smiled at him as if interpreting
His faint forgetfulness to call him back;
And for a moment she was like a mother

Bestowing an affectionate reproof
With silence. All she said was in her eyes,
Until she spoke—to startle him somewhat
With a composure more discomfiting
Than patience born of hate. There was no hate
That he discerned in her serenity,
Where it might all have died, for all he knew.
Here was his time to know.

                              "You come tonight,"
he said at last, "and almost from the end
Of everywhere, to see me. I suppose
I should have asked myself if I was worth
so much." The old low music was all there
In a few words, and years that were behind him
Were there before him for a little while.
He would not ask how long.

                              "I should have said,"
The voice continued, if it was a voice
That he was hearing, and it must be one,
When I was young, and saw it without seeing,
That our poor life that we so twist and maim,
And torture almost out of recognition,
Was friendly, and as easy to be tamed
As many another sort of easy creature
To follow at our call. When I was young,
You told me that you had me in your heart
Wherever you went. I may have been there always,
And I dare say it was no difference
When I was there so quiet that you forgot me.
Hearts are dark places. And if they were not,
There might be so much less for us to learn
That we who know so little, and know least
When our complacency is at its best,

Might not learn anything. I have not come
Like a wise spectre to lift any veils,
For you have eyes only to see the way
That you are taking, and not much of that.
You may be favored that you see no more,
Though my authority would be a lie
If it assumed a privilege to say so.
I have not come to fill you with new fears,
Or to make any darker for your feet
The road before you. You would not have that.
I can tell well enough by watching you
That you are anxious more than you are happy
To see me—which is only two and two.
For two and two, when they are less than four,
Are nothing, and are not for long endured
By nature. There was time for you to build
And reckon your account more cautiously,
And with a more considerate contemplation
Of loss by storm or fire or negligence.
You never thought of me so much at home
Before with figures and affairs, I fancy,
But women are compounded of surprises,
And in extremity may surprise themselves
In what they know. I knew, and never told you,
That your account would in the reckoning
Find you a lord of ruins, and no more.
It was all coming, and you let it come.
I was there too, and you should have remembered.
A dog, when he's forgotten, whines and cries,
Or looks and lets you know. Sometimes a woman
Will only smile and ask you to keep warm
When the wind blows. You do not see her face
When you are gone, or guess what's in her mind,
Or covered in her feelings, which are real
Beyond their reputation. It's a pity,

CAVENDER'S HOUSE

And a great shame, and a malevolent
Extravagance, that you should find that out
So often only when calamity
Comes down upon you like a broken house
To bring the news. Sometimes, again, suspicion
May take the face and shape of certainty,
And so be worse than truth and ruin together.
My penance is that I may say no more
Of life than that you are to learn of it
A best way to endure it to the end.
You are somewhat in danger, I believe,
Of making too much haste. For all I know,
You will not run much nearer to the end
By any such way as that. In Cavender's house,
As in the Lord's house, there are many mansions,
And some that he has not so much as opened,
Having so much to learn."

                                  Cavender stared
At her and her repose, and at her beauty,
Mobile, intangible, inscrutable,
And with a peril in it, or beneath it,
If he must have it there. Was ever a man
So grievously the fool of his possession
As to throw this away, and then himself?
If men before, knowing no more than he,
Had been as he was, why had God made such men
And let them live? If he was patient with her,
Possibly she might say; no man could know
What she might say or do. It was a grief
And a bewilderment to feel her there
So near him, and as far away from him
As when first he had held her in his arms,
A warm enigma that he would not read
Or strive to read. It was enough to have her,

And easy to forget she might not always
Leap when he called, or always dance and sing
For love of him. He should have seen her then
As now he saw her—and as she was then,
If he had known. If he had studied her
And all her changes, he might then have learned
That even in them there was a changelessness,
Performing in its orbit curiously,
But never with any wilful deviation
Out of its wilful course. He might, perhaps,
Have seen there was no evil in her eyes
That was not first in his. Seeing her longer
Before him now, he was not sure that evil
Had ever lived in them. They smiled at him,
Sadly, and waited. They would say no more
Until he answered them.

                         "When you began,"
He said, and faltered, "I was waiting rather
For more than I supposed there was in words,
Than for so many that I might have drawn
From the unpleasant well of my own thoughts.
It may have been your manner of surprise
That I was unprepared for. For yourself,
I was as ready as I am to die—
Or shall be soon, I hope. You are to say
How that shall be, or if it shall be said.
You have by right of justice now a range
Of many privileges. God knows I know it.
You have God's power tonight, compared with mine,
To lighten me of more than I dare ask—
For I dare ask you nothing. For a while,
Now that you and your words have made me sure
That you are here, where all is as it was,
I would do no more than just look at you,

970

And let you hear me saying how blind it was
Of me to lose my way, not yet assured
My way was wholly lost—or not to make one
In face of all assurance. For a while,
Having said that, I may be wise to say
No more of that—and I believe you shrink
To hear my name and that of wisdom uttered
By the same voice. Saying too much, or little,
Or saying it wrong to you, might make you go
Away from here for ever. Make me a sign
To say you will not go! Tell me a word
To say so. Laramie! Laramie! Do not go!
For God's sake, do not go. You did not come,
Only to go. Not if you came from hell,
Could you do that. Forgive me! I forgot
That I was there already. I do not dare
To look at you or look away from you.
Laramie! Laramie! Tell me what I am,
And what you are, but do not go away!
Not even if I were mad and you a dream,
Would you do that. And you are not a dream."

Laramie Cavender only closed her eyes,
And sighed like one weary of listening
Before she answered. "No, I am not a dream;
Although I may be dreaming of a time
When all this would have been a task for me
Outside imagination, and an insult
To comprehension. I shall not think of it,
Or more than you compel me to remember.
I was not hurt. You only frightened me,
And gave yourself a scar that will not heal.
My wish would be that you forget it all,
But my will is not yours. The best for you
Is to believe me always when I tell you

971

That hands harder than yours were helping you
To hurt yourself that night. I have no wish
For you to suffer more than properly,
Or more than your desert. The worst for you
Is not to see yourself with nature's eye,
And therefore know how much you are of nature,
And how much of yourself. I come forbidden
To light the way before you, which is dark
For you and all alive; and it is well
For most it should be so. So much as that,
At least, is yours in common with your kind,
Whose faith, when they are driven to think of it,
Is mostly doubts and fears. Not always—no.
There is a faith that is a part of fate
For some of us—a thing that may be taught
No more than may the color of our eyes.
It was a part of me when I was born,
But not of you; and I am sorry for that.
It would have helped you when you needed most
A shepherd to attend you. But that's over,
And I could wish you might forget. If not,
You may be happier if I leave you now.
You may be nearer to forgetting me
When I am not so near. And who shall say
That you may not survive your memories
To laugh and dance again? For why should not
A man of passion and address dance well
On a crushed life, and laugh? Many have done so,
And more to be will do so."

                      Cavender shook
With a new wretchedness. "Is there a God?"
He asked. "Is there a Purpose, or a Law?
I thought there was; or I should not have suffered
So cruelly more for you than for myself.

CAVENDER'S HOUSE

I am not half so much a fugitive,
As one doomed to eternity in time.
You have a right to smile, but there were dreams
Of mine that you might not. You come to me
With all your ways that made a slave of me—
Which is a retribution too remote
From mercy to leave any toy of hope
For me to play with. I was a fool to dream,
Who cannot sleep; and I was more than fool
To fancy there was hope."

                    "Yes, there is hope,"
She said, as if with a prepared reluctance,
"Always, except in those infernal words
Over the gates of hell—which, after all,
Are only man's invention. You may live,
Or die, to find them not so terrifying
In truth as in Italian. So, you see,
With all my ways and my appearances,
I have not come to you without some drops
Of mercy in my vial. I do not say
That you shall suffer always. I don't know."

Yes, there was evil surely in those eyes,
And he could see it shining. Then it faded,
And there was only sorrow there again—
A sorrow that was more a sort of wonder
For what had been. He rose and went to her,
Holding his hands out hungrily before him,
And would have touched her. But another look
At her dismayed him, and he hesitated
Until it was too late. He sighed for that
With trembling gratitude, and from his chair
Was seeing her once more. It was enough
To see her there, if that must be enough.

"You smile," he said, "as if you had averted
With kindness—you will let me call it so—
God knows what desolation. If my hands
Had felt you then to feel you vanishing,
If I had seen your place with you not in it . . .
I must not think, if I must think of that."

He shivered, and a mist was on his forehead,
Cold, as if death had touched him and withdrawn
His touch unwillingly. It was not time
For death, and death was vexed at his mistake,
Was Cavender's unformed thought. Laramie's eyes
Appraised him, but there was no message in them
But a calm shining of ironic sorrow
That only by God's mercy was not hate—
If it was not.

       "You may still think of it,"
She told him, "and why not? You are still you,
And Adam was your father. You would touch me,
Which is not any stranger than the stars;
For, though not much, I'm not untouchable—
Or time was when you found me not so dreadful,
And unsubstantial, as to find yourself
Afraid of me. I have no doubt at all
That if you dared, and were sure not to lose me,
You would come here and hold me in your arms
And kiss me, and so cry to be forgiven,
That I might—that I might forget? Well, hardly.
Hardly, perhaps. The queen of all forgetters
Would certainly be taxed and overladen
With excellence that would be noticeable
In heaven if she forgot what I remember.
If you should come to take me, I'm not sure
That in your arms I should find happiness,

Though once I found it there. But who shall tell us
What we shall find, or where? You might recover
In me the solid warmth of a small woman,
And in her kisses you might find the love
That you believe is dead. It should be dead,
By the world's easy measurement of ruin
And its inch-ruling of the infinite,
Yet there might still be left enough of it
To set your penitential wits at work
Till they were faint with wonder. If you knew,
Or if it were my power and will to tell you,
Who knows what answer might astonish you
For asking with your arms? It might be all,
Or it might be the end of all. Who knows?
While I have studied you, and seen you suffer,
I have been saying again how cruel it is
That love should entertain so many chances.
If you had weighed your faith more carefully
With me, when I was with it in your balance,
You might have saved your house, or possibly
You might. I cannot know so much for certain.
Or know how many houses are worth saving.
What if you came to me like Heracles,
Who fetched a lady from a tomb to please
A king? There are no kings for you to please,
And you might have the lady for yourself—
Assuming her to be no puff of nothing,
To vanish, or to laugh."

                                    Now in her eyes
There was a menace and a merriment,
Whether of evil or indifference,
Or both, or neither, he knew not. He rose,
And helpless, with imploring arms again,
He would have seized her. But her eyes met his

With frowning light that warned him, and once more
He stood with his arms empty. In her face,
A mingling of derision and reproach
Might have enhanced the beauty of the damned;
And in the room a stifling of unrest,
Accumulating curiously, was like
A sultry thunder-troubled afternoon,
Dark and surcharged with storm; and he could feel
That cold mist on his forehead, as of death.
"God help me not to touch you," he said, choking;
"I cannot—for I cannot let you go!"

II

CAVENDER, sure that she was there, could see
The room. It was the same as in years gone,
But for a baffling unreality
Which dimmed and insulated everything
Ineffably with change and accusation.
Nothing would ever be the same again,
For he was not the same; and the whole house
Was like a thing alive only with dying.
A nameless innovation was at work
In walls and corners; and all over it,
In all its darknesses and silences,
He could feel atoms moving and conspiring
Against him, and death rustling in the shadows.
Nothing was on his side; and certainly
Not the still woman who invited him
Indifferently to rapture or despair.
She was herself as he remembered her—
All but that emanation of his doubt,
Enshrouding and surrounding her tonight
With new mysteriousness; she was herself

976

CAVENDER'S HOUSE

One moment, and another she was the devil,
Dressed with her face and form, and in the clothes
That liked her best. He had not asked for them,
But they had come with her, coming as if
They had been called; and he remembered them
As if they burned him. She had put them on
To mock him, or he thought so, long ago,
When he was blinded by the sight of them
And of her wearing them as a child might,
Softer than lies, cleaner than innocence,
And asking to be praised. Now she was asking
For more than praise, more than forgiveness, more
Than life. She would not ask to be forgiven
While she had him to see. She would ask rather
To see him lying there dead before her feet.
There would be more of a consistency
In that than in submission; and far more
Of much-offended nature as he knew it
In men and things and time. He should have known
Before, not after; and he got of that
As good a compensation as one has
Of hoarding bottles that have held great wines
Of a lost vintage. She had been wine for him,
And of a power that had usurped his wits,
Once on a time, leaving of him a ruin
That was alive, a memory that could move.
Why should he look to her for less than harm,
Albeit she had brought with her, she told him,
Some drops of hope? He wondered where they were,
And in what vial of wrath she had subdued
Their wildness with her scorn.

                                        To shift his wonder
Another way, she was regarding him
With kindness now, and with a wistful care

977

That healed him while it cut. "I look about,"
She said, "and things I see are like old stories,
So many of them forgotten. They come back
To me like songs not heard since heaven knows when,
Or like forgotten odors, bringing with them
Pictures of old regrets and pleasures ended,
And of old places that would not be there
If we went there to find them. It is better
Never to go, unless the pain of seeing
No more old things and places as they were
Be pleasure for us—and not always then,
If habit follows. Dead hands holding us
Are dangerous, and may not let go of us
Until we strike them; and if we do that,
They seem to suffer, as maybe they do.
I say this with old sounds and images
Besieging me and telling me of you—
Which is a miracle, if you see it so,—
Before you saw me in a twisted mirror
That you might once have broken, but would not,
Which is another pity; for without it
To plague and change you, all the rest of me
Would have been perfect—or, if not so, quite,
Would have been near enough. You would have found
Your way home in the dark more pleasantly
Than with a light like yours, and would have found
A pleasant lady waiting—which is more
Than all men always find when they go home,
Or wish to find, as many of them would say—
Veraciously enough. But they were never
Of your exacting fancy and sad skill,
Dissolving doubts in their developments,
Regardless of the presence or existence
Of that which you must find. And now I see
More grateful things before me, or behind me,

Than you and your doubts at work together with me
In darkness; and I catch a better music
Than my words now are making for your ears.
Why should we not go back and hear again
Songs you have heard me singing in this room
So many and many a time? I have them still.
Perhaps if I should sing you one of them,
You would forget your doubts, and then be sorry
For what you did to me. For a short time
You might believe me, and then not believe—
Which would be more like waking from a dream
Of joy to misery, than like joy itself;
So maybe it were better not to sing,
Though I will if you ask. But what a child
I must be to consider singing to you,
With your face looking at me! What a way
We women have, having no foresight in us,
Of seeing time only as the minute given
For us to take, as a bird takes a worm,
Or as man takes a woman when his love
Prevails more in his blood than in his heart—
A subterfuge and a discrepancy
Ensured by nature not to be uncommon.
And there's where nature, having a plan for us
Too large for your belief or your evasion,
Has made us as we are, women and men;
But why with such a sad misapprehension
Of our acquaintance with ourselves, I ask
As you are asking, and I cannot tell you—
Except as I am told that we must learn
Of our defects and doubts, however they hurt.
Love is not vengeance, though it may be death,
Which may be life. You may know more of that,
Presently. But I'm far away from singing
Now, and I must remember what came first

With the old sights and sounds; for you came first—
You and your ways. You and your many ways.
I may have had a few you may have noticed,
But God forgot one, or omitted it,
In my construction. There should have been a way
Provided for a glimpse into your heart,
Where I was to be carried so compactly
And unobtrusively on all your travels,
And in your doings for your daily bread,
With a few luxuries, or perquisites,
Not to be shared with me. My vanity
Misled me to suppose that I should be
Enough, but there was never enough for you.
I should have foreseen that your daily bread
Was mostly to be change, and that your theme
Of being was wholly to be you. No doubt
My pride was in a panic when it first
Conceived how little for you there was of me
That was not either a body or a face;
If so, my panic had some precedents,
Which notably did not help. Why am I saying
All this, when all that's over? Let's go back,
And let me see you as you were at first:
You were a man of many promises,
With deeds enough already to warrant them;
You were a playful and persuasive man,
With power and will beneath your levity
To make a woman curious to be bent
A little, but not broken; you were a man
Who covered yourself with your vitality
So well that only another man might find you—
And he might not; you were a man designed
To change a woman to a desperation,
And to destroy her when your passion felt
A twinge of insecurity. I'll wager

CAVENDER'S HOUSE

You have not had so many compliments
In twelve years until now. Tell me you have,
And I shall know that you are lying to me;
And I will tell you more than you will hear
Of what you have been having—for I know."

There may have been some healing wistfulness
In her beginning, and some kindness too,
But none that was to last. No permanence
Was ever a part of her, nor was it now;
Not that it mattered now. She might enlarge
His errors, and a former few offences,
Into enormities and still be secure.
Holding a whip that was beyond his reach
And seeing, she could smile and strike him with it
Till he should cower, and with a smarting soul
Pray for her mercy—which was nothing slight
Or small, he knew, to pray for, whether or not
She struck him deeper still. She might not do it.
She might, knowing so much more now than he,
Tell him, or let him see, she found no joy
In smiting him, merely to see him suffer—
Without a word to say. It would be worse
To cringe and flinch and ache, having no word
To say, than it would be to curse and shriek
In protest, having at least a stricken right
Of protestation. Men were not born to meet
So much as this; and though it was their doing,
It was not they who did it. Some such balm
Assuaged him only for another onslaught
Of writhing certainty that he was held
In toils that he had woven for his long
Constriction and imprisonment alone.
If she was there to lacerate him, she
Could only be God's agent in the matter—

And so there must be God; or if not God,
A purpose or a law. Or was the world,
And the strange parasites infesting it,
Serpent or man or limpet, or what not,
Merely a seeming-endless incident
Of doom? If it was so, why was it so?
He could do nothing. He was in a trap.
Nothing was on his side.

            "To look at you,"
She murmured, with a slow unfeeling languor,
·As well as with a sort of lazy triumph,
"One could imagine that you have at last
Invested fate with an intelligence—
Which is a blow and a beneficence
Together, sometimes. What's to be done for it?
What's to be done for taking on yourself
The purpose, or the law, that puzzles you,
And troubles you, and makes you miserable?
What's to be done for trying to shake down
The stars? 'If you prevailed, and were successful,
I doubt if you could put them back again;
And that would be embarrassment indeed.
You were a man of many ways and means,
Of many infringements and necessities;
And you could smile away to grief and shipwreck
Those who annoyed you and impeded you
In your more secular performances;
But when you crushed a man and ended him
In your routine, you sighed and wished him well,
And first were sure that he was in the way
Of your more splendid gains and benefits.
You made the world an easier place, or said so,
For the rank and file to live in, or to die in,
As that might be. You should have made yourself

CAVENDER'S HOUSE

An easier way to walk in; and should first
Have been assured there was no darker way
Ordained for you than by your own self-blindness.
How could you always know that I was lying?
I never told you so. How sure were you
That all the costly flowers you bought for me
Were as intact in their enforced perfection
As I was in my natural innocence?
You should have known. Cavender, you should have known,
Before your stars came down."

                                        He could say little
To her defeating eyes; he could say less
To her white throat and arms, and her hands folded
So placidly and so conformed for torture
That he would not believe them hers. They waited,
Willing, in all appearance, to wait always,
While she sat watching him; and they were hands
Forbidden to be touched again by his.
They were remembered hands, and were so small
To hold so much. They could hold everything.
They could hold him, and crush him, if they would,
And fling him where they would. They were still hands
To say so much; and they were cruel hands
To be so silent. He would not look at them;
For there was peril in their gentleness,
And warning in their strength. He could say nothing
To them; but he could speak, after a time,
After a fashion, thickly:

                                "Was it easy
For you to smile at me while you were saying
That we had better not go back? Why not—
If we go far enough? You have no right
To let yourself be listening while I speak,

983

But since you too have spoken and heard words
Of mine already, and have not disappeared
At sound of them, as I believed you might,
I have a weak and most unhappy wish
To wander back, just for the sake of going,
Over some roads that were to lead to you,
Where they all ended—when I ended them.
I shall not ask you to go over them
With me tonight, for they were not your roads.
They were all waiting before I was born,
Perhaps, for me to take. Perhaps you know,
And will not tell me; or you may not know.
God knows I am not asking you to say.
I'm only wondering if along those roads
There was a devil ahead of me, unseen
And unsuspected; for there may have been one,
Because there must have been. You will see that,
If you will see me now. You will not care,
For that would be incredible—as you were
When first I found you, and as you remained;
As you remained too long. There are some women
Whose privilege is to treasure and conserve
Their mystery, and to make as much of it
As heaven may give them leave and means. But you,
Having so perilous an abundance of it,
Made for yourself a peril of its abuse—
Unconscious of how near you lived with madness
In one who could not know. If I had known,
I should be free, and you would not be here.
There would have been an end, but not the end
That was. I might be now as you are now—
Though I should not be here. If you are here,
And you must be, for God's sake, do not go!
Laramie! Do not go! I am not trying
To shake even what dust weighs from my shoulders.

CAVENDER'S HOUSE

Let them bear all there is for them to bear,
And lash me if you must. But do not go!
You have not said what you are here to say.
God will not let you go!"

                          Her folded hands
Remained as ever. Only her lips and eyes
Revealed a furtive and unhurried scorn
That was a promise but was not an answer.
Then she said, smiling, and with eyes half-closed,
"Your talk is rather as that of one forgetting
The size of life. But then, you never knew it,
Except as yours. The world was made for you,
And you were master of as much of it
As had your shadow on it while you stayed
At home. Your travels and advantages
Undid you and the freedom of your soul
And mind and body. You have not stepped since then
With the same enviable indifference
To the unwinking eye that's always watching
The mighty when they're tripped. I can remember
When there was not a way of mortal walking
So firm, and so erect and independent,
And so distinct in its authority,
As yours. But there was wickedness and waste
In your abused abundance (as you say
There was in mine, while saying you don't know)—
Which is so lamentably why it is
That you are here. I shall not go away,
So long as you are gracious and respectful,
Until you tell me, after good reflection,
Whether you wish to go with me, or stay.
I shall not have your life. I do not want it.
There is a purpose, or a law, you say,
That worries you. Well, one of them may use it,

For something. I doubt if God remembers it.
There have been so many since then."

                                        Her eyes were open,
Having in them a light that held no love;
And that which on her lips had been a smile
Became a slow short laughter. He could feel
Once more a moisture coming on his forehead,
And he was trembling in a cold dismay
Of unbelief. Whose words had he been hearing?
Was Laramie saying them? She must have said them,
For there she was; and she was smiling still,
Sleepily, once he would have called it, smiling
Himself, and valuing her with tenderness,
Because she was so beautiful to look at,
And comforting to touch. Now, if he touched her,
She might be nothing. He must not forget
That she had warned him, and he must remember
His place among men who have not a place;
And after that, if there was profit in it,
He might assay the dross of his deserving
To find there more than scorn or less than hate.
What should he try to find where all was dust?
If she had brought with her those drops of hope,
They were concealed with her identity;
And she had not yet promised he should have them.

He started at the sound of her low voice,
So low and soothing that he might have wept
Hearing it; and he saw now in her face
The coming of another gentleness,
A chiding, and a sorrow. "I am sorry,"
She said, "if I was bitter with you just then,
But your words before mine were not assuring:
There would have been an end, if you had known,

You said, but not that end. Why do you fly
So far away from me on the dark wings
Of your uncertainty? Why do you say the end?
If you had known, there might have been no end;
And you and I together might still be here,
Happy as children, with age watching us
From out of corners, but not touching us.
Oh no, not yet. We might be like two squirrels
Having a home in a large hollow tree,
More to be judged than those who had no tree
Like ours, and had not our exclusive store
Of nuts and acorns—which are necessary,
No matter how much the squirrels love each other,
Or with what loyalty. Why should it be,
With all the rest unfailing and abundant,
That loyalty should cultivate so little
Concern to save itself? Why are we made
So restless, and insatiable in change,
That we must have a food that is not ours?
And having poured the vinegar of suspicion
On food that once we found so appetizing,
Why in the name of heaven are we amazed
To find it not so sweet? And having soiled
Ourselves illustriously enough to serve
As migratory landmarks for the town,
Why must we look so viciously for spots
Where we must find them, even if we must make them?
The spots you found on me would have surprised
A leopard."

           Was she never to be herself,
He wondered; and he watched her watching him,
As one amused and weary of seeing him,
And unmoved by his wonder. Half she said
Had more the tenor of recrimination

Born of his long remorse and self-defeat
Than of her native way; and half she said
Was like her when he had adored and prized her
As an unmatched possession, which was all
There was in reason for a man to do;
And he was reasonable. Idolatry
Was never more so—never until there came
An evening when his idol swayed and mocked him,
As if to seize him and to strangle him.
He could not see what happened after that,
Or say what happened. He could only know
When the world stopped, and all the stars were dark,
And when the moon, the same moon that had seen
A steaming world before there was a man,
Gave no more light, although it was still shining.
And it was shining now—even as the eyes
Of Laramie were shining, without light
To guide him, or to show him where he was,
Or what was coming. If she did not know,
She might be merciful, and without mercy
Say that he was to suffer and to die
At fate's appointed pleasure. If she had come
Only for that, why had she come at all?
Why had she come so far without a reason?
It was a part of her to have no reasons,
And perhaps that was one.

       "You should have known.
Cavender, you should have known." Like drops of lead
Those words had burned a way into his heart,
Where they still burned. What manner of wife was this
To endure him in his guilt and ignominy,
And laugh while she endured? It was her way
Sometimes, and long ago, to laugh at him
When he was wise and solemn, but that was over—

CAVENDER'S HOUSE

Longer ago than ageless men remember.
He had been dead and damned again to living
Since then, and that was why he was alive.
One memory was between him and all time
Before it. All his time now was eternal,
And she was watching him as if she knew it.
"Cavender, why go back and try so hard
To bury yourself behind your memories?"
She frowned, he thought; and in her voice he felt
A pitying triumph that was worse than hate.
"You cannot hide yourself. There is for you
Only one memory left; and I can see you
Through it as clearly as through mountain air.
There's nothing in this going back of yours
But a sick hope to find some reason there,
Stronger than you, for what you did to me.
Some overwhelming heritage may have done it,
You hope; and so it may. I hope so, too.
Unhappily, you must die to find that out,
If ever you are to know. How shall I say
What you, who knew so little while you believed
Yourself a king of life, may learn of death?
You may learn all, or nothing. Why look to me
For wisdom that is not for man or woman?
Do you not see me as a woman still?
I should have said so. Cavender, Cavender, think
No more of going back, there's nothing there.
Twelve years ago it was all swept away,
And there your time begins—where your life ended.
The rest of it is only a long dying.
If you revealed yourself and told the law
Your story, you would not have so long a death,
And you might gain somewhat. The laws of men,
Along with older laws and purposes,
Might serve you well. Why not? Remorse and pain

989

May be the curse of our accomplishment
On earth, and may be our career, sometimes.
It may be, and it is. If there's a justice,
I have not found it yet, though I have hope;
And I have brought some drops of it for you.
I mentioned them."

                    "Good God in heaven!" he cried.
His wisdom and expediency forgotten,
He was a mendicant imploring her
To cease, and let him know. "Tell me the truth,"
He begged, "and you may let the dogs of hell
Follow and eat me. I shall not care then.
Tell me that I was mad for doubting you,
Or that a poison that was burning in me
Was truth on fire, as I believed it was.
I am not asking now to be forgiven,
Or dreaming of it. Laramie! Let me know,
And leave me then to die. I can do that.
Living and dying will be no more then
Than clouds on water. I have had death enough
To care no more for dying than for sleeping—
If I could sleep. I shall not sleep again
Until I know. And even if I be told,
I shall not walk again with men and women.
My God, that I should come to this—to this!
Laramie, give me the last drop of hope
That you will tell me, and then you may kill me.
Laramie, let me know!"

                    "Living and dying,"
She said, with hardness gleaming in her eyes,—
"Your living and my dying, for example,
Are nothing to your knowing whether or **not**
My freedom was a sin. Why do you ask,

                    990

I wonder." Her mouth was harder than her eyes
Now, and there was no pity for him in either,
While for a time of silence she sat there,
With her hands folded, always watching him.
"Why do you ask for what I cannot tell?"
She said; and seeing his face incredulous
With pain, and tortured with abject amazement,
She asked again, as anyone might, surprised,
"How shall I tell you, when I do not know?"

III

CAVENDER looked away from her cold eyes
To watch her hands again, folded and still,
As if at peace with time, and out of it.
He wondered how two hands could be so still,
And for so long; and a thought frightened him
Of all those hands had power in them to do
And to destroy. He would not look at them.
They were too small to be so terrible.
They were not hands.

        "You have the privilege,"
He said, with a dry tongue, "of your conceits,
And of your last obscurities. You have
A right to blind me with your mysteries,
And one to see me groping, as I am now,
Among them. You have only to say No,
To make of any question left in me
A prisoner to burn always in a fire
Of silence; you have only to say Yes,
To give it freedom so that I may ask
Once more of you that you will let me know.
Let your invention change my words to gold,

991

And you will see at last how poor I am;
I shall be destitute, having no words
That you need hear. Laramie, I have nothing.
No, I have nothing left in all this world
But one unanswered question following me
And leaping on me like a monster laughing—
A beast that will not die until I die,
If it will then. You know, and you may tell me,
Whether a madness tortures me tonight
With hope, or whether reason lives in it.
Even you may say as much as Yes or No
To that. Tell me if there be reason in it,
Or if it be so wrong and so outrageous
As only to be madness and an insult
To you and heaven, if you have come from heaven.
You do not tell me from where you have come;
You tell me nothing. But see how poor I am,
And see how little of me there is to kill!
Laramie, let me know—and let me die!"

He knew there was a woman with two hands
Watching him, but he saw no more of her
Than would assure him she was there. He feared
To see her face, and he feared not to see it;
And then he found it as it was before,
Languid and unrevealing. Her eyes closed,
And her lips moved as if repeating words
That had no meaning. Then, with eyes half open,
She said again, "Why do you ask, I wonder?
Moreover, there's a backward valuation
Of my commodity in all this anguish.
Have you not heard yet, anywhere, death-bells ringing
For Love and poor Romance? Biologists
And bolshevists are ringing them like mad—
So loud that Love, we're told, will soon be lost

992

CAVENDER'S HOUSE

With dodos, dinosaurs, and pterodactyls.
Has never a thought of this disheartened you
In your pursuit of pain? Has there not yet
Been sorrow enough for you in my destruction
To make you sorry for so many questions—
All to one end, and that one end yourself?
If I had sinned, and I should tell you so,
Would your account with me be cancelled then,
Balanced, and satisfactory? Your ledger
Was always in a tangle, Cavender;
But was it left like that? If it were mine,
And I were you, I'd enter myself as loss—
Profit and loss, and done with it. But no,
There's haste in that, and a forgetfulness.
If I was false, you set a price on folly—
For you to pay—that was outside the scope
Of your possessions or your expectations.
You are still paying, and for some time yet
You may still pay; and I am sorry for that."

There was no sorrow in the gleaming look
She gave him, no regret for what she said;
And after a forlorn effect of hope,
His answer was of one awaiting neither:
"You may say what you will. I took my doom
With ignorance for courage, fearing nothing
And knowing nothing. I was not there myself,
But one that had the name and face and body
Of me was there; and I am paying for him.
Laramie! Will you try to tell me now
If I had reason to be mad that night?"

"And why should I do that for you," she said,
"When all you want is to go round and round
Yourself, and to be saying endlessly,

993

'Laramie, let me know!'? It does no good
To comfort you with knowledge of new orders,
Or to assure you that you make too much
Of not so much; for you are not assured
Or comforted. You are old-fashioned there;
And were it not for what you did to me,
Your misery might be thought ridiculous
By sages who might laugh. Knowledge is cruel;
And love, they say, is cruel as the grave.
It's an old saying. All that's wrong with it
Is, that the grave may not be always cruel.
You will know more of that. There is a plan
Within me that's awaiting your acquaintance
And presently will be urging your approval.
It's an old-fashioned plan, older than you
And all your admirable ancestors—
Who may, unwittingly, have had to do
With our catastrophe. There are those laws
And purposes of yours, always at work,
And doing the Lord knows what with our intentions.
Eternity may have time and room to show us
How so transformed a fabric may be woven
Of crimes, corruptions, and futilities,
That we shall be confounded with a wonder
At our not seeing it here. Yes, there is hope;
And there is hope deferred by too much haste—
Or so there might be. It's all rather dark.
My plan may have a sort of nearness in it,
More in the measure of your speculation."

"What woman is this," he pondered, sick at heart,
"Who has the form and face of Laramie,
Her voice, her languors, and her levities,
Her trick of words—and half of them not hers?
Where has she been to find so many of mine

994

That have done service and have nourished me
Like a fantastic food, proving itself
Not to be food, but shadows? Shall our deeds,
And even our thoughts, be scrutinized hereafter
By any and all who have no more release
From follies here than to live still with ours?
If memories of so galled and sorry a life
As this must follow us when we go from here,
We are all damned indeed."

                       "I have not told
You yet, for certain, Cavender, that they will."
She laughed at him with her eyes, silently,
To see him stare at her. "I may have come,
Perhaps, by some celestial dispensation
To bring those drops of hope, if you require them.
My levity has outlined a sketch of you
Not wanting them, but we may rub that out
With no disaster and no difficulty.
You may still wish to savor them, and to feel
Replenished, as you may, with resolution
When you have swallowed them, and fortified
Beyond retreat. Some, having taken them,
Have turned their suffering faces to the sunrise
And waited for the light, careless of all
Unanswered questions that have haunted them,
And laughing monsters that have followed them,
And leapt upon them from behind and bit them,
And licked them with hot tongues. Others have not,
Preferring a blank hazard of escape,
With no especial surety of release
Thereafter for themselves. We'll go outside
Before long, Cavender; we'll go out together,
And in the moonlight see how it all looks.
I have a notion it would interest us,

And fill us both with memories and ideas,
If we should walk down, as we used to do,
To the old place. The cliff will still be there,
And the old seat, if years have not removed it.
We have had many happy hours down there,
And some of them with moonlight shining on us
Then, as it shines tonight, in the same way—
In the same chilly silver silent way
It had when we were there. But I was foolish
Then, for I let my love make me believe
Too much. I believed almost anything then.
You made me, and you let me. I was happy.
Then you would hold me close to keep me warm,
And I would watch clouds going over the moon,
Like doubts over a face—if I had known
Enough to think. I was not trying to think.
You said I was too beautiful to think.
You said that if I did, your quality
Might have a shrinkage. You were a playful man,
Cavender; and you played with me sometimes
As a child might, seeing it in the house,
With a superior kitten. It was careless
Of me that I was not much given to thought
While I believed in you and in your love,
Which was a sort of love—the sort that owns
And gloats, and prowls away complacently
For capture and a change. I had supposed
That I was bright and lively and adequate,
And even a match for your discrimination,
But I was not. I should have done more thinking.
I should have taught myself more amiable
And animal ways to make me surer still
That I should never be sure. But for the few
Who know, and in their hearts cannot but know
Security and content, women had best

CAVENDER'S HOUSE

Believe, or best believe they do not care—
Which is no harder than to know that wine
Is sweet when it is sour. If I transgressed
In desperation or in vindictiveness
At last, as fear inflamed you to believe,
I wonder when it was your avocations
Had first recess and leisure to find out,
And then to be disturbed. Poor Cavender!
The man who makes a chaos of himself
Should have the benefit of his independence
In his defection. He should wreck himself
Alone in his own ship, and not be drowned,
Or cast ashore to die, for scuttling others.
I have been asking, Cavender, since that night,
Where so malicious and inconsiderate
A devil could hide in you for so long time.
There may be places in us all where things
Live that would make us run if we should see them.
If only we could run away from them!
But, Cavender, we can't; and that's a pity.
I'm tired of sitting here and seeing you there,
As if you wished to die. Come down with me
To the old place, if there's a pathway left.
I want to see you when you see it. Come!"
With languid grace that he remembered well,
She rose and beckoned him. He followed her
As if on wheels, drawn irresistibly
And slowly, from the room where he had found her.
Through the dim hall, no longer dark, and filled
With its old furniture and ornaments,
He followed her.

"Open the door for me,"
She said, and smiled. Cavender opened it,
And followed her along a darkened way

997

Of weed-grown gravel, with encroaching boughs
Whipping him as he went, to the cliff's edge,
Barred with a fencing of long-rusted iron,
Which might not be secure. He stared at it,
And shivered in the moonlight as he stared,
As at a thing alive whose touch was death.

"Here is the place," she said; "and to be sure,
Here's the old seat again. I should have known it
At once and anywhere. Cavender, sit beside me,
But do not touch me. There's a distance yet
Between us; and you may as well respect it,
If only for form's sake. Form is important,
And has revenges, even as time will have them—
Though you forgot that, once. Yes, you forgot
Your manners, Cavender; and you are not one
To desecrate your code without remorse.
We must be born inferior and unfit,
If we shall so offend the Holy Ghost
As you did, and be well again thereafter.
You have not been very well since you looked down
Over this cliff that night. There must have been
Shadows down there that even a moon like this
Could not have made. They may have frightened you,
A little, I think. They may have made you shiver.
You may have shivered more than you are shivering
Now, for all I shall know. You were brave enough
In seizing your requirements, I dare say,
And in your game of living, as you played it—
Until that night. Men would have called you so,
Having no call for thought; and so you were.
Had a man injured or insulted you
Beyond all compromise or apology,
You would have knocked him down, the chances are,
Briskly and willingly, and without sorrow.

998

CAVENDER'S HOUSE

Granting you that, meanwhile, or more than that,
I shall believe you shivered and were sorry
When you looked down over this cliff that night.
It must have looked a long way down from here,
Cavender; and there must have been a darkness
Down there that even the best of moons could never
Have made for you like moonlight anywhere else.
I shall not ask you to look down there now,
For that would hurt you, and would not help me.
Besides, that iron is old. If you should choose
To trust it, and to lean so hard upon it
As to go down with it and learn what's there,
I should be powerless, I suppose, to hold you;
But let us wait. At least, there is no hurry.
You've not a notion of how much time there is,
Nor even if there be any such thing as time,
Save as you make it by the sun and stars;
And you may know so much more of all that,
One of these days, that you will almost laugh.
Tell me if you were not a little frightened
At what you saw down there, if you could see it,
Among so many shadows; and then tell me
If you had no remorse for what was there,
So surely there, whatever you may have seen.
It may be worse to know that a thing's there,
Not seeing it, than to see. Men have been scared
As much in that way as in any other;
And I should hate it worse than seeing demons.
I'd rather see a demon, Cavender,
Than a dead woman after I had killed her;
And I would rather see her dead before me
Than know she was down there, not seeing her.
You must have had a melancholy night,
Waiting for news of me. None of your friends,
Or mine, could tell you where I was that night,

999

For none could say till early workmen found me.
The town's had never so rich a mystery
Before or since to engage its hungry tongue.
It was a cream for cats; and all the time
They wondered why the woman they most envied
Should do it. It was peculiar, Cavender;
And you could answer nothing. You were broken,
And it was no more than in tune with nature
That you should bury me and then go away.
But why could you not so much as hesitate
That night, before you seized me and then threw me
Down on those rocks, a hundred feet below us?
I was not hurt; you only frightened me.
But still you should have waited and been sure,
And had at least the balm of certainty
To wash your scar. No, it would not have healed you;
Although it might have cooled you, in a measure,
And that would have been better than to ask,
And ask, and always ask, unanswered questions—
Impossible questions, and as dark to me
Tonight as they would be to the first child
That you may see tomorrow. There's a word now,
Cavender! Have you thought of it, sometimes?
For some of us who know that we shall die
Before another dawn for doing too much
In too great haste, Tomorrow may be, I fancy,
A fearful word. Are you afraid of it,
Cavender? I was not hurt, if you remember.
It will not hurt you if you throw yourself
Down there as you threw me, but it will scare you
Abominably. I'm sure you will not like it.
But as for that, there's nothing for you to like
In this life any more. You may go down
Where I went, and you may find comfort there;
Or you may cling to my few drops of hope

CAVENDER'S HOUSE

For more from your endurance. For such haste
As yours a certain slowness is exacted,
Or an uncertain plunge to find an end.
You may not find it, or you may. Who knows?
Cavender, you are locked in a dark house,
Where you must live, or wreck your house to die;
And I am sorry for that. No, do not touch me!
I am not here to feel those hands of yours
On me again. For God's sake, Cavender,
Try to forget your questions, and be decent.
If other arms than yours have had me in them,
What does it matter now? You may be dying
Tonight, for all you know. God knows it's time,
Unless he knows that you must go on living.
What do you say to that?"

                              There was a change
In the voice now that pierced and sickened him,
Like a sword going slowly into him.
It was not Laramie now that he was hearing,
Yet there she was, and she was Laramie;
Laramie in the moonlight. He could see her;
And he had never seen her quite so cold
And free of him before. He would have touched her
With all the tenderness and penitence
Imaginable, but she had thrust him off
With scorn stronger than hands, if not with hate.
Perhaps she did not even so much as hate him,
He thought; and such a thing as that was likely,
Considering what she was—if he could know.
He dared not look away from her cold face,
Fearing on finding her again to see her
Before him in another man's arms and laughing—
Laughing as Laramie would never have laughed,
Although she may have lied to him that night.

She must have lied; and he must learn of her
Whether she lied or not. He had paid for truth
By now, and Laramie would be kind to him
Tonight, and let him know. Let the rest come
For what it was to be. Let the end come;
And let the scales of retribution, heavy
With him and his offence, break with its weight
And hurl him into whatsoever pit
Should be prepared for him.

                    "I have no right
To touch you, Laramie; I shall not forget,"
He said. "It was the past in me, forgetting
How far away it was. I shall not ask
Forgetfulness of you, God knows. Although
You might afford it freely as the moon
Spares light, I shall not ask you for it now.
No, I shall only ask you for an answer
To one unanswered question. Tell me that—
Tell me if I was mad for doubting you,
Or if the fire in me was truth on fire—
And I will do as you say will be best;
Or I will do as you require of me,
Be it the best or worst. I'll throw myself
Down there to death—or, if you say to do it,
I will live on alone in my dark house,
With all its doors that I have never opened.
There may be something left for me to find
That you have hidden there. You were like that,
And you were always so—until that night.
Laramie! For the love of God, be kind
Once more, and let me know, and let me die!
Laramie, let me know!"

                    Laramie rose
Like fate, and stood before him like fate laughing;

And it was in fate's voice, or in a voice
That never in life could have been Laramie's,
That she was speaking now: "How many times,
Cavender, will it soothe or comfort you
To ask of me what I may never tell you?
There is in me no answer to your question;
There is in me only as much of me
As you have brought with you and made of me.
How shall I tell you what you do not know,
Knowing no more myself? Laramie's eyes,
If they are seeing you now, wherever they are,
Have pity in them, I hope. I do not see them—
Wherever they are—and so I cannot tell you.
I hope there may be pity in them for you,
And love. There is a love stronger than death,
Time says; and Laramie's love may have a life
Stronger than death. I should not be surprised.
It would be like her. You have had me saying
Her language to you out of time and tune,
And out of order most incongruously;
You have had life and death together so long
To play for you their most unholy music,
That you have not an ear left for another;
You are a living dissonance yourself,
And you have made of grief and desperation
Something of Laramie that had her voice.
There's yet another voice for you to hear
Before I leave with you those drops of hope—
Which are still real, if you believe in them—
Or you renounce them, and take on yourself
Your own destruction, to be rid of hope,
Real but uncertain. You may choose again
A sudden end, only to find no end.
So men have done before you, and so men
Will do. So men, sometimes, are made to do.

So men are made imperiously to act
For God, with only mortal apprehension,
And wish the act a dream. So men will do,
And do again, because a laughing monster
Has bitten them, and stung them with a doubt
That frets and bores like an undying worm
Through a disordered curiosity,
Like yours, and will not cease even while they blot
With death a furtive or an injured answer.
How are you to be certain, from now on,
That injury done to her was not itself
An answer, and evasion her revenge?
You do not know; you may be never to know.
She may have turned at last, and given your pride
A few incisions of experience,
To caution you that observation still
Attended her disgust and her endurance.
How do you know the stone you cast that night
Was not your fear, hammered to look like love
By passion and sick pride? Love would have been
The death of you far likelier than of her,
If there was to be death. Love, would you call it?
You jealous hound, you murderer, you poor fool!
You are listening to yourself now, Cavender;
And Laramie, let us hope, is where no sound
Of this will find her. She has had enough
Of you, and she has earned her silences,
Or what may be for her. If you are sure
Your silences are waiting for you there—
Down there, where she was—Cavender, why not
Go after them? She was not hurt, she said;
You only frightened her. Are you afraid,
Cavender, to go down where she was once?
Or is it another doubt that holds you here?
Well, there's a long time yet for you to think,

But there's not any, and there may not be any,
I fear, for your not thinking. I am sorry
For being so harsh, but you would have it so.
You have what you have made, which is not good;
And I am sorry for that."

                              A famished hope
Enforced him to look hard into her face,
Only to find it fearsome and severe,
And growing slowly into something else.
A clutch of horror seized him, and his head
Sank helplessly into his trembling hands;
And there was a dark silence everywhere
Until a voice that was not Laramie's
Began again inexorably to speak:
"Cavender, there is nothing for you now
But what your laws and purposes ordain;
For it appears that you believe in them.
If you did not, you would not stay alive,
Being what you are. You are not afraid to follow
Where she went once. You are afraid to live;
And where there is no fear, there's no more courage
Than faggots have in fire. You are afraid
Of time and life, and you are afraid of me;
But you are not afraid of dying, so long
As you shall have a mortal right to die.
Cavender, you are no such fool as that.
There are still doors in your house that are locked;
And there is only you to open them,
For what they may reveal. There may be still
Some riches hidden there, and even for you,
Who spurned your treasure as an angry king
Might throw his crown away, and in his madness
Not know what he had done till all was done.
But who are we to say when all is done?
1005

Was ever an insect flying between two flowers
Told less than we are told of what we are?
Cavender, there may still be hidden for you
A meaning in your house why you are here."

The terror that he felt, hearing those words,
Was more for hearing them as they were spoken,
And seeing, in fancy, who was saying them,
Than for their truth. It was intolerable
To know their warning told in his own voice,
But he must shrink, and hear them. It was foul
And perilous to be greeted by one's face,
But he must look. He looked, and there was nothing.

Into that house where no man went, no man
Would go again that night. The same white moon,
That saw the world before there was a man,
Would light an empty room until, in time,
There would be only darkness and a silence
Where man had been who had best not have been,
So far as he could know. If Laramie knew,
She was too far away even to care,
Perhaps, or to remember. He was alone,
And he was best alone. No man or woman
Would more than pity him, though a few might see,
As he believed that he might hope to see,
More than his eyes could hold while he was there,
Remembering what was done there. If he did it,
There was no more for him to do or say
Than willingly to slough a tattered mask,
And say what thing it was; and if hands stronger
Than his were more involved and occupied
Than his had been, there was no more to do
Or say than to cast out the lie within him,
And tell men what he was. He could do that.

He could do anything now but go again
Into that house of his where no man went,
And where he did not live. He was alone
Now, in a darker house than any light
Might enter while he lived. Yet there was light;
There where his hope had come with him so far
To find an answer, there was light enough
To make him see that he was there again
Where men should find him, and the laws of men,
Along with older laws and purposes,
Combine to smite. He was not sorry for that,
And he was not afraid. He was afraid
Only of peace. He had not asked for that;
He had not earned or contemplated it;
And this could not be peace that frightened him
With wonder, coming like a stranger, slowly,
Without a shape or name, and unannounced—
As if a door behind him in the dark,
And once not there, had opened silently,
Or as if Laramie had answered him.

THE GLORY OF THE NIGHTINGALES

(1930)

To the Memory of
Alfred H. Louis

THE GLORY OF THE NIGHTINGALES

I

WITH a long way before him there to Sharon,
And a longer way from Sharon to the sea,
Alone with an invisible companion
That was a valediction and a vengeance,
There were no further leagues or weary hours
Worth reckoning; for after years of hours,
And hours of years, the way ahead of him
Was like a line drawn surely, to be followed
With no great haste and with no hesitation,
Through time to silence. At the end of time
There would be Nightingale, and his last song—
A noxious and inevitable jest
That like a soft-winged insect at his ear
Fluttered and clung, or flew away from him,
Only to come once more. Weary of that,
And of a sun that burned the firmament,
He rested underneath a wayside oak
That he remembered. He was far from home
Or from a place that once had such a name,
Though not so far now as to be a stranger
To things familiar and so long forgotten
As not to be the same, or quite so large.
The way from here to there was not so long
As in his youth he would have measured it;
The trees and hills and houses that he found
Were not so high; and hours that once had held
So large a rationing of the time of life
Were not so large or long. He might perhaps

1011

Have counted them as longer than they were,
But for a fever in the certainty
Of what he sought. When once he had found that,
And had it, hours might have their way with him,
Or cease. With his work done so righteously,
Dying would not be much to pay for death,
Which was attuned and indispensable
To quivering destiny. No surer part
Was yet assigned to man for a performance
Than one that was for Malory, who must act,
Or leave the stage a failure.

For the present
All his wealth was in a purpose and a weapon,
All his purpose a removal of one being
Whose inception and existence was an error,
By fate repudiated and presented
To Malory for extinction. Nightingale
Had robbed him long ago of all the rest,
And with a smiling insolence not human
Had watched him crawling maimed out of a wreck
That had been life. There was no life since then;
For man, even if divine, is mechanism
While he is here, and so is not himself
If much of him be broken. Nightingale
Had shattered Malory, and as autumn waits
Unfailingly for summer to be done,
There was a story waiting to be told
By Malory, who believed he knew the peak
And issue of it—like so many of us
Whose knowing is belief, and whose belief
Is a determination to believe,
Whether in God, or in deflated friends,
Or in ourselves. If we believe enough
In something—none shall tell another what—

1012

THE GLORY OF THE NIGHTINGALES

That's ours to do, we are glad to be alive,
As Malory was, to do it. For some years
He had closed his eyes at night infallibly
On the same swift and satisfying picture
That in the morning would awaken him
Like a strong voice, or like a strong hand laid
Heavily on him, or like a bell struck once
To make him leap and think, and ask of life
What soiled and veiled necessity of space
Was there somewhere appointed and permitted
For one who must not live. Somewhere alive
He was; and when time whispered where he was,
Malory's part would be to smile and heed
And listen, and to follow and perform.
The larger doings of mortality
Must honor their importance to be done
Becomingly and right, as a seed grows
To a green shoot and so to a round flower.
The fiery-flying stars are in no haste,
And seen from here are still. So Malory's
Undying and unimpeded inspiration
Might have been watched and read by any of us,
As through the immeasurable distances
That are between the nearest and most known
Of loving and unfathomable strangers,
For patience, calm and kind. Patient it was,
As lightning is, or as volcanoes are
That are already alive with fire and death.

Patience under an oak, there by the road
That wound and climbed a silent way to Sharon,
Would then have been about what a wayfarer,
Passing him, might have said was Malory.
If he had paused, and tarried for a while,
He might have found a man somewhat the worse

1013

For wear within, and not unworn without—
One of the passable and unprosperous
To whom life clings; and might have said of him:
"There was a man I found one afternoon
Under an oak. He was a gracious man,
Who must once have had more to do with life
Than he was doing when I found him there.
He was a man of dreams more than of deeds—
Dreams that had not abundantly come true.
Disaster, manifest all over him,
Covered and held him like another skin
That was itself another nakedness,
To him, I trust, invisible. His eyes
Were kind, and bright enough; they were almost
Too bright for eyes that were so tired of seeing
No ships come in. For there was fire behind
Their light, and it would be there for some time
Before there was defeat. Meanwhile disaster,
Which is another name for something else,
Sat with him while we talked, under that oak,
And talked with me. Disaster was adept
In courtesy, and as I discovered soon,
In learning beyond mine. His history
He kept untold, more than to tell me once
He was a doctor—which was partly why
He sat in the shade. He smiled, saying that to me,
And saying it, smiled no more. And there I left him,
Alone, to ponder on the Lord knows what."

Could Malory then have heard and seen himself
So passively presented, and in words
That were so near to an obituary,
He might have conjured up another smile
To pay a stranger for his penetration.
Few would have seen so much as that of him,

1014

THE GLORY OF THE NIGHTINGALES

And fewer, seeing it, would have guessed how little
It was they saw. We should not all sleep well,
If night revealed to us our ignorance
Of others whose intents and evidences,
Errors and excellences, we have assayed
And tabulated. How many a one we meet
Would somewhat rather see us in a coffin,
Is not a thought for any far pursuit
On our part; and of all men, Nightingale
Would have disowned it and forgotten it
As an ingenious waste of meditation
In his impressive mansion by the sea—
A mausoleum that had been his dream
Until he had it. Now he had sea and mansion,
And having them had nothing. He had lost,
Like many in winning, more than he had won;
And he was lonelier there than one man left
On a well-furnished island. Nightingale
Had broken Malory, and was now alone
With his advantages and was believing,
Or saying so to himself, that he had acted
As a man must who is too strong to choose—
A pearl of his invention, therefore lustred
Not like a real one. He had always carried
More of a thwarted vision, and more wisdom,
Lost in himself, than an alluring world
Would let him use; and all being so adjusted,
It was ingratitude for Malory
To meddle with fate in any such thankless way
As his had been; for with his dream of healing,
And his foreshadowed confirmation of it,
He should have recognized, with no romance
Misleading him, his way that was appointed.
A man by nature dedicated only
To nature's hard submission, should have paid

The price of higher service—failing which,
Now there was nothing of him but a name
Of one forgotten. Where he was not forgotten,
He was among the most of all unenvied
Who have survived their dreams. It was a story
Of a worm boring in a noble tree,
And one there was no need of saying over:
Nature, that made the tree, had made the worm,
And Nightingale was not responsible.

Though his name, as a name treasured, was forgotten,
And his neighborhood was now not anywhere,
Malory felt that home was mocking him
In scenes and silences. He walked along,
Seeing everywhere familiar sights and landmarks,
And everywhere an insolence of change
That almost angered him, until he thought
How far change was from caring what he thought,
Or what he was, or whether he was alive
Or not alive. If there were a few left
To meet with more constraint than interest
An unimportant prodigal returning
In his adversity to the wrong town,
They would ask how he was, and having passed him,
They would look back at him and shake their heads;
They would remember how he had betrayed them,
And hurt their faith. Where friends have sown their faith,
And waited amiably for a late harvest,
Only success deceives; and one man gone
From Sharon would be tragedy as lasting
As one bee missing from a hive, perhaps.

But Malory sought neither faith nor welcome
From one alive, and he had none to give,
Or to inflict, in Sharon, on the living.
He had not come to parley with the living,

And he would not be long there with the dead—
Though she must hear him. She must know at last
That he was doing well, and hear him say so,
And she must give him thanks. Omnipotence
Had erred enough already in fashioning
His best friend as the devil, and would surely
Grant him a word with one the devil had slain
As venomously as any snake in darkness.
There was only Nightingale who came alive
Out of that darkness; therefore she must know
That fate was on its way to Nightingale.
Malory was too patient and sustained
In his malevolence to be mistaken.
He had not come so far to come for nothing,
He had been told the way for him to take.
Assurance, hovering like a benediction,
Had been his one companion. He was right,
Or nothing was right—in which complexity,
All might as well have the same end together.
It was almost a pity that in his arm
There was not power enough to dislocate
Creation. He felt and heard from silent places
A murmur as of all things mocking him
And his assurance as he moved along,
Which may have been a remnant left in him
Of an ancestral fear. He would not ask
Of silence what it was, for while his work
Was there ahead of him, it was not done.
When that was done, there would be nothing left
Worth asking, for the answer would be there;
The seed of a rich purpose would have grown
To the round flower of its accomplishment.

Agatha would be glad when all was over;
For even in that last hillside house of hers,

She must be troubled and humiliated
That he should wait so long, who had not known
At what precarious and intense a temper
The metal of his machinery was made.
Passion for what he sought had worn the face
Of patience, and had fooled him to endure
The wingless crawl of time in his pursuit
And conquest of invisible destroyers;
And when the mask had crumbled, and was gone,
Pursuit had gone mysteriously with it,
So that henceforward there was nothing left
Of Malory but some primitive wheels and springs,
Wound still to go till he was tired of them,
And of their ticking. Now there was no need
Of more oblivion, or excess, or nonsense—
Now that he saw, now that he was awake,
Now that he was alive. He was a king,
Whose word was life or death; and it was death.

II

With a wealth beyond a mortal estimation,
And not heavy, though it had the weight of doom,
He had come from other cities there to Sharon,
Where a woman had been left too long alone.
So it was time for him to think of twilight,
Before there was an end of a long day;
For the sun would soon be drowned in its own fire,
Like a burning ship that, sinking, burns the sea.
Now it was time to find the road below him,
Outside the town—the town he would not enter
Till Agatha had heard him and been happy
To know that ruin for him had not been waste.
Agatha must be told. They would be there

1018

THE GLORY OF THE NIGHTINGALES

Alone together, and science would have no eye
To censure them. There was no science left
In Sharon since her going away from him
So quietly, so forgetful of what life
Had done; and there was none left anywhere,
While Nightingale was left.

                With his arms folded,
And his eyes watching long across a valley
More than was there, and across more than valleys,
Malory would have had a brief regard
For any such foreign shaft of observation
As chance or curiosity might have aimed
At him in passing; and he would have felt it
As a post feels a fly. When he had watched
Enough, or seen that watching would reveal
Only what he had found, he moved along,
And soon was on a lower road that led him
Nearer than he could yet believe he was
To one of those three places he had come
So far to find. Two of them were so near
That he could see them, or see where they were,
For it was not a long way now to Sharon;
And even that last of ways would be no longer
Than a way there was from Sharon to the sea.

When he found himself a stranger in the silence
Of a city whose inhabitants were names,
He wandered, pausing, on his way to hers.
It was the last time he should ever see it,
And it was there. It would be waiting for him,
And it would understand why he came slowly,
For the last time. There was no science in that;
There was only a discreet benevolence
Of nature in his not having to make haste

Where death was leading him, and following him.
He could see death whenever he chose to look
Over his shoulder; for he felt him there,
And there was no need of seeing him too soon.
There were names all the way to Agatha's
For him to see; and death was, like himself,
Making no haste that day.

                Where it might come
Through many trees, there was late sunlight lying
On graves and grass; and everywhere a silence
Was like the coming of peace after pain.
He wondered if the dead were grateful for it,
And hoped they were. He was as far today
As ever he was from knowing more about it.
All that was best for him to know today
Was only that she was once a part of him,
And was a mystery that still humbled him
In his best memories. He was glad for them,
There in that silence, where he would not ask
How far he might be from deserving them.
He had not come to ask; he had come to tell her
What she must hear him say, and how his dream
Of long ago had latterly become
Another dream of now. The first had been
Of a long warfare in a field of death,
And of a noiseless victory; the second
Was one of those compelled necessities
Of righteousness for which the man appointed
Has God's mark on him and his work to do.
If Malory's God was not the King of Glory,
It was no less a king, whose voice foretold
Obedience where it fell; and it had fallen
Where manifestly it must be obeyed.
It was as plain as that to Malory,

THE GLORY OF THE NIGHTINGALES

And would be so to her, for whose repose
Obedience was exacted. Never in death,
More than in life, could there be such a sleep
As one that must not suffer some unrest
While one man was alive. If Nightingale
Were dead, and Malory dead, as Agatha was,
There would be peace. It was as plain as that
To Malory, moving there among the graves.

Now he could see time burning through the trees
With a slow crimson light that was, he reasoned,
The last of his last day that would be dying
Down to its end. Well, he was ready for that;
And it was better than a sunless day
Of clouds or rain would be. He could see now
A carved white name; and he began to see
More than a name, more than a shadowy face,
More than he came to find. For a flash of time
That was not measured she was there before him,
Between him and her house that had no door.
No shreds or clingings of a mortal change
Defiled or shadowed her serenity.
Her changing face and her mouse-colored hair,
Her solemn eyes that always laughed because
They saw so much that he was never to see—
Her mouth, and her white cheeks that were not white,
Her hands and feet, and all the rest of her,
Were there, and they were gone. But she was there,
And she was listening. So he told her all
He knew—which was abysmally not all
There was to know. How far he must go back,
And by what unimaginable guidance,
To find himself in all his origins
Was more than science knew—which was as well,
Also, as other knowledge not for man.

He had not come to ask of Agatha
More than he knew.

              "For one who has once had it,"
He told her, as an answer to her silence,
"Losing his faith in God is a disaster
By doubt still clouded and by nature made
Supportable. But to lose faith in man
And in himself, and all that's left to die for,
Is to feel a knife in his back before he knows
What's there, and then to know it was slimed first
With fiery poison to consume the friend
Who had no friend. It would have been as easy
To make me die instead of you, or with you,
But that would never have been enough for him.
He was not so enamoured of soft ways
As to do that. If someone else's neck
Was a good base whereon to set his feet
For a new spring to new vindictiveness,
There was no logic in his not using it.
Why else was a neck there? I warned him once,
That he might in some jungle of affairs
Tread inadvertently, and in the dark,
On a bad serpent, and it seems he did so;
Although his victim, then too much of a cripple
To sting him dead, has waited a long time.
Too long, as I can almost hear you saying,
Here in this dying light. I must leave all
To silence, and to justice after time—
Another justice that shall have its eyes,
As ours by time's necessity has not;
Which also may be well."

                Her name had now
A dimness in a light that faded slowly
Into a twilight that would not last long;

And in the west he could see no more crimson
Through darker trees that suddenly were changed,
And stiller than they were. They were too still
To stay with, or to go from. With her name
For a companion, they were like all there was
Of home for him, who had no home on earth,
Or need of one. The time of his desire,
And of one other man's iniquity
Had yet one day's diminished length to fill
Before it was complete, and that was all.
Or was it all? Her name, assuring him,
Would answer nothing, and he would not ask.
He was not there to ask.

                 "Now you have heard,"
He told her silently; "and having seen you,
I can see only one thing left to do.
I saw you for that moment, Agatha,
Which was enough, because it was no more."

He felt her glimmering name on the cold stone
With chilly fingers. There was only a name
There now; and he would leave it. On his way
From there, from Agatha, he was held a little
By two unhappy words that he could read
Where no trees blotted them: *Absalom Spinner.*
He scowled, and muttered; and for no new cause,
Felt to make sure of having in his pocket
His only wealth worth treasuring. He paused,
And in the dim light staring at that name,
Murmured, "It may not have been Nightingale,
So much as a too warm and willing bait.
There was a dereliction more primeval
Than his would be, and no affair of mine.
Spinner goes home to silence, as he went

Too many a time while she was fooling him,
And there may find some quiet. We don't know.
There is no quiet in life, and may be none
Till we may know that living is not dying.
There are two of us who may know more or nothing
Tomorrow. There is no room for us here.
There are two of us who are no longer wanted
Here at this cannibal banquet of man's life.
The word was given, and was not recalled;
And Agatha smiled."

     He walked on, wondering
Why he was saying that, over and over:
"And Agatha smiled."

     So on, and into Sharon,
He walked alone with night that had no eyes
To recognize him. He passed only strangers,
Nor many of them, though fifty thousand of them
Were not far off; and fifty thousand of them,
Or most of them, were only as many names,
Unknown to him. They might as well be names
On headstones, quiet as those he had left
Behind him in the dark, for all they were
To him; though he thought how each particular
Few feet and inches of unquiet life
That was a man or woman was for one
Or other, respectively, a more germane
And urgent work of God than was revealed
In others irremediably unlike it.
Annoyed that any such fond inanity
As that should be appointed to pursue him
And flick him like a moth along his last
Dark way through Sharon, he moved on unseen,
Or seen as nothing more felonious

Than a man going somewhere by himself
On a calm starry evening, harmlessly.

Now in a street with trees on either side
That hid the stars, he paused, seeing not far
Ahead of him a house with lighted windows,
Telling of life within—but of what life,
Or whose, or of what scope or quality,
Revealing only what a curtain drawn
May show; for there were shadows passing on it,
As of some phantasmagorial invasion
Of a place that once was his, and Agatha's;
He had come from far away to look at it
Once more, and there it was, and was not his.
He would not make a feast of seeing it.
He did not even so much as know whose house
He looked at; and his memory was not asking
What drama of home was played by shadows now
Behind those curtains. He was not there to ask.
He was there to see a house for the last time;
And having seen it, he had seen all there was
For him to see in Sharon. When he left it,
There was one way more to go; and that way taken,
There was a mansion somewhere by the sea.

III

With his last piece of silver disappearing
To pay for his last food in a retreat
That harbored other derelicts in Sharon,
Malory saw the glimmering end of time
Going out, even while he saw new daylight coming
Indifferently through dawn-defying windows,
Unwashed and unashamed. It was a place
Accommodated more to his departure

1025

Than to his entertainment or repose,
And one from which he went out willingly,
And gratefully, into the sunless light
Of a new morning that was not yet day,
And was not time. There was no longer need
Of time for him, more than there was of rest.
There was a way that he had come from Sharon,
And there was one from Sharon to the sea;
And there was nothing else on earth for him
Until he found the sea, and a new house
With towers and trees. That would be Nightingale's
New house; and Nightingale, he was informed,
Was in it, like a large and powerful worm
In a stone shell—a more pernicious mollusc,
With his hard house on land, than anything sunk
By God's foresight and love to live in the sea,
A stationary monster, doing no harm
And doing no good. Nightingale should have been
Like that—as God intended him to be,
And then forgot. So Malory must be fate,
Or more than fate, doing God's work, or fate's,
Or whatsoever the best name of it
Might be; for he was not pursuing words
This morning as he walked out finally
From Sharon towards the sunrise and the last
Of a long journey that would have an end
Where Nightingale was waiting in that house
Which he had always wanted, by the sea.

Like a fire to burn the world, with all its anguish,
And with all its evil evidence of man,
Malory saw the sun and saw it rising
For the last time, he said; and that was well.
In a world that would not burn there was no reason
Why a flash, and an immediate way out,

THE GLORY OF THE NIGHTINGALES

Should be delayed for two that were too many
To be alive and would be valued more
For being dead. He felt the gratefulness
Of nature for so right a thought as that,
And the approval of the rising sun;
He felt the spur of a good going forward
To the right end—a prize of realization
Withheld from all but the more fortunate
Whose dreams are preparations. Malory walked
In common shoes as Hermes might have walked
In wingèd sandals when he was not flying;
And every step that was away from Sharon
Was nearer to the sea.

                He tramped along,
Securely, with an onward earnestness,
And with a purpose in his expedition,
That might not from the curious be concealed.
He was not one of the world-nourishing
Unnoticeables who fit the place that finds them
And are not feverish to find another;
Nor was he one with any claim or station
Among the vagabonds, who would have marked him
As a man scratched, a gentleman gone down,
And going still. He would be one of those
Who in their unrevealed appearances
Are more distinguished than they are distinct,
And therefore are not welcome in the fold
Of the old brotherhood. It was not so
When Malory was himself, and now it mattered
Little, if anything, what a brother man
Might think of him. If there should be no thought,
So much the better. Malory would attend
To as much thinking of his own enigma
As was imperative or expedient;

1027

And a man saying that was not at odds
With his obscurity.

            An hour or so
Away from Sharon, none of the few faces
That were abroad so early would be one
To recognize, or to be reckoned with
In terms of amiable embarrassment
Begotten of mischance; and it was good
When he could say that such an hour or so
Was dead, and well behind him. It was early,
And he was free—with all the wealth there was
For him, in one small weapon that was his.
Croesus had nothing now but a rich name
That left him poor. Malory was like God.
So far as there was life to be considered,
He was omnipotent; and as for dying,
Death was another country where new light
Or darkness would inevitably prevail.
If there was hazard in his tearing down
This treacherous and imperfect house of man,
There was a moment of magnificence,
No less, in which the worst part of the world
Would make a piece of history best forgotten,
Along with his, that soon would follow it
Where history goes. It was as plain as that
To Malory, and so early in the morning
That hours to come were only coming names
Of time, the grave of names. This afternoon,
So far ahead of him, was only a name,
Because it was not yet; and what it held
For Malory was a picture that he saw
Because it should be there. The best and worst
Of pictures that we draw before we see them
Are there like that.

THE GLORY OF THE NIGHTINGALES

With none to challenge him,
And only few to stare a moment at him
As at a stranger too much on his way
To pay for salutation, he walked on
With more than half of Sharon still asleep
Behind him. There was only one more distance
Between him and the end. The rest were done,
And were among the journeys men have taken
So long ago that we shall see no roads
To say where those men went. As hours became
Forgotten but implacable recruits
Of his pursuing past, the name of Sharon
Was that of a dead city far behind him;
And as he walked the end was always with him,
And he was always nearer to the sea—
Till now it was full noon. He would soon have
The shadow of himself for company,
Not asking or imagining for how long
Some other shadows had attended him,
Or what they were. All he had seen of late,
All he saw now, was real—of a true form
And of a substance undeniable;
Or all but Agatha, and she was real.
There were no shadows or illusions waiting
In Nightingale's unnecessary mansion
To make him pause; for there was Nightingale,
Who was no shadow, and was deplorably
No phantom or illusion. He was as real
As reptiles, or as wolves are in dark places
Where men go perilously and unsuspecting
Of what else may be there till they are torn
By claws they cannot see. There were no doubts
Or reservations to be spent and wasted
On what he sought and was to find before
The sun went down. It was not going yet,

1029

And Malory knew the sea was not far off.
There would be more light left than he should **need**;
And when it was all done, there would be light
For those who came to see.

                             A giant elm,
Whose height from somewhere out of memory
Came back as yesterday an oak had come,
Told him how far away the desert wreck
Of a storm-buried past was from him now;
And a blank vision of oblivion
Chilled him with an irrelevance of regret
That he should never see that elm again—
As if a landmark had a language older
Than his, and a long eloquence that only
Ruin could understand. He saw behind him
Its height and silence; and as he moved on,
He could see all there ever was of Sharon
Fading into a distance that was death;
For there was no more time now than an hour
Between him and the sea; and afternoon,
Which earlier was a name for time unborn,
Was here, and it would soon be growing old.
Malory saw before him, drawn already
By fate, a place he need not hurry to see,
So long as it was there and was the place
Where he was going. Nightingale was there,
And any place where there was Nightingale,
Today, was a good place for Malory.

There was no need of asking whose it was
When Malory found it. Like a magician's work,
Or the small castle of a little king,
He saw it among trees, and saw the towers
Of which he had been told. He was not held
By them, or long impressed. He had not come

THE GLORY OF THE NIGHTINGALES

To study them; he had come to see the man
Who was inside, or in the neighborhood—
If such as he had neighbors. The whole place
Told of an empty wealth of loneliness
More than of hospitality and friends.
There might be satellites who deceived themselves
As friends, but they would never deceive the man
Within, who may have opened his heavy doors,
For conscience' sake, to anyone who might flatter
His host with an adroitness to be borne,
And help him to forget. He would soon forget,
Said Malory; and he waited for a door
To open, thinking of two other doors
That soon would open to an older house,
Where all men go.

                    Waiting inside, he saw
More wealth, attesting an intelligence
That was another lonely waste. He felt it
In all there was about him; and for surety
Of his possession and determination,
He touched, with fingers that were not afraid
To find it there, a more sufficient wealth
In his own pocket. He was a richer man
Than Nightingale. He was the richest man
In this poor world. He was a king, whose word
Was life or death, until another door
Was opened and the voice of a lost friend—
The voice of a dead friend, he must remember—
Called him as if a boy that he had known
And loved at school were calling him in pain,
For which there was no cure. Across more years
Than men had lived he heard it calling him,
With all but the authority of youth
To make it young. There was a humor in it

That had the sound of knowledge mocking hope,
And wonder sharing certainty with doubt;
And there was more in it than had a name
For vengeance to invent. And when it said,
"Malory, are you there!" it had the sound
It might have had if in the mills of years
Another life than Malory's had been broken.

IV

Like a desolating cry of an old music,
Long unheard, and falling strange in a new place,
Came again the searching voice of one appointed
To be voiceless; and an ache in Malory's heart
Was a poison that would soon be half a sorrow
If he waited; and he waited. He must act,
Or a folly more to be disowned and loathed
Than fear would slowly strangle resolution
With hands invisible and with silky fingers
Stronger than fate. And where was fate, meanwhile,
To leave him unresolved and hesitating
Till he was hearing "Malory, are you there,"
For a third time, and hearing it unanswered,
As if there were no answer? He was there,
At last, and opportunity was with him,
And he had yet no answer but his presence,
Which a few steps towards an open door
Revealed. With his hand clutching hidden death,
He stood and saw the man whom he had come
So far to kill, and waited, saying nothing,
As he gazed there at one who had grown older
Than time had made him.

                          In a velvet robe,
And in a prisoner's chair that was on wheels,

THE GLORY OF THE NIGHTINGALES

Nightingale was half sitting and half lying,
So nearly a pale prey of death already
That Malory's hand, still hidden in his coat,
Held nothing but his hate. The face he saw
Staring at his and waiting for some word,
Was that of one whom he had honored once
With love and trust, and with a grateful envy
That would have yielded all but life itself
To pay for such a friend. The same dark eyes
Were burning at him with a lower fire
From a white face that he had never seen
Before. The face that he had loved and hated
Was not the face he saw. The bones were there
That formerly were buried under power
And grace, and there was as much more of it
As time and pain together had not shrunk
To skin and death. In youth's idolatry
There was no possibility of this;
And in the fires of wreck and revelation,
Nothing had been foreseen that was like this—
Which was unfair. It was not even fair fate,
Said Malory; and he waited for an answer
To his appearance. He had not come to ask,
He had come to act; and as he was not acting,
He waited. There was nothing for him to say
That moved his tongue, and he had best be going,
If the rich gold of expectation yielded
Only a dross like this. He looked away
From the wan wreck before him to three walls
Tiered high with books that held the best of man's
Creation and reflection for the solace
Of this thing in a chair that went on wheels,
And to a fourth wall that was most a window,
Framing a sea and sky for Nightingale
To watch and contemplate, and to see pictured

1033

With shipwreck and remorse. He had always wanted
A place like this; and having a large habit
Of seeing as his what most it was he wanted,
Now he could have the sky and the wide ocean
Together, and in a chair that went on wheels,
He could sit still and see them all day long.
There was no need of killing him; he was dead
Before his name was called.

                    "Well, Malory,"
Said Nightingale, with questions in his eyes
And in his voice, "the old mariner's ashore;
Look at him, and you'll see him at the end
Of his last cruise. You may as well have a chair
And see him comfortably. If you have come
To shoot him, he will not be disagreeable,
Or argumentative. If I surprise you
With a mistaken levity, and a notion
That's all outside your proper meditation,
Forgive me. But experience, I have found,
Encourages an imaginative caution;
Though caution, I may guess, would serve me now
As a thin armor. I might ring a bell,
But who should answer it in time to save you
From a superfluous incarceration,
And me from a good sleep? I don't sleep well,
Malory; and if truth has painted you
As you look now, you are not of the seven.
I wonder what you have there in your pocket,
More than a hand. Again I'll ask your pardon
If my imagination is in error;
And then, if you may care, I'll tell you why
It was that you brought visions in with you,
And some that were not lovely."

THE GLORY OF THE NIGHTINGALES

                    Malory sighed,
As one discomfited by destiny
Too shrewd for chance, and said to Nightingale,
"I see no reason left why you should live,
Or why I should stay longer. You had always
Too much of an unused intelligence
To be as you are now; and you have still
Enough to need the word of no physician
To say where you are going. If there's hell,
Of one sort or another, and there may be,
You will not be much older than you are
Before you know. Or, it is possible
That yours was here."

               "I see," said Nightingale.
"A doctor, to be more than wind and hope,
Must have three eyes. Well, you may have your fee
For asking—or without."

               Malory moved
Along indifferently, and at the window
Stood looking at the ocean, which he saw
As men had seen it who were not yet men.
In ages lost in the long void of time,
It must have tossed and foamed as helplessly
As now, at the wind's will; and to the eyes
Of Malory's unimagined ancestors
It must have been a fearsome mystery,
Filled with infernal things in ancient fancy,
As it was now in fact. Look as he would,
Life was a fabrication of the demons,
On land, or in the sea, or in the air.
A snake, seeing a man, could frighten him
And sting him to quick death; and a small fly
Could sting him to slow death, and with no aid

Of dream or fancy. A far smaller thing
Than a small fly had shattered Nightingale;
And he was dying in his grand new house,
Which he had always wanted, near the ocean.
A tired bacteriologist, seeing him there,
Might say there was a God. Nature, at least,
Had never done her work so well before,
Or saved a man of science so much trouble.
A sense of rest, and of an unforeseen
Release replenished him with a new wish
To live—a wish that had in it more wonder
Than satisfaction. A new fear of living
Had come to him who had no fear of dying,
Or wish to die, or means to live. He wondered
How such a warfare of inept negations
Might end—when for a moment, having turned
Himself to look at Nightingale again,
He fancied he was in the way of knowing
Immediately of that; for the first sight
That held him was no invalid in a chair,
But a black weapon pointing silently
Straight at him. He considered the short barrel,
And then the square pale face of Nightingale,
Grinning mysteriously and ominously,
More like a living mask on a dead face
Than like a face alive. But Nightingale
Was living, and for the nonce, apparently,
Was finding life a privilege and a pleasure.

"Forgive me, Malory, if I'm curious,"
He said, "but I've a leprosy to know
What you have in that pocket where your hand is.
This thing of mine—it was not always mine—
Is educated and almost alive,
And might have speech. Now let me look at yours,
1036

And I will tell you then which implement
I like the better of the deadly two.
I may want both of them, if yours is pretty—
Like Absalom's. Are you surprised, somewhat?
Let me have yours, and I'll say how it was,
And why, and all about it. You are not going
To kill me in this chair and have a mess.
I can see that."

           "I came down here for that,"
Malory answered, "and I came too late.
Nature has beaten me. Nature, or God;
I don't know which. I have no need of this."

"I thank you, Malory." Nightingale, still grinning,
Had a flat pistol now in each thin hand,
And held them aimed at Malory. "Now sit down.
With your permission I'll say these are mine,
Although I do not use them. They are pretty,
And I have always loved the beautiful;
And the most beautiful of all there was
On earth you stole from me. But we'll go back
To that. Now this one in my other hand
Was given to me, and gladly, by a friend
Who came one day, as you have come this day,
To make an end of me. Yes—Absalom.
He had magnified himself with wicked gin,
And I was not like this. I was on my feet.
I smiled at him, and I said, 'Absalom,
You cannot kill me without having a drink
With me in my new house.' He hesitated,
And I held out my hand. He wanted rum
More than he wanted me, and did not know it
Until he was informed—though I'll not boast
Of any too brisk a sureness at the time,

Or say that I was happy to be waiting
So much at his not all assuring service.
I was not comfortable while I waited,
But I was calm. 'Absalom,' I suggested,
'There's a whole world of things for me to tell you,
But first we'll have a drink in my new house—
A tall, strong, curative drink made long ago,
An endless and illuminating drink,
Before I make of you a shining man,
A free man, and a merrier citizen
Than you have seen yet in your looking-glass.' "

"Yes," Malory said, "you could afford, perhaps,
As much as that, or more. I have not been
So far from news of life that not a word
Of you has found me. I have known more of you
Than a man has to know to be advised
Of honor wasted, as mine was on yours,
That I called honor. I leave men's affairs
That are not mine to men whose part it is
To manage them with a safe decency.
But when a friend . . . Why am I saying this?
Why am I here, with all I came to do
So nearly done before me. Absalom's wife—
Where is she now? I know where Absalom is,
For I have seen his grave."

                              "If you saw that,"
Said Nightingale, amiably, "you saw the stone
That I placed over him. Ophelia's father
Had a good end, or she believed he had,
And so had Absalom. As for his wife,
A moment of indulgence and attention
Will heal your implications in one error
That cries for healing. She was not a wife;

THE GLORY OF THE NIGHTINGALES

She was a fruity sort of Cyprian fungus,
With arms and legs, the brain-pan of a chicken,
And all the morals of a pleasant monkey.
God in his wisdom, which is infinite,
And is not ours, has always made such things
To be consumed. They are for nothing else,
And are good for nothing else; and if they could,
They would be nothing else. Send them to school,
And see what they learn there. Give them a home,
And see what's left of it when they have had it
Long enough to be tired of living in it.
They are not happy, or not so for long,
And that's a pity—or may be a warning
For all the others, who are interested
But not at large. When you ask where she is,
You may as well be asking for the story
Of all the rest of them. She's not in Sharon;
And Sharon has not seen her since a time
When Absalom, failing to assassinate her,
And losing half his face, did me the honor
Aforesaid. So for God's sake, Malory,
Whatever you do to me, or to my name,
Let Absalom Spinner's name be one to shine
As that of one man who had what he wanted.
Absalom came to make a feast of me,
And went away, or rather was carried away,
To sleep without a memory or a care,
Until he woke to find a longer feast
Awaiting him than I should ever have made.
I fixed a competent annuity
On Absalom, who made one splendid leap
From Sharon into paradise, and remained.
He was illuminated for three years
With light that never revealed him to himself
As a poor wick that he must saturate

Unceasingly in order not to see it.
He was a panorama and a pageant
That would have been an eminence in a city
Greater than Sharon. He was joy and color
Where nothing has been like him since he went.
As long as he could play, Spinner was trumps—
And always won. His only currency
Worth counting in his triumph was a freedom
To be a fool; and he had more of it
Than he could lose. Spinner had everything,
And had it for three years in tropic bloom.
Before it might have faded, or become
Only an occupation, or a duty,
Absalom died. He fell down under a dray,
And died. With his beginnings and ideals,
And the Lord watching him, giving him first
Some brief and beneficial misery
For joy to come, his cup was alabaster,
And it was always full until it cracked,
And the glad juice ran out. No, Malory,
Never defeat your sympathies or regrets
With Absalom. Lay roses on his grave,
But do not desecrate them with your tears;
For Absalom, wherever he is, may see you.
You may go round the world, and round again,
And after that you may go round once more
For sight of as inexhaustible a cask
Of happiness as Absalom, and not find it."

Malory sighed, and was almost asleep
With weariness. He had not known how tired
A weight that has at last been lifted leaves him
Who carries it too far. But he could say
To Nightingale, half hearing his own words,
"You are the last of men, as I know men,

To make so easy a simplicity
Of lives that are not yours. If your condition
Is a best evidence of your playful ethics,
You are less fortunate than Absalom—
Who, in his way, was as unusual
As you are, Nightingale. I have seen life,
And have not seen it easy. I have seen death.
Yes, Nightingale; I have seen death, also."

"Yes, Malory," said Nightingale, distinctly,
And with a resignation of assent,
"You have seen death. You are looking at it now,
And to your inexpressible satisfaction.
I know it; and I've had cataracts of ideas
Descending on me, and to some effect,
Since you came in. There's been a trickle of them
Before; and we'll say more of them tomorrow."

"I don't know. I am going," Malory said,
And rose, only to find that his knees bent
Like hinges in the legs of a lay-figure.
He sat, or fell, into his chair again,
And there forgot to say where he was going.
He did not know. He was too tired to care.

V

In the morning, in the light of a sun shining
On a million little waves that flashed and danced
With a cold primordial mockery there below him
And beyond him, beyond sight or thought of him,
Or of Nightingale, whose hospitality
Was like a venomous food that a blind man
Had eaten in his weariness, Malory looked
Away into the distance and found only

1041

Distance. He was an outcast long at home
With distances, but never with one like this
That was before him now. He was alive,
And was to have been dead with Nightingale,
Who sat with death already; he was awake,
And he could see too clearly and too far,
Or so he thought, over an empty ocean
Into an empty day, and into days
That were to come and must be filled somehow
With other stuff than time. There would be friends
In Sharon to acknowledge him so far
As on his word to see him on his way
To somewhere else. There was no fiery need
Of being a fool, and he must let the past
Serve as it would the present and the future;
Which was a way of saying that he must have
A few reviving dollars. He had eaten
Nightingale's food only to give him strength
To go without it, and would have no more.
"There's one thing in this Christian life of ours,
Which none of us could live, engages me,"
Nightingale said to Malory, coming down
To say some formal words and then to go.
"I mean the other cheek—in moderation.
You are a doctor, and that's why you know
What happens to a man who walks all day,
And doesn't eat till he's too tired to care
If anyone eats. I sent it up to you
Before you should see me. You called it tact,
Perhaps, but fear was nearer the right name.
I was afraid that you might emigrate
In anger when you found yourself awake
In one of my not execrable beds.
No matter what I've been, what's left of me
Is human; and if you have Christian faith,

Or Christian curiosity, sufficient
Unto some other evil day than this,
You may lay treasures up—if not in heaven,
Then here on earth, which is another matter—
Treasures not for yourself. I'm no such ass
As innocence like that would make of me,
Though I've been worse. I want you in this house
Until tomorrow. You are in no haste now—
Now you have seen that I am not worth killing,
And you will do yourself and me a service
If you will not run off immediately.
For, Malory,"—his mouth trembled—"there's not going
To be much time."

        "There will be time enough,"
Malory said, "to make you call to Christ
For less. I can do nothing about that.
I can say nothing that will give you hope,
Or happiness. I am sorry that you must live,
And think, until you die; and you have there
The sum of all the grief there is in me
For rather less than a fair reckoning.
Why, in God's name, should you be asking me
To stay, and watch? Am I so medieval
As to enjoy seeing even my worst friend
Suffer too long? I'd be no better for that."

Nightingale tapped the wheels that held his chair,
And looked across the waves. Then, with a smile
Of understanding that had no reproach,
He turned again to look at Malory:
"You have a right to say it with an edge,
And I have none to mind your saying it.
Some follow lights that they have never seen,
And I was given a light that I could see

But could not follow. There's the devil in that,
Always; and that's why I am asking you
To stay until tomorrow. If the food
That you have eaten here distresses you,
Pay for it, and forget it. It was yours.
I have a sum of money that is yours,
And I can see no honor-gnawing harm
In your belated repossession of it;
For you were robbed of it as viciously
As if you had been gagged and strangled for it.
But that's a tune that I was to play later,
If you would stay and listen. I saw your eyes
When you came yesterday to finish me,
And knew that you would stay. I don't know why
A man's condition makes a difference,
But so it is. Somehow it is not done,
Or not by Malory. For a glance at me
Told him how more proficient an assassin
Fate was than any doctor. You will stay,
If only for a suffering abstraction
Misnamed humanity. I don't mean myself,
And you are in no haste."

                              "I'm in no haste,"
Said Malory, "and I don't know what you mean—
Or all you mean. I know that I was robbed,
And share my knowledge willingly with you.
That was a part of it, but far from all.
You spoke of it, and may do as much more
As your interpretation of affairs
Compels or counsels. I had not come for that,
Or painted my bare walls with expectations."
"I see," said Nightingale. "You saw so far
Beyond a small recovery of the past
That all was in the present. Naturally

THE GLORY OF THE NIGHTINGALES

You had not come for that. I never fancied
That you were here for that. For when you came,
I saw you as you looked when we were boys
Together at school; and in a flash I saw
What you had learned of me in other schools.
I'm sorry, Malory, that the world goes round
The sun in such a way as to leave time
So far behind it; or I should be sorry,
If I saw less. I see more, possibly,
Than you see, Malory. If you had shot me,
You would have seen a finite retribution
That would have done no good. It's not like that.
You might as well have shot the flying earth
To kill a system—of which you are part,
And so the whole. But that's not Agatha."

His calm eyes for a moment were like those
Of an expectant and confessed offender.
But there was nothing done, and nothing said,
Till Malory spoke: "I will hear anything
That you may say to me of Agatha,
And your destruction of her. You destroyed her
With hell's deliberation in your method,
Or I'm as wrong as hell. You cannot say
That I am wrong. You may have been the devil,
But you were never a fool."

               "I beg of you,
Malory, to believe me when I swear
That I was more than one. I was a college
Of fools, under one scalp and in one skin.
But I was not myself. That's an old plaster,
And one that has been used till it will stick
No longer. You are right, for you were saying
Just about that." Nightingale closed his eyes,

As if a picture of his thoughts had hurt him.
Malory watched the sea.

                        For a long time
There was a stillness as of all things said,
And of a waiting for no other end
Than evident farewell. But Nightingale
Said quietly, at last, "No, Malory,
There were no diagrams of your disaster
Drawn to include what came, or half of it.
Yet, when it came . . ."

                    "Yes, Nightingale—when it came.
You were not there in Sharon when it came.
You were not there again till we were gone—
All three of us. They are not made of iron,
Women like her; though many of them are stronger
In stronger ways than ours. She and her child
Should not have gone so early, Nightingale.
If it was best for them to go together,
It was not then. They would be here today
If you had been—yourself. I can say that,
As well as you, for I was not myself,
And am not yet. There was a devil waiting
To steal me from myself. You are no part
Of that, although you may have been a devil.
I think you must have been one, Nightingale,
For you were not a man in a man's way.
It was some time before we found that out,
And you had not come back. If you had come . . .
I am glad not to know. If you had come,
We might not be here as we are today—
Which might be better. It could not well be worse
For you, or more ridiculous for me.

                    1046

THE GLORY OF THE NIGHTINGALES

It is almost a pity that you're not able
To savor properly the humor of this."

"God's right is yours," Nightingale answered, slowly,
And with no frown of protest, "to be bitter.
Yet, Malory, we'll see what there is left.
There may be more than you are willing to see,
If seen too near. I doubt if any of this
Is new, for I dare say it has all happened
In Samarcand or Celebes before us.
Should even a smouldering of apology
Be living in that, extinguish it at once
With indignation, hatred, or contempt.
You cannot hate me any harder now
Than heretofore, though you might find an anger
Somewhere in you that has not yet been used.
But I'll hope not; and I shall say but little
Of Agatha, and that only by your leave.
I said that when I saw you standing there,
When you came yesterday, I saw you first
As I had seen you long ago at school,
When we were boys together, never dreaming
Of what the coming men in us had waiting.
There was nothing then of mine that was not yours;
And you, if I had asked it, would have given
More than you had to give. You would have found
Outside your own possession what you lacked,
If possible, and you would have called it mine.
I should have done no less, and should have said
That a friend who so failed me was a liar—
A thing without a day's worth of remembrance
Left in him for my eyes. In those unfledged
Omniscient years of youth, I knew myself
Better, sometimes, than was a joy for me;
For there were premonitions then, and warnings.

I saw myself a part of a small world
Of traps and lies and fights and compromises,
And saw beyond it while I saw it coming,
And welcomed it—although I measured it
For what it was; and hating it, even then,
Precociously, I have not always loved
Myself. I had enough of other vision
To see the other side of selfishness,
But I had not the will to sacrifice
My vanity for my wits. I was the law—
And here I am. Here I am not the law.
I saw you, Malory, in those same raw years,
As far from me, in dreams and differences,
As ever you got; and that was a long way.
You were a thin-skinned prodigy of science
Before you had a whisker. You were never
A doctor; you had not the hide for it,
And you had no authoritative aura
To make a poor sick citizen glad for you
And God in the same room. You learned as much
Before you were too old; and I believe
My foresight and affection aided you
In your inquisitive enmity to microbes."

"You led me to a door that had no key
For me to use until you gave me one,"
Malory said; "and you made possible
A place where I might never have arrived
Without your foresight and your confidence.
Good God—your confidence!" Malory poured
A powerful drink of whiskey for himself,
And drank it with a purpose.

                                "You have lifted
Rather too much of that abused nepenthe,
Since you became a question-mark in Sharon,"

THE GLORY OF THE NIGHTINGALES

Said Nightingale, with his eye on the bottle;
"But it will do your body and soul no manner
Of harm today. You may not care tomorrow
Whether or no the ocean's made of it.
We'll see—or you will. So you found at last
Your niche of honor in the living temple,
Which is a place worth finding. I found one,
Also, in which I stood more gloriously
Mistaken for a beneficial hero
Than anyone else in town. I did some good,
And brought a sound and honorable name
Out of the dust and cobwebs of decay.
My father, a most melodious Nightingale,
Sang more songs than were good for a good bird,
And I was the indemnifying phoenix.
I was a youth of parts and promises,
Endowed with a convenient fluid conscience
That covered the best of me with a bright varnish,
And made me shine. If none had thwarted me,
I might be shining still, instead of dying
In this expensive nest. If I had learned,
In time, to know that I was not the law
That made me live, I should have done more shining,
And in a light more grateful to my eyes.
I was a sort of Saint George in the town,
However, as years went on; and I slew dragons
Habitually, having a spear of gold
Which I had fashioned of my own endeavor
And sharpened with commendable incentive.
That was all right, and it was all as easy
As it was right. I made a better town
Of Sharon, and I never sang outside
Myself the song in me that I knew best.
Why should I sing it? No one asked for it,
And only the envious and inefficient

1049

Would have enjoyed it. I was not so bad,
So long as I was having my own way.
It's a grave matter for the commonwealth,
Sometimes, when a good egoist goes down,
Whether he goes invisibly, as I did,
Or with the flags and tatters of defeat
Thrown after him. But that was all to be,
And I was waiting, eminent and unwarned,
Serene in Sharon. I was the dominant bird,
Outsinging and outshining and outflying
Everything else. I was informed one day
That in my doing what no one else would do,
I was a cold magician and a seer;
And that, for whistling, gold would follow me.
It did—though not till I had followed first,
While others whistled. It was easy then
For me to be magnificent and agreeable,
For I had still to learn how heavy a cake
A king may have to eat. Before I learned,
I was a lord of a small firmament,
Or almost that, with fifty thousand stars,
Most of them having a face that beamed on me,
We'll say, with more approval than reproof;
And that was right. I had robbed no man then,
And no man had robbed me. I was untried
In my submissions and humilities.
I was unquestioned of my qualities.
I was a friend to many who would have had
No eyes to see me had their place been mine.
I was a more approachable Maecenas
Than always had the license of his judgment.
I knew that I had played with the same cards
That were for all to use, and played them better.
I was a prodigal father's thrifty son,
With wisdom to be generous in my thrift.

THE GLORY OF THE NIGHTINGALES

I was a man the more to be admired
For tempering admiration with respect,
Or with a gracious imitation of it.
I was a man aware that each man carried
Only the lamp the Lord had given to him.
I raised myself no higher than others held me,
And therefore was a brother who understood.
I was a light that would be shining always,
A light for generations to remember.
I was a sort of permanent morning star.
I was the Glory of the Nightingales.
The sinful, well-intentioned Nemesis
Who said that first—it must have been a woman—
Should have had spiders in her marmalade,
And scorpions every morning in her stockings.
I was the Glory of the Nightingales!
Give me a drink, and don't say it will kill me.
You know damned well it won't.   Only too well
You know it won't—and don't say you're a doctor.
I told you about time, and the earth moving.
Arthritis and Ataxia—two Alphas,
And a malevolent long alphabet
Between them and Omega."

                    Malory stared
At Nightingale, partly in admiration,
Partly in helpless wonder and regret
For such a fusion of mortalities
To make one death.   Where was the use of power,
If a wrong element in the beginning
Was to make this of it?   Where was the use
Of satisfaction, hatred, or revenge,
If life avenged itself?   If it did, always,
There would be justice hidden somewhere in it;
But if the weak and headstrong and untried

1051

Paid for the rest to let the play go on—
If there was more fragility and defeat
Hiding in one disordered competence
Than in a thousand safe complacencies,
Having not much to hide or to reveal—
Why was it better not to be a dog?
A tired bacteriologist might ask
As much of Nightingale—or of himself.
He had not asked. He had not come to ask.
He had been tried, and had as little to say
Of one discrepancy as of another.
He was no longer critical. He saw
Too near the end—forgetting how many ends
There are that are not death.

                               "No, Malory,"
Said Nightingale, returning from a silence,
"I'm not composing an apology.
I was looking at the sea. Apology
Would be a worse offence to you than any
That you have suffered yet of my invention;
And I have been inventive, even as Cain
Was active. I've been drenched until I smelt
With praise of it. Fathers have made a show
Of my initiative for their dull sons
To copy, and have clucked at my foresight
In seizing what another could not see.
It is not always criminal to be first,
But there's a poison and a danger waiting
For him who will not hear, and will not listen,
While choruses of inner voices tell him
When to be second. That was the curse prepared
For me: I would not listen to my voices.
I'll only say it was not wholly strange
That I did not. When Agatha came to Sharon,

THE GLORY OF THE NIGHTINGALES

I saw what all my prowlings had been worth,
And what my restlessness had waited for.
It was not hard for me to find my way
To her acquaintance. I was not unknown,
Or notably unaccepted or unsought;
I was so far from that as to be shown
To strangers as one having everything—
Which was not so. The one thing I had not
Was everything, and she was Agatha.
But all was going well, and I believed
My triumph, long so empty of what most
It had so perilously lacked, would soon
Be filled, and all my turmoil and unrest
Be quieted. I should have everything—
In truth as in report; and that was all
I asked. The wonder of it, Malory,
Is that I should have had it, or I think so,
If in my self-destroying adoration
Of my divinity, I had not brought you
To see me at my worship, and see also
The object of it. Kismet, or Ananke,
Or melancholy chance, was following me
When I brought you, as a friend brings a friend
Into his treasure-house, to Agatha.
You were my king of friends, and Agatha
Was to be queen of all there was of me
And mine to give her. There was no fool's dream
In my delusion, for I was not a fool—
Not then; and Agatha was not a dream—
Not then. I was as near to paradise
As man may be. It was you who shut the door.
It was you who stood between me and the door.
Yes, it was you who made a knave of me,
When I was almost . . ."

"You were almost—what?"
Malory asked. "Are you the only knave
Who has—almost—made a good woman love him?
I fancy there are one or two before you
In the lost archives of iniquity,
For you are not unique in having a way.
You might, with all your batteries of allegiance,
Devotion, adoration, and insistence,
Have stilled within her for a while her voices—
Which were as many as yours—and I don't know
That in some web of pity and hesitation
She might not have been caught, to find herself
Your—queen, it was, you called her. Nightingale,
She would have been the most afflicted queen
That ever reigned, if she had reigned with you.
She never said to me as much as that;
A few infrequent and unwilling words
To which you might have listened, and agreed,
Told all her story. She was sorry for you,
Nightingale, but she saw too many of you.
All which would not have mattered, I suppose
If love had shared her caution, and told lies
Enough to her about it, but your Kismet,
Or your Ananke, had no power or skill
To do love's work for you. Love was not there.
You knew it was not there, but you would hear
No voice, or none at first, but vanity's.
Later, you may have heard God knows what voices;
For all your nonsense of my shutting doors
To your phantasmal paradise is worthy
Of a mad weakling. I'll be generous now,
When nothing comes of it, and call you mad—
Though you are not. If I have called you weak,
Say when it was, and ask your memory
If you are still inventive. I know traits

THE GLORY OF THE NIGHTINGALES

Of more malignities in mortal growth
Than you have heard of, and I know their names;
But not one of an ulcered understanding
That you possessed once, or that possessed you,
Of even the first of human rudiments.
You are the one physician, Nightingale,
For seizures, and peculiar paroxysms
That are not yet established or observed
In books or clinics. If you have healed yourself
Too late, you have done something for your soul
That even your stricken body will acknowledge,
If only with more pain. Why should I stay
To watch fate doing my work? I can do nothing."

"You might, by watching fate, do a deal more
Than you came here to do," said Nightingale,
With a long frown that held a weary smile:
"Unless you have a mind to drown yourself
In my commodious ocean, Malory,
You will do well to stay. You must, indeed,
For long enough to let me go on saying
What I began. You interrupted me,
And you were well within your injured rights.
You see how pliable and how mild I am,
And wonder, maybe, if it's all my conscience.
I should not say it was. I should say, rather,
It was acknowledgment and recognition,
Humility and surrender. It's more than that,
And has to do with more than you and me—
But that will come. You bit my words away
When I said I was almost . . . Well, I was.
I was, till you took everything there was
Alive for me to live for. You had science,
And I had nothing without Agatha.
It was the gash of that awakening

1055

That would not heal. Surprise and unbelief
Tortured it, and slow hate infected it.
A venom in me that I had not before
Believed in—one that I had said and sworn
Was not there—made its way infernally
Into the last and darkest crevices
That were concealed in me to be explored
And torn. I had not known there were such places
Anywhere, till a devil discovered them
With his contaminated little needle
Of hate. He may have visited you later,
Malory, and you may have come from Sharon
Down here because he sent you. If he sent you,
He was forestalled by power stronger than his,
And vengeance more sublime. Strong as he is,
The devil is only a part of destiny,
Doing the worst he may. He deceives man,
And makes an idiot shambles of the world
About so often, and for the joy of seeing
What fools men are; and whether he sees us here
At war or peace, he flies and strikes and stings
Incessantly, and has a name for peace
That pleases him. Men would have said, and women,
That I was, of all men, or should have been,
The most at peace and the least agitated
By the surprises of necessity.
That was my way of showing myself to men,
And women; and that was how I looked to you,
And Agatha. You had taken everything
Away from me, but that was how I looked.
All that I almost had was gone before
I knew who had it; and when at last I knew,
I was alone with my incredulousness.
I saw myself as one left robbed and stabbed
By friends who had betrayed him in the dark.

THE GLORY OF THE NIGHTINGALES

I wandered in the dark for many days
And many nights before I found my way;
And there was not a soul in Sharon knew
What I was finding; and I did not know,
At first, what I had found. I was to know,
Thoroughly, only when as a physician,
As you so unprofessionally suggested,
I made a proper search and diagnosis
Of what the devil within me had been doing.
When devils have driven their stings in deep enough,
And done their work, knowledge has time to mourn."

"But why the devil do you insist so hard
On devilish help in your duplicity?"
Malory asked, and scowled at Nightingale.
"You knew your work, and what was coming of it,
Or might come. I am leaving myself out,
This time, and I'm not saying what came to me—
Though I had devils enough assisting me
To my destruction—if you must have devils."

"If I'm impervious to insinuation,"
Nightingale said, "you called me a physician.
And if I shall appear to you, perchance,
More a physician than a penitent,
You will know why. If it would help the past,
I'd get down somehow on my knees to you,
And you would not like that; for it would make you
Merely a little sick, and be a trial
For me. I doubt if either of us would like
Ourselves as well for such extravagance.
I can afford, I fear, no more declension
Of my interior esteem, or dwindling
Of what there's left in me of dignity.
I had some once, and many may have said

I wore it with a comfort as becoming
As it was native. I don't know just what
They're saying now in Sharon. I'm not there.
About the time you left was the right time
For me to be away. When I returned
To find you gone, and Agatha gone before you,
I learned at last, as for the first time, wholly,
And comprehensively, what I had done.
There were no plans or diagrams, remember,
In my invention. How should I be certain,
I asked, of what might happen if I should knock
Some props away that held some walls upright?
There was no way of knowing. The house might stand
For ever, or might slant and sway a little,
And still survive, and stand. How should I know,
For sure, what houses were ordained to stay
Upright, no matter what storms broke over them,
Or what was taken away from under them?
Your legacy, which you needed, was for you
A large one. It was a gift out of God's hand,
Agatha said, and may have believed it was.
I don't know that it wasn't. My advice
Told you to sink it all, and more than all,
Where I was confident, and, as I saw it,
Magnanimous. I sank as much as yours
In the same hole, believing wealth would rise
And flow like golden lava out of it—
By far the worst inspired of my not many
Mistakes in seeing too soon below the surface.
Although I hated you as you did me—
Later—I could do that for Agatha,
And did it; and the gold flowed—for a while.
I was across the ocean, trying wildly
Not to wish both of you and your new home
Were dead. You had taken everything from me,

And I might have some peace if one of you,
Or both of you, were gone. Call it the devil,
Or not, but that's what was alive in me
While I was over there where I was warned,
Early, of what was coming. I sold all mine
For someone else to lose, which is finance,
And somehow failed—I'll hardly say forgot—
To show you the same seasonable way
Out of that golden hole. I must have known
Down in me, and with all my talk of houses
Falling or standing upright in all weather,
That I had thrown your world, and Agatha's,
Cruelly out of its course, and so far out
As never to return as the same world.
My only word to you from over there
Was an evasion and a temporizing,
Telling you nothing, offering you nothing
But a few shadowy promises. When you found
The truth, it was too hard for Agatha,
Who was not fit for shipwreck at that time;
For, as you said, all women are not made
Of iron entirely. I shall die not knowing
How near a madman I had then become,
Or whether there were devils. Tell yourself,
And let there be no doubt, that I destroyed her
While I believed I was destroying you.
It was too dark for me to see just then
What I was doing—for my only light
Was fire that was in me; and fire like that
Is fire that has no light. You hear me saying
That I did this, and that my first exploit
In Sharon, on returning, was to stand
At Agatha's grave and thank God she was there.
She was away from you, and as much mine
As yours—or my devouring self-defeat

Would so believe. I would go there at night
And talk to her. She was the only thing
I ever wanted that I could not have.
You took her from me, when she was almost . . .
Malory, if you care to open that drawer,
You will find in it the same implement
That you brought yesterday."

                                    Nightingale's voice
Was trembling for the second time that day,
And then was silent. Malory left his chair
And moved away again towards the window
That looked on those unceasing little waves
Which had no rest. They would have rest sometime,
And when they rested they would not be waves.
Should he be Malory when he was resting,
He thought, or only as much of earth and air
And water as there was of him to be moving
Again somewhere and to be something else.
He had almost forgotten Nightingale,
Who had said little to him that was new,
And nothing that was false. He had been false
Until it was no matter what else he was,
Or what he had to say, or what he did,
Said Malory; and that was easy saying
For one in whom even hate had now no home.

And was that all, and had he come in vain
So far to find where vengeance was not his?
Those flashing waves were life; they were not death,
Or sleep. The power that made them flash was power,
It was not nothing. It was like a wish
To live, and an awakening wish to serve.
It was not what he found in Agatha's
Untroubled smile or in her living eyes

1060

Between him and her grave; it was, perhaps,
More like what he saw now while she was coming,
With the same eyes, and the same smile in them,
Between him and a sea that had no rest,
And for another moment while she flashed
And faded between him and Nightingale,
Whose eyes were those of a man trying to smile
Because he was to die.

                  "Never forget,
Malory," said his ruminating host,
"What an unvisualized and writhing city
Of pain and fear a million men and women
Would make, who are not well and have too long
To live, and strangely are not ready to die.
I don't know what a million men and women
Are worth to you, yet I can estimate,
Remotely, what equipment and resource
Is in them of indignant uselessness,
And misery too merciless and too harsh,
And undeserved, to be explainable
To eyes of earth. I have the eminence
Of my deserts, and therefore am exempt
From your attention. Now go for a walk,
Down by the shore, where you may find some shells
That once were filled with unaspiring life,
And leave me to inhabit my grand mansion,
Which I have always wanted, by the sea."

VI

With his word that he would stay until tomorrow,
He obeyed; and with a willingness unknown
For so long that he was loth to recognize it
As a wish to breathe again the breath of life,

He could see, like fallen walls of an old city
In a plain where there was only sand and death,
Dead emptiness of hate and desolation
That he would not recall. He would forget it,
And by it be forgotten. He was tired
Of deserts, and had found at last that his,
Where he had groped and stumbled for so long,
Had been too barren a place even for death
To dwell in. Death had abandoned Malory,
Or was not yet his friend. There was no friend
Anywhere, and he saw no need of one.
If glimmerings that attended him today
Were intimations of a coming light,
He was to be alone for a long time,
And with no friends in sight. If he deserved them
Or if his light required them in his picture,
No doubt they would be there eventually.
But for the present they were far away,
And better so. He would have little for them,
Or for the solace of their wakeful ears.
Their presence would be kindness at his heels,
And underfoot, imploring to be stepped on
If in the way, and angry if obeyed.
There was a time for friends that was not now.
If he should find a way back to himself,
His enemies, long pursued and long forsaken,
Would be his friends; for death, living in them,
Would be his life. There was no answer yet.
His fancies came and went, and were as vain
As a dumb wave that he saw burrowing
Among weed-muffled rocks to find a sound
That was not there. From where he stood, alone,
A few rocks and the sea was all there was
Of a life-burdened world except himself;
And he was not yet small enough to carry

THE GLORY OF THE NIGHTINGALES

A whole world's burden. There was hope in that,
If there was none in those recurrent waves
That came and lifted always the same weeds,
Until they were like coarse and floating hair
Of giant women drowned and turned to stone,
And fell to rise again to the same end
That was no end, and always came to nothing.
In clouds that came and went, there was at least
A sort of promise, for they came and went;
But here there was a promise of nothing else
Than waves and waves, and then waves, and more waves,
That went and came. There was nothing in them for men
Whose imminent need to live was a parole
And a probation; and there was less for men
Who came from Sharon yesterday to die.
He found an inland way among the trees
More to his fancy. They would not go from him
And then come back. He was tired of things that moved
And did no more. He had been one of them
So long, for the achievement of so little,
That he would rest—who had no power to rest.
He should not rest again until he died,
Which was a thing to know. If Nightingale
Told him of what was his, he would deny it,
And say it was not his. Nothing was his,
Which was another thing for him to know.

In the afternoon, with Nightingale before him,
Silent, in the same room, in the same chair,
Malory found the task of saying nothing
Only a somewhat easier one than speech.
Having his wits, he was uncomfortable
With Nightingale, who was aware of more
Than would have been a pleasure to explain
Of Malory's constraint. If in his eyes

1063

There was a stricken willingness to smile,
With any encouragement, he could find none
In Malory's face, and said, indifferently,
"I'm glad you keep your word, and are to stay
With me until tomorrow. I like doctors,
Lawyers, and criminals, and all true men
Who keep their word; also those competent
Grand-nephews of Jehu who drive our cars.
If you are willing, we'll have one of them
Here now, and we'll go rolling. With two slaves
To put me in and take me out again,
I do a deal of rolling, and feel the world
Rolling away—though you may not believe it.
For why should you believe me, Malory,
Whatever I say? And yet, you may as well.
I'll say a little more while we are going,
And seeing the world the Lord has made so fair
For our defeats and victories. *Vae victis.*
Pronounce it as you think a noble Roman
Might once have uttered it, and say it twice.
I've an impatient and laborious ear
For listening while I ride, so you need say
Only those words, and say them to yourself.
We shall have time to scan familiar scenes
Again, and I shall not be long in saying
All I shall say."

        Nightingale's word was good,
And he was not long saying to Malory
As much as was required of him to hear,
And hear without reply. "I shall not know
What you are trying to do if you insist
On argument, or on immediate speech.
So, Malory, put yourself aside, and hold
Your scientific tongue. Imprison it

Behind your teeth and say it is a tiger—
A thing to do a fractious deal of harm
If it goes wild. Besides, I have no ears,
And I am rather helpless in some ways.
Remember that; also conserve a thought
Of millions who have never heard of you
Or me, and of more millions who are coming.
So for God's sake be quiet, and admire
The outside of God's world, which is not bad.
Perhaps we may as well not go to Sharon
Today. Perhaps we may as well not go
Tomorrow. I shall go there, before long,
For there the Nightingales have always gone
When they have done their singing."

                        Malory stood
Once more by the wide window, where he saw
Those tumbling and unceasing little waves
Until it seemed that he had seen them there
Since he was born; and they were not his waves.
Yet surely they were flashing with a language
That was important and inevitable;
There were too many of them to be dismissed
By one whose life was only a little more
Of time than one of theirs. If theirs were lost,
Why should not his be lost and be as nothing
In a more stormy and unsounded ocean
Than ever filled the valleys of a world
For men to weigh and measure? There was time
For living in himself and on himself,
Like a thought-eating worm, and dying of it
Unthought of, or for life larger than that,
Larger than self, and one that was not death.
There was avengingly not time for both;
And his was not the least of wavering lives

That had not stood when shaken. He was not
The least of summoned men who had served well,
And, having lost themselves in a great darkness,
Had not returned and were no longer sought
Among the missing, and no longer missed.
Had he returned? Was this the light again,
Or was a darkness worse than any other,
A darkness only felt, deceiving him?
He was not sure of anything since that ride,
Except that it was over, and that hours
Made days and years, and not so many of them
As there were waves.

                    "Well, Malory, by my soul!"
Said Nightingale. "If I've a memory left
Of anything pleasant, and a right to say so,
That was a pleasant ride. You like my ocean
Better, perhaps; yet even if it were yours,
You would not wear a window out with watching
The same one thing, and always the same thing.
I am the watcher who can swear to that.
We've had a ride; and since you are still here,
The prisoner of your word, we'll have some drink—
Which is forbidden. I shall not die of it.
If I should die just now, I should be going
A little too soon. You, a benign pursuer
Of hidden miseries, and of hidden means
To rid a more or less debatable race
Of their pernicious presence, are excused
From caring, or trying to care, whether I die
Tomorrow or today. There are more reasons
For your not caring than I'll reiterate;
There are more reasons than there may be days
For me to say them over and be sorry
For being as I have been. For a man with eyes

THE GLORY OF THE NIGHTINGALES

To see more surely what there was before him
Than eyes of the less fortunate may see,
I have not seen so well as men supposed,
And may be still supposing. Twice in my life
I have been blind; and that was a bad matter:
Once when I sank my judgment and your money
Into that most unhappy hole in the ground;
Once when I kicked my decency and honor
In after them. My purpose is to say
So clearly what I did that I shall never
Say it again. I'm sure you understand
Everything now, except that I should do it;
And sometime when you ask a streptococcus
Why it's a streptococcus, you may learn
All that I know of a dead Nightingale
That will not die. I'll say no more of devils,
But out of all this ruin, I'll save a few
Opinions and ideas for the small profit
Of having them. I have not seen the devil,
But I have seen sufficient of his work
Not to make light of him, or to invite him
Into my house again. The ruin I made
Is not all ruin, unless you make it so.
But if you ask why Agatha was chosen
To be the innocent means and sacrifice,
You will ask more than me before you know.
I shall not tell you. I am too blind for that.
I was not blind at first with Agatha—
I was almost . . . But what's the use of time,
If it will not be done when it's all gone?
We were not going back, but Agatha
Was calling me; and when she calls, I go—
And do not find her. There is little for me
To find, wherever I look. My blemishes
And evils now are mostly a sad trash

Of memory to be swept and blown away,
Or blown so as to leave you a clear path.
You and the world are in a partnership
Too large and too impersonal to include
A presence of sick hate. You owe yourself
To your unhappy millions in your city
Of cries and silences and suffering hope.
And there are many millions more to be,
And to be stricken. The world is not all pain,
But there is pain enough ahead of it,
And in it, to ensure the resurrection
Of you and your awakening faculties
For the few hours that we call years of life
That you may find remaining. There's a bell
Ringing, and not for you. We are not subtle
Today, Malory; there's hardly need of it.
I hope it's not another one come to kill me,
For you and Absalom, the Lord's appointed—
Who lived a while in heaven before he died,
And was a king of earth, having what he wanted—
Have so enriched me with an overplus
Of armament that I shall need no more
To scare my ghosts and enemies away,
If one day there should be too many of them.
I'll fancy rather it's a man of law—
This time; and it's as well for you to know him.
You are not fearing lawyers; not today.
Wherefore, we'll have him in. He's a good lawyer,
And does not know that I'm not a good man.
He knows too many others who are worse.
He has no knowledge of the lights I had
And could not follow; and if he knew of them,
And of the several ways where I've been lost,
Most likely he would not believe in them,
Having no time for visions or inventions.

THE GLORY OF THE NIGHTINGALES

Another day you may enlighten him
Somewhat, as you think best. When you are here,
You and your microbes, and your apparatus,
Your staff, your patients, and your God knows what,
You will know why it was this house was built.
A knowledge that was out of my possession
Till yesterday is a good knowledge now
For you, and who shall say how many more?
A pleasant home for microbes, I should call it,
Though it has never been a home for me."

The lawyer's entrance came to no long writing
Of a long story. It was all revealed
In words that held a latent increment
Larger than any estate. It was not land
And houses, and abundant maintenance,
That Malory found when he was given to read
The text of Nightingale's last composition,
But an imperious, fixed, and lonely way
Of life in service. There was no escape
From the long sentence of his usefulness.
He was a slave now in a city of pain,
A pullulating place that was all places,
And soon or late the last abode of man
Till his departure. There was no fear of joy
To be a stain on his inheritance,
Except the lonely joy of being alive
In a good servitude, and of not being
Obscurely and unintelligibly wasted.
Now he could say what Agatha may have meant,
Between him and her grave, when she was there
To welcome him with an untroubled smile
On his dark road—one that would still be gray,
For him, and endless, if he found no light

For others. He was alone, and would remain so,
Until he found more light.

                          "So much for that,"
Said Nightingale; and having signed his name,
He smiled at Malory and the man of law
With purpose and approval. "It's all done,"
He said, "and I've a planet off my shoulders.
I was tired of being Atlas; for my world,
Though it was no enormous one, was heavy.
And now that you two estimable agents
Of my deliverance are not unacquainted,
I should be glad if you would leave me here
A while to be alone, and not to talk.
Be sorry for an ominous example,
And let yourselves so live that you may not
Be living on wheels one day in a large house,
Alone—not even if you have always wanted
A large house by the sea. You will come back,
But I'll shake hands with you for your assistance,
And wish you a good ride. This is a day
For riding, and a good day for some thought
On my part. It is not like every day."

They left him smiling, and, as Malory knew,
In more pain than his body alone could feel.
They rode as easy strangers, having no food
For malice or mistrust. If one of them
Acknowledged inwardly a futile envy
Of such an unforeseen and unexplained
Cascade of shining fortune for another,
Nothing was to be done to a man's name
Written by him whose name was his to write.
They rode, and had but little to say of him,
Who, seemingly, had said everything for once

And all, and on a small array of paper.
For an hour they rode, in the late afternoon,
With trees and fields and houses on one side,
And with an ocean on the other, darker
As daylight faded, and with smaller waves
That had a slower motion as they rose
And broke more quietly now, and made less foam.
They told of a beginning of long silence
That night, and were somehow, for Malory,
Like toiling, weary people, who were soon
To have some rest before they toiled again,
And for a season were not to be waves.
Having each his personal fancy for companion,
They rode, saying what the old amenities
Required as best they might, and they came back;
And when they came to Nightingale's, they rolled
Quietly in on crushed blue stone to find
A strange house not so quiet, and a stranger
Within that was invisible, and a shape
Of someone that was no one, still in his chair,
With Malory's pistol on the floor beside him.
What Malory once had called his only wealth
Had given him wealth to serve, and without waiting.
Nightingale had said nothing about waiting,
And Malory had known why.

                    Alone that evening
With all there was to see of Nightingale,
Lying at last unharassed and untorn,
Malory sat with fate, and gazed at it.
"Well, Nightingale, you are quiet enough now,"
He thought; "and you have earned now, in your way,
Or in another way that was not yours,
The privilege of a sleep—if you are sleeping.
You have bound me hand and foot, body and brain,

1071

To service. I owe to Agatha, and to you,
All that I owe mankind. It's all an owing,
For me, and shall be one till I have paid
To man my sum of knowledge, which is little,
God knows, though not so little as I should be
For hiding it, or for throwing it away.
The light you could not follow is not mine,
Which is my light—a safer one for me,
No doubt, than if it threw a gleam too far
To show my steps. There is no grief in me
For your release, and there is no hate now
For Agatha's. If I could bring her back,
By calling her, to live and die again,
I should be silent; for I cannot know
The pain there was that was not hers to suffer,
Because she was not here. I cannot know,
For certain, that your way, dark as it was,
Was not the necessary way of life.
There was in yours at least a buried light
For time and man; and science, living in time,
May find at last a gleam nearer than yours,
For those who are not born to follow it
Before it has been found. There is, meanwhile,
A native light for others, but none born
Of penitence, or of man's fear to die.
Fear is not light, and you were never afraid.
You were blind, Nightingale, but never afraid;
And even when you were blind, you may have seen,
Darkly, where you were going, and where you are.
For where you are tonight, there was your place;
And your dark glass is broken."

　　　　　　　　　　　　　　　　He looked up
From Nightingale to see, against the wall,
Dimly, and on dim wheels, a dead man's chair

THE GLORY OF THE NIGHTINGALES

With no man in it. Here was the same room
Where fate was waiting for him yesterday—
With a presence now of death to make it empty,
And the difference of a day to make it his.
Here was a place where gold would buy no sorrow,
And the embellished rhetoric of regret
Would soon be words forgotten, and no more.
There was nothing left of Nightingale but silence,
And a cold weight of mystery that was man,
And was no longer man—as waves outside
Were cold and still, and were no longer waves.
There was nothing left for Malory but remembrance
Of the best that was behind him, and life struggling
In the darkness of a longer way before him
Than a way there was from anywhere to Sharon—
A darkness where his eyes were to be guided
By light that would be his, and Nightingale's.

MATTHIAS AT THE DOOR

(1931)

To
Ridgely Torrence

MATTHIAS AT THE DOOR

I

If years had been the children of his wishes,
Matthias would have wished and been immortal,
For so he felt; and he was only as old
As half a century of serenity
Had made him. As a man deserving them,
He glowed with honors earned. He was apart,
Because, being who he was, and as he was,
His natural station would inevitably
Be somewhat on an eminence, like his house.
Approachable, yet clearly at a distance,
Matthias was in harmony with his house,
And with all else that interested him.
He was in harmony this afternoon
Even with chaos; and from where he sat,
All he could see was his. There was no sky
In the wood-shadowed and forsaken gorge
Where he was now, but there would be a sky
When he came out. Matthias loved the sun
Better than shadows, and the more for them
When he came out. Down there it was impressive,
If not for long alluring. Mighty rocks,
Like a mis-shapen city that was dead,
Were monstrous and unreal. Trees were afraid
Of them, and to a straightness and a height
That would not elsewhere have been theirs thrust up
Their tops to find the sun. Somewhere above him,
There was his house; and somewhere in his house
Was Natalie. So Matthias had no fear
To contemplate a friendly retrospect

Of a good life with no disasters in it,
And no infirm mistakes. He had done well,
Wherefore he was a good and faithful servant.
God asked of him no more; and he would ask
No more of God than was already given.
He smiled with gratitude, not vanity,
To think of that. A brook somewhere unseen
Made a cold song of an eternity
That would be always cold, and always dark,
And far from his desire. Having a right
To smile at what he would, he smiled at that,
And was content—when he heard, suddenly,
More than a brook. He started and stood up,
Straining his eyes to see what he had heard;
For he had heard the sound of coming feet
That were the uninvited feet of man,
Prowling where none should be. Matthias frowned,
And with an eye not eager met a shape
Approaching him that was at first a stranger,
But soon was one that he might recognize
Without alarm or wrath.

                    "I'm not the devil,
Matthias. I am only a lost dog.
I was too tired to bark. Forgive my trespass.
You are not God, but you are more like God,
In a few ways, than anyone else I know.
Have you not thought so? All these rocks of yours,
Piled one upon another, if possible,
Would make a mighty monument, Matthias,
Fit for a mighty man. He might be You.
Who knows why not?"

                     Matthias made a smile
That failed him in the making, and sat down.
"Your compliments are not engaging, Garth,

MATTHIAS AT THE DOOR

And you are out of breath. I am not mighty.
It is your discontent that says I am;
Surely not your discretion, or your tact."

"My tact is a lost ornament, Matthias.
Do you see it shining on me anywhere?
I lost it fighting."

             "And just when was that?"
Matthias asked. "And for about how long?"
He gave his visitor another smile,
And studied him a little. He was bent,
As only one of those are who have carried
The weight of more than time. He was not old;
He was not older than Matthias was,
Though many would have said another decade
Might have been his to count. He was alive
More with indifference than with life. His eyes
Were all there was of him that was a part
Of the original picture, and they lacked
A lustre that was right. They had seen more,
Perhaps, than eyes of men are meant to see
Of earth and earthy works.

             "Never mind when,
Matthias. I shall not fight this afternoon.
My presence here today on your possessions
May be explained. There's a place here I like
Better than any other in the world.
I doubt if you have quite entirely seen it,
Though it is yours. Everything here is yours,
Matthias. I admire and envy you,
Some relevant reservations notwithstanding.
Your progress to all this has made a noise
That would resound in a biography.

1079

And have you never thought so? No, Matthias?
I wonder if you always tell the truth.
As near, I venture, as a man may come
To telling it without knowing it—which is harder."

"I cannot understand you, or your mood,"
Matthias answered, looking at the man
As at a gaunt and harmless animal
Performing a new trick. "You have a way
Of holding one to listen, which has been
The worst of your expense. You might have paid
For less, if only you had listened more."
The trespasser made no reply to that,
Save one of a slow nod and then another,
Till, after gazing at a vast square rock
That filled the distance with a difference,
He leaned and looked Matthias in the eye
With penetrating and obscure affection
That was not love. "Matthias, I believe
That if I were to make a book of you,
I should begin like this. Or, say like this:

"Men would have said Matthias was a man
For men to emulate; and in return,
Matthias would have said as well of them
As evidence and experience, and a tongue
Stiffened with truth, would say of anything
That was not of itself essentially
The living theme. If others were alive,
And had, for reasons hidden in themselves,
An interest and a pride in their endurance
Of an estate precarious and peculiar,
Matthias would not hurt them. He would smile
At them and their mutations and elations,
At their illusions and importances,

MATTHIAS AT THE DOOR

And wonder why they were so much in earnest
Over so little. He would not hinder them
In their pursuits or their proclivities,
Or thwart them in their pleasant homely ways.
His landscape would be lonelier without them,
And they did him no harm—knowing too well
Ever to try. And why should anyone try?
He had some enemies, and no fear of them;
He had few friends, and had the need of fewer.
There was nowhere a more agreeable bondage
Than his was to himself; and where he was,
He was not anywhere else. He was not one
To move unenvied or to fade unseen,
Or to be elbowed and anonymous
In a known multitude. There was that in him
That was not theirs; and that was all of him
There was for them to know. And had a scroll
Been his that held it all for him to read,
Would he have read it, or would he have burned it?
'A mystery might be worse if it were knowledge,'
Matthias might have said; 'and though unlikely,
There may still be surprise.' "

                                    Matthias, troubled,
Looked as a child might who had cracked a nut
And found it empty. On his guard again,
He smiled and answered: "Pleasant, if not profound.
If you go on with it some day or other,
I shall be here to listen. You are welcome,
Always, on my possessions, as you call them.
Whatever you are, or not, you are not common;
And that's itself a gift—or a possession."
He mixed with his indifference an indulgence
That made the other say:

1081

"Thank you, Matthias.
I shall remember that I'm welcome here—
And always. Always is not always long.
And I am not so sure of other days
As I am of today. I like this place,
Because it's like the last of everywhere."

Matthias nodded. "Yes, it is like that.
And I should not be here too frequently,
If I were you. There is not light enough.
It is a place to see, and then to leave."

"It's a place worthy of an observation,
Matthias. Do you see that square black thing,
Down there, that's dark and large and heavy enough
To be the tomb of God? Do you see it there?
Do you see anything Egyptian in it?"

"I can see what you mean," Matthias answered;
And a slow chill that was unusual
Crept over him like a thing not alive.
"If it's a tomb, it's an unholy one,
Where I shall never worship."

                              "And why not,
Matthias? If you would seek a present help
In worshipping the gods that are all gone,
Why not as dark a shrine as possible
For seeing nothing and saying prayers to it?
Tell me why not. You are as much in the dark,
Matthias, as I am. I know the dark."

"Imagine then the gods—or mine, at least—
Out of your knowledge," said Matthias, drily.

MATTHIAS AT THE DOOR

"Would you feed others with a fruit like yours?
You cannot; for dead seeds will never grow."

"I shall not try, Matthias; for you tell me
Only what I said first. I'm not so sure
Your God is not down there, for there's a door
Down there that's like an entrance to the end.
You have not seen it yet. There's a dark place
Down there, Matthias. Do you see from here
Two pillars—one on either side? Two shafts
Carved out of solid night, they are to me,
With darker night between them. That's a door
Worth watching; and I've been watching it, Matthias.
I shall go down to it some day and knock.
Shall we go down together and admire it?
Suppose we do. You should see all that's yours
While you are here."

            Matthias followed him,
But whether for a whim, or for protection
Of an imperilled soul, he never knew.
"There's a way where we go slowly now, Matthias,
But not a long one. If you follow me,
As once, you say, I should have followed you,
We shall go on together pleasantly,
And with no casualties. Do you see it now?
Only a little farther, and I'll show you
More than you see."

            Following silently,
Matthias felt impatience twitching him
To stop, and with it felt a warning fear
To leave this man alone. Alone too long
In such a waste of evil architecture,

A man too fond of ruins, and of betraying
Himself as one, might see more than was there.

"Here's a dark place, Matthias." He heard Garth
And shivered as one who was prepared to shiver.
"Here is a place I like. I live in the dark,
And for a year have done so. Do you see it?
One of these days I shall go there to knock,
And that will be the last of doors for me.
I have knocked on too many, and for nothing.
Why do you stay so far away from me,
Matthias? I am not going to injure you.
I shall not seize you and assassinate you,
And could not if I would. You are too strong.
You are strong in body and soul, yet I'm not sure
That you are sound in your serenity.
Your God, if you may still believe in him,
Created you so wrapped in rectitude
That even your eyes are filmed a little with it.
Like a benignant sort of cataract,
It spares your vision many distances
That you have not explored. I hope, Matthias,
That you may not pursue them ruinously,
For they may come to this—which you consider
Merely a scenery. You will come down here,
Sometimes, because you do not have to stay—
Much as a child goes into a dark room
Intending to be scared. If I were praying,
I should not pray that you be undeceived,
Or be discredited by revelation,
For that would be a waste of your God's time.
You are among the few that are contented,
Seeing the many scratch—as I have scratched,
Only to find an earth with nothing in it
But fool's gold, which is rather less than iron."

MATTHIAS AT THE DOOR

"I cannot say that you are doing more,"
Matthias answered, "than improvisation
That failure loves to sing. It's not good music
For one so far along as you to make—
And last, if anywhere, in a place like this.
Since you are candid, I'll be confidential,
And ask why such funereal interest
In my affairs has overtaken you.
Why should the blight of my discrepancies
Be shared so as to vex and agitate you?
Has envy bitten you, and so late as this?"

"Forgive me—I was looking at my door,
Matthias, or I should have answered you.
It's all a matter of shadows. Do you see it?
From here I see a dark Egyptian door—
Which, if it opened, as it will for me,
Might lead you to another. I don't think so,
And am no longer curious. Do you see it?
It's only a dark hole in a dark rock,
If you see only that. You will see more,
Matthias. You have not yet seen anything."

With what Matthias fancied was no more
Than cold annoyance, he said, rather sadly,
"I'm sorry to have bred in you the venom
That you have spattered so vindictively
Over my reputation—which, if guarded,
Will hardly die of it. I am sorry, Garth,
But I should have to be the God you scorn
Before I made you over, or young again.
When we began together, you had eyes
And ears; and you forgot that you had either.
Am I to blame that you are sorry now,

1085

Or if you talk of—doors? The more you talk,
The more will they be closed. Why are we here?
Why do you bring me here?"

                       "Why does a bat
Fly in the night, Matthias? Why is a fish
Ungrateful if you catch him? Why does a bird
Wear feathers and not fur? Why do you sleep
At night, not sure of waking? Why did you,
When we were young together, walk in your sleep,
And scare me in the moonlight when I met you?
Why do you wear that scar on your right hand,
Where you were burned when you saved Timberlake?
Are you sorry that you saved him?"

                           "Am I sorry?"
Matthias asked. "If words are only trash
For you to throw away, why not be still,
And throw them all away?"

                       "Well, I was asking,
Matthias. If you had left him there to die,
You might have spared a man a deal of living—
Which has not been too easy, I'm assured,
And has not been too fruitful, I'm certain.
It's all a matter of our congruities.
They make us as we are."

                    "Have yours made you?"
Matthias asked. "You have made yours, I'd say,
A cushion for your malevolence to lie on.
If you are wise, you will come up with me
And out of this—out of this into daylight,
If any such thing is left."

MATTHIAS AT THE DOOR

                              "You followed me,
Matthias, half afraid there was a door
Down here for you to see, and you have seen it.
My house is built, and so is yours, Matthias.
No, I'll stay here in the dark. I live in the dark.
I have been here so many times before
That once more is no matter. So go along
With God, and leave me here with only a door.
Tomorrow will be Sunday, which is good.
We shall not have to work."

                              "You will not work,
Whatever you call tomorrow," said Matthias,
Not oversure that he had said his best.
Feeling two eyes behind him in the gloom,
He clambered back, as he would from a city
Of tombs and shadows in a nameless land
Where there was left one living. As he moved,
A prickling chill pursued and captured him,
And held him—till he saw through trees again
The sky, and then his house that was alive.
The sight of anything then that was alive
Would have been resurrection; and the sight
Of one that he found living was like heaven.
"Is it you, Natalie? Are you alive?"
He asked; and held her shoulders to be sure.
"Whether it's you or not, don't go away."
He closed his eyes in gratitude for light
And love, and saw confronting him again
The silence of a dark Egyptian door.
He blinked, and brushed his eyes with a cold hand,
So to see real a more agreeable vision
Of a slim woman's easy stateliness,
Which never failed or faltered, or was false
To its design. An edible cleanliness

                    1087

Of countenance that hungry time forgot,
A straight nose, and large eyes that you called hazel,
And a firm mouth, made a face fair enough
To serve, or to be served. Over it all
Was a close crown of hair—a tawny bronze
Of shades and changes. Natalie called it red.

"Where have you been, Matthias?" Half amused
And half afraid, she waited. "I'd imagine
You have been seeing demons—or been walking
Where there are spirits."

                    He looked away from her,
Over his shoulder, where the shadows were
From which he had escaped, while Natalie stared,
Not knowing whether or not to be alarmed.
"I have," he said. "I have been seeing Garth."

II

A calm untroubled Sunday afternoon
Was always, for Matthias, a good hour
For thanks, and for acquisitive meditation
On who should feel him next and yield to him.
He was no worse than others not unlike him,
And he was worthier far than many of them
Who pelted him with envy or maligned him
With mirrored attributes of enmity
That was not his, but theirs. He did not hate them;
He measured and reduced them. They annoyed him
So little as only to admonish him
To a more capable humility
In his achievement; and a pleasant Sunday,
With daylight fading, was a time prepared
For peace, and for thanksgiving, and for rest.

MATTHIAS AT THE DOOR

But there was less today of any of these
Than he had known since he was born. Today
There were new shadows while it was too early
For shadows, and there was a recurring chill
While it was not yet cool or late enough
For any such thing to be. It was so warm
That Natalie, preoccupied and restive,
Was saying nothing till Matthias told her
Where her thoughts were.

                              "And why are you so still,
Now that he's gone? He was not much to you,
Or me, or anyone; and was least of all
To himself. He was a poor defeated soul,
And one for God to judge. I do not judge him.
I'm sorry for him."

                      "Why did you send men
Down to that awful hollow in the night,
As if you knew they were to find him there?"
Natalie asked. "When you came yesterday
Out of that place, you looked as if the dead
Had driven you out."

                        "Because I came from there
With two eyes following me, and a man's words
That would not leave my ears. They were not words
That we are here to say. I did not know,
Until too late, that one who was alive
Was dead already—which is not uncommon,
Or not unknown."

                      "It does not seem uncommon
To me," she said, and sighed. "There are so many
Who are like that, that I have wondered why.

But to creep into a hole and poison himself
In the dark—it was not nice. Were I to do it,
Should I be weak, or brave—in your opinion?
You have opinions."

       "And I hope, my dear,"
He said, with lips that smiled, "that when time calls
On you for bravery, it will be for more
Becoming and heroic proof of it
Than going into a hole in a dark rock
And dying there alone. I may have doubts,
And a few fears, but none of them are drawn
To make a picture of you doing such things
As that. O yes, I'm only a man living—
While God permits; and I must have therefore
My doubts and common fears. I have a fear
Of growing old that is unnatural—
One that I might believe my only fear.
I like to live. I would live on with you,
And always. Which a woman, if driven to it,
Might make herself believe a compliment."

She felt his warm proprietary eyes
Admiring and possessing her, and smiled.
"Or you might, after a few centuries,
Be tired of her, and have eyes for another,"
She said. "We are not old enough to know
All things; and I'm as happy that we are not."

"I have seen happier faces, if none fairer,
Than yours today," he said. "Your thoughts are living
Down there too long—down there in the dark, with him.
But he is not there now, and you had better
Be somewhere else. You had better be here, with me.
I like to see you here. You are so fair

MATTHIAS AT THE DOOR

To me, sometimes, that I'm afraid of you—
Or rather of the place my world would be
Without you in it."

     "It would be the same,"
She said; "or it would be so nearly so
That only you would see the difference.
The worlds we live in are not very large,
With room in them for only a few faces.
We meet the others, but we do not see them."

Matthias looked away over the trees
That filled the gorge below. "You will have moods
Until you die," he said, "and I am sorry.
They are like summer clouds that make us ask
If more are coming."

     "No, there are no more coming,"
Said Natalie. "It was only that poor man,
Down there alone, where you were yesterday."
She turned, hearing a sound more felt than heard
Of one behind her, and Matthias rose.

"So long as this poor man is out of it,
And unaccused, he'll have his innocence
To travel on," said a melodious voice.
"God help the homeless. I am glad to see you.
Matthias, you are solemn."

     "It's all Garth,"
He said; "and I was saying, Timberlake,
To Natalie that Garth will do no harm
To anyone now—unless she thinks of him
Unwisely."

    "I should not think of him unwisely;
And I should not forget him; or not wholly—

Or not at once." This man who had arrived
So quietly found a chair, and with the others
Looked off across the trees. He had blue eyes
That held a kindly sparkle, not so bright
As it was once, and a face made of wrinkles.
The story of the world was in his wrinkles,
Natalie said, if one could only read them;
Yet they were not the manuscript of age,
Or of decrepitude. He was built straight
And tight, and with a tree's economy
Of slender strength. His face would have been hard,
But for a gentleness that softened it
Somehow to a thin sort of living leather,
Browner than red—a face for women to see,
While other faces waited. "I came home
And heard of Garth," he said, "and was no more
Surprised than you are. I have outlived surprise—
Which is my symptom of antiquity;
For which I beg your pardon."

                           "You had better,"
Natalie said, and made a face at him:
"If I should find myself without an age,
And crying for one, I could almost wear yours."

"No, I am not surprised. I am only sorry."
Matthias looked at Natalie, whose answer
Was nothing that she said.

                           "And why be sorry?"
Timberlake looked at each of them in turn,
Saying his question over silently.

"I am sorry more for leaving him alone,"
Matthias answered, "than for his leaving life

1092

MATTHIAS AT THE DOOR

Behind him. There was no purpose left in it,
For him; and I'll assume it was God's way,
Not his, that he was taking when he left us.
I can afford forgiveness, I dare say,
Of all he said to me."

          "And what was that?"
Timberlake asked. His blue eyes held a laugh
That all his vigilance would not conceal,
And all his wrinkles listened.

          "It was more,
If I may say so, than was necessary,
And more than I've a reason to remember.
It was the old confusion failure makes,
And will make always—or as long as men
Prefer to fail. I am not judging him;
I'm only sorry that he should make a show
For me, at last, of an undying envy.
I should have said, indeed, that in his envy
There was, till yesterday, a friendliness
That was almost affection. I was friendly,
But I was not his guardian, or torch-bearer.
My own torch was as many as I could carry,
And trim, and keep alive. Seeing him so bitter
In his contempt of God, and man, and me,
I might have wondered that he was not angry;
But now I see that his intent was only
To put me in my place. Poor soul! Poor soul!
When I see folly that has pawned its wings
Hating itself because it cannot fly,
I'd rather turn my eyes the other way."

"You always do, Matthias," Natalie said,
And smiled with a demure impulsiveness
Of one not meaning to be critical.

1093

Timberlake held his lips together tightly,
So that he might not grin, saying at last,
"That was in ways an able argument,
And in ways mostly music. I'm like you,
Matthias, in my not judging those who leave us,
Or those who are still here. Natalie says
I'd better not. And now that Garth is gone,
I'll say to you it will be safe and friendly
On your part to believe that he was friendly—
As I believe he was. In his last hours
He may have lost himself, and his proportions.
For all I know, a fellow may swerve a little
In his diplomacy before he swallows
At once what's left of life. Having heard Garth,
And seen him, yesterday, you may know more
Of that than I. For me, I'll trust the chances.
I shall not go until my name is called."

Matthias, with a sudden inward flinching,
Saw fronting him again, as in a darkness,
A dark Egyptian door. He sighed, and smoothed
His forehead with his hand. "No, Timberlake,"
He said, "we are not waiting for an end
In any dark hole for you. You are not wise
In all ways, and you are not silly enough
To see yourself dishonored and destroyed
By needless failure and futility."

"My sovereign sometimes has a tendency
To the sententious. And why say 'dishonored,'
Matthias?" Natalie asked.

                    "Matthias means
'Unfortunate,' maybe," said Timberlake.
"Our words have our complexions, like our skins.

MATTHIAS AT THE DOOR

Accomplishment and honor are not the same,
Matthias; and one may live without the other."

"Yes, Timberlake. A man may throw himself
Utterly to the dogs and say to them
That his accomplishment is less than honor.
The dogs would be impressed." Matthias chuckled.

"Of course," Natalie said. "He should say, 'Dogs,
I am not much, but I am honorable.
So wag your tails at me, and do not bark.'
That would soon quiet them."

                        "Perhaps it would,"
Matthias muttered, after a long breath.
"My God! I'm tired of all this easy greasing
Of rusted wheels with soft apology.
Do you think that will make them go again?
If Garth was honest—and I'll go as far
With you as to say that—am I not honest?
Men who are soft will say that I am hard,
Only because they can't make holes in me.
I can see nothing so miraculous
Or damnable in my not being a fool."

"You are not judging him," said Natalie;
"You are doing with him as he did yesterday
With you. You are just putting him in his place."

He came as near to scowling at his wife
As a man should, and said, respectfully,
"Forgive me if I have a few convictions
As to what we should make of what we are."

"You have a right to them," said Timberlake;
"Though as an errant brother I'm not feeling

Any too sure today of how my doings
May look to a stern eye. If you, Matthias,
Were not a friend of mine, I might by now
Be cheered with your unprejudiced estimation
Of my deserts. I am as honorable
As possible, but you have not seen my house
Which I shall never build."

                     Matthias gazed
At Timberlake and, smiling, shook his head:
"We can do nothing with a man like you
But leave you as you are—to go your way."

"To the same dogs, you think, that followed Garth.
It may be so. Sometimes I'll hear a barking,
And ask how far away the brutes may be."

"Not the same, Timberlake. You are not Garth.
There are dogs, and dogs. If Garth had kicked the first
Out of his way, he would have scared the others."

"Perhaps the others would have bitten him,
And not been scared at all," said Natalie;
And her words had a sharpness for Matthias
That he had never felt before: "I'm not
So sure that you know all there is to know
Of dogs, and dogs. It may be that we'd best
Not know too much of what their teeth may do
Till we are bitten. I can fancy them
Following us without our seeing them
And tearing us to death. It's not their barking,
Matthias, that mangles us; it is their teeth.
Garth could have told you. He had felt their teeth,
And he had bled where they had bitten him.
None of us know for certain when the dogs
Are on the watch, or what they are waiting for.

1096

And as for Garth, I doubt if it's as easy
To write his life in saying he was a fool
As you imagine. I can find other names
For one who did much good, and did no harm.
I find a sort of bravery, if you like,
In his way out. Try it yourself, and tell me."
She laughed at Timberlake, who stared at her,
And at Matthias, and in a wonderment
Of premonition. "Never mind me," she said;
"I'm in a mood. Matthias knows I have them,
Or should know; and he knows how to forget them."

"Twilight will be around us before long,"
Said Timberlake; "and I don't see in the dark.
I've had for some time an uneasiness
Of one who has arrived at a wrong hour.
Garth has upset your hive, and all your bees
Are flying about your heads and about mine,
As active as they are invisible.
You may not hear them, but they make a noise
Like thunder rumbling in another world—
Which may be one where Garth is. So good night,
And wish me joy, for I am going home.
My home is where I take my collar off,
And presently my shoes."

                    Natalie flashed
A look at Timberlake that he remembered;
And then, remembering it, she laughed. "Good Lord!
Don't go away," she said, "leaving us here,
Or Garth may come between us, like a sword;
Which would be awful, and unnecessary."

"Some of your language is unnecessary,"
Matthias warned her, gently. "Why is Garth

A burden for you now? He won't come back;
And I can show no better friendliness
To him than in my joy he may not;
For the same life would be awaiting him,
And one more death. For cause that was apparent,
Dying was his career. When a man says
Unceasingly what things he is to do,
Until he says at last he can do nothing,
He meets a desperation."

          "Or a dog,"
Said Natalie, "whose name is Desperation.
I shall shriek, certainly, if this goes on.
Women are funny, but there's nothing alive
So funny as men when they are telling others
How to put fate in a cage—as they have done."

"I'll set mine free and follow it, and go home,"
Timberlake said, and rose. "When fates are restive,
They let us know. Natalie, you had best
Believe Matthias, and say no more of Garth.
He has gone forward, and that's well for him."

She seized him with a long inquiring look
That was not happy. "How do you know," she said,
"Where Garth has gone? I'd fly for such a knowledge."

He waited there, with his eyes held by hers,
Till all three in the twilight, though together,
Were like three strangers who were there alone.
"I don't," he said. "Good night." And he was gone.

Natalie turned her face to find Matthias
Observing her with eyes that had a light
As kind as twilight. "He might be as far

MATTHIAS AT THE DOOR

Away from us," he said, "for all we see,
As Garth has gone. He leaves a loneliness."

"It might be so," she said, "if it were so.
A lonely chair, a match, and a few ashes,
Are like a death, saying where friends have been—
Friends who may not return. They will be there,
Sometime, for the last time. That's Garth again,
Giving me fancies. I must have liked that man.
I'm sorry if I was too unsociable,
Matthias; and if I was, it was all Garth."
She tapped his cheeks and kissed him on the nose,
Which had for years been her best way of saying
That everything was right.

                  She would have moved
Away then, but she failed. She felt his hands
Like iron that held her without hurting her,
And her arms yielded. She looked up at him
With a serenity that bewildered him,
Smiling with eyes in which he could see twilight,
And waiting for his hands to let her go.
She laughed at him, and then she said, "What is it?"

For a long time she waited for an answer
That would not come. Only his tightening hands
Told her that he had heard, until he said,
"Women like you are not demonstrative,
And men like me may not be always vocal."

"If I were too demonstrative, Matthias,
I might surprise you. Now it is you, instead,
Who are surprising me. I'm rather patient,
And have been cherished for my disposition;
Yet, I suppose, if it should have no end,

I might be weary of this. What have I done?
What is it?"

             With eyes unwilling to leave hers,
He watched her while his hands, reluctantly,
Released her prisoned arms. "Nothing," he said.
"Nothing," he said again. "It was all Garth."

III

Natalie, playing lightly with an envy
Of almost anything not herself alive,
And everything not alive, saw the years coming,
And having seen more of them than were important,
Smiled at herself and wished herself extinct—
Or said so to the cat, who pondered it,
As if in doubt, and went to sleep again.
She sat where they had spoken yesterday
So carelessly of Garth, who in time gone
Had sat there with them and as carelessly
Promised himself the wealth that was for him
His pillow and his dream—not that he cared
For wealth, but for the quieting of some tongues.
Matthias, long familiar with it all,
Had been for years indulgent and amused,
But now for years had nodded, and sometimes
Had yawned. It was his tongue, more than another,
Garth would have quieted. Now Garth was quiet,
Natalie thought, and missed him. She had liked him—
Partly for his futility, perhaps,
Having one something like it as her own
To nourish and conceal.

             From where she was
She looked down on the tops of the same trees
That had been there when she had told Matthias

1100

MATTHIAS AT THE DOOR

She loved him—which was temperately true.
She did not hate him, and had married him
For reasons old as history, and as good
As reasons mostly are when they are found.
"I might have married Garth and starved to death,
Or Timberlake, if he had seen it so,
And maybe poisoned him," Natalie said,
To herself and to the trees. The trees and rocks
Down there were calling her. There was a place
Below those twinkling peaks of oaks and birches
Where men who had been sent there by Matthias
Had found Garth in a square hole, like a door
In a square monstrous rock that she remembered
As one too large to be. More like a tomb,
Where man's hand for a time had followed nature's,
Than a thing there by chance, it would be there
When Egypt was forgotten, and was calling
Natalie to come down to the dark place
Where they found Garth. She was afraid to go,
Which may have been a reason why she went.
"I wonder why we go to see the places
Where those we liked have died," she thought, "and why
We feel as if there must be something there.
I wonder if I'm different from the others
Who are like me."

                    Down where the gorge began,
Leaving the sky behind her, she could feel,
Like an embrace of an unpleasant stranger,
The chilliness of an untimely twilight
Surrounding her, and holding her at first
With no heart to go on. Yet on she went,
And down; and on again and down again,
Until there was a rock that filled the distance

With a square darkness. On she went, and down,
And down, and down, till she could see a blot
That might have been a door, with two dim pillars,
Carved out of night, on either side of it.
And she saw now, knowing before she saw him,
That she was not the only one alive,
There in that place of death.

                    "So it is you,"
She said; "and it was in there they found *him*.
Why don't you say you are surprised to see me?"

"I have outlived surprise, I told you so
Last night," said Timberlake, regarding her
With a sad pleasure that belied laconics
Until her silence warned him, and he smiled:
"A normal morbid mortuary impulse
Brought me to see this place, as it did you.
Why should I be surprised? Are you surprised?"

"Never, by you. If they had found you there
Instead of Garth, I should have shed some tears
Of nature, none of wonder."

                    "Am I worth,
To you, the moisture of a natural grief
After these years?" He shrugged, and turned his eyes
To the square darkness in the giant rock
Before him. "If I said it the wrong way,
It was because the past got hold of me—
When you and I and Garth, and good Matthias,
Were young and uninformed. Matthias thinks
That he was informed always, but he wasn't,
And is not yet—which is good providence

For him, and a good security for you.
The more I think of it, the less I'm certain
There was not too much joy on Ararat
When they all sat and watched the water falling.
It must have pleased the animals."

                                    "If it's Garth
Telling you that," she said, "we'll go away.
I'm not a skylark lately, and that hole
Is too dark for a door; and your bright words
Make it no lighter. I have seen the place,
And seeing it is enough. He was in there.
I wonder where he was and what he suffered
Before he found his way there. We don't know,
And so had best be still. Matthias says
Garth was a fool."

                    "Matthias may be right,"
Said Timberlake. "So many of us are waiting
To wear the mark of some such name as that,
That he may throw it where he will, almost,
Assured that it will stick. He's a good man—
Matthias—and you know what else he is.
I love him none the less; I love him more
Than you do, Natalie. He saved my life,
But that's not why. You see, I'm sorry for him,
Which is one reason. There are other reasons,
And they are things of nature—like those tears
You might have shed for me. Matthias needs
As many friends now as there are commandments,
Or more than any man has. Once he had two,
One of them being Garth—for what he was;
Now he has one—for what he is—in me.
The miracle is, he cares. Why should he care
For what is left of me? . . . What—who is this!"

Natalie, while he asked, was in his arms—
Where she would stay or fall. He felt her there,
Clinging and shaking in a desperation
So long imprisoned that escape at last
Was only to another. Timberlake
Held her and wondered what her life had been
To break like this, while a great helplessness
Humbled and stung him. She was his to take
Or fly with, if he would. He had known that;
And there was more than that. He kissed her mouth,
And face and eyes, and held her closer to him,
Remembering why it was he was alive,
And at whose peril. Then she freed herself,
As if in anger, and stood looking at him,
Her mask of resignation all washed off
With tears. "You know," she said, "we are two ghouls,
Coming down here like this to watch a hole
Where a man died. Worse yet, we are two fools.
I hope you are beginning to know that."
She sat down on a rock and laughed at him
Like an unhappy witch, with a warm face
That was itself a witchcraft.

                "It's not easy
For me to be a scholar, with you near me,
And never was." He leaned against a boulder,
And for a time saw nothing but a face
Below him, looking up, and seriously
Said nothing, till he found a few poor words
That had a wealth of melancholy truth:
"There was too heavy a credit on his side,
And there was little on mine; we'll say enough,
When added carefully, to make a sum
About as large as ordinary honor—
Which, if it's all we have, is more than . . ."

1104

MATTHIAS AT THE DOOR

"Say it,

Say it," she said. "Say it is more than love,
Say it is more than happiness, more than life.
Say it is more than everything else together;
And I'll say, when you're done, we are two fools.
Down in me somewhere I'll agree with you,
And then I'll say again, we are two fools.
It does me good to say it, and I enjoy it.
You should have married me, and tortured me,
And got drunk, and left me for other women,
And then come back when you were tired of them.
I should have been the devil and hated you,
And scratched, and made fur fly all over the house,
And loved you, and one day I might have killed you,
And then myself. That would have been all right.
We should have killed each other, and so known
That we had lived a little before we died.
Can you see there no comfort? What do you see
In this? It looks to me a waste of being,
And a more desolate foolishness for knowing
Just what it is." She looked up at him, smiling,
With tears running unhindered from her eyes
And down her cheeks, like little brooks. "Matthias
Would be surprised at this, if you are not;
And I should tell him. There isn't so much to tell,
More than to say we are three fools together,
Each in a crumbling foolish human house,
With no harm done—save two of them in ruins,
And one of them built happily on a lie.
He thinks I love him, and so throws away
No time or pride in asking why in the name
Of heaven and earth I shouldn't. That's his way.
He married me and put me in a cage
To look at and to play with, and was happy—
Being sure of finding me, when he came home,

1105

With my face washed and purring. Poor Matthias!
He says I'm not demonstrative, God bless him,
And he says prayers because I'm not a fright.
He's a good man, and has been good to me—
But what if many a man like him should learn
Somethings that many a man must never know?
Now look at me, and say, to comfort me,
That I'm a fool. You know that you are one—
Honor or not." She made a face at him,
And rubbed her eyes with a wet handkerchief
That was by now almost invisible.

He watched her, fancying she was like a child
Who had been crying and was tired of it;
But that was no long fancy. "I'm afraid,"
He said, "that he may soon learn some of them.
Garth, I've a notion, tore a few farewell holes
In the rich web of his complacency,
Letting some truth come in. Whether Matthias
Would see the truth, or would see only holes,
Is a new question. I'm not answering that,
But there's an answer, or say half an answer,
For one of yours—if yours was ever a question.
You know the story in a distant way,
And I would rather never bring it nearer.
I don't mind what you call me, or mind saying
That all your names will be as true as tar;
Yet in my wilderness I'd like to save
One refuge for reflection and escape.
While you were speaking I saw only your face;
For there was nothing else—until it melted
Into time going back, and I was there
Strangling, in that accursed house again,
Roused out of heavy sleep by knocks and yells
To find myself there swimming, it seemed. in smoke

MATTHIAS AT THE DOOR

Too thick to breathe. I knew there was a door
Where I should never find it; and I drowned
There in that ocean of death-heavy smoke
While it was battered in. All I could see—
While I could see—was red light and more smoke,
And hardly much of either. Light went out
Entirely then, and all remembrance of it,
Until I was awake in a dark room,
And heard Matthias. He was asking for me,
And there was friendship trembling in his voice,
As memory will in music we have heard
Somewhere before. I forget many voices,
But not that voice of his, or what it said,
There in the dark."

         "No, you must not forget it,"
Natalie said; "and you must not forget,
If ever you learn, to tell me why it is
Our fates and ways are so malignantly
Mixed up that it's a miracle to me
So few of us die crazy. I can see
What's coming for you to say. It's all I've seen,
Or guessed, for twenty years."

         "I know," he said,
And with unanswered eyes he watched the place
Where Garth had been, as if in envy of him.
"There's a malignance in the distribution
Of our effects and faculties. It is nature,
And our faith makes it more. If it's no more,
Garth waited longer than was logical
For a good atheist who believed himself
And life a riot of cells and chemistry—
If he believed it. You say you believe it,
But in that curious woman's apprehension

1107

Of yours there broods a doubt that frightens you
More than annihilation."

       "The last thing
To frighten me would be that," said Natalie.
"It's only that I have never been quite ready."

Timberlake only smiled. "Well, to go back,
When I awoke there was night everywhere.
If I had eyes, I knew they were on fire,
And of no use to me. I heard Matthias,
And only wished that he had never found me;
More of me than my eyes had lost all seeing;
And when my eyes returned I saw Matthias,
All scorched and swaddled, and so happy to see
That I could see, that I was sorry and sick
For wishing in the dark. Don't wish in the dark;
Or never until you know there's no more light,
Which is a difficult knowledge. If you tell me
You know what's coming of what I'm trying to say,
I'm willing enough you should. I knew Matthias
Had found that my unworthiness of you
Was like an apparition stalking always
Between him and your love. Yes, you are right:
I made myself more worthless than I was—
For his sake, and, as I saw then, for yours.
I don't know what it is that I see now.
If you were not the world and heaven together
For him and his complacent faith in you,
There might be some escape, or compromise
With fire-born obligation even like mine;
Or a maybe-beneficial cataclysm
Might be the best way out, but I don't know it.
Whether my one way then was folly or fate,
Is more, no doubt, than I deserve to know;

MATTHIAS AT THE DOOR

Only, I know that I am glad somewhere
Within me, where so little deserves a wreath,
For one thing right—or not. Fire leaves a mark
On friendship that would be a brand on love,
Always in sight; and even without Matthias,
You might have paused. If you had come to me
For happiness, you might well have murdered me,
As you so playfully have intimated.
I should have tripped and slipped and broken the eggs
Until you might have starved yourself to madness.
There's no slight fire in you, my child; and time,
Developing combustion, might have achieved
An earthquake, or a woman-quake, within you
That would have blown our problematic house
To chips and flinders, and ourselves as well;
Which would have been more picturesque than pleasant,
More ruinous than unique. The same has happened;
And I have helped, and burned my fingers helping,
To rescue out of hot and smoking ruins
A few things yet worth saving. It's dark work,
And mostly smoke and ashes. Half the grief
Of living is our not seeing what's not to be
Before we see too well. You have Matthias,
And a safe nest. I'm ready enough to know
How far that is from nothing."

                       Natalie laughed,
And dug holes in the air with nervous fingers.
"When you poor men look in from the outside
With your well-meaning and unmarried eyes,
And see so much, and tell us all about it,
What has a woman left to do but laugh—
Unless she cries? I'm tired of crying now,
And tired of this unearthly place. Come here."

1109

She reached up for his hands and drew him slowly
Down on his knees, and having him there, surprised him,
Who had outlived surprise, by seizing him
And holding his hot lips with hotter lips
That had alive in them the fire of death
To burn him till he knew what he had lost,
And might have thrown away. Slowly at last
There was an end of that, and she sat gazing
At the black rock that she had come to see,
A rock with a dark entrance like a door.
He lifted her and held her while she pointed,
Like a child frightened, at the place where Garth
Had entered and had stayed. "He was in there,"
She said; and they went silently together
Away from there, together and each alone,
Climbing to find a sky.

                Another twilight
Found Natalie, still alone, where she had seen
Matthias in his chair, and Timberlake,
Who would not come tonight. Matthias came,
As always, and as never before; for silence
Came with him, and attended him along
The dim veranda, where he passed her twice,
And twice again, before he stopped and said:
"You chose a merry place for love, you two,
Down there this morning. You should have gone in
Where Garth went—where there was more privacy."

Natalie waited, but he said no more
"I see, Matthias." Hesitating only
A moment, she stood up, and without fear
Or care for any danger or disaster,
Said calmly: "You had better know, Matthias.
I'll be direct, and so not like a woman

MATTHIAS AT THE DOOR

As to astonish you, but you will know me.
It's not so dark here that you cannot see me.
Whether you went before me, or came after,
This morning, is no matter. You were there.
Whether you saw me distantly or clearly,
Whether or not you heard me, is no matter.
So long as you were there, that's everything.
I went without a wish and with no fancy
That I was not alone, and found him there.
He was there to see that place. He was drawn there,
As I was; and what followed was my fault,
If it was anyone's fault. You saw me there;
And if you heard me, you heard all there is.
There is no more; there'll never be anything more.
There was a man I would have married once,
And likely to my sorrow, but you saved him
Out of the fire—and only saved yourself
By mercy of a miracle. You were brave,
Matthias; and because he was your friend,
That man gave me to you, first having given
Himself to folly, and to waste worse than crime.
I don't know yet whether he loves me really,
Or if it's in him to love any woman
Save as a game and an experience.
I know that I'd have given myself to him,
Not caring whether or which. But it was you
Who saved him from the fire, and he remembers,
As he remembered then. He is your friend,
And sometime you may know, wherever he is,
Your need of him. I married you, Matthias,
Because I liked you, and because your love
Was too real to be tortured, and because
There was no better thing for me to do.
Houses are built on more infirm foundations
Than ours, and some of them are standing well.

1111

I would not have you walking in your sleep—
Not after this—as you have said you walked
When you were young. Were we ever young, Matthias?
It must have been a long, long time ago.
You see me as I am, and have been always.
I am not lying to you. Do you believe me?"

Matthias, like an image in the gloom,
Stood silent, looking only at the floor,
While Natalie felt creeping from his eyes
Tears that she could not see. It might have been
For minutes or for hours that he stood there,
And she stood watching him. "Yes, I believe you,"
He said, and stumbled as he walked away.

IV

Natalie, now alone with hours and days
And nights, found a soul-wearing company
For loneliness in their continuance
To no end she could see. There was no quiet
In silence that was only a slow dread
Of when it should be broken, and no comfort
In waiting for the coming of a man
Whose joy of long serenity and content
Her words had killed. It might as well be so,
She reasoned; for the best and blindest faith
Is dead when it may be deceived no more.
There was no purpose left in her not saying
She was alone; for when Matthias came,
Sooner or later, she would be as far
From him as she had been from Timberlake,
When they had climbed that morning, and together,
Out of that perilous place to find a sky
Above them and a world that never should be

A world of theirs. Now she had found another,
And one that would be hers, and cruelly hers,
While she was in it. Timberlake had left it;
Matthias would never recognize or find it
When he came back. His was another place,
Not hers to enter—and a lonelier place,
Perhaps, than hers; and she had made it so.
Matthias had been told, and he was gone—
Not saying how far away, or for how long,
And his new world was with him where he was.
Natalie thought of that, and of a love
Too real, she had informed him, to be tortured,
And all for this. He had not soiled his love,
Or made possession cheap, or flaunted rights
Of ownership that would have smeared respect.
He knew his way with her amenities,
As with men's power and worth in his affairs
And traffics. There was much good in Matthias—
If only one could love him. One man did,
In his man's way, and Timberlake was gone.
He was not coming back. The mark of fire
Was on his friendship, and was on his love
For Natalie—if it was love. She doubted
If he knew what it was, and would have given
Herself to doubt—her love being more than doubt,
Or death.

        Matthias, coming silently,
As he had gone, found Natalie as fair
And undisturbed and undemonstrative
As he had left her. The one change he found
Was in his world, which he had taken with him
And brought home with him. It was an incubus—
A thing to be acknowledged and endured,
Like an incurable new malady

1113

Without a name, an ill to be concealed
And never mentioned. Once on a time a world
With one man in it might have been amusing
And harmless in imagining, like a sea
With one fish in it somewhere; but he found
No peace or privilege now in contemplating
Any such world or sea. He was alone—
Alone as he supposed no other man
Was ever alone before. He had read books
About the foiled and the unsatisfied,
Who should have had more sense, and he had known
Many, like Garth, who had succumbed and fallen
Rather than work and climb. But never before
Had he perceived among the foiled and fallen
An adumbration of one like himself,
And would not yet perceive it. He was apart,
As he had always been; and though alone,
He would be always on an eminence.
Natalie should know that.

                    Like one who knew it
By listening unrevealed and hearing him
Through silence, he could see her coming now,
All as if nothing in the world had happened
That had not always been. "I think, Matthias,"
Natalie ventured, "patches are better than holes.
I'll ask you if my notion is a good one,
Or just a preference—or an intuition.
I feel it as a good one. A ship sinks
If it has holes in it that are not patched—
And even in calm weather, like today.
I should hate shipwreck on a quiet sea,
Matthias; and heaven defend us from a storm.
If I had wronged you or been false to you
In more than thought, there would be reefs and havoc

All round us, for I know you. But is thought
So fierce and unappeasable a monster—
When it is only thought? How many good men,
Like you, are told of all their wives are thinking?
Most wives are full of thoughts. O yes, they think,
Matthias, and mostly nothing comes of it.
I don't say always. I'm saying that my wishes,
If they are strong enough, will hold our ship
Together for some time yet, with only ourselves
To know that underneath, where none may see them,
There are some patches to keep death away.
Matthias, if only your bewildered pride
Would lend its eyes to your imagination,
You would see ships afloat with patches hidden
That would be worse and larger far than ours
Would have to be. Meanwhile I see dark water
Filling our ship; and it's for you to say
Whether or not we sink. I'd rather we sailed,
With a flag flying."

           Matthias, who had scowled
And looked away while he was listening,
Saw facing him the picture of a woman
No longer his. Her body and her face
Would always be as fair to see as ever,
And only fair to see. The woman herself
Was not for him, and never had been for him;
And it was to that woman he had said
Garth was a fool. A knife was hurting him,
But he made out to smile: "Yes, I suppose
We'd better sail, with a flag flying—somehow.
To sink would be conspicuous and dramatic;
And drama is a show that's always played
By someone else. Yes, we had better sail."
His face grew hard again, and he was gazing

Over the shining tops of oaks and birches,
Growing out of a gorge that held a darkness
That was like memory.

               "I am glad you say so,"
She said, and with a sigh repeated it,
Wearily to herself. "If I could find
Your God, or what you call it, to believe in,
Matthias, I could praise him for creating
A world no worse than this. He might have done it,
If he had tried, and how much worse a mess
We mortals might be making of ourselves
Is only for him to say." With a faint music,
Like that of a cold shadow-hidden brook
Down there that he remembered, she was laughing.

He turned, and after frowning, smiled at her
With a sad patience. "If my faith went out,"
He said, "my days to be would all be night—
A night without a dawn, and with no lamp.
You should know that. God knows you should know that."
"Praise him for what there is, then, if that's true,"
She said. "We might have lost our arms and legs,
And then our eyes and ears. There's possible fate
Far worse than this, though you believe there isn't,
Or make believe. If I know anything well,
I know you'll praise your God, in retrospect,
That all there was of me surviving truth
And revelation was as clean as ever.
No other man has had it, you will say,
And walk the straighter for it. Is that nothing
To you, and your Olympian pride, Matthias?
Is it not even a patch for our poor ship?"
She said it with a quick commiseration
That was a quick regret. Some other man

Might have said vanity was not compassion,
Envenoming an error with a pity
That might be worse.

                With nothing else to do,
She gave herself to time, and lived with it
As a child might have lived with a dumb mother,
Present, yet never seen. She went no more
Down there, but she would see from where she was,
Darker for shadows always over it,
A black and giant rock that made her think
Of Egypt, and lost sorrows in the night
Of ages, where defeats were all forgotten,
Dreams all a part of nothing, and words all said.
There was a man she had found watching it
That morning, but he was not watching now—
Not there. She would not find him there again;
And Natalie, in a broken way, was glad
For one thing in him that she might admire,
While she could only love the rest of him
More than her life. If there was folly in that,
Greater than love, folly stronger than death,
Her penance was to nourish it alone
With cold estrangement and a patient sort
Of rage. If Garth had been a fool, she thought,
What name would poor Matthias find for her?
Had he known all she knew of her deceits
To please him into loving the defects
Of her necessities, he would have lost his wits
Finding a name for her. If he knew all,
He might know more than was in any name
To tell him, and be sorry for all women
Who lie because they live. No friend of hers,
Or garrulous acquaintance envying her,

Would have said everything was not as always;
And time went by.

          And as it went, Matthias
Upheld a dignity that had a distance
Becoming in his new part, which he was playing
Because there was no other. He sustained
His eminence as he might, and to the town
Presented as untroubled and unaltered
An aspect of achievement and address
As ever, and with only himself to know
The sorry toil it was, and Natalie
Partly to know. He might have played for years
To men's indifference and to Natalie's
Unheard applause, if time had honored him
So long. Time was a traitor to Matthias,
Who had believed in time and trusted it
Without a fear of its betraying him,
As faith will trust a grave without a promise;
And in their way Matthias and his pride
Were traitors—if an insurrection sleeps
While its indignities and inspirations
Are moving and awakening in the dark.
Meanwhile Matthias and his pride progressed
With time through hardness and civility
Into a mellowness that Natalie
Felt was unripe. An early-fallen fruit
With a worm hidden in it might have had it;
Or a determination to be kind,
After long injuries and indecisions,
Might have been like it. Call it this, or that,
Or welcome it, it was not like Matthias.
It was too smooth and soft on the outside
To be Matthias. It was not Matthias,
Natalie said; nor was it, mercifully,

MATTHIAS AT THE DOOR

A variation of a mortal silence
Which had so long resisted and ignored her
As to be like death dwelling in the house,
Waiting his hour to be revealed and feared.
It mattered less to Natalie what it was
Than that it should be visible, and be change.

"If it had looked at me, and said something,
I would have held my hands out to a ghost,"
She said, with a sharp humor, "and embraced it."

"I say with an experience," he said,
"It might have been a disappointing armful."
He took her in his arms for the first time
Since his awakening; and he found her there
No less responsive than a ghost had been,
Nor more for being real. "You are no ghost;
And that's as far today as I have knowledge.
Will you say what you are?" He would have held her
More closely, but she stood away from him,
While he was holding her.

                              "If you surprise me,
Matthias, I may not like you, or believe you.
Like someone else, we have outlived surprise,
Or surely should have conquered it by now."
She smiled a little sadly at herself,
And looking up, saw passion in his eyes—
Passion and sorrow, and a burning pain
That found her memories.

                              "Nothing in you," he said,
"That was, and is, will be outlived in me.
No, nothing." Breathing hard, he let her go,
Leashing her with his eyes, and holding her

1119

From going far. She was too sorry for him
To leave him there alone, or so she thought.
She fancied, for a moment, she was seeing
Their melancholy drama as he saw it,
And pitied him. Pity is like a knife,
Sometimes, and it may pierce one who employs it
More shrewdly than the victim it would save,
And with a wound unhealing.

                                        Natalie,
Weighing herself with justice, found a void
Between her and uncompromising earth,
Whereto she had returned, reluctantly,
With pity, and with renewed acknowledgment
On her side of defection and deceit—
Not of itself so much an injury
As a convenience, and a way prepared
By circumstance to make Matthias happy.
That was at least a way of saying it.
She needed him, and there was nothing new
To an old world in her not loving him;
And all would have gone well if Garth had lived,
Or gone more quietly through another door
Than one down there that she was always seeing—
Before her, in a darkness. Time would have held
Timberlake and Matthias and herself
Always the same as they had been before,
And they would never have been down there together,
Down there among the shadows, where disaster
Was hiding to destroy them.

                                        Natalie cried
One day, as never before since Timberlake
Had vanished; and her misery, she discovered,
Had in it more of rage and self-contempt

MATTHIAS AT THE DOOR

Than sorrow. She had seen more with her eyes
Of late than with her pity or resignation;
And after two years with another man
Than one that she had married as Matthias,
She had come surely and unwillingly
To see how much of her was left for him
To cherish or believe since he had learned
How little there was before. She could see change
Writing a sordid story on his face,
And she was hearing now another language
That he was learning. An intangible,
Untarnishable seal of something fine
Was wearing off; and in his looks and words
A primitive pagan rawness of possession
Soiled her and made her soul and body sick.

After another year, she felt impending
More than was hers to bear. All she had left
Was a long-vanished presence of a man
Far off, if anywhere, who remembered her,
If he remembered, only as one forsworn
And far behind him. He was not coming back.
There was inviolate fire between his life
And hers; and she was never designed for flight,
Alone, to a new loneliness.

                    Matthias,
With a full, flushed, deteriorated face
That made her shrink, invaded moodily
Her thoughts and fears, and her uncertainties
Darker than any fear. "What's it about?"
He asked; and smiling like a sultan, watched her,
While she sat watching him. "You are not playing
So well—not half so well now—as at first.
You are not so proficient with your cues,

Or with your lines, as when you married me.
I don't see why. You are playing the same part;
And if you are pretending it's a new one,
If you are trying to see yourself a martyr,
You might consider a few famished thousands
Who would go miles tonight to find an egg."
A latterly familiar reek of spirits
Followed his words, and seemed, to Natalie,
To fill the house.

              "No, I am not a martyr—
I am a fool," she said. "I'm not complaining.
I'm only asking you to go away."

He scowled at her a moment, and came nearer,
Watching her with a smile she did not like.
"For me it's not so easy to go away
From you—sometimes," he said. "You were not made
For me to go away from. If you had been,
I should have gone before, and given you this—
All this you see—to live in. There's a plenty
For me without it, but there's not enough—
Not anywhere—without you. I'll go away,
But that's no reason for not coming back.
That would be rather—rather ridiculous."

He laid his hot hands on her shrinking shoulders,
And would have kissed her, but she sprang from him
Wildly, and stood before him, pale with hate.
"My God!" she cried. "What do you think of me?
What manner of chattel have you made of me?
I know, and I could say. But while I lived
Under your roof with you and ate your bread,
I was a wife. I should have run away,
But was too much a coward, and too weak.

1122

MATTHIAS AT THE DOOR

I had been here with everything soft and safe
Too long for that. I had been hidden too long
From all those tiresome things there are to do,
With nothing to do them for. You have your God—
If you have not forgotten him and lost him—
But I have nothing. Do you hear me? Nothing.
I was born spoiled, perhaps—or perhaps not.
You have not spoiled me. You have spoiled yourself.
I should have run away, or should have died,
But never was ready for that—never before.
You reason, I suppose, that without love,
You may as well have my body while it lasts.
Well, it will not last always."

                    "Neither shall I,"
He said, and laughed at her. "He gave you to me,
You said, and you knew then, if I did not,
What he was keeping; and you married me
Because you liked me, and because my love
Was too real to be tortured, and because
There was no better thing for you to do.
You recognize your own remedial words."

"Don't fling that in my face tonight," she said.
"There are things decency says only once.
You have known that, for you were decent—once.
Now you are drunk. . . . Why won't you go away!"

Matthias felt a new knife cutting him,
In a new place. He stared, and his lips twisted
Before he laughed. "You said you loved me—once;
And I remember that you said it slowly,
As if it hurt—and probably it did.
But why should it hurt now? You sold yourself
More to your satisfaction and advantage
Than to your disappointment or surprise,

1123

And must have known what you were selling. Love?
I have enough for two. There is more love
In half a minute of my looking at you
Than twenty of you could hold or comprehend.
If you have treasured it for your convenience,
Don't wonder if it seems a bit confused,
Or possibly forgetful. The trouble with you,
And me, and a few millions who are like us,
Is that we live so long to know so little,
And are not willing then to know ourselves.
Where are the mysteries in us that require
So much dramatic fuss? Now we are sorry
For all we've said." He buried her mouth with his,
And held her while she fought and choked and struggled
Till she was free.

    "God—get away from me!"
She cried, and struck his hot face furiously
With an unguided hand that seared with fire
His pride and his belief. Calming her rage,
She saw him there, like a man standing blind,
And found no words to say. There were no words.
And after she was gone he was still there,
Like a man standing dead.

    Hours after that,
Matthias, by dull degrees of realization
That sought oblivion, slowly drank himself
To a dead sleep. When he awoke, the sun
Was in his room, and everything else was there
That should be there; and there was one thing more—
A white thing, a white paper. He reached out,
With fingers trembling, and unfolded it,
Only to find five words. He read them over
Until they had no meaning, and then read them

Until a meaning that was never in them
Pierced him with hope that broke itself in him,
And was no more than pain. Again he read them:
Matthias, I am sorry. Natalie.
Only five words; and while they were so few,
He wondered why those words were so much more
Than nothing at all. At last he rose, not knowing
Why he should rise, or who was alive to care.
He fortified his hope with a brave drink
That once had frightened him, and if no braver,
He was accoutred for a brief endurance
Of what was at the best a long beginning.
He would not ask how long, or of what end.
A stillness like an end was all he found
In Natalie's room; and downstairs it was all
That he found anywhere, till a servant said
That she was last seen going down towards the trees.

Matthias would not eat; he was not well.
Whereat the maid bowed her acknowledgments,
And having left him, smiled. Matthias found
More courage where he found it first, and watched
The twinkling tree-tops while he hesitated.
He would not go, but he should have to go.
Wherever he looked the sunlight tortured him
With shafts of memory till his eyes were dead
With desolation, and he had no eyes
To meet the pitiless beauty of the world.
But he must go, and he must go alone—
Down to that place. He stumbled as he walked,
As once before, but he moved on, and on,
And down—down among trees and rocks and shadows,
And silence broken only by a brook
Running unseen down there where he must go,
And go alone, knowing what he must find.

V

Matthias, when he saw that Natalie
Was dead, saw nothing else. For a long time
His world, which once had been so properly
And admirably filled with his ambitions,
With Natalie, with his faith, and with himself,
Was only an incredible loneliness,
The lonelier for defeat and recognition.
There was no going back where there was nothing
But memory choked with dust. There was no joy
In gazing at a desert of dead sand
That held above its terrors of endlessness
No more mirages; and there was no refuge
In a retreating faith as unsubstantial
And thankless as a wasted adoration.
There was no reason in such ruin as his,
And no design in any such havoc of pride;
There was no system or serenity,
And no incentive, or there was none for him,
Where there was error without recompense.

It was October now, a chilly Sunday,
And a gray afternoon. Matthias, alone
As always on his desolate veranda,
Sat watching, while he shivered, the bare spikes
That were the tops of oaks and birches growing
Out of a gorge where now he never went.
The place was dead now. Garth and Natalie,
And Timberlake, had made a tomb of it—
A tomb of life and love, and of his God.
There was a rock down there that Garth had said
Might be the tomb of God, as now it was.
Matthias wondered now if ever his faith
Was more than a traditional convenience

MATTHIAS AT THE DOOR

Taken on trust, a plaything of a childhood
That with his ignorance had survived too long.
Let that be as it might, he was lonelier
Than perished life or crumbled love had made him;
Yet he was on an eminence, and would stay there
Until it fell, and carried him down with it.
His pride of unbelief had strength in it
Of a new tonic that must give him strength
Because it was so bitter. There was pride
In bitterness for him who must be proud
Of one thing or another if he would live,
And for Matthias pride was more than life.
So, on a chilly Sunday afternoon,
Alone there with a winter-laden wind
Whirling dead leaves over a darkening floor,
Matthias heard their message and was proud
That he could meet with patience and high scorn
A life without a scheme and to no purpose—
An accident of nameless energies,
Of which he was a part, and no small part.
His blindness to his insignificance
Was like another faith, and would not die.

December went, and with it went a year
That he would never have to live again;
And the new year brought with it nothing new,
Till on a silent evening, in late March,
There was a bell, and then an apparition
Of a lean visitor, wearing clothes almost
As worn-out and as wrinkled as his face.
Matthias rose, while a great wave of joy
Submerged his courtesy and his gratitude,
And he was inarticulate.
                                    "Matthias,

1127

You do not have to talk," said Timberlake;
"There's too much talking in the world already.
Give me a drink, and then a beggar's morsel,
And if I'm eligible, a place to sleep.
I have done you no wrong, and little good;
And after that, Matthias, I'm as you see me."
His face and all his wrinkles, and his eyes,
Were smiling at Matthias with a doubt
That held a memory and a wistfulness
Of one who might be welcome, or might not.
"When you have looked me over, and appraised me,
You will be saying without my hearing you,
Matthias, that I'm done. We'll say I am,
And wait for what will happen to the stars
When the news reaches them. I'm tired, Matthias.'

He coughed, and held his thin hands to the fire.
Matthias watched him, and again that joy,
Which had so much of fear in it, possessed him.
For the first time since Natalie had spoken
That evening after Timberlake had gone,
Matthias was not alone. He said that over
Until he smiled and was almost ashamed
Of so great happiness. How much was left
Of Timberlake was all to learn. Meanwhile,
Matthias was not alone.

             When Timberlake
Had warmed himself with fire and food and drink,
And told a story that will not be new
Or old while there is man, poured out more drink,
Chiding Matthias for his abstinence.
"Nothing since Natalie died? That's an odd form
Of eulogy, or commemoration, surely,
For one so measured in his indulgences

MATTHIAS AT THE DOOR

As you, Matthias. Do you believe she cares,
Where she is now, what you and I are doing,
Or saying?"

       "I don't believe she cares, or knows,"
Matthias answered; "and I hope she doesn't.
What is there to believe? I believe nothing;
And I am done with mysteries and with gods
That are all gone. Garth was intelligent,
And had found reason, when he told me that."

"So that is what he told you." Timberlake
Smiled at the fire, and thought. "Hold fast, Matthias.
There's not a man who breathes and believes nothing.
So you are done with mysteries. If you are,
You are the one elected and fulfilled
Initiate and emeritus of us all.
You are a man worth a long journeying
Over cold roads to see. I'm not amazed
That you see only folly and false vision
In such a fraudulent and ephemeral
Disguise of life as this." He raised his glass,
And after drinking what was left in it,
Sat musing. "And you tell me this is all
Since Natalie died."

       "All this, and more than this,
And still more. Natalie told me who I was.
You loved her, Timberlake, and she loved you;
And you must love her still."

       "I do, Matthias.
Now she is dead, I love her desperately;
And that will do no harm, now that she's dead.
I doubt, with you, if she knows now, or cares;

1129

And if she knows, I dare say she discovers
In my unworthiness of her remembrance
One of those things infinity forgets.
We're more than that, or nothing—as you believe
Since you have torn the veil and have forgotten
Just what it was you saw. Never mind me,
Matthias. I'm warmer now, and full of thanks
That I can't say for seeing you here again.
Yes, I am warmer now, and reconciled—
Which is important in our preparations.
The time we sigh for what's left out of us
Only gives age to what was always there.
We don't increase ourselves with our regrets
Unless there's action in them. Let us act."
He coughed while he poured out another drink,
And saw Matthias frowning.

                                    "It's a blemish,
Matthias, and a maleficence," he said:
"I mean that sad and saurian eye of yours
That's glowering now so cold on my employment.
Now that God's in his grave, where you have laid·him,
Are you to set your dogs on Dionysus?
You know those dogs. They were all waiting for me
That afternoon, when they were on your mind.
Though I said little, I could hear them coming,
And not far off. As you observe, they got me,
Tearing the garment of my soul severely,
But not with this that you are giving to me,
To make me warm. It was their teeth, Matthias,
That did the work. This was a balm for that—
For Babylon suddenly fallen and destroyed.
Howl for her; give balm for her wounds, if so
She may be healed. So Jeremiah says—
In substance, or effect. Turn your sad eye
Away from me, Matthias. Be not afraid.

MATTHIAS AT THE DOOR

All things that are worth having are perilous,
And have their resident devil, respectively.
There's this that I have here, there's love, pride, art,
Humility, ambition, power and glory,
The kingdom itself, which may come out all right,
And truth. They are all very perilous,
And admirable, so long as there is in them
Passion that knows itself—which, if not hushed,
Is a wise music. Howl, ye ships of Tarshish,
, Sang once a Jew. In days of the drunkards of Ephraim,
The Jews had their Ezekiels and Isaiahs,
Solomons, Davids, and a fellow on fire
With Job; for there were howlers in those days.
Now they have power and learning, and quick ears,
And eyes, and hands; yet somehow they aren't howling.
There's mystery there, Matthias. It must be water—
Which is material and insidious,
Prolific in small monsters that are lethal,
And arrogant in its multiform negations.
Our tortured benefits are our worst of demons,
Bleeding us while we sleep."

                              "You aren't asleep,
Timberlake," said Matthias. "I wish you were."
He gazed into the fire and tapped his knees
Uncomfortably. "Your demon's at your service,
Along with anything else of mine you like;
Yet I've an interest in your—your employment.
You are the only friend that I have left;
And if you die, I shall be here alone.
Here in this world—alone. If that's by chance
A thing significant as another drink—"

"Or two, Matthias. You said two, certainly.
I heard you, and I have a squirrel's ears.

'Good God,' you say? You told me God was buried.
Matthias, you may have buried him alive."

Timberlake honored with an abstinence
That he averred was vain and ostentatious
The fears and wishes of a grateful friend,
And for three days was quiet, save when he coughed
On the fourth morning he reproached himself
While he reproved Matthias: "Your affairs
Are calling you with tongues of gold and silver,
While I'm an obstacle here of no report
Or worldly consequence. I cannot tell you
What infinite progressions and expansions
May or may not be waiting for the end
Of this you see before you in my shape—
Or rather what you don't see. All I can say
To cheer you is that your return tonight
Will find me here, intact and honorable.
You will remember Garth was honorable.
But I'll not follow Garth. I shall not go
Until my name is called. Now, good Matthias,
Go catch a golden fish. You have my word
Of honor, if only for not mentioning it."

The day was harsh and raw, with a wet sky
Preparing coldly to drench everything
With a cold rain. Soiled islands of old snow
Not washed away or melted were not winter,
And unawakening grass that had no color
Was not yet spring. But heedless of a season
That had no name, Matthias in his car
Rode smoothly with a gladness warming him;
For he was not alone. He had one friend—
A frail one, but a friend—a sure possession,
A treasure threatened only with a fear

1132

MATTHIAS AT THE DOOR

That having found and sheltered it so late,
He might not have it long. But worry for that,
Or worry too soon, would be a thanklessness
For one who was safe now in a warm house,
With all his economic woes behind him,
With books to read, and with a smouldering hope
To guard and to restore. He was not old.
His wrinkles were not years; they were a life,
Written for all to see and none to read.
"We are not old at fifty any longer,"
Matthias thought; "and there's a place for him
As long as I'm alive, and afterwards—
If so it is to be. I do not know him,
And never shall. No man has known another
Since men were born. It is enough to know
That he is in my house, and is my friend."
The swollen sky broke in the afternoon,
And it was raining while Matthias rode
Through storm and early darkness to a house
That for so long had been the tomb of life.
He thought of that, and smiled as he went in
To find a waiting friend who was not there.
No one had seen him, or knew where he was.
He had been sitting mostly by the fire,
And watching it. They had not thought of him
As anything stranger than a quiet person,
Who coughed too much, and had considerate words
When there were words to say. For an hour or two
Perhaps, before it rained, he was not there.
If he was not upstairs and in his room,
He must be gone. Now it was five o'clock,
And for an hour or more a deathly rain
Had deluged all outside with a cold flood
That would have chilled and driven a lunatic
To shelter; and the man was not in the house.

There was no longer any doubt of that.
He was somewhere; and he was not in the house.

At six o'clock Matthias and two men,
Arrayed against a tempest, went with torches
Down to the one place that was darkly left
As an abysmal possibility—
Or rather went halfway down. There was no need
Of going farther; for where Garth had found
Matthias, they found Timberlake, dumb, drenched,
Exhausted, and with only his eyes at first
To say that he was living. When he spoke,
It was to cough and whisper, while he smiled,
That he could go no higher, and was sorry
For being a fool. That was like Timberlake;
So like him that Matthias could almost
Be glad there for the rain that washed his tears
Out of existence before Timberlake
Could see them—as if pride stronger than death
Was his, like Natalie's folly.

                              The next day,
Timberlake, with Matthias watching him,
Lay waiting for the fiends that were assembling
To fight with him for breath. "I did not come
For this, Matthias." Half whispering, he said it,
Implying grimly that it mattered little
What he had come for. "I sat yesterday
There by the fire and saw Natalie in it—
And there was Garth. I saw them both down there,
Where each had gone alone, for the last time.
I saw that place where Natalie was alone,
Until you found her there. I would not see her,
In there, but she was calling. She was calling
For me, for the last time. And I went down,

MATTHIAS AT THE DOOR

Say what you will. 'She was in there,' I said,
And sat before the place where she had been,
Trying to say that she had not been there.
I sat there till it rained, and while it rained,
Because I could not move. I was too cold.
Too much of me was dead for me to care
Whether I came up out of there or not.
I was not thinking of how cold I was,
But rather of you and Natalie, Matthias,
And of what we had made of our three lives—
Or life had made of us. It seemed a waste
Of more than should be lost, until I thought
Of nature's way and of how small we are
In our performances, and how infinite
In our futilities and our ignorances.
They are as many and various as we are,
Always in our degrees, which are not ours
To choose, yet may be ours to recognize
And occupy more profitably—sometimes.
If I have made my best of my not much—
And God knows you believe that I have not,
Matthias—I am sorry it was no better.
You saved me from the fire; and you saved more,
Conceivably, than you see. There should have been
Far more for you to save; and why there wasn't
Is one of those long questions we don't answer.
So do not ask me why so many of us
Are more like sketches of ourselves, half done
By nature, and forgotten in her workshop,
Than like a fair or tolerable fulfilment
Of her implied intention. Implications
Of more than is revealed in our defeats
Are targets always for the many who trust
And emulate, and crown with confidence,
A self-enveloping uniformity

1135

Of compromise. That's how the world was made
Before my lost omniscience came too late.
Why are we as we are? Don't ask, Matthias.
Why do we come to nothing who have more,
We'll say, than most? What is our value here
Unless we fit? To make a mould that fits us,
You'd like to say, Matthias, but aren't going to.
Read a few years of history, and you'll see
The stuff is not so pliable as all that.
If it were so, we should all be each other—
So great that nature would be on her knees, ·
Which is not nature's natural attitude.
Why are we.as we are? We do not know.
Why do we pay so heavily for so little?
Or for so much? Or for whatever it is?
We do not know. We only pay, and die.
To a short-sighted and earth-hindered vision
It would seem rather a waste, but not to mine.
I have found gold, Matthias, where you found gravel,
And I can't give it to you. I feel and see it,
But you must find it somehow for yourself.
It's not negotiable. You have to find it—
Or say it must find you. Even you, Matthias."

He paused, and coughed, until Matthias turned
His eyes away, and sighed. "Forgive my not
Remembering, Timberlake. You must be still.
There will be time for this."

                              "God knows, Matthias,
Whether there will or not, or if it matters.
If I've done one thing well, I have not meddled,
Until today, with men's inheritances
And acquisitions. But men like you, Matthias,
Believe that if you stumble the world trembles.

1136

MATTHIAS AT THE DOOR

Try to believe now, as a friendly favor
To me, that it does nothing of the sort.
If you had eyes inside you, and you may,
To read a little further into your book—
Well, you would be surprised at what is there
For you to find. If it had not been there,
I might have hated you for saving me,
When we were young, out of that burning house.
There was a price for that, which I have paid
As well as I was able. Natalie paid,
And you are paying still. We are like stairs
For one another's climbing, and are never
Quite told which way it is that we are going
While we are climbing higher, or think we are.
I have not always thought so; but you have,
Matthias, and I have watched you going up
While you were going down. You are down now
As far as you will go—if you remember
That you are like a book with pages in it
You have not read, and cannot read in the dark.
Some of us would be happier in the dark,
As you have been, and cannot be again.
More darkness would have been a balm for me,
But not a cure. There is no cure for self;
There's only an occasional revelation,
Arriving not infrequently too late.
For me it was too early—which is granted,
Sometimes, to the elected and the damned.
I don't suppose that I was all a fool,
Or that I was all bad. There have been worse
Who have aroused more reverence and more noise,
And shown more colors to the common view,
And I'm at peace with them. If I whined now
For benefits that I may have lost or wasted,
I should lose only more. Spare me all twaddle

Of what I might have been; for you don't know,
And would still be Matthias if you did.
No estimate or retrospect of me
Will save you now. There's a nativity
That waits for some of us who are not born.
Before you build a tower that will remain
Where it is built and will not crumble down
To another poor ruin of self, you must be born.
You are not old, Matthias; you are so young
That you see nothing in fate that takes away
Your playthings but a curse, and a world blasted,
And stars you cannot reach that have no longer
A proper right to shine. And that's no way
For me to say it to a friend who cares.
A friend who takes me in out of the cold,
And sees me on my way, and will be sorry,
Merits a more communicable reward
Than talk of towers that will be built sometime,
Or of lives wasted that will not be lost—
Not even if thrown away. Say to yourself
That if some wreck that was not Timberlake
Were telling you to go back, you would arise
Refreshed and better for having strangled him.
Don't listen to me, Matthias, for I'm tired;
And I don't half believe what I am saying."

"Yes, Timberlake, you believe it," said Matthias;
"And why not? I don't know that we are wasted.
Since Natalie spoke to me when you had gone,
That evening, I've had no knowledge, or belief.
Perhaps I never had it. Why do you smile?
And why do you never mention Natalie?"

Timberlake said, "I mentioned her, Matthias.
I mentioned when I came that now she's dead,

I love her desperately. You must have heard.
You were supposed to hear."

                       "Yes, I heard that,"
Matthias answered. "And I am never to know
What my life was with her. My knowledge fell
One day, and broke like glass on a stone floor."

"Don't try to know, Matthias," Timberlake said,
And held out a weak hand. "Say that's all over,
And that illumination would light nothing
Where there is only dust. Don't ask, Matthias.
A happy woman may be understood,
Or near enough, but there is no man living
With eyes or intuitions to interpret
A woman hiding pain. Don't try, Matthias."

Again, with his blue eyes and all his wrinkles,
Timberlake smiled. Matthias looked away
And heard him coughing. All that night he heard him,
And for three days and nights heard nothing else,
While doctors came and went and shook their heads
At Timberlake, who, having outlived surprise,
Had seen them when they fancied he saw nothing.

VI

Matthias in his dreams would have a glimpse
Of Natalie sometimes, but never a word
Until he found himself alone with her
One night in regions he could name as only
Nowhere on earth. Natalie came to him
Robed all in gold—a film of heavenly wealth
To make him gasp. There was gold everywhere.

Matthias had loved gold for what it gave him,
But never had asked for this. Natalie laughed:
"I know, Matthias. I know all your thoughts,
As you will soon know mine.. They are good thoughts.
Everything here is good, as your God made it.
You died, Matthias; and now you are in heaven,
With me, for ever; and I shall never change.
My soul and body are yours, and will be yours,
And always, which is now. There is no time
To make us old, for there is nothing but love,
Nothing but you and me." He felt her breath
Warm on his face, and her warm body clinging
To his until it seemed a part of him;
And he was trembling for the wonder of it
When she began, still in his arms, to shrivel
And change, unspeakably and abominably,
While all about him became dark and foul,
And only darker while infernal fires
Lighted what once was gold. Natalie's face
Was now a demon's, and her breath was fire;
And she was like a skeleton strangling him.
"You are in hell, Matthias," she was saying;
"Your God has changed his mind"—when suddenly
He was in darkness that he slowly felt,
And knew, and recognized. He was awake.
He was awake, but he still heard her laughing
As woman cannot laugh. He was awake,
Somewhere, and he was on his feet somewhere;
For he was standing in the dark, alone,
With a sweat chilling him. He groped a little,
Only to find black air, till gradually
Blackness became a room that was not his,
With outlines in it of still things that once
Were Natalie's. He had come there asleep,

To find her in a dream of heaven, and then
To lose her in another dream of hell.
His life with Natalie had been like that,
He thought; yet he could think no ill of her,
Though she had struck him. He could not forget
The blow, and he could not forget his love,
Which had been real, if blind and unreturned,
With Natalie a stranger in his house,
And in his arms. But Natalie was gone,
And there was little use in saying that over.
Trying to sleep once more, he found himself
Still saying it, over and over, against reason
And against fate. The foodless luxury
Of a dry truth was all it had for him;
And it was all that life had while he felt
The memories of a nightmare stinging him
To a sick wakefulness. There was no sleep
Till daylight came, and then there was so little
That it was easier not to wait for more.
For days the taint of that perfidious dream
Was like a smell of death following him—
A death that would not die. At last it faded,
Leaving him as he was before—alone.

A longer loneliness, with no friend coming
This time, and none to come, compelled Matthias
Half-heartedly to search the darkness in him,
Hoping to find surprise where Timberlake
Had said it lived in unsuspected ambush,
Patient and there to wait. But no surprise
Had yet revealed itself except a small
And useless one of his not finding any.
All he could find was an unsatisfied
Conviction of no room for anything new—

A certainty that had concealed in it
Somewhere a question that was like a midge
In a man's eye. He sought for it in books
That were like heavy keys for doors not his
To open, and doubted if they fitted even
The doors of those who had invented them.
Some of the newest of them had already
Richer accumulations of more rust,
Matthias fancied, than the oldest of them;
And there was nothing in any of them for him.
The best of them were moonshine without light,
Or news of an ingenious mechanism
That must have built itself mysteriously
And infinitely out of infinite nothing.
His brain ached, and he went back to himself,
As he had gone a thousand times before,
To see what there was there, still hoping faintly
To find surprise. But all he found was doubt,
Insoluble and impregnable as ever,
And the same man. He must be the same man,
For he was still Matthias. If he had built
His life like a tall tower to see it fall,
There were no failures in his masonry,
Nor in the safe precision of his plan;
He had built, with all his foresight and selection,
On undivined and insecure foundations
Deeper than all security and precaution
Had whispered there was reason to explore.
He saw it lying about him, shafts and arches,
And shattered walls, in fragments on the ground,
And for no fault of his. The only eyes
He had were those that his inheritance
Had given to him, and he had seen with them
Only what he might see. He saw that now,
And asked his eyes, hoping there was no answer,

MATTHIAS AT THE DOOR

Where they had seen a ruin like this before,
And turned them on himself to ask again
What they were seeing. It was the same man—
A man with nothing left but money and pride,
Neither of which was worth his living for,
If there was nothing else. To live alone,
A captive in a world where there were none
Who cared for him, and none for whom he cared,
Was a dark sentence and might be a long one.
Digesting that, he thought of Garth saying once:
"You'd save a man from drowning, or from burning,
And tell him then that he was not worth saving—
Unless you liked him. I like you, Matthias,
And so does Timberlake; and God knows why.
We are outside the wall that you have built
Around yourself and Natalie—or I am.
Timberlake may climb over or crawl through,
Once in a while, and you had better let him."

"Well, Garth, I should be glad enough to see you
Tonight, if you were coming to my door,"
Matthias thought; "and I might say to you
A few things more to your desire and liking
Than many I may have said. You will not come,
And would not if you could—if Timberlake
Saw truth before he died. If he was dreaming,
We are all dreaming, and it's all the same
To him now, and to you. When towers are fallen,
The tallest are no loftier than the lowest.
Falling so far, they drive the ruin only
A little deeper into original earth.
Tonight I'm not so free with your last folly
As I was while I gazed at my tall tower
Before it fell, and was so ready to fall.
No, Garth, I'm not so sure you were a fool,

Now that I see you in a clearer light.
It was undignified, but not ignoble."

Matthias did not know that in his garden
There were some perilous seeds of sympathy
That he had found and planted, unaware
Of what they were or what they might conceal,
Until another Sunday afternoon
Found him, in August, watching the same tops
Of oaks and birches growing out of a gorge
That held so many memories. The veranda
Where he was sitting was a silent place,
And so was the whole house. With his permission,
All its inhabitants were away somewhere,
Leaving him like that last man in the world
Whom he had seen in fancy—as in truth
He saw the last man living in his world,
Which he was leaving. From the shining tops
Of those familiar and indifferent trees,
He turned and looked into a lonely chair—
Natalie's chair. She was not in it now,
And never was in it. There was a woman in it,
Once, and a woman he was never to know.
He was never to know anything. He was lost.
He had explored himself so many times
To find surprise where there was only darkness
That he was tired of darkness. He was alone,
And he was tired of that. He was alive,
With pride for company, and now pride was tired
Of groping with Matthias among shadows,
Where for three years they had been prisoners.
Matthias was a man who must have light,
Or darkness that was rest and certainty,
With no fool-fire of an unfuelled faith
Invading it and losing its own spark,

MATTHIAS AT THE DOOR

Such as it was. Matthias was alone,
And there was only loneliness before him,
Because he was Matthias, and had failed.
He would have prayed for less intelligence,
But there were no prayers in him any longer.
It was too late. He looked at his calm hand,
And saw death lying there. "Why not?" he said
To Pride, who said, "It is undignified,
But not ignoble." Matthias winced at that,
And said to Pride, "You think I am afraid?"
"No, you are not afraid; you are Matthias,"
Pride answered; and Matthias, with a sigh
Of satisfaction, lay back in his chair
So comfortably that comfort was itself
Surprise. He knew that he was not afraid,
And there were days enough. There were too many,
If many of them were to be like today.

Sighing, he wished that he might hear the steps
Of Timberlake again and see him coming,
With all his wrinkles and his twinkling eyes,
Which had seen farther and found more, somewhere,
Than his were ever to find. With all his waste,
And his uncounted losses, Timberlake
Had died the richer man, having found gold
Where there was only gravel for Matthias;
And that was strange. Timberlake was a ruin,
But he was not alone. He was always a ruin,
But never alone. Matthias had felt that
From childhood, and was feeling it today
So finally that a waiting for more days
Disheartened him, although there was no haste.
Besides, he was too indolent to care,
And one day meant another. Garth had said
Sunday was good, and had not waited for it.

Garth had done well. Why should Matthias wait
For Monday?

        He was asking, with no answer,
While hours went by and a long afternoon
Became a twilight and an end of time—
A twilight, or a darkness, where Matthias
Could see confronting him, invitingly,
A dark Egyptian door. Now it was closed,
And silent, but a touch would open it,
Giving him entrance. He would leave all behind
That he was glad to leave; and once inside,
There was to be no coming out of there.
It was as easy and as ordinary
As going to bed. There was no hesitation
Longer defeating him; there were no doubts
Delaying him. His hand was on the door,
Which he felt moving, slowly, when a voice
Within said, warningly, "Not yet, Matthias."

There was decision and authority
Not native in that voice. Matthias frowned,
But he was not surprised. It was like Garth
To say that, and to be there in his way,
Matthias thought, though he could not say then
Why it was like him. "Garth, is it you," he said,
"Telling me I should wait? Why should I wait?
If you knew all that I have known of waiting,
Alone, you would be glad to let me in.
Whose power is yours to say what I shall do?
What if I show you that my power is mine?"

"Not yet, Matthias. No matter what you do,
You are not coming. A way was found for me
To meet you here and say you are not coming.

1146

MATTHIAS AT THE DOOR

You cannot die, Matthias, till you are born.
You are down here too soon, and must go back.
Don't be annoyed, or be disquieted,
Or more than necessarily surprised
At any change. You will still be yourself
When you are born. There is no cure for self;
There's only an occasional—"

                          "Yes, I know it.
So I have heard before, from Timberlake.
Where is he now? And where is Natalie?
Why are they not with you, to meet me here
And tell me to go back? Where are they, Garth?"

"What the world had for them is theirs, Matthias,
Wherever they may be now. They are not here,
And I shall soon be gone. But you were coming,
And I am saying that you are going back.
I'm sorry to dishearten or to vex you,
But you might still go back if you came in.
It's all a matter of seeing which way we go;
And it's imperative that you shall be born,
Whether you will or not, before you die.
I am an emissary of the shadow
In this, Matthias, and I'm nothing more.
I see a little, but I'm still in the dark."

"But this is folly. This is all folly, Garth—
Like some occasional words I may have said
Of your procrastinations and shortcomings.
They were so easy to say, that—well, I said them;
And I am sorry. Your lessons were too hard.
Now I begin to see that your instructions
In the world's exigencies were not mine."

"Terrestrial exigencies are the devil,
Matthias, and others exist; and other devils.
Your generous language, and its implications,
Although a little delayed, will not be wasted.
Nothing is wasted, though there's much misused—
Like you and me, Matthias, who failed together,
Each in a personal way. You, having more
To fail with, failed more thoroughly and abjectly,
But that was not the end. I shall go on,
Where you'll not follow me. You will go back,
Where I'll not follow you. And in that fashion
We shall go on unconsciously together,
And consciously apart, to the same end.
It's all a matter of our not going too fast."

"And what same end is that? I am down here
To find the only end, and you forbid it—
Or say it is forbidden. Who says it is?
What if I push my way in while you tell me
Where I shall go? There can be nothing worse
For me in there than death; and if I'm here
For that, why should I listen or hesitate?
So far as I know, you are only a voice
Between me and oblivion. I have come
Too far through dark realities to be scared
At last by buried voices. You are dead,
And the dead cannot hurt."

                    "There's no regret,
Matthias, with a sorrier sting in it
Than for a word that cannot be withdrawn.
The dead have weapons to pierce all defiance
Of pride and vanity, which are flimsy shields
For those who must remember. You know that,
Or you would not be fumbling at this door

MATTHIAS AT THE DOOR

To find an entry. Push with all your power,
Matthias, and we shall see how strong you are.
I shall not hinder you. The door does that
To all who are not ready enough to move it,
Or are not desperate enough to break it.
It moved for you a little to let you hear
My voice, but you will see it moves no more.
I broke it once, and I am here to meet you.
The others are not here. Make what you will
Of that," said Garth.

          "Natalie broke it once,"
Matthias said. "Could her poor little hands
Do heavier work than mine? Where is she now?
What does she say of me? You will not answer."

"I cannot tell you where she is, Matthias.
She is not here. Her way was hers, not mine.
Make what you will of that. There are differences
Of desperation as there are of ruin
And uselessness; and you have found this door
Too soon. It will not open, and would be here
If you should wreck it. It's a peculiar door;
And when you are assured it will not open,
You will not come until your name is called."

"I have heard that. There's more of Timberlake
In you than of yourself. Is it you, Garth?
It is your voice."

          "No matter whose voice it is,
Matthias. It may be yours. It may be Cæsar's.
All voices are one voice, with many tongues
To make it inexpressible and obscure

1149

To us until we hear the voice itself.
We are prisoners now and pupils in a school
Where often our best rewards appear to us
To be our punishments. There's no escape.
To sleep with earth between you and the sun
Is not escape from earth, or from the sun.
It seems a mystery that so many should live
Who are not born, but that's the infinite way,
And one that is not altered or improved
By protest or denial, or by rebellion.
It's an old-fashioned way, older than fashion,
And it will serve your need better than any.
You have not yet begun to seek what's hidden
In you for you to recognize and use.
There's more of you for you to find, Matthias,
Than science has found yet, or may find soon.
Science that blinds its eyes incessantly
With a new light that fades and leaves them aching,
Whatever it sees, will be a long time showing
To you, Matthias, what you have striven so hard
To see in the dark. You will not see it there,
Though you may find it there if a door opens.
Not this door, but another one in yourself."

"In me, in you, and all to the same end,"
Replied Matthias, with a rueful breath
Of weariness that was answered amiably,
And with no accusation or resentment:
"You will be happier to forget the end,
Or more than revelation or conviction
Tell you to see, and to make what you may
Of your apportioned means. The end will wait
For all your most magnificent and protracted
Progressions and expansions, and be still
Sufficiently far away."

1150

MATTHIAS AT THE DOOR

          "Why do you laugh,
When you had better tell me," said Matthias,
"If these untold progressions and expansions
Of yours, or Timberlake's, begin with us,
Or if worms, armadillos, and hyenas
Have them as well. Where may the soul begin?
And why not grass? There's mystery living in grass
As dark as any in me."

                "Language, Matthias.
With a few finite and unfinished words
That are the chips of brief experience,
You restless and precipitate world-infants
Would build a skiff to circumnavigate
Infinity, and would find it, if you could,
No more sufficient or more commodious
Or comprehensive in its means and habit
Than a confused, confined phenomenon
Prisoned within a skull, with knowledge in it.
There's not much knowledge in it; and less wisdom.
How are you sure that some of you, Matthias,
May not be grass? And why not armadillos?
Men have done well with coverings hard as theirs.
I have seen men with more hyena in them
Than man; and I've seen others with more worm.
If you could know, Matthias, you would be free.
But you are far from knowing, and are not free;
You are not even free to open this door,
Or broken enough to break it. Only defeat
Born of disintegration and despair
Does that, Matthias. Your pride would only break
Its hands, and be ashamed to see them bleeding
After so blind a fight. You will go back
To build another tower—a safer one
This time, and one for many to acclaim

And to enjoy. It will be yours to build—
As towers, in your opinion, should be built;
It will be yours to admire while it is rising,
And yours to dedicate, when it has risen,
To whom it shall serve best. You have no friends,
And when you have seen deeper you may learn
That friends, for you, might be impediments,
Or luxuries, or counsellors in the way
Of your convictions and your certainties.
You will have occupation all your days,
With none to tell you this or that about it,
Or how it should be done. It will be done
About as your desire and your decision
May visualize and sanction its emergence
Out of a slumbering thought. You are not old,
And will be younger still when you are born.
Most of us are half-born, with only self
To cheer us with a promise of importance
Until it is all over—in appearance—
And one by one we're down here at this door,
Some frightened, some indifferent, some content,
And a few frantic, or experimental—
Like you, Matthias—in anticipation.
Forget that, and anticipate your tower;
And sometime, when you see it and have leisure
To look away from it, you may remember,
And gratefully, that you came once down here,
Where I came first, and Natalie not long after.
Your right remembrance of her will be gladness
That she is not here now, waiting outside,
And fearful to come in. You would not see her
Out there with her face white and her hands shaking,
And all to do again. She was a creature
Caught in a trap she thought was only a cage
Of many comforts with an open door—

1152

MATTHIAS AT THE DOOR

Until she knew; and she is farther now
From you and your concerns and preparations
Than words of yours have eyes or feet or wings
To follow her. She wants no following now,
And no recall. Say that she was not wasted,
And you may see your tower a little stronger
For no vast sacrifice. And for myself,
You will excuse a few diseased remarks
That made a mean farewell. I was not there,
Maithias; it was mostly fear and envy
That you observed and heard—fear of myself
And of what I was doing, envy of you
And of what you had done. We did not know—
Not then—how little that was. Good-bye, Matthias,
And let the best of us that you remember
Serve as it may. The worst is good oblivion.
There's a ship waiting for you; and when dawn
Begins to let you know, you will see then
That you are outward bound, with all your ruins
And all your old mistakes on board with you—
With you, and your regrets, and your possessions,
And with yourself, and all that makes a tower.
There may still be surprise. You are so far
From sure tonight that you and all before you,
And after you, are nothing, and here for nothing,
That you are curious. You are smiling now.
Yes, I can see in the dark. Good-bye, Matthias."

Matthias, in a light that was a darkness
More than a light, saw the door shut itself
Inexorably; and there was only silence,
Saying he must go back. There was no door
There now, and there was nothing for him to see.
There was a cloak of night that covered him
So heavily that he felt the weight of it.

He held his eyes wide open to see that door
Again, but all was black. He might have been
Buried and dead, if he had not been breathing.
He breathed, and moved, and slowly satisfied
His doubtful sense of being that he was alive,
And that he was awake. He had been awake
Like this in Natalie's room, after that dream,
But he was not there now. He moved his hands,
And then his arms, but they found only darkness
That was too cold and heavy to be in his house.
He was not there; he was in no man's house.
He took a searching step and felt dark earth
Under his foot; and suddenly he heard
A tinkling in the night like a small music
That had been always and would always be,
And was a brook; and there was only one brook
Running like that. With both his hands before him,
He groped a short way forward and was halted
By rock that he could see with his eyes open
Or closed. He was down there where Natalie
And Garth and Timberlake had been before him;
And they were all gone now. He had come down
To follow them, and found he was not wanted.
He must go back again; he must be born,
And then must live; and he who had been always
So promptly served, and was to be a servant,
Must now be of some use in a new world
That Timberlake and Garth and Natalie
Had strangely lived and died to find for him.
He had no friends, and his not having them now
Might be as well for him and his new tower.
To say that it was his and see it rising,
Would be enough. And while he saw it rising,
It would be his; and it would be himself
Behind him when he died. Even Timberlake

MATTHIAS AT THE DOOR

Would grant him that; and if his eyes agreed,
And all his wrinkles, they would do no harm.

Groping away, with his hands out before him,
And his feet going cautiously, Matthias
Moved as a blind man moves, with memory
Guiding him as it might, until he found
An unseen place to rest. The night was cold,
And in the darkness was a feel of death,
But in Matthias was a warmth of life,
Or birth, defending and sustaining him
With patience, and with an expectancy
That he had said would never in life again
Be his to know. There were long hours to wait,
And dark hours; and he met their length and darkness
With a vast gratitude that humbled him
And warmed him while he waited for the dawn.

NICODEMUS

(1932)

To
Edwin Carty Ranck

NICODEMUS

If held and questioned amiably, no doubt
Caiaphas would have said he was a priest,
And not a prophet; and he might have said
That his eyes rested well on what they saw,
And that his ears required no crash or murmur
Of innovation for their daily music.
There were some rumors, but he smiled at them
And all who heeded them, and shook his head
Reprovingly, as at uneasy children;
And so he smiled tonight at Nicodemus,
Who had come late. More like a fugitive
He looked, in a long cloak that covered him
With dark humility that composed itself
Conveniently with night, than like a lord
At home in his own city; and Caiaphas,
Greeting him, asked him why.

                    "Why do you wear
Your shroud while you are living, Nicodemus?
And a black shroud at that. Why do you pay
For noble robes and cover them with a sack?
Are you afraid of robbers?"

                    "No—not robbers."
And sighing as he said it, Nicodemus
Sat gazing at a darkness on the floor,
Where the black cloth had fallen. "No—not robbers."

"You are afraid of something, Nicodemus.
I have had fear myself, and know the signs.
I was afraid once of an elephant.
There are no elephants in Jerusalem.
What is it then that ails you? If I know,
There is no need of asking; for your coming
Like this would be an answer. Was he pleased
With your accommodation of your graces
To the plain level of his lowliness?
I have been told he was a carpenter—
Before he was a . . ."

                  "You may go as far
As that, and frequently," said Nicodemus,
"And find yourself as far from the same word
As you are now. He was a carpenter;
But there are men who were dead yesterday,
And are alive today, who do not care
Profoundly about that. What the man is,
Not what he was to unawakened eyes,
Engages those who have acknowledged him
And are alive today. Though he has wrought
With common tools, he does not ask of us
That we be carpenters."

                Caiaphas laughed unheard,
And curled a quiet lip. "I am glad of that;
For you might cut your finger, Nicodemus.
And what's all this that you are telling me
Of men dead yesterday and still alive?
I do not know such men, and would far rather
Not meet them in the dark."

                    "It is not there
That you are like to know them, Caiaphas.

NICODEMUS

They have come out of darkness—where we are,
I fear, and where I fear we may remain.
High men, like you and me, whether by worth,
Or birth, or other worldly circumstance,
Have risen to shining heights, and there may still
Rise higher, where they shall be no higher than earth.
Men who are braver may forgo their shining,
Leaving it all above them, and go down
To lowliness and peace, and there find life.
Caiaphas, you and I are not alive.
We are two painted shells of eminence
Carried by two dead men. Because we move,
And breathe, and say a few complacent words
With tongues that are afraid to say our thoughts,
We think we are alive. But we are dead."

Caiaphas laughed: "Small wonder, Nicodemus,
That you conceal your death in some such rag
As that there on the floor when you go calling
On carpenters at night. How strong, I wonder,
With his assumptions and assurances,
Must a man be to be a carpenter
And honor your condescension without laughing."

"My fears and vanities are confessed. He smiled,
If that will comfort you, and then assured me
That he had more than once himself been driven
Not only to expediency, but hiding.
Yes, Caiaphas, good men like you and me
Have driven this man, if he be man, to vanish
Beyond the laws that hate him."

                      "Why not say
Beyond the laws he hates, and done with it?
What's wrong with them? Would his be any better?

1161

Our laws and Caesar's are enough, God knows,
To keep the safest of us occupied
With not forgetting them. This man is mad.
Believe me, Nicodemus, he is mad,
Or such an overflowing charlatan
As never was before. I have not heard him,
But waves of his high language have made echoes
All through Jerusalem. Beware of him,
I say to you, and stay at home o' nights.
I can see peril waiting, Nicodemus,
For this man—and for you, if you pursue him.
I am not given, or over much, to meddling,
But if you love him and would tell him so,
Tell him his home is not Jerusalem,
And hasten him away. You have the power
And place to save him. Save him, and you save more.
If he is what your folly says he is,
Why should he hide from powerless things of earth
Like us, who cannot hurt him? What strength is ours
To injure him? What can we do to him?
No, the whole story shakes. It's like a house
That creaks too soon—one that he might have built
When at his trade."

             "You may destroy his body,
Which is an instrument whereon the spirit
Plays for a time—and not for a long time,
He tells me. He must hold it as he may
From harm till there is no more use for it.
Meanwhile he is a man, with a man's end
Awaiting him. There is no fear in him,
But for the blindness that is ours who fear him."

"I am no more than man," said Caiaphas,
No longer smiling. "But I do not fear him;

NICODEMUS

And saving your regard, I am not blind.
Whether or not I am the painted shell
Of something dead, requires a contemplation.
I had not thought so, and had not been told
Until you spoke. Your vocal ornaments
Are not all complimentary this evening.
Are they the carpenter's?"

                "No, they are mine,"
Said Nicodemus briefly, with a sigh.
"And they are past retraction or improvement.
You may forget them, but I'll not unsay them;
And spoken words that are unsaid are said
Only a little louder than at first.
No, Caiaphas; we are dead, and we are blind;
And worse than either, we are both afraid.
You don't like that."

             "I treasure it so little,"
Caiaphas answered, rather quietly,
"That from another I might not receive it
Without a word in kind. But you are mad;
You and your carpenter are mad together,
And God sees what's to come. My office owes
A few indulgences and obligations
Even to madness, and I'll say no more—
No more than one more warning, Nicodemus,
That you provision your seditious prophet
Out of Jerusalem, and with no lost time."

"In God's name, Caiaphas," cried Nicodemus,
Rising and holding out his hands as if
To clutch two hands unseen, "is one poor string
The sum of all your music, and one word
Your only song? Because you are afraid,

1163

Must you see nothing in the world but fear?
There is no fear in this man, Caiaphas.
He shuns a little while a coming death,
Which he foresees, that you and I may live;
And your fond warning now that I may save him
Is like a child's unwillingness to read
A book of easy letters that are life,
Because they are new letters, and not death.
You are a priest of death, not knowing it.
There is no life in those old laws of ours,
Caiaphas; they are forms and rules and fears,
So venerable and impressive and majestic
That we forget how little there is in them
For us to love. We are afraid of them.
They are the laws of death; and, Caiaphas,
They are the dead who are afraid of dying.
So do not say again that I may save
This man from death. There is no death for him."

"There may be something comfortingly like it,
If he is here too long," said Caiaphas;
"And I may soon be weary, Nicodemus,
Of hearing you repeat that I'm afraid.
The laws that were our fathers' laws are right
For me, and I can see no death in them,
Save death itself—which is the only death
I know. I know it, and I do not fear it;
Or not more than another. Only the mad
May welcome it, so long as life is better.
Have you a finger to lay on a law
Of ours that says to us we shall be mad?"

"No, Caiaphas; I'm not saying that we are mad.
I'm saying that we are dying while we are dead.
He tells me of light coming for the world,

NICODEMUS

And of men loving darkness more than light.
He is the light; and we, who love the dark
Because our fathers were at home in it,
Would hound him off alone into the hills
And laugh to see that we were rid of him.
In darkness we might see as much as that,
Not seeing what we were doing for ourselves
In doing ill for him. He will not die,
Though he find death where we have driven him.
The pity and waste of it is our not living,
With life so near us, and to take as ours,
Like shining fruit from an undying tree.
The fruit may fall, and we may crush the pulp
And blood of it, but it will not be dead.
It will replenish and increase itself
Immortally, because it is alive—
As even the lowly are, who love him first.
The lowly are the first inheritors
Of his report, the first acknowledgers
Of his reward—having no fame to lose,
No brief and tinsel perquisite of pomp,
Or profitable office, to renounce.
They are not politicians, Caiaphas,
Like you and me, who tremble when we step
An ell's length from the middle of the road;
They are not sceptred slaves of precedent
And privilege, who must buy their breath of life
With fears and favors and hypocrisies
That would, if recognized, make honor sick.
I say this, Caiaphas; for I have heard you
Citing the riff-raff that he feeds with words,
Telling them words are food till they believe it.
You have not heard and tasted them to know,
Or not to know, the food that lives in them
And quickens them till they are words no longer,

But are the Word. We tenants of high places
Are too high now to hear them, or to see
From where we are the inevitable harvest
Of this eternal sowing. Come with me,
But once, to see and hear him, Caiaphas;
Or, to be more courageous than I am,
Be once an item in the multitude,
And let yourself inquire, for once, how much
The lowliest, in his primal composition,
Would look, if you were God, like Caiaphas.
You don't like that, but there's a time for man
When he must speak, or die, or follow himself
To deserts where men starve and are forgotten.
I could starve here as well, and hate myself,
No doubt, a little harder for so doing.
I could sit starving in these noble robes,
As you have called them in your pleasantry,
But they would not be noble—not for me.
Truth is a sword of air cleaving the air,
Sometimes, to make it bleed; and here am I,
Armed, you would fancy, with a sword like that.
You smile to see me strike, drawing no blood—
Though blood may follow, and may God say whose,
And all so needlessly and against fate,
Except it be his fate that his worn body
Shall perish that he may live. So many have died
Before their work has lived that one more dying
Will not be new on earth; and this man's dying
Will not be death. What has truth done to us
That we must always be afraid of it,
As of a monster with a shape unknown
To man, prowling at night and breathing fire?
The truth is not like that; we are like that—
Or would be so if we were not so little.
Not all Jerusalem creeping in one skin

1166

NICODEMUS

Would make a monster for this man to fear.
One fiery word of truth would pierce and frighten
Jerusalem then as now. We are afraid,
Caiaphas; and our flawed complacency
Is a fool's armor against revelation.
Why must we turn ourselves away from it?
If you and I together should stand with him,
For all to see, who knows what we should see!"

"We might see stones flying to find our heads,
For one thing, Nicodemus. You are mad.
Say to your carpenter that he is mad,
Or say what else you will. Take him away
While there is time, and hide him where the law
May lose him, or forget him. Telling you this,
I'm trying to say that a long suffering priest
May love a madman who has been a friend."

"Caiaphas, you are sorry to say that,
But will not own your sorrow, or your fear.
When sorrow hides itself in sophistry,
It might as well be scorn. I should have known.
I should have gone alone to my cold house
That will be colder for my coming here.
God knows what ails us in Jerusalem.
You cannot wash the taste of your misgivings
Away with wine, or rub the fear of them
Out of your face with an unquiet finger.
There's no security in a subterfuge
Where truth is marked a madness. I am not mad,
Unless a man is mad who brings a light
For eyes that will not open. I have been
A burden for your patience, Caiaphas.
I shall not come again."

"Yes, many a time,
I trust, and always welcome, Nicodemus.
When this absurdity has overblown
Its noise, and is an inch of history
That a few may remember, you will come.
There is a covenant that has not changed,
And cannot change. You will not go from us
For a mad carpenter; and as for him,
I am afraid for him unless you save him.
You may do that, but he will not save you—
As you would say it; for you are one of us,
And you will save yourself at the last hour;
And you will be as wary of Messiahs
Henceforth as I am. You may take yourself
Alone to him at night and feast with him
On dreams till you are drunk with his evangel,
And when your frenzied head is clear again,
You will rejoice, like a man dug from ruin,
To find the sun and stars, and the old laws,
Unfailing and unchanged and firm as ever.
You and your carpenter, while you have eyes,
Will not be seen as man and man together
Where there is daylight in Jerusalem.
Some things are not, and this is one of them.
When he is chained, or stoned, or crucified,
As like enough he will be if you let him,
You and your sorrow may be seen, too late,
Mourning where safety and necessity
Have buried him. But you will never be seen
With him beside you in Jerusalem.
I know you, Nicodemus."

Nicodemus
Trembled and held his cloak with clutching hands
As if it were his life. "Safety, you say?

1168

Necessity, you say? Panic, I say!
Panic, and ancestors, and desperation!
Rabbits and rats! God help me, Caiaphas,
If I am what you see. If you are right,
I am not worth my name."

               "As one of us,"
Caiaphas answered, and his words were calm—
"As one of us, I see you, Nicodemus,
True to our laws and hearts, and to our God,
Who chastened even Moses when he faltered,
And held him out of Canaan. Am I right?
Why, surely I am right. I am always right.
If I were wrong, I should not be a priest."

Caiaphas rubbed his hands together slowly,
Smiling at Nicodemus, who was holding
A black robe close to him and feeling it
Only as darkness that he could not see.
All he could see through tears that blinded him
To Caiaphas, to himself, and to all men
Save one, was one that he had left alone,
Alone in a bare room, and not afraid.

SISERA

FROM Taanach to Harosheth, by the river,
Barak had driven Sisera and his thousands
Till there were only a last few of them
Alive to feel, while there was time to feel,
Jehovah's hand and Israel's together,
Smiting invincibly. A slave of Canaan
For twenty years, now Israel was a slave

No more; and by the waters of Megiddo,
King Jabin's army was a picture drawn
Of men who slept. Sisera felt the dead
Behind him, and he knew the sound of death
Pursuing him—a sound that sang no hope
Or mercy for the few that were alive
Of Israel's enemy, and the last alive
That were to sleep that day, and for so long
As to be loved and trumpeted no more
By time and man than all who are forgotten.

Sisera, soon to see himself alone
Among the slain, or soon as one of them
To see not even himself left of his host,
Suddenly from his chariot, to rough ground,
Leapt as an animal from a flying cage
That plunged and rocked and staggered might have leapt,
Blindly, to wild escape and a short freedom.
Prone for a moment on hard earth he lay,
Bruised and amazed to find himself unbroken,
And with a quicker leap was up again,
And running—running as he believed no manner
Of man had run before—to the one place
He knew that might receive him yet and save him.
Heber the Kenite had no world to lose
Or win with either side, and was not fighting.
He was in Canaan frequently, moreover,
King Jabin's guest and friend; and his wife Jael
Was Jabin's adoration and desire,
And Sisera's despair. She frightened men
With her security, and she maddened them
With dark hot beauty that was more than woman's,
And yet all woman—or, as Jabin said
To Heber, enviously, perhaps all women
In one. If Sisera's fear remembered now

SISERA

That there was more of Israelite in Jael
Than Canaanite or Kenite, he was running
Too fast and furiously and ruinously
For memories to be following him so far
As to the tents of Heber, where he prayed
For Jael and sanctuary. Her smile would save
A captain, as her frown would blast a king,
If she but willed it so. Sisera's feet
Flew as he thought of that, and his thought flew
Before him like a promise that he followed,
And followed flying. For an insane hour
He flew, and for another, and for a third,
And then fell helpless at the feet of Jael,
Who smiled at him unseen—which was as well
For Sisera; for her smile would save no captains,
Or none today.

              "If this comes out of Canaan
For me to save, then Israel must be free,"
She thought; and a thought slowly filled her heart
With music that she felt inflaming her
Deliriously with Deborah's word fulfilled.
Again she smiled, and went for cloths and water
To wash his heated face and his closed eyes,
Which, having seen her and been sure of her,
Saw nothing else until he felt the touch
Of her cool fingers and of her warm breath,
Incredible and together. His eyes opened
And found hers over them, shining at him
With a protection in them that he feared
Was too much like a mother's.

                        "Speak," she said,
"And tell me who has fallen in this battle,
And who fares well. We Kenites are peace-lovers,

1171

Not mixed with either camp—yet we must know.
Tell me, and sleep."

       "Yes, if you let me drink,"
He whispered, "I will tell you. Let me drink,
Or let me die. Let me die here with you,
If I must die. Not many of us are left
To die. This day is Israel's. Let me drink,
Or let me die. Let me die here with . . ."

          "No,"
She said, and smiled at him mysteriously.
"We are alive; and while we live—who knows?"
He reached with a blind hand for one of hers,
And held it while she said, "No, you must drink,"
And smiled: "Is there in Israel or in Canaan
A bowl of sleep like this for one so weary
As you? I have seen weariness before,
But never a man so made of weariness
That he shall not be flesh and bone again
Till sleep has made him so. Is it not cool
And healing as you feel it on your tongue,
And in your throat, and through you everywhere—
Like life itself? It is the milk of life
That you are drinking. It will make you leap
Like a new lion when you are awake.
Yes, when you are awake. Now, now, my friend,
Now is your time to sleep."

        "Before I sleep,
Hear this," he said: "There will come after me
Some ravening fiend of Israel to destroy me.
They will have nothing left of us alive.
For twenty years they have worn Canaan's yoke,
And always, in their dreams have known Jehovah,

Still watching them. They have believed in him;
And their belief will be the end of me—
Unless you say to them no man of Canaan
Has crossed your sight this day. If I say this
Asleep, or still awake, I am not here. ·
No man was here . . . No man . . ."

                          "No, Sisera,"
She said with lips that moved without a sound,
"No man was here that will depart from here,
Except as weary meat for scavengers.
Was that what you were saying? It must have been,
For that was what I heard." She waited, crouching,
And watched him with exalted eyes of triumph
That were not any longer woman's eyes,
But fixed and fierce and unimagined fires
Of death alive in beauty and burning it.
"No, Sisera; when they come, if they do come,
No man will be awaiting them. No man
Is here today who has not seen his last
Of Israel, and feared all there is for him
To fear of Israel. You are asleep
As only trust and weariness together
Makes a man sleep; and you will not feel this."
She laid an eager finger on his temple,
And pressed it, satisfied. Still watching him,
She moved away; and searching among shadows,
Found all she sought. "No, Sisera," she said,
Crooning above his face like a mad mother,
"There is no fear of Israel, or of earth,
Or of men living on earth, or things not men,
That you need fear today, or more tomorrow.
When they come here for you and say to me,
'Where is he?' I shall say, 'He is not here.
All that is here is yours. Take it away.'

See, Sisera! See what I have found for you.
Here is a nail as long as a man's life—
And sharp as death; and here is a brave hammer.
I found them there in the dark, where I remembered
Seeing them once. We had all best remember
Things we have seen, for soon or late we need them.
So, Sisera!"

          Slowly she drew away
The pillow she had lent his head to lie on,
And left his head lying sidewise on the floor.
Still crouching, she surveyed him, saying softly,
"So this is Canaan, who for twenty years
Believed that he was more than Israel!
Who is he now? What is he, Sisera?
You will not answer; for where Canaan sleeps
This day and night, there will be sleep indeed.
I can see thousands of you lying quiet;
And one will be one more."

                    The nail, sure-driven,
Transfixed a silent head that would not move
When she would see its face. And with him there,
What was a face? She had seen Sisera's face
Before; and it was no more Sisera now
Than were his fingers or his feet, she thought.
A face was not a man; and a man dead
Was less, or so it looked, than was a nail.
And she had driven the nail to make him dead,
For Deborah to celebrate, and for Barak
To see, and for all Israel to see.
Her life within her body was like fire—
A fire that healed in her the wrongs and sorrows
Of Israel sold in Canaan to a king
Who made a sport of his malignity,

And Sisera's; and now Sisera was dead.
All Israel would be told in a few hours
That Sisera was dead.   And Deborah then
Would say to Barak: "The Lord's will be done!
Jael has killed Sisera—sing!—sing to the Lord!"

Still crouching over him, and watching him
Like an avenging image, she could hear
The coming sound of horses, and soon with it,
Confirming it, a murmur of men talking.
"Barak!" she told her heart; and her heart said,
"Barak!"   And Jael arose in her rejoicing.
Outside she saw them, Barak and his men,
Who had known where to come.   With arms aloft,
And eyes afire with triumph and thanksgiving,
She stood awaiting Barak.   "Yes, he is here,"
She said; "and he is yours for no more seeking.
He will not fly away from you again."

"Hardly, if he is here," said Barak, halting.
He smiled at her with battle-heated eyes,
And met the fire of hers with admiration,
Mingled with weariness and victory,
And with a searching wonder.   Then a spasm
Of silent laughter shook him and his voice:
"If he is here, you must have promised him
More than a man may give to make him stop.
We might have seized him, if necessity
Had said we must, and we might have him now
To count with his lost thousands; but we knew
That Heber's tent would hold him, if such running
As his might last until you took him in.
At first, and for some time, we only watched him;
And all the horses watched him.   Never since man
Was born to run has there been such a running

1175

As this of Sisera's here today in Canaan.
Children who are unborn will emulate it;
And aged men will rise up out of chairs,
Remembering Sisera, and sit down again.
There's not a curse's worth of Canaan left,
Nor more than Sisera left of Jabin's army;
And Sisera's only safety is between
Jehovah and a woman—which is good,
If Jael is the Lord's woman. Well, where is he?"

Jael, who had partly heard him, turned and said,
"Follow me, Barak. I will show him to you.
And you, having seen how quiet and safe he is,
Will praise me. I shall have praise of Israel,
And of Jehovah shall have praise and glory,
For this that I have done. Since I remember,
I have heard voices of high prophecy,
Telling me to fulfil myself with patience
And readiness against an untold hour.
Now is the hour. The chosen of the Lord
Are told, if they will hear; and when the Lord
Has need of them they serve him—as they must.
My way to serve him was magnificent,
And will be praised for ever . . . See him, Barak!
Tell Deborah what you saw. Tell Deborah
That he is dead! Tell her that he is dead!
Tell her that everything that she foretold
Has come to pass. Tell her that he is dead!"

Barak, abrupt in battle, and in slaughter
Not subtle, till now had always made of war
A man's work, and of death attending it
An item necessary for a total.
So long as he should live, and live to fight
For Israel and for glory of the Lord,

1176

Others would cease to live if they opposed him;
For that was the Lord's way, and Israel's way.
But this was not. He stared at Sisera's head,
Where the nail was, and slowly shook his own
Before he spoke: "I am not sure of this,"
He said, and looked at her uncertainly,
As if to ask for the first time, perhaps—
Whose hand held death for him. She who did this
Might one day flout her fealty to Jehovah
And lust for Baal. She might do anything.
So Barak only scowled and said to Jael,
"I am not sure of this. How was this done—
If he was not asleep?"

                    "He was asleep,"
Jael said; and her eyes measured him with scorn
For one so artless and inquisitive;
"The Lord put him to sleep, and gave me strength
Of more than one small woman to destroy him.
So there he is. Tell Israel to rejoice.
Tell Deborah to rejoice. Tell Deborah
Where you saw Sisera dead, and bring her here
That she may see him. It was she who said
That Sisera was to die—and he is dead.
What is one man, or one man's way of dying,
So long as Israel has no more of him!"

Taut and erect she stood, and her possession
Bewildered Barak and astonished him
Into an awkward silence. All he did
Was to look down at Sisera, and once more
At Jael, not sure that he was looking at her.
At last he sighed, and made as if to throw
His hands away, having no use for them;
And having sighed again, he said to Jael,

"A world that holds so much for men to know
Must have been long in making. The Lord pondered
More than six days, I think, to make a woman.
The book of woman that has troubled man
So long in learning is all folly now.
I shall go home tonight and make another.
The wisest man alive, wherever he is,
Is not so wise that he has never wondered
What women do when they are left together,
Or left alone." He stood with folded arms
And with shut jaws, gazing at Sisera's head,
And at the driven nail piercing his head.
Scowling and thoughtful, he considered them
In silence, and then said, after some time,
"The tiger's wife, we're told. . . . I've all to learn.
Is this what women do?"

              "Tell Deborah,"
Jael answered, as if answering a voice
Farther away than Barak's, "that I killed him.
Tell Deborah, who foretold it, that a woman,
A woman filled with God, killed Sisera
For love of Israel, and that you have seen him,
As he is now, with no more harm in him.
Tell Deborah this right hand of mine was God's
That hammered in the nail—while Sisera slept.
Tell her my hand was God's that held the nail—
While Sisera slept. Say Jael and God together
Made Sisera what you see. Sing to the Lord,
Barak! And say to Deborah, 'Jael says,
Sing to the Lord!' For now there shall be peace
In Israel, and a sound of women singing—
A sound of children singing, and men singing—
All singing to the Lord! There is no king
In Canaan who is king of Israel now!

TOUSSAINT L'OUVERTURE

This day is ended—and there is no King
In Israel but the Lord! Sing to the Lord!
Let Israel see the dark·of a day fading,
And sing!—praising a day that has an end.
Let Israel see the light of a day breaking,
And sing!—hailing a day that has a dawn.
Sing to the King of Israel her Thanksgiving!
Sing to the King of Glory! Sing to the Lord!"

TOUSSAINT L'OUVERTURE

(Chateau de Joux, 1803)

Am I alone—or is it you, my friend?
I call you friend, but let it not be known
That such a word was uttered in this place.
You are the first that has forgotten duty
So far as to be sorry—and perilously,
For you—that I am not so frozen yet,
Or starved, or blasted, that I cannot feel.
Yes, I can feel, and hear. I can hear something
Behind me. Is it you? There is no light,
But there's a gray place where a window was
Before the sun went down. Was there a sun?
There must have been one; for there was a light,
Or sort of light—enough to make me see
That I was here alone. Was I forgotten?
I have been here alone now for three days,
Without you, and with nothing here to eat
Or drink; and for God knows how many months,
Or years, before you came, have I been here—
But never alone so long. You must be careful,
Or they will kill you if they hear you asking

1179

Questions of me as if I were a man.
I did not know that there was anything left
Alive to see me, or to consider me,
As more than a transplanted shovelful
Of black earth, with a seed of danger in it—
A seed that's not there now, and never was.
When was I dangerous to Napoleon?
Does a perfidious victor fear the victim
That he has trapped and harassed? No, he hates him.
The only danger that was ever in me
Was food that his hate made to feed itself.
There lives in hate a seed more dangerous
To man, I fear, than any in time's garden
That has not risen to full stalk and flower
In history yet. I am glad now for being
So like a child as to believe in him
As long as there was hope. And what was hope?
Hope was a pebble I brought here to play with,
And might as well have dropped into the ocean
Before there was a bitter league of it
Between me and my island. It was well
Not to do that. Not that it matters now.

My friend, I do not hear you any longer.
Are you still there? Are you afraid to speak?
You are the first thing fashioned as a man
That has acknowledged me since I came here—
To die, as I see now—with word or motion
Of one man in the same world with another;
And you may be afraid of saying to me
Some word that hurts your tongue. Have they invented
A last new misery fit for the last days
Of an old sick black man who says tonight
He does not think that he shall have to live
Much longer now? If there were left in me

1180

TOUSSAINT L'OUVERTURE

A way to laugh, I might as well be laughing
To think of that. Say to Napoleon
That he has made an end of me so slowly,
And thoroughly, that only God Almighty
Shall say what is to say. And if God made him,
And made him as he is, and has to be,
Say who shall answer for a world where men
Are mostly blind, and they who are the blindest
Climb to cold heights that others cannot reach,
And there, with all there is for them to see,
See nothing but themselves. I am not one
To tell you about that, for I am only
A man destroyed, a sick man, soon to die;
A man betrayed, who sees his end a ruin,
Yet cannot see that he has lived in vain.
Though he was crushed and humbled at the last
As things are that are crawling in man's way,
He was a man. God knows he was a man,
And tells him so tonight. Another man
Mixed fear with power and hate and made of it
A poison that was death, and more than death,
And strangled me to make me swallow it—
And here I am. I shall not be here long
To trouble you; and I shall not forget
Your seeing in me a remnant of mankind,
And not a piece of God's peculiar clay
Shaped as a reptile, or as a black snake.
A black man, to be sure; and that's important.

I cannot tell you about God, my friend,
But in my life I have learned more of men
Than would be useful now, or necessary,
If a man's life were only a man's life.
Sometimes it is, or looks to be, no better
Than a weed growing to be crushed or cut,

Or at the most and best, or worst, to live
And shrivel and slowly die and be forgotten.
Others are not like that; and it appears
That mine was not. Mine was a million lives,
And millions after them. Why am I here!
What have I done to die in a cold hole
In a cold land that has no need of me?
Men have been mightier than in doing this thing
To me, I think. Yet who am I to say it?
An exile, buried alive in a cold grave
For serving man, as men may still remember.
There are diseased and senseless ways of hate
That puzzle me—partly because I'm black,
Perhaps, though more because of things that are,
And shall be, and for God may say how long.

Hear me, and I will tell you a strange thing—
Which may be new and of an interest
To many who may not know so much of me
As even my name until my name shall have
A meaning in this world's unhappy story.
Napoleon cannot starve my name to death,
Or blot it out with his. There is an island
Where men remember me; and from an island
Surprising freight of dreams and deeds may come,
To make men think. Is it not strange, my friend—
If you are there—that one dishonored slave,
One animal owned and valued at a price,
One black commodity, should have seen so early
All that I saw? When I filled sight with action,
I could see tyranny's blood-spattered eyes
That saw no farther, laughing at God and fate,
Than a day's end, or possibly one day more,—
Until I made them see. Was it not strange?
Drivers and governors of multitudes

TOUSSAINT L'OUVERTURE

Must be more than themselves, and have more eyes
Than one man's eyes, or scorn will bury them,
Or leave them worse uncovered; and time will pass them
Only to kick their bones. I could see that;
And my prophetic eyes, where God had fixed them
In this black face, could see in front of them
A flaming shambles of men's ignorance
Of all that men should know. I could see farther;
And in a world far larger than my island
Could see the foul indifferent poison wreaking
Sorrow and death and useless indignation
On millions who are waiting to be born;
And this because the few that have the word
Are mostly the wrong few in the wrong places.
On thrones or chairs of state too high for them,
Where they sit swollen or scared, or both, as may be,
They watch, unseen, a diligent see-saw
Played by their privileged and especial slaves
On slippery planks that shake and smell of blood
That flows from crushed and quivering backs and arms
Of slaves that hold them up. There are more slaves
Than have yet felt or are to feel, and know it,
An iron or a lash. This will go on
Until more slaves like me, and more, and more,
Throw off their shackles and make swords of them
For those to feel who have not felt before,
And will not see. It will go on as long
As men capitulate who feel and see,
And men who know say nothing. If this means
It must go on for always—well I have done
All that one man—one black man, I should say—
Could do against a madness and a system
And a malicious policy, all rotten
With craft and hate. It will be so again:
Humanity will hear the lash of scorn

1183

And ignorance again falling on hope,
And hearing it will feel it. Ignorance,
Always a devil, is a father of devils
When it has power and fire and hate to play with,
And goes down with the noise of its own house
Falling, always too late to save itself,
Because it has no eyes. That's power, my friend.
If you are sorry to be born without it,
Be sorry for something else, and answer me:
Is power a breaking down of flesh and spirit?
Is foresight a word lost with a lost language?
Is honor incomprehensible? Is it strange,
That I should sit here and say this to you—
Here in the dark? . . . Nothing to eat or drink,
Nothing to do but die? This is not right. . . .
Hear me, and I will tell you what I saw.

Last night I saw Napoleon in hell.
He was not dead, but I knew where he was,
For there was fire and death surrounding him
Like red coals ringed around a scorpion
To make him sting himself rather than burn.
Napoleon burned. I saw his two hands flaming;
And while I saw him I could see that hate
For me was still alive in his blind eyes.
I was no happier for the sight of him,
For that would not help me; and I had seen
Too much already of crime and fire at work
Before I made an end of it—for him
To make of peace a useless waste and fury.
I have not yet gone mad, for I have known
That I was right. It seems a miracle,
Yet I am not so sure it is a mercy
That I have still my wits and memories
For company in this place. I saw him there,

TOUSSAINT L'OUVERTURE

And his hands that were flaming with a fire
They caught from the same fire that they had lighted.
So fire will act, sometimes, apparently.
Well, there he was, and if I'm not in error,
He will be there again before he dies;
And that will not be medicine here for this.
There is no cure for this, except to die,
And there is nothing left that is worth hating—
Not even the hate of him that kills with hate.
Is it that I am weak—or am I wise?
Can a black man be wise? He would say not.
Having his wisdom, he would have to say it
To keep his hate alive; and without that
He would soon hate the sound of his own name.
Prisons have tongues, and this will all be told;
And it will not sound well when men remember.

Where are you now? Is this another night?
Another day—and now another night?
I do not hear you any more, my friend.
Where are you? Were you ever here at all?
I have been here alone now for too long.
They will not let you come to see me again
Until you come to carry a dead man—
I see it now—out of this cold and darkness
To a place where black and white are dark together.
Nothing to eat or drink—nothing to do
But wait, and die. No, it will not sound well.
Where are you now, my friend? I cannot hear you;
I cannot feel you. Are you dead, perhaps?
I said to you it would be perilous
Not to remember that I'm not a man,
But an imprudent piece of merchandise
To buy and sell—or this time rather to steal;
To catch and steal, and carry from my island

To France, and to this place. And in this place,
Is it not strange, my friend, for me to see
So clearly, and in the dark, more than he sees
Who put me here—as I saw long ago
More than a man could do, till it was done?
Yes, it is done, and cannot be undone.
I know, because I know; and only those
Whose creed and caution has been never to know
Will see in that no reason . . . Yes, I know,
My friend, but I do not know where you are.
If you are here, help me to rise and stand
Once more. I cannot sleep. I cannot see.
Nothing to eat or drink—nothing to see
But night. Good night, my friend—if you are here.

Nothing to see but night—and a long night,
My friend. I hear you now. I hear you moving,
And breathing. I can feel you in the dark,
Although I cannot see you. . . . Is this night?
Or is it morning! No, it is not night—
For now I see. You were a dream, my friend!
Glory to God, who made a dream of you,
And of a place that I believed a prison.
There were no prisons—no Napoleons.
I must have been asleep for a long time.
Now I remember. I was on a ship—
A ship they said was carrying me to France.
Why should I go to France? I must have slept,
And sailed away asleep, and sailed on sleeping.
I am not quite awake; yet I can see
White waves, and I can feel a warm wind coming—
And I can see the sun! . . . This is not France—
This is a ship; and France was never a ship.
France was a place where they were starving me
To death, because a black man had a brain.

PONCE DE LEON

I feel the sun! Now we are going faster—
Now I see land—I see land and a mountain!
I see white foam along a sunny shore—
And there's a town. Now there are people in it,
Shouting and singing, waving wild arms at me,
And crowding down together to the water!
You know me—and you knew that I was coming!
O you lost faces! My lost friends! My island!
You knew that I was coming. . . .

                                   You are gone.
Where are you gone? Is this the night again?
I cannot see you now. But you are there—
You are still there. And I know who is here.

PONCE DE LEON

(HAVANA, 1521)

IN Florida, the fair land he had named
In admiration of its many blossoms,
And for its opulence of promises,
De Leon, with an arrow in his thigh,
Lay stricken on the shore of his new world,
Cursing it while he groaned and heard the sound
Of water washing always on the sand.
Around him, in a circle, all his men,
Burning in armor hardly to be borne,
Stood sweltered in defeat, and in despair
Of what was next to do; and high above them,
Blazing as if to melt them and their master,
The tropic sun rose higher. A look of thanks
For their protection and their loyalty,

Was all he had for them while arrows flew
From ambush, like fierce insects, and found iron
Instead of flesh.

              Only when they were all
Afloat again, and safe away from arrows,
Was there more time for words: "If this thing here
Is venomous, you had better pray for me,
For you may do no more. I know its method,"
He said, and scanned the arrow that he held
Now in his fingers. "Take me away from here.
There is a man of learning in Havana,
A sage and a physician, an old man,
Whose ways are famous. Men have said of him
That he reads all that we have written on us
Of what we are within, and has a genius
In all obscure things that are physical,
To make them right and well. It may be so,
But I am bitten deep; and I am older
Than a man is who tames a wilderness
For sport of being the first. I should have known
Before that my home now is in my house,
Which I have left behind me, and may see. . . .
Well, we shall see."

              Time and a silent voyage
Brought a slow ship and its unhappy freight
At last into the harbor of Havana,
Where the man was who might explore and heal
De Leon's wound, if there was healing for it
In mortal knowledge . . . And when all was done
That might, for even the most magnificent
Of invalids, be feasible, the physician
Would only smile and say, "You are too old,
My lord, for such a perilous game as this.

1188

PONCE DE LEON

Have you not fought and toiled and found enough
For one man's appetency, without this?
Why has a man a fair wife, and a house
Of state, and famous wealth, and a grand name,
If he must only sail away from them
And let one vicious hidden angry savage
Do this? Is Midas less than a mosquito?
God save you men of action, who will never
Be done with acting. Be a child again
In spirit, and our Saviour will reward you;
But if you be a child again in deeds,
He may be overtaxed, and leave to nature
Those who offend it. He left nature with us
That we should recognize it and observe it,
And through it find a wiser way to grace
Than we are finding yet."

                   De Leon, lying
In a wide room that was as cool as rooms
Could be in Cuba, said with a twist of pain
That might have been a smile, "I see the drift
Of your evasions, or believe I do;
For I have been a sinner in this world
Of sin too long, and heard too many lies,
And told too many, to receive as healing
Your playful way of covering a last hope
With colors that I fear are mostly made
Of dust and water."

               "You are making words
Into a poultice for your pain, my lord;
And I have seen strong men who have done less,
And with less fortitude. If speech is hard,
Lie with your eyes closed for a little while,
And let some valorous pictures of yourself

And your performances inspirit you
More than I may. To you that shake the world
And change it, and have never enough of it,
We that are only scholars, or physicians,
Are so like books with faces, books that walk,
That we must let you do our living for us,
And thereby be the mightier. You are mighty;
So close your eyes, and let the past come back."

"There is too much of it that will come back,
My friend, whether I close my eyes or not.
There are no valorous pictures of myself
That will inspirit me, as you will have it,
And there are few of my performances
That are good memories, or good food for souls.
You say the arrow was not venomous,
But that another venom has come in
To make my wound a flame and a damnation.
You know, not I. I don't know that it matters
What fire it is that burns. For I am burning,
Burning; and this poor fuel that I am
May not last long. Unless the fire goes out,
I shall weigh more as ashes than as man.
Doctor, are you my friend? You say you are,
And your eyes are an answer. If you are,
How long have I to live?"

                    "Could I say that,"
The old man answered, partly with his shoulders,
"I might be questioned as an evil spirit,
And burned alive. Is it not God's first mercy
To suffering man that he shall not know when?
Why do you ask for more than you would know?
Will you in your distress, and your disaster,
Forget what you have made of these wild islands,

1190

PONCE DE LEON

Or what your royal mother, royal Spain,
Will say of you? Nor Spain alone, my lord;
For there's a world will say it. So take heart
Of glory, and be glorious over pain.
Your deeds are yours, and what is yours is you.
And what of all the gates that you have opened,
With your name shining over them in gold?
Is there dominion without victory,
My lord? And is there victory without price?"

"Doctor, I see so little to deceive me
That your deceit is innocence. Forgive me—
I mean your kindness to a stricken man,
Who sees more gates with his name over them
In blood now than in gold. Or why not both?
When were they not blood-brothers and allies
In this 'dominion' and this 'victory'
Of yours? Are they my comfort and reward?
Dominion, is it? There was more of it
In one small arrow than there was in me.
You know; and all your skill and all your science
Will give me only words to make me well."
The old man smiled: "I say to you again,
Unlock the casket of your memories
And gaze on what is in it. You will see
Jewels of conquest there, rich and intact,
And indestructible; and you will see
Treasures of effort and accomplishment
Waiting for time's account."

                              "Yes, time's account,"
De Leon answered, "will indeed appraise them.
The only jewels of mine that I would see
Today are my wife, Ines, and her children.

I left them all, a man too old for folly,
For a fool's voyage to find in Florida
God knows what sort of gain.   Jealous of time,
Or Cortes, I must have a world unknown
To conquer and call mine.   When does a man
Become his years, and see that these new doings
Are not for men at rest and in the shade,
With deeds enough behind them to remember,
And to be sorry for?   I practised evil
Sufficient for one man's alacrity
In Boriquen, or call it Puerto Rico,
And should have been content.   Now I can see,
And read the wisdom of a wiser God
Who hid from me that fountain I was after,
In a lost island that I never found,
That I might flourish always.   Had I found it,
I might have walked with iron feet for ever
Over the maimed or slaughtered flesh and faces
Of those who trusted me.   Are we the worst,
We Spanish, of all who might have been appointed
For the blind occupation and the ruin
Of this new land, or are we as we are
Because we are here first?   Are the first always
The worst?   Are they, being drunk with ignorance
And opportunity, by God's will ordained
And pampered for their ultimate undoing?
Does history say so?   I am not a scholar,
And have not read so deeply as to know.
Meanwhile I fear me, and for proper cause,
There may stay after us, here in these islands,
A mortal odor that will smell of slaughter,
And will be slow to die, being death itself.
I wish to God that we who have done this
Had not forgotten time in our time-service."

1192

PONCE DE LEON

The scholar shook his head, and laid his hand
Affectionately on De Leon's forehead.
"My lord, there is no hope in this you say,
Although God knows there may be truth in it.
Truth is not always hope; nor, as we learn,
Is anguish always death. There are surprises.
Listen, and you will hear a sound of hope
In those slow waves below us on the shore.
They break, and end; yet they are always there,
And they are never ending. Do you hear them?"
De Leon sighed, glad for the touch he felt,
Cool on his forehead: "Doctor, your poor wallet
Of words has not much left in it for me.
Have you an ear so out of tune with truth
As to believe that there was ever a sound
Of hope in any waves on any shore?
My living hope is where you know it is,
And it is not in waves. Are you so dry
With desperation as to make me drink
The sound of water, saying there's life in it?
Here's water, at least, and not the sound of it;
And water warm as blood. Is God's whole world
Itself burning alive, as I am burning?
Your hand is cool, doctor; yet if those waves
Down there have any hope in them for you,
You are the father and mother of hope. For me,
They are the music of time's funeral,
Which is a long one, and appears to have
No end. My friend, your eyes accuse your tongue,
And they say truth to one whose place and fame
Are two delusions, founded and established
On tricks and treacheries and exterminations.
God!—must a man be looking at his grave
Before he sees of what his house is built
That he is leaving?"

>   "No, no! You are speaking
> As one of your despairing islanders,
> Who sees extinction in a slow eclipse—
> Until the shadow vanishes."

>   "No, no,
> My friend. And mine is a more potent no
> Than yours, for I have memories, and my eyes
> That see where yours do not. There was a land
> Where destiny had been asleep for ages
> Until I came to shake it, and my reign
> Began. There was no going away from it,
> Or leaving it unused, for time had spoken;
> But there are farther seeing ways than ours
> Of cutting nature's throat. I was the end
> Of nature for those children of the earth,
> Who hailed me as they would have hailed a god—
> With joy and welcome, and with adoration.
> They more than half believed that I was God,
> Until I was revealed and was a devil—
> Far worse than any of theirs; for theirs at least
> Were native, and were understandable.
> My ways were not so devilish, if you like,
> If you insist, as were Ovando's ways
> In Haiti, but I'll say no more for them.
> You are a doctor of our minds and bodies;
> You have read many books, and have left men
> To die, knowing your knowledge could not save them—
> Which is not much to know. To know yourself
> Incarnate and inviolate in God's image,
> You should be noble. You should be the flower
> Of man, with a new world for you to ruin,
> And ruin it, to see things that we have seen.
> Then you and others like you, and like me,

1194

PONCE DE LEON

Might see men drown themselves and hang themselves,
And women leap with children from high cliffs,
Rather than see your faces any longer,
Or meet another sunrise. If they knew you
As a physician, and as one of us,
They might avoid you, or might be too sick
To care."

    "Oh, this is bitterness, my lord!
You may be feeling wounds you never made.
I have heard many legends of Ovando,
Of Roldan and of Esquival, and others,
And their extremities, but fewer of you
And yours. There may be gratitude unspoken
For you in some dark hearts, and silent thanks
For thoughts and acts that you may have forgotten;
And you may still go back, and find them there."

De Leon smiled, and frowned—feeling a tear
Tickle his cheek. "There is no gratitude
Awaiting me, nor silent thanks, I fear,
Save in my house, where they may well be silent.
For I shall not go back—or not without
Some flags and cannon to say who is coming.
We noble knaves and worshipful bloodhounds
Must have processions and reverberations
When we are dead, or men may not believe
That we were noble. I shall be heard, not hearing
The sound my going makes. I only hope
When I am out of this, I shall not hear
Some cries, and other sounds, that I have heard
Above the music my renown has made
For my magnificence. I have heard sounds,
Doctor, not to be heard—not even in hell."

"You are saying this to me alone, my lord;
And you are wiser for not hiding it
Within you, to become another poison.
The marks that you are making on yourself
Are more the brand of a bad fellowship
And of a seething fever, drugged with gold,
I fancy, than of ingrained willing evil.
If we knew more of our self-clouded means
And privileges, I might say more of this.
Being man, I say no more—saving a word
Of thanks to God, and of congratulation
To man, for your not coming to your fountain."

De Leon smiled again: "I have said that,
My friend, and with no lightness of defeat,
Or cynical deliverance. I believe
There is a time for man that has been measured,
By a wise God, and measured mercifully.
When I asked that old woman from Luquillo,
Who came once to my house with a long story
Of water that would heal man of his years
And hold him here for ever, if she herself
Had tasted it, she laughed at me, and said,
'No, master, I am doing well without it.
But it is there, and I will send you there,
If you are sure that you are thirsting for it.
Be sure that you are sure. I have lived well
For more years than I need to live again,
And I don't want it.' I conceive suspicion,
Doctor, when I set out on that north voyage,
That I was looking more for a new land
That I had never seen, than for a fountain
That I should never find. I never found it;
And while you look at me, I am not sorry.

For there is peace and wisdom in your eyes,
And no fear for the end—which is worth more
To me now than all fountains. Tell me something.
Tell me—what does it mean?"

                               "Some of it means,
My lord," the old man answered, easily,
"That hidden voices are in some of us,
And, when we least would hear them, whisper to us
That we had better go the other way.
And other voices are in some of us,
Telling us to go on as we are going—
So long as we go sensibly and fairly,
And with a vigilance. There are voices also,
Saying that if this world is only this,
We are remarkable animate accidents,
And are all generated for a most
Remorseless and extravagant sacrifice
To an insatiate God of nothing at all—
Who is not mine, or yours. And there are voices
Coming so far to find us that I doubt
If you, my lord, have yet an ear to seize them.
They may be near you now, unrecognized,
If not unwelcome, and like unseen strangers
In a dark vestibule, saying in vain
That they are always there. You cannot listen
To more than you may hear; you cannot measure
More than is yours to comprehend."

                               "No, doctor,"
De Leon said, holding his pain as hands
Of island slaves held fire, because they must,
"But you may see me lying here on this rack,
And pierce me with hot wires until I die.

Forgive me. All you say is excellent
For my nobility, but no cure for me.
What else I may have earned, I may know soon.
Now it will not be long."

              There was a pause
That was not hesitation. "No, it will not
Be long, my lord." The old man said it kindly,
And without sorrow, and without regret
That was revealed: "I shall soon follow you,
For I am old; too old to be afraid,
Or to care tragically where or when—
So long as there are voices."

              "There are voices,
Doctor, which I am glad you do not hear.
And I am glad your eyes are watching me.
They say more than you told me. Without them,
Your words might all have crumbled, or been lost
In that long sound down there of broken water,
Where you found hope. I can see more in them
Than I can see in all the sixty years
That I have lived. I don't say what it is;
I don't know what it is; and shall not ask—
So long as it is there. It may be voices."

"I doubt if they will hold or show so much
For you as that, my lord," the old man said;
"Though surely my old eyes, which have seen more
Than they will see again, or wish to see
Of this torn world and its infirmities,
Should have some wisdom in them by this time,
And some forbearance. There is no cry for haste,
Yet when you have revealed your memories

PONCE DE LEON

To your confessor, and have made your peace
With God, you will be wiser, and be done
With fear, which I see written on you still.
Your pain will then be less your enemy
Than fear is now. You do not look to me,
My lord, so black as you have drawn yourself
In your defeat. Ambition forgets time,
And opportunities are mighty forces;
And we are not omnipotent, or all-wise.
I am not very wise; but I am old,
And I shall follow you in a few years,
Or a few days—or I may go before you.
Our minutes are all arrows. If one strikes,
There is no balsam for it, and we go;
And Time has a last arrow for himself."

"Doctor, if you were God, I should believe you;
Since you are mortal, I can only thank you
For saying not too much truth. If I might live,
I might exalt you, and give you a name
Larger than mine. You would not care for that—
Or for my fountain. It was best for me,
And for all men, that I was not to find it.
Now let me say to God all that He knows
Of me that I may say. I hope He knows
A little more of me than I remember."

De Leon sighed, and felt the old man's hand
Cool on his forehead, as it was before,
And closed his eyes to be alone with pain.
Yet he was not alone, for the same eyes
Were there. He smiled, knowing them to be there,
And opened his to say that he was ready.

ANNANDALE AGAIN

ALMOST as if my thought of him
Had called him from he said not where,
He knocked. I knew him through the door.
And Annandale was waiting there.

Nothing of years or distances,
Or deserts that he may have ranged,
Betrayed him. He was Annandale,
The only man who never changed.

"Do as you must," he said, "and God
Will say that you have done no wrong.
Begin by disappointing me,
And ask where I have been so long.

"What matter's it where I have been,
Or on what mountain or what star?
All places are as much alike
As all men and all women are—

"Which is not much. The best of us
Are curiously unlike the worst;
And for some time, at any rate,
The last shall never be the first.

"Wherefore I leave them, having done
No harm to them, or none to show."—
There was no liking such a man;
You loved him, or you let him go.

"Dreamers who crave a common yoke
For bulls and ewes and elephants
May have it; and my having mine
May be a soothing circumstance

1200

ANNANDALE AGAIN

"For you and me, and for my wife;
I mean my new wife Damaris.
I'll tell you, if you must be told,
The sort of woman that she is.

"When Miriam died, my former wife,
I wept and said that all was done;
Yet even as long ago as then
My darkness had a smothered sun

"Behind it, trying to shine through.
More like a living voice of light
It was, than like the sun itself,
And my night was not wholly night.

"And my world was not wholly gone,
As I had feared. Well, hardly so.
I wonder we should learn to live,
Where there's so much for us to know.

"For that, we don't. We live meanwhile;
And then, with nothing learned, we die.
God has been very good to him
Whose end is not an asking why.

"But I'm astray, beginning ill
To lose myself in setting out;
It was my new wife Damaris
That you were asking me about.

"Your interest was an innocence,
And your concern was no surprise.
Well, I have brought her home with me,
And you may find her in my eyes.

"In general, there's no more to tell;
Yet there's this in particular:

She knows the way the good God made
My fur to lie; and there you are.

"And that's enough; you know the rest.
You know as much as I may learn,
Should we go to the end of time
Together, and through time return

"To now again. I should like that,
Ad infinitum. So you see
How graciously has fate prepared
A most agreeable trap for me.

"For where we stay because we must,
Prison or cage or sacrament,
We're in a trap. This world is one,
Obscurely sprung for our ascent,

"Maybe, till we are out of it,
And in another. Once I thought
My cage was dark; but there was light
To let me see that I was caught

"For always there, with Damaris
In the same cage. It's large enough
To hold as many as two of us,
With no constraint worth speaking of.

"The Keeper, who's invisible,
Reveals himself in many a sign,
To caution me that I shall read
And heed the benefits that are mine—

"I don't say hers. Still, if she likes
Her cage with me, and says it's home,
And sings in it, what shall I say
That you may not find wearisome?

1202

ANNANDALE AGAIN

"You doctors, who have found so much
In matter that it's hardly there,
May all, in your discomfiture,
Anon be on your knees in prayer

"For larger presence of what is
In what is not. Then you will see
Why Damaris, who knows everything,
Knows how to find so much in me.

"She finds what I have never found
Before; and there's a fearsome doubt,
Sometimes, that slumbers and awaits
A day when Damaris finds out

"How much of undistinguished man
There is in her new destiny.
When she divines it, I shall not
Be told, or not immediately—

"Nor ever, if I'm as amiable
As her attention apprehends.
I'm watching her, and hiding tight
Within me several odds and ends

"Of insights and forbearances
And cautious ways of being kind,
That she has dropped like handkerchiefs,
Conceivably for me to find.

"But one shall not acquire all this
At once, or so it would appear.
I've lain awake establishing
Her permutations in a year—

1203

"Not always indispensable,
You say; and yet, for recompense,
Revealing, when it looks like rain,
A refuge of intelligence;

"Which, with all honor to the rest
That makes a cage enjoyable,
Is not the least of ornaments
That every woman may as well

"Inherit as an amulet
For disillusions unforeseen—
Assuming always that for her
May still be some that have not been.

"Meanwhile, perfection has a price
That humor always has to pay
With patience, as a man may learn
Of woman when she has her way.

"While Miriam lived, I made a book
To make another woman wise.
Blessed are they who are not born
Above instruction by surprise.

"But there was wisdom in it too;
And there are times her eyes are wet
With wonder that I should foresee
So much of her before we met.

"Again, when her complexities
Are restive, or she may have bruised
An elbow on the bars of home,
I may be for a time confused;

1204

ANNANDALE AGAIN

"But not for long. She gratifies
A casual need of giving pain;
And having drawn a little blood,
She folds her paws and purrs again.

"So all goes well; and with our wits
Awake, should go indefinitely—
Sufficient without subterfuge,
Harmonious without history.

"You'll find us cheerful prisoners
Enough, with nothing to bewail.
I've told you about Damaris;
And I'll go home."—Poor Annandale!

Poor Damaris! He did not go
So far as home that afternoon.
It may be they offended fate
With harmonies too much in tune

For a discordant earth to share
Unslain, or it may just have been,
Like stars and leaves and marmosets,
Fruition of a force unseen.

There was a sick crash in the street,
And after that there was no doubt
Of what there was; and I was there
To watch while Annandale went out.

No pleasure was awaiting me,
And there would have been none for you;
And mine was the one light I had
To show me the one thing to do.

Sometimes I'll ask myself, alone,
The measure of her debt to me
If some of him were still alive,
And motionless, for her to see;

Sometimes I'll ask if Annandale,
Could he have seen so far ahead,
Had been so sure as I am now
Of more than all he might have said.

I'll ask, and ask, and always ask,
And have no answer; or none yet.
The gain that lives in woman's loss
Is one that woman may forget

For a long time. A doctor knows
The nature of an accident;
And Damaris, who knows everything,
May still be asking what it meant.

THE SPIRIT SPEAKING

(CHRISTMAS, 1929)

As you are still pursuing it
    As blindly as you can,
You have deformed and tortured it
    Since ignorance began;
And even as you have mangled it,
    The Letter has killed man.

Because a camel cannot well
    Go through a needle's eye,
No jealous God has ever said

YOUNG GIDEON

The son of man must die;
Only the God that you have made
Has mocked you from the sky.

No God has in his mightiness
Told you that love is fear;
And some of you, who are almost
Too mighty to be here,
May fancy that you are not so—
If only once a year.

As long as you contend with it
For longer fear and pain,
As always you have injured it
And angered it again,
A grief and a malevolence
The Letter will remain.

YOUNG GIDEON

(JUDGES, 6)

YOUNG Gideon would have threshed his father's wheat
With no more words, and as obediently
As other sons were toiling in Manasseh,
Where toil was tribute and a vanity.

Another day would be another day
For Gideon now; and round him everywhere,
Whether he toiled or slept, there would be always
Eyes watching, and a presence of despair.

There were too many presences with eyes,
Invisible and alert; they were like fire,

1207

Piercing his heart and brain, till anger made him
A slave without ambition or desire.

Why toil so long to feed a Midian mouth,
With shame his only wages? Why not make
Jehovah's wrath aware of one who feared him
Less than he feared dishonor for his sake?

If this was life, why not be done with life?
The means at hand was his, and his the choice.
So Gideon waited for the word within him,
Hearing it not. He heard instead the Voice.

The least of a small nouse in a poor land
Until today, he shook, and feared to raise
His eyes to see the common things around him
That looked as far off as old yesterdays.

He knew, and still he feared—as prisoners fear
The weariness of waking. Yet he knew;
He knew that his one doubt was a thing dying
Before it should be born. It was all true.

God found him young, and in his youth had found
Faith to mock knowledge, knowledge to mock fear.
Why then was he afraid if he feared nothing?
God knew his Gideons, and the way was clear.

He would have danced and sang there where he was,
With Israel pitying him, for all he cared.
Meanwhile he pitied Israel for not knowing
How many were soon to perish, or be spared.

Now that he knew the man that in himself
Had been a stranger, freedom, like a bell,

Sang through him; and he knew that while he trembled
His fear was only joy for Israel.

He trembled while he felt the Midian yoke
Releasing him; and there was in release
No fear, until a second morning found him
Fearing to find the dew upon the fleece.

THE PRODIGAL SON

You are not merry, brother. Why not laugh,
As I do, and acclaim the fatted calf?
For, unless ways are changing here at home,
You might not have it if I had not come.
And were I not a thing for you and me
To execrate in anguish, you would be
As indigent a stranger to surprise,
I fear, as I was once, and as unwise.
Brother, believe, as I do, it is best
For you that I'm again in the old nest—
Draggled, I grant you, but your brother still,
Full of good wine, good viands, and good will.
You will thank God, some day, that I returned,
And may be singing for what you have learned,
Some other day; and one day you may find
Yourself a little nearer to mankind.
And having hated me till you are tired
You will begin to see, as if inspired,
It was fate's way of educating us.
Remembering then when you were venomous,
You will be glad enough that I am gone,
But you will know more of what's going on;

For you will see more of what makes it go,
And in more ways than are for you to know.
We are so different when we are dead,
That you, alive, may weep for what you said;
And I, the ghost of one you could not save,
May find you planting lentils on my grave.

HECTOR KANE

If Hector Kane at eighty-five
Was not the youngest man alive,
Appearance had anointed him
    With undiminished youth.
To look at him was to believe
That as we ask we may receive,
Annoyed by no such evil whim
    As death, or time, or truth.

Which is to doubt, if any of you,
Seeing him, had believed him true.
He was too young to be so old,
    Too old to be so fair.
Beneath a snowy crown of curls,
His cheeks that might have been a girl's
Were certainly, if truth were told,
    Too rose-like to be there.

But Hector was a child of earth,
And would have held of little worth
Reflection or misgiving cast
    On his reality.

1210

HECTOR KANE

It was a melancholy crime,
No less, to torture life with time;
And whoso did was first and last
   Creation's enemy.

He told us, one convivial night,
When younger men were not so bright
Or brisk as he, how he had spared
   His heart a world of pain,
Merely by seeing always clear
What most it was he wanted here,
And having it when most he cared,
   And having it again.

"You children of threescore or so,"
He said, "had best begin to know
If your infirmities that ache,
   Your lethargies and fears,
And doubts, are mostly more or less
Like things a drunkard in distress
May count with horror, while you shake
   For counting days and years.

"Nothing was ever true for me
Until I found it so," said he;
"So time for me has always been
   Four letters of a word.
Time? Is it anything to eat?
Or maybe it has legs and feet,
To go so as to be unseen;
   Or maybe it's a bird.

"Years? I have never seen such things.
Why let your fancy give them wings
To lift you from experience
   And carry you astray?

1211

If only you will not be old,
Your mines will give you more than gold,
And for a cheerful diligence
   Will keep the worm away.

"We die of what we eat and drink,
But more we die of what we think;
For which you see me still as young
   At heart as heretofore.
So here's to what's awaiting us—
Cras ingens iterabimus—"
A clutch of wonder gripped his tongue,
   And Hector said no more.

Serene and inarticulate
He lay, for us to contemplate.
The mortal trick, we all agreed,
   Was never better turned:
Bequeathing us to time and care,
He told us yet that we were there
To make as much as we could read
   Of all that he had learned.

THE MARCH OF THE CAMERON MEN

An autumn twilight on a quiet lake;
A silent house, with more than silence in it;
A boat, and a man resting on his oars;
A woman with him, looking at the shore,
And inland where the house was, and the trees.

Since that was all there was to be a picture
That she was tired of seeing so long, she said:

1212

THE MARCH OF THE CAMERON MEN

"Row me into the middle of the lake,
Where there shall be no eyes, or possible ears,
To watch or listen. We are alone, you say;
But we are not alone who are so near
A shore alive with silence. I can hear it,
And feel it holding me. It has cold arms,
Like one of those unnecessary monsters
That God must once have hidden in the sea
Because he was afraid of his own work.
He has done much to make himself afraid,
And more to make us wonder why he does it.
No, I am not afraid. I am only saying
We are too near that house where silence lives."

"A most unlovely fancy, nevertheless,
For one so lovely as you are," he said,
And smiled at her: "Well, it will not be noisy
Out there where we are going."

            "We are going
So far," she said, "that we may not come back;
Or not as we are now."

            "I'll pray for that
While I am rowing; and you may as well
Pray also. There will be no harm in it,
And I shall see you—which is always prayer
For me, and prayer enough. . . . So here we are,
With not an ear to listen, or an eye
To watch. My eyes are occupied with you,
But yours are always looking at the water—
As if to see a monster with long arms.
You will not see him—not unless you find
His image in your fancy. By this time
You must have heard an inward little voice,
Saying that you are free."

"It is too soon,"
She said, "for me to hear too many voices,
Though I can hear a few that follow me.
And there are still our mortuary manners
To be remembered. We are not yet so free
That custom has forgotten us."

"Not yet;
And I deserve a ribbon and a cross
For not forgetting that. You know by now
A love as careful of its counterfeit
As it was careless of its cost. You know
By now, and with all said, how much there was
Not said—and all for manners. That was right,
And we shall hold ourselves a little closer
For not outreaching death. There was a lapse
That I regret. There was no more than one;
And there was one only because . . ."

"Be careful—
Or you will say it badly and be sorry.
And I can see no right that sorrow has
To follow us out here." She sought his eyes
With hers, and smiled as if to punish him.

"If I was careless once, it was because
Life made you as you are. How, I don't know.
No more have I a knowledge to define
A few not all celestial elements
That I would not see elsewhere than in you.
Although a doctor, I would not remove
Their presence, or transmute them. As you are,
You are more perilous than snakes and lions,
Or anything in the sea; and as you are,
You are more than a man's life; mine, or another's.

THE MARCH OF THE CAMERON MEN

You drove me away once, but I came back.
I came because you said you needed me—
Because you called me. I could hear men marching,
And I was all those men. I was an army,
And you the banners that were over me.
In a forgotten tune that you were drumming
On dim keys, aimlessly, in a dark room,
I could hear drums and pipes down all the ages
That I had waited. I had come home again,
Where no home was for me. I could not stay,
And could not go; for there was a man dying,
Unless my skill should save him. It was you
Who called me back again; and we were there,
Together where darkness was. If you had willed it,
You might have driven me into this lake to drown—
Or possibly not quite. We'll say, perhaps,
You might have driven as much of me to die
As would have been worth living, and left the rest
To go on as it might, ingloriously.
Sparing me that, you drove me back to life.
You might have driven me then to anything.
You drove me once to song."

                       Waiting, he smiled,
And watched her fingers touching the cold lake
As if it scalded them. "If I did that,"
She said, "there must be power unfound in me,
Deserving a discovery. I daresay
If only more physicians would bring songs,
And sing them to us, they would save more lives.
What song is this of yours that I inspired?
Sing it, or say it. Was I playing it?"

"You played for me unseen; and as you played,
Music made words. I have not written them,

Or said them until now. Their only worth
Is in whatever there is of you in them—
Which, if assayed and analysed, appears
A little playful and equivocal:

> '*Any tune in the world would have told him as well*
>   *As another of all that was there,*
> *For a beggar with only a story to tell*
>   *And a woman with nothing to spare.*
> *But you called, and a king who believed he was dead*
>   *Was alive and undying again:*
> *It was you, and the night, and the stars overhead,*
>   *And the March of the Cameron Men.'* "

"Yes, I remember—now," she said. "I played it
There in the dark. I don't know where it came from.
Where do things come from that are so forgotten
That we have lost them and the names of them,
And are not sure we had them? You were coming,
And I was calling you with an old tune
That must for years have hidden in my fingers,
Waiting for you to come. Were the stars hidden
From you until you heard it? I hope not."

He gazed at her uncertainly, and answered
As a man willing still to be assured:
"There was more hidden from me than the stars,
And you know that. All that I'm seeing now,
All that I waited for, and has been waiting,
Was hidden; and I was hidden from myself.
God, what it is for me to see you here—
You here, alone! I said there was an army
Marching along with me to find you there
That night, and so there was. It was an army
Of new days to be born of joy and hope,

1216

THE MARCH OF THE CAMERON MEN

A phantom regiment of realities
That now are—almost real. I hesitated
For the same reason that bewilders me
In seeing you here and saying it is you.
It may be well for us that we know slowly
What sorrow teaches; we know better then
What peace and freedom are when they are ours.
And freedom now is not for us alone;
For there's another free, there in that house—
The same house where I came and found you waiting.
You had been angry and implacable
So long before, and for so long been silent,
That I was nothing till I was a king:

> *'In your smile was a gift of ineffable things,*
> *And of more than all scholars have learned.*
> *In a palace where beggars were richer than kings*
> *There was more to be given than earned.*
> *Not a murmur remained of a storm that was past,*
> *Or of why it had happened, or when.*
> *You had called, and he came; and he found you at last*
> *In the March of the Cameron Men.'*

"You are still giving, and more than I shall earn
If I live always. Love has a way sometimes
Of giving and of hiding what it gives
Until it withers and is not the same—
Yet this is not an hour for telling you
So much less than you know. It seized me then,
Much as another stanza that I made
Came out of nowhere—and, as one too many
Has always done, troubled the other two
Until it recognized itself and vanished,
Leaving the two sufficient. Now you know
The sort of minstrel I might be, if urged,

And honor me the more as a physician.
You may as well rejoice within you also,
For your sake and for my sake, and for his,
For what has come to be . . . God, is it you—
At last! A smile would make me sure of you.
I am not asking you to laugh, you see—
Not now. Are you afraid I do not know?
Are you afraid that I'll forget myself
And be a fool—with him there, in that house?
No, I shall not do that."

                          "I'm not afraid,"
She said, and smiled for him. "But I am hearing
The marching feet of all those Cameron Men.
They are going, I suppose, to kill somebody,
Or to be killed themselves. I wonder why
So many of our songs and melodies
That help us to forget, and make us happy,
Are born of pain, and oftener of defeat
Than victory. I believe those lines of yours
Told all you knew, all you will ever know,
About the melancholy why of things—
Out of which hope was born."

                          "They were not made,"
He said, "to make you melancholy. Rather
I fancied you might recognize in them
A triumph coming to you from a distance,
Through a long darkness, to an open door
In your unhappy house. If you had been
Away from there, there would have been no house
Worth coming to; and if you had not smiled,
I should have gone again. Did you hear nothing
In those poor lines of mine to tell you so,
And make you happier for not sending me

1218

THE MARCH OF THE CAMERON MEN

Away from a closed door? Nature has done,
Since then, only as much as you have prayed for
With all but words. There was no need of words
To speak a wish or make a purpose clear
While you had eyes to ask. Did you get nothing
Of joy, or of release, or of thanksgiving
Out of those lines of mine?"

                                        "Surely I did,"
She said, "But you said only some of them.
I shall be surer when I have them all
Of what it is they say, and of what music
It was that I was making when you came.
Men marching all go somewhere—some to freedom,
Some to captivity, and some to death.
The dead are free, I hope. I wish we knew.
Or—no, perhaps, I don't. Tell me the rest
Of that so joyful song you made for me
About those marching men. You should have said
It ended there, or should have given me all
There was of it to hear. Never since God
Made the first heart and ears that felt and waited,
Was anything not revealed less perilous
For leaving it half said."

                                        He studied her
And tried to laugh, but his accomplishment
Was only a small broken sound of doubt.
"Was it a woman who was saying that?"
He asked; and with a shrug that was a sort
Of answer to himself, he hesitated.
"There was an end of it that went like this,"
He said, "but it was meaningless to me,
As it will be to you. When a thing's done,
Only a novice goes on doing it:

1219

'When he left you again there were stars in the way
Of his eyes, and he wandered alone
In a dream that would mock him for many a day
With a music unheard and unknown;
Till at last he awoke, and remembered, and found
All there was that remained of it then.
There was only the sound of the world going round,
And the March of the Cameron Men.'

"Nothing, you see, to scare you or disturb you.
Nothing—or no more than a footed fancy
Chasing its tail. I would have let it go
And lost it as a vagrant—willing enough
To see no more of it. But I'll obey
My lady's humor when she bids me serve,
Although her whim may whistle me to danger.
There is no danger now. Why do you gaze
At everything but me? Why do you look
So long across the lake to see that house?
You cannot see it. There are too many trees.
And even if you should find it, and be in it,
You would be there alone. He is not there.
There's only an old garment all worn out—
A body that he was glad to leave behind.
What is he now but one far more a theme
For our congratulation than our sorrow?
There was no happiness in him alive,
And none for you in your enduring him
With lies and kindness. It was a wrong knot
You made, you two; and one knot more or fewer,
In a world where there are still so many knots,
Will be forgotten and will not be found
In the large histories. Why are you looking
At that place, always? Men will come tomorrow
And carry him away to his last home,

And to his first. There was no home on earth
For him, and none for you while he was here.
What is it makes you seek so curiously
For what you would not see if it were there?"

"Nothing. I thought I heard those Cameron Men. .
Are they to march as long as I'm alive—
And over my grave, perhaps? . . . Yes, I remember.
You asked a question that has had no answer.
Nothing—except that once I married him,"
She said, and waited with inquiring eyes.
She touched again the cold lake with her fingers,
And shivered as if she were there alone.
"A woman's fancy would go back to that,"
Said he, "and make her say it as a duty.
Her way of never letting go a thing
That's gone would make of healing and escape
A pleasant incubus to bite her dreams.
I have known prisoners, free at last, not wholly
At ease with freedom, or at home with it."

"What had your lawless friends been at," she asked,
"To be so loth to walk abroad again?
Had they been killing men? Had they been doing,
Not quite with our precaution and finesse,
What you and I have done so delicately?
Why start? We are free now, and are alone
On a cold lake; and a lake has no ears."

She pierced him with a look that blinded him
Until he saw that she was humorous,
Whereat he smiled at her uncomfortably,
And partly laughed at her. "My faults," he said,
"Are numerous and acknowledged, and are mine
For penance or for pardon, as may be.

1221

COLLECTED POEMS

I have seen opportunity like water
Flow through my fingers when I might have held it;
I have been told the word I should have said,
And have been silent when I might have said it;
With a short road before me, I have followed
Trails that have ended only in the long
Forlorn way of return; with my eyes open,
I have walked into brambles and been scratched.
I am not blameless; I am not unsinged,
Or spotless, or unbitten. Have I said so?
Yet there is more of me than my mistakes,
Or you and I would hardly be together
Here in the middle of this chilly lake,
With night soon covering us. There's more of me,
Be sure, than a man asking for a woman
Who would not have him if she doubted him.
I'm farther from the pliocene than that;
And you would soon see in my care for you
How much of care there is in a man's love
When it is love—which is a little more
Than any myopic science isolates
With so much carnal pride. Now you are smiling—
Either because you doubt me, or believe
My doubts are talking. There is more of me,
I hope, than a pathetic mechanism
Grinding itself to nothing. Possibly not,
But let me say there is; and let me feel
Inside me that I've done more good than harm,
With my mistakes and opportunities
All marked against me on the other side.
Leaving an inventory to your fancy,
I'll only say that I see many alive
Who might be dead if I had never lived.
Some I have saved who might have loved me more
If I had let them go as they were going.

1222

THE MARCH OF THE CAMERON MEN

Sometimes I have imagined I was God,
And hesitated. I have seen the end,
Before their trial, of last and desperate
Experiments, and I have not suborned
The best of me in hastening nature's worst
Indignities of anguish and despair
To nature's end. I have done this before;
And if again—I shall have killed no man."

Once more she touched the water with her fingers,
And in the twilight smiled admiringly.
"A man's precision in extremities
Would say all that," she said, "and would forget
How it might sound if on a judgment day
Some God, or some inflexible magistrate,
Without your genius in the differences,
Might hear it and then make you say it over.
Your chivalry says 'I'—and mine says 'we.'
We have not killed him. We have let him die.
And we shall find him as we left him there.
He will not hear the sound of our return,
But we shall hear those Cameron Men, I think,
Still marching, always marching. I can hear them
Where we are now. You may have summoned them
With those last lines of yours—that meant so little
To you that you would rather not have said them
Aloud to me. Why do you think you made them?
Or, if they made themselves, what right had they
To make a music that in you already
Was marching when I called for you to come?"

A laughter for a moment in her eyes
Was like a flash of cruel triumph passing,
At which he scowled and wondered, and then smiled—
As the betrayed and the defeated smile.

"You have not scored so unapproachably
As to be laurelled or to live in song—
Or not for that," he said. "Am I the first
Who has confessed unwittingly misgivings,
Or premonitions, or the still small voice
That a man hears when he stakes everything
On Fate—whose name is yours? In face of all
The fairness of your magnanimity,
I'll still say that I did it. You are free.
I did it more for you than for my love—
Or so I did believe . . . God—is it you
That I am looking at! Are we alone—
Here on this lake together, and at last
With all that was intolerable behind us?
You are not thinking. You are only free,
And are not yet aware of what it means."

"Yes, I am free—if women are ever free;
And I am thinking—if a woman thinks.
You men, who from your scalps down to your toes
Are built of thought, are still debating it.
But I'll commit myself to your misgivings,
Your premonitions, and your still small voice,
And tell you what I think. . . . Horrors—hear that!"

The unearthly ululation of a loon
Tore the slow twilight like a mortal yell
Of madness, till again there was a silence.
"Fate punctuates our words and purposes,
You see, and that was a full stop," he said:
"It may have been a way of warning you
To say no more—except that you are happy,
Or that you will be when all this is over.
Tomorrow they will carry him away,
Out of that house, to sleep and to be done

1224

With all his persecutions. You are free
Of them all now. And you are free to think—
Of what you will."

         "I'll tell you what I think,"
She said; and her calm eyes were like a child's,
Waiting for the reward of his approval:
"I think that when a woman and a man
Are on their way to make of their two lives
Deliberate and ceremonial havoc,
There's folly in going on if one of them
Sees what's ahead, knowing the other sees it
And shuts his eyes. I have paid once for ruin,
And once will do. I thought, before I thought,
Before I knew, that I could see fair weather
For you and me, and only friendliness
In every natural sign that led me on—
Till I found nature waiting like a fox
For an unguarded pheasant. But I saw it
In time to fly away and save myself,
And, for my flying wisely, to save you.
There are some promises of mine, I know,
And they are best forgotten. If remembered,
They would be treasured more if broken and lost,
Like placeless remnants that are in most houses,
And in most lives. We stare at the old things,
Until they are all blurred with memories
That move and hum for us monotonously,
Like old ghosts playing on forgotten strings
We cannot see or hear. Your sound of the world
Going round is not unlike it."

                 A new chill
Now falling on the lake was not so cold
Or certain as a freezing realization

That gripped his heart. What sort of ignominy
Was this that pierced·him with an innocence
More venomous than contempt? It was not that,
But might as well be as be what it was.
"You thought, before you thought," he said at last;
"And when you sent for me, was it before
You thought, or was it after? You should know,
And I should know. Nothing in life appears
To me of more importance than my knowing
Just when it was you called me, and for what.
I saw you, on my journey, in my arms
At a long journey's end, and saw you smiling;
And so you were—and you were in my arms.
Why was all that? Why should I let him die,
But for a vision of lost years filled only
With you, and one of other years before me
That were not to be lost—with you in them.
Was it all shadows, then, before and after,
And all the time? Was it a shadow playing
For me when I came back there in the starlight?
Was it a shadow that inveigled me
To serve as agent of a weariness
That owns no purpose and has no remorse?
I say remorse, for nothing is that's ours,
Not even the gift of love like mine for you,
That has the refuge of too sure a credit
Against the price of time. We gambled there,
And are we both to lose? By God, my lady,
If I have heard you and have learned your language,
A quieter place for you than in his house
Would be a place with him where he has gone.
You should have silent earth, or say the bottom
Of this benevolent lake, where all is quiet.
You will not like that house when he's not there,
More than when he was in it."

1226

THE MARCH OF THE CAMERON MEN

                    "No," she said,
And shivered. "I have had enough of it.
I have been there too long. He was a devil,
And should have gone before. God was afraid
To let him live. You would have been afraid,
If you had made him. As for you and me,
You would have nothing, if you drowned me now,
But sorrow for your work. I should have peace,
But you would only have those marching men
To follow until you tired of them and died.
Would you have that, and would you call it wisdom?
Is it not better to be wise tonight,
And free tomorrow? To be wise and free
Has always been a dream for most of us,
And will remain a dream. Yet for a few—
For you and me—it will be real and easy,
If we will be ourselves. For your heart knows
More than it lets you say—as mine did once,
Before it let me think. His going away
Has left a clearness where it was all fog
While he was here. We shall see better now,
And there will be a time for you to bless me
That all has ended well. Some time or other
We shall see backward to this quiet hour,
Praising our wits because it was so quiet.
There is that loon again!—reminding us,
He says, that we have had his lake too long."

He sat with his head heavy in his hands,
Gazing at shadows. There was cold within him
Where triumph once alive had no life now.
There was not even anger to arouse it
Into false life again. "God—is it you?"
He said, and was not asking anything:
"And has it come to this? Is this the end?"

"Many have died for less than this, my friend,"
She answered; and her smile was like a blow
Dealt softly on his heart and staying there,
For time to cool and heal. "Now row me back,"
She said: "We must not be here in the dark.
He will be waiting for us, and will do us
No manner of harm. He will be there tonight,
But not tomorrow. We shall all go tomorrow.
I shall remember you, and pray for you;
And I shall always hear the Cameron Men."

TALIFER

(1933)

To the Memory of
Gamaliel Bradford

TALIFER

I

Althea, like a white bird left alone
In a still cage of leaves and memories,
Sat watching summer, seeing no more of it
Than scattered sunlight—which was better at least
For her to see than rain. There was no sound,
Or sight of sound, to say that even a leaf
Had left in it a whisper. The last voice
Had spoken, and said all there was to know.
The man whose voice it was that she had heard
There yesterday was now as far from her,
And was a phantom as intangible
To capture, as remembrance would have been
Of her first knowledge that she was alive.
Her world was dry and silent, and green vines
Around her where she sat, watching her thoughts,
Glimmered in vain to say their light was not
A darkness. If she looked away from them,
She might see other light for other women,
But they were all too far for much of that,
This afternoon; and she was only one
Of the Lord's playthings—if there was a Lord
Who lighted lamps only to put them out.
The sun might be a lamp, or the white furnace
Itself of life on earth, and it might burn
Earth and all on it slowly to a cinder,
Before Althea saw where she was going,
Or where there was to go, or what there was

Worth finding if she went. Calamity
Bewildered and outraged reality
Within her so completely, and profoundly,
That sorrow fought with rage to find a name
For nothingness. She made a little image
Of crumbling arrogance and desperation,
Saying its name was pride, telling herself
That if she held it fast and prayed to it,
And trusted it, she would be saved at last,
And satisfied. But while she fondled it,
Clutching it with an unavailing hope,
She felt and watched it falling dismally
To pieces; and she saw the pieces falling
Relentlessly to dust. Women in books
Had made of pride a guidance and a magic,
And walked with it through fire and desolation
To strength and safety. Women alive, also,
With only pride for sorrow's mask and armor,
Had suffered charmingly; for she had seen them,
And seeing them she had wondered not a little
How it was done. Now it was hers to know
More than a babbling tells. Never till now
Had she foreseen herself assailable
And appetizing to the common tongue,
But now she was, or was to be tomorrow,
A diet and a sustenance of talk
For an immortal hunger that began
In Eden, when Eve told the animals
All about man. There were tears blinding her,
And she could only smile at a brave fancy,
Forlornly with her mouth; and her mouth shook
In a new way that was not humorous.
There was no mirth in Eden. There was fire;
And she was driven alone into the dark,

1232

Where there was no way back. She must go on
Alone; and there was no place anywhere
For her to go. It was all old enough,
Or so tradition sang; and she supposed
That there were women enough who might have told her
That it was always new, and very strange.

There was no sound until her heart heard steps
Of someone coming. Was he coming back?
Never, she said; and she prayed, saying it,
That he was coming back. Hidden by trees
That once had shaded her lost ancestors,
A man, with a man's feet, was coming nearer,
Soon to be visible, and now recognized
As one of all men, saving always one,
Who might not be unwelcome. Unannounced
And unexpected, here he was again,
After another foreign wandering,
Deploringly to find only himself
Attending and awaiting him, he said,
Wherever he went next. Althea's house
Was always the last house he left behind him,
He said, and it was always the first house
Before him sailing home. Always, he said.
Althea might explain it or forget it,
But so it was. It was her fault, not his,
He said, that she was perfect.

                              "Where," she asked,
"Have you been hiding for a hundred years?"
She said it with a smile at which he stared
With doubt that would have been unmannerly
Anywhere else. "When you are sure you know
My face—well, you might ask me for my name."
And then she bit her lips.

"I know all that,
My child," he said. "I know you never meant it.
Moreover I have asked for it already,
More times than you have trees. Just why, I wonder,
Am I, a man of merit, always asking
At the wrong door? And about when, if ever,
Are you to pleasure my nobility
So far as to believe me, and to trust me?"

There was no cloud or question in her eyes
When she said, "I have always trusted you.
I shall believe you too, some day or other.
When you have carved for me an amulet
Of quicksilver, perhaps, I shall believe you.
And I shall say to it how sorry I am
For having let you go. But don't go now!"

His round untroubled face, alive with charm
That would have neutralized an ugliness
Not there, and with a weakness underlying
A solemn counterfeit of easy strength,
Was that of a safe counsellor—for her,
At least. If there was nothing else in him
For sorrow to be sure of, there was love—
A love that was uncertain of its name,
And for its best endurance better so.
"I shall not go—not yet," he said. "Not yet—
Not even if you throw ornaments at me."
And after a small comment on his absence,
Uttered and heard indifferently, he laid
His warm hands like a father's on her shoulders,
And fancied he could feel her soul and body
Trembling together under a thin shroud
Of summer white. He frowned and shook her slightly.

TALIFER

"Now sit you down and tell good Doctor Quick
What most it is that isn't as it should be,"
He said, letting her go like a man losing
More than was his to hold. "So. Here we are.
I had supposed there would be joy-bells ringing
By this time, or before. But I don't hear them.
And as for joy, what thief has hidden it,
Or frightened it away? It has not gone
For always. And where's Talifer, meanwhile?
He is not dead. You would have told me so.
You said it would be June, and time says June
Is half a part already of time's ashes.
And if he is not dead, what means all this
That I don't see? If ever a man pursued
One woman only, and that woman you,
And worshipped her, that man was Talifer.
Why are you here? Why have you not his name?
Why is the last of all the Talifers
Alone in his old house? And why are you
Alone in your old house? Do you love houses
More than you love yourselves? I should have known
A few more men and women by this time
Than would have been enough to make amazement
A stranger to their most egregious doings;
But I saw wrong—and where? Until you tell me,
My wits will have no pivot, and my friendship
Will have no exercise. I am working hard,
You see, to make your way an easier one
To find, if not to follow. Follow it now,
And you will have me with you to the end;
For I am Doctor Quick, your humble servant,
Respectful and obedient, and for ever."

"I know you are a friend," Althea said,
"And I am safe with you in word and person.

1235

With June half gone, I cannot be amazed
That you are here, with all your knives, to cut
Sick answers out of me to make me well.
I felt you cutting me, and may have suffered—
Although no cry came out of me, or none
That you could hear. Before I heard you coming,
Rumors or news of me must have been waiting
To seize your ears and fill them. You heard something."

"I heard what I believed was only nonsense
Unparalleled," he said. "You aren't confirming—
Regretfully I say it—my belief.
There was a time when two and two meant four;
Now they mean zero. And there was a time
When everything meant room for nothing else,
Or need of it; now it means ravening folly
For those who are elected to possess it.
These are new times, and there are new diseases
To make new invalids and imbeciles
Out of the soundest and the worthiest.
Now tell me what in hell's unhallowed name
Ails Talifer."

Althea moved her shoulders,
And laughed at him—as well as she could laugh;
And he sat watching a small piece of light
Lying on her soft orange-colored hair
Like a pale flame. "You know the only answer,"
She said; "and like so many a man of healing,
You have no more to say."

"Oh yes, I have,"
He answered. "I have more than would be sweet
For you to hear. I have not heard the truth;
I have heard early talk. If, as I gather,
Talifer told you only yesterday

Of his compelled descent to the ninth circle,
The town must wait, feeding on inference—
A food, alas, on which a town may feed
And fatten for some time. We can't help that;
Yet I may still help you."

               "Yes, possibly,"
She said; "or you may say green leaves are crimson;
Or you may push that shadow on the wall
Back where it was when I was here alone;
Or you may rub it out. I'll never deny
Your powers till I have seen them all at work.
And will you please forgive me? You are kind,
And you are my good friend. But kindness fails
When fate cuts off its hands. You are sincere,
This time, and I can ask of you no more.
If there were decency of hope or sense
In asking you for more, you might be sorry—
For I might ask too much. Women are greedy,
So long as there is hope, and may not always
Count what hope costs, or where. But you are safe;
All you possess is yours. I cannot use it,
For it would buy me nothing—which is mine
Already in abundance. All the rest
Went yesterday."

            "We'll say so, and forget."
He said it with a slow security
That puzzled her, and made her stare at him,
And wait for more. "We'll say so, for your sake,
And for the sake of harmony. Why bring in
Too soon the discord of a contradiction?
We do not need it yet, for I am hearing
More than your story tells; and I am seeing
More than a child who dreams. So Talifer

Came yesterday. I should know more of him
For knowing what he said. I know his theme,
But not his variations. Keren-Happuch
Was one of Job's three daughters, a fair damsel,
The fairer for a full inheritance.
This Karen here, our neighbor, Talifer's Karen,
Inherited a face, and little else
Than a cool brain. Let her be boiled or frozen,
Her feminine temperature, if she has any,
Would feel no change."

                             "If Job had three of her,"
Althea said, "he would have had enough
Without his boils. O Lord, what am I saying!
Don't listen. I don't know. I only know
That she has always hated me politely,
And flattered me because I have a house
That has an atmosphere and a tradition.
I do not need her envy or her learning—
You are not hearing this—to fathom that.
And now I have a man's word—yesterday
I had it, from his lips—that he has found,
At last, in *her* . . . No, I'm afraid to say it;
For I can't laugh today. And if you laugh,
I shall be sorry that you are my friend,
And that I cannot kill you. Well, then, listen:
Unless you listen you will never learn
What he has found in her. What do you think?
He has found—Peace. At last, he has found Peace.
I say it with a capital because
I see it written so on everything,
And everywhere I look. He was not sure,
With all that he believed was loyalty,
That he found Peace with me. And honor says
Hypocrisy can hide itself no longer

Within his heart. He feels it rankling there;
And where it rankles there may not be Peace.
Never, he says. He will be true and kind
Before it is too late for truth and kindness,
He says—to me! He will be kind to me
Before it is too late! What has she done?
And how, with her waxed language, has she done it?
Where is that wealth of sense and truth and wisdom
I gloried in because I called it his,
Till it was partly mine? Where's all that strength
Of his that made me strong, and humbled me
To such a comfort of security
That I loved life because he was alive?
What's a face made of strength, if it's a false one?
And what's this new necessity of honor—
This Peace? Am I a firebrand, or a whirlwind?
I thought he needed—me; and I was happy,
And wrong. Have I so little in my poor head
That he has pounded it and found it hollow?"

"Since that was in you to be said," said he,
"Let the past welcome it. For you must wait.
Now you are lost, and you are going nowhere.
There's more in this than has a definition.
If this were all an educated malice
On her side, and a silliness on his,
And a weak readiness to share disaster,
Most of us might be hanged and the world better
Without us. As for Talifer, we must wait.
I have seen men with jaws built to eat iron,
With eyes to scare you, chins invincible,
And royal noses; and I've seen them doing
More foolishness than you may dream of seeing
In forty nights. From all you say of him,
The man is bitten and the venom has him.

I do not say that Karen is a serpent,
Or any such easy trash of melodrama
As that. She is more like an ivory fish—
If you have seen one. They are fascinating,
For reason of their slimness and their skins,
But they are not proliferous, or domestic,
And are not good to eat."

         "Has one a right
To wonder, and to ask," Althea ventured,
Not struggling to conceal an interest,
"When you made such a progress in your knowledge
Of her and her best qualities?"

         He laughed:
"She felt a fever coming to consume her,
Once on a time, and sent for Doctor Quick,
Who found she had not fire enough inside her
For a combustion. She is still alive.
My lamp would still be going if she were dead."
He blew smoke at a walking grasshopper
On the porch-rail beside him, and was quiet.

"You and your nonsense are on friendly ground,"
Althea said; "and while you play together,
You will not be molested. I like children,
But not so well, sometimes, when they would make
A child of me. I am to wait, you say.
When a ship sinks, do those on board step out
And wait there for another?"

         "No," said he;
"But sometimes there are life-boats, hen-coops, belts,
Or furniture afloat that may be useful.
We do not mostly drown if we can swim,
Or drift, somehow, to shore."

"What do you mean,
Chiefly, by that?" she asked, with an unguarded
Sharpness edging her words. "I shall survive,
Undoubtedly. I shall not drown myself;
And I shall never find the shore again
That once I thought so firm. Now it is there
No longer: there is only darkness now,
And a black ocean where an island was
That was my little world. O God, how little
It was—if I had known! You do not see me—
You are not looking at me. Don't forget."

He rose, and with his quiet strength again,
Held her and felt her shaking in his hands.
"I shall forget," he said, "and so will you—
Sometime. Now listen, while I tell you . . ."

"No!"
She cried, and laughed. "Don't tell me anything!
For I know everything! He has found—Peace!
Peace! Peace!" . . . She would have fallen to the floor,
Still laughing, if his hands had let her go.
At last there was a trembling time of silence
Till he released her, and stood watching her
With eyes of sorrow and uncertainty.

"Now that's all over." He sat facing her,
And smiling from his chair. "We'll have no more
Of that sort, if you please. Now, if you listen,
I'll tell you something that you never knew.
I can see things. *La ci darem la mano.*"
He turned her hands, and while he studied them,
He sang until she smiled. "I can see change
Before you, like a friend who can do nothing
Until he comes. But you will see him coming,
And I shall see you waiting—learning to wait,
We'll say at first; and you are quick to learn.

You always were—though you have never learned,
Entirely, what you lost in leaving me
To grope alone and unappreciated
To a forgotten grave. But that's outside
The mark of our attention, which is time.
Learn to believe in time, if not in me."

"I might believe in you, my friend," she said,
"And praise you, if I knew what you were saying."

He rose to go: "My dearest friend alive,
Believe in time—which holds for many, I fear,
Only itself and emptiness. For you,
You know not what it holds. But you must wait,
And save yourself to wait. Patience will help
To save, but will not come if not invited;
And your significant red head will help
To save. I hope to God there is no woman
Who could love me as you love Talifer.
And so farewell, my child—but not for ever."

II

Leaving Althea and her trees behind him,
He found his way into a drowsy street
Where progress and improvement and raw change
Had not yet entered. There were trees here too,
If not a forest of them like Althea's,
On either side, sufficient and unchanged.
Among them, two tall oaks that he admired
Were like two giants always at the door
Of an immortal princess in a cottage,
With white walls and green shutters, and green grass
Growing all round it. He had said to Karen
That she must be immortal, for he knew,
As one who studied them, no general ills

TALIFER

Or shocks that might invade or dislocate
The comely realm of her serenity
And her repose. He found her reading Greek,
In a room cooled as if her presence cooled it,
And found her as exotically fair
And as impeccable for contemplation
As ever. A saint's face of ivory white,
So moulded as to be almost unholy
In its immune perfection, with dark eyes
Always impassable, and with darker hair
Never disturbed, awaited him and smiled
At him, with no surprise, as at a friend
Who had come yesterday, or every day,
At the same hour.

            She rose and welcomed him
With unexcited hands, and felt his mouth
Warm on her cheek, where it found, as expected,
No interest or resistance. "You asked once
What good it does," he said, "and I'll be damned
If I've an answer yet. How do you do?"

"As always, as you see," she said. "Sit down,
And tell me all about it."

              "Willingly,"
Said he, "but I would rather you said first
What you must have to tell. Suppose you talk,
And tell me all about it. Karen, Karen,
In a land burning certainly to ashes,
You are as cool and lovely as a trout.
Of just what unimpassioned particles
Are you composed, I wonder. In this weather,
How do you show yourself so heinously
Refrigerated, and so heavenly clean?
Yes, I have heard a little, inevitably."

1243

"There's nothing in me that is out of nature,
I hope," she said. "I have no wings, or scales.
You mean that you have seen Althea first.
Quick, you are not opaque."

       "Who says I am?
Yes, I have seen Althea. I heard news
That left a fatherly curiosity
Unable not to see her. From all signs
That she revealed to my transparency,
And from her language, I should make of her
A woman with a wisdom to meet fate,
And recognize it—which, as you have found
In Aristophanes and Adam Smith,
Maybe, is not a woman's first enjoyment
Of all those intuitions. I'm not affirming
That she is happy, for you know she isn't.
Since you know that, you may as well decide
That she will have no joy in hating you.
She will not make a banquet of her heart,
Or whistle for a vulture. What's all this
Offensive and irrelevant intellect
Inhabiting your table? Bacon—Locke—
Plato—Plotinus—Hermes Trismegistus—
Herodotus—Hume—Cicero—Lucretius—
Greek—Latin—Greek—more Greek. What do you mean
By making love to man? You are not nature."

She shook her head at him forgivingly;
"I am not sure that in Althea's place
I might not be less generous, and see fate
More as a monster, as you say I am,
Than as my portion of uncertain life.
Althea and I are friends—I hope we are—

But we are not, we'll say, inseparable.
We are not quite . . ."

                "I know you are not quite,"
He said. "Not at all quite. You have not lapped
Your cream from the same saucer. That's a figure."

"Your compliments and implications, Quick,
Are fringed with an unfading elegance.
I treasure them. You are calling us two cats."

"Well, aren't you—rather? In a way of pastime,
Aren't you? If not, I'm not importunate
To carry you two together in one basket
For a long ride. I can feel strangulations
Of a soul-terror worse than seeing the devil,
Seeing in fancy what might be uncovered.
Praise God, that's not to be. And this that happens,
This news of you and Talifer, makes me ask
What you are doing; and why, in the Lord's sight,
You are disowning and abandoning
Your freedom—which has always been, you say,
The well-spring and the fountain of your life.
I know; but implications agitate you,
And facts are tiresome food. What I don't know
Is what you may see coming. You read logic
With one eye, while ambition blinds the other;
Which, I suppose, is one way to be free.
Karen, O Karen, you are the Lord's despair.
You say, as you would say what time it is,
That manners, or conventions, are no more
To you than creeds or rituals; and you say
That if so minded you would throw your cap
Sky-high; and I, being figurative myself,
And in extremity no obstructionist,

Have done my possible to inveigle you
Along the path where roses, and primroses,
And such like, are indigenous and perennial.
You say that you were never a botanist;
You always look up from Thucydides,
And tell me to go home. I can't go home.
Damn it, I have no home. I've only a house—
My uncle's house it was—and I'm an orphan.
Before he died, my sinful uncle said
That I should never attain. I was like Reuben,
He said, because like him I was unstable,
And told me where to find him in the Bible.
He died, leaving all to me—and to my honor.
He must have enjoyed that. And since he died,
Honor has only made me miserable,
And worn to weary grief my fiery spirit;
Honor has been the cross that I have carried,
Unseen and unrewarded, all these years.
Don't wish that you might have it. Karen, Karen,
I look at you sometimes with a sad fear
That you are mostly made of beauty and brains—
A coalescence rarer than green robins,
Yet not quite all there is that's in a woman.
And while you laugh, that little house in Wales—
You know about it—is there waiting for us,
Above a lovely jingling little river
That you will not believe until you see it.
You would be happy there, and be as free
As a wild mountain bird. You could read Hume,
And Hermes Trismegistus, all day long;
You could have goldfish, and a marmoset.
Karen, I don't believe you have a cap;
Leastwise, I've never seen you with one on.
No, you have only hats. Karen, O Karen,
Why do you break my heart?"

"If you are patient,"
She answered, laughing quietly, "one reason
May soon be seen and heard." A velvet crunch
Of a car coming ceased, and the car stopped;
And out of it came Talifer. "Now look,"
She said, "and tell me if you see a reason."

He turned and saw, and said, "Yes, I can see it.
I can see Samuel Talifer, Esquire,
With white new trousers and a Leghorn hat,
And a blue coat. Lord, how he shines! I mean,
With his own light. Karen, how in God's name
Are these things done?

"Your compliments again,"
She said, "but never mind. I shall be jealous,
For I shall see his eyes forgetting me,
And seeing only you. Finding you here,
He will be thrilled, for reasons more than one,
And will say words, perhaps, that may as well,
And may as easily, be said now as ever."

Commanding and erect—an admiral,
At least, if not a monarch, in appearance—
Talifer, with himself and with his presence,
Filled instantly the doorway. Standing there
A moment, he was like Quick's picture of him,
Drawn swiftly for Althea to remember
Too clearly and too well. A power to bend
Or break was in his face, and in his eyes
The conquering gleam—which is a gleam sometimes
Of more fire than is there; and in his voice
There was a ripe repose—which might, without
Its honest warmth, have been complacency.
To Karen, having smiled admiringly

And passionately at her cool perfection,
He said, "So he comes here to see you first—
Before he comes to me. Well, I forgive him.
I cannot be offended or surprised.
Quick, you are welcome. What have you brought home?"

The doctor shook his head, and with a sigh
Displayed his empty hands: "What you have seen,
What you behold. Only myself, God help me.
My sinful uncle should have lived for ever,
And left me penniless. Then I might have toiled
And won some praise of Aesculapius,
And for myself some credit. I have merit,
Though few perceive it. I shall roam this world
No longer, for there's nothing in it now
But places—only places. You have robbed
Them all of glory and life. Persepolis
Is now as jolly a town as Paris was
Before the war. I'll roam the world no more,
For you have stolen the beauty and the brain
That once it had for its illumination.
Now there is only twilight. This is all
As true as you are glad you are not dead,
And you have made it so."

                              Talifer beamed.
"I have not stolen," he said, with a warm eye
On Karen—"I could never have done that,
And could have done it only less for trying.
No, it was fate—or name it as you may—
That gave me vision while time promised me
That I was not too late, if I made haste.
At first I doubted, and at last believed—
Though I must wonder still." He found a chair,
And filled it splendidly.

TALIFER

            "I dare avouch,"
Quick said, "that you have done some wondering.
In your place, Talifer, I should say my prayers,
And be a child again. Why should one man
Have all, when there are legions of the worthy,
Like me, who are inglorious and forsaken?
I can see one who sees me now as large
In glory as a large Angora cat,
Who brings a mouse and blinks at her for praise."

"Where is it?" Karen asked. "You roam the world,
You tell me, and you don't bring even a mouse
For me as a remembrance. I suspect
That you have as much more to learn of cats
As women have of men—which, for our good,
Is a great deal." She smiled, with eyes half open,
And watched him while he thought.

                              Talifer coughed
Indulgently at these irrelevancies,
And with a restive surety of intention
Secured a silence: "We are friends together,
By chance here at this hour; and at this hour,
As well as at another, for aught I know
Against it, I may say, to our friend here,
Truth he has not yet heard; and to you, Karen,
For whom alone I have a nearer name,
Truth you have partly heard, before and after
My telling it. You are not two women, Karen,
With even your knowledge. And I am less at ease
Than once I was with an assumed acquaintance
With unrevealed experiences not ours
To share; and I am humbler for the warning.
There's a humility for the fortunate,
Which, if acknowledged, profits and exalts him.

I shall not be deceived, or not in this.
Here are no mysteries. For in every heart,
I fear, there lives a wish that has a life
Longer than hope; and it is better there
Than an undying lie, and is far safer,
And has more kindness in it. If I felt
Or feared in this the presence of a loose
And easy reasoning, I should not be happy;
And surely not, so far as I'm the measure,
The happiest man alive. But even the first
Among the chosen of the undeserving
May wish there were no price of pain for those
Who may not be forgotten. You, Quick, return
To us unchanged and welcome, and surprised—
Immoderately, perhaps, and pardonably;
And as you are surprised, you will believe;
And in believing will remember always,
That after a wise fight with first illusions,
And after their inevitable surrender,
And while there was still time, I have found Peace."

"He says it also with a capital,
As I supposed he would, and he believes it,"
Quick thought; and then he said, "If the Peace-makers
Are truly to be called the Children of God,
And Scripture says they are, I see a place,
A pleasant place, not far away from them,
For the Peace-finders. You are there, Talifer—
Or if not yet, you will be. I have listened,
Admiring your reserves and your repressions,
And with a trained ear for your modulations;
And while I may be still a bit bewildered,
May truth forbid that I should be astonished.
Who could see Karen there and be amazed
At man's defeat and his capitulation?

1250

You are a sensitive citizen, Talifer,
And are a decent man. The which being so,
You have your feelings. Now my wicked uncle
Was a dry-languaged man, who boiled his words
Down to the bottom; and sometimes he burnt them—
Or they burnt me. And his incisive habit
Taught me a brevity that I may forget,
Except for solemn and important moments,
When words are mostly steam. You mean to say,
That while you only thought you loved Althea,
You know that you love Karen, and are glad
That you found out in time to save yourself,
And all three, from disaster and the devil.
And while you are the happiest man alive—
You always were exclusive—you are sorry
To leave Althea down there, and all alone,
Thinking of you. That's well, and to your credit,
And about all there is; and neither joy
Nor sorrow has ever changed a calendar.
The sun will set tonight and rise tomorrow—
And peace be with you all. Can I say more?"

"Well, no," said Talifer. He said it slowly,
And he smiled while he scowled. "I dare say not.
Or not in your allusive uncle's language."

"Then why say more, when more would only mean
Good wishes and good fortune for you all?
May joy await you, and may time forget you.
God knows if I were God, you would be happy,
And there would be no pain for any of you.
If choice were mine, I should walk always laden
With living seeds of joy, in a large sack;
And I should sow them so promiscuously
That all should have a portion. When I died,

1251

The world would miss me; and you, Talifer,
And many another, would soon be visited
By canvassers, all sorrowful, for money,
Wherewith to build anon a monument
For Doctor Quick. Alas, I say, no glory
Shall sing to men the good that I have done—
Which yet may be a little."

                    Karen smiled,
Appraising him again with eyes half shut
That held a captive gleam. "And why a little,"
She asked, "when you have seen so many changes,
And in an hour or two? How do you know
That other changes are not on their way,
Or that you may escape them? There are women
Whose hair and eyes are not so dark as mine—
And who care more for manners."

                    Talifer
Caressed his iron chin with knowing fingers,
And contemplated Quick with knowing eyes.
"Karen has learning that we cannot read,"
He said; "and she has wisdom beyond beauty—
If there may be such wisdom. You had better
Think more than twice, my friend, and solemnly,
Of her least urgent word."

                    "By chance," Quick said,
With Karen's eyes, unchanged, assisting him,
"My thought was following, if not solemnly,
The path of your advice. Now I have come
To a grim wall, with a locked entrance in it;
And I read over it, *Che sarà sarà*—
Which means, we are to say no more of that.
My prepossession is to be the sower

TALIFER

Of joyful grain, that none of us may starve.
Would you forbid me? Not for your two noses.
I knew it. So farewell, but not for ever."

Talifer laughed, if not with all his power:
"While I'm on wheels, no friends of mine shall walk
On such a day as this; and last of all
Two that are with me now. Come, both of you."

"No," Karen said, "take this physician home
With you, and give him something cool to drink.
Some of the same they gave to Socrates
Will be the best—for him. He speaks in figures."

When they had left a silent mile or two
Of heat behind them, Quick said, gratefully,
"Now I can see why Karen is for you
A treasure not of earth, a gem celestial.
There was a comprehension more than woman's,
A foresight more than man's, if I may say so,
In her command that you take me alone,
And show me why the blue bells ring in Scotland—
With lots of bubbles and ice. You owe as much,
If only in a way of celebration."

"Her thought was in my mind," said Talifer,
Who steered without a smile through a small forest
Into a spacious field of green, where stood,
Vine-grown for years, the mansion of his fathers.
He was the last of a decrescent line
That now reproached him; and though he had found,
And in one body, all the beauty and mind
Of woman, accumulated and perfected,
And though he was today the happiest man
Alive, or should have been, he was not smiling.

"You have more trees, Talifer, than Althea,"
Quick said, when they were sitting in a shade,
With the whole paraphernalia of refreshment
Before them on a table. "They are like me—
Except that some of them bear fruit. Without them,
You would not have your beechnuts, or your acorns.
And so the Lord provides."

                    "Yes, I have trees,"
Talifer said, and for a while sat thinking.
"Quick, we are friends. You will not mind my saying
That once or twice your words this afternoon
Were, possibly, more pointed and explicit
Than they were necessary—or, say prepared.
A meaning may be present without showing
Its head and shaking it, or showing its teeth.
You know this world. You know the ruin that lies
And fond hypocrisies have wrought in it;
And you must know it was more honorable,
Although there was a price of sorrow and pain
Involved, and more considerate, and more manlike,
On my side, not to fail when I was tested.
I thought I knew myself, but I knew nothing
Till Karen found and taught me. So no more
Of that. You are my friend, and will forgive me,
And wish us all the joy that will be ours."

"Prepared? Or necessary? Why, God bless you,
And shield you, Talifer. Was I ever prepared?
My sinful uncle was my preparation;
And when he said that I was necessary,
I was not there. Now let's go back a bit.
For ten years you have hardly seen this place—
This place where you were born. Two years ago
You came back—finally—and found Althea,

Still waiting; and you would have married her,
If you had not found Karen, who came later,
And fallen before her beauty and her brains,
And—well, her God knows what. I cannot name it.
The skeleton facts are there—for you, and me,
And a few thousand more, to recognize.
And if they are, what of it? You are not fate.
Why then be so mysterious and secretive,
When all's as plain as two men under a tree?
You look at me as if reproach, or doubt,
Might still be tickling you, but that's a fancy.
There's nothing in that but a few memories
That won't die all at once. They may die slowly;
They may not wholly die. If they do not,
No more shall Talifer die, says Doctor Quick.
And as for honor—why do you mention honor?
Is honor not your breath and your complexion?
Is honor not the color of your eyes?
And as for joy, you must know more of it
Today than most of us are ever to know—
Although I'm praying that you may live to read
Your knowledge of it now as men may read
Old school-books found forgotten in an attic,
And smile at sight of them as they remember
How hard it was to learn what looks so easy.
That's how I wish you happiness, my friend.
Now I shall say no more. I'll drink the rest."

"And Karen, Quick? Have you, perhaps, forgotten
Karen?" Talifer scanned him piercingly,
And with a sort of smile.

               "Karen? My God!"
Quick answered, and he waved an empty glass.
"Forgotten? Forget Karen? Do men forget

1255

To die when they are drowning? What's the matter?
You scare me when you look at me like that.
Talifer, you are a damned basilisk.
Your eyes burn holes in me. Karen—of course!
By heaven, we might have thought she was left out,"
He said, and laughed as merrily as a child.

III

"Another summer brings another June,
With August on the way. When August comes,
Our friends will have an anniversary,
And celebrate, maybe, their overflowing
First year of ecstasy. They have come back
As frisk from their delirious honey-moon
As two bedraggled spaniels tied together
Out in the rain all night."

                     Althea frowned
On Doctor Quick, who pondered with an air
Of one who was not telling everything.
"I cannot say," she said; "I have not seen them.
I hope they like each other."

                     "Well, they don't,"
Said he; "and I'm at work on a prognosis—
Which is a medical word, my frowning one,
Meaning their chance or probability
Of getting well. Their case is not a nice one.
No pills or tinctures that I know about
Will cure them, and I'm sorry; which is to say
I'm sinful glad. Why so? It serves 'em right.
And I speak with a heart swollen so large
With kindness and insatiable good will
To man and woman that I'm short of breath.

TALIFER

I'd be a better doctor if my heart
Were not so large. I should have been a priest;
For I might then have comforted the wicked,
If not the selfish and infatuated,
Who are God's own to save. His laws are said
To be obscure; yet my belief in them
Uncovers them, and sees them occupied
Not far from where we live. They are outside
The kingdom of our wits, and frequently
Are inconsiderate of our best mistakes.
They wake us up and make us hate ourselves
Till we cease hating them. Sometimes we can't;
And we are for the scrap-heap, to be wasted.
We dread the sound of our deliverers,
And shut them out, because we like to starve;
Or say because we cannot face ourselves
In a true looking-glass. Few of us can;
But that won't save our neighbors, who are shaken
Out of a silly dream that won't come back
To punish them again. They are awake
Today in a cold prison, which has a door
That has no bolt. And there's a looking-glass;
And there's our old friend Time. You may remember
When I presented him, a year ago,
And asked you to believe in him. He knows you,
And he will not forget you. He remembers
Your shameless estimation of my merit
Because of my large heart—which is a menace
To eminence and applause. My godless uncle
Knew it, although he said it differently—
In words less tempered with extenuation,
And so the more profanely to the point."

Althea smiled, with a satirical
Affection in her eyes: "You like your voice;

1257

You like your voice more than you like your friends;
Or you would tell them, confidentially,
What you are trying to say. What has your heart
To do—you mention hearts as if you had one—
With our imprisoned neighbors? I am sorry
For all who are in prisons. I am in one,
And I am just as sorry for myself,
And doing myself no good. About the best
That I have done is not to have done worse
Than to lose all that I believed was mine,
And to be disillusioned and deceived
Unspeakably in what I have supposed
Was my importance. When the Bible says
No chastening for the present seemeth joyous,
I don't say that it does. Is there much left
For me to say?"

     "No, not much—for the present,"
He said; and he repeated, "for the present.
But fix your diligence hard on those three words,
And hold them well. Don't let them get away.
Don't play with them. I doubt if in our language
There are three other words that will say half
To you that they are saying. For your life's sake,
Seize them. They are the best words in your book."

"There are not many," she said, "that are worth reading.
I see so many pages that are empty,
Or blurred with memories that have lost a meaning,
That nowadays it looks best in the dark;
And if I touch it, I've a dusty finger
To pay for my indifference."

      "You are not
Indifferent; you are desperate," said he;
"And that's not good for ladies living alone."

She sighed, and writhing slightly under her clothes,
Laughed at him with a melancholy pity:
"There never was a doctor in the world
Before who knew so much. If desperation
Is a mistake, and a wrong medicine
For loneliness, have you an easier one
To swallow, or a sweeter one to taste?
If you have in your pharma-what-you-call-it
A drug for memory that will make it sleep,
And has no evil in it, for heaven's sake,
Bring me as many blessed pounds of it
As you may carry and not break your back."

"My back will carry mountains. It is yours,
Not mine," said he, "that is in danger now.
For it has carried all that it should bear,
And for as long as would be necessary
If reason were the king of circumstance,
And could wear folly's crown. But since it isn't,
And can't, it can do only what it can—
Which is occasionally not a little.
It may be well for you and your impatience,
Before you wear another pillow out
With your indignant head, trying to sleep,
First to get down on your two little knees
And thank the Lord that folly, with all his power,
Is not yet absolute."

                    "It will do no good,"
She said, "to tell you twice how fond you are
Of hearing your own voice. It's a good voice.
But it is not the Lord's, or an archangel's.
And why be suddenly so concentrated
On folly? Am I a fool? You dwell on it
As if you had just found a new disease."

He smiled, and smoked. "No, it is not a new one.
Indeed, I do not know of one that's older.
I saw the Talifers—I mean Talifer
And his exotic helpmate—yesterday;
And that may be why folly follows me
Like a wet dog today. The law may call her
A wife, but she was never a Talifer,
And never will be one. So there remains
Only one Talifer; and who shall say
That more than one might not be a profusion,
A prodigal duplication, if you like,
Or a majestic error. For one of him—
And you will surely say it after me—
Will serve, at least for one community,
Better than two. Would you have, if you might,
Two Talifers in one town?"

       "There are not two,"
She snapped, "in this town, or in any other.
If I don't sleep tonight as once I did,
When I was two feet long, never suppose
My fear of hearing there's another like him
Keeps me awake. There's not another like him.
You know there never was, and never will be."

"The biologic odds are all against it;
Yet I don't know, for sure," he said, and laughed
Inside; and feeling his laugh, Althea scowled.
"There may be one somewhere; and where he is,
He will be notable, and will be observed
And envied, and will not escape, not wholly,
The qualifying eye and the true tongue.
For truth will say that no man has a right
To look so great and still be not so great.

When all is said, you know, this Talifer
Is not a Julius Caesar—which is well;
For with a Julius Caesar in your house,
You might not be so tranquil as without him.
Talifer would be more to your desire.
And yet, you know, this Talifer, on occasion,
May weigh an atom heavy. While he looks
To be made only of magnificence,
And race, and grace, there may be, on occasion,
A few too many mortal ounces of him;
And on occasion—I go timorously—
When he is not too sure of his foundation,
He might appear to the malevolent
A little owlish and oracular—
As when he told, with Karen listening
Like an oblivious kitten, how it was
That he awoke (he must have been like Saul
Before he became Paul) and found—what was it?—
Peace, with a capital. That's what it was,
And a good thing to find. Yet, all the same,
He was, you know—he was, he was, you know—
Well, I said heavy."

              "I dare say he was,"
Althea cried, with her eyes flashing anger.
"And if he was, it's a great shame and pity
That there is nothing to be done about it."
She rose and looked away, rubbing her eyes
In disappointed rage. "Why do you tell
These things to me?" she said, turning at last
To see him. "I thought—I thought—you were a friend.
If there's a grain of tiresome useless truth
In this, are you supposing that I care?
Why do you say this now? What does it mean?"

He was already there, and his warm hands
Were on her shoulders, holding her securely.
"Only to see the sparks, my fiery one,"
He said, and laughed. "Only to see them fly,
And to be sure the fire has not gone out.
And as for Talifer, you are right, my child,
You are quite right. There's an elected remnant,
A scattered one, a small one, far to seek,
On whom accomplishment, as the word goes,
Might be a blemish—like a price-mark scratched
On a jade vase. They are themselves enough.
Their being alive is their accomplishment,
Their presence and urbanity their service.
They are more loved than envied, never hated,
And are so few that they are never scorned.
I have known two of them in forty years,
And one of them is dead. Now I have told
As much as need be told of Talifer,
And may as well get out. The wedding guest
Here beats his breast. Farewell, but not for ever."
He drummed himself like an orang-outang,
And disappeared. Althea, trembling, watched him.
Long after he had vanished and was lost
Among the trees, Althea could still see him,
As he was when he left her. He was laughing,
As if he did not care whether she trembled
Or not. And trembling still, she wondered why
He laughed—or why an anniversary
In August was amusing. Still she trembled,
And still she wondered why.

                             There were no signs
In August of an anniversary
More festive than today's of yesterday,
Or none to be discerned. Quick, leisurely

Approaching, found them where not long ago
He had congratulated Talifer,
He feared, somewhat evasively. Today,
Evasion would have hung its head and hidden
Behind a tree. There was nothing to evade;
And there was less to mourn or deprecate,
Since all was going well.

                    Talifer rose,
And with a carved smile on an older face,
Composed a welcome that would serve; and Karen,
With eyes half shut, gave him some languid fingers
To do with as he might. "Where is the band?"
He asked, with a grimace after a pause.
"If you are so indifferent and informal,
And so inured to joy that you don't feel it,
My small attention, Karen, and remembrance—
Don't forget that—I fear, may not excite you.
I hoped it might. But I was always hoping,
And am addicted still to certainties.
If you, whom God hath joined, don't understand it,
I'll tell you that his purpose, dark sometimes,
Was never clearer. Karen, you are lovely,
But you are not alert. Open your eyes
Wider, and try to purr, and put your paws
Out nicely. For this time I've brought a mouse.
Regard him: Apollonius Rhodius.
You said that you had never tasted him,
And I remembered—as I'm doing always,
And having not so much as a kind word.
He looks a bit forgotten and long-tailed
To me perhaps, but I don't have to eat him.
Now he is yours; and with my compliments,
And with my most agreeable intimations
Of your contented coming retrospect.

Nothing is lost, or it is best to think so;
And life, if not unduly maimed or stretched,
Is not too long. You are both doing your best.
Why do these trees, who are all strength and wisdom,
Grow up, with roots in earth, instead of down,
With roots in air? Think for an hour of that,
And find your thoughts becoming beautiful.
Think for an hour of how and why things grow.
If there's to be no music, or thanksgiving,
There may be hidden drink. Will Talifer
Please clap his hands and see?"

                                 "I will," said Karen.
"If you must pay for hearing yourself talk,
You have my thanks for Apollonius.
I'm purring them. There are not many cats
Today who are pursuing him."

                                Talifer's mouth
Deformed his countenance till it became
A face that was as homelike and engaging
As a bronze Dante smiling. "Quick," he said,
"You are the crowned among the fortunate.
You know what women want."

                               "I do," said Quick—
"Sometimes; and I have lost a world of sleep
For what they do not want. They don't want me,
Talifer. There are two at least who don't;
And elsewhere there are probably some others.
I don't know why. I'm cheerful; I can talk;
I have a studious eye for small attentions;
I pick things up; I'm kind to animals;
I dance with feet that are not too ferocious;
I can shift busily from the wrong note,

And fade from argument imperceptibly;
I can be childlike when they flatter me,
And tell them lies that they like best to hear;
I can be gracious when they say I'm going
To places where I'd rather be damned than go;
I can avoid reminding them that men
Are sometimes restive and preoccupied
With trivial claims and interferences
Of life and death. But they, not knowing my worth,
Make light of me. A sigh for merit wasted
Says I am not the man. I don't know why.
Althea's thumbs are down at sight of me—
While Karen here would pour petroleum
All over me, and sing to see me burn.
I don't know why."

                    "You might think for an hour,"
Said Karen, who rose drowsily and yawned
Behind her Apollonius Rhodius.
"I'll send out what you creatures think you need,
And take a nap. You will do better alone.
Cats can read signs."

                    "An anniversary nap,"
Quick said, "is always a brave evidence.
It argues that a year of discipline
Has not undone the present or laid waste
The future. You will live for a long time,
And may as well prepare." He followed her
With eyes that asked and answered an old question,
And watched her all the way into the house.

"Well, Talifer," he said as he sat down,
"You are not voluble this afternoon.

You leave to me and to my reticence
The normal occupation of three tongues.
I miss today the measured eloquence
That I heard once—only a little more
Than one brief year ago—in Karen's cottage
When I came back and was to be surprised.
You told me then that I was your best friend,
And I believed you. I believe you still—
As you do. For you must, or you would never
Have listened the other day when I set out
So painfully to prove it. Where's the use,
When a thing's here, for men like you and me
To say it's warm, or that September's coming,
Or so on? When I told you, for your knowledge,
Only what you told me when you were silent,
You had your reason for not showing me
The short way home. You are about the last
On whom the uninvited would intrude
Without a warning and at least a small
Response. Was I misled when I was here
Last time—last week? When I do less than well
I shall have doubts, or qualms, and hesitations.
But hark—do I hear tinklings in the distance?
By heaven, I do. Karen, though cold herself,
Remembers warmth in others. Or doesn't she?
I may be going too fast."

                              "What in God's name,"
Talifer said, relaxing desolately,
And all but angrily, "do you know about it?
You know as much as you have read in books,
Written by those who know no more than you
Of what it means to live, as I have lived,
For twelve months, and each longer than the last,
In an—in a— . . ."

"In an aquarium,
May be, perhaps, what you are trying to say,"
Quick answered, filling slowly a tall glass.
"And if I don't know everything about it,
I do know two determining good reasons
Why you are to escape—over the top,
Flop, flop, down to the good warm earth again,
And solid on your feet. Where, and oh, where . . .
Not far from here, my friend, if I guess well."

Talifer sighed, watching a frosted glass
With clear eyes that saw nothing. "I don't know,"
He said, "that I shall ever escape—from her.
I found her yesterday, lying asleep,
With sunlight shining on her like warm glory
On a white saint with hair as dark as night.
She was too beautiful to be a woman.
She was like nothing I had seen before,
And had a saint's appearance, or a child's—
I don't know which. Her face was partly turned
Away from me, and there was her white throat—
A small thing to mean life. For just a moment
I thought how pleasant it would be to seize it,
And hold it; and I was sorry and ashamed.
For though it was at worst a bitter fancy,
I wished it had not been."

                          Quick, who was drinking,
Chuckled and choked. "When I was young," he said,
"I could have slain at least three schoolmasters,
Who lathered me when I was not absorbed,
And been a merry child. I was not merry,
Because my uncle was not imaginative.
He would begin sometimes where the schoolmasters
Left off. My uncle was a sinful man,

Who left me everything. When I was older,
He said I was like Reuben, son of Jacob,
Because I was unstable—and so I am,
Somewhat, though I have merit. No, Talifer,
I am not fearful of your isolating
Body and soul of anything that's alive—
Not even of a wasp—or never unless
He stings you twice. If there is nothing worse
In you than an incipient willingness
To strangle Karen, you are sound and safe,
And far from crime's alarms."

                         Talifer tapped
His glass with idle fingers, and said, grimly,
"I'll venture to believe it, if you say so.
Nevertheless, I could say things to you
That in a meaningless and friendly way
You might believe you partly understood.
But they are best not said."

                        The doctor poked
His cubes of ice: "You do not have to say them,
Talifer, for I know them. Disembarrass
Your brain of its indelicate preparations,
And finish that drink before it is all water.
For you have lived a year too long on water,
And your discretion will be inundated
Unless you act. In ages unrecorded
You may have been aquatic, but your fins
And gills are gone, and you have two legs now.
You are not even amphibious, Talifer;
And you are not to drown because a woman,
Who is in habit more than in appearance
A watchful trout or an elusive eel,
Has made you to believe you might as well.

1268

TALIFER

It is not so. No more are you to perish
For a sphinx-eyed Greek-reading Lorelei,
Or philosophic siren. God knows best
Why she was born, or why she must be here,
From nowhere, to become the chatelaine
Of your unhappy castle. At first sight,
And by the nameless law that lets you know,
Karen appraised Althea and envied her,
And hated her with her best graciousness—
Which is, if you still notice it, a thing
Considerable—and was repaid at once
With hate as gracious, and with more sparks in it.
If Karen saw them, and with her perceptions
There is a possibility that she did,
She may have made of them partly a reason
For teaching you to swim. Is it not strange
That one right woman, dowered with fate for you,
Should be left waiting while you might possess
And cherish, in an amatory trance,
A changeling epicene anomaly,
Who sleeps, and finds her catnip in the classics?
Is it, or is it not, remarkable?
I don't say. All I say is, your release
Will not wait for next year, or the year after."

Talifer shrugged his admirable shoulders,
And answered first with a forgiving smile:
"I cannot follow if you go too fast.
We Talifers have always found ourselves
A little behind—or, if you like, old-fashioned;
Or feudal, if you like. Feudal, or foolish,
Or what you will, and maybe never in step
With a world hurrying after a brass band
That plays—yes, rather too loud. We are inclined
To let the world go by, and doing no harm,

1269

To stay for a while longer as we are—
'We' being only one, the last of us.
I do not know that we are right or wrong,
Or what is wrong or right, or how much longer
We shall go on—if we go on at all.
Assuming a short view, it looks today
As if in me might be the end of us.
But there are still some providential clouds
Between now and tomorrow, and I'll wait.
An ancient fancy has passed on to us
An old man with an hour-glass and a scythe—
Which, with him always mowing, may reduce
My tangled weeds and grass to a clean field.
I have had glimpses, though I see just now
Nothing impending. There has been no stain
On our name yet; and Karen, whatever she is,
Has done my name no wrong. There is a duty,
It seems to me, that I owe to my name,
And to the voices of my ancestors.
I may not always think so. And the voices—
Time and events may drown them."

                                    "Talifer,"
Quick murmured, pouring not quite half a pint
Of amber spirit into his large glass,
"If my descriptive and incisive uncle
Were now alive, and sitting with us here,
He could say everything aloud to you
That I can only whisper silently
To a sad heart. If I am stimulated,
And say things to you that I do not mean,
I mean them all the same. You are my friend,
Talifer; and you are, if you don't mind,
At times a rather splendid sort of ass—
A nobler sort, we'll say, than should be nibbling

TALIFER

Where there is nothing but dead leaves to eat.
You are the last of all the Talifers;
And you might yet be monstrously in tune
With your inertia and your temporizing,
If you should drown yourself for one of those
Incurable stupidities of duty
That would be wept in heaven. Time and events?
God help us, Talifer. If I go home
From here inebriated, and scare women,
Or make of merit a fell spectacle
For curious and contaminable youth,
It will go on your books. For you have done
A sinful thing in rifling, as you have,
The last and inmost pocket of my faith,
Which held a jewel that will be lost to me,
And to far more than me, unless, by heaven,
You give it back and promise never again
To stir my sorrow and wrath, or make me cry
Into my drink, or make me wring my hands,
Or, like a wounded and forsaken hound,
Howl all night long, as I shall, presently,
If you should say again, in one relation,
Time and events. To hell with time and events,
And first with time. And you know what I mean.
Your eyes do, if you don't. For both of them
Are shining with a bright benevolence
That augurs well. You will not drown yourself;
And you may still find Peace. Who shall say no?"

Talifer, startled for a moment, stared
At Quick, whose countenance was not unflushed,
And smiled. "There may have been some temporizing
In my last words," he said. "I have forgotten
Just what they were, or what they may have meant.
There are so many words that mean so little.

1271

If I know what yours mean, you will have patience.
Sometimes I do not know what anything means;
And you might not, with my last year behind you."

IV

There came at last a shining afternoon
In late September when his trees all sang,
For Talifer, a fiery dirge together
Of lights and silences. Leaving his house,
Ivied half over with a still vermilion,
Behind him in the sunlight, he walked slowly
Along a darkening road, with trees all round him
That hid the sky with red and yellow leaves,
Of which a few, as he went on alone,
Fell warningly, and in their falling whispered
Relentlessly of time. Time and events,
He muttered, with a twinge of reminiscence,
Had wrought no miracle yet; and he moved on,
Where many a Talifer had gone before him,
Till he was outside his inheritance
And on the world's highway, where still he owned
His human and inalienable right
To walk and do no harm. So Talifer walked,
And did no harm, and had no premonition
Of what a few next hours of life may hide
From man or woman.

                    He walked until he paused,
Like one compelled to pause, where two stone posts
That were at once familiar and forbidding
Told where he was. A curving road, soon lost
Among remembered autumn-colored trees
That were like his, lay silent there before him,
Like a deserted way to things all gone,

TALIFER

Until a moving shape that was a woman
Came as if called; and seeing Talifer there,
Below her at the gate, where she had seen him
So many times, paused like a frightened ghost
Before she came to greet him.

                "Is it you?"
She asked, and let her trembling hand remain
In his until he let it go. "They told me
That you were here again. I hope you are both—
Happy."

        Talifer knew there was no truth
In that, for her large eyes and trembling mouth
Told what a liar she was, and left him asking
If this could be Althea there before him,
After so long. She was almost like one risen
Out of a grave where he had buried her
Alive, and she was not reproaching him.
Sorrow and joy and hope were in those eyes
That would not look from his; and there was fear,
Which might have pierced him deeper with remorse
If hope had not withheld it. He felt most
That she was there, that she was touching him,
And that she was alive, and was Althea.
There might be time for more when he knew more,
And she knew all. So he stood watching her,
And searching with a fearsome exultation
A face not ruinously beautiful,
Yet fair as a face need be to reveal
A beauty that is made of more than faces,
A mobile and a multiple confusion
Of humor, truth, and passion, and of love
That outwears time. Talifer knew them all,

And saw them all again as he had left them.
Sorrow and pain had only softened them;
And anger, which he knew, knowing Althea,
Must once have been a tenant of their house,
Was not there now. There was no trace of it;
And in its absence his humility
Found more room to be felt—as her eyes told him,
And soon her shaken smile. Talifer tried
To talk, but her accusing wonderment
And fear, and half-emerging happiness,
Were made of questions that were now too many
And large for him to answer. He must wait,
And while he had it might as well not let
The moment go.

        "You hope that I am—happy?
You said so." Then he paused, waiting for time
To give him language to go on with it.
"Before I answer that," he said, not trying
To hide the truth, which in his hungry eyes
Was hers to read, "may I not ask you first
If I have come to nothing in your sight
That you should ask me that? If I deserve
No answer, you deserve no persecution,
And shall have none—from me. If I deserve,
Sometime, a time that is imaginable,
More than another moment of your kindness,
You will not quite forget? Althea, tell me.
Althea, do you hope that I am happy?
If in your heart you do, no matter what things
You say, I shall have no right to be sorry,
And I shall never come this way again."

"If I believed you never would," she said,
"I should have many reasons to be sorry,

1274

And a few rights.   You have not taken them
Away; you cannot have them.   They are mine."

"I came today because day follows night,
Althea—which may not be, if we knew all,
The least of reasons.   At a future time,
It might be charity, if you cared enough,
To say where you believe the best of me
Is buried in me; for it is in me somewhere,
For what it may be worth.   Once I believed
That I was not a fool—till I became one.
Today I have a yearning to go back
And find myself again, to recognize
Today in yesterday—which may be asking
A man's whole world too much.   How shall I know
Whether I'm there or not, if none shall tell me?
It is important that I find myself;
For we that are no more than ordinary
Are more for that the creatures of our lapses.
They make us—or unmake us.   Erring man
Has a cold eye for other men's mistakes,
And women a colder one—which is as well,
Most likely, for a world so full of traps.
If this is unexpected, or prolonged,
You are permitted to interpret it
Alone when I am gone, and as you may.
Althea, if my wishes are worth keeping,
I wish that happiness may still surprise you,
And that you may not damn me to the dust
Until you know.   Quick would applaud me now,
And say *bravo*.   If you do, I can bear it.
God gave the moment and I merely seized it.
Tell me, Althea.   Tell me—are you sorry?
You have not told me yet to go away,
And your large eyes have still a kindness in them.

If it is only pity, never say so;
Leave me in ignorance, and let me follow
The way that I must find. I have said this
Because time whispered softly in my ear,
And said I might as well. Whether or not
The moment is a trusty counsellor,
We cannot always know. Sometimes it is."

Althea, whose large eyes were seeing just then
Nothing too clearly, could not see the smile
Of hope in Talifer's. But she could feel it
In the warm melancholy of his voice,
And then she did not care. She rubbed her eyes
Industriously and thoroughly, till she saw him
All as he used to be; and then she laughed
In a doubt-haunted way as if afraid
He might not still be there and was a spirit.

"Well, no," she said, "I may not have been ready
For time's advice—or for so much of it.
I'll trust that he was kind. He can be kind,
And he can be as cruel as a tiger
That waits in places for what comes along—
Which might not be so bad if he were not
So fierce and so terrific, as your eyes are
When you don't know. But they are not so now;
Now they are kind. I might say they were sorry,
If I knew more of what is hidden in them."

"Unless I have been looking at a stranger,
With voice and eyes and features of Althea,
You know enough," he murmured, and looked hard
At a red leaf that had come fluttering down
While he was listening. He took it up,

TALIFER

And after holding it as if uncertain
Of whose red leaf it was, said, like a boy,
"Will you keep this until I come again?"

A warmness, like a sudden wave of healing,
Touched her and filled her and brought happiness,
Unwarranted or not—she did not ask—
Into her eyes, where she could feel it shining.
"I will," she said; "and I may keep it longer.
Have I no rights? It came down from my tree."

He smiled, and seizing her small hands, forgot
That his were strong. "God knows you have a right
To more than I have yet to say is yours.
You may have that as well as your red leaf—
If you have room for both, and have a notion
That they go well together."

                              "It is good,"
She said, "to find a glimmer of yourself,
In the same face I knew. For when you looked
At me last year, there was no mercy in it.
You don't know how you looked, or how you talked.
You were so solemn and so terrible,
So sure that you were done with me for always,
That I believed—no, I can't lie to you;
One part of it I'm sure you must have heard
In someone else's house before you said it.
I can't believe you found it. 'Peace,' I mean.
I shouldn't have said that, and so I said it.
Only a thoughtful and sweet-natured ferret
Like me, would do it." She made her large eyes larger,
While from his coat she plucked invisible threads
And held them in the air for him to see.

Talifer fixed his eyes on the red leaf,
And then on her changed face: "If what you mean
Is what I see, you have already said it.
But we had best not be here any longer,
Or we shall soon be news. You will not lose it?"

"No, I shall always have it, and I'll watch it.
If rightly kept, they last for a long time—
I shouldn't wonder if a hundred years.
Good-bye, and thank you for it."

                        Talifer's world
Was larger as he wandered slowly back,
And autumn held a glory and a warmth
Of colors that had shone nowhere on earth
An hour before. The tunnelled road he found
Through his own trees and foliage, waiting for him,
Was none that he had followed in his life
Till now. It was all new and unexplored,
And was beyond remembrance or belief,
Till suddenly, half-covered with the same
Vermilion, his house told him with hard silence
That here was home. It did not look like home,
And felt less like it as he entered it
And found the same things he had always known
Awaiting him—still there as they had been
When he was born, and some as long before him
As there were Talifers who had lived and died
Within those walls. He was the last of them,
And he had bound himself by church and state,
In a blind lapse of pagan turbulence,
To a soul-frozen disillusionment
That was not woman and was not for man.

A breathing silence and a western light
Was on the couch where Karen lay asleep

While he came in unheard. He felt Althea
There with him, like an injured wistful spirit
That might be with him for as long as life,
And injured for as long, unless he made
Of his not yet humiliated name
A target and a plaything for the town
To pelt with ignominy, and to laugh at
As a high-flying game brought down at last,
And sadly spattered. If it must be so,
He reasoned, he had made the way for it.
So far as man alone made anything here—
A master-question that his pride evaded,
Save in appraising others—he had made
His bed, and here was what he found in it—
One of an ancient God's wise mockeries,
Perhaps, and a right punishment for a fool.
So he might think so long as his eyes rested
On anything not that face. No man could watch
A face and form so harrowingly divine
As hers and tell himself it was all folly
To be its famished prey. But what of that?
There was no sustenance in repeating it,
And no especial sense. The more he gazed
In vain upon that seeming heaven-wrought sheath
Of ice and intellect and indifference,
The more he felt the presence of Althea,
With a forgiving and amused reproach
In her expectant eyes. What was a name,
A shield, or a tradition, or a legend
Worth now, he thought; and in Althea's eyes
He found the only answer. And once more
He gazed at Karen, sleeping. "God in heaven,"
He groaned—"God, fate, or nature, or mischance,
Why was this woman born!" Unconsciously
He raised his arms in angry supplication,

Clutching at nothing with indignant hands
That would have torn the veil between man's folly
And fate. His will was his alone no longer,
And he could only ask, and ask unanswered,
"Why was this woman born!"

                     With upraised hands
That had no purpose, and with eyes ablaze
With fire that was not his to feel or know,
He stared at her; and while he stared, his words
Were answered with a terror-laden shriek,
A writhing, and a moaning, and a leap
From where she had been lying to the floor,
Where now she stood with hands holding her throat,
Like one who had seen death. She seemed to wait;
And when he made a forward step to save her,
Covered her eyes and swayed. He lifted her,
And felt the frightened warmth of her soft body
Trembling in helplessness. She was alive,
And was awake; but life was horror breathing,
And consciousness a terror without speech.
He laid her softly on the couch again,
And stroked her cold white fingers while a slow
Unfolding of incredible comprehension
Chilled him with her mistake.

                  "Karen," he said,
"What fearful dream is this that I have broken?
And why were you afraid to find me here?
I have stood here and seen you lying asleep
Before—because you were so beautiful.
There was no other reason. Did you dream
That I could hurt you, Karen?" He could feel
His words drawn out of him like heavy weights
Of uselessness, and now he felt the sweat

Of cold despair for having spoken them.
They were not words, although they were the truth,
For Karen to believe.

                        "Don't look at me!"
She cried, and snatched her fingers out of his
As if the touch and sight of them were fire
And death. "Don't touch me with those hands!
Don't look at me! It was your eyes! Your eyes!
It was your hands—it was your hands and eyes!
It was your eyes! Your eyes!" She threw herself
Upright, and groped away like a blind child
Until there was a chair that she could feel
Between him and her fear. She clung to it
As people sinking cling to sinking things
At sea before they drown. "Don't look at me!"
She cried again. "Don't tell me anything—
It was your eyes! Your eyes!"

                                Talifer sat
Amazed and helpless, fearing if he arose,
Or moved, or spoke, nothing would come of it
But that mad shriek repeated. So he sat
With sad eyes looking at the floor, and waited—
For what, he did not know. The only sound
He heard was of a quick and fearful breathing,
Which hurt him as a stinging lash would hurt,
And made a pain of silence. He looked up
To find her facing him, with her dark eyes
Fixed on him with an unbelieving fear,
Which had a darker and a wilder light
Than fury would have had, or woman's hate.
It was a fear that had no thought of him,
Save as a nameless horror watching her,
And holding her, he fancied, as a serpent

1281

Would hold a bird. And there was pity in that,
And sorrow that was not to be endured
Longer with nothing said.

                So he said, "Karen,
You poor bewildered and unhappy child,
You poor mistaken child, what have I done?
I'll tell you, if I can. You were asleep,
And woke up suddenly to find me there,
With my hands raised in hopelessness above you.
I raised them, and not knowing why I did it,
Held them above you and your loveliness,
And your deceiving and unearthly coldness,
And said to God, 'Why was this woman born?'
You may have heard. If not, you hear it now.
There was no anger in me when I said it;
There was just wonder, and a long despair.
I would not injure you to save my life.
And when you saw me there, there was in me
No thought or furthest wish to give you pain,
Or to molest your sleep. You might have slept
Until you woke to find the sun gone down;
And I should have gone softly somewhere else.
I should have gone like Ahab. He went softly."
He smiled at her with only a drawn hope,
And thought of nothing better.

                After a pause
That each long second lengthened painfully,
He spoke again: "Will you believe me, Karen?
You would not have me telling lies to you,
For somehow I believe that you would know them.
You know so much that I'm afraid of you—
And yet so little as to believe your life
Unsafe with me. This is all comedy,
Karen; and with your knowledge you must know it,

Or must believe that I'm a scurvy fiend,
And liar; and you will never believe that,
Strive as you may. A tortured evidence
May torture truth until it has no features
For even itself to recognize. But—Karen!
You must believe me, for I said the truth.
It was not easy. And we, not being two fools,
Must own the presence of an error somewhere,
And at a better time—not now, God knows—
Acknowledge it, and find what's left to do
With our mishandled lives. I am not mighty,
And when my life is done, so few will know
Or care, that I might sigh to think of it,
If sighs were seeds of glory. I'm not glorious,
Karen, nor am I eminently vicious;
For I can swear to you that I am decent,
And swear again that I am not a liar;
And I'm not much for swearing. If my word
To you were not sufficient, all my oaths
To God would be no more. You saw my hands
Uplifted in a solemn desperation
That may have had a sort of humor in it.
I don't know what it was. I looked at you,
And saw you sleeping there, so beautiful,
So inaccessible and impossible,
That I—well, I forgot what I was doing.
You are enough to make a man forget
That earth is not a tomb—where the dead live,
All reading only what the dead have written,
And all as beautiful as . . ."

                              "Don't!" she cried.
"I have read everything—and in your eyes.
I saw your eyes—and there was death in them.
No!—stay away—don't touch me!"

Talifer, rising,
Like a man battling with a last despair,
Would have restrained and held her, and with words
Of sorrow and assurance pacified her
Into a right belief. But she escaped,
And like a frightened fox eluded him,
This way and that, crying "Quick! Quick! Where are
    you!"
Out of the room and through the hall she ran,
And through the open doorway to the road
That ran like a long tunnel under trees
Into the town. He did not follow her,
Nor could he have said why. He only knew
There was a will not his that hindered him,
And held him there alone. She would come back
Before she had gone far, and would be sorry
For what she said. If she did not come back . . .
He shook his head, and found that he was smiling,
Because two mighty and invisible hands
Imprisoned him from action. And he knew,
And would have known if she had never told him,
Where she was going.

And while Talifer,
With trees that might have been the walls of time
Between him and the truth, was asking fate
What a red leaf was saying to Althea
In a new language, there was Doctor Quick,
Reading at home serenely a new book
About the universe, and learning from it
Knowledge as far beyond phenomenon
As brontosauruses had known before him.
Yawning, he stretched himself, and saw the sun
Above a distant hill. The day was going,
He thought, and would be gone with nothing done

1284

Deserving a red letter; and he sighed,
With an untroubled comfortable envy
Of mightier men than he, who had performed
Or thought immortally, and had left their deeds
And thoughts behind them for mankind to cherish.
He sighed again, fearing that he would leave
Only what undiscriminating fortune
Had left to him; and if his pride was quiet
Because of that, his grief to be unwritten
Among the mighty was an easier pang
To bear than endless pain and destitution—
Of which in lives around him he had seen
Far more than was a pleasure. On the whole,
He fancied he was not the most accurst
Of men, and was about to yawn for that,
When someone running, while a startled maid
Stood watching, found a way to where he was,
And stood there panting while she looked at him
With scared, beseeching eyes.

                "For God's sake—Karen!"
He said, and shut the door. She ran to him
As to a sturdy father—which may never
Have been quite his imaginary status
In her proximity—and with quivering arms
Around his neck, held herself close to him,
And was held closer still. "Take me away!"
She moaned: "If you meant anything when you said it,
Take me away from here, where I shan't see them—
Where I shan't see his eyes!"

                    For the first time
A dream that had been his, mostly the whim
Of a luxurious curiosity
That loyalty had for a year disowned,

Was granted. He had not expected it,
But here it was; and what the devil it meant
Would in its time be told. When she looked up,
He kissed her, and her warm lips answered his
As if she cared. He wondered if she did,
Or if she could have told, or if it mattered,
Whether she knew or not. For there she was,
The loveliest biological achievement
That his prehensive eyes had yet approved,
Or that his arms had held. If Talifer
Had lost his wits and thought he had found peace
In finding her, he was to be forgiven,
Though Quick was at a loss for Talifer's
Envisagement of peace. He lifted her,
More for the sake of holding her, perhaps,
Than for her visible need of being lifted,
And left her in a chair. "Drink this," he said,
"And tell me all about it. Talifer,
Unless another man has had his name,
Would have it so. Tell me, in your own way,
What has been said or done; and in my way,
I'll tell you how it looks."

                              "I was asleep,"
She said; "and when I woke I saw his hands,
High in the air above me, like great claws.
And then I saw—and then I saw—his eyes!
I saw death in his eyes—and then I screamed.
I leapt away from him and almost fainted.
He carried me, as you did now, and laid me
In the same place where I awoke and saw him—
And saw his eyes. He talked about his hands,
And said that they were only asking God
Why I was born. But he could see his hands,
And may have told the truth. He could not see

His eyes, or what was in them that I saw,
And could not tell the truth. I saw his eyes—
And I saw death in them. His eyes! His eyes!"

Quick rubbed his chin, and said assuringly,
"It sounds to me more like a benediction,
Or a farewell. He raised his hands to heaven,
And asked why you were born? He might do that,
You see, if you forgot that you were married;
And if you did, it's too late to remember.
There are too many forces you don't know.
Or do you? The Lord knows just what you know,
And why you gave yourself to Talifer—
If ever you did. You never wanted him;
You only wanted what Althea wanted;
And with your face and your anatomy,
And your pied-piper voice, and your quaint learning—
Which, in a crazy way, made all the rest
The more unreal and indispensable—
You stole him, as you might steal priests and bishops,
If you set out. You are the devil, Karen;
And you must not go back to Talifer.
You could not if you would—though, I'll assure you,
Talifer's eyes are not so terrible
As you believe them. If a good old dog
Had wakened you as he did, suddenly,
And you had seen his eyes examining you
Too curiously, you might have found in them
Death and hell-fire together. You might have yelled;
And the good dog, not knowing what else to do,
Might have stood up amazed, on his hind legs,
And barked as if he'd bite you. It was all
A wild misunderstanding on your part,
Yet one we don't regret. You can't go back."

"I know I can't," she said. "I am afraid.
I can't go back. You know I can't stay here.
What can I do? What is there left to do?"
He smiled—or grinned: "Oh, there are lots of things.
So far as I can see with your sphinx-eyes
What's left for you to do, I should say first
That you might best imagine yourself running
Out of a burning house, Talifer's house,
And that by now the whole manorial mass
Is no more than a seething crumbling ruin,
Roaring and smoking, with brave firemen spouting
Water all over it that will do no good.
For now it is too late. Nothing of yours
That you're not wearing on your body and bones
Is left. So where's the use of going back?
You don't want Talifer; and from your account,
He doesn't want you. He may have burned, also;
And ashes may be all that you and sorrow
May find of him to mourn. Now there's a thought
Worth polishing and holding to the light.
And all this might have happened. Since it hasn't,
You'll need a few discreet commodities,
More personal and more individual
Than I have here. I shall see Talifer,
And he, with a few prompt and willing words
To your obedient maid, will give me all
You'll need for a few days. And in ten minutes,
Or maybe twenty, I shall be here again.
And all the while I'm gone this world of ours
That was here yesterday will have been whirling
Around the sun—because the sun, being stronger,
Will have his way. And there is a law stronger
Than all the suns that has you in its keeping—
But we'll forget that now. You know it better
Than I can say it—and you can't go back.

You are afraid to go, and you are right—
Though not for the wrong reason you have given.
Even so, you can't go back."

               Karen, who heard him
As an imprisoned victim of a siege
Might have heard murmurs of encouragement
Above the roar of a surrounding battle,
Stared at him with despairing eyes wide open,
Pounding her knees with her two little fists.
"But you are blind!" she cried. "I can't stay here.
I won't stay here! The town would laugh for ever
At me—and I won't be ridiculous.
I'd rather be dead than be ridiculous."

He stilled her quickly, with a lifted hand
Commanding quiet, and with a patient frown:
"Child of anticipation and illusion,
Not more than one of those invisible ears,
Which might be seen, could have been listening,
Or you'd not say with any such violence
That you will not stay here. I know you won't.
And I know you will never go back again
To find the webs of Talifer's traditions
Entangling and delaying you for nothing.
And you don't dare to go. I forgot that.
You will not flout fate's opportunity,
Which is a part of an immortal progress
In which you are a pilgrim, whether or no.
Now let us yoke our brilliant wits together
And find out, by geography at first,
Just where you are. You are three hours from New York,
And there's a tavern there; and there's a ship
That sails away sometimes. If I know more
Than owls—reputed falsely to be wise—

1289

All you may ask will be sent after you
Before you sail. Nothing of yours that's here
Will be withheld or misappropriated.
Your things, your trinkets, and your dictionaries,
Your Plato, and your Hermes Trismegistus,
And your new Apollonius Rhodius,
And all your little friends, will follow you.
I shall not hold you to your invitation
Till you are more composed. Only, remember
That I'm still here, and your inveterate slave.
Don't be delirious, don't be agitated,
And don't forget that little house in Wales."

V

One sunny Sunday morning, two years after,
Talifer came down stairs and found Althea
Laughing. When asked what she was laughing at,
She said, "At you, and Quick, and everything
That makes a creature pleased to be alive,
To see what comes. There was a time she wasn't—
Or wasn't particular. Are you more resigned,
And ready for your endurance to the end?"
She watched him with amusement in her eyes,
And he could see that she was throbbing with it,
Although it was not audible: "If you are,
I'm grateful. For you see if you were not,
Good Doctor Quick's untiring services
Might have a sad reward, and his return
Show for him nothing but a blighted harvest
Of all the joyful grain he has been sowing.
But if you're happy, and I'm laughing at you,
It could not all have fallen by the wayside,
Or upon stony places, or been mildewed
Before it fell. Surely it must have been

1290

Good grain, or it would never have come up."

"Resigned? Of course I am." He laid his hands
Carefully on her head, and pulled her ears.
"Resigned, and reconciled, and undefeated
By a few obstacles and reservations.
I knew that if I married this red hair,
Sorrow would come of it, and servitude.
Yet I was not prepared or fortified
For any such unbecoming levity
As yours. Perhaps you are not quite aware
That this will be the first home-breaker's welcome
In my remembrance—and I hope the last."

"I'll hope so, certainly." She poked a part
Of a pink tongue out at him, and withdrew it
Suddenly, with a frown at his appearance.
"But you had best be watchful, and hereafter
Never wear one like that."

                              Talifer cast
A downward look upon himself, and said,
"You call me too conservative, and have fits
To find that I've a memory. What's wrong with it?
Is it not cheerful, and inspiriting?
Is this day an occasion of no color?
With our deliverer—for whose intercession
We should have proper thanks and gratitude
In preparation—coming this afternoon,
You laugh and shake yourself. If you should laugh
Yourself to death, what would become of me?
Have you no self-repose? Have you no morals?"

"I don't know," said Althea, "but I rather
Expect I haven't. And we'll call this thing
One of my lord's mistaken elegances—

Which mercifully are not habitual,
Or frequent. Now I have it; and I'll hide it
Where you will never more be dazzled by it
Into temptation. In a secret manner
That we'll invent, we may, if we are crafty,
Give it anonymously to the orphans.
When brides wear tiger-lilies, you may get you
Another just like it. I've a slow suspicion
That you had best remain conservative
For a while longer. Quick, if he should see it,
Would say that any woman who could watch it,
And be unmoved, would carry the cat to church.
Have you forgotten the grave hours of thought
He must have given to our complexities
Before he smashed them—as he might a clock
Because it wouldn't go? Now do you see?"

"I see why you can't help yourself from being
The seemingest red-headed Rose of Sharon
That ever blossomed on a Sunday morning,"
Said Talifer: "If I put on a red one,
Harmonious and agreeable with your hair,
Quick will appreciate the inspiration,
Giving you all the praise. I shall not mind.
Sorrow has taught the family worm to smile
And suffer, and to see no use in turning.
How is young Samuel?"

     "He is happy and well."
She said; "and for as long as heavenly mercy
Protects and shelters him, no clouds to come
Will dim the sunshine of his ignorance.
He is not old enough to know his father."

Talifer, with a fond joy in his eyes,
And a forgotten collar in his fingers,

Stood like a schoolboy taller than his mother,
And helplessly transfixed with happiness
For getting himself praised. The more she laughed,
The more he beamed with a beatified
Paralysis that was unassailable;
And when with a reluctant resignation
He left her standing there, still laughing at him,
He made a violent and unusual face
That warmed her with a grateful reassurance
Of an unspoken code. If he should break it,
He would break everything, and himself with it,
And she knew that he knew it. She was born
To be like that, and Talifer should by now
Know what he wanted. She believed he did;
And comforted with her belief, she tied
A long cravat into a careful ruin
Of hard and irremediable knots,
Each in itself a pleasing piece of work,
And all a gratifying morning pastime.
When it was done, she sat there dangling it
Like a too-many-colored knotted snake
That she had slain. When Talifer returned,
He might say that a resident snake-killer
Would have been useful earlier. If he didn't,
He might still think so without saying so.
She held it up again to see it hang
And swing, and watched it as contentedly
As if it had been Karen.

                    That afternoon,
Alone under a tree, Althea played
With memory, as in childhood she had played
With a loose tooth, and so relived an hour
At home, three years ago, when Talifer,
Like a man changed into another man,

Had come, as he had made himself believe,
To set her free, and to be honorable,
Before it was too late. She felt the same
Sick chill going through her; and this time she wondered
If she enjoyed it, now the past was over,
And finally decided that she did.
All this that she had now, it seemed, was more
Than even God gave for nothing, or chance offered
Once in a hundred years to mortal choice
Because it happened so; and she knew better
Than to believe that her being miserable
Would heal the common wound. She might, indeed,
Be of more use upright and fortunate
Than supine and rebellious. She was doing
Some good, and if the world would not behave
More as it might if jungle-minded knaves
And patriots were not always playing with it,
Her tears would do no more. If Quick should come
Prepared for happiness, and should find a woman
With a world on her shoulders, he might wish
That he had never chosen or encountered
The task of her salvation.

                              She looked up,
And there was Talifer, who had come unseen,
And with a meditative solemn step
That made no sound. He sat and looked at her
As at a loved one who had stolen something,
Or at a dead friend whom he had offended
Before he died. And then he said, "I wonder
If all men have inside them little tombs,
Where squirming memories are like jacks-in-boxes
Pressed under covers that will not stay down.
Most likely all have several. But there's one
In me that has a small mean demon in it,

Whose head it will not hide for longer time
Than to prepare to pop it out again
When least announced. I have sent reason down
To plead with it, and humor to engage it
With its own method; but they both come back,
One with no language left, and one in tears.
It might be worse if Quick were not your friend,
And mine; for he was there in Karen's cottage
When I explained, and said I had found—peace;
And that's what I'd eat lizards to forget.
I am not naturally an imbecile,
Or you would not be here; and Quick would not
Have seized the moment when he had it with him,
And held it for your sake. It was for you
That he concerned himself so diligently
With my well-being. What are you laughing at?
You have been laughing ever since you got up.
Your Pilgrim Mothers would have spanked you for it."

"No doubt," she said. "Conditions and opinions
Prevailed then of a nature to make ladies
More vigorous and severe in their devotions,
And their observances, than they are now,
And men more stern and awful. In those days,
A faith in something hard and horrible
May have been necessary to transform
A forest wilderness into this place here,
Which looks as if the vikings might have seen it,
Just as it is. But I'm afraid they didn't.
Somebody must have worked. And we must hope,
For their sake, they were happier for believing
The more they toiled and the less fun they had,
The more God loved them for it. I can see,
Without being metaphysical in the least,
Why they believed no easy-going God

1295

Could have made men to fell so many trees,
And lift so many rocks, and women to bear,
As needful rest and incidental change,
From twelve to twenty children between sweepings
And garnishings. A woman must have some rest.
It may be weakness and a shrinking sin
For me to say so, but I'm pleased no less
Not to have come so early. I am proud
Of what was done by those who were before me,
But not for life itself would I go back
To be my great-great-grandmother—who, I'm told,
Wore herself out at ninety and died smiling,
Sorry to go so soon. I'm still uncertain
That I've a sinless right to think of her
Except down on my knees; yet all the same,
I'd rather be where her bones are than be living
Her life instead of mine. You never supposed
That I could be so truthful, but I can—
On Sunday. In the world that's on its way,
We shall be only ornamental remnants;
We shall be curiosities—or we should be
If we were here. It's well to know the worst,
And face it like a Roman—or a Spartan,
If you like Spartans. I have hated them
Intensely, always. When you married me,
You married a thing clinging to the past
With a tenacious pride, something like yours.
You married a proud limpet—though I say it
Only to you and your ferocious eyes,
Which have a peaceful and domestic shine
Just now that doesn't scare me. If you knew
What you were doing when you brought me here,
We should go on, with only normal bloodshed,
Until we are no more."

TALIFER

"I don't account,"
Said Talifer, laughing at her with his eyes,
"For all these powerful thoughts of yours today.
You must have read a book. In any event,
I am not unimpressed; I have, in fact,
Done some unspoken thinking recently,
In which I have some pride. You can't have all
The pride there is; and here is the right moment
For your new estimation of my brain.
Here is young Samuel in his chariot,
Coming to listen. He must know sometime
His useful doom; and if he hears it now,
Being his father's son, he will not flinch.
When he grows up, we'll make the scion work
Unceasingly, and save the family honor
From any such disrepute and execration
As your forebodings may anticipate.
Today the only vision, except yourself,
That haunts me is the coming of our friend,
About now, from experiment and exile—
Two years of it. Well, he is wiser now,
And soon should be in sight, with his round face
Haggard and hardly to be recognized.
He will need spirits to invigorate him,
And sympathy not much easier to express
Than to experience. You are still deceived,
I see, with a false presence, or pale phantom,
Of something you insist is humorous
In my calamitous lapse and aberration,
But if you try to find it with my eyes,
You may search harder than you do with yours,
And see it indistinctly. If you were not
A sanctified and precious vessel of sin,
You might restrain your mirth. If you had morals,

You would remember that you have a son,
Who may, as he develops and observes,
Be more and more like you than like his father.
Have you considered that, and all it means?
And here he is. Remark him, and remember
That he is yours to ruin."

                The son and heir,
From his perambulator, scanned his father
Somewhat as if in doubt of his importance;
And having striven in vain to change his mind,
He fixed a beaming gaze upon his mother,
And with a language of one syllable
And of two hands, made himself understood.
She lifted him from his imprisonment
And held him as if he were naturally
A part of her, and was no trouble to hold—
Which was a mystery still to Talifer,
Who found him fearsome and irregular,
And of no constant length or magnitude.
Like one who had read somewhere in a treatise
How it was done, he touched his infant's nose
With an abrupt unfaltering forefinger,
And sat back with an air of one who knew
What was expected and could always do it—
All with a shrewd smile of encouragement
And confidence between him and his son,
Who promptly welcomed and rewarded it
With a malignant scowl.

                "I can hear steps,"
Althea said. "I hear him—and I see him.
And I see nothing haggard or decrepit,
Or different. I should call him the same Quick
That went away from us two years ago.

He walks, if anything, with a firmer foot,
And with a surer freedom in his legs
Than ever. He looks happy."

      "There might be,"
Said Talifer, with a dryness, "if we knew them,
Some reasons why he should—reasons apart
From seeing you and me. He knows more now
Than he did once, and that may be sufficient
To make him happy; although the happiest
Are nowhere the most learned. You might ask him."

"Well, well, my children! What have you been doing?"
Now in a chair, with a large glass before him,
Quick smiled upon the scene of his return
With retrospective eyes: "God bless my soul!
Babies, and everything. His father beams
As if he thought the race, with him to save it,
Might still go on. I've seen the same before,
And always have accepted and respected,
Impartially, its import and assurance.
A face like Talifer's is like a sunrise
After unhappy days of gloom and rain.
I can remember when that face foretold
Only disintegration and despair.
Look at it now. And who is this new person,
Who sees more than he thinks he'd better say?
Give him to me. Children and animals
Know they are safe with me, and they alone
Appreciate immediately my merit.
No, I'm not going to drop him. Once I knew
A gentleman who was dropped in infancy
Out of a window, inadvertently,
By a red-headed mother. He was never
The same man afterwards. And what would be

This giant's name, perhaps? Micajah? Manfred?
Or Samuel would it be—after his father?"

"Yes, Samuel would it be—after his father,"
Althea said. "And if his name and station
Command no more respect than they are getting
From you, his patient father may be heard from."

The doctor looked up from his infant burden
At Talifer, and then looked down again:
"You hear that, Samuel? Your patient father.
My God, but he was patient, Samuel—
If that's the word—and for some months too long.
But he was nothing to your patient mother,
And she was not so patient. No, it is not
The word, but let it pass. I'll tell somewhat
About it, if you listen. You should know it;
And if your father tells me I'm a liar,
I'll tell you more, for he'll be one himself.
Your inferences may not yet have dimmed
Your knowledge, Samuel, with a suspicion
That somehow this obscure phenomenon
Of ambulant mortality called man
Pays variously, with more than coin of earth,
For more than his terrestrial apparatus;
And you are not to suffer, or shoot yourself,
If you don't know. There are things I don't know.
I don't know why your mother should have paid
So heavily for your father's education.
But if she's happy with him, and satisfied,
He may be worth the price. We shall not ask
Your mother to go back for confirmation.
You must have learned by this time, Samuel,
The folly of that. You show it in your face
You are presumably omniscient now—

At least you look so; and it has been argued
That we are all omniscient at your age,
And year by year are sillier till we die.
Sometimes it would appear so, certainly.
But that's an unproductive argument,
Like most, and we will not pursue it now.
Leaving it out, your father, Samuel,
Was manifestly for a time foredoomed.
He should have been. If I may seem severe,
Ask him one question for his meek assurance
That there's a genius in my moderation:
Ask him if he was not for a sad season,
Common to men who, having all God may give,
Cry for the unpossessed, considerably
An ass. Ask him, and he will not deny it,
For he knows better. You see, Samuel,
I say to you what I say to your father.
I am not ambidextrous in my friendship;
When I have gifts in one hand for my friend,
I have not in the other a sharp knife
For my friend's back. I'm rectitude all over,
And yet unstable. Your mother always knew it,
And weighed me with a lightness undeserved.
When she is old, and I am here no more,
She'll plant a little flower where I am buried,
And she'll sit watching it for hours and hours.
And then there was my uncle, a stern fellow,
Who said I was like Reuben in the Bible,
Who was no good at all. He might have broken
His father's heart if it had not been Jacob's,
Which was a rather tough one. So was mine;
It had to be. And yet I too can suffer.
I've suffered pangs and spasms seeing your father
Led helplessly to cold incarceration,
Where he believed was Peace—with a capital.

He told us he believed it. Now your mother,
Who has good manners when she thinks of them,
Is going to be amused. Whenever she frowns
Or glares at you, or takes you over her knee,
Samuel, you have only to say 'Peace,'
And all will be forgotten. Observe her now:
Her most unworthy thoughts are slinking back,
Maliciously, just to remind your father
Of all he should have seen."

                              "You can do nothing,"
Talifer said. "She was like that this morning.
She still believes that there was something quaint,
Or funny, in my misfortune. She had better
Do so than make a fireside viper of it,
For that's a serpent not so easy to kill.
I thought first it was pathological,
But now it appears harmless—mere illusion.
She will not die of it."

                    Quick only smiled
With a calm satisfaction while Althea
Shook with unmanageable memories
In struggling silence. "You see, Samuel,
She will not die of it. It's mere illusion.
How do you know that you are not illusion,
Samuel? No, your mother won't die of it;
She can't. She was prepared by destiny,
Samuel, to fulfil your father's life
With more than he deserved; with so much more,
Indeed, that a probation was created
In the false image of an Ashtoreth,
Or Lilith, or Fish-Venus, or some sort
Of perilous reptile fashioned as a woman.
She had ambitions, and a learned eye

TALIFER

For the necessities of impending years,
And a sweet hatred of your gentle mother,
Who would have salted her while she was frying
Alive, and would have turned her with a fork,
And fanned the fire at times. Wherefore your father,
Not being so strong as fate was, married her;
And then his wits came back. Quite as a man
Wakes in a sweat from a malefic nightmare,
Your father came to daylight and saw truth—
By which I mean your mother—but the Fish
Was with him still. Now God knows what affliction,
Disaster, or destruction might have followed
Your father's hesitations and traditions,
And his forgetfulness that there's a knife
For more knots than are cut, if Doctor Quick,
His good friend and your mother's faithful slave,
Had not lived in this town. Strange as it sounds,
Your father, Samuel, might still have his Fish,
And you might be more surely an illusion
Than you are now; and with a blasting peril
Unparalleled haunting him and his house,
He might at last have cursed all out of him
The courage and sense to let your mother know.
But for the foresight of good Doctor Quick,
Your mother might never have known—though I'll be just,
And we will not believe it. Time and Events,
Your father's team of galloping tortoises,
Who arrived suddenly one afternoon,
Would have come sometime anyhow; and your mother,
Not fitted for the part of an impatient
Griselda, would have frowned unfeelingly
On numerous men of merit, like myself,
And still would have been waiting for your father,
Who is not nearly so remarkable,
Or so celestially worth waiting for,

As she believes he is. But fate said yes,
And so it was. And so good Doctor Quick,
As always, did the work and had no pay.
There's a word waiting on your mother's tongue
To be a wasp."

         "You always liked your voice,"
Althea said: "I've always told you so.
Go on, please. You are company."

                  "I will,
For Samuel's sake, if you are so insistent.
Well, Samuel, as it proved, Time and Events
Were of a sudden service, as your father
Believed they might be. But if Doctor Quick
Had been elsewhere than here, or naturally
Had been less prompt and loyal in his habit,
I am not saying, Samuel, or surmising,
What might have fallen. At a sad sacrifice,
And a large inconvenience and expense,
He ferried the Fish-Venus and her playmates,
Her Plato, and her Hermes Trismegistus,
And her new Apollonius Rhodius,
Over the ocean to a little house
In Wales, which he had most erroneously
Supposed would hold her. But she wouldn't have Wales.
She said Wales was too chilly and too remote—
Which, had they been the last two adjectives
Alive, would never have been her two to use.
There was a magic river to make music,
And there were trees and hills and dictionaries,
Philosophers, and all the Greek and Latin
That any normal monster would require
For heavenly bread to feed her and her beauty,
But when October came she smiled and flew.

TALIFER

She was so beautiful that many believed
She was not real; and, Samuel, they were wrong.
She was unusual, but was not illusion;
She was no more illusion than you are,
Samuel. If you doubt me, ask your father;
And if he fidgets and stays reticent,
Ask anyone who's from Oxford. She's in Oxford,
Samuel, where she's had, or so I gather,
A fur-lined assignation with the past
Since her first sight of the Greek alphabet.
At any rate, she is there, where she is happy,
And harmless, too—unless to curious youth,
Who, seeing her suddenly, may forget their Greek
And metaphysics, which, could they only know it,
Is about all they see. If you and I,
Samuel, were out walking over there,
We might observe, with schooled serenity,
Dons following her like dogs, and ancient sages,
With a last gleam of evil in their eyes,
Watching her and forgetting their arthritis.
Your father, free, and far away from her,
Forgives her; and as long as his remittance
Has wings, she will have paradise in the bank."

"I think young Samuel may have heard enough,"
Althea said, still quivering silently
With a recurrent mirth of reminiscence
Not shared by Talifer, nor indignantly
Reproved. "Give him to me," she said.

                                    "All right,"
Said Quick, "but you will scare him, and he'll hate you.
Have you no sort of reverence or regard
For what a mother means? How sure are you
That you have not a wrathful Julius Caesar,

1305

Beginning to make faces while you shake him,
And meaning soon to howl?"

                              Talifer nodded,
With an agreement of one not annoyed:
"At first I was alarmed," he said, "but later
Became cold-hearted and resigned. So now,
When it comes on, I wear the face of patience,
And wait till she returns. If she had manners,
Or morals, her obliterative instinct
Would urge her to conceal, or to forget,
Her joy in my remorse. If she had mercy,
Or decent sympathies, or a character,
She might, with years, be an agreeable helpmate.
But while she lets her memories and inventions
Rummage the past, more like a thankless cat
In an ash-can than an obedient wife,
What has a man to say? What has a man
To do, but wear the face of patience?"

                              "Take him,"
She said, and gave young Samuel to his father,
Who fancied for a minute he was nursing
An insane centipede. But no complaint
Came out of him, while with efficient hands
He mastered and compressed his struggling son,
And listened with a smile to the slow tone
Of peaceful bells that sounded from afar
Through the late afternoon. Althea, watching
Alternately the two contented faces
Of two admiring men, quivered and shook
Unfeelingly, until she moaned and choked
With an accumulation of impressions,
And had from Doctor Quick no more attention
Than a barbaric laugh. Young Samuel,

1306

TALIFER

Too long misused, employed his power of sound
As an elected and clairvoyant martyr
Might publish the injustice of his birth,
With none to notice him. Talifer, smiling,
With eyes that were no longer terrifying,
Saw now around him only quiet and rest,
And realization; and with grateful ears
That were attuned again to pleasant music,
Heard nothing but the mellow bells of peace.

AMARANTH

(1934)

To the Memory of
H. Dean Robinson

AMARANTH

I

AFTER a sleep and an awakening
That only freedom earned of servitude
And error may deserve, Fargo saw first,
As always now, before him on the wall,
The one of all his pictures he had spared
When wisdom, lashing heart-sick heroism
To mortal zeal, would let him spare no more.
They were all gone now, and the last faint ghost
Of an unreal regret had followed them.
A voice like one of an undying friend
Whom he had always known and never seen
Had pierced and wounded him till he was warned
Of only one escape; and he was free.
An oily-fiery sacrifice one day,
With nature smiling at him as if pleased,
Had left him contemplating gratefully
A wealth of smoke and ashes. He had heard
The voice until its calm reiterations
Were no more to be stifled with denial,
Or longer to be borne; and he was free.
There were ten years between him and those ashes
That were behind him now to make him young.
At thirty-five he had been cleansed and cured;
At forty-five he could look back and laugh—
Or sigh, if need be. With a sleepy glance
At his accusing remnant on the wall,
He rubbed his eyes, and thought. It was not bad;

It was about as good as a few thousand
That hands no worse than his would do somewhere
Before the day was over. Sunday morning
Would never stay those hands. Art has no rest
Until, unlike the old guard, it surrenders,
Or, like the old guard, dies. He had surrendered,
So not to greet himself among the slain
Before he should be dead. He was alive,
And was content. No bells of destiny
Frightened or vexed him with recrimination,
Or with remorse; no trumpet of loud reason
Told why he should not cherish and encourage
An unforbidden willingness to sleep.
So Fargo slept again and had a dream.

Now there was nothing that a world awake
Would have called light, or darkness. Where he stood
He could see wharves and ships that he had seen
Somewhere before, where there were lights and sounds
And stars, and the cold wash of a slow tide
So far below him that he had not looked
Too long to see it there. All this had been
Before, but never a silence like this now
On ships and wharves and water could have been
Since moving time began. He had come back
Once more to a lost world where all was gone
But ghostly shapes that had no life in them,
And to the wrong world he would once have left
By the wrong door. The old door was now open,
And he had merely to gaze down again
To know the darkness of its invitation,
There in that evil water. Without sound
Or motion, there it was. There was no sun
Or moon to make him wonder whether day
Or night revealed it, and there were no stars;

And that forbidding water was not the same
That once had called him. It was calling now;
And all the silences, stiller than time
Between the stars, if anywhere there were stars,
Were calling. The awakening and escape
For which he had thanked God, the sacrifice
For which God had apparently thanked him,
The world that he was born for and had found
Before it was past having, all were gone,
And were remembered shadows. It was here
That he had been before there was a voice
To stop him and to ask him if the cross
He carried was the cross that fitted him.
A cross, like many another misfit burden,
May be thrown off—sometimes, the voice had said;
Throw it, and you are free. He had been free
Only in fancy. He was here again
By the same water that was not the same
As one that once had waited to receive him.

He made a slow step forward and looked down
Despairingly at a black flood of silence
That had no ripple of life. The world was dead
That held him; and so far as he could fathom
The depth and end of its past vanities,
No clearer way was anywhere left for him
Than a swift one to darkness down before him,
And waiting for him. If he had for years
Carried a cross that was not his to carry,
Believing it was art, and had been dreaming
Of years when it was done with and behind him,
Why should he wait? If he had only dreamed
Of a transformed and sound accomplishment,
Imaginably the sounder for delay,
Why should he pause or faintly temporize

Where there was nothing left? He gazed again
Below him, and the water was still there.

And there was more than water. Near behind him,
He could hear steps, and slowly a low voice:
"You heard me once, and once you heeded me;
And in my words you found deliverance.
I did not ask you then to look at me,
But you may see me now. I have come down
To tell you that I cannot let you sink
So quickly and so easily from my sight.
I have come down here to the end of things
To find you, as I found you here before—
Before you heard my voice. Why are you here,
When you must know so darkly where you are?
Why, friend, have you come back to the wrong world?"

He listened, without power or will to turn,
And only by enforcement hazarded
The sight of what was there. Had this been life
That he was living, and had this been earth
Where he was standing, he would have been shaken
No more than by the voice of any stranger
Saying strange things. But as he heard, he knew
That whatsoever presence there might be
Behind him, there was more there than a man;
And though no more a coward than another,
He knew that fear had found his heart. He knew
Also that he must turn, that he must know.
Too much that was mysterious had already
Amazed him and oppressed him. He must know
More of this place that was a place of death,
And more of what was in it still alive,
And with a tongue to speak. He made himself
Turn round, and saw why he was not alone.

AMARANTH

If it was man, it might have been all men
And women there as one. All who have been,
And all alive and all unborn were there
Before him, and their eyes were watching him
Out of those two that might have been the eyes
Of death, if death were life. He looked at them,
But only as a fool looks at the sun,
And for about as long. More fire was in them
Than he could meet, though he felt glimmerings,
And shadows that were less than memories,
Of having met them once and welcomed them
Incredibly, and their appointed purpose.
If that was true, they could not then have been
So flaming or so fierce. Meanwhile the face
That held them, and held him, was more the face
Of man than of his maker; and the more
He looked at it, the less was it the face
Of one unknown. If it was man before him,
Not even a presence so unnamable
Was unapproachable. If it had no name,
And still had speech, it might say things to him
That he had better know.

                    "You meditate
Only the truth, for you had better know,"
It said; and a sad shadow of a smile
Said too much more: "So you will follow me,
And leave this willing water far behind you.
You sought it once, and would have none of it,
When you had heard my voice. For I was here
To see, my friend, as you were here to listen.
You heard; and then there was no need to see me—
Not then. But since you have come back to me,
To the wrong world whence I delivered you,
Now you shall see. For those who damn themselves

By coming back, voices are not enough.
They must have ears and eyes to know for certain
Where they have come, and to what punishment.
Only the reconciled or the unwakened
Have resignation or ambition here;
And I have here no power that I call mine;
The power is more than mine."

                  "If that be so,"
Said Fargo, "and if you are not the Devil,
What means are yours to make me follow you?"
He trembled as he said it, and half feared
The blast of a divine annihilation
As a last answer. But a sadder smile,
Betraying an approval that was useless,
Followed instead, and silence. "Why do you care
Whether I go with you, or go the way
That I came here to take? What matters it
To you, whatever you are, which way I go?
I thought once I was free, and far from here.
I dreamed all that."

            "Freedom is mostly dreams,
My friend. As for your coming and your going,
I should not care—if it were not my doom
To save, and when discredited or feared,
To quench or to destroy. I do not say
That for some exigencies of my office
I am less grieved than I am gratified,
Or that I am more loved than I am hated.
Only, I say that you will follow me
Because no other road is left for you;
For the same law that holds the stars apart
Holds you and me together. Come with me,
And you will come to nothing wholly strange.

AMARANTH

I wish you might not come. But since you must,
We may as well progress. It is not far
From here, and you are not afraid of graves;
For we are in a land where there are many,
And many to be made. Shall we go now?"

Resentment, recognized and disavowed
As a futility not worth fighting for,
Made Fargo plead for parley—as one will,
Even when he knows: "Before I follow you
May I pray, briefly, for the privilege
Of asking what you are? Are you a man,
Or are you spirit? If you are a man,
There is a name for you. I'm never at ease
When a man tells me I shall follow him,
And has no name."

        The stranger's face betrayed
A weariness: "But you would follow him,
Perforce and of a surety. Man or spirit,
He has a name. The name is Amaranth—
The flower that never fades. Where we are going
You may hear more of it; and among the graves
Around you now, my friend, nothing insists
On pleasantry. For those who are down in them
Went mostly with no smile. Some looked at me
And cursed me, and then died. Some looked and live,
And are indifferent. They are the reconciled,
Who neither live nor die. Now you may see
Before you the gay Tavern of the Vanquished,
Which has been here so long that no man says
Who carried the first stone."

        More with a feel
Of having flown or floated, with no motion,
Than of remembered steps that he had made,

Fargo surveyed a place illuminated
By the same changeless light that had revealed
Still wharves and water and fear-laden ships
That had no life on board, and was not light
That shines on earth. It was a place so old
That all who entered it remembered it.
Dark walls and darker shadows, and dark rafters,
Looked always to have been there; and old floors,
Hewn of a wood that was unwearable,
Might never have been trees. Tables and chairs
Of an unspoilable antiquity
Were dim with centuries of welcomings
And shadowed with farewells; and with no end
That was to see, the long place was alive
With nothing that was any longer there.

"Where have I seen all this before, I wonder,"
Said Fargo to himself; and Amaranth,
Appearing, answered: "There are times and scenes
Which for so long have been the life of you
That they are melted in the veiling mist
Of years behind you. You were here before,
But you had then your zeal and ignorance
Between you and your vision of it now.
Since you are here to stay, you will see more:
You will see memories that you may have felt,
And ecstasies that are not memories yet;
And you will ask of me in vain to tell you
Why the rest cannot see. Some of them will;
And some of them, caring no more to live
Without the calm of their concealed misgivings,
Will die; while others who care more for life
Without a spur than for no life at all,
Will somehow live. I do not ask of any
To meet the mirrors that are in my eyes;

1318

AMARANTH

But if they must, they will. You see the place
Is filled now, and you mourn to see so many
In the wrong world—some young and unsubdued,
Some older and untold, some very old,
And mercifully not to be disturbed
Or undeceived. And why must you be here?
After my saving you, so long ago,
There by that water where you were today,
Why, why, must you come back?"

                                 Before he sought
The first word of an answer, a lean stranger
Called him. And in a moment, without walking,
He made himself informally a guest
At a round table, where they welcomed him,
And found without confusion or commotion
A place for him, although there was none there.
"Because we saw you," the lean stranger said,
"With Amaranth, and because we know him better
Than you, if the Lord cares, will ever know him,
I beckoned you. Beware of Amaranth;
For if you look too long into his eyes,
And see what's there to find, you will see more
Than a good God, if not preoccupied,
Would let be known to the least diligent
Of his misguided and ambitious worms.
I am one Evensong, a resident
For life in the wrong world, where I made music,
And make it still. It is not necessary,
But habit that has outlived revelation
May pipe on to the end. Listen to this:"

The stranger suddenly produced a flute,
And played while his companions heard and smiled
Resignedly as at a story told

Long since to death. "A theme for a quintette,"
Said Evensong. "It sounds like nothing now,
But once it sounded as if God had made it.
Therefore I say, beware of Amaranth,
If you are not the mightier. You are not,
Or you would not be here. Your name is Fargo—
Which is a good name, and has overtones.
Permit me to present the rest of us:
This disillusioned fellow-citizen,
Whose coat needs ink and scissors where it frays,
Is Edward Figg, whose eyes, like yours and mine,
See backwards. There is more in him to worship
Than has come out. He would not strangle you;
He would not steal your money, or your wife;
But he saw wrong, and is a good man wasted.
Once, in a cruel trance of aberration,
He thought himself enamored of the law—
The last of all employment possible
For one of his construction.—Our next friend,
Who sees also behind him, will assuage
Your qualms and aches that are not memories,
Or of the spirit. He is Doctor Styx,
Who might, perhaps, God knows, have been a diver,
A silversmith, or a ventriloquist,
But not, as you behold, what playful fate
Misled him to attempt. Error prevailed,
And here he is. The springs of interest
Are broken in him, and you hear him creak.
Yet lesser men than he, in the right world,
Are crowned for staying there.—You see beside him
A worthy friend who has a crying conscience
Because he knew before he was informed.
The Reverend Pascal Flax, from all we learn
Of his decline, became a clergyman

1320

AMARANTH

Because he liked to talk, and to be seen
As one anointed for an elevation.
But he saw nothing that he could believe,
And one day said no more. He left his flock
To a new shepherd, and you see him now—
A man of rust, and of a covered worth
Never to shine again since Amaranth
Withered him with his eye. But he still talks,
Unless he drinks too long, and younger men
Who smile, and do not yet know where they are,
Will buy his knowledge with a condescension
That one day will be sorrow. Two of them
Are with us here, and they are not so young
Now as they were at thirty. The slight one
Who sits erect, impervious, and secure,
Is Pink the poet. He cuts and sets his words
With an exotic skill so scintillating
That no two proselytes who worship them
Are mystified in the same way exactly.
All who believe themselves at one with him
Will have a private and a personal Pink,
And their unshared interpretation of him—
Which makes him universal for the few,
And may be all he wants.—Now there remains
One more of us. This giant with a beard
Blacker than paint, and with his red shirt open
To show us what it is to have a throat,
Is Atlas, who was a king stevedore
Before he was a painter. Now he paints
Because he must; which is, it seems, the reason
Why there are painters, poets, or musicians,
And why so many of them come here to drink,
If you see what I mean. You are a painter,
And must have eyes. Whatever you see with them,

Don't pity us, for you are one of us—
Unless he lets you go. Once in a while
Not even the eyes of Amaranth will hold
A victim to his doom, but that's not always;
For the most part we stay. As you may guess,
Barring our well-illusioned visitors,
Who still enjoy the comfort of their scorn,
We have encountered Amaranth face to face,
And eye to eye; and as we are, you see us.
We are the reconciled initiates,
Who know that we are nothing in men's eyes
That we set out to be—and should have been,
Had we seen better. We see better now."

"You do not see so well," the poet said,
"That you are not all burrowing in a past,
Where there is mostly darkness and dead roots
That you believe are juicy. If you like them,
Eat them until you choke."

                              "Dear, dear," said Flax,
"Why such a violence? If the roots are dead,
Why for so many stormy centuries
Have the trees lived? If you are tired of them,
Young man, you might resolve to have them down.
We shall not fail, we old ones, to be present."

"I am not young," Pink said: "I am as old
As art; and where death has a life in it,
I can see living death. If you don't see it,
You old ones are the children, who have nothing
To play with but a few poor dusty toys
Left in a garret by your grandfathers.
And when you're tired of them, you have your roots.
Good God, I'm sick of roots."

1322

AMARANTH

"I fear, young man,"
Said Doctor Styx, "that you are sick of more
Than roots. There are misgivings eating you,
Like borers in a tree—and in its roots."

"And you had best remember," said the lawyer,
"That we are more acquainted with misgivings,
And more resigned to them, than you are yet.
Ours have all hatched, and are consuming us
Inside, young man. We set ourselves to grow
In the wrong earth, and soon we had no roots.
If there's no shade beneath our foliage,
There's evidence to say why."

                              "I shall exist
Without the tonic of your sad example,"
The poet said. "And not so much 'young man.'
If you four are the foliage and the fruit
Of your world, I have longings for another;
And so, if there's a foresight in his frenzy,
Has comrade Atlas."

                        "I don't know," growled Atlas,
"What you are saying. And if Pink cares, let him.
I'm sorry to agree with him, but once
I'll have to. There are too damned many roots.
I don't know poetry, but I do know paint;
And if you'll spare me, I'll go back to it.
You don't need me—for I was here to drink,
And hear the Reverend talk. But he's not talking
Today; and I don't talk unless you tell me
Things about paint that you don't know about."
He coughed, and with a massive confidence
That had no falterings, he lounged away.

"You may be safer if you follow Atlas,"
Amaranth said to Pink: "I came in time

To hear you, but your vehemence obscured me.
In art you must esteem yourselves or perish,
Which is not saying that esteem is genius,
Or violence independence. I have still—
And I am older than the youngest poet
Who has no more to learn—to recognize
And worship, as a man more than divine,
One who is independent. I am not,
Or I should not be here. If I had will
To make me wings, and power to fly with them
So far away from this insidious place
That all here might forget me, none of you
Should have to quail again at my approach,
Or fear to meet the mirrors in my eyes.
For most, there is more joy, if not more wisdom,
In seeing not too well."

                        "Who fears—or quails?"
Pink asked of Amaranth; who closed his eyes,
And with a weary smile of helplessness
Opened them slowly: "Do you think, young man,
That you, of all the many who have hoarded
Strength to say that, will prove yourself elected
Never to quail? Now I should avoid quailing
To my last hour of arrogance on earth;
I should not rush to see myself too well,
Or to behold myself too finally,
If I were you. Dreams have a kindly way,
Sometimes, if they are not explored or shaken,
Of lasting glamorously. Many have lasted
All a man's life, sparing him, to the grave,
His value and his magnitude. In this
One sees, or feels, if so attuned and tempered,
An ordered prudence, or an adumbration
Of more than we arrange. If I were you,

1324

AMARANTH

I should not wrench or scorch myself unduly.
Why not let these injurious agitations
Go pleasantly to rest and be forgotten?"

Pink rose, and trembled: "For you, Amaranth,
I do not know you, and I do not like you.
And you would not be missed if you should shrink
And fade for ever."

                "The flower that never fades
Will not do that, young man," said Evensong:
"You cannot scare him, and you cannot kill him.
Four of us here have seen him eye to eye,
And we are still alive. We are not kings,
But still we live. You are afraid of him,
And you had better stay so. There's no shame
In wisdom; and there's often, if we knew it,
A deal of healthful and grief-saving fear."

"Damn it, I was not asking you," said Pink,
"For your assistance or commiseration.
When I shall see no longer where I'm going,
I shall not ask the dead."

              "I drink reproof,"
Said Evensong: "My frailty copes in vain
With fevered youth. If your new flowers and trees
Require no roots, why vex and scald the soil
With so much acid? May not the new truth sleep
In a new bed, and still be comfortable?"

Pink smote him with a scowl, and then he said,
To Amaranth, "All this may end as well
At once as ever. I have seen your face,
And have not shivered at the sight of it,
Or not inordinately. If you fancy

1325

That I'm afflicted with a fear to meet
Myself, and what I am and am to be,
I'm at your service. Let me see what's hidden—
And now; and let me learn how far my sight
Outsees the truth. If your friends here have seen
The face of God—your pardon, my mistake—
And still sit here alive, if not renowned,
I fear no shrinkage."

                    "You will have it so,"
Said Amaranth. "Come here, then. Look at me;
Look in my eyes. . . . Now tell me what you see,
And whether you should pay for staying here
Your price of dust. Is it a lawful price?
I should say not, but I am not the Law
That says what men shall do—though I may wish,
Too late, that you had gone when Atlas went."

The poet held his hands against his eyes,
And for a while stood rigid. Then he spoke:
"Forgive me; this is more surprise than terror,"
He said to Fargo: "But it rankles always
To share a disadvantage with a stranger.
You need not look at me, or look away.
The rest of you may look, for all I care,
Back to yourselves as you believed you were,
And then regard yourselves as you are now.
I wish you a long life in the wrong world,
Where you seem well-adjusted and at ease.
I shall go on as well without your comment
As I have lived without your comprehension.
Amaranth has no reason for remorse,
Or self-reproach. I asked, and I received.
The bowl is broken, and I'm not afraid.
Excuse me, while I go and hang myself."

AMARANTH

"He will hang hard, I fear," said Doctor Styx,
Who watched him as he walked away, erect
And unsuspected by the multitude,
Who drank and sang and saw him only as one
Among so many. "Poets are of a toughness,
And they are slow to kill," the doctor said
To Fargo: "Shall we drink to his departure?"

"Before we do," said Evensong, "permit me
To play for him the burden of a dirge—
An elegy, as it were—which I prepared,
Anticipating an event like this.
It is not long, and it is not immortal;
It is not overwhelming, or supreme.
Listen to this." He played, and they all smiled
As at another story told too often.
"You don't extol it, or not noisily;
No more do I. Now let us drink to Pink,
And may our new companion Fargo join us.
He's not yet reconciled, and has the manner
Of one unwilling to be one of us.
Time will attend to that; for he is here,
The Lord knows why, and has been here before;
And here he must remain—which is a pity.
So then, to Pink—and to an easy voyage
Over a lonely sea that shall be ours
In turn to cross. If when our voyage begins
There may not be much weeping on the wharves,
We shall not care; and those we leave behind
Will suffer less than if they needed us."

"There's more percipience in you, Evensong,
Than there is music," said the doctor, rising;
And they all stood erect, with a precision

That was abrupt and ceremonial.
And soldierly: "Since our young friend has paused
And faltered on the wrong road to Damascus,
Having seen too much light, we'll drink to him,
And to ourselves, and to our new friend Fargo.
Let our new friend regard us, and see twice
The end, before he says he is our brother;
For we are here by ways not on the chart
Of time that we read once as ours to follow.
Time here is all today and yesterday,
For in the wrong world there is no tomorrow.
We stayed and lingered, only to be lost
In twilight while we saw where we were going;
We slept and rested, and we slept again,
Till we awoke where there was no returning.
So let us drink to all we should have been,
Telling ourselves again it is no matter;
The more we lie, the more must we believe.
Similia similibus curantur."

II

Now there were streets and houses. There was nothing
But empty streets, and houses that were still.
There was a tavern far away somewhere
Behind him, but without a guide or sign
To lead him, there was no way back to it.
He could remember what had happened there,
But now he was outside, and was alone.
A door that was forgotten must have opened,
And must have shut itself irrevocably
Against him; and all that was long ago.
He was alone again. By the same light
That was not light, in which he had seen first
Those wharves of silence, and the silent ships,

AMARANTH

Now there were only unfamiliar streets,
And houses that were strange. If there were men
And women hidden in them, they were silent;
And if they were aware of a man walking,
Lost and alone, they were not occupied
With his identity, or with his presence
Or destination. Fargo, had they asked him,
Could not have said to them where he was going,
For he was going nowhere. He knew that;
And with a certitude that was abysmal,
And in a manner fearsome, he walked on,
Hearing his aimless footfall on the pavement,
And hearing nothing else—till all at once,
And round a corner that was imminent,
Came suddenly the sound of other feet,
Heavy and hard, and of harsh laughter mixed
With words not good to hear. Surprise and rage
Assailed him at the sound of his own name,
Spoken with ribald and unwholesome scorn
By one that with a mouth and with a mind
That was unclean foretold ambiguously
Disaster and extinction.

                Fargo stopped
As if a wall of glass had hindered him
Invisibly from going farther forward,
And waited, more in anger than in fear,
For what might be approaching. No long time
Was gone before he saw surrounding him
Their soiled and uncouth shapes, and their lewd faces
Watching him with a glee that had no mercy;
And he saw picks and shovels on their shoulders
Before he saw their eyes; and he saw clay
Upon their feet before he heard his name
Spoken again.

"So Fargo has come back,"
Said one of them. Had each not been as foul
As all the rest, he might have been the foulest,
And so a sort of captain, Fargo thought,
Or noisome foreman. "Yes, he has come back,"
Said a voice farther off. And then the first:
"Yes, Fargo has come back to the wrong world.
He left us, but he loves the sight of us,
And cannot die without us. Shall we tell him
How long he has to live, and how far down
We bury them, who come back? There is a place
That's waiting for you, Fargo. Come with us,
And see what happens when a man comes back.
It's a good place to see—if you are blind;
And most are blind who go there."

                                Fargo felt
His arms held bestially by noxious fingers;
And weaker for the fury that was in him,
Found himself pulled and pushed and dragged along,
His opposition only cursed and laughed at,
And all persuasion vain.

                    "No more of that,"
Came then as a command; and Amaranth
Appeared as God might among torturers.
"You ghouls and scavengers that would possess
The dead before they die, scuttle and hide,
And wash your skins; or the next graves you make
Will be for you your beds."

                        With a low snarl
That said surrender and obedience,
They faded and were gone, as if the wrath

1330

AMARANTH

Of Amaranth had made a vapor of them.
"What are you doing with the grave-diggers?"
He questioned; and he came as near as ever
He came to smiling: "Why resolve so early
On dissolution? Why have you forsaken
The good companionship that I prepared
For you there in the Tavern? If you saw them
Only as derelicts and castaways
Unworthy of your larger contemplation,
I shall not urge you now to contemplate
Your picture in my eyes. There will be time
For pictures more detached and recreative
Than yours may be, and with more drama in them.
Whether you see me as your friend or not,
You will be happier not too far from me,
And wiser for no ranging. To be lost
In the wrong world is twice to be astray,
For you are lost already. Come with me,
My friend; for you are shaken and amazed,
And are still fearful of the grave-diggers.
So some with me. You are not theirs—not yet."

Now there were stairs. "Be careful," Amaranth said,
"For some of them are gone. This house is old—
So old that many tenants have as children
Ascended here in sport, and are still here
As children. If you must be one of them,
Accommodation that will be sufficient
May soon be made for you. Out of this house
There's always going; and those who go, go far.
There are physicians here who cannot hold them,
Or cure themselves of an incessant wound
That now no retrospect of their tuition
In a wrong school shall heal; there are divines

1331

Who long ago lost their divinity,
And are still feeling for a solid station;
There are philosophers who delve and starve
To say again what others have said better;
There are wan moralists and economists
Who write with screaming blood to save a world
That will not read them and will not be saved;
There are lost lawyers who have never pondered
Until too late, the law that was their sentence
To serve where they were never born to serve;
There are deceived inventors who still grope
For bridges that were never built for them
Between their dreams and their discrepancies;
There are spine-weary gardeners who are foiled
Because their fruits and flowers are not their friends;
And with all these there are as many others
As there are lives that are not to be lived—
Not here—but should have been, or many of them,
And well enough, had they been lived elsewhere.
Oh, this is an old house; and all the streets
You found and wandered in, and with no guide,
Are walled with houses that are populous
With tenants who have never found a home.
You have come back, my brother, to a city
Where there is nothing firm and nothing right.
Have you come back to it because you love it?
Was it for nothing that I set you free?"

"I see no answer shining in the dark,"
Said Fargo. "All I know is, I am here.
I have no other knowledge than a dimness
That is not quite remembrance, yet remembers.
I am not here because I would be here;
And God knows why I must."

AMARANTH

Now there were doors.
At one of them, half open, Amaranth,
After a pause that might have been a warning
Or a command, led Fargo silently,
And with a downward eye, into a room
Where there was Evensong, Atlas the painter,
The Reverend Pascal Flax and Lawyer Figg,
And Doctor Styx—all gazing curiously,
And without anguish or astonishment,
At Pink the poet, who was hanging straight
And silent from a rafter. The dim wall
Behind him was more like a painted silence
Than like a wall; and the man hanging there
Was more a picture than he was a man
To his examiners.

"Well, here we are,"
Said Evensong, who had produced his flute,
"And we may do no less for our late friend,
Whose love of us may not have been alone
The leavening of his unsustaining loaf,
Than play again the burden of my dirge—
My elegy, as it were—for his departure.
I pray for the collusion of your silence,
Which I'll interpret fondly as your patience.
I thank you gratefully. Pink, listen to this.
It's not ineffable, it's not absolute,
But it's at least a balm of harmlessness
For me in my defeat. So, Pink, be kind—
If so you may."

While Evensong had blown
Reluctantly his funerary last,
The poet's eyes had slowly partly opened
And now his lips had moved: "If, Evensong,

1333

I am worth only that for having lived,
I should have hastened and come earlier
To my condition here. If Amaranth
Had been less merciful, or indifferent,
He might have served as a more useful spirit
In forcing me to know. And here is Atlas,
Grinning at me because I told him once
What a crude opulence of mortality
There was in what he did. Did I not so,
Atlas? And is not that why you are present,
And happy to be here? Atlas, I weep
To know there is extinct in you the giant
That you repudiated and betrayed,
And so destroyed, when you began with paint.
God, what a sorrow for the stevedores,
I said, beholding you, and then your work.
Smile, if you must. Farewell now to you all.
Please go away."

                  "But how, if you are hanged,
And you are dead, and you are still alive,
And are as complimentary as ever,"
Said Lawyer Figg, aware of a new point,
"Are we to act? If you are dead, so be it;
But if you are somehow deceiving us,
And are not irrecoverably deceased,
And if we leave you hanging here alive,
We are accessories."

                      "No, you are not,"
Said Pink. "Will you but leave me as I am,
You will be saviors and Samaritans.
Not even in heaven itself, which is not here,
Would there be welcome for the uninvited.
Where are your graces? And in what forgotten

1334

AMARANTH

Puddle of dullness have you sunk your tact?
After a decency of hesitation,
And with a tribute of enforced respect,
Two of you might have come; and had you been
Restrained and delicate, and considerate
Of my amelioration and progression,
I should have been as mute and unrebellious
And portable as clay in a wheelbarrow.
When I sought only quiet and privacy,
Why should I be distressed and celebrated
By this obscene inquisitive convocation
Of dry rot walking? I have not summoned you,
And cannot save you. There is more law, Figg,
Than you have on your shelves or on your conscience;
There is more law than all the colleges
Have heard of, or could make you, if they had it,
See to be law. There's music, Evensong,
That might, if you should hear it, overwhelm
The sense of your necessity on earth—
Or all that Amaranth has left of it
For you to trifle with—and humble you
At once to a small heap of sudden dust.
There's a divinity so different, Flax,
From any that man has drafted from the sun,
Or from the seasons, or from the profound
And healing wisdom of his desperation,
That you need sigh no longer for a shadow
That has no substance. You'll be going one day
From this place, which was never the place for you;
And when you go, Evensong will assist
With a new elegy that will be no worse
Than any of its innocuous predecessors.
For you, Styx, there's not yet identified
And captured the correct elusive juice
Of action that will combat and extinguish

1335

The potent worms of doubt and indecision
That congregate and feast and multiply
In you as you grow old. In the wrong world
Will you remain till you are carried from it
In a long box; and you will not mind that,
Which is as well.—Will you all go away?
I am not warmed, I am not comforted,
My friends, in your superfluous attention.
Since uninvited you have honored me
With your respective presences, and heard me,
Honor me once again and go away.
For me this visitation is a task
And an embarrassment; and if you discern,
At last, the measure of my disadvantage,
You will not lacerate me to say more.
If this is not enough, and words are nothing,
And a man's final cry to be forgotten
Is less than nothing, you may all be damned.
And Amaranth, in this I'm not omitting
Your new friend Fargo, who has grace at least
To be uneasy and uncomfortable."

"I am not comfortable," said Doctor Styx,
"If that will earn your praise. I am annoyed,
And uninformed. As one supposed to know,
I ask: Are you alive, or are you dead?"

"I am as dead as I shall ever be,"
Said Pink; "and that's as near as a physician
Requires to know.—Now will you go away?"

"Suspicion," said the Reverend Pascal Flax,
"Whispers to me that in our poet's eyes
We are not heroes. It may well be so.

AMARANTH

My lost assurances of right and wrong,
Of true and false, are like a mist that glimmers
With hidden light. Poets, whatever the end,
Should know a little more than most of us
Of our obscurities."

              Now there were streets again,
And houses—the same streets and the same houses
That in his earlier lost wanderings
Alone, Fargo had seen as a place dead,
Or unawakened, till the grave-diggers
Had been a smirch of life that was itself
A sort of death. But now he could see people,
Women and men, who were not horrible,
Or smeared with special evil. Some were young,
Some older, and some very old; and all
Were going somewhere without saying where
Or why to one another, as men went
In lighter places, and with no more sound
Or pageantry of purpose. Amaranth,
Who knew them all, but was unknown to them,
Said presently to Fargo: "At the Tavern,
Where they forget to think, or to count hours,
Their world is right; but thoughts are fickle sleepers,
And hours come round. But hours and thoughts together
Are not enough to tell them where they are:
They must hear *me;* and only a few do that,
And few that hear will dare an absolution
Of error that is not unsufferable,
For truth untried. My friend, you heard me, once,
And dared escape from here. What have you done
To fate since then that you are here once more?
There are men so disordered and wrong sighted,
So blind with self, that freedom, when they have it,
Is only a new road, and not a long one,

To new imprisonment. But you, my brother,
You are not one of them. You caught yourself
Once in the coiling of a wrong ambition,
And had the quickness to writhe out of it.
You heard me, and you acted, and were free;
And you are here where now there is no freedom.
I shall peruse this mystery to the end;
For some infirmity that sleeps in me
May be a part of it."

                              Now there were stairs
Again for them to climb. By the same light
That was not light, and in a swifter way
Than walking, they were in another house.
It was an old house, older than houses are,
Yet somehow not so near as was the first
To always-coming ruin. "All these houses
Will be, as long as there are men and women
To live in them, and die," Amaranth said;
"And that will be as long as there are men
And women." While he said it, they had entered
Another room. There was a woman in it,
Who had white hair, and a young face not young,
And beauty enough to last. Attending her
Was Evensong, who sat and held her hands,
And Ampersand, who was a large black cat.
His name was Ampersand, she said, because
He looked like one when he sat still and held
His tail around him. Amaranth observed
The man and woman who were there together,
And humored them with his unhappy smile;
And Ampersand, who became suddenly
As large as two cats, flung maliciously
A whispered hiss of hate at Amaranth,
Who frowned as if he felt it. Evensong

AMARANTH

Let go the lady's hands; and while he held
Her face, he kissed her mouth with all his heart.
"Watchman," he said, "if you and I were young,
We should know better than to be here now.
Was it our doom, or was it our good fate,
That we were not to know?"

                    For Evensong
She had no answer but a laugh. She turned
Her face to Amaranth and smiled agreeably,
Though not as if she must, if she would know
The best of being alive, see more of him.

"Elaine Amelia Watchman, gentlemen,
Who writes, and writes, and writes. You know her work,"
Said Evensong; and then to her, "This man
Is Amaranth—which means he is the flower
That never fades. He may sometimes have murmured
Things in your ears. He is a mighty one
For murmuring; and he murmurs all the time,
To all of us. But most of us who hear him
Believe we are mistaken and hear nothing
But the false voice of doubt, common to man.
You smile because you are afraid of him;
Ampersand spits at him because he hates him—
All for your sake. So the best friend we have
Shall have no thanks, or few. This other fellow,
Who's not here to be happy, is one Fargo,
Who made himself believe he was a painter,
Till Amaranth murmured one day in his ear
And he escaped. In his right world he learned
That God's good purpose was to make of him
A spring-clean unimpeachable pump-builder—
A foe to phantoms, and a man attuned

1339

To his necessities. And so he was,
Until the free thread of his fate was broken,
Or tangled with another so in a knot
As never to be untied. Now he is here,
And wonders why. And Amaranth wonders why;
And when he sets himself to questioning,
Order is hurt, and there are wheels not whirling
Quite the right way. Fargo, it seems, is here
With a perplexed remembrance of his coming,
And with no wish to stay. He has forgotten
How the place looked when he was living in it,
And wonders now if he may not be dead,
And on a sort of halting-ground between
His world and hell, maybe. But he sees wrong,
If that's his picture of us. I may say so,
For I know where we are. Watchman, I wish—
I wish—I do, indeed . . . But no, I won't.
What shall I wish? For I know where I am,
And shall remain. Watchman, ask Amaranth
If you and I were not worth more than art
Before it was a wall we built between us.
Amaranth knows. Whether he tells, or not,
Is his own music. Watchman, I wish to God
That you had never learned to read and write,
And I had never heard of counterpoint.
We might by now be sailing where the whales
Of grief would never catch us."

                              "If it's music
That makes you as you are, play some of yours,"
She said, "and you may suddenly feel better.
Make a sad theme for me—a dismal one
That will be heard when you and I are dust,
And our poor woes are nothing."

AMARANTH

                          "As it happens,"
He answered, brightening, "I have done just that;
All but the part of it that shall be heard
When we are dust—which is deplorable,
Though more for the frustration of your wishes
Than of my hopes, which lie where they are buried,
And feel already grass-roots tickling them
In a cool sort of way that doesn't hurt.
Amaranth knows; and so does Doctor Styx,
And his uncoffined friends who live because
They know the Tavern and don't know the grave.
Here they are now. This Amaranth is a doctor—
A wiser one than Styx—though I suspect
That you had best not make him think of you
Too hard, or let yourself be long concerned
With his prognostic eyes. If they are sorry
For seeing too much that's ominous and lonely
In this place, don't imagine the maternal
In you is to be summoned or excited:
Amaranth is not hungry for a mother,
Though he may be at times preoccupied
With other mothers, and some fathers also,
Who would live longer with their sons and daughters
Anywhere else than here—which is a place
To go from with your luggage yet unopened,
And with a ticket that may still be used.
The sorrow of it is that only rarely
Are we to know, until we are too old
Or too unstrung to care, that we are here.
Fargo learned early, and had wings to fly,
But here he is again, without his wings,
And has no story for us. Amaranth
Will have no sleep—I question if he needs it—
Until he knows why Fargo has come back.
If you should ask him, Watchman, you might steal

His answer, for you have a stealing voice.
First, here's an elegy for you and me
That may as well be played while there is time
For you to hear it. It is not transcendent,
But you will not forget, if I go first,
That I it was who made it."

                    "Yes," she said,
Smiling a little when it was all over,
"I shall remember it was you who made it.
You will not mind, for I'm not musical,
If that's all I remember."

                    "You have ears
That hear with mine, my snowdrop," he said, sighing,
And put away his flute: "My wish is only
That you had eyes to see with mine behind you
The lives we two have lost. If I offend,
You learn at last what rancid acrimony
May stew in a sweet nature. It's as well
For you that you are not to visualize
The two we should have been."

                    "I see behind me
What I have done. There is my life, up there,—
Almost a shelf of them," she said, and smiled
At Evensong, who looked at Ampersand,
Who glared at Amaranth: "Let others live
And let me write. You must soon go away,
And let me write; and you means all of you.
There's more than has been written."

                    "Are you certain
Of that?" asked Amaranth. "Do you know all
That has been written? If you know, your knowledge

AMARANTH

Might be a pleasure for the unforewarned—
Or possibly might not, if it were printed.
Meanwhile, so far as you are to be read,
You are not marked or stricken with misgivings
More than are many here. I see no purpose
In our not going. May contentment always
Be near to your command. Farewell; we go."

"Farewell," said Evensong; "and do not see
Too far before you, or too far behind.
God must have made me rather generous,
Or I'd be silent there. Time had the whip,
And you have heard my elegy. Do not say
That it will make death sweet, but say I made it.
So write, and write. See not too far ahead."

"But that's where I will see!" she cried, and rising,
Fixed all her fearlessness on Amaranth,
Who said, "But why?"

              "And I," said Lawyer Figg,
"Can only say with Amaranth, But why?"
"And I," said Doctor Styx, "say only, Why?"
"And I," said Evensong, "say only, Why?"
"And I," said Flax, not caring if he confessed
Accumulating fear, "am asking, Why?"
"I also; I ask, Why?" said Ampersand;
"I can scent presences that you may not,
And emanations that are menacing;
I can feel peril waiting in this room,
Unless you are discreet. 'Twas so in Egypt."
Fargo said nothing, but remained apart,
A stranger trembling with expectancy
And sightless apprehension.

1343

                              Lawyer Figg
Implored her with a look, and said, "Dear friend,
You have heard Ampersand. Will you hear me?
Four of us here you know, and you know well
What time has made of us. What you behold
Is not ourselves, but whims and caricatures
Of our mishandled heritage. We may say,
And with no unsubstantial arrogance,
Or thin defense of our lost usefulness,
That in the proper light of our beginning
We shone for more than this. And as we are,
There may be more of us than we reveal;
We make a tinkling jest of the wrong road
That brought us here, but when we are alone
We put the bells away. Say, if you will,
That we are for a moment here alone
Together, and do your wisest to believe.
Believe that you do best in seeing as far
Before you as tomorrow; and tomorrow—
As far as one day more. Ask Ampersand,
And he will tell you so."

                         "My learned friend
Says well," said Doctor Styx. "Your life, you say,
Is in your work. Why then, in God's name, Madam,
Should you not have your life, and leave to others
The joy of twisting and tormenting theirs?
There are no enemies present, or abroad,
I dare affirm, to thwart you or molest you.
Why then should you be curious, or impatient?
And why not leave the pool unvisited
Until the angel comes? Why trouble it now?
Peril is here, but only if you seek it;
There's no distinguishable jeopardy
That's imminent in your mortal organism;

                         1344

AMARANTH

You have, or so it looks, a competence;
You have a place to live; you have your tea;
You have your books; you have a stately cat;
You have, in sum, so far more than is frequent
In this infected realm, that I beseech
And beg of you to see as far before you
As you see now, and say no more about it.
Ask Ampersand, and he will tell you so."

"Dear lady," said the Reverend Pascal Flax,
"You have heard physic, you have heard the law.
Now let this humble and unworthy tongue
Tell solemnly to you a piercing message,
Which I have heard and have interpreted,
Perforce and clearly, as the voice of God.
Of late I seldom hear it as it sounded
Once on a time, but now I'm filled and ringing,
I swear, as I am here, with truth not mine.
My words, I fear, would be for you as chaff,
Or like a dust of language. Pray forget
Remonstrance, and believe a voice that warns you
That you will see no farther. Be at peace
With time; for in this region where we are,
There is no other peace. Ask Ampersand,
And he will tell you so."

                    She laughed at him,
But a brave terror living in her eyes
Would not be mirth: "You are all trying to scare me,
And that's not why I like you. If you ask him,
Evensong, who has no persuasion left,
And will be happier for not having it,
Will tell you that although I am not large,
There's in me an insistent little spirit
That holds and shields me from life-eating trifles-

Love, doubt, regret, or fear. I'm never vague;
I never cloud myself with airy vapors.
When I am dust, my work will say all this,
And against all your doubts. I should not say it,
But I can see not one here to assure you,
Except myself, that I'm beyond a fear
Of Amaranth, or of anything in his words,
Or in his eyes. Come—let me see those eyes
That are so famous. I like things that are famous,
If only they're not frauds. Where's Pink the poet?
I felt one that I missed."

       "We left him hanging,"
Said Evensong. "He told himself, as you do,
That he was not afraid of Amaranth's eyes;
And so he looked, and saw himself in them
As he was really."

      "I am not surprised,"
She said, "and in a manner am not sorry.
I could have told him his enameled words
Were dead while he was making puzzles of them.
Sometimes, when I was tired, I played with them,
But never read them twice in the same way.
And some of them were beautiful. Poor fellow!
He never found his world."

       "I am not certain,"
Said Doctor Styx, "that there was ever a world
For him to find. If so, I have not seen it.
He saw me as a stripped materialist,
And may have known. And Amaranth, if he knows,
Will never tell us. If we knew too much,
And the bright armor of our own esteem

1346

AMARANTH

Were torn from us, we might all be embarrassed.
Madam, remember that."

                   "I'm tired of *that!*"
She cried; and rushing at Amaranth, she seized him.
"Who are you! Look at me—look—look!" she said,
And sought his eyes with hers. His arms were folded
While she was looking, and his arms were folded
While she came staggering away from him,
With Evensong to guide her as he might
The blind and silent. She would see no chair,
But stood taut and erect against her table,
Pressing with her cold hands the edge of it.

"Nothing is half so hard," he said to her,
"As learning first to know. Think of what's left.
Here is the book of yours that you like best.
Listen: I'll read a page that will be read
When you and I are dust."

                           She turned her face,
And watched him with a fear that made of it
Almost a face that never had been hers,
While he removed a volume, richly bound,
And held it, waiting. "Listen," he said, "and smile."
He opened it, and found between the covers,
Where leaves had been, only gray flakes of dust
That fluttered like thick snow and on the floor
Lay silent. A thin scream came out of her,
And there was nothing more. She was not there.
Where she had been there was a little mound
Of lighter dust, and that was all there was.
"I think," said Evensong, "that she had always,
Hidden somewhere within her, unacknowledged,
A sort of love for me. With your permission,

I'll say she is mine, now." With careful hands
He put it all in a small envelope
And sealed it with his ring. And then he said,
"If she had stayed, she might have learned too soon
Where she was living, and why she was here.
There was no resignation born within her.
Truth, coming first as an uncertainty,
Would have said death to her, and would have killed her
Slowly. Now I shall have her with me always.
Forgive me if I go away, my friends,
And for a while am silent and alone."
He paused, and with a last look at the place
Where she had been so long, he walked away;
And after him walked Ampersand the cat,
Crying as if bewildered and forgotten.

"Well, Fargo, my new friend, my new old friend,"
Said Amaranth, "what do you make of this?
Are you not sorry to be here again?
For this is where you were before you heard
My voice and fled. But that was years ago,
And there's no going now. Well, if you must.
We understand you, and are not amazed
That you and Evensong should for a time
Seek a seclusion and a retrospect.
But have a memory and a care, my friend;
Remember there are still the grave-diggers,
And do not go too far from here alone."

III

Now there were graves. There were so many of them
That they were like a city where tall houses
Were shrunken to innumerable mounds
Of unremembered and unwindowed earth,

1348

AMARANTH

Each holding a foiled occupant whose triumph
In a mischosen warfare against self
And nature was release. "If I had stayed,"
Said Fargo to the desolate still acres
Between him and a line that might have been
His last horizon, "I might be by now
The wrong inhabitant of a cold home
As dark as one of these." He thought of that,
And hurried fast along. "I fled the place,
And was for years safe and away from it,
With only memories of a young mistake
To make it real. Then why am I here now?
For I am here—still here." He thought of that,
And hurried faster. Where he might be going
He did not ask, and there were none to tell him;
There was no sign to show him. There was nothing
But graves, which he had passed·with Amaranth
Before they found the Tavern, and those houses
That never could be far enough behind him
Until he knew that Amaranth and his eyes
Were nowhere watching him.

                          But he must fix
His will, with no more waste of memory
Or thought, on his one purpose of escape
From this insidious region of illusions
That once had made of him their prisoner,
And then had let him go. He had come back
For reasons unrevealed, and had been driven,
Out of time's orbit into a lost chaos
Where time and place were tossed and flung together
Like an invisible foam of unseen waves;
He had come back to a doom recognized
As one to fly from, and now he was flying.
As he rushed on he felt his heart within him

Pounding as if with a foreboding joy
For liberty that was not yet to be his;
But surely somewhere far ahead of him,
If he pursued it and saw not behind him,
Nor thought of what there was that followed him,
Nothing—not Amaranth even, he conceived—
Would hold him in his frenzy for return
To his right world where he had learned to know
That he was living there, and was not dying
Of slow deceit—which, even while it killed,
Whispered and leered, and pointed still the way,
So rarely taken, to deliverance.
But he had seized it; he had heard a voice
Above the whisper, and he had obeyed it;
And in obedience he had found release.
Why then should he be here among the dead?
Was it all graves—this half remembered home
Of ghosts and young ambitions and regrets?
Was he the only fugitive thing alive
Among so many dead? He paused enough
To wonder, and then heard an aged voice
Beside him, as if someone buried there
Were speaking to him.

                "Come with me," it said;
"Or better, remain with me a while, and rest.
There'll be no sailing yet. We shall be early,
And still have time for rest. Your name is Fargo.
I know you. You are the nimble prisoner
Who fled from here while time would let you go.
I saw you in the Tavern, where they told me
Of your return. Why in God's ancient name,
My hurrying friend, have you returned? And where
Would you be going so fast among the graves?
In this one lies a woman. If I killed her,

AMARANTH

She suffered on a slow and loving rack
That hid from me its name. For I was blind—
Until it was too late; and then I saw.
I was a long time learning where I was,
Though I heard murmurs."

                          Fargo, looking down,
Saw sitting at a mound, long overgrown
With negligence, a figure less infirm
Than it was indigent of enterprise.
Gray-haired and wrinkled, he looked up at Fargo,
And smiled at him with eyes that held a fire
More like the shine of burnt-out stars far off,
And shining still, than it was like man's life.
"You do not know me; and there's no remorse
For you in that," he said. "Your ignorance
Of my oblivion is excusable
As one more of those planetary trifles
For which we are not scorned or persecuted.
I'm Ipswich, the inventor. I have never
Invented anything that you have heard of,
But God, the dreams I've had! When I was young,
Visions already of quick miracles,
That would be mine, were like a fire inside me,
Set there to burn with God's immortal fuel
Till all my dreams were deeds, and my ambitions
A time-defying monument of glory
For me and for my science, and for my toil
In darkness where the light was always coming
For men, my brothers. But as one by one,
After soul-wrenching search and repetition,
And after years of it, there would come rays
That almost would be light—so, one by one,
The rays would always fade; and somewhere else
There would be crowns and wreaths and pilgrimages

1351

That were not made for me. Another man's flame
Would have been kindled with accomplishment,
And in the path of its illumination
Would quench my gleam for ever. And so it was—
Not once, but for as many times as fire
Within would burn my doubts to sodden ashes.
A stranger, burning with more fire than mine,
And seeing with eyes that had more light behind them,
Would find at last, where my eyes were not searching,
One waiting treasure more for the world's crown
Of common glory. She who is lying here
So quietly, and with no untold reproach,
Never complained. She only smiled and starved—
Partly for constant and too far prolonged
Frugalities of home, partly for me.
I loved her more than life, but less than science.
She knew the last; the first I never told her—
Although she may have known. I think she did,
For I remember how she looked at me,
And found no fault. I can remember too
A doubt that had an ambush in her eyes,
And would peer out at me when she forgot;
Which was all natural. For a woman's view
Of heaven at home is not one of her waiting
Always, and on the watch, for a concealed
Fulfilment that she knows will never come.
I know it; and if I had known it then,
I do not say my sorrow for it now
Would show me it was not the fate of nature
That I should have been Ipswich. There's a casting
Of too much hallowed and long-honored nonsense
Over the names and skeletons of all those
Who might as well have been George Washington
As not. But this, I fear, accuses me;
For truth on crutches is a mendicant,

AMARANTH

Though God be at her side supporting her.
But there's another glimpse I get of her,
Wherein she stands imperious and intact.
I do not say she points a finger at me,
But there's a frowning that I cannot like
On her calm face, and there is in her eyes
A look that penetrates and troubles me;
For always when it finds me I must hear
Remembered murmurings of a still voice,
Less pleasing and less welcome than a sound
Of anything seen could be. For the long years
It followed me, I stifled it with lies,
Trying to tell myself there was no voice;
But there it was. There was an ear within me
That always heard it, if these ears would not.
I cannot hear it now; and silence tells
To me the reason, which is old and easy:
The voice believes that I'm already dead,
And seeks the living who would still be warned.
But I know better. There's a ship that sails
Today, and you and I shall be on board,
Soon to be leaving, far and far behind us,
A world of graves that are the fame and harvest
Of reaping what should never have been sown."

"I know the murmur of the voice you heard,"
Said Fargo, "and I know whose voice it was;
For I was one of the permitted few
That out of a loud chorus of delusion
Sifted and heeded it. I fled this place,
And found another, where I found myself.
Why am I here? God knows. I have not done
Large evil in the world where I belong;
I am not here for that; I am not here

1353

By wilful choice, by call, or by command
That I remember."

            The inventor smiled,
And rising, winced with age: "No matter now,
For we shall soon be sailing. It's as well,
Sometimes, that we leave reasons in the darkness
Where they like best to live. We do not know
So many forces that are moulding us
That we must have a word we call a name
For more, say, than a few of them." He laughed
At Fargo silently, and without sound
He disappeared; and there were no more graves.

Now there were ships and silent wharves again,
And a black water lying like a floor
That he might walk away on till he found
The freedom he had lost. Fargo at first
Saw naught that had a motion or a shadow
Of life. Where there was neither night nor day,
There were no shadows; and where life was not,
There was no motion. He could see below him
The dark flood that had once invited him,
But did not now. If there was any escape,
He knew it was not there; and in his knowing
He owned unwillingly a nameless debt
To Amaranth. He wondered what it was,
And might have tired his wits not finding it,
Had he come not so near to losing them
Just then, when faintly from a rusted funnel
Not far away from him he saw smoke rising
Into an empty silence. There was life
Somewhere; and it was in a battered thing
Of rust and iron that had been a ship,
And here in its last port had floated only

AMARANTH

Because it had not sunk. Now the smoke rose
And rolled itself into a solid soot
That scattered and spread imperceptibly
Into a distant cloud; and out of cabins,
Which he had fancied might have been the home
Of sleeping demons, there came noisily
A swarm of superannuated men
Who sang with shattered voices, and of women,
Obscenely decked and frescoed against time,
Who shrilled above the men deliriously
A chorus of thanksgiving and release.
Each man and woman held a shaking goblet,
From which there dripped or spilled a distillation
Of unguessed and unmeasured potency,
Which had already vanquished any terrors
Attending embarkation, and all sorrows
Inherent in farewell.

          Fargo, alone
With his amazement, felt lost recollections
Of words returning that were spoken once,
And were forgotten. An old man had said
A ship would sail away, and he had vanished.
No, the same man was here. Ipswich himself,
The old inventor, was approaching him,
And holding with an outstretched trembling hand
A dripping goblet. Fargo pushed away
The fevered invitation and said, "Ipswich,
What are you doing with a drink like this?
I do not know it, but your frenzy tells me
It is no drink for man. Throw it away,
And come with me."

             "Come where with you—and why!"
The old man cried. "No drink for man or woman,

You say, and you say well. We are not men—
We are not women. Since I made this drink,
We are the souls of our misguided selves,
And our lives are no longer our disasters.
We are immortal now, and we are going
Where life will cease to be the long mistake
That we have made of it. We have no captain,
But we have a rejuvenated sailor,
Who never loved the ocean, to command us;
After a measure of this drink of mine,
He sings to me of a world built for us
Dim leagues away, and says he can hear billows
Roaring on undiscovered promontories.
And we have an indignant engineer,
Who should have been a surgeon, driving us
Out of this world anon and to another,
Where long ago, could we have seen ourselves
With eyes that we have now, we should have lived
And grown to glory that shall still be ours.
Come, come with us! There is no other way.
Drink this that I have made and brought for you,
And come! Oh come, for we shall soon be sailing,
And we shall not come back. Praise be to God,
We are not coming back!"

                         The old inventor,
Suffused with an ecstatic saturation,
Proffered again the trembling glass to Fargo,
Who learned, with an incredulous reluctance,
That he was worse than tempted; he was helpless.
There was a diabolical bouquet
Enveloping and intoxicating him,
As if a siren that he could not feel
Or see were breathing in his arms. He faltered;
But when the old man smiled again, he saw

1356

AMARANTH

The wisest and the most affectionate
Of guardian fathers reassuring him,
And urging him to drink if he would live.

"Take it, my son," he said, "and come with me,
Where we shall be defrauded never more
By the grief-plundered and pernicious dreams
That have defeated us. Drink it, my son.
Trust Ipswich, the inventor. Do you see me
As a false comrade, as a man of peril?
Or as a vicious remnant of disaster
Who might inveigle, for his wretched pleasure,
Others to his damnation? There are many
Who sink so far that they may go no lower,
And there may be content. If they are so,
May God reveal to them what they have done,
I say, and let them suffer what they see.
Have I the features or the inward manner
Of an insatiable depravity?
I should be inconsolable to believe it.
Drink, drink, my son!"

                Fargo seized eagerly
The dripping glass and its infernal fragrance,
And would have swallowed the perfidious draught
It held, believing it the wine of life,
Had not a power like that of a calm hand,
Holding him and compelling him to pause,
Touched him and driven a chill of knowledge through him
That made him see. He saw the old inventor
Now as a poor decrepit frail fanatic,
With gentle madness gleaming out of him
Instead of pleasant life. He threw away
The glass, and heard it breaking.

                        "No," he said,
And laughed at the old man indulgingly:
"I'd rather be the last fool left ashore
Than be afloat with you. What wits are mine
Will be some company; and if I conserve them,
There may be a way out. If there's a way
Without a wreck before the end of it,
There's also, and for all there is of me,
The task of finding it. If your invention
Has crowned itself at last with desperation,
Say it is yours and leave to me despair.
For me it is the safer of the two,
And is not always a fixed incubus."

The old man shook his head at him, and wept:
"My son, it is the very fiend and father
Of lies who makes himself invisible
Before he tells you this, and lets you say it.
Despair, or desperation—what you will—
There is no safety here. Come, come with me,
Before it is too late! Come, and be saved!
For we are going now—far, far away
From this imprisonment that was our folly,
And was almost our grave. You will not come?
God save you, then. You know not what you do.
Farewell, farewell, my son. I gave release
For you to drink, and I could give no more.
Farewell, farewell."

                    The old man sang those words
To Fargo for as long as he went shaking
Back to the crowded hulk where men and women
Still waved their hands and sang. There was a puff
Of white steam and a sound of a thin whistle,
And then that ruin of what was once a ship

AMARANTH

Struggled and groaned like a sick beast of burden
That asked of man only some solitude
Wherein to sleep and die. Driven to move
By some last artifice of mind and action,
It left the desolate wharf where Fargo waited,
Watching it as it labored helplessly
Away with a sad clanking, and more groaning,
And a great hissing. Smoke and steam were leaking
Infernally and impossibly through plates
Where time and rust had eaten them; and now
There was a dark eruption all at once
Of smoke and sudden flame from a tall funnel
That leaned before it fell; and all on board
Were singing so that Fargo on the wharf
Could hear their sound of joy—till a dull roar
Became a silence, and there was no ship,
And no more sound.

          "Their voyage was not a long one,
Though longer than we might have prophesied,"
Amaranth said, behind him. Fargo turned
And found a patient face, familiar now,
Watching as if no more had happened there
Than a man going home: "It seems a pity,
My friend, but there is no way out of here
Alive like that. There's no such easy stealth,
Nor such abrupt and festive exodus
As your mad friend foresaw. You would have drunk
Your doom in his invention, had I let you,
And would have gone with him where others went
Who are gone now indeed. Their vanities,
And their Plutonian amenities,
Were not long to endure. Are you not glad
That I was here in time?"

                      "I don't know that,"
Said Fargo, after thought. "If I am here
To stay until I die, and for no reason,
I am not sure that my friend's last invention
Was not the true release he said it was."

"Was that his name for it?" Amaranth asked.
"I wonder how he knew. How do men learn
To know, and where the light is none too clear,
The language of so much that's unrevealed
And ultimate in the books they have not read?
I see that here I must have some instruction."

"Is that why you are smiling—if you call it
A smile that you are wearing?" Fargo asked.
"Do you smile always when a crazy ship
Is blown to pieces, and all those on board
Are blown to death, or drowned?"

                            "Not always—no,"
Amaranth said, and gazed away from Fargo
To where the ship had been: "But I see now
Nothing that holds us longer where we are.
This is a place that I have never sought,
Or fancied. There is no escape this way;
And you, if you are shrewd and sound, will hasten
Away from here with me."

                      Now there were ships
And silent wharves no longer, and no music
Of those intoxicated emigrants
Who sang no more. Now there were only walls
And web-hung rafters, and a patched north window
That was half covered with as much as time

Had left of a stained curtain. On a floor
More famous than the man who never swept it,
There was an easel with a picture on it,
And a few sorry chairs. In one of them
Sat Atlas, with his red shirt and his beard,
Admiring audibly a last achievement,
Which of itself would be a revolution
When the world heard of it. He said it would;
And pouring a stout drink from a full bottle,
He said it twice. He swore at Lawyer Figg
With a voluminous harmless blasphemy
That ended innocently with a laugh
Of patient pity, whereat the lawyer smiled
For sudden lack of words to fill the moment.

"The gifted have their obligations, Atlas,"
He ventured, "and are lenient when a lawyer
Requires a breath of time to stroke his chin
And hesitate. I don't know what I think,
And you don't care. Your manner makes a riot
For an uncertain eye. It agitates
And dazzles; and I'm only a poor layman,
Too old now to be learning a new language
That has no roots. You say it is a horse,
And I have never called it a volcano.
You say the sky is blue, and so it is,
And a horse has a right to some of it;
But when you make him indigo all over,
And then forget that you leave out of him
Everything that I've always called a horse,
A lawyer wonders why it is a horse,
Whatever the sky may be. Green trees are blue,
Sometimes—I know they are, for I have seen them—
But even blue trees have roots."

                        "Oh, damn your trees,
And damn your roots," roared Atlas, angrily.
"You'll eat a poisoned rat if you say 'roots'
To me again, by God!"

                      "Dear, dear," said Flax.
"Why such an animal accent? By your leave,
I'll ask for silence while I drink to peace,
Atlas, and its concomitant, good will.
When you are on the westward side of life,
Which man's imagination has for ages
Configurated aptly as a mountain,
You will have learned, and by some sore tuition,
That peace, if you are chosen to achieve it,
Is worth a world of noise. Sinners of old
Believed if they prayed once or twice to God,
He would prepare for them an easy march
To heaven without good works; and nowadays
Sinners in art believe there are short roads
To glory without form. I drink once more
To peace and to good will, and to you, Atlas;
And now it is a horse. If lesser men
Deny it, say the Reverend Pascal Flax—
A clergyman decayed, who might have been
A lawyer, or perchance a politician—
Beseeches them to tell him what it is
If it is not a horse."

                      "I was not raised
In your world, Reverend," Atlas answered, growling.
"And I can't tell you all that's in my heart
To say to you. I could tell Styx and Figg
Where they might go, together or separately,
But there's a broadcloth line that I respect—

AMARANTH

Though I don't see that you, with all your roots,
Have a plantation on your side of it."

"Your pardon, gentlemen"; said Amaranth,
"But there are waves of latent indignation
Coming from Atlas that you may not feel.
He may be large and dark and powerful,
But strength and size have sensibilities
That may deceive."

        "There are so many in him,"
Said Doctor Styx, who now possessed the bottle,
"That color with him is all, and needs no line.
He says there is one line that he respects;
And I wish, Atlas—here's to your long life—
I wish to God that there were more of them.
I am less exercised and less excited
Because your horse is blue, than I am, Atlas,
Because you see it and still see a horse.
Like my contemporaries, Flax and Figg,
I lean to less rebellious innovations;
And like them, I've an antiquated eye
For change too savage, or for cataclysms
That would shake out of me an old suspicion
That art has roots. Atlas, why do you flash
A look like that at me for not yet saying,
In friendship, that a blue horse, or a green one,
Should have at least a buried line somewhere
To say it is a horse? Creators ache,
I fear, for growing too fast; and I am sorry
For you, that in your frenzy to attain
You have found only one line to respect—
The which, being broadcloth on a clergyman,
Is rather a step away from a blue horse.
And what am I, meanwhile? A stranded leech,

Of no announced importance or repute,
Whose word has an authority in art
As large as yours in physic. To you, Atlas,
I drink, and to the swelling of your fame
For centuries, till it says farewell to earth,
And floats above it like a firm balloon.
The more I drink, the more I see a horse,
And love him none the less for being blue.
What do I see, if it is not a horse?
If anyone says it's not, say Doctor Styx
Challenges them to call it anything else.
I shall remain here neighing until I know
Why it is not. If it is not a horse,
What else, in God's name, is it?"

                              "Hear him, Atlas,"
Said Evensong. "Hear him, and humor him;
And heed him as you would the silver noise
Of poplars in a breeze. I take your word;
And when you say to me it is a horse,
To me it is a horse. Why call a storm
From nowhere, when we may as well have peace?
Our reverend friend is right in prizing it
Higher than controversy. For myself,
I'm a too long unwanted votary
Of old and overworn deficiencies;
I thought once that a multitude of notes,
Because they were my creatures, must be music.
I should have been perhaps a naturalist.
Had nature won, I should know more of horses;
And of art, possibly."

                           "Good God!" said Atlas,
Pouring a giant's drink and gulping it,
"Your soft way of not saying what you're afraid

AMARANTH

To say, and your sweet throwing of your own failures
Into my face to keep me company,
Will not go down. Your motive, I dare say,
Is to be kind. Well, put your kindness back
Into your windpipe. Someone else may want it.
There are some hungry souls that are so sick
With having nothing but the past to live on,
That like as not they'll eat the withered skins
Of cant you throw to them, and thank you for them.
Now I begin to see. If God's alive,
He must be laughing to watch Evensong
Pouring his patronizing oily pity
On Me. My God, on Me! I've pitied you
Too long, and I have never let you know it."

He shook himself like a large dog and laughed
With inward indignation and amazement;
Then, swallowing what was left, he disappeared—
Soon to arrive again triumphantly,
Emerging fiercely from behind a screen
With a new bottle. With a nervous hand
He drew the cork, and paused before he drank:
"Now I begin to see. You, Evensong,
Are not alone. There's you, Figg—and you, Styx—
And, Reverend, there's you. I've always liked you;
I've liked your talk, and I've liked your not seeing
The difference that I felt. I don't forget,
But that's no use today. I know you all
Today, and should have known you long ago.
You're all alike. You all think I'm a fool.
Because God gave me vision to see more
Than you know how to see, there's nothing left
For you to do but laugh. The fool's old laugh
At everything that's not yet cracks and cobwebs
Will never frighten me. It's the true cross,

And always has been, that we have to bear.
Was I a stevedore? Well, if I was,
Once on a time there was a Carpenter;
And some of you have heard what happened to him.
It was a portion of my preparation
To be a stevedore, and that part's over.
I was a good one, if that's any matter,
And I've a strong arm still. If I should use it,
I might throw all of you, and never feel it
Afterwards, one by one out of the window—
All but you, Amaranth. I don't know you.
I don't know what you are, or what you think.
But if you fancy I'm afraid of you,
There'll have to be some showing. You and your friend—
Your new friend Fargo, who tried once to paint,
And then, in answer to God's call, made pumps—
Are silent over there. You are all silent . . .
Well, Reverend, have a drink, if you won't talk.
I thought so. It was not my fate, when young,
To go your delicate ways, but I know men;
And, Reverend, I know you. And I know paint—
Which is what you don't know. I mean all present—
All but you, Amaranth. I don't know you;
And I'm not certain . . . Maybe I'll stop there.
Pink said he didn't like you, to your face,
But I'm not saying just that. Only a poet
Would have such a divine be-damned assurance.
It's not that I don't like you. I don't know you . . .
Evensong, have a drink, and let's forget it.
I see that I'm not done with Amaranth,
Who still believes that he can feel inside him
A sort of squirming notion, or suspicion,
That I'm afraid of him. I'll drink to him,
Just to convince him that I'm not afraid—
Of him, or any man."

AMARANTH

                  "I have not heard
The sound yet of one timid syllable
From you," said Amaranth. "If you uttered one,
I should be disconcerted and reduced
Unpleasantly to many questionings.
To make myself unwelcome, I could wish,
Meanwhile, and only for your peace and reason,
For thunder not so loud. Faith, if assured,
Will ride without a cannon or a banner—
On a blue horse, if it be necessary—
As far as there's a way. I like to fancy
That your explosive note of confidence
Today has more the tone of celebration
Than of a sounding habit."

                          "You have words
That I can't play with," Atlas answered, thickly;
"I went to my own school, and have some reading
Locked up in me that I don't advertise;
For I've a rough tongue still. I know it's rough;
But I can make it say, and without oil,
That I'm as ready as a rat for cheese
To meet whatever it is that you are hiding,
And see myself today among the masters.
Where are they? Bring them on. I'll say to them,
Or maybe to as many as I've an eye for,
That we are brothers. And they'll say to me,
'Brothers we are.' And they'll shake hands with Atlas."

Amaranth looked a long time at the bottle,
And then away: "I wish, for your sake, Atlas,
That your vociferous demon had his being
Only in what you drink. But he was in you
Before the grain that angers him was planted.
Well, peace be with you, Atlas. If I stay

Till you may know me better, there's that matter
Of liking me, remember. For my part,
I would have only peace—if peace were mine
To make, or share."

           "Stay where you are!" growled Atlas.
"You are not going away with your conceit
To keep you warm and to leave me a fool
Behind you. Where are those damned eyes of yours
That Flax and Figg and Styx and Evensong—
And Pink, poor devil—have seen, to see themselves?
Let me look into them and find what's there.
You are afraid—for me? My God!—for Me?
You are worth living for. If I don't laugh,
I'll need a drink to keep myself polite."

He took an ample swallow, and then laughed
At Amaranth, who stood with folded arms
Against the wall, and said: "I have not asked
For this; and Atlas, it is not too late
For me to go . . . You will, then?"

                Atlas laid
His large and hairy hands on Amaranth,
And gazed into his eyes. There was no need
Of words when the collapse of everything
That had been Atlas fell into the chair
Before the picture—to sit there and shake
And be a speechless wreck till it arose
And said to Amaranth: "Who is this God
That I have heard of who saves men? Where is he?
Let me look once into his face and tell him
What he has done to me! If you are God,
Amaranth, you had better have been the Devil.
What are you? Are you . . ."

AMARANTH

        "No, I am not God;
And I am not the Devil," Amaranth said.
"And you, in your first waking, are not Atlas.
You are a stranger, still to meet yourself,
Alone and unafraid."

      "Afraid? By heaven
And hell! Afraid of what!" Out of his clothes
He drew a sailor's knife, and opened it:
"See this; and try to see now, as I shall,
The blood run where I strike. The blood you see
Will be my life, and all that my life means."
He slashed the picture lengthwise and crosswise
Till there was nothing but shreds left of it.
"Now say that I'm afraid."

         "Why make me say it?"
Amaranth asked. "This is no joy for me.
If you were not afraid of me, my friend,
Your faith would not have cared enough to look
Into my eyes—and you would not be here.
If doubt had not been living like a worm
Within you, Atlas, you would not be here.
You would be in a world where clearer voices
Would be less mine than yours. Clearer, because
Men hear mine to forswear it and forget it,
And say it never was—which is not, Atlas,
The same as knowing they have never heard it.
There is still time for you to go from here.
Many awake to learn that they are born
Out of a dream. There may be a new region
Waiting for you outside, and far from here,
Where I shall have no power to trouble you."

"Good God, is there no truth left anywhere!"
Cried Atlas. "How many times have you been born,

1369

Amaranth? Six or seven? The pain, they say,
If we remembered it, is worse than dying.
I don't mind death. I mind the falling down
Of a tall monument that I was building
Higher than lightning, and as everlasting
As man on earth. To your health, Amaranth! .
And may you live to be the curse of man
As long as earth breeds life."

                       So saying, he poured
A fearsome drink, and laughed when it was gone.
Then he said, swaying. "Where is your new world
For me? The only world that I have had
Is gone now. You have made a desert of it,
Amaranth; and the rest of you are liars—
You and your learning, and your ways of saying
To me that I'm an outcast and a fool.
What are you all to me? I know you now.
I know you, and I see you—all alike.
You are not much to see. The fire of lies
That lit the way for me to find no more
Than you here at the end of it was wasted.
I thought it was the lamp of God. What was it?
And what was I? I don't know who I am.
I haven't even a name. Does anyone care?
Now see what I shall do. And if you say,
Before you see, that I'm afraid to know,
Say it—and see!"

                   He seized another canvas,
Slashing it madly, and then seized another,
And still another, until not one of them
Was left unsacrificed. "Good-bye," he said;
And now he was half hidden by the screen.
"Amaranth, you have done a good day's work.

1370

Good-bye, and damn your soul." He disappeared;
And there was nothing seen or heard of Atlas
Till there was an explanatory sound
Of weight that fell down heavily on the floor.

"You, Styx, are a physician," Amaranth said:
"And if your various means and implements
Of restoration are not here, no matter.
There is no need for more of us than you
To see him; and you need not stay with him
Longer than you are pleased with his appearance."

"I shall regret for life," said Evensong,
"My footless notion of preparing him
For resignation—or for God knows what.
Pity and condescension dress themselves
Adroitly in humility's old clothes,
And may as well be naked."

                              "Let your motive
Be more the salvage of your memory there
Than your mistake. Your qualm is not uncommon,"
Said Amaranth: "Well, Fargo, my old friend,
Where do you go this time? The grave-diggers
Are never so far from here but they may find you;
And they remember. If you like my counsel,
You will avoid them; for I may not always
Be where you are when you have lost your way."

IV

Now there were glimmering walls that were to Fargo
At the same time familiar and unknown.
Once he had worked in such a place, he knew,
But this room was not his—though it revealed

1371

Appearances that had the ghostliness
Of old possessions that were memories;
And here, against the protest of his being
And will, he was compelled again to paint.
He wondered why; and Evensong, who sat
On high there with a willing weariness
Of one who would do anything for a friend,
Was asking with a still defeated smile
Fargo's unanswered question.

                  "If, like you,
I had escaped from here when first I heard
The voice of Amaranth, I would more than rather
Have worn my feet off running than come back,"
Said Evensong: "If I had built my house
In the right world instead of no house here,
I should have locked it so that no invaders
From a deceiving past, like yours and mine,
Should have crept in to drag me out of it,
And carry me back to this. If I had found
Myself where I belonged, and not too late
For my indifference to be interested,
I should have stayed. I should have let the Devil
Do his own tinkling, and been satisfied
Not to be scoring for him, with him grinning
Here in the dark. I should have been content
With hearing what there's more than life has time for
Without the blameless help of my small offspring.
If I'm in any measure truculent,
Or too censorious, they are not suffering.
Did they not give me hours and years enough
Of indecisions and uncertainties
Before I told them I was not their father,
And that their mother was the Devil's playmate?
Unlike some accidents of ecstasy,

1372

AMARANTH

They made me think they clamored to be born.
You know their argument, and their revenge.
Wherefore, I fear that I'll ask endlessly,
My valued and unfathomable friend,
Why in God's name, having got once out of this,
To the firm highways of deliverance,
Have you come back? If you should paint me, Fargo,
For twice as many days as there are hours
In this one, you'd have then, as heaven's wages,
A failure maybe not so nullifying
As death, nor yet so luring that even love
Would climb a mountain more than once to see it.
Fargo, if I could put my tongue to sleep,
It would still talk, and say, Why, Why, and Why
Have you come back?"

                 "If I could answer you,"
Said Fargo, painting on with a compulsion
That had no pleasure in it, and no faith,
"I could say whose offense and whose resentment
Has will that I have not. It's like a dream
Of going back to school, and to old lessons
That once we thought were learned. There is no place
Left here for me. Has Amaranth any name
For labor that compels an execution
Because it wills itself against our wits?
I've toiled where effort was intelligible
In circumstances I would not have chosen;
And I have chosen error that afterwards
Rejected me and let me save myself;
But here there is no choice. There is no heart
In me for this; and there is none in you.
When I am seasoned and acclimated
Like you, beyond escape or thought of it,
I may know why it is that you are smiling;

I may—if death forgets me for so long."

"It comes all to the heart, and to the treasure—
Which is adjacent, or synonymous,"
Said Evensong. "I knew a fellow once,
An ablest of the ineffectuals—
One of the brotherhood, and extant yet—
Whose qualities had so many focuses
That there was never a sure centre for them.
So he became impatient and unruly,
And fixed upon a last determination
To finish it all with drink. But there he failed,
As always; for his heart was never in it,
He said. He still lives, and he drinks enough,
But not sufficient for incineration;
And all because his heart was never in it.
So, Fargo, now you know why you must fail
In painting me. Your heart is somewhere else,
And there your treasure is. It is not here."

"No," Fargo answered; "it is far from here.
Yet Atlas would have said that his was here.
If not, where was it? There was nothing in life
For him but art; and when he saw the end
That had been waiting for him, there was not life."

"Better say paint than art," said Evensong.
"Color with him, when he discovered it,
And learned a little of its perilous ways,
Was a long drunkenness—which he conceived
As new, and revolution. While it rumbled,
He should have learned to draw. But like some others,
Assured of more than they possessed, he flung
His first bomb to annihilate for ever
Those ancient superfluities of line

And form that were an obstacle between him
And his desire. There was a blast of color,
And Atlas never knew that he was blind
Until he knew the eyes of Amaranth.
It may have been as well. He might have seen
His end too soon; and his awakening
Might have been longer torture for the man
Than Amaranth and his eyes. His wits were sharp,
And though they were untempered by the world,
They still possessed an edge that would have turned
Itself against him as it did today.
He was a victim, or a sport, of glory
That would have laughed him mad. Amaranth said
His doubt was living in him like a worm;
But I should have said sleeping. Does it matter?"

"I'm searching my last archive to find out
What matters, or what doesn't," Fargo answered,
"If I am to stay here. Have you not found
One door yet that will open? I'm so far
From all I left behind me that was right,
That I'll be wondering somewhat if I'm dead,
And in a sort of twilight purgatory
That I should not have said was merited.
I gave myself indeed a sprig of honor,
Or satisfaction, for the pride I found
In having redeemed myself from a taskmaster
Who only laughed at me and used his whip
When I defied him. Atlas called him paint;
I called him art; and Amaranth called him death—
Unless I fled from him and set my steps
Away from here for ever. If I'm here long,
I may go prowling down again alone
To those dim wharves where that unholy boat,
With Ipswich and his crew, all singing drunk,

1375

Steamed off to sink; and then I may go farther—
If Amaranth will let me."

     "He will not,"
Said Evensong. "For recondite good reasons,
He means to keep you here for a long time—
I fear for always, though I mourn to say so.
There's talk abroad of Ipswich and his vessel,
And not much grief. There's no such playful way
Out of the past as theirs; and since they foundered
Shouting, with Ipswich's imperial drink
Warming and permeating their perceptions
With a wrong promise, we should be fools, or worse,
To wish them back. We don't know where they are."

"I was near saying that I know as well
Where they are as where I am," Fargo said,
And paused. There was a clear sound of a scratching
Outside the door; and Evensong said, "Ah,
My friend and fellow-lodger. By your leave,
I'll ask him to come in."

     "How do you do,"
Said Ampersand. With a superior tread
Of ease and ownership that made no noise,
He walked along to Fargo and jumped up
Softly into a chair not far from him,
And sat there like his name—with his tail round him
Like a black serpent. "I came in," said he,
"To see the picture."

     "If you came for that,"
Said Fargo, "there'll be one more disappointment
For me to count in my long list of them
Since I came back. But I'm past all reproach,

1376

AMARANTH

Which has no current worth or meaning here.
I thought you might be coming to see me."

"Not so," said Ampersand, with a red yawn,
"I came to see the picture. Men go hungry,
And travel far, leaving their homes behind them
And their wives eating scraps, all to see pictures
That hungry men have painted. Art is cruel,
And so is nature; and if both are cruel,
What's left that isn't?"

                    "I don't know," said Fargo;
"I'm hungry to find out. We'll talk about it.
Well, here is your new master, or new friend,
On canvas, and awaiting your opinion.
And what is your opinion?"

                    "I don't like it,"
Said Ampersand—who promptly caught a fly
And anxiously chewed air until he found it.
"Excuse me. He was flying to his fate,
And here was I, ordained to swallow him.
You call it nature's law. I, being a cat,
Call it a problematical free will.
If there's a difference, no philosophers,
I'm told, have caught it yet. No, I don't like it—
I mean the picture. And if you have eyes
That are not liars, you are not proud of it
Along your back. There are no crinkles in it.
Why do you do it? You were here before,
I am informed; and why are you here now?
You must know where you are. Miss Watchman knew,
Although she never said it—not even to me.
And there was not much that I didn't know

1377

About Miss Watchman. She told everything
To me—except that she knew where she was.
But she liked writing more than she liked truth,
Or life, and I'm not saying that she was foolish,
Or self-destroyed, in doing what she liked best.
When I can seize the possibility
Of doing what I like best, I always do it;
And I have no devouring aspirations
Consuming me with unacknowledged lies.
The more I learn of men's and women's folly
In trying to make their wishes their belief,
The more I'm rather content to be a cat;
And cats, you may have guessed, are not without
Their ingrained and especial vanities,
For which there is no cure. Nature in us
Is more intractable and peremptory;
Wherefore you call us feral and ferocious,
Which is unfair to us; for the same God
Who sees a sparrow on the ground shows us
The way to catch him, and we cannot choose.
You can, you say; and you have certainly
An instinct that appears more flexible
And less confined and less inexorable
Than ours. And if you have one, I mean really,
There should be freedom in you to explain
Why, for God's infinite sake, you are still painting,
And why you have come back."

                "If you are asking,
As well as Amaranth and Evensong,
And all their friends, I shall undoubtedly
Go down to those dim wharves and drown myself,"
Said Fargo; "for I cannot answer you.
Almost I wish that Ipswich had prevailed
In luring me on board his hissing ship,

And blown me with it into the black water
That you will find down there."

     "I shall not find it,"
Said Ampersand. "You may have all the water
That I can't drink, which will be most of it.
Water was necessary, I was told,
To make me clean, but there was always blood
Before I would believe it."

    "So it is here
I find you, Fargo," Amaranth said, behind him.
"Well, you are safer here with Ampersand
And Evensong than with the grave-diggers.
And you are not so hostile, Ampersand,
As heretofore. Unless your face tells nothing,
You have been meditating and repenting."

"I have been ruminating and revolving
Ultimate thoughts, and had forgotten you,"
Said Ampersand. "If all had eyes like mine,
The darkness of our disappearances
Might have a transience and a diminution.
There's Atlas. Would you bring him back to us,
For rage and revelation to slay twice?
Since Evensong has given me a new home,
And all is changed, I'm full of afterthoughts
And inferences. Have you seen Fargo's picture?"

"I see it," said Amaranth; and Lawyer Figg,
Appearing imperceptibly, said "Yes,
I'm seeing it now."—"And I," said Doctor Styx.—
"And I," said Flax.

    "You are all seeing it,"
Said Fargo; "and so far as I'm the martyr,

There's no more to be said. I have no thirst
For praise that is not coming—and if it came,
Would only be salt water for the shipwrecked.
Your faces are your news; and I have read it
In headlines heavier than your reticence
Before you came. I ask with Ampersand,
And with you all together, why am I here?
It is my turn to ask."

        "We are all here,"
Said Amaranth, "to pay a pilgrimage—
The least we owe—to Atlas, who is now
The profanation of the grave-diggers.
Before oblivion blots and mingles it
With dreams of kings and slaves who are forgotten,
His reckoning of an increment not there
Merits a breath of our commemoration.
I shall go charitably to the grave
Of one for whom ambition was a monster."

"And I," said Evensong. "Incidentally,
I have composed for him an elegy
Of sorts, and will play there, if you are patient,
The burden of it. Atlas will not mind.
It will not ruin us to remember him
And his discrepancies for a few minutes.
Always excepting Amaranth, who murmurs,
Forgive me if I see not one of us
So bent with eminence that he cannot walk,
And cannot spare a twinge of it for Atlas.
I shall go meekly to the funeral
Of one whose exultation so betrayed
And wasted him."

        "And so shall I," said Fargo;
"And I shall go with no commiseration

1380

AMARANTH

Of one whose way from here, if I stay here,
May still be mine."—"And I," said Lawyer Figg.—
"And I," said Doctor Styx.—"And I," said Flax.—
"I also; I like funerals, and promote
Mortality myself—as when, perchance,
And on occasion, an elected mouse
And my compulsive predatory instinct
Combine and synchronize with my desire,"
Said Ampersand.—So there was Amaranth,
The Reverend Pascal Flax, and Doctor Styx,
And there was Lawyer Figg, and there was Fargo,
And there was Evensong, and Ampersand,
All going to the funeral. Evensong,
Descending, led the way; and after them,
The picture now forgotten, Fargo followed.

Now there were graves again surrounding him,
And everywhere as far ahead of him
As vision followed sight. He saw them now
Like waves, interminably motionless
And held by some unnatural command
In solid calm upon a sea of earth,
Where there was never to be storm or change,
Or a sun shining. Fargo moved alone,
Painting himself in hues of a new fancy
As the last man alive, and without fear.
He knew that where there were so many graves
To see, in that same light that was not light,
If he walked on, and on, and far enough,
There must be one somewhere that had been waiting
Too long. If it was here that he must live
Till death remembered him and set him free,
There was no more to ask of Amaranth,
Or time, than to forget. But where he was
There was no time. And where was Amaranth,

And all the rest who had gone out with him
From that old room?

               Yes, here was Amaranth,
And here was Evensong, and all of them;
And on the ground, like things that had emerged
Unwillingly from where they lived in it,
Munching unsightly food, and tearing it
With earthy fingers, were the grave-diggers.
The foulest of them Fargo recognized
As the malignant one that first had hailed
And seized him in the street; and now he heard him
Laughing uncleanly and with ribald scorn
To his foul neighbors: "Fargo has come back.
He knew enough to run away from us,
But not enough to stay. We'll have him yet!
We'll throw him down alive into a hole
Deeper than this one we have made for Atlas.
We'll have him yet. Only a fool comes back
Who has been here, and gone. We'll have him yet!"

"Be still, and eat—you necessary vermin,"
Said Amaranth. "There's work still waiting for you,
And then your pay. There's pay for everything;
And your existence is a part of it—
For you, and for all near you."

               "If you died
Without us, we should hear bells ringing for us,"
Said one; "and we should then have better names.
We know the dirt that's on us, and we like it."

"You do not know it yet," said Amaranth,
"And that is why you like it. Now be quiet
Until this man is buried, and then be gone.

AMARANTH

If you were clean, you would be miserable;
Which is too much for you to comprehend
Till you are born again—if ever you are."—
"Yah, yah," said one of them; and they were quiet.

Before there was a last pounding of earth
On Atlas, Evensong played his elegy
With earnest execution to an end
That was a rueful silence, and then sighed.
"It is not seizing, it is not celestial,"
He said, "but once it would have shaken me
All up and down myself with ecstasy,
And prayerful thankfulness to the Almighty,
That Evensong should do it. But Amaranth,
With his remorseless if unwilling habit
Of showing us, if we let him, where we are,
Laid ecstasy and thankfulness together
With me in the same grave where days are buried;
And when he found that I was here securely,
Without incentive and without invention,
Too dream-worn and indifferent to escape,
He gave me resignation or destruction
As a cold choice. Slower than Pink and Atlas
In my pursuit of the omnivorous Why,
I am still here, and in a manner tuneful.
But I am not deceived. I wish to heaven
I were, but Amaranth would not have it so."

"You would not have it so," said Amaranth.
"I murmur in men's ears invisibly
My warning, and I wait—mostly in vain;
And even with you that are aware of me,
I do not hold a mirror to your faces
To make you see, or die."

"Or both, maybe,"
Said Lawyer Figg. He gazed in retrospect
Where the grave-diggers, who had done their work
With chuckling curses and insinuations,
Had left a mound on what had once been Atlas:
"There was a time when for a few first years
I could have seen myself as Atlas is,
And wished indeed that I saw more than fancy.
But that was not my way; and I doubt yet
If Pink and Atlas have achieved release—
Though I am not an artist or a poet,
And I have not yet ridden a blue horse
Beyond my observation over the hill.
If I'm a sorry lawyer, that's because
I should have been seized early and submerged
In forethought chilly enough to make me shiver
And think. I was too docile and too warm.
I followed others, and you see me now;
I followed them because I saw them shining;
And without asking whether or not the fuel
In me was one to make their sort of fire
And light, I came to learn that it was not.
There was a proper flame that all the while
Was burning in me, but I stifled it
Slowly with indolence and indecision.
One day I fanned it with a breath of hope,
And found that it was out. Since then, and now,
My knees and sleeves are all of me that shines.
But they are mine, and I have no reproach,
Or verdict, or vain censure for this man,
And none for Pink. I have not lived their lives.
I have not shared their pangs or felt their terrors
On their awakening here in the wrong world
That unassayed ambition said was right.
My only contribution at this hour

1384

AMARANTH

Is my suspicion that a mortal haste
Like theirs may not have hurried them on so far
As they foresaw. I do not see them here,
And cannot follow them to tell you more.
I am not mystical. But there's a jarring
Somewhere in this for me, and for the most
Of mankind, I believe; and I suspect
Without it there would not be trees enough
To make the paper that would hold the news
Of those who might no longer stay with us."

"Our friend and eminent horse-leech, Doctor Styx,
Owes you his next imperative attention,"
Said Evensong: "Your jam has all gone sour,
And you have covered your bad bread with it
Too heavily. The unlovely sight of Atlas,
Before we buried him, has turned everything;
But it will fade, as we shall."

                Doctor Styx,
After the time of an inquiring glance
At Amaranth, who said nothing, looked at Figg
To reprimand him with a stern grimace:
"My bilious and invincible torch-bearer,
Listen to Evensong. Attend him shrewdly,
And you'll see shadows that are not so black
For some of us. If you must have black things
To see, why not see Ampersand, who sits
Ungrieved and with a firmness on the grave
That we have made for Atlas? There's a lesson
In him, and for us all, of independence,
If there's not one of courtesy. He's not saying
That all cats who have no-one to call Father
Should therefor curse their birth and drown themselves.
He looks away where there are distances

That are unknown and unimaginable,
And maybe for the reason of their dimness
Are more profound for him in their perspective
Than Atlas, in the ground there, is for me.
He looks to me as if he had forgotten
All about Atlas; and he may have learned
In Egypt, where his import and importance
Were stated and established, that his rights
Are to sit where he will, if not removed,
And see what things he may. I cannot see them
With your eyes, Figg, more than I can with his;
And on the whole, if mine were to be lost,
I'd rather see them with his eyes than yours.
Things I can see with mine I know are there,
And should have known their purpose long ago.
If I had known them where they waited then,
My hands and faculties would be grateful now
For grasping them. Pink, in his diagnosis
Of my complaint, was nearer the physician
Than I was; and his candle might have burned
Longer, and with a wider light around it,
If Amaranth had waylaid him in his youth,
And held him and compelled him till he saw.
Figg feeds himself with mystery that he feels,
And cannot name. No man that I have met
Has ever named it with a word that tells me
More than a clock says. As for seeking it,
Or flying from here in a malignant rage
Of disillusionment—well, I suspect
I'm too indifferent, or we'll say too lazy.
Say what you will; I shall not writhe, or suffer.
I'm so inured to uselessness, maybe,
That moral torture and eternal doubt
That others feel leave me uninterested.
Let a man come to me with a disease

That I've a name for, I'll try not to kill him;
But let another man say the man's alive
When he is dead, I shall know what to call him."

"You mean," said Evensong, "if indirectly,
That you believe yourself, and all who live,
To be in essence, and in everything,
Identical in revealed futility
With what we buried when we buried Atlas.
The rest, you say, is nothing. Some would say
The rest is Atlas."

         "And I have to say it,"
Said Flax, the clergyman. "But if you pursue me
For more than I may tell, I shall be silent.
In the forgotten graveyard of the gods
There are so many that have come and gone
That I am lost among them. Most of them
Had better be called dead than their inventors—
Who must once have had life to fashion them,
As Pink said, of their fears. There is no God
For me to fear, or none that I may find,
Or feel, except a living one within me;
Who tells me clearly, when I question him,
That he is there. There is no name for him,
For names are only words. There was a time
When I thought words were life. There was a time
When I might have calumniated Atlas,
Branding him as a culprit and a sinner
To let himself be crushed under the weight
Of his house falling round him. But the God
That is within me tells me now that Atlas
Lived in another house that was not mine,
And that I am not told what might have happened

1387

If my house had been his. We are too brisk
In our assumption of another's lightness
Under a burden we have never felt,
And too remiss in calling ourselves liars
For saying so well so much more than we know.
Theology fell to pieces on my pulpit
Before I learned that I was telling lies
To friends who knew it. But my God was left
Within me—to be stirred there more by sloth,
Perhaps, than by revealed iniquity.
So, friends, I cannot answer you for Atlas.
All I can tell you is, that when I found
My house was falling, I fled out of it;
And that if I should fail to fly again,
The God within me would be felt and heard—
Although it might be quiet if it was there
Alone with only pain waiting for death.
I leave you to your several estimations
Of what I mean. We shall be here once more
Together, nor long from now, with Pink to bring us;
And I shall tell you only the same story—
Or better, none—when we are done with him.
There are complexities and reservations
Where there are poets, for they are alone,
Wherever they are. They are like Ampersand;
They do not like us if we harass them
Unseasonably. I think it would be safer,
And more for our well-being and for our peace,
If we should let him hang for a while longer.
Our visitation, coming unforeseen
And unsolicited a second time,
Might only vex him. Though he fail, or die,
The poet somehow has the best of us;
He has a gauge for us that we have not."

AMARANTH

"Pink had a gauge for me," said Doctor Styx;
"I could see that, but not his reading of it,
For I'm an indifferent reader in the dark.
'I am as dead as I shall ever be,'
He said; and that's what men who hang themselves
Do not say generally to a physician.
If I can't tell you whether a man's alive
Or not alive, don't ask me why I'm here,
Or why I should be anywhere. I don't know."

"And he had one for me," said Evensong;
"And while I mean to mourn appropriately,
And for some time, his going away from us,
I shall endure devotedly the scission
And rift, I think."

                        "You are not thinking now,"
Said Amaranth; "you are struggling not to think.
The stings he left in you would not be itching
Without the lingering acid of some truth.
When Pink is here, you may be here sometimes,
To ponder on his end and to ask whether
Or not it is the end. Your friend the doctor,
Whenever he says to you that Pink is dead,
Will tell you that it is. Your friend the preacher,
So far as words are his interpreters,
Weighs evil in more discriminating scales
Then heretofore, and says he cannot say
For certain what is evil. Your friend the lawyer,
Not yet assured of his illumination,
Would rather conserve the glimmer he thinks he has
Than blow it out. I hope you may all live
Until you are all sure you are not sorry,
Even here in the wrong world, that you were born.
And you, Styx, have a reason to live longer,

1389

For you have more to learn. If I should answer
Your last unhappy question, you would still
Be asking; for the words that you may hear
Are like small shot that fly with a large noise
To shatter stars and bring them down to you
In dust for you to study. And if you had it,
You would have dust like this you cannot read
Where you are now. Fargo, the time has come
For you to tell me that my eyes have in them
Nothing for you to fear; for now you know
That once having heard my voice and heeded it,
Henceforth you are the stronger of the two.
Now it is clear that you have come to us
Unwillingly, and by no command of mine,
To see, and to be sure. When you are gone
From us, and are a memory here behind you,
We shall all know that you are coming back
To this place again never. So remember
A little, once in a while, of what it was
That you were leaving when you went from here.
If you are looking down now to find Atlas,
He is not there. You don't know where he is,
Fargo; and there is more doubt haunting you
Than sorrow. Never be sorry for the dead—
Lament them as you may, or treasure them;
And never build a stairway for a swallow."
Reluctantly, and with a premonition
Of change without a name compelling him,
Fargo, employed with his unanswered thoughts
Of Atlas, raised his eyes and found himself
Alone with Amaranth and Evensong.
Figg, Styx, and Flax, and Ampersand had vanished,
And there were no more graves. He looked again,
And even the grave of Atlas was not there.
Mist, like a moving carpet on the ground,

1390

AMARANTH

Was over everything; and through the sky,
That for so long had been a veil of gray,
There was a coming of another color.

Amaranth said, "My eyes have nothing in them,
For you, that you may not see now with yours.
They did not summon you, but it is well
For you that you came back. Now you are sure,
And you are free. I cannot hold you here."

"Farewell," said Evensong. "If I had known,
I should have made a music of departure
That might have followed you for a short way.
Its eminent element would not have pierced
Or thrilled or melted you especially,
Though I should have enjoyed inditing it,
And with no injury to muse or man.
Farewell, and may your pumps unceasingly
Pour strength and blessing on you, and no paint.
Think of me as one fixed here in this place
Because he saw too late to go away.
Think of me as a friend who is remote,
Yet real as islands that you cannot see."

"Farewell," said Amaranth. "Remember me
As one who may not measure what he does,
More than fate may. If it were possible,
I should hold only pleasure in my eyes
For those who see too late. You heard my voice,
And heeded it, not knowing whose voice it was.
Many have heard it, and have only covered
Their fears and indecisions and misgivings
More resolutely with their vanities;
And under such an unsubstantial armor
Against the slow rust of discovery,

1391

Must choose rather to strive and starve and fail,
And be forgotten, than to feel their names
In my pursuing murmur—which is mine
Because a mightier voice than you have heard
Is over mine the master. To a few
I murmur not in vain: they fly from here
As you did, and I see no more of them
Where, far from this miasma of delusion
They know the best there is for man to know;
They know the peace of reason. To a few
I show myself; but only the resigned
And reconciled will own me as a friend.
And all this you have seen. You are not here
To stay with us; and you are wiser now
For your return. You will not come again.
Remember me . . . The name was Amaranth . . .
The flower . . . that never . . . fades . . ."

                                    "But you are fading!"
Said Fargo. "You and Evensong are fading.
Where are you going? And where has all this light
Come from so suddenly? Both of you are fading—
Into a mist—a white mist. You are crumbling.
Your faces!—they are going."

                          While he spoke,
The world around him flamed amazingly
With light that comforted and startled him
With joy, and with ineffable release.
There was a picture of unrolling moments
In a full morning light, and out of it
Familiar walls and windows were emerging
From an inscrutable white mist that melted
Transparently to air; and there were fading
Two shapes that had no longer any form.

1392

AMARANTH

Fargo, partly awake, with eyes half open,
Saw sunlight and deliverance, and all through him
Felt a slow gratitude that he was hearing
Outside, somewhere, at last, the sound of living—
Mixed with a quaint regret that he was seeing
The last of Amaranth and Evensong.

AMARANTH

Farao, partly awake, with eyes half open,
Saw sunlight and deliverance, and all through him
Felt a slow gratitude that he was hearing
Outside, somewhere, at last, the sound of living—
Mused with a quaint regret that he was seeing
The last of Amaranth and Evensong.

1933

KING JASPER

(1935)

KING JASPER

I

HONORIA, by compliment the queen,
Would have been royal anywhere, and apart
With her distinction in a multitude
Or on a throne. Whether a queen or not,
And wilfully or not, she would have drawn
Around herself invisibly a circle
For none to cross without a smile or sign
From her to say they might. If there was joy
Or glory in this for her, there was tonight
No shining record in her eyes of either;
Nor in her face, where time had faintly won
A negligible skirmish with her beauty,
Was happiness to spare. Yet everything
That other women would have suffered for,
And many enough would ardently have sold
Salvation and intelligence to possess,
Was in appearance hers. So has it been
Since envy, like a foundling, hated first
Its name, and sighed because it had no other;
Though envy, gazing in a window there
Tonight, and seeing well, might have seen less
Worth stealing there than in a toiler's cottage
Where no queens ever came. Honoria
Might have been happier had she never felt
The touch of hidden fingers everywhere,
On everything, and sometimes all but seen them.
For they were there, they were all over the house;
They followed her unseen wherever she went,

And stayed with her unseen wherever she was,
As there now by the firelight where she sat
Alone, and waited for she said not what.
Surely for nothing new. The massive wealth
Of house and home was armor too secure
For change to shake or pierce. Or, were those hands
That she felt everywhere on everything
Blasting already with unseen decay
Walls, roofs, and furniture, and all there was
For her to feel and see and never to know.
She watched the flame and wondered why it was
That she was always waiting, and for what.
The king would soon be coming down the stairs
To praise her and to worship her discreetly,
And probably to say again to her
That time, whenever he stole a year from her,
Replaced it with another loveliness
Fairer than youth—all which would have been true,
And would have been a comfort undenied,
If there were not those hands always at work
Somewhere. If she could see what they were doing,
Or say more certainly what hands they were,
Doom, when it came, would be endurable,
And understandable, as death would be.
The world outside, and with abundant reason,
Would say she was the last of things alive
To play with death, or make a picture of it;
And many would see themselves, and with more reason,
Already pictured. The queen considered that;
And hearing the king coming down the stairs,
Arranged a smile. The king deserved a smile,
And there was always one awaiting him.

Jasper the first, King Jasper generally,
By compliment also—and by some right,

Which all might not acknowledge as divine—
Came softly in to where the queen sat waiting
For more than Jasper. Had she told him that,
And had she told him of those unseen hands,
He would have laughed at her and kissed her twice
Instead of once—which now, if not enough,
Was all that was expected. So she smiled
At him obediently and beautifully,
And the king smiled. He was a small, tight man,
With eyes that should have seen you in the dark,
And a face moulded hard and handsomely
To a deceiving candor—a face made
For men to study twice, and one for women,
If able, to forget. It was a face
Of amiable deceits and pleasant dangers,
And was withal—or would be for as long
As there were on it no annoyances—
An unoffending and a patient face.
"You may throw billiard balls or bricks at it,
And they will leave no mark," one citizen
Had said; and several had agreed with him.
The queen would have heard nothing to resent
Had she heard that; and those invisible hands,
For ever at work, might have let something fall
That was not built to fall. If one thing fell,
She had long fancied, always with a shiver,
That all would follow. She was thinking now
Of that; and while she thought of it, she smiled
At the king watching her across the hearth
With piercing gentleness that never changed,
Or never except infrequently to pierce
Deliberately, that she might not forget
Who ruled and answered only his own questions
Of what a king had mostly on his mind
When he was silent or was not at home.

1399

Without those eyes that were his heritage,
He might not have been king.

                    "And so, my dear,"
The king said, "we may count the coming down
Of one more night on us, and on the chimneys—
For now we cannot see them; and that means
That we are one day older. If your face
Were the one calendar available,
There would be only as many days and nights
As we might live; for there would be no years.
You are miraculous."

                   "Oh no," she said.
"Your chimneys are the miracle. Without them,
I might have one face, or I might have two;
Or I might have no face. It wouldn't matter.
Your chimneys are the landmark of your power.
Without them, I know best what I should be.
Why do you wait so long? I said all that
Only to make you say it was not so."
She laughed, and had a momentary triumph
To play with.

             "You're the more miraculous,
The longer you're alive. So make the most
Of that before I swear I never said it.
But all the same, and not for the first time,
I'm wishing that your eyes were finding more
For mine to share with them, and less that's hidden.
God gave you eyes to make the world affirm
That you are not supremely among women
The most unfortunate or disconsolate.
I think so, but I like your saying so;
And that was why I waited. I'm no worse

Than when you married me; and you said then
That I was wonderful. I see no change,
Unless we say I'm older. As for you,
Astronomy and addition are both liars
When they say you are fifty. You are thirty.
If there are more years in your doubts tonight
Than thirty, they are there and nowhere else.
Who puts them there? Or what? For all I know
It's that incalculable only son
Of ours. What are we going to make of him?
Answer me that, and I'll go on my knees
To you, and make you blind with diamonds."

"Jasper, if diamonds would make me blind
In one direction, or in one respect,
I might be on my knees, imploring you
For baskets of them. No, it is not our son,
Although I grant you there's a problem in him.
What shall we make of him, you ask? I ask,
What shall he make of us? If you are strong,
And the world says you are, he may be stronger,
And with a wilder strength. He is still young,
And so must have his visions. If you fear
He sees today too far beyond your chimneys,
Why be alarmed? Be quiet, and let him grow.
The chimneys are still there."

                              "Thank God they are.
And in a proper course of time and reason
He may discover them and consider them
As more than hollow trees that are on fire—
Down where the dragon lives. His filial pride
Sees in what others have called supremacy
A smart abstraction that he calls a dragon.
Meanwhile his occupation is a woman

He calls his wife. She is too free and holy,
Or so he says, to let herself be bound
Or tangled in the flimsy nets or threads
Of church or state. So far as I'm informed,
Or have inferred, she seems to be a sort
Of charming and transfigured wasp, equipped
To sting the mightiest spiders of convention
And fly away from them as free as ever.
In my son's place—well, well, I'd rather not say.
She has enraptured him past intercession,
And I've a notion how—for I have seen her;
And you, this evening, if you will, may gauge her
With all your motherly judgment and affection.
For better or worse, you may as well accept her;
For I'm afraid you must, or lose your son.
If she is false, and I am sure she isn't,
He'll scorch himself and be a little wiser,
And will not be the first. If you see better
Than I see, let me share with you your picture
Of his improvement and his transformation.
He needed both, if ever youth needed sight;
And you, my dear, may not have seen, as I have,
New terrors that have overtaken us.
You feel them, but you do not know their nature."

"I know, though mercifully I'm a novice,
The nature of an insult. If my son
Tells me to suffer, I suppose I must.
And your new terrors, Jasper, are not new."

"Some of them are," the king said; "and she is—
Although I should have known, and so been ready
For any such apparition as might arrive,
Early, or later, as I feared—or knew.
You cannot know, as I do, what the years

1402

Are bringing home, but you are soon to learn.
Never mind, now. I'll sit here and see—you;
And with a son's eye try to see the stranger.
Why must you women, you pernicious ribs,
Make havoc always of awakening man?
I've not forgotten what you made of me,
After one sight of you. And I'm aware
That this fantastic and elusive sprout
Of ours would hear from us no thwarting sort
Of counsel. If I told him, as a father,
What he must do, he'd find, without a pause,
A way to make me scan with a new care
The size of my experience. If assurance
And aimlessness are strength, your hero has it.
I think it must have been your contribution
To his exuberance. It was never mine."

"Am I then so exuberant?" she asked.
"I might recall innumerable names
Of yours for me, but none would have that word.
Am I exuberant?"

                    "No, you are not—tonight.
The distance here between us is the same
As always, yet you seem so not quite here
That I'm uncertain that I'm not astray
In someone else's house, and you a stranger.
Say it's a fancy; for I'm one of those
Who thrive indifferently on mysteries.
Say it is fancy. Then say what it was
That set my fancy ranging. For you know,
My dear, and there is no-one else to tell me.
I have not watched and measured men so long
That I have not remembered there are women
One woman I've remembered so intensely

1403

That I may not have told her—which is wrong,
And may for many a man be perilous.
My sense of having you has like as not
Misled me, as it has a million others,
To saying not enough. If that's the matter,
Scratch me and see how instantly I bleed.
You must have an unseen sufficiency
Of little knives; and I'm of the elected
In having never felt them. Won't you tell me,
And with no slaughter, what it is you see,
Or would see if you might? If it's a ghost,
I'm chilled with interest. I have never seen one.
A ghost in a new house where none has died
Is out of order."

          "And why so? Some houses,
Newer than this, may well be full of them."

The king looked hard at his Honoria
Before he laughed. "And have you seen one here?
If not, you may have heard him; and if so,
You should have been asleep. Nights are alive
With noises if you lie and listen for them."

"No, Jasper, I've not seen him, nor yet heard him;
And maybe only my imagination
Has let me tell myself that I have felt him.
Not only in the night; for there are ghosts,
I fancy, at all hours. When I'm alone,
By day or night, I feel mysterious hands
Doing a silent work of slow destruction.
I feel them here; and if I went down there,
And waited, I might feel them in the chimneys.
Someone is here at work, or more than one,
With hands that I shall be afraid to know

So long as they are silent and unseen.
Have you an enemy, or a friend, who died,
And might return to you to be unwelcome?"

"What thread of language is it you are spinning
As if you mean to weave a shroud of it
For all that we have been—for all we are?
What have I done so deadly different
Of late that I remain a stranger to it?
If you are too much alone when I'm away,
God knows it is your choice. I should have said,
If questioned, it was a clever way of yours
Of staying alive sometimes. But if it serves you
Only as a new way of seeing demons,
I recommend activity and fatigue—
And sleep."

       She smiled. "It is your memory now
That sleeps. I never told you that I saw them.
I told you that I felt them."

       "I've a doubt,
My dear, if you've an inkling of what ails you.
World-weary nerves, I'll wager. If you say so,
We'll go to sea and sail around the world,
With freedom and free air for company.
There's nothing for you to ask that I'll refuse,
If it will change those anxious eyes of yours
That feel, but cannot see."

       Again she smiled:
"No, Jasper. You are kind; you always were—
To me. But we might sail ten thousand miles
Away from here, and I should feel those hands,
Always invisible, always at work."

1405

"God help us, then," the king said; and he sat
Like a still image, gazing solemnly
At a slow-burning log that smoked and hissed
And whispered. And the thing was listening.

Without a motion, or a glance at her
Who sat there silently, "And you," he said,
"Are not alone permitted or condemned
To know there are somewhere some hands at work
That may destroy us if we live too long.
I feel them, as you do; but there's with me
A difference. Mine are not those of a ghost."

"I know them; and I know whose hands they are,
Jasper; and I have known for a long time."

With a slow sigh that said less of relief
Than of lost hope restored, he studied her
With eyes that held a warmer confidence
Than had for long been hers to find in them.
A smile of an inquiring gratitude
Softened them strangely while he sighed again,
Contentedly almost. "Well, if you know them,
You know there's nothing that is here for always.
There may be a long madness on the way
To shatter a mad world that may deserve it.
I cannot answer if you ask me now
To tell you what it is those hands are doing.
Only remember, and be satisfied,
That you may fear no ghost. Only God knows
How gladly I'd exchange for a ghost's hands
The living and invincible hands I feel
All around me. For I feel them, and I see them;
And you might, if you knew them as I know them."

The queen, with a monotony unaltered
And with no smile, said, "Jasper, I am sorry.
But mine are a ghost's hands, if yours are not.
I know your purpose, and I know those hands
Down there, and everywhere, that may have power
To crush us. If they do, I shall not care—
So long as I'm permitted not to touch them.
No, mine are the cold hands of an old ghost
That will not rest unfelt. But for the while
He stays invisible, we'll not mention him.
Let us imagine that he never was,
And say no more of him."

                    They said no more.
He sat there, with the face of a man baffled,
And found in hers no answer. Silently
They sat alone, the king and queen together;
And silently they turned, hearing at last
A new sound, and a murmur of young voices.

II

Jasper the second, commonly the prince,
By compliment again, came radiantly
Into a room where radiance, rightly brought,
Might have been welcomed and appreciated
With less of an inclement hesitancy
Than was to meet the prince and his companion,
For whom was no escape. A strong young hand
Held hers and brought her along confidently;
And strong young arms, had she been obstinate,
Would instantly have seized and carried her
Into that room where now the king and queen
Sat quietly and stared. The prince, with eyes
Alive with laughter and rebellious joy,

1407

And with a pink face crowned and animated
With golden hair that was unruly always,
Came leading in with him a slight young woman,
Impredicably firm, fair to behold,
And more amused than scared.

                          "Father and mother,
I have brought Zoë home with me tonight,"
Said the prince, happily, "for you to see.
Zoë's a lazy name, but not so Zoë.
Zoë is intricate and industrious,
And sees all through you. So be kind to her,
And make her one of you, so far as wisdom—
Or prudence, if you say so—may permit.
When she was young, the wisest man alive,
Before he died, gave her a little knife
That's like a needle. But she doesn't use it,
And you need have no fear. Zoë's a prophet,
And wishes you no evil. Zoë's an angel,
Which means a messenger. All there is of her
That's not a wonderment to be observed
Is mind and spirit—which are invisible
Unless you are awake. Yes, we are married,
Mother—under the stars and under God,
As we see deity, and have bound ourselves
Therefore as loyally and sacredly
Together as if two bishops and their wives
Had tucked us in. Zoë, don't scowl at me.
It's well for mother to be agitated,
Occasionally, for she draws and follows
A line too fixed and rigid, and too thin
For her development. Mother, will you see Zoë,
And say if there came ever, except yourself,
Anything half so near to the divine,

Or anything half so satisfactory
Out of God's crucible."

                  The queen said nothing.
The king said, "Will you children please sit down;
And while your mother and I prepare ourselves
For gravity, will you say a little more?
My words are now for you, my son. The lady,
Later, may tell her story. We shall hear it
With a becoming interest."

                    "I shall not,"
The queen said, trembling. "If this means the end
Of my world, and if I have lost my way
In a new wilderness, with no road back
To where I was, I'd rather be there alone,
And die there, than go on. If you two strangers
Tell me this house is yours—and it seems now
No longer to be ours—your father, Jasper,
Will answer as he will. I have no voice,
And I have been content, as it appears,
To be without one. If I leave you now,
I shall say nothing that I might regret."
She rose, and the prince laughed affectionately.
"Mother, your manners are immaculate,
Majestical, and somewhat serpentine."

"Whatever they are to you, others have borne them
With no complaint," she said. "If they have served
And are outworn, new manners will forget them."
And quietly, with a pallor-covered rage
Half-blinding her, she walked out like a queen.

The prince looked at his father ruefully,
And laughed again: "I should have said, and sworn,

There was a curiosity in all mothers
That would have mastered her, even though she burned
Inside until she died spontaneously.
Don't worry, Zoë. She is not going to die—
If I know mother."

          "You don't know anything yet,
My son," the king said; and he shut his jaws
Until his teeth ached, while he gazed at Zoë
With half-shut eyes that had a smile in them,
Which was acknowledged with no trepidation,
Or manifest surprise, by one in hers.

"I'm glad you like me—if you do," she said;
"For I shall not remain where I'm unwelcome
To Jasper's father. I could never do that."

"You might not," said the king. "And Jasper's mother?
In chemistry there are several elements
That will not yet combine—though I suspect
They must; and when they do, they'll all be one.
But that's far off; and we are still the slaves,
I fear, of our ingrained affinities.
We may not say, 'Now this one I will love,'
Nor may we say, 'Now this one will love me.'
I doubt, my child, if you and Jasper's mother
Will ever combine. It's not your chemistry."

"I know that," she replied, "and I am sorry.
But there's a world far larger than your house
For us to live in. Jasper knows already
That I should not improve here, or be happy,
With your frown watching me. You are not frowning
Now, and you should not. I am not wicked.
I am only as I came, as Jasper says it,
Out of God's crucible—although I'm not so perfect

As he has painted me. If I'm not evil,
And I am not, it is your chemistry
That shows me clearer than it has shown those
Who wrought it, the long monstrousness of life
That most have suffered and a few been crowned for.
You have been crowned, and that is why you like me."

King Jasper stared at her until she laughed,
And then away from her and at the fire
A while. At last he laughed at her, and then,
Not knowing what else to say, he said,
"I like you, but I'm still afraid of you;
And I'm not one much given to being afraid
Of man or woman. If that's a compliment,
Say it is yours. I shall not cancel it."

"Hear, hear!" the prince exclaimed. "The old one sees.
Zoë, I said he would. If you ask father,
He'll say that I was always a bit crazy
For not having eyes like his to see as his do
More in his chimneys, where the dragon lives,
Than in the nearness of a younger dragon.
He'll say that I am headstrong and ungrateful,
And then be penitent; for he knows better.
He knows more than he tells. Now tell me, father,
If I did well or ill in fetching Zoë
For you to see. I'm sorry about mother."

"My son, there's many a question safer left
With silence," the king said, and gazed at Zoë,
Whose dark eyes challenged his with hidden triumph.
"An answer, if I made one, might resemble
One of those decimals that extend themselves
And end nowhere. A repetend, we called it,
When I was sent to school. Am I still there?"

"I can see pupils, father, older than you,

Going to Zoë to be educated,
And fast as rabbits go. If you learn only
A little from her of all she knows of you,
You'll say, 'Who's this?' to the first looking-glass
Wherein you see a stranger."

                    The king fixed
A gaze of indecision on the prince;
Then one on Zoë, who commanded it,
Mostly with her warm eyes. "With you for teacher,
I might go back to school again," he said,
"And might be punished."

                    "You might," said the prince,
"Be rulered on both hands until they bled,
And come again next day for more of it.
Zoë can be ferocious, if incited;
She can be merciless, and all for love;
And not for love of one, or two, or three.
Father, be careful. It is not too late
For you to drive us out and shut the door
Against us and the dark, and make believe
That you have seen and heard the last of us.
We shall be here, and you may feel our presence.
We may still touch you with invisible hands.
Whether or not you see us here again
Is not the immortal point, for we are here;
And if we stay, you will know more of Zoë,
And more of me. I'm sorry about mother."
So the prince finished, laughing at his father
With an affection unmistakable,
For which the king was glad. But while he listened,
His eyes were tethered and held invincibly
By those eyes of a woman—laughing eyes,
Of which he was afraid. The fears he felt

Were not the tinglings of inveiglement;
They were unsought inept awakenings
Of truth he long had fancied was asleep,
Knowing truth never sleeps. And why, he wondered,
And why at this unreal disarming moment,
Must he be told once more of hands at work
That were invisible? And the more he wondered,
The more his house was a place filled with hands
That were invisible. Did the woman see them?
And was that why her eyes were laughing at him?

His eyes were asking, and she answered them:
"Invisible hands are not so comforting
As hands that we may recognize and hold.
I'd rather see them. I should be terror-sick
For days if I should feel them and not see them—
Especially all alone and in the dark.
The mightiest are the blindest; and I wonder
Why they forget themselves in histories
They cannot read because they have no sight.
What useless chronicles of bloody dust
Their deeds will be sometime! And all because
They cannot see behind them or before them,
And cannot see themselves. For them there must
Be multitudes of cold and unseen hands
That reach for them and touch them horribly
When they're alone. If I were Queen of the World,
And had no eyes, I should feel cold hands always,
And certainly die shrieking; for those hands
Would strangle me."

     "If you were Queen of the World,"
The king said, with a wry laugh that accused him,
"Beauty and love would reign—though probably
Not for so long as you conceive they might.

1413

If years have taught me more than a child knows,
That world of yours would soon be a red desert
Of the same bloody dust that you have seen
So confidently coming. I see no man
Who looks to me as if the crown of the world
Would not come down so quickly over his eyes
That he would soon be blinder than he was
Before he wore it. And with a right respect
For you, my child, and for all restless women
Who'd see this world turned neatly upside down,
I fear that you might find the same absurd
And abused atom that was here before.
Sorrow and admiration, and esteem,
Forbid my seeing a woman wearing it
For more than a few days."

                     "Zoë, hurrah
For father!" cried the prince, applauding him
With joyful palms. "He has said everything
That every other king with a top-hat,
And a wrong understanding of the part
That he was given to play, has said no better.
Father's an old dog, Zoë. If you stroke him,
He'll treasure the attention, for he likes you,
And value it the more because he fears you.
But you may teach him nothing. He knows more
Than pride and habit and uneasy caution
Will give him tongue to say; and he knows you—
More than he dares. So, Zoë, don't annoy him;
And for the sake of all who are too old
To see the coming of what they have called for,
Don't prick him, for the joy of seeing him wince,
With your old wise man's knife that's like a needle.
Now father's wondering what we mean by that.
So, don't excite him. I'll sound an older theme,

KING JASPER

Father—a thing your memory may have lost
Among the noises of your coronation.
I'm trying, and vainly, to find anywhere,
On any wall in this commodious house,
A picture that so far as I have sought
Is nowhere here. After a sad sojourn—
Till I found Zoë—among the ruins of time
In ancient cities, and among more pictures
Than are alive, there's one I've not seen yet
That follows me. You said a thousand times,
When I was young—Zoë, don't laugh at me—
That you would have old Hebron hanging here,
Because he was your friend. I saw young Hebron
Down there among your chimneys yesterday,
Measuring them with a sardonic eye
As if they were not yours. I did not know him.
He has been long away; and I'd have prayed
He might have stayed there. But he did know me,
And was no happier for the sight of me.
His eyes, as I went by him, held for me
As much love in them as a bulldog's hold
For rats—yet he was patient, and restrained
His tongue from saying he wished that I was dead.
Father, why not hang Hebron—the old man—
In a good place, where you may look at him
And say he was your friend? You owe him that,
And there's a rumor that you may owe more."

"My son, when you are older," said the king,
Smiling a scowl away, "you will have learned
That all who have climbed higher than the rest
Owe the dead more than pictures. If the dead,
And the long-dead before them, should return
With ledgers telling us where our debts are cast,
We should know more than fate sees necessary.

1415

If Hebron was my friend, I was his friend.
He died, I lived. And there was no crime there—
Unless you say there's crime in being alive;
And I'm not certain you might not say that,
If you might startle someone. When I die,
As I shall, soon or late, you will survive
Surprisingly. I want you to be sorry,
But not to wither away; for then my works
Would all be lost and scattered. So preserve
Yourself, my son. With Zoë, I think you will."

The king felt Zoë's eyes, and felt once more
In them the far-off laughter of a language
That might have been Etruscan or Minoan,
For all he made of it until she spoke:
"I mean to make the best I can of him,
But when am I to know how much of him
Is his, or mine, or yours, or maybe Hebron's?
I cannot read your ledgers of the dead."

The king compressed his mouth into a line
Of careful thought. "I'm not so sure of that,"
He said. "Who was your father—and your mother?"

"I don't know," she said, smiling. "I was found,
Once on a time; and someone called me Zoë."

The king appraised her as he might the grace
Of an escaped and unafraid wild thing
That sought his love, and yet might one day bite him
After some time he said, "Well, well. So, so.
It may not be important. Your two eyes,
And what you see with them, and what's behind them,
Are more for you, and for your preservation
Than are the names of unremembered parents.

Parents are everywhere, and incidental.
If you had known yours, they would never have known
Their child. I wonder, when I look at him,
If I know mine."

        "Who knows a child, knows God,"
She said. "Yet even if you and he were strangers,
You must have been companions—which all fathers
And sons, alas, are not. For he has told me
Of times, which he believes were long ago,
When you would hold him on your knees and read
'Sindbad the Sailor.' He remembers best
The Old Man of the Sea." She laughed at that,
As if the story, or the name, concealed
A source of untold mirth.

        "Yes, I remember,"
The king said; and she fancied that he trembled.

"And you remember, father," said the prince,
Like one excited unexplainably,
"How Sindbad finished him. He cracked his head
With a large rock, while the old fellow slept.
If ever you feel him on your shoulders, father,
Remember Sindbad's way. If that should miss,
One of your chimneys may fall down on him;
And that would crush him surely. Good night, father;
Zoë and I are going upstairs to sleep—
Unless you change your mind and banish us
Outside, into the dark. There is still time.
I'm sorry about mother."

        "Good night—father!"
Zoë said, smiling; and she kissed his lips
With a warmth too compelling and long-clinging
To be the seal of home.

"Father, beware
Of Zoë's ways and means. Unyoke yourself
Immediately—and, if you must, by force;
Or God knows what may happen in this house."
The prince's eyes were flashing with delight
Unqualified, and his words had the tension
Of an unfilial glee.

"Good night—my children,"
The king said. When he found he was no longer
The prisoner of those arms and lips and eyes,
It seemed a privilege never felt before,
Nor estimated, merely to stand there,
Unshackled for a moment, and forget.
Because he was a king, he could afford
The dispensation of at least a smile:
"Good night," he said. "Good night—and go away.
I cannot send you, Zoë, into the dark.
I don't know what you are, or what you mean—
But here you must remain till I know more.
And you, my son: I don't know what I'm doing,
Or if your mother was right."

"She is no mother
For me, I fear," said Zoë; "and I'm wretched
That I should be an outlaw, if no worse,
In her too swift and fierce interpretations.
But there are some of us who cannot change;
And as we were, we are. And the world turns
Like a mill grinding minutes into years,
In which we live until we are no longer,
And can do no more harm. Father, sleep well."
She laughed; and when he looked up, they had vanished.

Like one who for the first time in his life
Knows that he is alone, the king sat watching,

1418

And seeing not what they were, nor why they were,
The few last sparks of a forgotten fire.
They died; and there was nothing but white ashes,
And the king watching them. When he stood up,
And stretched himself erect and absolute,
A clock struck two. The lighted room was cold,
Too large, and empty; and the king was cold.
He shivered as he moved himself away
To the dim-lighted hall, and at the door
He stayed—as if that large and lighted room
That was there now might not be there tomorrow.
The Old Man of the Sea, King Jasper said,
Unheard; and like a man who was afraid
To be alone, he put out the last light.

III

King Jasper lay for lonely hours awake
That night, turning himself incessantly,
As kings will when their crowns are troubling them.
For well he knew, and latterly too well,
That age, as it came on, was giving him eyes
To see more surely the dark way behind him
That he had climbed, with opportunity
And enterprise to drive him, and to mock him
Whenever he looked back. If they had been
Two giants lashing him to his attainment
Of high desire that was a fever in him,
They would have been for that no mightier drivers
Than their two voices were. So the king told
His listening doubts until it was all true;
And his doubts told the darkness and the hours,
Who had no mercy, or may not have heard,
Until a clock struck five. There was no hope
Of sleep deceiving him; for there was more

Tonight than those diminishing small voices
Of opportunity and enterprise
To trouble him. There was a new voice now
That had a warning in it, and a laughter,
Which might be carelessness, or might be scorn,
Or both—or might be triumph, holding him
As a cat holds a bird. There in the dark
It might be death. He heard it, and he felt it;
And still remembered a clock striking five.
With sleep no longer even a theme of hope
To save him as a doom-defying refuge,
He counted those lost hours until he saw them
Like dead friends he had slain; and then he slept.

Not even a king may say what he shall dream,
Or what his dream shall tell. And so it was
For Jasper there asleep. His years behind him
Were like a desert now, and were before him—
A fearsome endlessness of rocks and hills
That he must climb, and climb, and climb for ever.
Here there was no beginning, and no end;
And here there was no life. Nothing alive,
He knew, could stay and live in such a place;
And it was then he knew that he was dead.
Not even a lizard or a leaf could live
Where no life was; and here not even the dead
Would stay. He was alone, and he was lost.
There was to be no friend or guide or servant
For one who in his life had climbed so high
That he had been a king. No suffering shade
With sins innumerable to expiate,
And fouler far than Jasper's, would have earned
So lonely and laborious a damnation
As this that had no end. No vicious God
Conceivable to mortal fears or throes

Could have found joy in this enormity
Of a king toiling endlessly along,
Alone and aching, and to no arrival
Or last release. Yet so it was all written,
And in a language ineradicable,
For Jasper's anguish, though he read nowhere,
And heard nowhere, the sentence that he knew
So fearfully was his.

     So the king toiled
Along, alone and aching, and forbidden,
By some command that was immovable
And unrevealed, to rest or even to pause.
If high rocks had no level way around them,
He must climb up, and up, and at the top
See more of them ahead, and more and more,
As far as there was distance. On and up,
And down again, and up again he labored,
His one companion a perfidious hope
That after time from some eventual summit
Hope might appear revealed, though far before him,
As more than a false torture that so long
Had whipped and failed him. No, there was nothing there;
There was no hope. He groaned again for gazing
Too far ahead of him, and for too long.
And then a joy that of a sudden smote him,
Until it was a fear, so blinded him
With fear and joy at once that had he then
Been given the power and will, he would have fallen,
And on his quaking knees would have cried out,
"For God's love, do not vanish! Whatever you are,
Wait—if you only wait for me to kill me.
If you may kill the dead, you will do well.
But wait, and stay for me—if you are there!"
He could not say the words, but now he felt

At last the sound of hope like deafening bells
Within him while he gazed and wept and strove
To make his feet go faster. Where he looked,
There was a growing speck that presently
Became a shape that had the form of man;
And now it had two arms that waved a welcome.

Once more the king would shout, but had no force
To sound the joy that filled him. He could only
Half lift his heavy arms, and in such wise
Make as he might a sign that would say little
Of a divine delirium, past belief
Or record, that suffused and stupefied
Credulity that might still be illusion,
Leaving him lonelier than he was before.

As a forestalling of malicious truth
Too terrible to be met with confirmation
Of more than blasting loss, he shut his eyes
For the few steps that he could make without them;
And sick with hope, and with a cruel fear
Of seeing, he dared slowly to open them.
He raised them, and with joy that was by now
A sort of madness in him, he strove on,
Until a gaunt frail shape that was a man
Whom he remembered hailed him with a voice
Of welcome that was like an accusation,
Or like affection with a venom in it.
King Jasper, listening, looked at him and shivered,
As if a snake had smiled.

                                        "I saw you coming,
And here we are," said Hebron. In his voice
There was a poison of calm enmity
That was not there when Hebron was alive;

And on his face there was a crafty scorn
That was no part of Hebron. Death had changed him.
Or was it a king's fear that wrought the change
In one the king had crushed and left infirm,
To starve on lies and perish? Jasper quailed
As no king should; and while those eyes were on him,
He was a king no longer.

                "It's a grief
Beyond a name," said Hebron, "that we two
May not sit here together and rest ourselves,
And talk of old years that are drowned in time,
Till your poor feet might cease to swell and ache
And your poor legs have comfort. But as long
As you are doomed to climb, I'll follow you
And talk. You must be tired of going alone
Over these rocks that are so much like mountains;
And I was always one of those who drew
Refreshment, like sweet water from a spring,
From unrestrained and easy conversation.
Jasper, there was a time, and many a time,
When you and I had more to tell each other
Than a long night would hold; and I remember—
Yes, Jasper, more than once—dawn coming in
To find you still alert, assuring me
Of peace renewed, and health, and independence,
And God knows what incalculable gold—
All to reward my genius, and repay
The price of those diseased and foodless years
That were to cost my life. Don't suffer, Jasper,
Or seem to be distressed on my account;
For I can climb as well as you, and listen
As well as I may talk. And if my feet
Should fail, you would not leave me here alone.
Jasper, your heart would be a fiery coal

Within you, should you leave me twice behind you,
And let me die. I have died once for you,
And that should be enough. If it is not,
You hate yourself more than you hated me
When you had finished me and seen me safe,
As you believed, and buried. Never believe,
Jasper, that when you bury us we are safe;
For more than sometimes it is only then
That we are truly known as things alive—
Things to be feared and felt, with unseen hands
That reach for you and touch you in the dark.
You do not love us then."

                  "Hebron, I swear,"
The king began, not with a royal voice,
And then began again: "Hebron, I swear
That I have never hated you alive,
Or dead. I may have been afraid of you,
But that was not from greed—"

             "May the fiends have him
Who tells me it was that! Who says it was?"
Asked Hebron; and his question sent with it
A laugh that was for Jasper like a blow.
"Your words are faster than your feet, old friend,
And have a surer sense of destiny.
O king, beware of words. When they are said,
They are like minutes that have ticked and gone,
And are still ticking. Men have died hearing them.
And I've a son somewhere who may be heard.
He never loved you, Jasper, for he knew you—
Long before I did. You were afraid of him,
Far down inside you, without knowing why.
I never knew him. He was a dark child."

KING JASPER

King Jasper, groaning while he climbed, said, "Hebron,
It was for power that I neglected you—
So selfishly. It was for power, not gold.
Between the two there was, could you have seen it,
The difference there has always been between
Daylight and lightning. You could not have known
My demon of ambition; for in you,
Hebron, he never dwelt."

                "I hear you, Jasper;
And I still follow you, albeit my feet
Are now less lightsome than I said they were.
I'll tell you something, Jasper. First of all,
You are a liar. You have always been one;
Wherefore, by logic and chronology,
You must have been a liar when you were born,
And probably before. I can forgive,
With my accretions of new comprehension,
Jasper, all such incriminating trifles;
And as for that, or leastwise in a measure,
I forgive everything. I'm only showing
To you the picture you have never cherished
Of you and me together before I died.
By then, old comrade, we were far along—
Or you were, Jasper—yet you never said so.
You never made me see, or let me guess
What you were doing with what I had done.
Did you know what it was that you were doing
While you enlarged your dream, and swelled and changed,
Till you were more a monster than a man?
When I was gone, men said you were a king;
But you were more. You were almost a kingdom;
And you forgot that kingdoms are not men.
They are composite and obscure creations
Of men, and in a manner are comparable

1425

To moving and unmanageable machines,
And somehow are infernally animated
With a self-interest so omnivorous
That ultimately they must eat themselves.
You cannot eat yourself very long and live,
Jasper; and that's about what you were doing
Before I found you here. There's not much left,
And the prince knows it. He's not alarmed;
For he has Zoë, and seeks no other crown.
Jasper, could you go possibly more slowly?
I'm faint with a fatigue, or a prostration,
That will no longer let me follow you;
And I was never strong."

                     "God help us, Hebron!
If I might rest, I should be glad to sleep
On these eternal rocks and rise no more,
Nor wake again. I'm like your mechanism,
Driven by some command that is not mine
To mount, with hardly strength in me to move,
One height and then another."

                        "That's a pity,"
Said Hebron, with a humor not amusing,
"And a sad hindrance I had not foreseen;
Yet for the sake of old associations,
And for some gratitude that's in arrears,
Necessity, too frequently a tyrant,
Forbids me, Jasper, to climb unassisted
This huge and hard upheaval here before us
Of cruel granite. Hell must have quaked here, Jasper;
For there was never on earth a desolation
Like this, or one so foreign or forlorn.
We might be on the moon. Make ready, Jasper,
For I can limp no farther. I'll spring up

As lightly as a bird, and on your shoulders
I'll ride so comfortably and quietly
That you'll say I'm a squirrel. I was never
A man of weight, for I was always lean.
You made me so; and with a private zeal
That I was not to share, you kept me so—
Until I died. Be thankful now for that,
And praise your fate that I'm not corpulent;
For that would be the devil."

       "For God's mercy,
Hebron, if there's a place in you for mercy,
Take your damned weight away!" King Jasper reeled
And swayed and staggered, praying that he might fall;
But soon he knew, more cruelly than before,
That he was not to fall. He must go on,
Upholding as he went, and with endurance
More terrible to confess than death would be
To greet and recognize, the crushing load
Of malice that he carried.

       "No, no, Jasper;
You are not saying that. You have been here
So long, and you have gone so long alone
Over these rocks, that your tongue, too long quiet,
Says the first word that moves it. It's your tongue,
Jasper, not you, that holds no gratitude
For this convenient privilege, long denied,
Of lifting your old friend from where you left him,
Ditched and half way to death, and helping him
Over these difficult hills. It's your turn, Jasper.
Did you suppose you would have all for nothing?
With Hebron in his grave for lack of gold
That was already gleaming, and was his
To share, did you believe that he would stay there?

Say no, or nothing. If you tell more lies,
Jasper, to me, I'll tickle you under the chin
With my rough heels, and urge you to go faster."

Sick with a torture and a weight of pain
Beyond the grasp of fancy, Jasper staggered
And stumbled while he climbed with aching feet
Those endless hills, up one and down another,
And always, with a mute and anguished prayer
That he might fall and die. But while he slipped
And swayed and reeled, half blinded and half mad,
With Hebron's weight a clinging misery
Never to cease, never to be thrown off,
He knew as well as he knew Hebron's voice
The quality and the source of his endurance,
And that he must climb on, and on always,
Over those hills and those eternal rocks.
So Jasper, like a demon-driven beast,
Under a yoke too heavy to be borne,
Suffered and answered nothing; for in silence,
Even while he strove and ached, there was a respite
That was a sort of rest, but not for long.

"Jasper, I fear that you forget your friend,
And with your friend your manners. I remember
When words came out of you so copiously
That my two ears were not enough to hold them.
Had the Lord given me three, I might have heard
Some that were never said—the most important,
As I learned when too little was left of me
For use or care. You reckoned well your time,
And mine. You knew then that your need of me
Was done; and that another sick year or two
For me would not be long for you to wait.
There was no more of me that you required

1428

KING JASPER

For your development and ascendency
Than my accommodating disappearance.
To kill me outright would have been imprudent
And hazardous, and was not compulsory.
Your lies assured me there was nothing then
Forthcoming or in view for either of us;
And so I died for lack of means to live,
And you became a king. For there was brain
Under my skull, richer than yours. You knew it,
Jasper; and you sustained it on your promise,
And on your lies, till all of it was yours
That you might use. That was unfriendly, Jasper;
And there's a waiting debt of explanation
That clamors to be paid. Come now, the truth.
I know the truth, but I shall know it better
When you distress yourself enough to tell it.
I know it will be hard—as hard for you
As you made death for me. Have you forgotten?
You groan as if you carried on your shoulders
More than one trivial man's ill-nourished weight;
And I've a fear you do. You stumble, Jasper,
Like one who has had wine."

                        "Hebron, have mercy!
Leave me, and let me see no more of you.
Was I not paying in full before you found me?
Leave me, and let me die. I lied because
Your way was never mine. If you had lived,
Your freaks of caution, and your hesitations,
And your uncertainties—if once you saw
Before you what was only yours to take,
And hold, and say was yours—would have been clogs
And obstacles that would have maddened me,
And might have tempted me to worse than lies.
I told you lies that were akin to truth;

1429

And I believed there was for you a glory
In your accomplishment that neither power
Nor gold would buy. And I believe it still."

"Jasper, if there's in you another jewel
Of balderdash as precious and as rare
As that one was, save it and treasure it
Against an imminent hour of last despair.
From now to then, I think we might go faster."

"Hebron, if anything left of you is human,
Will it not hear me, and at last have mercy?
Now that you have the truth you knew before,
What else are you to torture out of me?
Tell me the name of it when you have found it,
And then it will be yours. You know the truth,
You would have been between me and my fate,
Which made of me a king."

                              "A king of what,
Your majesty," asked Hebron, "are you now?
If you're a king, long live the king, say I;
And let me ride as a contented subject
On the king's back. I'm not uncomfortable;
And if I'm heavier than I was at first,
Do you guess why? It is because I'm changing,
Jasper. Yes, I am changing into gold.
I am the gold that you said would be mine—
Before you stole it, and became a king.
Fear not, old friend; you cannot fall or die,
Unless I strangle you with my gold fingers.
Now you may feel them, and how hard they are,
And cold. They are as cold and hard as death,
For they are made of death."

1430

KING JASPER

          "Hebron, have mercy!
Leave me—or strangle me, and let me die!
Kill me—for I can carry you no farther.
You are as heavy as the world is, Hebron!
Hebron! Have mercy! Leave me, or let me die."

"No, I am not so heavy as the world is.
Jasper, you magnify me, and exalt me.
I am as heavy as no more of it
Than you said would be mine. Had you been king
Of the world, Jasper, you might be carrying now
The world's weight, maybe, and be far worse off
Than you are while you're carrying only me.
Jasper, I don't know what the world would weigh
If it were made of gold. It would be heavy,
And it would hurt you. I don't know how much.
I only know that you were a blind king,
And that your burden is no more than I am.
Jasper, suppose we go a little faster.
You cannot fall yet, and I'm riding nicely.
If only we might have the sight of water,
We'd say that I'm the Old Man of the Sea,
And you Sindbad the Sailor. If I should kick
Your ribs a bit with my gold heels, who knows
That we might not ascend this hill before us,
Which is a rough one, like an antelope,
Or like a young horse, for the love of running.
Yes, here we are. I said so. And who's that?
Who is that woman waving her white arms,
And laughing at you, Jasper? Is it Zoë?
And who is he that laughs to see his father
A kingly beast of burden? He's your son,
Jasper. Are you not sorry that he was born?
They call for you together, beckoning you
To cross this narrow chasm. It's narrow enough

To tempt you, and yet wide enough to swallow
And hide you if you leap. With me to carry,
You know the burden of your worth, and feel it,
As it accumulates with every step
An overpowering slow solidity
That clings, and cripples you the while it grows.
You said I might have crippled you, and I will."

"For God's love, Hebron, let me go to her!
I feel a meaning flaming in her eyes
For me that I must read. And there's a promise
Of more than I possess. Hebron, have mercy!
Leave me, and let me leap across this place
And hold her in my arms and say she's mine."

"And why not?" said the prince, with a grimace
That was not his before. "Come, father, come!
Shake off that living load of death you carry
That was your life and your philosophy,
And here you are. One jump, and she is yours.
Come, father, come!" The prince danced up and down,
And Zoë danced; and the two danced together,
Each with a beckoning glee that chilled the king
To fury and despair.

                    "Yes, father, yes!"
Cried Zoë, calling him with her arms, and laughing.
"Throw off the monster that is holding you
And crushing your poor shoulders to the ground.
Throw him away—and let him fall down screaming
Into the darkness that you see between us.
He'll fall for a long time, and never come back—
Or not as he is now. If you could see him
As truly as you feel him, just as I do,
You would see then your kingdom and your power
1432

And glory—and as it is, and is to be.
He does not love you, father. Come to your son
And daughter, and be loved."

                                    "You hear her, Jasper,"
Said Hebron, rowelling with his heels of gold
The king that carried him. "Her implication
Would be that I am gross and treacherous,
Malicious and vindictive. And if I am,
Who made me so? Answer me that, my king,
Before you leap. You may still feel her arms
Around you, and from the promise in her eyes
Decipher your salvation, though I doubt it.
You cannot leave her; and there's yet a chance,
Almost as large as a mosquito's ears,
That you and I may clear this chasm together.
If you leap with a free forgetfulness
Of me, and with a faith, and fervently,
We may not fall—though I suspect we shall;
For while we wait, moments accumulating
Are making me a load that is no lighter.
The prince and Zoë, I see, are occupied
And entertained while you are marking time
With anxious feet that are a toil to lift.
The more you wait, the mightier you must be
For your performance. And time has a voice
That says to me that you may wait no longer.
So let us leap, and hope. Jump, Jasper, jump!
If we go down together, I shall not die—
For you have killed me once, though I'm alive
In spite of dying, and heavier than you dreamed
The growing ghost of a dead friend could be.
You did it slowly, but you did it well,
And so that's over. One of life's awkward laws
Forbids my dying again for a friend's pleasure."

1433

By now King Jasper knew for what it was
That awful weight of gold that was alive
And breaking him. Below him he could see
That narrow gorge of darkness, and imagine
Unfathomable depth and emptiness
Wherein to fall; and he heard Zoë calling,
Barely two steps across from where he stood
And swayed and staggered, and raised painfully
One foot and then the other, because he must.

"Come, father, come!" the prince cried; and his eyes
Flashed with a stinging glee that pierced the king
Like an unseen hot sword.

          And Zoë, holding
Her hands halfway across from where she laughed
And waited, said again, "Come, father, come!
You know you are my father, and you knew it
When first you found that I was in your house,
And there to stay, because you are my father.
Without you, I should never have been born.
Without you and your folly, and your shrewd eyes
That saw so much at once that they saw nothing,
Time would have had no need or place for me,
Or for the coming trouble I must behold
Because you gave to me unwittingly
My being. You should have thought of that before
You buried your brain and eyes in golden sand,
And in your personal desert saw the world."

She danced and laughed, and the prince danced and laughed;
And both held out their hands to him and cried,
"Jump, father, jump!"

          And Hebron, heavier still
Than ever, said, "Jasper, there is no more time.

1434

There's only enough for you to say to Zoë
That you are Zoë's father. Are you, Jasper?"

"Yes, I am Zoë's father," Jasper groaned.
"My folly and I together, for centuries,
Have been the forebears of her parentage.
But I can say no more. Hebron, have pity!
For you are breaking me. My bones will hold
Your cursed weight no longer. Zoë! Zoë!
Tell him to let me die!"

                She laughed at him,
And holding out her arms again, said only,
"Jump, father, jump!"

              King Jasper's eyes met hers,
Which held him like a charmed and helpless prey,
Without a will to choose, and without power
To stand there longer on the sickening verge
Of a bleak narrow cleft that he was never
To cross—never with Hebron's deadly weight
So crushing him that he could only plunge
And fall. Dashing away the last of hope
As he might a weak insect stinging him,
King Jasper shut his eyes for the vain leap
That even for one in hell must be the last.
He plunged, and instantly felt Hebron's weight
Releasing him from its intolerable
And awful clutch; and with a joy like none
To be believed, he found he was not falling.
He was alive and upright on safe rock
That he could feel beneath him, and should see
When his eyes dared to open. He had crossed
Incredibly that chasm; and where he stood
He was no more the slave of weight or motion.

1435

All but his eyes believed. They would not open
Until the prince explained—maliciously,
And with a cynic jeering in a voice
That half was his and half was no man's voice:

"Well, father, after all 't was but a matter
Of seeing what might be done, and doing it first.
If you had waited longer, someone else
Might have come first, and might have **stolen Zoë**
Away from both of us. Open your eyes,
Father, for God's sake. Don't say you are blind.
You are old enough to see."

                      King Jasper felt
A shaft of cold go through him, and forgot
That he was free once more to stand alone,
And that the weight of Hebron grown to gold
Was off his breaking shoulders. Indecision,
Worse than no hope, still held him until, slowly,
He looked and saw. He saw the prince before him,
And feared him, knowing not why; and he saw **Hebron**,
A shape of living gold that once was his
And was now hating him; and he saw Zoë,
Fairer to see than woman born of woman
Was yet on earth to be.

                    "You do not know me,"
She said, with a calm hatred in her eyes;
You never shall. Why did you not go down—
Down there, where you belong? Why are you here.
No,—come no nearer, for I've this to save me.
The wise man, when he gave it to me, told me
That one day I might use it—against you,
Perhaps, or one not you, yet of your making,
As I am. Are you trying to make me love you?
If I am beautiful and desirable,

Evil and ignorance have made me so—
Evil not mine, but yours. No—come no nearer.
This knife, you see, has a blade like a needle
To pierce you and your folly unless you hear me."

"I hear you—but I cannot let you go!"
The king cried, leaning towards her, his arms hungry
To seize her and to hold her . . . "Zoë! Zoë!"

He saw the knife upraised in her small hand
And he saw fire of anger and malignance
Burning in her bright eyes; and then he felt
Steel in his heart, and sank there at her feet.

"Poor king! Poor fool!" she said, and laughed at him
As once he clutched the edge of that cold chasm,
Before he fell. For he was falling now
Into a darkness that was colder still;
And while he fell, he could see far above him
Three faces mocking him; and while he saw them,
He could hear Zoë's laughter singing down
Like vengeance down from paradise to the damned.
There was a falling long and horrible
Into a darkness where he felt the death
Of time beneath him; and then, suddenly,
There was an end of that; and there was daylight
Where now the king lay trembling on his bed,
Not sure at first that he was there alive.
He was not sure that he was there at all—
Till pain apprised him sorely of a wound
That ached where Zoë's knife had found his heart.

IV

The palace of a convalescent king
Who eats and drinks and takes his air again,

1437

Yet knows he has a wound that will not heal,
May show itself, to those who are not in it,
The same today as it was yesterday.
When told the king was ill, a few were sorry,
More were indifferent, and the rest, rejoicing,
Prayed for the worst because he was a king,
And therefore better dead—but not so clearly
Because a righteous envy may have called him
A criminal or a knave. They could be knaves
And criminals inconspicuously themselves,
And quietly, and without being kings.
So there was indignation and chagrin
In many a bosom when King Jasper's face,
Though pinched and worn, was evidence undismayed
That he still reigned the master denizen
Of his uncertain and inquiring realm,
Which had the sound of more unheard vibrations
Than a king cares to feel.

Honoria,
The queen, sat watching at a window for him
Till he came riding home in lonely state
And with his unshared thoughts, which had so long
Been visible doubts, and had for no brief time
Been graven and ineradicable fears,
And were not his alone; for their slow virus
Had found its way to her before the prince
Brought Zoë home. She had felt unseen hands
All round her long before those eyes of Zoë's—
Those cruel, wistful, scornful, pitying eyes—
Had said to her so plainly what they saw,
And what those hands were doing; for Zoë, she knew,
Saw what the king saw, and she hated Zoë
The more for seeing so much that was to be
Because it must be.

When the king came in,
"Jasper," she said, "I have been slow to tell you
That this great house of ours, which once I thought
So safe and ample and inviolable,
Is too small for two women. Jasper's wife—
If that's what you encourage him to call her—
Must go, or I shall. I have said everything
To her that fear and sorrow and decency
Permit, and a world more to her in silence
That only scorn or triumph or contempt
Would suffer twice."

           "I'm sure that Zoë suffers,
In Zoë's way, because you cannot love her.
God knows, Honoria, that I have suffered,
And you know; and the worst you have to say,
To scare yourself, is nonsense. She has told me,
Time and again, and for your sake, my dear,
That Jasper's father's house is the wrong home
For both of them with one of them unwelcome.
But I have told her that I find in her
The one among the daughters of the world
That I would have called mine. She will not go;
She cannot go. I shall not let her go.
And this that I have said to her, my daughter,
I'm saying to you, my wife. You will not go;
You cannot go. I shall not let you go.
You are the queen; and queens have obligations.
The king would have a wrecked and empty reign
Without his queen; and there's the world as well.
The world, with an eye always for the worst,
Would not spare Zoë. So long as there's a woman,
The world sees what it will, and says the rest."
The queen's eyes flashed: "I am not Zoë's mother.
I should leave her to you. She calls you 'father,'

1439

And laughs at you, and fears and honors you,
As a cat fears and venerates a mouse."

"A king—and now a mouse. These transmutations
Of mine should be a somewhat lively trial
For one so little in love with change as you.
Be what they will, you are not going away.
See where you are. Take one full look, and see
This one place that is yours. Take one more look
And say how long you would live anywhere else,
Or wish to live, without it, and all alone.
It is your home, your world. You cannot leave it.
Nor could I leave it either, unless to die;
And if I died, you would still cling to it,
Because it is your world. It is not Zoë's;
And you need have no fear of her usurping
A world that makes her weep when she's alone."

"How do you know so well why Zoë weeps
When she's alone? If you're not her confessor—
And I've a notion you are not quite that—
There must be peep-holes, or a place where sighs
And whispers are made audible unawares.
I am not spiteful; I am incredulous
Of a king seen so pliable all at once;
And that's what I'd be fearing more than changes,
If Zoë, whatever she is, were not the source
And evident inspiration of it all.
If you have built your kingdom on a quicksand
Of self and fate, why should I fear the truth?
And why should I fear Zoë, wishing the while
That I might whip the creature from the house?
You know, as I know, nothing would come of that
But a catastrophe. Yet—I must hate her.
I am not jealous; I am afraid of her;

1440

And you are more afraid of her than I am.
That's why you love her; and that's natural.
There is a fear that loves, and one that hates."

"Honoria," the king said, "there are times
When I could hold you in my arms and love you
Alone and inexpressibly for your brain."

"That's not one of our more volcanic notions
Of love on fire, but it's a compliment,
Of sorts, and we are never too cold for them.

"Well, don't throw acid at me. If you do,
You will not like my face—which, I confess
Was never too beautiful. It is well for men
That women love the man—or what they learn
Too often was not the man, but their mistake—
More than they love Apollo. As for Zoë,
She does not love me. No, for she pities me
For what she knows that I'm afraid to learn.
But even a king may love the one he fears,
And have her in his house and wonder what
She is, and why he cannot let her go.
Honoria, unless you wish this house
To fall, be not so merciless to Zoë.
You cannot hurt her, and she might help you
To meet what's coming. You only waste yourself
In hating her because you fear to love her.
If you must hate, why not as well hate me?"

"No, Jasper, there may not be time," she said,
And thought; and leaning forward held his hands
And looked into his eyes until tears rolled
From hers. "Today we'll say no more of hating.
Your reign was more a system than a sin,

1441

And I've a fear that it is almost over.
And I am not so sure as I supposed
That I shall go away. Those little voices
That live within us all are saying to me
That neither of us shall be alone here long.
Don't think—not even of me. You are not well.
Long before Zoë came, you waited for her.
We are not stricken so swiftly as you were,
Or seldom are, without some warning touch
That may for love or kindness be concealed,
Or scoffed away. You are the sort of monarch
Who would have told me nothing. Be quiet now,
And for a while forget that there are kings.
Do not forget that we have had each other.
I like to fancy that I'm still at least
More than a decoration, or an item
That happens to be alive and to wear clothes.
So let me know it, or at least believe it.
We have no longer the same wealth of time
To spend that once we measured as too large
To count. If that was folly, there's none, surely,
In having not quite the last of what remains.
If you should want me and not find me here,
You would not like the change that I should leave
Behind me, or the ghosts, or the new silence.
Think only of old hours now that were pleasant,
And they'll almost come back . . . No, they will not—
Not yet. I can hear someone at the door—
Someone, whoever he is, I wish had waited,
Or had not come. I cannot tell you why."

She frowned and rose, and left him watching her,
Unhappily, until she was not there;
And soon a new face was confronting him,
And one so much not hers that for a moment

KING JASPER

His eyes betrayed him, and a stranger smiled.
King Jasper knew the smile, if not the man;
It was a dark and understanding smile,
With contemplating and consuming eyes
That gave it a slow fire of confidence;
It was a smile of pleasure without honor,
Or the right kind of joy.

                              "My name is Hebron,"
The stranger said. The words came consciously
Through sensual hard lips that slowly twisted
Into a colder smile.

                    "Your name was brought,"
The king said.   "It is one of the few names
That would have been an entrance for its owner.
I'm still not half myself, and so to many
I cannot be at home. Your name is Hebron—
Which is indeed the last of names that I,
Of all men, should forget."

                          "I thank you, sir,"
Young Hebron said. "Your chairs, like all about you,
Are thrones of comfort and magnificence.
It is a privilege and a rarity, sir,
For me to sit so near you in this one,
And to see you—at last. I have been long
Away, in other lands, but never so far
But that your name has followed me, or met me,
And had for me the promise of a welcome
That I may have imagined, or invented.
My father, as I dare say you remember,
Was also an inventor, and too intense
And too ingenuous for our vicious world,
Which might have overthrown him with surprise

And sorrow, if he had lived to know it better.
You and my father, if I'm not astray,
Were friends, and in a manner—in some manner—
Were partners; and I may have said in haste,
Or carelessly, some light words of his dying
Before he found life out. The more I see
Of this that's yours, and think of what was his,
The more it seems a pity my father died.
If he had been allowed to live, who knows
That he might not have owned as grand and vast
A place as any? For almost thirty years
I have been old enough to ask myself
What ails this world; and I have found an answer."

"Then you are the most enviable young man,
Perhaps," King Jasper said, with hesitation,
"Of all men, young or old, who are alive
And asking. You have learned more in thirty years
Than I have learned in more than twice as many.
Oh, no offence. For I have heard before
The voice of honest and eternal youth
Before it fades away, and its illusions
Are found and served again for the same issue."

"I see what's here to see," young Hebron answered,
In easy tones that might have been the voice
Of patience pardoning an interruption,
"And ask, being somewhat of a philosopher,
Which of you two is the more fortunate:
Whether it's you, King Jasper, having all this—
Or whether it's he, my father, having a few
Dark feet of earth, forgotten and undisturbed,
To call his house? That's a cold question, sir,
That has for centuries been debatable.
I doubt if even a king would have an answer

1444

Prepared and certified. If I might press
One of those buttons, and so bring my father
Back to share what he lost, and live again,
And die again, I should know how God feels
When he can't sleep o'nights."

                              Young Hebron smiled,
And waited. The king said, "If I were where
Your father is, and you should bring me back,
I might go far to find my way to thank you
For doing what God saw fit to leave undone.
And since I was your father's friend, and you
Are my friend's son, one pleasantry, I trust,
May be left out: it irks and humbles me
When you say I'm a king. I am no king;
And I'd rejoice if you might have my knowledge
Of an uneven sport of circumstance
That gave all this to me, and to your father—
Well, you have told me, and I have no heart
To use your words, and after thirty years.
I knew you only as a watchful child.
You were dark, even then; and you were mostly silent."

"Silent—or maybe sulky. For I felt
Precociously that ill fate had my father
Marked, for no fault, indelibly for disaster.
Now why should a child, before he could use words
That were not his, feel such a thing as that?"

King Jasper might not have been listening:
"I have been searching you, your face and eyes,
To find your father in them. He was fair,
And slight. Your mother was dark. Yes, I remember."

"She must have been. But she was dead before
My memory was alive, or born. My father

Said once that my complexion and my eyes
Were hers; and that's as far as I dare lean
On heritage, for my mother was beautiful.
She would have liked this house—if she had lived,
And father had lived. I'm not sure that I shouldn't
Myself—if it were mine, or if my wits
And qualities were like yours. We cannot all
Be kings. I beg your pardon. Forgive me, sir."

King Jasper laughed, though not with royal joy:
"Your modesty disowns you, and I question
If there's a need of it. You have the air
Of a strong son—who might build, if he would,
His house to his own taste and preference."

Young Hebron made a new smile with his lips:
"I shall embalm your compliment. My father,
I'm sure, would have been cheered and stimulated,
Could he have heard his old friend saying it
So late as this to a son so undeserving,
Whose house will be the world. He cannot own it;
And what he cannot own he cannot lose."

"The vision of youth is never to be dismissed
Too lightly or too soon," King Jasper said.
"Yet if the years were mine to meet the wager,
I'd give you odds that would astonish you
Against your seeing at sixty half so clearly
What seems today so fixed and feasible,
And on the side of nature. The more sound
And solid it feels now to your conviction,
The more, I fear, will be the wound it leaves
When wisdom crowds it out. There's always then
A festering, at the best; for I have seen it,

1446

And for a season fancied that I felt it.
Yes. I have had my dream, and had my sun
And stars to light my phantom of a world
That was not God's and never shall be man's.
And I was nearer then to being a king
Than I shall be again. And you, young man,
Are nearer the mirage of your desires
Than a few years will find you. See the most
Of a deceiving picture while you may,
And while it shines."

    "I shall not fail in that,"
Young Hebron said, "or fail to thank you, sir,
For your co-operation and your counsel.
Not all men on your eminence, I suspect,
Would so indulge the groping or the lowly,
The disinherited, or the unworthy.
He who sees only evil in high places
Has not employed his eyes. With a new range
And focus, he might see less; he might see more.
Only God knows what he might see and learn, sir.
It may be well for us that we learn slowly.
So long as we are safe and insulated
Against the fire of lightning, if it strikes,
We are at ease with restless elements
That are at large as never they were before.
When we have met next time, I shall have weighed
And tasted your prescription carefully."

Young Hebron, smiling, rose; and the king rose,
More as if pulled erect by strings and wires
Than by his will: "I'm sorry that your father,
Who saw the child, might not have seen the son
And man. He would have treasured the son more
Than all this trash of mine that you call power."

"I have not called it power, though I believe
The world would name it so, and with a reason.
Would you not call it power?"

                              The king laughed,
And with an effort beamed uneasily:
"Call it what name you will, and come again.
Infirmity forbids an open door;
Yet a few have an entrance, and are welcome.
My old friend's son will never find it locked."

"I thank you, sir," young Hebron said, and fixed
His hot eyes on the king until they burned him.
"If I have wearied you with my intrusion,
Surely you will forgive and understand me.
My native curiosity, and my pride
In seeing my father's friend here in his palace,
Would warrant—or, I might say, would command—
One pilgrimage at least to this that's here,
And is all yours." His eyes resumed their leisure
In their renewed appraisal of the place,
And his lips changed into a colder smile:
"I came, and saw—like Caesar, you remember;
And I shall go away from here amazed
With admiration, and with some regret
That I might not have brought with me my father
To meet his old friend in his old friend's house.
"Besides," he said, still smiling at his host,
"And as was only fair and natural,
I came to see the king. I thank you, sir."

He turned, and he was half-way to the door,
When a sound made him tremble, and a face
With two dark startled eyes in it transfixed him.
"Your pardon—oh, your pardon, if you please!"

Said Zoë to King Jasper. "I heard voices—
I thought I recognized . . ."

                    "Zoë is lying,"
The king said to himself, "and with a purpose.
I shall know more of that." Then he said, "Zoë,
This is my old friend's only son, young Hebron.
Zoë is my son's wife."

                    "I know," said Hebron.
Driving a smile into his flaming eyes,
He fed his admiration till she wondered
If all her clothes were on. "I should have known
The lady Zoë with no presentation.
Praise beyond language, yet inadequate,
Had left me skeptical and unprepared.
Beauty, I learn at last, was only a word
Until today—a toy for tongues and ears
To trifle with because they were not eyes.
If you devour me longer, Madam Zoë,
I shall become fantastic, and your slave;
And you might pardon that."

                    "When you were born,"
Said Zoë, not caring what else her eyes might say,
"I think the gods endowed you with more words
Than one man's portion. I dislike you, sir,
And will devour no more of your attention."

He smiled as if no barb had entered him:
"Yet I dare say that we shall meet again.
Auf wiedersehen. Commend me to the prince.
I'm sorry that my sorrow leaves with you,
And with the king, a portrait so remote,
So false and clouded and intangible.
Once more, I thank you, sir."

                    1449

When he was gone,
The queen came swiftly from another door,
With eyes wild, and her majesty forgotten.
"Who was that man!" she cried. "I saw his face,
And heard his voice; and I'm afraid of him.
Jasper, who was that man?"

"That man was Hebron—
Young Hebron," said the king. He waited then
Till pain had mercy on him, when he smiled
As a king should. "And Zoë, it would appear,
Is not the victim yet of his persuasions.
At last you two have achieved harmony.
I shall do better in a chair, I think . . .
Zoë, it hurts to tell so lovely a work
Of God's that it's a bright-eyed little liar,
But why did you come plunging in just then,
To say what most it was that wasn't so?"

"My Jasper saw him first. We were upstairs.
He called me to the window and said 'Zoë,
Here is young Hebron coming. I fear the Greeks,
And even if they bring nothing but themselves.
Go down, and somehow have a look at him,
And hear him speak, and tell me what he is.
I know before you tell me, but go down,
And then come back, and say if you smelt sulphur.'
I did, and so did you. Why was he here,
Father, and what was he so long in saying?"

"He brought his incubated filial tribute
Of my friend Hebron's only son."

"I hate him,"
The Queen said; "and if I had heavenly strength
To smite him with a wish before he goes

1450

One step from where he is, my God would thank me
For doing his work so promptly and so well."

"So, so," the king said; and a lonely smile
Crept over his wan face into his eyes.
"Well, well. And I believe you would, my darling.
Young Hebron has a grievance; and for those
Whose eyes are lighted with a brain on fire,
A grievance is a mission, a religion,—
Very much like yours, my love. For where's the use
Of Christ dying on a cross, and you being told
To love your enemies, if you'll only hate them
Harder, and worse and worse? . . . No, I don't hate him."

"No, you don't hate him," said the queen, and laughed
Her scorn into her words. "You wouldn't do that.
You are too gentle, and too magnanimous.
You would not injure an anemone.
No, you don't hate him; you are afraid of him.
And so am I."

                    "And so am I," said Zoë,
Now calmly, to the queen. "Also, I hate him—
His ignorance, I should say—and his inflamed
Assurance of his power to serve the world
When he is doing his ruinous worst in it;
Which is his way, and the world's way, of growing.
Madam, forgive me—and don't answer me
Unless your reason lets you. Just a fancy—
A vain one and a wild one, probably—
Has touched me, and has left a memory
That's like a pleasant sting. It might be folly;
It might be hope. Madam, I cannot give
My hand to you until I have had yours—

Yet I might hope. With the same thing to hate,
We might—almost—be friends."

                              The queen subdued
A smile by the old way of biting it
Before it happened. For a wavering instant
She hesitated. "You are a skilful child,"
She said, and would have laughed, if she had dared,
Before she disappeared, leaving the king
And Zoë alone together.

                    Zoë sat watching
The doorway where the queen so quietly
Had passed and vanished. "I may call you 'father,'"
She said, "and you don't care; and if I might,
I'd call her 'mother.' But how shall I do that,
While she sees only the bad serpent in me
That is not there, and she knows is not there?
A pride like hers, with its unwillingness
To see, may be as long a woe for women
As women are for men."

                    "Are you a woe
For men? You might be, the Lord knows," he said.
"It may be well for me that I'm not younger,
And that you are the savior of my son.
Without you, he might one day climb a rainbow,
And hurt himself severely."

                              "I might be one.
I might be, if you ask, a woe for men;
I might be, and I may be. The wise one,
Who found me lost in a morass of men
With eyes like Hebron's, and in danger there
Of doubting all eyes and of losing mine,

1452

Told me, when he had carried me away
And opened them, and made me see with them,
That I must always be alone with them.
But now that I have Jasper, who sees also,
I wonder if the wise one always knew."

"He may have known," the king said, with a frown
Of thoughtfulness: "He might, if he were here,
Tell me just why I was afraid of you
When first you came. Was it a month ago?
It seems a year ago—ages ago—
And seems no time at all. Are you released
From time? Or, where you are, does time forget?
I think that's it. I rather fancy, Zoë,
That I have found it. You may call me father,
If you don't mind my calling you my mother.
How old are you! . . . Forgive me—you don't know."

"I don't know; and I'd say it was no matter.
The wise one never cared enough to ask.
Now tell me something, father. Must the queen
Punish her soul for ever to make herself
Believe she hates me? If she did at first,
There's no dark reason why. But now—she knows."

"She knows, but she must wait; and while I wait,
I'll tell you of a dream that I had, Zoë,
All about you. I dreamed you had a knife—
You have one, Zoë—and you struck me with it,
Into my heart. Now why should you do that?"
He smiled, but she found sorrow in his eyes
That made a mist in hers.

                    "All about me—
All—all?" she asked. "I don't believe you, father.
1453

Not quite." She looked at him insistently,
And with untiring silence while she waited:
"All about *me?* And was there nothing else?
Father, was there no more of it—than me?"

"Yes, there was more of it than you," he said.
"You are too comprehensive to be happy
In such a world as this. We men have made it;
And we have made, to now, a shambles of it."

"And you will see it worse than it is now,"
Said Zoë. "And wrong prophets, like this Hebron,
Will sing of blood while others bleed for them.
They cannot know. Only a few may know;
And they, the wise one said, must go alone.
He may not always have been absolute
In his foreknowing of time and man and me,
Though he believed he was; and I did, then—
Till Jasper found me. . . . All about *me,* you say
The dream was? I forget. You say it wasn't
Was Hebron in it? Your old friend, I mean—
This Hebron's father. And you say that I
It was who struck my knife into your heart?
It was not I who struck you to the heart,
Father; it was yourself, and with my knife.
It's all as clear to me as a new moon.
You laughed, and said you were afraid of me,
Father, when first you saw me in your house.
Why did you laugh? You knew there was a knife
That I was hiding."

     "I knew that you hid something.
Should I have said I was afraid of you,
If I had not known that? And if I laughed,
Tell me what else there was for me to do."

"We were all laughing, and were all afraid,"

Said Zoë. "I was afraid for you and Jasper;
He was afraid for me, and for his mother;
You were afraid of time, and you still fear it.
Is it worth fearing, when so little is left?
I'm not afraid of it. I'm only incensed
With destiny somewhat, and sorry for man
Always; and for the curse of time on man
That shrieks to him unheard from history.
All a man sees is less than what he is
Without it, if he knew. Is he ever to know?
Look, father, look. You see down there below you,
And far from you—you cannot know how far—
Your chimneys, and your kingdom going in smoke.
Father, when they are gone, as they will go,
Where will your kingdom be? When they are gone,
There's not much else of it that will be left
To be a monument. Your kingdom creaks
And shakes while we are talking. I can feel it;
And you had felt it long before I came—
Long, long before. Father, are you afraid
Of me because you know I have a knife?
The wise one had it once; now it is mine.
Father, you should not be afraid of knives,
For you have used too many. If one of them
Has wounded you unseen, and in the heart,
Is it unnatural? And are you surprised?
Now look at me, and laugh, as you did first,
And say you love me; for I know you must."

"I love you; and I fear you," said the king,
"And for I know not what. Why do you say
The chimneys will be gone? Why should they go?"
"Father! O Father! A king should not say that.
He should know better than to ask an answer
That aches in him already, and in his heart.

1455

Now laugh at me again, and go to sleep;
And please have no more dreams—or none of me.
It is all Hebron's work . . . Which Hebron, father?
There are two Hebrons, and there always will be."

V

The king had no more dreams. He saw without them,
And with no useless need of asking longer
What they were doing, those unceasing hands
That long had haunted the foreboding queen,
Warning her of their work. He saw them now,
Pulling his world around him, and his house,
Dimly and irretrievably to pieces,
Leaving on everything an unclean dust
That he could feel and could not wash away.
Here where he sat he saw them; and far down
Below him, where the chimneys had so long
Been changeless, and as near to the eternal
As he had striven to see, there were those hands
At work that wrought by no command of his,
But for an older and a mightier master.
Once in a while, as he sat gazing down
Upon his power today, he felt a thrust
Sharper than Zoë's knife; and it would be
Just then that he believed a chimney trembled,
And may have shaken. If he gazed again,
And saw them firm, he would sigh thankfully
For peace that was like hunger for a food
That he had not yet found, and had a price
He could not pay, and was too far from him
For ships to bring it now. To know it was,
Was of itself a refuge. Though denied,
It served—until another chimney trembled,
If all but imperceptibly, while those hands

1456

That had no age or number multiplied
And wrought on mercilessly because they knew
There were no kings of earth mighty enough
To make them rest. There would be kings always,
Crowned or uncrowned, or all would be alike—
A thought so monstrous that King Jasper shivered
As long as it was in him. But no kings,
Crowned or uncrowned, would have now, or in ages
Unpictured and unshadowed, power to stay
Those hands, if they were given their work to do.
Now he could see; and he could ask in vain
If earlier sight would have seen far enough
To read for what they were the fire and gold
Of shining lies that opportunity
Had held and waved until they were all true.
He did not know. Zoë had come too late
To make a new king of a stricken one
Whose retribution was a world's infection.
He gazed, and far away, and far below him,
The chimneys were unshaken and unchanged.
They were as firm as they had always been,
Since they were built. He knew they were alive;
He knew they were still breathing; and he knew
Their breath was fire and life. But all the while
He saw them, there were those hands, never ceasing,
Never to be appeased. Zoë had come
Too late; yet he was happier with her near him,
Although he knew that with her in his house,
Beauty and truth and death were there together,
Watching and pitying him, and laughing at him
Because he was a king. He wondered why
Her scorn that she had buried in gentleness
Till it was almost love might not be love;
And he believed it was. He must believe it;
Or, with his heart still bleeding where her knife

Had struck him, he must crumple, or go mad.
If he sat staring longer at the chimneys,
One of them soon would shake, and then another;
Or one of them might fall; or all of them
Might fall, and go down horribly with a crash
That might shake even his house down on his head.
Would anyone weep for that? King Jasper sighed
For gratitude to Zoë that she had come
So far to tell him the best way to learn
That his indomitable reign was ending.
Without her presence, and without the wound
Of his awakening that her knife had made,
Approaching hours would be enormities
Of a slow and unendurable dissolution
That would be fire to feel and death to know.
But Zoë had come, and that was best. He feared her
But not as men fear death, or women years.
In his mind there was a turmoil of endurance
That would save him till his kingdom was a grave;
In his heart there was a wound of revelation
That would ache until his triumph was a name.
In a future that he fancied there without her
There were silences that soon would be a rumbling
And a music and a marching of destruction
Destroying itself and him in storm and folly;
In his fear there was a numbness of defiance,
Like a spell to foil an onslaught of illusion;
In his pride there was a calm and overwhelming
Recognition of irrevocable changes.

"Well, father," said the prince, a fortnight after
Young Hebron's apparition, "this world of your
Is with us yet. We don't say for how long,
And that's why I am here with this to tell you:
I'm your begotten son, Jasper the second,

By compliment the prince; and it's like this:
I said to Zoë that it might be as well
For you and mother to remove yourselves,
With items appertaining to your comfort,
And a few bits of raiment and adornment,
All in a trunk or two, away from here
Till we know more. There are bad wings in the air
That might be wings of hell-birds watching us,
Themselves unseen; and there's a breath of sulphur
That Zoë and I don't like. I said to Zoë,
'Father and mother must go away from here;'
And Zoë said, 'Yes, they must.' So there you are.
Your late ophidian visitor, I suppose—
Young Hebron—has not honored us again."

"Not yet, my son," the king said. Far below him
He saw the chimneys that were still alive,
And still were life. "Why should he come again?
I know he will, but why? Has not the world
Room for that man without his coming to me?
I do not want him, and I told him so
While I was asking him to come again.
I know men best when I can see around them,
As well as through them. . . . Yes, I can hear the wings,
And I could wish your mother might not hear them."

"If you can hear the wings that Zoë and I
Have heard, and still believe you cannot see
Around this man—father, I'll take your crown off
And wear the thing myself, while there is time.
Zoë, come in, and listen. Father can hear
The wings, yet cannot see around young Hebron.
Father and mother must be sent away."

"Your mother must be taken away, my son,"
The king said, sadly. "As for you and Zoë,

If I had wishes that would say aloud
That they would let you follow her, and leave me
Alone to listen, and to hear the wings . . ."

"And smell the sulphur, father. Don't forget
The sulphur, or the place from where it comes.
Down there they blend it so insidiously
With heavenly fumes and vapors of all sorts
That we inhale it in this air of ours
As if it were sweet breath from endless fields
Of roses; and we think those fields were planted,
By the Lord's orders, for what we have done,
And for ourselves alone. You have done well,
Father; and you have done a deal of evil
In doing it handsomely. But a king, father,
Whose roses have long roots that find their way
To regions where the gardeners are all devils,
May as well know there is a twilight coming,
When roses that were never so sweet before
Will smell for what they are. Nothing in this
Is more revealing or more terrifying
Than any man's life—could we but know the seeds
And roots and branches of it that have lived
And gone, and are forgotten. It's not you, father;
For you are passing, and you cannot change.
It's not you, father; and it's not your crown
That matters now. If Hebron comes again,
Hear him, and learn from his red rhetoric
How little he knows that millions who know less
Might yet be taught by kings—if kings were not
So royally occupied in their not seeing
Sometimes an inch or two ahead of them.
Oh yes, I mean you, father—but obliquely,
Or say inclusively, or indirectly,
Or some such word. Whichever commends itself,

Be certain, father, always, that I love you;
And all of you that is most honorable
I'll cherish for as long as I shall Zoë;
And that's as long as life. If Hebron comes,
Regard him as you would a coming curse
That you and your defections have invited.
I do not know the way now to avoid him.
Young Hebron is the Young Man of the Sea."

King Jasper, nodding his appreciation
As with a doubt, made a forgiving face:
"Strange music for a father from a son,
Perhaps, and yet a music that has in it
A tune that even the worldly and unworthy
May recognize, and more or less remember.
I have heard one much like it in my life
Before, somewhere, my son; and I still hear it,
Humming above me like an earnest bee,
Who cannot find his way out through a window
That will not open for him. If your Zoë,
Who knows her task—and it's a lonely one—
Has fixed herself on you as the best thing
There is of extant youth for her to mould
And animate, I'll pray, and in her presence,
That she may quicken this awakening brain
Of yours with less intelligence or more tact."

"Very well, father. That was on its way,
And it was easy said, and there's no scratch.
Now there's another tune that is worth hearing,
Father, and it's the one that I'll play next.
Listen: are you to go away with mother,
Or are you to stay here—with Zoë and me?
You know your mind. This flower of extant youth,
So far as you may credit him with owning
A sort of dormant or potential vision,

Sees here a question of how little or much
It's worth to live. The price and value vary,
I'm told; and there's not one may tell another
Whether it's always best or not to pay."

King Jasper sat as if he had not heard,
And saw below him, far away, the chimneys
That had been there so long. For the first time,
And with a new fear that was like a beak
That burrowed in his heart, he thought of them
As a tall forest where wild fire had raged
And swept, and left them there to be no more
Than cold memorials with no life in them.
He saw them, and he saw they were not dead—
Not yet. They were alive, and were still breathing.
He knew that; for he saw their smoky breath
Over his kingdom like a peaceful cloud
Wherein there were no storms that he could see,
And surely was no lightning. All there was
To frighten him was an innumerable
And ceaseless multitude of shadowy hands,
Always at work, doing he knew not what,
Yet always and mysteriously at work.

"You do not answer, father," said the prince;
"And if you tell me there's no more to show you,
I shall not be unfilial or obnoxious.
If Hebron comes, ask him how old he is,
And say that Zoë knows; and ask him next,
As once, in your first error, you asked Zoë,
If he believes the world would heal itself
Of all its inward sores if it were turned
Suddenly upside down; and ask him last
How many hours he thinks he'd be a-walking
From here to Sirius if his eyes were out

And facing the wrong way. Your asking him
Will make no difference, and will do no good.
I mention it as a way to pass the time.
There may be still some time."

                  "You come to me
Too late with your inspired advice, my son,"
The king said wearily; "and as you yourself
Observe, there may be no deliverance in it.
Hebron was here again this afternoon;
And having wished me well so venomously,
And with such unction, that I might have shot him
Had I the means at hand, he soon produced
A friendly trap that he had made for me
Of hate's last word that he calls compromise."

"Father, I wonder whether it's best or not,
Sometimes, to tell a fellow that he's a liar,
And see what comes, or to be gracious with him,
And hope that nothing comes of being a liar
Myself for listening and for hearing more.
He means capitulation and surrender."

"Yes, I know what he means," the king said, smiling
Remotely, as if nothing mattered now;
"But these abrupt discoveries of hot youth
Must not be thrown at me too suddenly,
And not too frequently. When a man hears
The scythe of time as I do, only Zoë
Knows how it sounds to him. Safely aside,
She may not hear it; yet she feels and sees it,
With sorrow for me, and pity, and some love;
Not much, but still a little. Zoë, my son
And you, together, may be the king and queen
Of a new kingdom that will be far larger
Than mine, than many of mine, if both of you

1463

Should live; and to my son I owe today
Homage and honor for your finding him,
And for his knowing you. There's more in this
Than kings who know their crowns are counterfeits,
And cannot die without them, will confess
To any but you. I was afraid of you
When first I saw you. Be so kind then, Zoë,
As to remember that I told you so.
You know the vengeance hidden in my words,
And you know they are true."

                          "Father, I know
That if you were to strive with all your soul
And skill, you could not lie to me," said Zoë.
"Now rest; and if you can, sleep for a while,
And have no dreams of me. Too many dreams
Are dangerous; they are not good for kings."
She laughed and kissed him quickly on his forehead,
And singing softly led the prince away.

After an hour the king could not have told
The queen if he had slept or had been dead:
"Yes, I have rested—if you call it rest
To feel your kingdom crumbling down all round you,
And yourself buried in the dust of it.
There's always rest in burial, I suppose,
If we are dead, but there's a difference
If we are still alive. A sprightly note
Like this, now you are here, will serve as well
As a lugubrious or ambiguous one
To say how swiftly we may change our minds.
For a long time—it seems long, if it's not—
I have been dandling, like a worn-out plaything,
A shapeless hope that somehow you and Zoë
Might love each other a little; or, failing that,

That you might hate her less. But now I'm grateful,
Harsh as it sounds, that you are what you are,
And that you cannot change. For you knew best
What you were saying when you told me once
That this house was too small for both of you.
That's one sharp reason, and a fortunate
And ample one, why you must go from here.
You said you must, and now I say you must.
It may not be for always; but for now,
Here is no place for you. I cannot go;
I'm fixed here like a tree; and all my life
Is planted here as firm as are my chimneys.
They are there, and still alive; and I am here,
And I am still alive. Our son and Zoë
Are here; and if they stay, they choose their peril.
They are beyond the range of my protection,
And are as free to die, if they like dying,
As you are free to live. There is death here,
Honoria; and that's the other reason
Why you must listen, and must go away.
God knows it will be lonely and unreal
Without you here, but nothing has been real
Since Zoë came. There is no sorrow for me
In that; my sorrow is her coming so late—
So long too late. But there's time yet for you—
For you to go away; and you must go.
Honoria, you must go."

                              "You say I must,"
The queen replied, smiling invincibly,
"But saying is not compelling. I shall stay,
Jasper. Zoë has made me change myself.
A changing woman is not so fabulous
That a man has to gasp. If Zoë at first
Offended or misled me with a freedom

That may have seemed an insult or a challenge
To me and to tradition, yet was neither,
Offence is nothing now but a small cloud
That's hardly to be seen. There's a clear sky
Today—so clear a sky that a mist coming
To cover it would be welcome. But no mist
Or fog that I can find is on its way
To comfort or confuse me any longer;
There are those unseen hands, and more of them
Than ever, at work while I am saying this.
Now I can hear them; I can hear things breaking;
And I can almost see the dust they make
Where they are falling. You too are hearing them,
Jasper; and that's why you are telling me
That I must go away. I shall not go.
No matter by what secretive or avenging
Or vicious means it came, here is my house,
My home, my world; and anywhere else than here
There is no place for me. I have prepared
And sworn myself to stay. I shall not go.
And if you say I must—well, we shall see."

King Jasper looked at her as only once
Or twice, or maybe three times, he had looked
In all his life before, and felt the same
Defeat that, when she willed it, would be there.
When it was there, he tried always to laugh,
And always failed. "I'm sorry, my dear," he said,
In a slow frozen way that frightened her,
As if it came from him and was not his,
"But you must go. I'm sorry, but you must go."

"And where?" she said; and saying it, smiled at him
As only women who know before they ask
May dare to smile. She waited for no answer,

But threw herself against him, and her arms
Around him, and so held him while she kissed him;
And then she said, "Jasper, whatever you are,
Whatever you may have done that men will do
To crown themselves, you have been good to me;
And I believe that you have loved me, Jasper—
All a king can. Zoë knows more than you
Of where we are, and I am sorry for her;
For there is a great loneliness in knowing.
She and our son together may live to see
Firmer and higher forms rise out of ashes
Than all your chimneys, which to you are temples,
Built high for your false gods of a small heaven
That is not going to last for you much longer.
You knew from the beginning of your ascent
How false they were; and many a time at night
You may have heard them telling you in the dark
All that you never meant for me to know.
But there were those hands, always. Never mind them;
There's only a little more for them to do.
Jasper, I love you. I have always loved you.
You are not paying for that."

                Before he felt
That he was left alone, he saw his wife
Already on the stairs, and going slowly
Upward—until there was no more of her.
Racked with an indecision worse to know
Than anguish in the flesh, he was alone;
He was alone as he had been but once
In life before—when Zoë had laughed at him
And left him by the fire the night she came
To change and frighten him, as if one king's
Illusions going while his throne was trembling
Were no distress for her, and no more news

Than a tree falling. But his thoughts were far
From Zoë while he watched those quiet stairs
Where the queen was before she paused and vanished.
There was a voice that whispered, 'Follow her';
And then there was another that asked, 'Why?'
And sounded to King Jasper like God's voice,
That was to be obeyed. So he went back;
And in a room where there was a new silence,
He sat alone, forbidding himself to think,
When Zoë and the prince came in together,
Intolerably at ease, and with no sorrow
Or fear on their young faces.

                            "Well then, father,"
Young Jasper said, giving himself a chair,
"What think you of the good God and his works?
Or do you believe the Devil is all there is,
And we are phases of him? Zoë and I
Believe in both. We say the Devil is here,
And shall be here so long as kings insist
That he is God, and bend their willing knees
In adoration of his omnipotence.
Father, you have been rather adept at that
For a long time. Zoë knew all about it—
So don't reproach her. Things that are gone from us
Are not worth mourning for unless we miss them
Because we owe them tears. Now there's a dragon
Down there among the chimneys. He lives there,
And has of late been restless and unwell;
And Zoë knows why. Father, if we should lose him,
How much would there be left?"

                            "Nothing, my son,"
His father said; "or enough not to starve on.
You know. Why do you ask?"

KING JASPER

                    "Zoë, hear that.
Father has loved the dragon all his life,
And has admired and exhibited him
Since he began to grow. But now he knows
The dragon is sick, and has not long to live;
He knows the dragon is eating his own tail.
Is he undone for that? Has he forgotten
To smile? Not father."

                  "Now will you, for God's sake,
Be quiet awhile!" the king cried; and he groaned
In helplessness. "If you know what you are doing,
You might remember that a few still live
Who are not dancing yet with you on ashes.
No, Zoë, I was not saying that to you,
And I should not have said it. Please forgive me."

He rose and slowly walked away from them
Out of their sight; and then there was a silence.
"I don't like that," the prince said, finally.
"Something is here that I have not found out.
There are more things and meanings in this house
Than I have yet a name for."

                "And there's one thing,"
Zoë said, with fear and sorrow in her voice,
"Of which I'm not so sure as you are, Jasper.
Are you so certain you could leave all this—
That you could leave your dragon, as you call it,—
That you could leave your father and your mother
When they might need you most? It's all too soon,
And all too far from those last words of one
That was my master, and my only father.
I'm like a child trying to be at home
In the wrong house. The wise one said to me
That I must always go my way alone;

1469

And I have hoped, with you, that when he said it
He was too old to know. Was he too old?
I tire myself with asking, and still search
Myself for more than I dare find in me.
For you are one—you are the only one—
With heart and sight to feel and see with mine.
Your wisdom and your vision were asleep;
And then I found you—and was not alone.
Somehow you knew; and only God knows how
Or why it was, and is. We two together
Might be an instrument alive with music
The world has yet no ear for, but may learn.
Are you still sure that you will leave all this,
To go alone with me?"

               "Zoë, this house
Was never my home, and it must not be yours.
My only home is where you say is best
For you and me. Is there no knowledge in that?
No heart, no sight? The wise one was adrift
With his last warning. Are we not here together?
You are distraught; and this is no right air
For you to breathe; and it's as wrong for me.
Home is not in this house for either of us.
Something has happened here since yesterday,
And father knows. I have it. I'll ask mother."

"No, you will not, my son; you will not ask."
King Jasper had come slowly down the stairs,
No sound announcing him. "You need not ask;
For I have brought for you your mother's answer.
Here is this letter that she left for you
And Zoë to read. Your mother, her life long,
Said sorrow had no other friend than silence.

It was her way—and may have been the best.
You will not ask. Your mother is dead, my son."

VI

King Jasper, for a month incarcerate
In his own castle, and without a queen
To serve him with her grace and her cool beauty,
Sat waiting, as the prince and Zoë knew,
And he knew, for the night that must come soon,
And with it the reward of his last freedom,
Which he hoped would be darkness, and no dreams.
When he told Zoë that, she said, "No God,
No Law, no Purpose, could have hatched for sport
Out of warm water and slime, a war for life
That was unnecessary, and far better
Never had been—if man, as we behold him,
Is all it means. Father, if I were you,
I should not think too vigorously today
Of what it means. Your doing it only shows
That even a king, when he is vexed and worn,
Is a bit fearful of his imperfections.
You cannot have the past, and cannot want it;
You must have what's to be, and cannot help it.
If it is all, there's nothing to be feared;
If it is nothing, it is not worth fearing."

"Your pliant logic forgets compensation,"
King Jasper said. "No, Zoë, it's not the price
I'm paying, that I resent; it's the worse folly
Than mine, that mine shall have to suffer for
When I'm forgotten. There would be no kings
If there were none to suffer."

                              "There might be,"
Zoë said, smiling. "We should all be kings,
1471

Or queens, if we could see ourselves in others.
But that's a long, long way from where we are;
And a few suffocatings and blood-drenchings
Of helpless heroes who will not know why,
Or what it means, will show the devil's ahead,
With banners and with music of all nations.
The devil is an impartial patriot,
Unprejudiced as he is promiscuous.
Today the devil is more than God. Tomorrow
He will be more, and more. Out of it all
He'll come with crutches, and not the devil he was.
Father, don't ask me when, for I don't know.
Suppose you go to sleep. You're laughing at me,
And that's as well as saying you aren't afraid.
You call it compensation, but how many
Resplendent and more shining sinners than you
Have had their sainted end, and, unsuspected,
Gone gloriously, and with heart-shaking strains
Attending them to their small paradise
Of worms without a king. If retribution
Were general and inevitable, and assured,
Our bleeding progress upward from the mud
Might have been longer had there been no kings,
Or queens, or other ambitious anthropoids
Without a conscience before history.
If I were you, I should give Hebron's ghost
My crown of glory, and leave the rest to God.
I don't say what God is, but it's a name
That somehow answers us when we are driven
To feel and think how little we have to do
With what we are."

                    "If I were a sick cat,
Zoë, I might not mind your stroking me,
And smoothing me," the king said: "Go away."

So Zoë stroked the king, and went away—
But only as far as to another room,
Where the prince greeted her with a lost look
Of conflict in his eyes, and with a smile
For sight of her. "Zoë, if all my thoughts
Were deeds," he said, "I should take you and father
Away from here. But force would only kill him.
Father will never go."

              "And you," she said,
"Will stay with him as long as he is here.
Nature is more than love, more than all knowledge.
If you should leave him to die here alone,
Nature would bind your knowledge with hard knots
That neither my love nor your philosophy
Would ever untie. He cannot go from here.
His kingdom and his power and his glory
Are with him still, and here. He cannot go—
Nor you; but I must go, for I must live.
My father—my wise father, not the king—
Told me I must, and saw for me the means
To live when he was gone. 'For you must live,'
He said to me, 'and sometimes wonder why;
And you must always go your way alone.'
And those words follow me. If we have found
Ourselves, and in each other, why should nature
Sunder us—just for that? I'm like a child
Trying to find the answer; and all the while
I know it, and am afraid because I know it.
With you, because I love you, I'm a waif
Afraid of nature, and of going so far
Alone—if I must go."

              "You are not going
Alone," he said, seizing her ravenously;

1473

"For you are going with me. If not at once
Well, shall we love each other any better
If we sit scared and shivering while we wait
For what's to come, and only watch the clock
And count its hours until my father dies?
Your wise one, even with eyes all over him,
Could not have seen so far as to see that."

"No," she said, thoughtfully, "he never saw that.
I love you, but I cannot love your picture.
Please leave me out of it. There are some others
That we had best forget; they are too vague
To name, and too malevolent to remember.
They are like fires that once were lights, but now
Are smoke and embers. So forget everything,
Except your father."

                    "Are you to be forgotten?"
He was still holding her and searching her
For more than she would say.

                    "No—nor your mother,
Nothing was left for her. So, like your father,
And like yourself, she could not go from here—
Save only by one door that she could see;
And that was a closed door. She opened it,
And now she is not here. She was not made
For changes; and wherever she is today
Is better for her than this. Your father waits,
And even smiles a little. He says my knife
Found his heart first one night while he was dreaming,
And left him as he is. But he knows better:
He knows my knife had found him long before
I came. All that he did not know before
Was whose knife it might be that he had felt

1474

Before he dreamed of me. He knows me now,
And wishes I might love him as a father.
He says he is my father—which is more
Than I supposed he knew. I hope he goes
Before us—for if we are here too long
We may not fare so well."

           "Zoë, I think
If you were led one night by skeletons
To a new grave, and saw yourself there dead,
You would not be distressed or interested.
You'd only say to them, 'You call it Zoë,
Yet I'm still here alive; for I must live.
Cover that up, and let's go somewhere else.'
I think that's what you'd say. . . . But tell me, Zoë,
What's under this? If we have found ourselves,
As you say, in each other, you might say more."

"Jasper," she said, "you know that place of ours
Outside, above this house, where we look down
And far away to where we see the chimneys,
And where your dragon lives. I was up there
This afternoon alone and found a rock—
Just a flat rock that lay there, for no reason;
And I said to myself, and for no reason,
'What's under it?' I could not lift the rock;
And what was under it I cannot tell you.
And like as not there was not anything . . .
What have I said? Why do you look at me
As if you were afraid?"

           "Because I am,"
He said, and held her closer while he gazed
Into her silent eyes and felt her trembling,
For the first time. "Zoë, if you should die . . ."

She smiled, as if to pay a debt she owed,
And drew his face slowly to hers and kissed him
Until he could not see. "I shall not die,"
She said, letting him go, "for I must live.
The wise one said I must."

       "The wise one said
That you must live, Zoë, and go alone,"
The prince replied. "Have I forgotten that?"

"There may have been a blemish in his wisdom,
For we are still together, and still breathing.
So are the chimneys. They are still alive,
But less alive than they were yesterday.
Jasper, I fear the dragon is no better,"
Said Zoë.

    "The dragon is dying," said the prince,
And sat there, staring absently away,
Far off and far below him, at the chimneys;
And while he stared at them he did not see them.
"I was not thinking of the dragon, Zoë,"
He said, and drew her towards him till she sank
And rested in his arms. And they were silent
Longer than there was light; and after twilight
They were there still, and silent.

        After dark,
King Jasper, with a restive wilfulness
That would not yield either to pleas or warnings,
Went back to the same place and the same chair
That he sought always to find solitude,
And a king's privilege to be left alone,
If so he would. He was alone tonight,

With only a dark window fronting him
For company. He watched, and saw the chimneys
Although they were invisible in the gloom
That lay now on his kingdom like an ocean
Holding an unseen and mysterious life
That he could feel was near, and coming nearer.
"But it may not be life; it may be death,"
He thought, and smiled, remembering Zoë's reasons
Why dying was not worth fearing. He believed her—
Until he saw, far down and far away,
A shining and a rising of wild light
That never was there before.

              "You see it, father!"
The prince cried, rushing in. "I should have said
It was not coming yet—as we all say,
After it happens."

              "Yes, your father sees it,"
Zoë said, calmly; "and he sees nothing else.
Why should he, when his kingdom is on fire,
See you, or me? If you and I were lying
At his feet dead, he would not see us yet—
Or, seeing us, he would say that for some reason
We were there dead. He would know what we were.
But this thing that has come, even though he knew
That it must come, in one way or another,
Is more than a king's fear to see too soon
The least invisible of things imminent
Will recognize at once as Nemesis.
And if our voices found their way to him,
He would hear only sound somewhere behind him,
Like a rat grinding, or like hands unceasing
That he has heard before."

              1477

                              If the king listened,
Or heard, there was no sign; for in that light
He could see chimneys that were no delusions
Of a nostalgic fancy. One light followed
Another, wherever the planted spawn of doom
Bloomed into flame and rose to find the sky
And burn the firmament. He had forgotten
Zoë, and all that she had said of death.
Here was a death worth dying; here was a pyre
Of life worth dying for. He glorified it,
And reverenced it, until he saw himself
The body and fact and apex of it all,
And a world humbled by the noise and shine
Of a king leaving it. Silent he sat,
And saw. There was a nameless exultation
In having all this alive, not leaving it
As a memorial and an after-show
For friends and strangers. Joy and fear together
Filled the king's cup till only fear was left
For him to taste—fear and astonishment
And revelation that must be a lie,
Or an insane illusion. While he watched
His glory going, and so magnificently,
And trembled as it went, a shaken chimney—
The tallest and the mightiest of them all—
Fell with a crash and insult of lost sound
That must have agitated and deranged
Earth and the stars. All else that he could see
Might be a dream, or a majestic fiction,
With Hebron, like a wizard in his grave,
Inspiring it; but in this fall and ruin
And end that was epitomized and real
Against that fury of light, no kings alive
Could not know what was falling.

KING JASPER

                              "You saw it, father,"
The prince said, "and you might almost have heard it.
If it must come, it may as well come tonight;
For this will be as apt a night as any,
Maybe, for blindness to be burning itself
Alive—but not to die . . . There goes another.
Don't see it, father, unless you, as we do—
Zoë and I—believe, since they are going,
That all of them had best be down at once,
And done with. They are not worth watching, father.
And if their falling so inevitably,
And finally, is no sight for a king's eyes,
Shut them, and do not see it. Nothing is left
Down there for you, or me; and surely nothing
To let me leave you here alone with Zoë.
And if I should go down, and were seen there,
There's a vast chance that I might not come back—
From doing no good."

                              The king replied, and calmly,
"No, it would do no good. I should not love you,
My son, or prize you more, for being a fool.
Trouble, I knew, and had foreseen, was coming—
But not so suddenly, and with no sign."

"Father, because you are a king, perhaps,
Your words are not your thoughts. They have had always
A sort of covering lightness to conceal
The most of what they meant when they said least.
Habit is much like love—stronger than death.
This is not trouble, father; this is war."

"Yes, I know what it is," the king said, faintly:
"I'll say no more. There is no more to say."

1479

The prince, with hesitation chilling him
With sorrow and uncertainty, said, "Father,
I waited before saying it, but this house
Is empty—save for you and Zoë and me—
And might as well be a forgotten island
In a forsaken ocean. How it was done,
Or when, or by what miracle of deceit
And treachery, I know not. There is no calling
From here; and if we called, and someone came—
What then? You cannot go away from here;
And if ten giants were telling you that you must,
You would not understand them. You would say
That mother's way out was right. It may have been.
See, father—or don't see. There goes another.
They will all go . . . Father—what is it! Father!"

"Zoë," the king said. "Zoë—Zoë—my son, . . .
You found him, and you knew him. . . . You together . . .
I don't know . . . You know . . . Zoë—Zoë—the knife!
Zoë—and you—together . . ."

                                That was all
The king said, and the prince said nothing more;
And that would have been strange, had not just then
The sound of a loud shot shaken the room
With noise that might have been the crash of judgment
On a dishonored world where only Zoë
Was left with ears that were alive, and eyes
To see the prince lying still where he had fallen
Between her and the king, with not a word
For either, and with a bullet through his brain.

The king heard nothing, and saw no more fire
Below him, and saw no more chimneys falling.
No matter how many of them were still to fall,

The king would not have cared. He was asleep;
And on his face there was a gratefulness
For a last wound that he no longer felt;
And on as much as death had left of him
There was a final peace.

                    Zoë found time,
Before she learned that she was still alive
To sorrow and to passion, for thanksgiving
To change and fate that there was neither king
Nor queen now in the house to know what else
Was there. The prince, lying silent at her feet,
Was more than she would see, while on her knees
She touched and felt him, and knew what it was
That once had held her in its arms and laughed,
And loved her, and was happy having her there.
Now it was long ago. The wise one knew
That she must go alone, waiting for time
And life to blind themselves in finding her,
And sometime to have eyes. Tears, filling hers,
Were merciful at first, and for a spell
Made her forget that while she was alone
With two that would not answer if she spoke,
She could feel eyes of one somewhere behind her
Who might not wait.

                "You see him," said Young Hebron,
"There where I laid him for your majesty
The king to see. Is he not beautiful?
Look, look, your majesty. Have you no eyes
To see the son and heir of all your power
And glory that you have stolen? And, down there,
Do you see the fire and light that you have kindled
So slowly and so thoroughly? Do you see it,
Your majesty? Oh, yes, you must have seen it.

Now look away from it, and see this thing
Down here that would have carried your torch along,
And maybe lighted with it merrier fires,
Larger than yours. Look, look, your majesty!
Have you no interest? And have you no pride?"

Young Hebron, coming forward, found the king
Indifferent in his chair, and Zoë kneeling
Over the prince, whose torch was hers to carry
Unseen by time and man. "You are too late,"
She said from where she knelt. Her eyes, now clear
To shine with all the grief and fiery scorn
That lighted them, saw leering there before her
The stained and heated face of a lust-drunken
Demoniac, who in his task and frenzy
Of twice-avenging hate had not forgotten
The one sight he had had of Zoë's face,
Or the untold enigma of her beauty,
Or the clear scorn of her supremacy,
Or Zoë's last word one day.

                    "You are too late,"
She said to him again. Now she had risen,
And was erect and unafraid before him,
Her eyes afire with scorn, and had he known it,
With a despairing pity. "And you have done
Your work so well that I see nothing for me
To do but go. Leave me, and let your madness
Be the one medicine that will ease a little
Your blistered hatred of all things there are
That are not you, or yours, and cannot be.
Leave me, and let your poor, sick, stricken soul
Suffer until it feels; and let it feel
Until it sees. You will have died meanwhile,
But who knows death? Why am I not afraid,

With death all round me, and with you before me?
You are not far enough yet out of the jungle
Of poisoned heat where you have groped and grown
To be the thing you are. Leave me, I say.
I said your work was done. Did you suppose
That I was lying to you, or was mistaken?
I have made my mistakes, but none so large
Or gross as yours would be in your delusion
Of doing worse wrong to me than fate already
Has let you do. Now I see partly why.
But even fate has its ends, as roads and rivers
Have theirs; and if we gaze ahead for them,
Sometimes, if all is clear, we may foresee them.
What more than death is left here in this house
For you to gloat on or to linger for?
The father and the mother and the son
Have had their tribulations and are gone.
When all are buried, there will be three graves
For you to visit and blaspheme unhindered—
If you will let me go. They will not care.
Will not three be sufficient—with all the others
That you are filling and are yet to fill,
Without a fourth?"

            "One more mistake of yours,
My lady Zoë, and an unworthy one
For such a piece of nature's work as you are
To waste your time and fire and eloquence
In making. Your three graves will be enough—
Oh, quite enough. If you are teaching fear
To tell you that a fourth will be for you,
Tell fear to sleep in it, and to stay dead.
Let fear be as dead as these two things are dead,
Which only by God's negligence had life.
Let fear be the least echo of a thought

That has no voice. Are you afraid of me?
God! If you are, you do not know me, Zoë.
You do not know that you and I together
Are God's elected who shall fire the world
With consecrated hate and sacrifice,
Leaving it warm for knowledge, and for love.
You are too tender, Zoë, to know knowledge.
You have it, and it only frightens you;
You have it, you are overflowing with it;
And there are gleams of it that I must have.
Nothing that's only one was ever itself.
You do not know that yet; you are too young.
You may have had your dolls, and a few playthings
You may have thought were men. That's one of them—
Down there; and you may say what he is worth.
Zoë, you read without your alphabet.
You do not yet know love."

                    With a quick plunge
He seized her; and before she could resist him,
He smeared her lips with his hot mouth, and laughed,
Holding her at arms' length and leering at her
With uninformed assurance of possession
That only sickened and awakened her
To calm necessity. She did not shriek,
Or struggle, or swoon; she stood and looked at him,
As a child frightened might look innocently
At a mad, prowling stranger who had found her
In a still house alone.

           "So then," he chuckled,
Pinching her shoulders with his greedy fingers,
"My lady Zoë is not unteachable.
Your knowledge is your safety and your armor
Against impatience and irreverent haste.

You don't know yet how gentle a man like me,
So long as he's not misinterpreted,
Or thwarted by she-devils or she-saints,
May show and prove himself. Which of the two
You are, we'll see. You may be saint or devil—
Or both. We'll see."

        "Which of the two I am,
She said, "is more than you may learn of me
When you have crushed my bones till I can't speak."
She said it slowly, and with what he thought
Was the beginning of a yielding smile
In unrevealing eyes. She felt his hands
Relaxing, and stood silent while she felt
Possession in his laugh. . . . "Why do you watch
The clock so thoughtfully? Are minutes precious?
What are your minutes worth tonight?" she asked.

He left her free: "Yes, in this house they are.
Your clock is true—as this is that I tell you:
In a few minutes there will be no house.
The servants of his late damned majesty,
There in his chair, were all my slaves and agents.
This house is mined and woven with doom and flame
That hides and waits for no more than a spark.
So, come with me; and when you know me, help me
To light for blinded man the fire of truth.
Yes, you must come with me; for I must have you.
One glimpse of you said that."

        She moved a little
Away from him, and held him with a look
That angered him with fear of the unknown
In her that mocked him while she said, "My dream,
And only distant vision of a purpose,

Has always been to make those who are blinded,
Like you, begin to see. Before we go,
Give me one lonely moment with these two
Who loved me. One of them was too old and worn
To change, or live; and one of them was too young
And wise to die. In him that you see lying
So quiet, there's half of me that you have killed.
Why would you kill the rest of me, I wonder."
She knelt beside the prince, and falling on him,
Fondled his upturned face for the last time,
And laid his hands together. And then she went
To the king's chair; and for a moment hidden,
Was only heard. "Poor king!" she said; "poor father!"
And then, appearing with her hands behind her,
She waited while she said, "Poor prince! Poor love!
I loved you, and he killed you; and I must live,
And go alone—all as the wise one said."

"Come!" cried a wolfish voice. "No more of this.
You are not going alone. You go with me.
You will forget this carrion of the past,
And pity yourself for the lost pride and tears
That you have wasted in remembering it.
Come—there is no more time. . . . What have you there
Behind you? Will you speak? Damn you, I think
You will."

            "Yes, I will speak, and you shall listen.
I am a woman, and have changed my mind.
I am not going. I am not going—with you."

"You are not going? You are not going—with me?
God—are you mad! Would you rather stay here and die—
With me?"

    "No, I should not like that," she said.
"I'd rather die here alone, if I must die.
But I must live."

            He cursed, and rushed at her,
And hardly saw the narrow flash of steel
Before he felt it in his throat and sank
Like a slain weight of hot mortality
That still had breath to speak. "Zoë," it said,
"For God's sake, go away. . . . You cannot die—
With me . . . Zoë! . . . I know . . ."

                 "You do not know,"
She said. "You cannot know. You think you know,
But only because you hear death telling you.
If you should live, time would have room for you,
And folly worse than this. It's well for folly
That centuries are so many, and far to count.
Fools against fools have a long time to fight."

"Zoë—I know," he groaned. "Look in my eyes—
Look once—and go . . . Zoë, for God's sake, go!
Go—go—for you must live . . ."

           Zoë looked once
Into his eyes, and said, "Yes, I must live—
And I believe you know. And I believe,
If you should live, that you would soon forget.
Poor fool! Poor clamoring soul! It says it knows,
Only because it feels too late the knife
Of knowledge it has lost."

          "Zoë—I know . . .
I know, and you must live . . . because I know.

There's no time . . . Go away—out of this house.
For you must live . . . I *know!* . . ."

                                   At last outside,
And half-way to the place where many a time
She and the prince had felt a shadow on them,
And on the king's house that was under them,
And on the chimneys, breathing power and smoke,
Below them, far away, Zoë, alone,
Fled upward through the darkness. She was hearing
Crashes and rumblings in the house behind her
That she had left; and over her shoulder now,
She could see flame within that filled the windows
With more than fire and light. More than a house
Was burning; and far below her more than chimneys
Were falling. . . . Now she could rest, and she could see
Two fires at once that were a kingdom burning.
In one of them there was the king himself,
The prince, and their destroyer. In the other,
With chimneys falling on him while he burned,
There was a dragon dying. . . . Nothing alive
Was left of Jasper's kingdom. There was only
Zoë. There was only Zoë—alone.

INDEX TO TITLES

1489

INDEX TO TITLES

INDEX TO TITLES

INDEX TO TITLES

INDEX TO FIRST LINES

1493

INDEX TO FIRST LINES

INDEX TO FIRST LINES